BRITISH ARMY BADGES

BRITISH

Lieutenant Colonel ROBIN HODGES

ARMY BADGES

Published by Lt Col & Mrs Robin Hodges ⁎ 2005

First published in Great Britain in 2005
by Lt Col and Mrs Robin Hodges
Court Hill Farm, Potterne, Devizes SN10 5PN

ISBN 0-9551463-0-5

Design and layout by Lyn Davies at *designsection*
(part of Butler and Tanner Ltd)
Printed and bound by Butler and Tanner Ltd
Frome and London
www.butlerandtanner.com

JACKET ILLUSTRATION Foot Guards RSM Full Dress rank badge (see p. 91).
HARD COVER ILLUSTRATION Crossed crusader swords with lion and crown adopted for the Army flag in 1938, not worn as an official badge but both gold and silver examples are sold by the Army Benevolent Fund 3.5 × 2 cm (see p. 480).
TITLE PAGE ILLUSTRATION Foot Guards RSM No1 and Mess Dress rank badge (see p. 91).
ABOVE ILLUSTRATION Foot Guards RSM No2 Dress and working dress rank badge (see p. 91).

Contents

ORDER OF PRECEDENCE

The organisation of this book is based on the Order of Precedence of Corps and Regiments, laid down in Queen's Regulations. The Royal Armoured Corps and Infantry Regiments are deemed to have equal precedence and take precedence amongst themselves as shown in *The Army List*. Squadrons and other sub-regimental units can be found via the index.

Foreword

Professor Richard Holmes CBE TD JP

This is a mosaic of the rich iconography of the British Army at a particular stage in its development. The book's enduring merit springs from its extraordinary breadth and depth. In breadth, it deals comprehensively with all regiments and corps, regular and reserve, existing when it was completed. In depth, it examines the lineage of individual units, and has photographs of cap badges, collar dogs, buttons, shoulder flashes, badges of rank, hackles, tartans, belt buckles – all those 'tribal markings' which play such an important part in soldiers' lives.

I am sure that it will delight collectors, and that soon 'Hodges' will become for contemporary badges what 'Westlake' is for First World War shoulder titles and 'Parkyn' is for shoulder-belt plates. But its importance goes beyond the antiquarian. The British Army is founded on a regimental system which, despite understandable controversy at times of change, evolves to reflect fresh requirements, new structures and shifts in recruiting patterns. At its best the system links past achievements to present organisations; brings together men and women of shared regional origins or functional specialisms; and encourages links between military units and local communities, helping to spread understanding of the army into civilian society.

A few of the insignia in this book will disappear even as it goes to press. Some infantry regiments are amalgamating, and the Territorial infantry, largely organised as multi cap badge units reflecting the amalgamation of Territorial battalions of regular regiments, is restructuring to conform to the Regular army's regimental structure once again. But if there are snapshots of the recent past, there are also images of a thriving present. The badges of the cavalry regiments amalgamated in 1993 bring together a heady mixture of old and new, and in harking back to a name which pre-dates the raising of hussar regiments in the British Army, the Light Dragoons gave an elegant example of how to use past glories to buttress future accomplishments.

Military readers will leaf through these pages in search of their own badges. There will be more smiles than frowns, for it is good to see just how many of the symbols that glinted on the caps of yesteryear have, with a variety of transformations, survived to the present. I was a private in the Essex Yeomanry, and there is its badge, motto proclaiming 'An ornament and a safeguard' although in truth I was neither. I wore the badge of Cambridge University OTC, though mine was bronze, not those lustrous beauties shown here. I commanded 2nd Battalion The Wessex Regiment: its fine Wyvern, such a striking piece of heraldry, now worn by the cadets of Exeter University OTC. Finally, the badge I wore in The Queen's Regiment lives on, with the addition of a Royal Hampshire rose, in The Princess of Wales's Royal Regiment. This has existed since 1992, but in 2004 it gave a remarkable display of sustained courage in Iraq, where Private Johnson Beharry earned the Victoria Cross. Its members have the nickname Tigers, and their tiger arm-badge originates in an award to the 67th Foot in 1826. Ancient virtues, modern valour, change and continuity: the proud symbols of a great army in a wonderful book.

© David Graeme-Baker

Introduction

As soldiers, we are often asked to stand in harm's way for others. It is what we do, be that in Sierra Leone, Afghanistan or Iraq. Soldiering in these operational situations demands a great deal and it would be wrong to assume that it is easy or even a natural act.
Major General Graeme Lamb CMG DSO OBE

The British Army is busier now that at any time since the Second World War. At the beginning of 2004, when research for this book began, 27,000 soldiers were on operations, reinforced by almost 3,000 reservists. In 2005 troops are deployed on operations worldwide; Northern Ireland, Kosovo, Bosnia and the Former Yugoslavian Republic of Macedonia, Afghanistan and Iraq; with United Nations missions in Cyprus, Sierra Leone, Georgia, the Democratic Republic of Congo, Liberia and Sudan; and in Garrisons in Brunei, Cyprus, Falkland Islands, Germany, Gibraltar, Nepal and in Great Britain. As I complete the book the Army's operational effort remains firmly focused on Iraq, centred on the UK-led Multi-National Division (South East). At the same time the Infantry is beginning a process of reorganisation that will result in the formation of new regiments and the loss of many of the current cap badges.

This record of British Army badges worn in 2004 is therefore dedicated to the British soldier. We serve our Regiment, our country and The Queen but we reflect society. If proof were needed that we reflect the best in society then one has to look no further than our young soldiers. Trooper Christopher Finney was awarded the George Cross and Private Johnson Beharry the Victoria Cross whilst I was researching this book.

THE BADGES

The best known military book of the 18th century, and one whose advice was widely respected (by the French, at least) was *The Continuation of the History of the late war in Germany between the King of Prussia and the Empress of Germany and her Allies* by Major General Henry Lloyd, published in London in 1781. With wide experience as a mercenary with Marshall Saxe at Fontenoy, with the Jacobites in 1745, the French army, the Austrian army, with Prince Ferdinand of Brunswick and finally in the Russian army, Lloyd wrote: 'I would recommend that a plate of brass be put on the hat, signifying the name or number of the regiment, battalion, and company, all of which would contribute to enforce discipline and valour'.

The type of cap badges worn by the Army in 2004 were introduced around 1897 in response to changes in uniform and headdress. In 1913, when the regiments of the Household Cavalry finally adopted khaki uniform for training in Great Britain, all regiments had a cap badge. Collar badges had generally been adopted in 1872, and shoulder titles in 1881.

The present anodised aluminium badges, known as Staybrite, are a by-product of the motor industry. In 1958 with discussions about the ending of National Service it was clear that an all-regular Army would not need to be kept busy with 'bulling' and a search began for low-maintenance items. Anodised aluminium was replacing chrome decoration on cars and seemed a natural choice. But the motor industry

Warrant Officer Class 1 wire embroidered rank badge for Mess Dress and a personalised version with added daffodils belonging to a Royal Signals Regimental Sergeant Major with Welsh connections.

has moved on, anodised aluminium is no longer manufactured and only a small stock remains. New bright metal is replacing anodised aluminium and some regiments either require or encourage soldiers to buy and to polish unofficial badges manufactured from nickel and gilding metal.

THE WEARERS

The British Army is composed of arms, corps and regiments from which units combine to supply the operational capabilities required. The number, types and organisation of arms, corps and regiments changes according to the guiding principle of fulfilling operational need. They also change role and structure; they may amalgamate, multiply or disband. Yet despite such changes, corps and regiments have, from the reputation of years and in many cases centuries of success in battle and other operations, acquired tremendous spirit and distinctive, often geographical, identity. In addition, British soldiers usually remain in the regiments and corps they joined as recruits, in many cases returning to the same operational units throughout their service, resulting in depths of familiarity and comradeship which give a unique edge to the morale and teamwork of the British soldier. The spirit is manifest in distinctive uniforms, emblems, music and other outward signs which contribute to the special pride British soldiers have in their corps and regiments.

ORDERS OF DRESS

Full Dress Worn by the Household Division and the Corps of Army Music, and (often purchased from Regimental funds) by Corps of Drums and Pipe Bands.
Number 1 Dress Blue Patrol jacket and regimental trousers or overalls.
Number 2 Dress Service Dress jacket and regimental trousers.
Barrack Dress Number 2 Dress or lightweight trousers with pullover or shirtsleeve order in place of the jacket.
Number 3 Dress White patrol jacket and regimental trousers.
Number 4 Dress Lightweight, stone coloured, Service Dress.
Number 6 Dress Lightweight, stone coloured, Bush jacket and trousers.
Number 8 Dress Combat 95.
Number 10 Dress Mess Dress.
Number 11 Dress Mess Dress with white Drill Jacket.
Number 12 Dress Coveralls.

The usual order of dress for the Army in 2005 is 'working dress', interpreted by most units as the loose light jacket and trousers made of disruptive pattern material (DPM) known officially as Number 8 Dress, and by soldiers as Combat 95. It has also unofficially replaced

Private Johnson Beharry VC The Princess of Wales's Royal Regiment (The Queen's and Royal Hampshires).
Photograph *Army*

Number 2 Dress, the khaki suit, for more formal duties to the extent that it is now commonly worn in offices and for parades, including the presentation of campaign medals. As a result the habit developed of wearing badges on Number 8 Dress which were in many cases designed for wear on Number 2 Dress.

Number 8 Dress includes a field jacket, or combat jacket. When the combat jacket is not worn it is usual to wear the sleeves of the shirt folded up which effectively removes the lower sleeve on which certain non-commissioned ranks wear rank badges. Number 8 Dress does not include epaulettes; rank badges for officers have been removed from the shoulder to the centre of the chest in the French style. Initially Warrant Officers, who did not have a lower sleeve on which to display their rank badges, and later all ranks, began to wear rank badges on officer style 'slides'. This caused some confusion between the ranks of major and Warrant Officer Class 2, both of whom wear a crown as a rank badge, though in most cases of different sizes. One notable exception is the Parachute Regiment whose field officers' crowns are as large as some warrant officers' crowns.

Number 2 Dress, known by officers as Service Dress, remains the usual dress uniform but is rarely worn other than for pass out parades

Trooper Christopher Finney GC The Blues and Royals.
Photograph *Army*

Soldiers enjoy wearing their qualification badges. The order to remove badges from Combat Dress has led some units to have rank slides woven with instructors' badges. Rank slides of a corporal skill at arms instructor and of a sergeant signals instructor.

at training units. In Number 2 Dress collar badges and officers' rank badges are usually metal; silver and gilt for officers and either anodised aluminium or the new bright metal for soldiers. Arm badges are usually woven, although there are some exceptions.

For those not in the Household Division but on public duties, Number 1 Dress, sometimes known as Blues, is worn, in which case arm badges are usually made of wire embroidery.

Mess Dress is worn by officers, warrant officers and senior NCOs and, in some regiments also, by junior NCOs. Badges, whilst following official patterns, sometimes reflect regimental custom to the extent that some regiments and corps wear wire embroidered badges whilst other regiments do not wear any insignia at all.

TYPES OF BADGES

Cap badges are worn on the regimental headdress which consists of the beret, the coloured Forage Cap and the regimental side hat, although Scottish regiments wear the Glengarry and Tam o'Shanter, and Irish regiments, the caubeen. A few regiments and corps, usually those dealing with horses, also wear the khaki Service Dress Cap.

Collar badges are worn by most regiments and corps on the closed collar of Number 1 Dress, and on the lapels of Number 2 and 4 Dress.

Rank badges are worn by officers on both epaulettes of Number 1, 2 and 4 Dress. Soldiers rank badges are worn on both sleeves of Number 2 Dress. In other orders of dress they are usually worn only on the right sleeve. The exception is Number 8 Dress where badges of rank are worn on a slide in the centre of the chest.

Shoulder titles are not much worn except by those who wear shirt-sleeve order. Rank slides, which often include the regimental or corps title, have replaced shoulder titles in common use.

Two new badges have been generally introduced since 2003. The Union Flag is being worn on the upper left sleeve and a regimental or corps-pattern Tactical Recognition Flash, or TRF, on the upper right sleeve of Number 8 Dress. In June 2002 the Chief of the General Staff gave direction on the wearing of badges on Combat 95 'the only qualification badges which may be worn on Combat 95 are Parachute/SAS wings on the upper right arm, Commando dagger on the upper left arm below any Formation badge, Explosive Ordnance Disposal (EOD) badge on the lower left arm and Ammunition Technician (AT)/Ammunition Technical Officer (ATO) badge on the lower right arm, and finally an Army Flying badge – wings – on the chest.

The Union Emblem is to be worn on the upper left arm above any Formation badge.

Only one Formation Badge – as authorised by the Army Dress Committee (ADC) – is to be worn at any one time, be it divisional, brigade, NATO or UN as appropriate and as directed by the Formation Commander. These badges are to be removed by individuals on posting, or on formal detachment from the formation concerned.

One regimental or corps-pattern Tactical Recognition Flash (TRF) – as authorised by the ADC – may be worn on the upper right arm below any Parachute/SAS qualification badge at the discretion of commanding officers. Drop Zone (DZ)/Landing Zone (LZ) flashes may continue to be worn by 16 Air Assault Brigade personnel in lieu of TRFs, providing authority is given by the Brigade Commander, agreed to by the respective regimental/corps Dress Committee and endorsed by the ADC. Apart from the Parachute Regiment, DZ/LZ flashes (when worn) are to be replaced with the appropriate regimental/corps TRF on posting out of 16 Air Assault Brigade.

The current arrangement where regiments and corps have the choice between issued disruptive pattern material (DPM) slides and customised or regimentally-procured slides may continue, except that only DPM slides are to be worn in the field on training and operations.'

CGS further directed that 'Stable belts may be worn with No 8 Dress at the discretion of individual units but not in the field on training or operations, this accords with the dispensation given for the wearing of customised rank slides, and that gorget patches (red tabs) are not to be worn on No 8 Dress at any time.'

Acknowledgements

ADVICE TO BADGE COLLECTORS

Many Regiments will sell badges through their PRI, the regimental shop, but are reluctant to give items away as stocks are bought from regimental funds for the benefits of soldiers. Write to the regiment's PRI rather than to the Quartermaster. Most regiments have their address on a website.

ROBIN HODGES
Headquarters EUFOR Althea
Sarajevo 2005

My thanks go to all the officers and soldiers who have assisted in compiling this book. Many of them have allowed their badges to be photographed, others have allowed me to quiz them on their knowledge of regimental history. Those who have given me extra time, and often entrusted badges to me for recording, are acknowledged on the various regimental pages.

The Commander in Chief, General Sir Tim Granville-Chapman KCB CBE ADC Gen offered me his support and advised on the first draft of the book.

General Sir Tim Granville-Chapman
KCB CBE ADC Gen.

Captain Morgan O'Neill, formerly of the Irish Guards, has been spectacularly helpful in allowing me access to his amazing collection of cloth badges. Cloth badges have been worn since at least AD 286–305; a mosaic from that period survives showing a Roman soldier wearing the ivy leaf shoulder patch of the Imperial Herculii Legion. As far as I can tell it is about the only badge Captain O'Neill does not have in his collection.

Mr Tony Kelly of Firmins, the company which has held a warrant from the Crown since 1677 to provide insignia, was terrifically helpful in allowing access to the company's patterns of hard-to-find badges. (Incidentally Firmins holds the second-oldest warrant to the Ministry of Defence. The oldest is apparently an engineering firm which has held a warrant to make cannon balls since the reign of Henry VIII in the 16th Century).

Mr James Scheck of Toye, Kenning and Spencer Ltd allowed me access to the Company's pattern room where I was able to photograph a wide variety of cloth badges early in my work when I was still casting around trying to define the left and right of arc for the research. Collectors should be warned that, from what I saw, there is a wide variety of military-looking badges produced for other organisations, including the mercenary units created to be combated by James Bond!

WO2 Paul Spafford based at the Defence Logistics Organisation, Caversfield was invaluable in providing access to many of the Full Dress badges which the Army holds in stock and Mr Steve Cooke at RMA Sandhurst allowed me to photograph the officers' cap and collar badges he issues to tailors for the new subalterns' uniforms.

Mr Robert Lamble of Intramark Limited and the Honourable Artillery Company allowed me access to the Company's stocks of wire-embroidered badges and warned me about the 'bullshit brigade', those individuals with a tenuous link to the Army – or no link at all – who have badges privately manufactured. Collectors beware.

As I was completing the project Mr Gary Gibbs the Editorial Director of *Regiment* magazine and author of 'Badge Notes' published in the quarterly *Bulletin of the Military Historical Society*, was unreserved in offering advice and allowed me to photograph some of the Territorial Army badges which I had not tracked down elsewhere.

Most of all my thanks go to the ladies of the Hodges family who have supported their men through two world wars and innumerable tours of duty in Northern Ireland. My wife, Sarah, has always been the model of an army wife and my perfect supporter whilst researching this book as in everything else. My mother, a war widow, my father having died as a result of his wounds, has seen both her sons and both her grandsons become soldiers in their turn, and has always encouraged me even to the extent of acting as proof-reader.

Finally, to all those Regimental Quartermaster Sergeants who have said, 'You'll never get them all sir':

I'm sure you're right.

BRITISH ARMY BADGES

Household Cavalry

The Household Cavalry consists of The Life Guards and The Blues and Royals. In 1992 the regiments formed a union; Squadrons from both regiments now man the Household Cavalry Regiment, or HCR, which operates as a force reconnaissance regiment, and the Household Cavalry Mounted Regiment, or HCMR, which carries out ceremonial State and Public Duties.

All ranks of The Life Guards and The Blues and Royals wear the Household Cavalry cap badge in the Forage Cap. Regimental badges are worn on the Service Dress Cap and beret except by officers of The Life Guards who wear a wire embroidered Household Cavalry badge on the beret.

The Household Cavalry cap badge was introduced in 1913 with the cypher to be changed with the accession of each sovereign. The crown changed from the Tudor (or King's) Crown to the St Edward's (or Queen's) Crown on the accession of Elizabeth II in 1953. The badge issued to recruits is anodised aluminium, on joining the Household Cavalry Regiment soldiers are required to buy and polish a gilding metal badge.

During the Second World War the Household Cavalry followed precedent set in earlier wars and formed composite regiments. The 1st Household Cavalry Regiment served with 2nd Polish Corps under General Wladyslaw Anders in Italy and was awarded the distinction of wearing the Syrena from the Arms of Warsaw as an arm badge. The badge was to be worn only by those who had served in the regiment. It appears to have survived worn by Major Eric Sant, who joined the regiment in 1943, until he retired in 1977 (see The Queen's Royal Hussars p.30).

1

2

3

4

5

In Review Order, officers' rank badges are fitted to the shoulder cord of their plaited aiguillettes, made from 15 Ligne Gold Wire Basket Cord, which end in two coils and gilt Trophy Tags. They are backed with scarlet cloth for The Life Guard officers and black cloth for officers of The Blues and Royals.

For soldiers, the aiguillettes themselves indicate rank. Warrant Officers wear plaited aiguillettes made from 11 Ligne Gold Wire Basket Cord which, as for officers, end in coils and gilt Trophy Tags.

Ranks from Lance Corporal of Horse to Staff Corporal wear plaited aiguillettes with shoulder cords ending in gilt Trophy Tags without the coils.

Lance Corporals wear plaited aiguillettes without shoulder cords. Troopers do not wear aiguillettes.

The soldiers from the Household Cavalry Regiment assigned to 16 Air Assault Brigade wore a blue-red-blue Landing Zone (LZ) Flash, originally introduced as a Drop Zone (DZ) Flash for parachute trained troops. It has evolved into a better quality badge worn by all-ranks as the Household Cavalry's Tactical Recognition Flash. It is the same design but larger than the TRF worn by The Guards Division.

opposite

Forage Cap badges

1 Officer's gilt and enamel badge 2.5 × 4 cm.
2 Soldier's anodised aluminium badge 2.5 × 4 cm.
3 Private purchase gilding metal badge 2.5 × 4 cm.

4 Tpr Paul Jones The Blues and Royals and Tpr Ritesh Raj The Life Guards wearing Mounted Review Order Dismounted, their ranks indicated by the absence of aiguillettes.

this page

5 Officer and warrant officer's helmet plate worn curved to fit the helmet 18.5 × 16.5 cm.
6 Soldier's helmet plate curved to fit the helmet 15.5 × 17 cm.
7 Soldier's gilding metal waist belt clasp 8 × 5.5 cm.

6

7

8

9

10

11

12

The Household Cavalry has unique non-commissioned ranks:

* Lance Corporals (LCpl) wear two chevrons and the Crown,
* Lance Corporal of Horse (LCoH) (equivalent to corporal) three chevrons (khaki – known as Gold – for the combat rank slide) and the Crown,
* Corporal of Horse (CoH) (equivalent to sergeant) three chevrons (black for the combat rank slide) and the Crown.

All three ranks wear their badges of rank 'above the elbow' and are called 'Corporal' whilst those who wear their rank badges below the elbow are called 'Corporal Major'.

Staff Corporal (SCpl) (equivalent to staff sergeant) four inverted chevrons and the Crown.

As the Household Cavalry does not use the title of sergeant, Warrant Officers Class 2 fill appointments such as Squadron Corporal Major (SCM) and regimental Quartermaster Corporal (RQMC), whilst Warrant Officers Class 1 may be appointed Regimental Corporal Major (RCM).

The rank of Lance Corporal of Horse was approved in 1971 when all Household Division recruits began training at The Guards Depot, Pirbright. The Foot Guards lance sergeants (equivalent to corporal) had membership of the Sergeants Mess whilst Household Cavalry corporals did not. The rank of Lance Corporals of Horse conferred membership of the Sergeants Mess.

Household Cavalry ranks are little known to the majority of the Army and it is said that when Private Driver, a driver in the Royal Logistic Corps, was behind a Household Cavalry non-commissioned officer booking in at Sennelager Training Centre in Germany. The non-commissioned officer reported himself to the sergeant major as 'Corporal of Horse'. Private Driver found himself locked up when he announced himself as 'Driver of Truck'.

13

14

15

16

17

18

opposite

8 Soldier's Full Dress cartouche. Issued with a shaped red felt backing to the Royal Arms badge, The Life Guards trim the backing to the exact size of the badge whilst The Blues and Royals remove the backing completely.

HCMR employment badges worn by soldiers below the rank of Corporal of Horse on the upper right arm on Number 1 Dress. The badges are also woven in brown on khaki and in anodised aluminium for Number 2 Dress (see Royal Horse Artillery p14).

9 Class B1 Mounted Dutyman 6.5 × 5.5 cm introduced in 1944 and authorised for all Class B Trades and therefore it should be the most common of all employment badges but it is rarely worn by units other than the Household Cavalry.

10 Class B3 Mounted Dutyman 6.5 × 5.5 cm introduced in 2002.

11 Farrier 5.25 × 5.5 cm, originally worn as a cap badge by farriers. The Blues and Royals wear the badge on a red background.

12 Saddle and Harness Maker 5.25 × 5.75 cm originally an RA and RE badge introduced for the Household Cavalry in 1923.

this page

13 Riding Instructor badge 5.25 × 7.25 cm introduced in 1865.

14 CoH Des Payne wearing the Riding Instructor badge.

15 Obsolete DZ Flash 7 × 7 cm.

16 TRF 7 × 7 cm.

17 WO2 Dean Gray and SCpl Wayne Burton wear maroon berets as qualified parachutists, and parachute wings above the Household Cavalry TRF on their right sleeves.

18 Gold rank badges worn by officers on the blue epaulette and silver badges on the gold epaulette.

19

The official London residences of the Sovereign, from Henry VIII to the present day, have been the Palace of Whitehall (to 1699), St James's Palace (to 1762) and Buckingham Palace, originally known as Buckingham House. The only access to St James's and Buckingham Palace before 1841 was through Horse Guards; The Mall was closed at both ends until the opening of Trafalgar Square in that year.

Horse Guards is named after the troops who have mounted the Queen's Life Guard on that spot since the Restoration of King Charles II in 1660. Horse Guards remains the official entrance to St James's and Buckingham Palace and is why The Queen's Life Guard is still mounted there. Apart from members of the Royal Family or cavalrymen on duty, everyone needs the Sovereign's permission in the form of an Ivory Pass to either drive or ride through Horse Guards.

When The Queen is in London, the Long Guard consists of an Officer, a Corporal Major (who carries the Standard), two Non-Commissioned Officers, a Trumpeter and 10 Troopers.

When Her Majesty is not resident in London, the Short Guard is reduced to two Non-Commissioned Officers and 10 Troopers. In early times the Guard could be up to 100 strong and provided Escorts to accompany the Sovereign if travelling by road.

Gold Stick was first appointed in 1678 from one of the Captains of his Horse Guards as personal bodyguard to the Sovereign. His assistant, Silver Stick, was appointed at the same time.

The token of office is an ebony staff with a gold head engraved with the Royal Cypher and Crown. Since the 18th century, the appointments of Gold Stick and Gold Stick-in-Waiting have been shared in rotation by the Colonels of The Life Guards and the Royal Horse Guards, now The Blues and Royals. Gold Stick for Scotland, first appointed in the 1820s, is invariably the Captain-General of The Sovereign's Body Guard for Scotland, The Royal Company of Archers.

With the elevation of the Royal Horse Guards to Household Cavalry in 1815, the Commanding Officers of the regiments took turns holding the office of Silver Stick. Since the Second World War, the office has been held by the colonel commanding the Household Cavalry.

20

19 CoH Chris Newell and Nigel Saunders escorting the Sovereign's Standard of The Life Guards carried by WO1 (RCM) Kev Poynter, and WO2 (RQMC) Chris Elliott carrying the Sovereign's Standard of The Blues and Royals escorted by LCoH Bob Blackwood and LCpl Chris Eade.

20 Captain Charlie Trietline wearing the Frock Coat with the Household Cavalry cap badge worn on the Forage Cap.

Acknowledgement
Lt Col Christopher Anderson, Captain Julian Speers, WO1(RCM) Kev Poynter, WO2 (RQMC) Darren Carter, CoH H Halfhide and LCoH Geno Watkins

The Life Guards

The Life Guards was raised in 1660. A and B Squadrons The Life Guards serve with the Household Cavalry Regiment as Force Reconnaissance squadrons, and The Life Guards Mounted Squadron serves with the Household Cavalry Mounted Regiment carrying out State and Public Duties.

The Life Guards, or LG, cap badge was introduced in 1913, with the cypher changed with the accession of each sovereign, and crown changed from the Tudor (or King's) Crown to St Edward's (or Queen's) Crown on the accession of Elizabeth II in 1953. The badge is worn on the Service Dress cap, and on the beret when it is worn on a square of Household Division silk. The Household Cavalry badge is worn on the Forage Cap.

Until 1913 the Household Cavalry were distinguished by their uniform and did not require cap badges. They were issued khaki service dress for annual training that year and a bronze cap badge was chosen. In 1915 2nd Life Guards polished their badges, a practice which was continued by The Life Guards on amalgamation of 1st and 2nd Life Guards in 1922.

Non-Commissioned Officers, or NCO, wear a St Edward's (or Queen's) Crown above their rank badges; anodised aluminium for all ranks except Lance Corporals of Horse, who wear a worsted Crown. The custom may date from 1815 when Lord Harrington, the Colonel, ordered that Crowns be worn by the NCOs of the 1st Life Guards after the victory at the Battle of Waterloo

There is no title on the rank slide. Squadron officers wear black Garter stars and Field officers wear the Tudor (or King's) Crown. Lieutenant Colonel Anthony De Ritter, the last Commanding

1

2

3

4

5

6

7

8

Officer of The Life Guards, introduced the rank slide in 1991 in order to differentiate from the slide worn by The Blues and Royals. The black rank badges were previously worn by the Regiment in Borneo between 1962 and 1964.

The Household Cavalry traditionally provided soldiers to the Guards Independent Parachute Company which acted as Pathfinders for the Parachute Brigade. When the Company was disbanded The Life Guard's Commanding Officer, Lieutenant Colonel James Ellery maintained a parachute capability.

One squadron of the Household Cavalry Regiment is now allocated to 16 Air Assault Brigade for operations and all ranks wear the brigade's maroon beret when deployed, at other times the regiment's blue beret is worn except by those who are parachute trained who always wear the airborne forces maroon beret.

Household Cavalry, rather than regimental, badges are worn in Review Order with the exception that officers wear a regimental waist belt clasp with both the gold and buff belts, and the officer's cartouche is ornamented with a regimental badge. The soldier's Household Cavalry cartouche has the Coat of Arms badge mounted on a red felt backing.

12

13

9

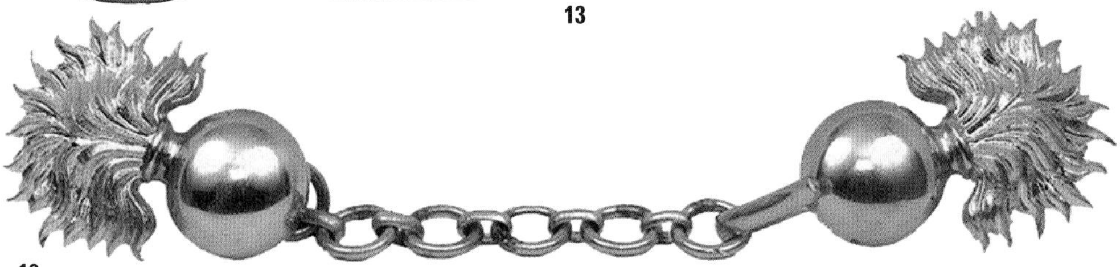

10

11

previous page

1 Officer's wire-embroidered beret badge 2.75 × 4.5 cm.

2 Soldier's anodised aluminium cap badge 2.5 × 3.75 cm.

3 Private purchase gilding metal badge 2.5 × 3.75 cm.

4 Lt Nicholas Bacon wearing the embroidered beret badge on the Household Division silk backing.

5 LCoH Swiny Swinburne, a regimental Policeman, wearing the gilding metal badge on the Household Division silk backing, and the Household Cavalry TRF. His rank slide, for a rank equivalent to a corporal, includes a regimental Police badge.

6 Cloth shoulder title worn by soldiers on Number 2 Dress 12.75 × 4.5 cm.

7 The Life Guards button.

8 Sand coloured cloth shoulder title. It is reported that samples were produced for all Household Division regiments in the 1990s but not issued although examples of those for The Life Guards, Grenadier Guards and Welsh Guards are available.

this page

9 NCO's anodised aluminium regimental rank. Crown 3 × 2.75 cm worn by all ranks from Lance Corporal to Staff Corporal except Lance Corporal of Horse who wear the cloth Crown.

10 Officer's cloak chain. Grenades 4 × 5.5 cm.

11 Officer's cartouche 22.5 × 9.5 cm, badge 13.5 × 9 cm. Soldiers wear the Household Cavalry cartouche with the badge backed with red felt.

12 LCpl Mikey Partridge parades in Dismounted Review Order wearing the Household Cavalry helmet and waist belt clasp. His scarlet tunic and white plume indicate his regiment. His rank is indicated by plaited aiguillettes without shoulder cords. Photograph *HCMR*

13 Lieutenant Colonel's worsted rank slide with the Tudor (or King's) Crown and captain's obsolete combat slide with coloured insert.

14 Officer's waist belt clasp 8.25 × 5.5 cm worn with both the gold and buff belts. Soldiers wear the Household Cavalry clasp.

Lineage The Life Guards (1661).

14

The Blues and Royals

Royal Horse Guards and 1st Dragoons

The Blues and Royals was formed in 1969 by the amalgamation of the Royal Horse Guards (The Blues) with The Royal Dragoons (1st Dragoons). C and D Squadrons The Blues and Royals serve with the Household Cavalry Regiment as Force Reconnaissance squadrons, and The Blues and Royals Mounted Squadron with the Household Cavalry Mounted Regiment carrying out State and Public Duties

1

2

3

The Blues and Royals bronze cap badge, based on the design of the Royal Horse Guards badge, was introduced on amalgamation in 1969. The badge is worn on the Service Dress cap and on the beret, when it is worn on a square of Household Division silk. The Household Cavalry badge is worn on the Forage Cap.

Non-Commissioned Officers, or NCO, wear the same St Edward's (or Queen's) Crown above their rank badges as The Life Guards; anodised aluminium for all ranks except Lance Corporal of Horse who wear a worsted Crown. The badges differ from those of The Life Guards by having black cloth backing adopted from The Royals, which had followed that custom since at least 1900.

Until 1913 the Household Cavalry were distinguished by their uniform and did not require cap badges. They were issued khaki service dress for annual training that year and a bronze cap badge was chosen. In 1915 2nd Life Guards polished their badges, a practice which was continued by The Life Guards on amalgamation of 1st and 2nd Life Guards in 1922, leaving the Royal Horse Guards as the only Household Cavalry regiment with bronze badges. The Blues and Royals continued the practice on amalgamation in 1969.

There is no title on the rank slide. Squadron officers wear the Garter star and Field officers wear St Edward's (or Queen's) Crown.

In the Household Cavalry Regiment, or HCR, soldiers wear the waist belt clasp with a white plastic belt and with the buff belt in the Household Cavalry Mounted Regiment.

5

6

The Royal Horse Guards trace their origins to Colonel Unton Crooke's Horse of the Parliamentarian New Model Army raised in 1643. In 1661 the regiment was accepted for service by Charles II under the command of the Earl of Oxford who dressed them in blue uniforms; gaining them the title The Blues.

4

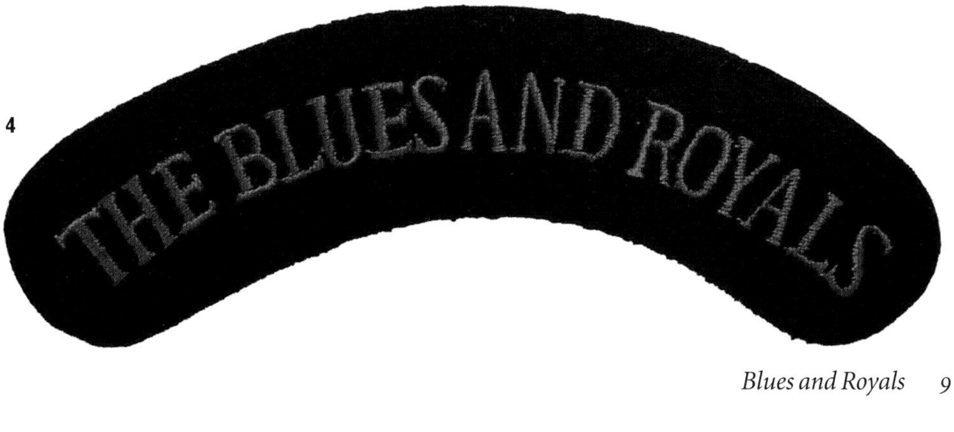

7

8

10

12

The Blues were appointed to the Household Cavalry for their conduct during the Battle of Waterloo in 1815, and their Colonel, The Duke of Wellington, appointed Gold Stick in 1820.

9

The black cloth backing to the regimental Rank Badge and rank badges is said within the regiment to commemorate the defeat by The Royal Dragoons of a regiment of 'Black Muskateers' at the Battle of Dettingen in 1743.

The regimental museum suggests that whilst the black cloth backings could be worn in memory of these killed at the Battle of Dettingen, there was a belief in The Royal Dragoons that the backing was in memory of Second Lieutenant John Spencer Dunville VC who died of wounds in 1917.

Alternatively, and possibly the most likely reason, is that the black cloth reflects the black plume worn on the helmet by The Royals in full dress.

11

During the Battle of Waterloo in 1815, Captain Clarke and Corporal Stiles of The Royals captured the Eagle of the 105ème Régiment d'infanterie de ligne. The Royals were granted the Eagle as a badge in 1838 and it was adopted as the officers' collar badge in 1887, and for soldiers in 1898. In 1948 the Eagle was adopted as The Royal Dragoons cap badge.

All ranks of The Blues and Royals wear a wire-embroidered Imperial Eagle badge on their left sleeves. (See Royal Scots Dragoon Guards p22).

13

14

15

16

17

18

Lineage The Blues and Royals (Royal Horse Guards and 1st Dragoons) (1969), from the Royal Horse Guards (1661) and The Royal Dragoon (1st Dragoons) (1661).

previous page

1 Officer's wire-embroidered beret badge 2.75 × 4.25 cm.

2 Soldier's issue cap badge 2.75 × 3.75 cm in a bronzed finish.

3 Soldier's private purchase bronzed cap badge 2.75 × 3.75 cm with polished highlights.

4 Cloth shoulder title worn by soldiers in Number 2 Dress 12.75 × 4.5 cm.

5 Cornet Lorian McCallum wearing the wire-embroidered beret badge.

6 LCpl Craig Trencher, wearing Parachute wings and Household Cavalry TRF, wears a maroon beret at all times as a qualified parachutist, whilst CoH David Carrington, identified by black chevrons, wears the regiment's blue beret.

opposite page

7 NCO's anodised aluminium regimental rank badge on a black backing 3 × 2.75 cm worn by all ranks from Lance Corporal to Staff Corporal except Lance Corporal of Horse who wear the cloth Crown.

8 Officers rank badges – Tudor (or King's) Crown and Garter Star.

9 Tpr Kev Doran wearing Mounted Review Order on Queen's Life Guard.

10 Imperial Eagle wire-embroidered arm badge 4.75 × 6 cm.

11 Tpr Jeff Capes wearing Dismounted Review Order on Queen's Life Guard. The Blues and Royals Eagle badge is worn on his left arm.

12 Corporal of Horse rank badge worn in Barrack Dress and Coveralls.

13 LCoH Andy Anderson wearing No 2 Dress with the Household Cavalry Forage Cap badge. His regimental rank badge, the Crown, is on a black background and worn below the Imperial Eagle badge.

14 Lieutenant colonel's rank slide

15 Blues and Royals button.

this page

16 Officer's cartouche 16.25 × 8.5 cm, badge 10.5 × 7 cm. The cartouche is issued with the badge backed with red felt, which has to be removed. Soldiers wear the Household Cavalry cartouche (see The Household Cavalry).

17 The Blues and Royals officer's buff belt waist belt clasp 8 × 5.5 cm and gold belt waist belt clasp 6.5 × 5.25 cm. Soldiers wear the Household Cavalry clasp.

18 Officer's cloak chain. Roses 3.5 cm.

Royal Horse Artillery

Two troops of Horse Artillery were formed in 1793 to support the cavalry. In 1924 the Royal Regiment of Artillery was reorganised, and the title and precedence of the Royal Horse Artillery were retained.

The Royal Horse Artillery, or RHA, cap badge, the Sovereign's Crown and Cypher, was taken into use by Batteries in India in the 1930s. The present anodised aluminium badge, surmounted by St Edward's (or Queen's) Crown, was introduced in 1958 for wear in the beret. The Royal Artillery badge is worn on the Forage Cap. Non-Commissioned Officers serving in 1st Regiment, or 1 RHA, are encouraged to wear a private purchase silver cap badge.

There is a belief amongst some Gunners that The King's Troop wears pre-1953 Tudor (or King's) Crown badges. However The Troop is issued the standard Royal Artillery and Royal Horse Artillery badges, although a blind eye is turned towards those who wear old badges.

Officers' wear wire-embroidered beret badges with different coloured centres, 1st and The King's Troop blue, 3rd red and 7th maroon.

Soldiers also wear the Royal Horse Artillery cypher as a collar badge. Officers wear Royal Artillery collar badges.

1

2

There is a belief in the Royal Regiment that the coloured backings of the officers' embroidered badges reflect the underlying material that can be seen through the void centres of the soldiers' metal cyphers. However informed sources suggest that whilst the blue backing is the natural colour, the red backing of the 3rd Regiment is in recognition of the action by J (Sidi Rezegh) Battery in 1942 during which Second Lieutenant George Ward Gunn won the Victoria Cross. This is disputed by other authorities.

In 1977, 7th Regiment, which traces its history to the Second World War 33rd Airborne Light Regiment RA, became a Field Regiment and consequently replaced its maroon airborne beret with a blue beret. In recognition of its service as an airborne regiment it adopted a maroon backing to the officer's embroidered badge. In 1984 the regiment again became a parachute unit and readopted the maroon beret, retaining the maroon backing to the officer's cypher.

3

4

5

6

1

2

3

4

5

7

8

6

opposite page

1 RHA soldier's anodised aluminium cap and collar badges 2.5 × 3.75 cm.

2 LBdr Kerry Fletcher 1 RHA wearing combat dress.

3 1 RHA private purchase silver badge 2.5 × 3.75 cm

4 RHA ball button.

5 Shoulder title 2.75 × 1 cm.

6 Cloth shoulder title 12 × 4.5 cm thought to have been produced to match the cloth titles worn by other Household troops on No 2 Dress but not yet issued.

this page

RHA officers' bullion beret badges 3 ×4cm.

1 1st Regiment and The King's Troop – blue centre.

2 3rd Regiment – red centre.

3 7th (Parachute) Regiment – maroon centre.

4 Officer's red backed side hat badge 3.25 × 4 cm.

5 Bdr Kate Russell wearing the RA cap badge with RHA collar badges. The metal spur badge indicates that she qualified as a riding instructor in The King's Troop.

6 Waist belt clasp 7 × 5.75 cm.

7 Warrant Officer Class 2 rank slide

8 Gnr Eddie Lilo 1 RHA wearing the RA TRF on his right sleeve and the 1st Mechanised Brigade badge below the Union Flag on his left.

Lineage Royal Horse Artillery (1793)

The King's Troop Royal Horse Artillery

For many years before 1939 the Royal Artillery maintained a battery at St John's Wood Barracks in London to carry out ceremonial duties, wearing Full Dress uniform, which had become obsolete in 1914.

After the War in 1945 King George VI asked for a battery again to be assigned to ceremonial duties. The Army was completely mechanised and therefore a new horsed battery had to be formed which was given the revived title The Riding Troop Royal Horse Artillery. The Troop had originally been responsible for training cadets in equitation at the Royal Military Academy Woolwich. On his first visit to The Troop in 1947 the King crossed out 'Riding' in the visitors book and wrote in 'King's'. On acceding to the throne Queen Elizabeth II asked that the name, The King's Troop, be retained in memory of her father.

6

1

4

7

2

3

5

8

1

2

3

4

5

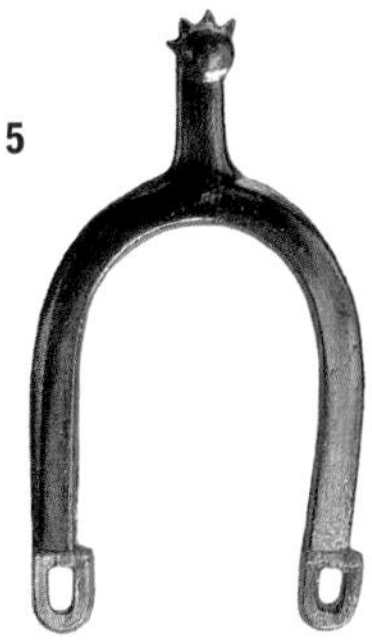

6

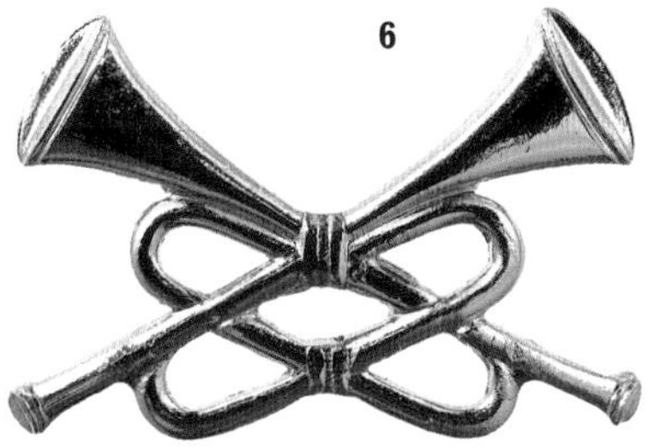

7

opposite page

1 Trumpet Major appointment badge 8 × 5.25 cm.
2 Trumpeter's appointment badge 8 × 5.25 cm.
3 Trumpet Major Rod Jeffries MBE MSM in Full Dress.
4 RHA staff sergeant's rank with the Crown and Gun embroidered together.
5 Captains Rob Batson and Ed Botterill, the Full Dress busbies have prominent plumes which are used as visual signals when the head is nodded.
6 Riding Instructor's appointment badge 5.25 × 7.5 cm.
7 Farrier's appointment badge 5.25 × 5.75 cm.
8 RHA staff seregeant riding instructor full dress rank badges.

this page

1 RHA officer's shabraque badge 16 × 6.75 cm, worn on each side with the gun facing forward.

RHA No 2 Dress Appointment Badges.

2 Saddle and Harness Maker badge 3.5 × 3.75 cm introduced by 1865.
3 Farrier's badge 3 × 3.25 cm, originally worn as a cap badge by farriers, introduced by 1865.
4 Wheelwright badge 3.5 cm, introduced by 1886.
5 Riding Instructor badge 2.5 × 4.5 cm introduced by 1865.
6 Trumpeter badge 5 × 3.25 cm introduced by 1865.
7 RHA officer's Full Dress pouch 17.5 × 11 cm.

Acknowledgement
SSgt (BQMS) Graeme Innes

7th (Parachute) Regiment Royal Horse Artillery

7th (Parachute) Regiment, or 7 RHA, wears the maroon beret with the Royal Horse Artillery cypher cap badge; in the case of officers, wire-embroidered on a maroon backing.

Originally officers and Non-Commissioned Officers wore the Pegasus badge on the left sleeve of Number 2 Dress. The badge was adopted in 1977 when the regiment left 16 Independent Parachute Brigade to become a field regiment. The badge is now worn by all ranks.

The regiment wears a Drop Zone flash, which has been adopted as the Royal Artillery Tactical Recognition Flash and was worn by 1st Regiment Royal Horse Artillery in Iraq in 2004.

1

3

5

1 7 RHA and 21 Air Assault Battery DZ flash 7×7 cm adopted as the RA TRF.

2 Major Gerry Porter MBE wears the 7th (Parachute) Regiment RHA maroon beret and RHA ball buttons. The Commando Fighting Knife badge shows that he has also served with 29 Commando Regiment RA.

3 WO2 Neil Radford wearing 7 RHA No. 1 Dress. He is wearing the RMA Sandhurst waist belt clasp often worn by instructors.

4 Bdr Dean Daley wearing the DZ flash, and Gnr Paul Cast, both 7 RHA.

5 Airborne Forces Bellerophon astride Pegasus badge worn by all ranks of 7 RHA on the upper left sleeve of No. 2 Dress 4.5 ×4.5 cm.

2

4

ROYAL ARMOURED CORPS

The Royal Armoured Corps was formed in 1939 as an administrative grouping of cavalry regiments and the Royal Tank Regiment.

The Royal Armoured Corps badge was introduced in 1941 and worn by war-raised regiments of the Royal Armoured Corps. After the end of the Second World War it was worn by a succession of units including the RAC Junior Leaders, the RAC Parachute Squadron and latterly the Special Reconnaissance Squadron RAC. At present the anodised aluminium badges remain available but unissued to a unit, although the Armour Centre has used them for presentations.

1

2

1 Royal Armoured Corps Special Reconnaissance Squadron anodised aluminium cap badge 4 × 5 cm and collar badges 3 × 3.75 cm.
2 RAC button.

Acknowledgement Mr Terry Chapman

Armour Centre

The Royal Armoured Corps and the 9th/12th Royal Lancers, or 9/12 L, share the red and yellow diagonal square as a recognition badge. In 1995 the 9/12 L were in Bosnia Herzegovina and had brassards with the coloured square manufactured for what was known by NATO as BRITCAVBAT, standing for British Cavalry Battalion. Similar recognition flashes had also been worn by the former RAC Junior Leaders Regiment. The Regimental Police at the Armour Centre wear the obsolete badge as a Tactical Recognition Flash.

Non-commissioned officers selected as 'Schools Instructor' wear the highly prized instructor's nametape on the edge of a slide.

1

3

4

2

5

1 Armour Centre Regimental Police TRF 5 × 5 cm.
2 Armour Centre 'Schools Instructor' name tape worn sewn onto a slide 18 × 3 cm.
3 Schools Instructor appointment slide.
4 Regimental Police appointment slide.
5 Tpr Nicki Smith in training and SSgt 'Ted' Heath Youd a 'Schools Instructor' at the Armour Centre.

1st The Queen's Dragoon Guards

'The Welsh Cavalry'

1st The Queen's Dragoon Guards was formed in 1959 by the amalgamation of the two senior regiments of the Cavalry of the Line, 1st King's Dragoon Guards and the Queen's Bays (2nd Dragoon Guards).

The Queen's Dragoon Guards, or QDG, adopted the Imperial Eagle, formerly the badge of the 1st King's Dragoon Guards, or KDG, on amalgamation in 1959. The cap badge is the double-headed eagle taken from the arms of Emperor Francis Joseph I of Austria who was Colonel in Chief from 1896, when cap badges in their modern form were being introduced, until the outbreak of war in 1914. The KDG exchanged the Eagle badge for a simple star design badge between 1915 and 1937 because of anti-German feeling during and after the First World War.

Soldiers are issued badges produced in anodised aluminium but they are required to buy a silver metal badge and to polish off the Coat of Arms on the Eagle's breast. The reason given being that it is an attempt to remove the dishonour of having a German Colonel-in-Chief during the First World War.

The collar badge is the same design as that worn by The Bays from about 1884 until 1959. The wreath is officially described as laurel but is of bay leaves; bay belonging to the laurel family.

The regimental rank badge, worn by corporals and above, is based upon the design of that worn by The Bays. At least one 'family' Bays rank badge is still worn by a serving Warrant Officer on Number 2 Dress. Four chevrons distinguish Staff Sergeants holding the appointment of Squadron Quartermaster Sergeant. Lance corporals are distinguished by wearing two chevrons.

A Tactical Recognition Flash in the regimental colours, Royal blue, white, Royal blue, was approved in 2000 but has not yet been taken into use.

1

2

3

4

5

6

The name 'Bays' originated as a nickname for the regiment in the mid-eighteenth century when it was mounted on bay horses. The name became so fixed that it was the name by which the regiment was universally identified and in 1870 'Bays' was incorporated into the official title.

During operations in Iraq in 2003 C Squadron supported 3 Commando Brigade. The commandos referred to the Squadron as the 'Commando Light Horse'. In recognition of their service they were awarded the 3 Commando Brigade Flash to be worn on the right sleeve.

From about 1943 The King's Dragoon Guards had a nice custom of permitting sergeants commanding Troops, when there were no subalterns, to wear an officer's cap badge as a rank badge.

9

15

7

8

10

11

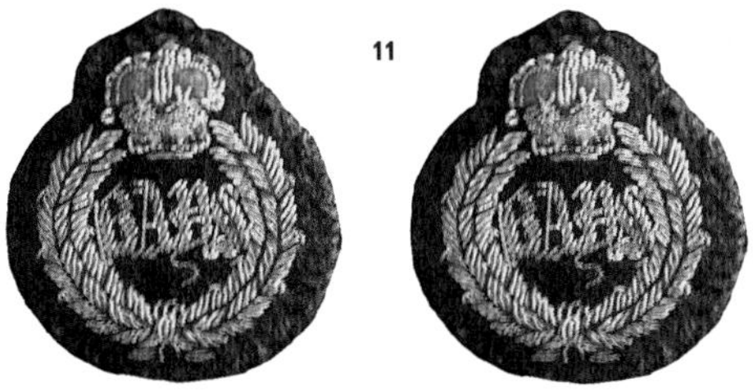

12

13

14

opposite page

1 The Queen's Dragoon Guards soldier's anodised aluminium cap badge 3.25 × 3.75 cm and collar badges 3 × 3.25 cm.

2 Officer's silver cap badge 3.5 × 3.75 cm and bronze collar badges 3 × 3.5 cm.

3 Sgt Paul Jones wearing No 2 Dress with the regimental rank badge above his chevrons. On his right forearm is the crossed rifles badge of a Skill-at-Arms Instructor. He is wearing a sword belt whilst under instruction on the Drill Course.

4 Officers and Senior NCO's woven title, 5 × 3.25 cm.

5 Anodised aluminium shoulder title 2.5 × 1 cm.

6 QDG button.

this page

7 Private purchase white metal badge 3.25 × 3.5 cm.

8 Officer's silver badge with the Coat of Arms polished off 3.25 × 3.75 cm.

9 Lt Col David Norris OBE wearing No. 1 Dress with silver cap badge, wire-embroidered collar badges and metal shoulder title.

10 Officer's wire-embroidered beret badge 4 × 4 cm.

11 No 1 Dress wire-embroidered collar badges 3.25 × 4 cm.

12 WO1 (RSM) AD Bowtell wearing the wire-embroidered beret badge.

13 Captain Simon Farebrother MC wearing No 1 Dress.

14 Corporal and lance corporal's rank slides differentiated by the regimental badge.

15 Sgt Robert Chubb wearing combat dress with the polished cap badge.

Lineage 1st The Queen's Dragoon Guards (1959), from 1st King's Dragoon Guards (1685) and The Queen's Bays (2nd Dragoon Guards) (1685)

16

21

22

18

17

19

20

16 Sgts Ian Rees and Christopher Edwards escorting WO2 Ian Coles carrying the regimental Standard.

17 SSgt Giles Powell wearing the four chevrons of a Squadron Quartermaster Sergeant below the regimental rank badge.

18 QDG No 2 Dress regimental rank badge 5 × 5.5 cm.

19 Sgt Mark Faux wearing Combat Dress.

20 QDG No.1 Dress and Mess Dress wire-embroidered regimental rank badge 6 × 6.5 cm.

21 QDG soldier's plastic pouch mounted with the regimental rank badge.

22 QDG officer's silver pouch 17.7 × 7 cm.

A Squadron, whilst supporting 1st Battalion The Royal Northumberland Fusiliers during operations in Aden in 1967, fastened the Fusiliers distinctive red and white hackles to their vehicle antennas. Because of the close bonds which developed A Squadron was invited to perpetuate the distinction when on parade, although the privilege has not been exercised for some years.

Acknowledgement
Captain Dominic Roberts and WO1 (RSM) AD Bowtell

The Royal Scots Dragoon Guards
(Carabiniers and Greys)

The Royal Scots Dragoon Guards was formed in 1971 by the amalgamation of the 3rd Carabiniers (Prince of Wales's Dragoon Guards) with The Royal Scots Greys (2nd Dragoons).

The regimental badge of The Royal Scots Dragoon Guards, or SCOTS DG, combining the Napoleonic Eagle of The Royal Scots Greys superimposed upon the crossed carbines of the 3rd Carabineers, was adopted on amalgamation in 1971. The Eagle commemorates the capture by Sergeant Charles Ewart of the Eagle of the French 45ème Régiment d'infanterie de ligne at the Battle of Waterloo in 1815. The crossed carbines had been used by the Carabiniers since the 1770s, the title having been awarded for its service in Ireland in 1690 and 1691. The issue anodised cap badges are worn on the Forage Caps by ranks up to Staff Sergeant. Trained soldiers are required to buy metal cap badges and to polish the feathers off the eagle's breast. Some officers wear hallmarked silver badges. Officers wear their badges on a black outline backing whilst soldiers wear a 2" black square backing.

Officers' collar badges are worn on a black domed (or 'tombstone') backing, soldiers wear an almost square, 1" × 1¼", black backing.

In memoriam for Tsar Nicholas II, Colonel in Chief of The Royal Scots Greys from 1894 until his murder in 1918, a black cloth backing was placed behind the regiment's cap and regimental rank badges in about 1925. In the late 1940s the black backing was extended to collar badges. The Royal Scots Dragoon Guards continue the custom. Soldiers wear a square backing, with officers' backing being cut to the shape of the badge.

1

2

3

4

5

6

7

8

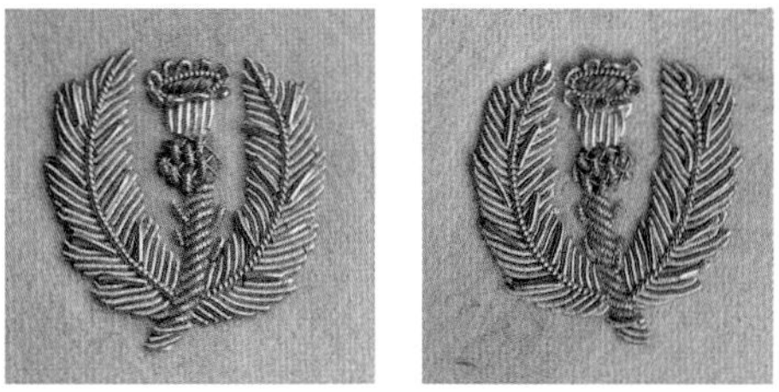

The Prince of Wales's feathers, which had been granted to the 3rd Dragoon Guards in 1765, are retained and worn on the upper left sleeve.

Lance corporals are distinguished by wearing two chevrons whilst ranks above lance corporal also wear the regimental rank badge, similar to the cap badge but without the title scroll.

During the Battle of Waterloo The Royals, The Royal Scots Greys and The Inniskilling Dragoons charged together. The Royals captured the Eagle of the 105ème Régiment d'infanterie de ligne emblazoned with the Battle Honours II Jena, Eckmuhl, Essling, and Wagram.

The 2nd Dragoons captured the Eagle of the 45ème Régiment d'infanterie de ligne with the Battle Honours Austerlitz, Jena, Frieland, Essling, and Wagram.

Both Eagles had been presented to the regiments by Napoleon.

9

10

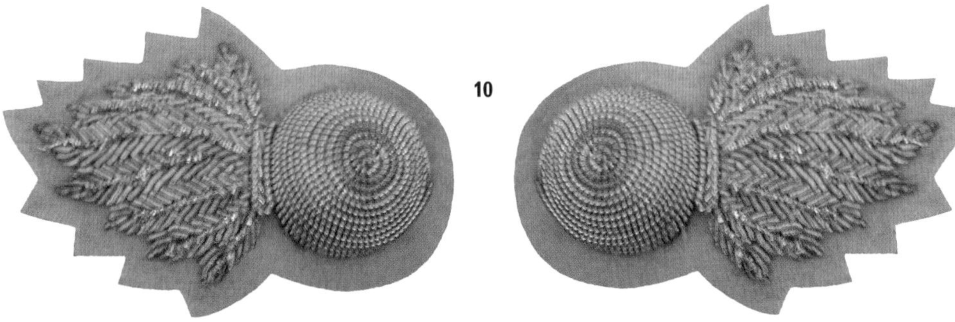

11

12

13

14

15

16

17

18

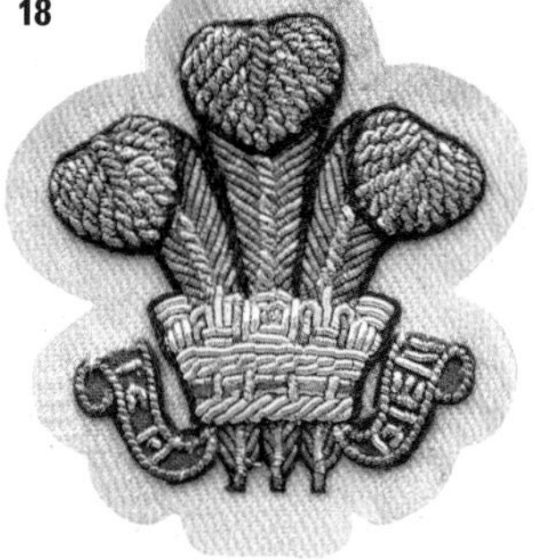

19

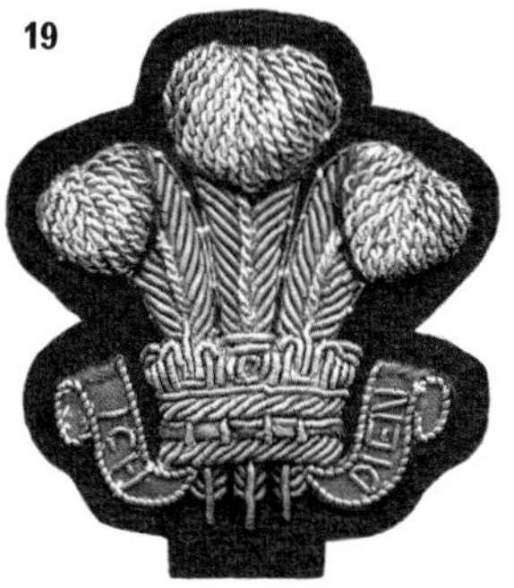

20

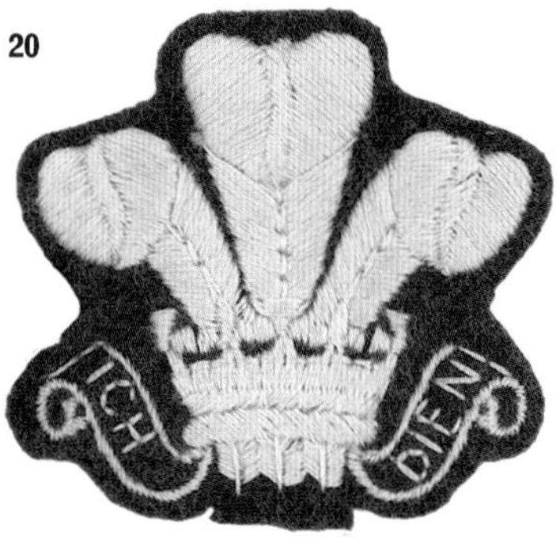

The red lion rampant was chosen as the badge for the Regiment's tank crews competing in the Canadian Army Trophy gunnery competition in 1983 and again in 1985. In 1986 Lieutenant Colonel Marcus Coombs adopted the badge for his tank and Land Rover crews. The red lion is taken from the Scottish Royal Standard. The regiment retained the privilege given to The Royal Scots Greys of flying the red lion rampant over regimental headquarters and as the Commanding Officer's pennant. The pennant is flown from a radio antenna on whichever vehicle the Commanding Officer is in.

The regiment was the first to be issued with Challenger 2 tanks. To mark their delivery Vickers, the manufacturers, provided a Challenger 2 Crewman badge to all those trained by Vicker's instructors, only a few remain in use.

21

22

23

24

previous page

1 The Royal Scots Dragoon Guards soldier's anodised aluminium cap badge 4 × 4.5 cm and collar badges 2.5 × 3.25 cm.
2 Bimetal badge purchased and worn by soldiers with the eagle's chest polished smooth after recruit training.
3 The shaped black backing on the polished badge indicates a Warrant Officer Class 1 or officer 4 × 4.5 cm.
4 Scots DG button.
5 Captain Ali Gemmell wearing a silver cap badge on black outline backing on the regiment's distinctive grey beret.
6 SSgt Bobby Campbell wearing Combat Dress with the Regiment's distinctive grey beret.
7 Anodised aluminium shoulder title 4.75 × 1 cm.
8 Officer's Mess Dress waistcoat badges embroidered directly onto the cloth 3 × 3 cm.

opposite page

9 Officer's silver and gilt cap badge 4.75 × 5 cm and collar badges 3 × 3.5 cm.
10 Officer's Full Dress wire-embroidered collar badges 5.5 × 3.5 cm.
11 No1 Dress and Mess Dress regimental rank badge 5.5 × 6 cm.
12 Sgts Jim McGhie and John McKelvie wearing No2 Dress with the regimental rank badge, the Prince of Wales's feathers and the anodised aluminium shoulder title. The Forage Cap is unique in having the van Dyke band.
13 Soldier's waist belt clasp 6.5 × 5 cm.
14 No2 Dress bi-metal rank badge worn on a black felt backing 4 × 4.75 cm.
15 Officer's No1 Dress collar badges 4 × 4 cm.
16 Sergeant's Mess Dress collar badges 3.25 × 4 cm.
17 TRF produced in 2004 before deploying to Iraq 5 × 3 cm.

Prince of Wales's Feathers badges.

18 Officer's No1 Dress wire-embroidered badge 4 × 4.5 cm.
19 Officer's No2 Dress and soldier's No1 Dress badge 4 × 4.5 cm.
20 Soldier's No2 Dress badge 5 × 4.75 cm.

this page

21 Commanding Officer's tank and land rover crews' arm badge 6.75 × 8 cm.
22 Obsolete Challenger 2 Crewman arm badge 6 × 5 cm.
23 Officer's waist belt clasp 6.5 × 4.5 cm, also worn by the Drum Major.
24 Officer's No2 Dress leather pouch 16 × 11 cm, gilt badge 5.5 × 6.5 cm.

25

27

26

The regiment has a Pipe Band which was formed in The Royal Scots Greys in 1946. King George VI granted them permission to wear the Royal Stuart tartan and advised on the design of much of the uniform. The regimental badge is worn as a plume clasp on the side of the feather bonnet, and as a sporran badge, whilst the regimental rank badge is worn as the cross belt badge. The regiment's traditional White Horse of Hanover is worn on the plaid brooch.

The Royal Scots Dragoon Guards is the only cavalry regiment to wear a bearskin cap in Full Dress. It evolved from the grenadier cap authorised for the Royal Regiment of Scots Dragoons in 1706 in commemoration of the defeat of the French Régiment du Roi during the Battle of Ramillies, 1706. The honour was also granted to the 5th Dragoons which was disbanded in 1799.

Lineage The Royal Scots Dragoon Guards (Carabiniers and Greys) (1971), from 3rd Carabiniers (Prince of Wales's Dragoon Guards) (1922) and The Royal Scots Greys (2nd Dragoons) (1681). 3rd Carabiniers (Prince of Wales's Dragoon Guards) from 3rd Dragoon Guards (Prince of Wales's) (1685) and 6th Dragoon Guards (Carabiniers) (1685).

28

32

33

29

34

35

30

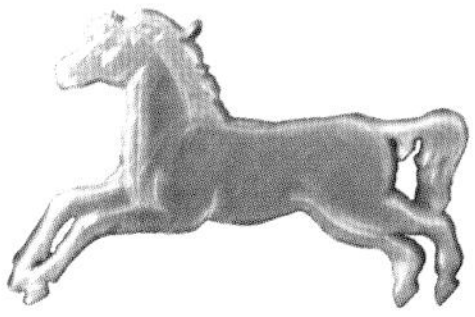

31

opposite page

25 Soldier's leather pouch with white metal badge.

26 DMaj Gary Rieley, Tpr Mark Lovell and PMaj Derek Potter. The kettle drummer's white bearskin is unique in the British Army.

27 Tpr Stephen Matthies, as a piper he wears the cap badge on a Glengarry.

this page

28 Warrant Officer Class 1 rank slide.

29 Regimental rank badge on black backing 4 × 4.5 cm worn polished as a shoulder belt badge by pipers.

30 Pommel badge on the dirk 3.75 cm.

31 Regimental badge on the Dirk 3 × 2 cm.

32 Piper's plaid brooch 9.25 cm.

33 Piper's kilt pin 4.5 × 5 cm.

34 Pipe Major's waist belt clasp 10 × 7.75 cm.

35 Pipe Major's kilt pin 4.25 × 9 cm.

36

37

38

36 Pipe Major's sporran cantle.
37 Piper's waist belt clasp 10.5 × 8.25 cm.
38 Pipe Major's appointment badge 11 cm.

Acknowledgement
Major Henry Cummins and WO1(RSM) Ian Millar

The Royal Dragoon Guards

The Royal Dragoon Guards was formed in 1992 by the amalgamation of the 4th/7th Royal Dragoon Guards with the 5th Royal Inniskilling Dragoon Guards.

The regimental badge of The Royal Dragoon Guards, or RDG, is the Star of the Order of St Patrick from the badge of the 4th/7th Royal Dragoon Guards, with a 5th Inniskilling Dragoon Guards' Inniskilling castle mounted on the centre. The badges include the Roman numerals MCMXCII, (1992), the date of the amalgamation. The 4th/7th Royal Dragoon Guards had similarly placed the date of its amalgamation, MCMXXII, (1922), on their badges.

The original badges issued in 1992 were silver anodised aluminium; the present version has a coloured centre, but is only worn by recruits. The obsolete uncoloured badge is occasionally recycled and issued to recruits in error. All trained soldiers purchase officer quality badges. The badge is worn on the beret on a maroon diamond backing, and by officers on a green backing when worn on the Service Dress cap.

The regiment wears two arm badges. A wire-embroidered representation of the cap badge on a black background is worn on the lower left sleeve by senior ranks in Number 1 and Number 2 Dress and Mess Dress. The star shape was originally the Star of the Order of St Patrick, authorised by the Marquis of Buckingham for the 4th (Royal Irish) Dragoon Guards on being granted the title in 1788. The Star was altered on amalgamation as the 4th/7th Royal Dragoon Guards in

C Squadron, 4th Dragoon Guards was the first to be engaged during the First World War, with Corporal Thomas firing the first shot and Captain Hornby the first to draw blood with his sword. The 7th Dragoon Guards claim the last cavalry action of the War when they captured Lessines on the 11 November 1918, just before the armistice came into effect at 11 o'clock.

1

2

3

4

5

6

At the Battle of Salamanca fought in Spain in 1812, the 5th Dragoon Guards captured the Drum Major's staff of the 66ème Régiment d'infanterie de ligne. The Staff is carried on parade by the regimental Quartermaster Sergeant (Technical).

7

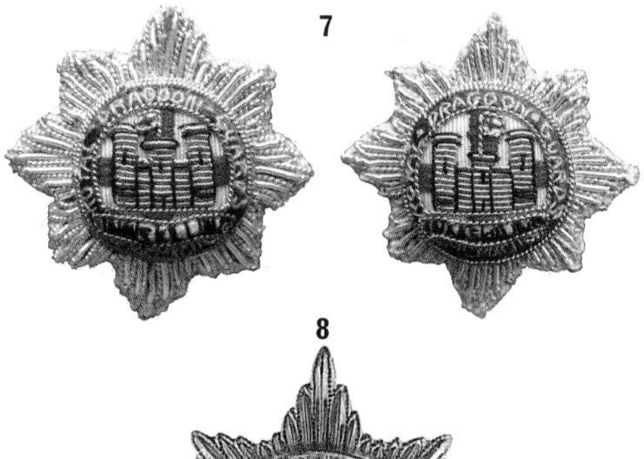

8

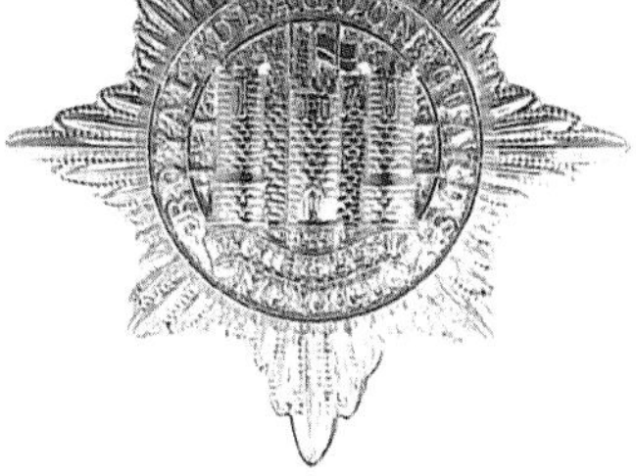

1922, but possibly not taken into use until 1930, and further altered to the present pattern in 1992.

Senior ranks also wear the 5th Dragoon Guards White Horse of Hanover arm badge, which had been taken into use during Lord Baden-Powell's tenure of command, 1897–1899, and retained after amalgamation by the 5th Royal Inniskilling Dragoon Guards. In 1898 Lieutenant Colonel RS Baden-Powell had written from Meerut, 'Given to the Regt. By George III on its return from the campaign in Holland 1796 in recognition of its gallant conduct especially at the battle of Catean 1794.'

The Horse is worn on a green backing by Warrant Officers in Number 1, Number 2 and Mess Dress, but on green backing only in Number 2 Dress by sergeants.

The regiment wears the 'D Day flash' on Number 2 Dress. The badge was originally worn on the sun helmet by the 4th/7th Royal Dragoon Guards, and was reintroduced before the Regiment deployed to France in 1939 as a recognition badge worn on the sleeve. The Royal Dragoon Guards retained it on amalgamation worn on the left sleeve of Number 2 Dress.

A Tactical Recognition Flash in the regimental colours, maroon, primrose yellow, and bottle green was approved in 2000 but has not been taken into use.

9

10

11

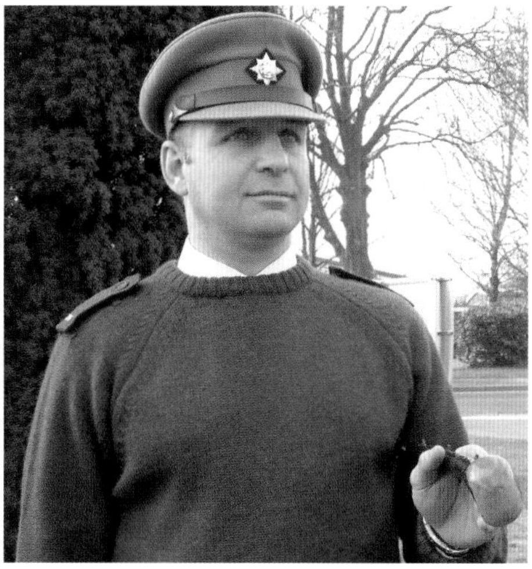

13

15

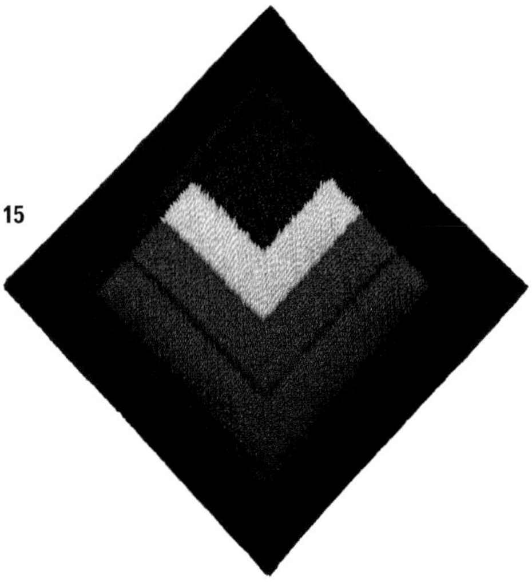

12

14

16

17

18

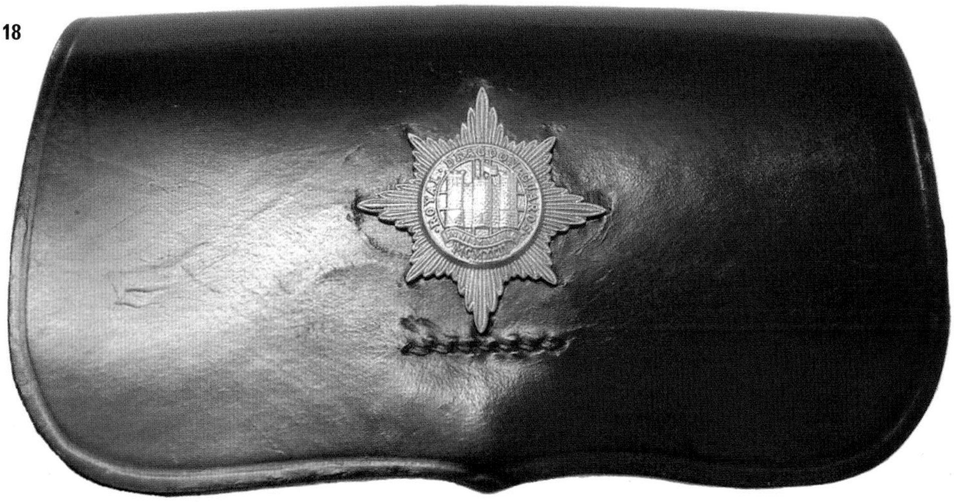

previous page

1 The Royal Dragoon Guards soldier's anodised aluminium cap badge 4.5 × 4.5 cm and collar badges 3 × 3 cm.

2 Senior ranks beret badge 3 × 3 cm.

3 Officer's silver beret badge 3 × 3 cm.

4 Anodised aluminium shoulder title 4 × 1.5 cm.

5 Royal Dragoon Guards button.

6 Sgt Heath Tyson wearing No1 Dress with the regimental rank badges on both sleeves. He carries the regimental blackthorn.

7 Mess Dress collar badges 3.5 × 3.5 cm.

8 Obsolete cap badge issued to a few recruits in training 4.5 × 4.5 cm.

opposite page

9 Officer's silver, gilt and enamel cap and collar badges.

10 Private purchase bright metal cap and collar badges.

11 LCpl Richard Fearnley and Cpl Steve Yates wearing the metal cap badge on the maroon diamond backing.

12 Wire-embroidered regimental badge 5 cm.

13 WO2 Norm Fowler wearing the cap badge on a green diamond backing.

14 Officer's Service Dress cap badge on a green backing.

15 No2 Dress 'D Day Flash' 6.75 × 7 cm.

16 Regimental rank badge 5.75 × 3 cm.

this page

17 Officer's leather pouch. The same badge is mounted on the soldier's pouch and on the officer's silver pouch in Full Dress.

18 Soldier's No2 Dress leather pouch.

19 Standards of the 4th/7th Royal Dragoon Guards and 5th Inniskilling Dragoon Guards carried by WO2 (RQMS(T)) Barney Virr and WO2 (SSM) Geordie Best, escorted by SSgts Eric Kenyon and Graham Willis. Photograph *RDG*

20 Staff Sergeant's rank slide.

19

The 22nd Dragoons were raised in 1940 from cadres of men from the 4th/7th Dragoon Guards and the 5th Royal Inniskilling Dragoon Guards. By a happy coincidence the sum of the regimental precedence, 4th, 5th, 6th and 7th is 22.

Lineage The Royal Dragoon Guards (1992), from 4th/7th Royal Dragoon Guards (1922) and 5th Royal Inniskilling Dragoon Guards (1922). 4th/7th Royal Dragoon Guards from 4th Royal Irish Dragoons (1685) and 7th Dragoon Guards (Princess Royals) (1688). 5th Royal Inniskilling Dragoon Guards from 5th Dragoon Guards (Princess Charlotte of Wales's) (1685) and The Inniskillings (6th Dragoons) (1689).

20

Acknowledgement Colonel Frog Freeman and SSgt Agi Agar

The Queen's Royal Hussars
(The Queen's Own and Royal Irish)

The Queen's Royal Hussars was formed in 1993 by the amalgamation of The Queen's Own Hussars with The Queen's Royal Irish Hussars.

The cap badge of The Queen's Royal Hussars, or QRH, is a miniature of the Royal Crest above the Irish harp similar in format to the original 8th King's Royal Irish Hussars regimental arm badge. The device is backed by the monogram of the 7th Queen's Own Hussars.

The collar badge is taken from the design of the regimental arm badge worn by the 3rd The King's Own Hussars in about 1906.

The Polish Syrena is worn on the left sleeve in Number 2 Dress.

Lance corporals are distinguished by wearing two chevrons whilst ranks above lance corporal also wear the regimental rank badge, similar to the cap badge but without the title scroll.

A Tactical Recognition Flash in regimental colours, Garter blue, primrose yellow, Brunswick green, primrose yellow, Garter blue was approved in 2000 but has not been taken into use.

1

2

4

3

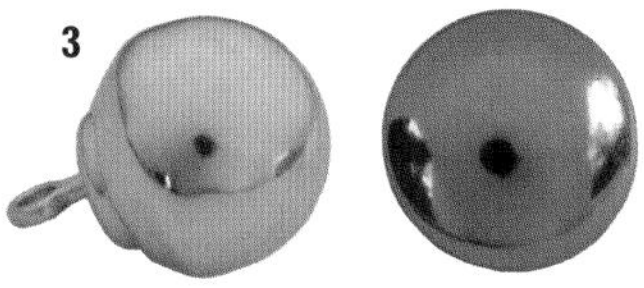

5

6

The 7th Queen Own Hussars supported the 2nd Polish Corps under General Wladyslaw Anders in Italy from 1944 to 1945. As a Battle Honour the regiment was granted the Syrena, or Mermaid of Warsaw, badge. The badge was chosen at it typifies the fighting spirit of the people of Warsaw. A woven badge is worn by soldiers on the lower left sleeve in Number 2 Dress, whilst officers wear a bullion embroidered badge. B Squadron, who have an artist in the squadron, have the badge painted on to their vehicles. The 'Maid of Warsaw' badge is also worn by 10 (Assaye) Battery Royal Artillery and by 651 and 654 Squadrons Army Air Corps. It was also awarded to personnel of the 1st Household Cavalry Regiment, a war-raised unit.

7

8

9

10

11

12

In 1685 The Queen's Consort's Regiment of Dragoons, later the 3rd The King's Own Hussars, wore the Queen's livery with Garter Blue feathered hats. The colour has been handed down to the RDG and is reflected in the Garter Blue backgrounds to officers' badges of rank and non-commissioned officers' regimental rank badges.

Sir Winston Churchill was commissioned into the 4th Hussars in 1895. He became Colonel of the Regiment during the Second World War and remained in post until his death in 1965. The Commanding Officer's tank is named Churchill, and The Churchill Cup is awarded annually to the best gunnery troop in the regiment.

13

14

15

opposite page

1 The Queen's Royal Hussars soldier's bright metal and enamel cap badge 3.75 × 4.75 cm and collar badges 4 × 2.25 cm.
2 Soldier's anodised aluminium shoulder title 2.5 × 1 cm.
3 QRH button.
4 Soldier's woven Syrena Battle Honour badge 4.25 × 5 cm.
5 Officer's wire-embroidered Syrena badge 3.75 × 4.75 cm.
6 Officer's silver, gilt and enamel cap badge 3.75 × 5 cm and silver collar badges 4 × 2.25 cm.
7 LCpl Simon Bluff wearing No2 Dress with the Syrena badge on his left sleeve. On his right sleeve is a regimental police brassard.
8 Officer's wire-embroidered beret badge 4 × 6 cm.
9 Major Keith Deakin wearing Service Dress with the Syrena badge on his left sleeve.

this page

10 Cpl David Cook wearing Combat Dress and the regiment's unique beret with its wide sweat band.
11 Lt Tom Auld wearing the regiment's unique beret in Iraq. He has the 20th Armoured Brigade badge on his sleeve below the Union Flag badge.
12 Captain Max Maxwell wearing the QRH unique Tent Cap, worn without a badge. His rank badges are mounted on Garter Blue backing.
13 No1 Dress and Mess Dress wire-embroidered regimental rank badge 4.75 × 6.5 cm.
14 No2 Dress regimental rank badge 3.5 × 5.25 cm on Garter Blue backing.
15 WO1 (RSM) Euan Johnston wearing No1 Dress, the regimental rank badge on his right sleeve.

Cross belts fitted to a pouch are worn on parade. Soldiers wear a leather pouch mounted with a two part badge. There is no officers' Service Dress leather pouch, officers wearing any pouch from the former regiments. However leather pouches unofficially ornamented with regimental rank badges are available in training units. Silver pouches are worn by officers with Number 1 Dress.

QRH pipers' uniform is based on that of The Royal Irish Rangers. On the saffron kilt are green cloth shamrocks mounted with the obsolete anodised aluminium cap badges of The Queen's Own Hussars and The Queen's Royal Irish Hussars.

16

17

18

19

The principle purpose of Cavalry Standards and Infantry Colours was to act as a guide and rallying point in battle. The word *guidon* is a corruption of the French 'guide homme', or guide man. They were therefore jealously guarded in war and peace. Their loss was unthinkable and many soldiers have died to protect their Guidons. Regimental guidons are no longer carried in battle but emblazoned with the Regiment's battle honours are venerated as the Regiment's proudest possessions; a reminder of a glorious past and an inspiration for the future.

20

Winston, the regimental drum horse was presented by Prince Philip. By command of King George II the silver kettledrums captured at Dettingen in 1743 are borne by a Drum Horse at the head of the regiment. In 1771 Lady Southampton, wife of the Colonel, presented a silver collar to be worn by the Kettledrummer. It is also worn by the Orderly Officer when dining in the Mess.

21

22

23

24

opposite page

16 Piper's cap badge 4 × 7 cm.

17 Tpr Stevie Keay wearing the piper's cap badge.

18 Lt Col Andrew Cuthbert wearing the Tent Hat originally adopted by the 8th Hussars in 1909. On his left sleeve he wears the 20th Armoured Brigade badge.

19 SSgt Andy Acton and Nigel Pearce escorting WO2 Ian Coles carrying the regimental guidon.

20 Cpl Lee Miller wearing the QRH Full Dress escorting Tpr David Philpott riding Winston, the regimental drum horse.

21 LCpl David Wilson wearing piper's Full Dress.

this page

22 Captain's white embroidered rank slide worn in barracks, dark green rank slide worn in the field, and a Trooper's rank slide.

23 The Queen's Own Hussars and the Queen's Royal Irish Hussars kilt badges on their shamrock-shaped backing worn on the piper's kilt.

24 Pipe Major's appointment badge 11.5 × 12.5 cm.

26

27

28

The New Zealand Fern Leaf
Lieutenant General Freyberg VC commanding 2nd New Zealand Division awarded the Fern Leaf to 9th Armoured Brigade following its outstanding attack on the German position during the Battle of El Alamein in November 1942. The Fern Leaf was the Division insignia and was painted on all the vehicles. It was awarded to 3rd The King's Own Hussars, The Royal Wiltshire Yeomanry, The Warwickshire Yeomanry, 14th Battalion The Sherwood Foresters and 31 New Zealand Anti-Tank Battery. In The Queen's Royal Hussars the Fern Leaf is used as a vehicle recognition sign.

Lineage The Queen's Royal Hussars (The Queen's Own And Royal Irish) (1993) from The Queen's Own Hussars (1958) and The Queen's Royal Irish Hussars (1958). The Queen's Own Hussars from 3rd The King's Own Hussars (1685) and 7th Queen's Own Hussars (1689). The Queen's Royal Irish Hussars from 4th Queen's Own Hussars (1685) and 8th King's Royal Irish Hussars (1693).

26 Soldier's leather pouch with distinctive badge with detached Crown, 7 × 6.5 cm.
27 Officer's unapproved leather pouch worn in some training units.
28 Officer's No1 Dress silver pouch.

Acknowledgement WO1 (RSM) Euan Johnston

9th/12th Royal Lancers
(Prince of Wales's)

The 9th/12th Royal Lancers was formed in 1960 by the amalgamation of the 9th Queen's Royal Lancers with the 12th Royal Lancers.

The badges of the 9th/12th Royal Lancers, or 9/12 L, based on the design of the 12th Royal Lancers badges, were adopted on amalgamation in 1960. Both the 9th Queen's Royal Lancers and the 12th Royal Lancers had converted from Light Dragoons to Lancers in 1816 and crossed lances had featured on both their badges.

All warrant officers and non-commissioned officers of the 9th/12th Royal Lancers wear a chromed Prince of Wales's feathers badge on Number 2 Dress, with the exception of the Regimental Sergeant Major who wears a silver badge presented to the regiment by Mr BW Cox. Wire-embroidered badges are worn on Number 1 Dress and Mess Dress, although chrome badges have also been worn on Number 1 Dress. King George III presented the Prince of Wales's feathers to the regiment in recognition of their 75 years service in Ireland from 1718 to 1793.

1

2

3

4

5

6

7

8

In 1928 the 12th Lancers was mechanised, exchanging their horses for armoured cars, and all non-commissioned ranks adopted a brass arm badge depicting a Rolls Royce Armoured Car. It was retained by the 9th/12th Royal Lancers on amalgamation in 1960, worn on the lower right forearm. It was discontinued in 1963 and reintroduced for Class 1 Tradesmen in 1972, worn on a black cloth background.

All Regiments and Corps put particular effort into recruiting. The first challenge is to make potential recruits aware of a particular regiment within the Army. The 9th/12th Royal Lancers Regimental Recruiting Team have done so by awarding a special badge to Army Cadets who successfully complete the annual Cadet Recce Cadre Course run by the Regiment. The cadets are principally from detachments in Bedfordshire, Derbyshire, Leicestershire and Northamptonshire.

The crossed lances badge is of the design originally authorised in 1881 for the best lancer in each Troop.

The 3rd Dragoon Guards, 10th Royal Hussars and 12th Royal Lancers all wore the Prince of Wales's feathers as an arm badge. The 12th Royal Lancers had worn an embroidered version for many years prior to 1834, but from 1881 to 1929 all three regiments had the same issue badge. From 1928 the 12th Royal Lancers in Egypt wore the badge on a black (or very dark blue) cloth backing, possibly in memoriam for the exchange of their horses for armoured cars.

Lineage 9th/12th Royal Lancers (Prince of Wales's) (1960), from 9th Queen's Royal Lancers (1715) and 12th Royal Lancers (Prince of Wales's) (1715).

9

10

11

12

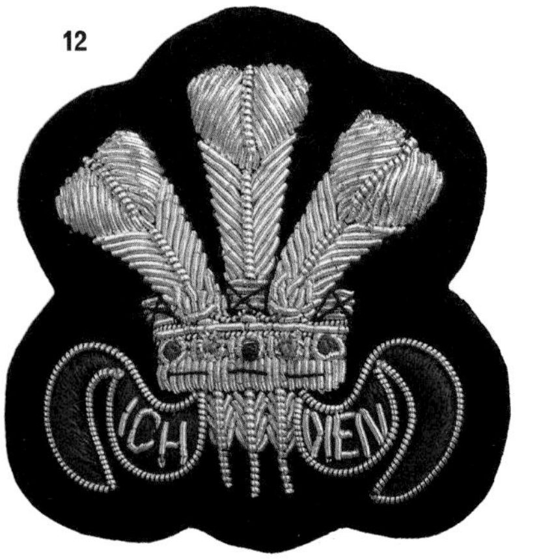

13

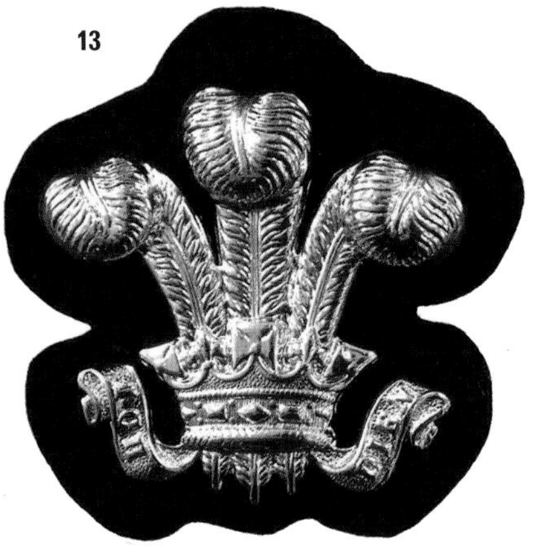

14

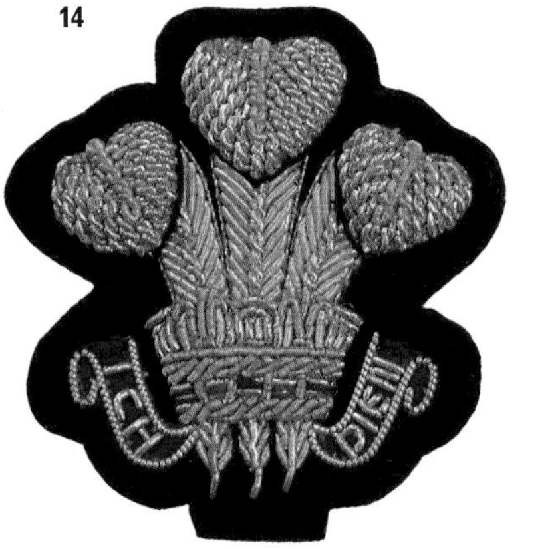

15

16

17

18

19

20

previous page

1 9th/12th Royal Lancers soldiers' anodised aluminium cap badge 3.5 × 4 cm and collar badges 3 × 3.25 cm.

2 Anodised aluminium shoulder title 4.5 × 1.5 cm.

3 9/12L button.

4 Officer's wire-embroidered beret badge 4.5 × 5 cm.

5 Soldier's cloth beret badge 4 × 4 cm.

6 Captain's rank slide.

7 2Lts Will Richmond, William Rollin and Ed Short wearing Combat Dress with wire-embroidered beret badges.

8 Sgt Madge Major wearing Combat Dress with the cloth beret badge.

opposite page

9 Officer's silver and gilt cap and collar badges.

10 9/12L regimental guidon carried by WO2 Des Hennerson escorted by WO2 (RQMS) Mark Gorman who has his rank badge above the Armoured Car which is above his regimental rank badge, and WO1 (RSM) Steve Buckley who wears his rank badge above his silver regimental rank badge.

11 WO1 (RSM) Tony Price wearing officers' insignia and also the regimental rank badge on his right sleeve.

12 Wire-embroidered regimental rank badge 5.75 × 5.5 cm worn by all Warrant Officers and NCOs on No 1 Dress.

13 Chrome rank badge 5.75 × 5.5 cm worn on No 2 Dress.

14 Mess Dress wire-embroidered rank badge 5 × 4.5 cm.

this page

15 Class 1 Tradesman badges wire-embroidered for No1 Dress and Mess Dress 6 × 3.5 cm.

16 Bright metal badge for No 2 Dress 5.5 × 2.75 cm. The embroidered badge may be produced on an oblong backing, which is trimmed by the tailor. The gilding metal badge is backed by a piece of felt cut to shape.

17 LCpl Tim Daisley, a regimental policeman, wearing the regimental rank badge on his right sleeve. The 1970s shape to his Forage Cap is said to be an affectation amongst the regimental police.

18 Guidon belt plate 8.5 × 10.5 cm.

19 Cadet's arm badge 3.25 × 4.5 cm.

20 12th Royal Lancers officer's silver cross belt boss originally worn in the 1880s.

21

22

23

21 12th Royal Lancers officer's silver and gilt pouch originally worn between 1902 and 1914.

22 9th Queen's Royal Lancers officer's silver pouch originally worn between 1902 and 1914.

23 Soldier's plastic pouch 16 × 8 cm, chrome badge 5.5 × 5.5 cm.

Acknowledgement
Major Bill Fooks and Phil Watson and WO1 (RSM) Steve Buckley.

The King's Royal Hussars

The King's Royal Hussars was formed in 1992 by the amalgamation of The Royal Hussars with the 14th/20th King's Hussars.

The cap badge of The King's Royal Hussars, or KRH, is the Prussian Eagle formerly the badge of the 14th/20th King's Hussars and known in the regiment as The Hawk. The Regiment point out that the principal difference between the badge of the 14th/20th King's Hussars and the present badge is that the new Hawk has an open beak. Slightly easier to see is that the Hawk is larger than that previously worn and has the letters FR on its chest. It was adopted on amalgamation in 1992.

The 14th King's Hussars had been granted the Prussian Eagle as a badge in 1798 when Princess Frederica Charlotte of Prussia married the Duke of York and the Regiment became 'Duchess of York's Own'. The badge was not worn from 1915 to sometime between 1924–1926 because of anti-German feeling during the First World War.

The Hawk is produced in three qualities. The issue badge is lightweight black and gilt anodised aluminium. Senior Non-Commissioned Officers are required to purchase a much more substantial blackened brass badge with the highlights relieved (or polished). Junior ranks are also allowed to wear the more substantial badge if they wish. The badge has an attractive well-worn look, which is not popular with some senior NCOs (said to be former 14th/20th King's Hussars soldiers) who paint their badges black.

Officers wear a black and gilt version of the badge on the Service Dress Cap and Forage Cap and a wire-embroidered version on the Regiment's distinctive brown beret. There are two other versions of The Hawk. A gold anodised aluminium version is worn on the soldier's pouch and a silver version on the Pouches of Royal Gurkha Rifles officers. The Regiment is introducing a new gold coloured Hawk as a beret badge before deploying to Iraq in 2005.

1

2

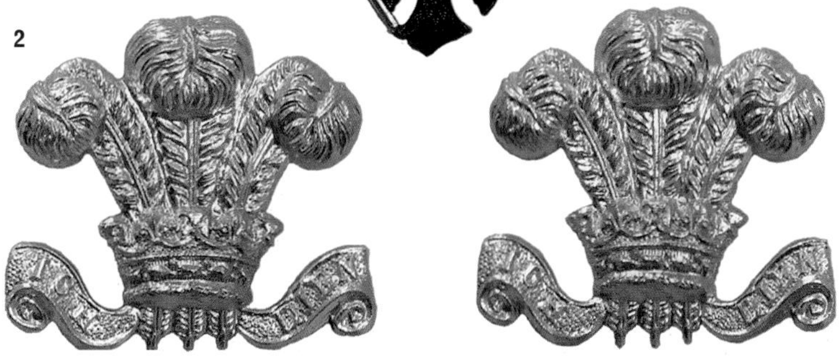

3

4

5

6

7

The Prince of Wales's plumes of the Royal Hussars are worn as the collar badges. The pattern worn on Number 2 Dress is relatively small, whilst that worn on Number 1 Dress is much larger.

To commemorate the service of the 14th/20th King's Hussars with 43rd Lorried Gurkha Brigade from February 1943 in Italy, and in particular the capture of Mercina in 1945 during which six members of the regiment were awarded rare immediate awards for gallantry, the Regiment adopted a pair of crossed kukris in 1947 worn on the left sleeve, and 6th Gurkha Rifles similarly adopted The Hawk. The successor regiments, The King's Royal Hussars and The Royal Gurkha Rifles, maintain the custom, with the exception that the crossed kukris are worn on both arms by The King's Royal Hussars. The issue kukris for Number 2 Dress are produced in silver anodised aluminium, and wire-embroidered for Number 1 Dress. The embroidered badge is also worn on Mess Dress whilst officers wear brass badges on Service Dress.

8

9

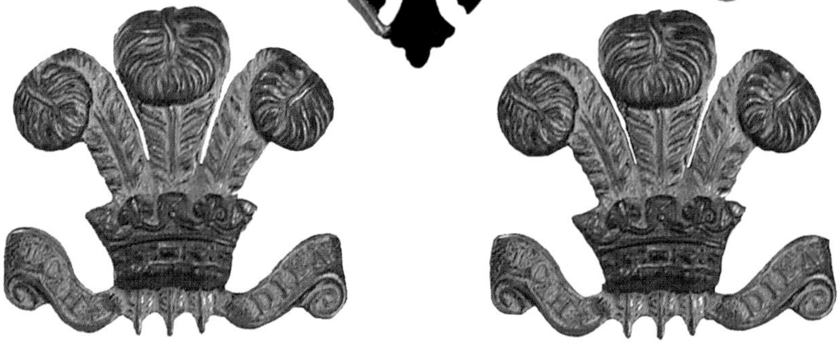

10

11

12

13

14

15

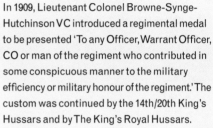

In 1909, Lieutenant Colonel Browne-Synge-Hutchinson VC introduced a regimental medal to be presented 'To any Officer, Warrant Officer, CO or man of the regiment who contributed in some conspicuous manner to the military efficiency or military honour of the regiment.' The custom was continued by the 14th/20th King's Hussars and by The King's Royal Hussars.

The Regiment wears a brown beret, introduced in 1928 by the 11th Hussars when converting to armoured cars. The Service Dress Caps worn by the cavalry were found to be unsuitable and the RTR style beret was introduced in the colour of the officers' Busby. It was worn without a badge until amalgamation with the 10th Royal Hussars.

The 11th became Hussars in 1840 and were extravagantly dressed with blue jacket and pelisse and crimson overalls. Crimson was the colour of the house of Saxe Coburg Gotha and may have been adopted when the regiment was given the title of 11th or Prince Albert's Own Hussars after escorting him to marry Queen Victoria. The regiment and its successors has been nicknamed 'The Cherry Pickers' which may originate from the colour of the trousers or from an incident during the Napoleonic War when a patrol was apparently surprised in a cherry orchard.

NCOs of the 14th King's Hussars wore an embroidered crown above a black Prussian eagle arm badge from 1832, and possibly from 1830. The arm badge was retained on the formation of the 14th/20th King's Hussars in 1922 and on the subsequent formation of The King's Royal Hussars in 1992.

In 1995–1996 The King's Royal Hussars deployed on an operational tour to Northern Ireland. 1st Battalion The Argyll and Sutherland Highlanders operated in the adjoining Tactical Area of Responsibility and their distinctive arm badge prompted The King's Royal Hussars to adopt a similar sized arm badge, which was nicknamed 'rhubarb and custard'. A larger Tactical Recognition Flash in the regimental colours, crimson, primrose yellow, crimson, replaced it in 2003 with the instruction that the original smaller badges were to waste out rather than be replaced.

Cross belts fitted to a pouch are worn in Number 1 Dress. Soldiers wear the universal pattern plastic pouch mounted with an anodised aluminium Hawk badge. There is no KRH officers' pattern pouch, officers wearing any pouch from the former regiments.

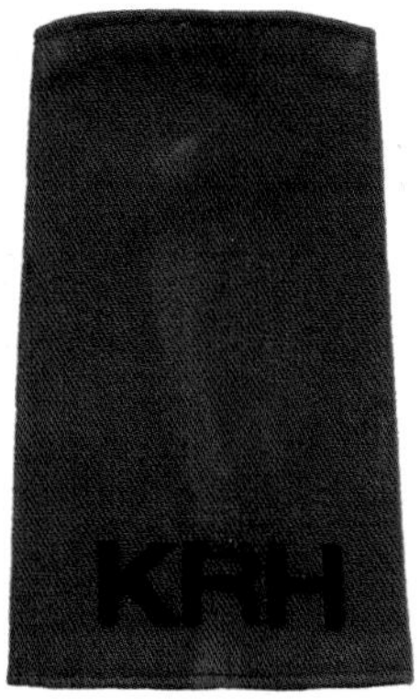

16

17

19

18

20

21

22

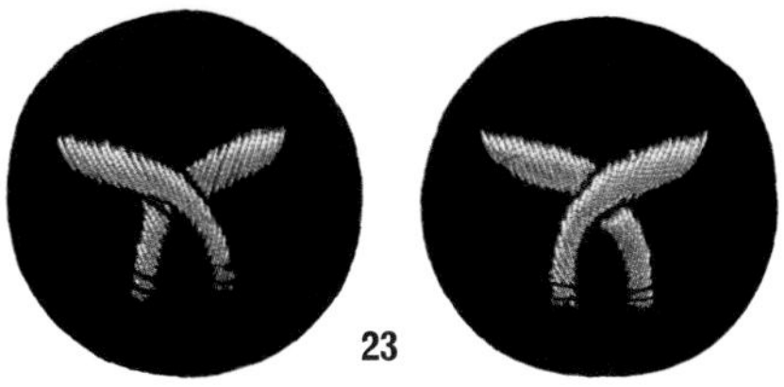

23

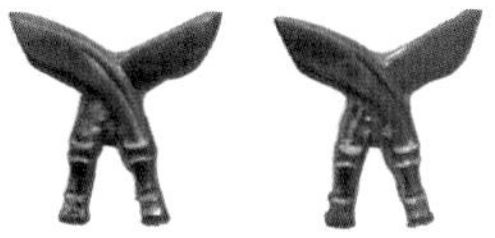

24

25

previous page

1 King's Royal Hussars soldier's anodised aluminium cap badge 4.75 × 3.25 cm, small No2 Dress collar badges 2.25 × 2.25 cm.
2 Larger No1 Dress collar badges 3.75 × 3.25 cm.
3 Soldier's anodised aluminium shoulder titles 2.5 × 1 cm.
4 KRH button.
5 WO2 (SSM) Ploppy Sloane wearing No 1 Dress with the large collar badges. He wears the crossed kukris and the regimental rank badge on his right sleeve.
6 Private purchase relieved metal cap badge 3.25 × 4.75 cm.
7 Officer's wire-embroidered beret badge worn on the regiment's distinctive brown beret 7 × 6cm.

opposite page

8 Officer's black and gilt cap badge 3.5 × 4.75 cm and silver and gilt No 2 Dress collar badges 2.25 × 2 cm.
9 Silver and gilt No 1 Dress collar badges 3.75 × 3.25 cm.
10 Officer's collar badges are worn polished.
11 Sgt Michael Wood and WO2 John Donald wearing the private purchase relieved cap badge.
12 Officer's brass shoulder title 2.5 × 1 cm.
13 Officer's rank star.
14 Captain Anthony Sharman wearing Service Dress with the Side Cap.
15 Anodised aluminium beret badge 3.75 × 4.75 cm introduced in 2005.

this page

16 Regimental rank slide.
17 Second Lieutenant's shirt sleeve order rank slide.
18 Regimental rank badge 3.5 × 4.25 cm and wire-embroidered Mess Dress badge 4.25 × 5.5 cm.
19 'Rhubarb and custard' arm badge 4 × 2 cm.
20 TRF 5.25 × 3.25 cm.
21 Major Jules Buczacki wearing No1 Dress with cloak.
22 Sergeant Tony Hill, on the right sleeve of his Number 2 Dress he has the Regiment's crossed kukris badge above the crossed swords of an All Arms Physical Training Instructor above the regimental rank badge.
23 No1 Dress and Mess Dress wire-embroidered kukri arm badge 3 cm.
24 Officer's brass kukri arm badge 1.5 × 1.5 cm.
25 Soldier's anodised aluminium kukri arm badge 1.5 × 1.75 cm.

Lineage The King's Royal Hussars (1992), from The Royal Hussars (Prince of Wales's Own) (1969) and 14th/20th King's Hussars (1922). Royal Hussars from 10th Royal Hussars (Prince of Wales's Own) (1715) and 11th Hussars (Prince Albert's Own) (17115). 14th/20th King's Hussars from 14th King's Hussars (1715) and 20th Hussars (1862).

26

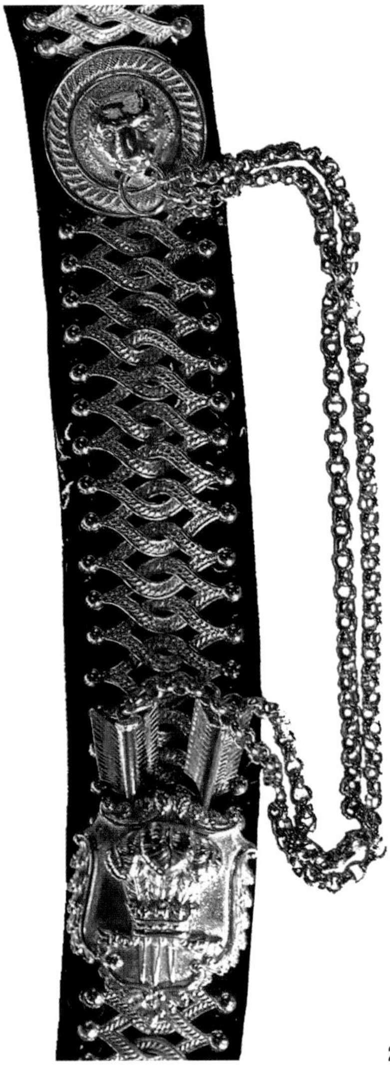

27

28

29

30

26 10th Royal Hussars refurbished cross belt.

27 The Royal Hussars officer's pouch. Pouch 15.5 × 10.5 cm, badges 3.5 × 4 cm, Crown 3 × 3 cm.

28 Soldier's pouch mounted with an anodised aluminium badge.

29 Guidon carried by WO2 (RQMS(T)) Mickey Caulfield escorted by WO1 (RSM) Gary Wills and SSgt (SQMS) Mark Witham.

30 10th Royal Hussars officer's pouch refurbished for The King's Royal Hussars. Pouch 15.25 × 11.5 cm, badge 5 × 7.5 cm.

The Light Dragoons

The Light Dragoons was formed in 1992 by the amalgamation of the 13th/18th Royal Hussars with the 15th/19th The King's Royal Hussars.

The cap badge of The Light Dragoons, or LD, was a new design introduced at the amalgamation in 1992 and based upon the Maltese Cross design of the shako plates worn by Light Dragoon regiments before their conversion to Hussars in the 19th Century. The badge was designed by Lieutenant Colonel Alan Mallinson, who as Brigadier has gone on to write a series of popular books about Matthew Hervey, a Light Dragoon officer of the Napoleonic wars.

The 15th/19th Hussars Royal Crest was combined with the 13th/18th Hussars distinctive Z scroll to produce new, and comparatively large, collar badges.

1

2

4

3

5

6

7

8

The 13th Hussars adopted a white and dark blue diamond badge halved vertically for wear on the Wolseley helmet in 1899 during the Boer War. Known as the 'South Africa Flash' it was worn, white to the front, on the left sleeve of Number 2 Dress. The Light Dragoons retained it on amalgamation but the colour was changed to black and white. In order to conform, tailors in training units made up new flashes from felt for recruits. The Regiment is returning to the correct dark blue and white flash. It is said that the change was made by a Regimental Quartermaster Sergeant who as a Newcastle United Football Club supporter was pleased to see his Club's colours worn by his regiment. A woven badge is worn, also white to the front, on the right sleeve of combat dress as the Tactical Recognition Flash.

The Royal Crest had been used as a badge by the 15th King's Hussars since before 1768 and was a natural choice when arm badges were authorised in 1888. The arm badge was retained on the formation of the 15th/19th King's Royal Hussars in 1922 and on the subsequent formation of The Light Dragoons in 1992. The embroidered badge replaced the original metal badge in 1963 in order to avoid piercing holes in the sleeves of the new Number 2 Dress. The silver wire-embroidered badge for Number 1 Dress was changed to St Edward's (or Queen's) Crown on formation of The Light Dragoons in 1992, whilst the woven badge for Number 2 Dress retains the old Tudor (or King's) Crown.

Cross belts fitted to a pouch are worn in both Number 1 and Number 2 Dress. Waist belts are only worn by the regimental police. Soldiers wear a brown leather pouch mounted with a white metal Elephant badge, which had been awarded to the 19th Light Dragoons for its conspicuous gallantry at the Battle of Assaye in India in 1803. In Service Dress officers have worn any leather pouch from the former regiments mounted with a silver Elephant badge, and similarly any silver pouch in Number 1 Dress.

9

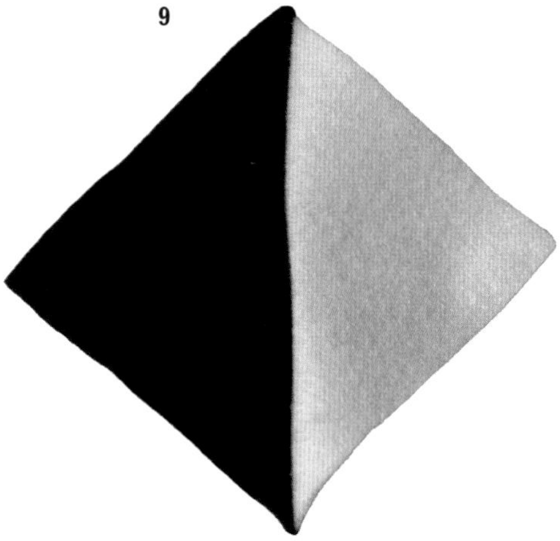

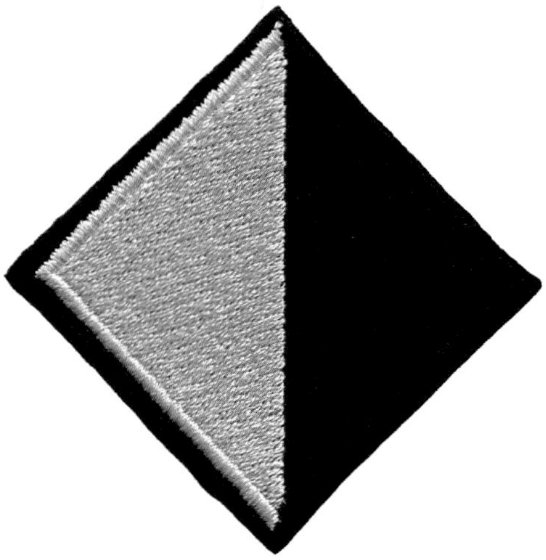

10

Lineage The Light Dragoons (1992) from 13th/18th Royal Hussars (Queen Mary's Own) (1922) and 15th/19th The King's Royal Hussars (1922). 13th/18th Royal Hussars from 13th Hussars (1715) and 18th Royal Hussars (Queen Mary's Own) (1858). 15th/19th The King's Royal Hussars from 15th The King's Hussars (1759) and 19th Royal Hussars (Queen Alexandra's Own) (1858).

11

12

13

14

Light Dragoon officers pattern leather pouches are now available and silver pouches and cross belts combining features of all four regiments should be available in 2005.

On amalgamation The Light Dragoons followed the 19th Royal Hussars practice of wearing boxed shoulder chains on Number 1 Dress. The practice involved cutting down the issue 'arrow-head' chains and was wasteful. Soldiers will continue to wear boxed chains because Number 1 Dress is not an individual issue and all those in stock have boxed chains fitted. Officers, who are required to own Number 1 Dress, are now adopting the arrowhead chains.

15

16

17

18

previous page

1 The Light Dragoons soldier's anodised aluminium cap badge 4.5 × 4.5 cm and collar badges 2.5 × 3.5 cm.
2 Officer's silver gilt and enamel cap badge 4.5 × 4.5 and collar badges 2.5 × 3.5 cm.
3 Officer's wire-embroidered beret badge 4.5 × 5 cm.
4 Lt Kieran Atkinson wearing combat dress with the wire embroidered beret badge.
5 Anodised aluminium shoulder title 5.25 × 2 cm.
6 LD button.
7 Captain Edwin Lawrence wearing No1 Dress with obsolete boxed shoulder chains.
8 Private purchase a bright metal cap badge 4.5 × 4.5 cm.

opposite page

9 Light Dragoons 'South Africa' flashes worn, white to the front, as an arm badge on the left sleeve of Number 2 Dress 5.5 × 6 cm, and as a TRF on the right sleeve of Combat Dress 5.5 × 5.5 cm.
10 Cpl Howie Howard wearing No1 Dress with boxed shoulder chains and the wire-embroidered regimental rank badge above the crossed rifles badge of a skill at arms instructor.
11 Sgt Stotty Stott wearing No2 Dress with the woven rank badge. He wears a belt whilst on the Drill Course.
12 Warrant Officer Class 1 rank slide.
13 No2 Dress woven and padded regimental rank badge with Tudor (or King's) Crown 4.25 × 5.75 cm.
14 No1 Dress wire-embroidered regimental rank badge 4.25 × 6.5 cm.

this page

15 Captain Steve Summerscales wearing No1 Dress with boxed shoulder chains.
16 Full Dress cross belt.
17 SSgt Stotter Baston wearing the South Africa Flash on his left sleeve.
18 LCpl Wardy Wardle wearing No2 Dress with cross belt.

19

20

22

21

19 Officer's Full Dress silver pouch of the 13th/18th Royal Hussars worn with No1 Dress 18×6.5 cm.

20 13th/18th Royal Hussars officer's leather pouch worn with No2 Dress.

21 Soldier's pouch 16×9, badge 4.5×35 cm, scroll 4.5×1.25 cm.

22 Captain Sharkey Wiles wearing No1 Dress with the new pattern shoulder chains.

Acknowledgement
Captain Sharkey Wiles and WO1 (RSM) Lenny Newcombe

The Queen's Royal Lancers

The Queen's Royal Lancers was formed in 1993 by the amalgamation of the 16th/5th The Queen's Royal Lancers with the 17th/21st Lancers.

The Queen's Royal Lancers, or QRL, cap badge had been the badge of the 17th Lancers from its formation in 1759. Known in the regiment as The Motto, and by soldiers who originally served in the 16th/5th Queen's Royal Lancers as The Chad, it was adopted as a cap badge in the modern sense in 1897, retained by the 17th/21st Lancers on amalgamation in 1922 and by The Queen's Royal Lancers in 1993. It is now worn on a red pre-cut backing on the beret. Officers wear a slightly reduced sized badge on the beret. In 1984 the 17th/21st Lancers deployed to Northern Ireland and the regiment blackened its Mottos. Officers adopted a gunmetal badge, which continues to be worn by a few officers. Officers serving with the regiment, rather than on the Staff, readopted the original silver beret badge in 1998–1999.

The collar badges are those of the 16th/5th Queen's Royal Lancers, which had been introduced in 1922. The badges link the Garter and the cypher of Queen Charlotte, Consort of King George III, from the 16th The Queen's Lancers, with the Order of St Patrick, from the 5th Royal Irish Lancers.

The Death's Head Badge was, according to tradition, chosen by the first colonel of the 17th Lancers, Lieutenant Colonel John Hale, after he carried the news of General Wolfe's death to England in 1759. The Death's Head emblem was a traditional symbol used on graves.

The red backing to the Motto commemorates the 16th The Queen's Lancers who were known as the Scarlet Lancers, having been the only regiment of lancers to avoid changing their uniform from scarlet to blue in 1846.

1

2

3

4

5

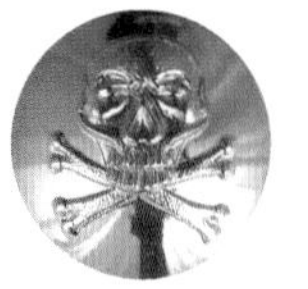

6

7

8

A silver embroidered badge combining the crossed lances of 16th The Queen's Royal Lancers with the 17th Lancers Motto is worn as the regimental rank badge by senior ranks on the right sleeve of Mess Dress.

Warrant Officer Class 1 (Regimental Sergeant Major) Dave Winner reintroduced the 5th Royal Irish Lancers Maid of Erin Harp arm badge worn by senior ranks on Mess Dress. The 8th Hussars had adopted the Maid of Erin Harp as an arm badge before 1834. The 5th Lancers adopted it in 1860 and it was retained following the amalgamated by the 16th/5th Queen's Royal Lancers in 1922, although until 1930 it was only worn by senior Non-Commissioned Officers of C (5th Lancers) Squadron.

The 21st Lancers arm badge is worn by all ranks on Numbers 1 and 2 Dress and Mess Dress.

A Tactical Recognition Flash in regimental colours, Crimson, French chalk, crimson, French chalk, crimson was approved in 2000 but was not issued. Instead in 2004 a Tactical Recognition Flash combining the crossed lances of the 16th The Queen's Royal Lancers and the Motto of the 17th Lancers was introduced.

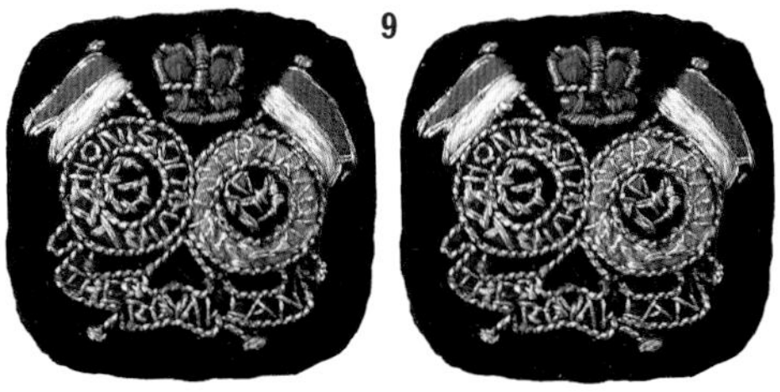
9

10

11

12

13

14

15

16

17

In 1822 at Bhurtpore in India the 16th Lancers were the first regiment to use the lance in action. In 1846 at Aliwal during the First Sikh War the regiment returned from the charge with the pennons on their lances so caked in blood that they appeared to be crimped. Since then the regiment has crimped the pennons.

Lineage The Queen's Royal Lancers (1993), from 16th/5th The Queen's Royal Lancers (1922) and 17th/21st Lancers (1922). 16th/5th The Queen's Royal Lancers from 16th The Queen's Lancers (1759) and 5th Royal Irish Lancers (1689). 17th/21st Lancers from 17th Lancers (Duke of Cambridge's Own) (1759) and 21st Lancers (Empress of India's) (1858).

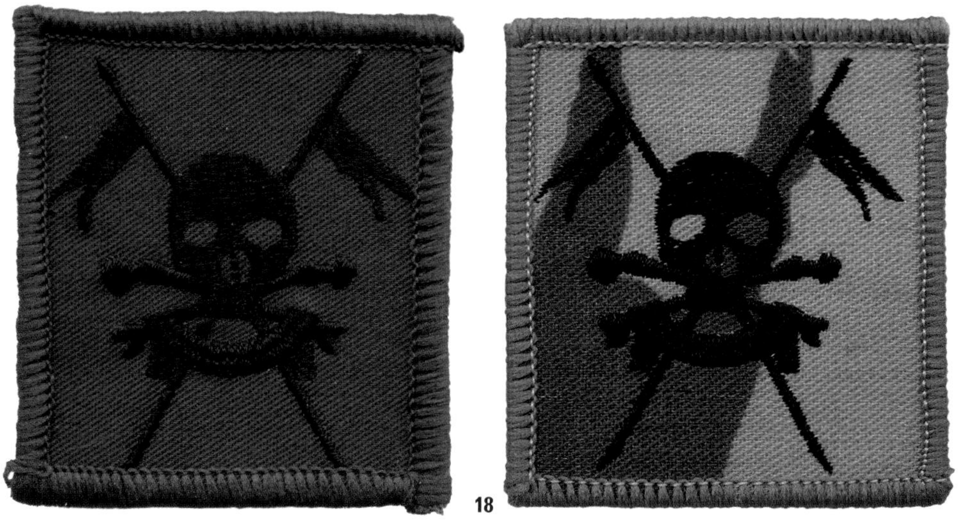

18

19

20

previous page

1 The Queen's Royal Lancers soldier's anodised aluminium Motto 4.75 × 4 cm and collar badges 3.25 × 3 cm.

2 Officer's silver Motto 4.75 × 4 cm and silver and gilt collar badges3.25 × 3 cm.

3 Private purchase nickle Motto 4.75 × 4 cm.

4 Soldier's anodised aluminium shoulder title 3.5 × 1 cm.

5 QRL button.

6 Officer's bronze shoulder title 3.25 × 1 cm.

7 WO2 (SSM) James Scattergood wearing Barrack Dress with the Regiment's distinctive pullover.

8 Officer's gunmetal beret Motto introduced in Northern Ireland in 1984 and now replaced by a silver Motto 4.5 × 3.75 cm.

opposite page

9 Sergeant's Mess Dress wire-embroidered collar badges 2.5 × 2.5 cm.

10 Sergeant's Mess Dress rank badge is worn on the chevrons.

11 Sergeant's Mess Dress regimental rank badge 5.5 × 6.5 cm.

12 Sergeant's Mess Dress 5th Royal Irish Lancers arm badge 3.5 × 5.25 cm.

13 21st Lancers arm badge 3 × 3.5 cm worn by all ranks on No1, No2 and Mess Dress.

14 Warrant Officer Class 1 woven rank slide.

15 Lieutenant Colonel's gunmetal rank badges and shoulder title worn in shirt sleeve order.

16 QRL regimental guidon carried by WO2 John Southam escorted by SSgts Rob Smith and Ronnie Briggs.

17 Major Neil Oswin wearing Service Dress with the 21st Lancers arm badge on his left sleeve.

this page

18 TRF 5.5 × 5.5 cm and desert version worn in Iraq.

19 LCpls Dave Smith, Mick Vann and Bill Leaning, 2Lt Edward Wainright-Lee, and Cpl Geordie Burnett wearing combat dress.

20 Officers wear silver pouches from constituent regiments whilst soldiers wear neither belts nor crossbelts.

Acknowledgement
WO1 (RSM) IC Money, WO2 (RQMS) John Southam
SSgt Arni Cowans and Sgt C Harrison

Royal Tank Regiment

The Royal Tank Regiment, formed as The Heavy Branch The Machine Gun Corps in 1917, consists of two separate regiments, 1st Royal Tank Regiment, which forms the nucleus of the Joint Nuclear Biological and Chemical Defence Regiment, and 2nd Royal Tank Regiment, an armoured regiment.

The design of the cap badge of The Royal Tank Regiment, or RTR, is based upon the rhomboid shape of the first battle tanks. The badge itself is based upon the design of the arm badge, designed by Colonel Sir Ernest Swinton and still worn, which had been approved for wear on the upper right sleeve by all personnel of The Heavy Branch, The Machine Gun Corps in 1917. After four months The Heavy Branch was redesignated The Tank Corps and a cap badge designed to replace that of The Machine Gun Corps. In 1922 the present cap badge design was introduced with a Tudor (or King's) Crown, which was altered to St Edward's (or Queen's) Crown in about 1955. Soldiers' badges have been produced in anodised aluminium since 1958. In recent years it has become common practice for soldiers to buy metal badges, and issue frosted white metal badges are now replacing the 'staybrite' examples.

There is an extremely rare RTR wire-embroidered beret badge which was worn on the officer's astrakhan beret in the 1960s and is now worn by only one or two officers close to retirement on the beret.

1

2

3

4

5

6

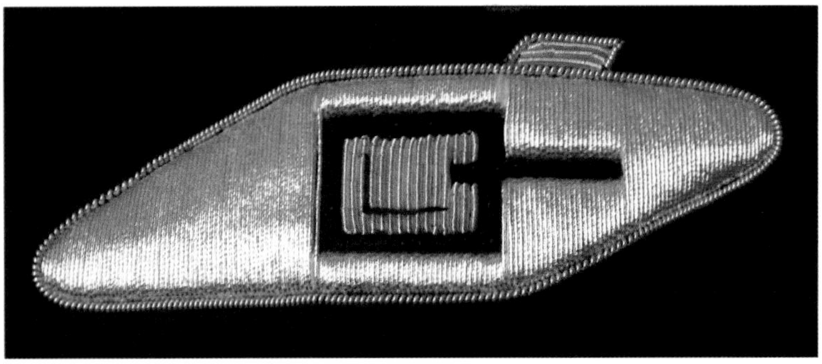

7

The Tank sleeve badge, in silver bullion for Number 1 Dress, khaki and tan cotton for Number 2 Dress and Working Dress, and gold bullion for Mess Dress is worn by all ranks except on Number 12 Dress, the black coveralls, when the Tank badge is worn only by officers and Class 1 crewmen.

In Number 12 Dress, the black coveralls, Non-Commissioned Officers serving with 1st Royal Tank Regiment wear their ranks on a brassard, whilst those serving with 2nd Royal Tank Regiment wear the badges sewn directly onto the coveralls.

The issue rank slide is black embroidered with a brown, red and green flash. The traditional colours of The Royal Tank Regiment are said to represent 'through the mud and the blood to the green fields beyond.'

The Tactical Recognition Flash in regimental colours, green, red, brown, was approved in 2000. 1st Royal Tank Regiment was to wear the TRF with a red border and 2nd Royal Tank Regiment with a saffron border. In the event the regiment has decided not to wear a TRF, retaining instead the green, red, brown border to the rank slide.

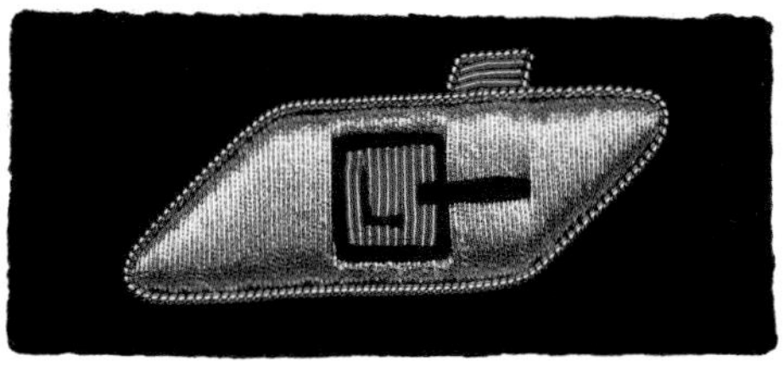

9

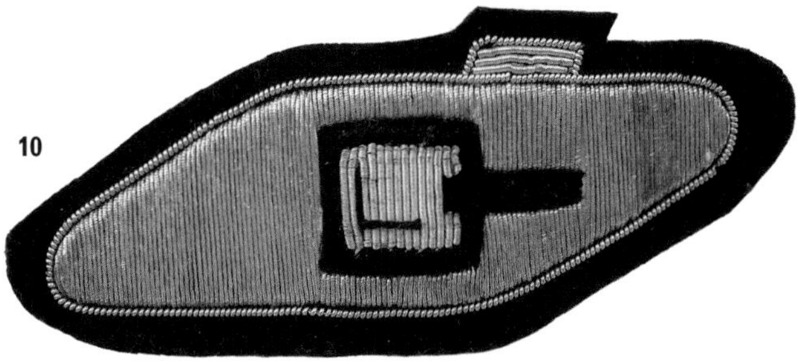

10

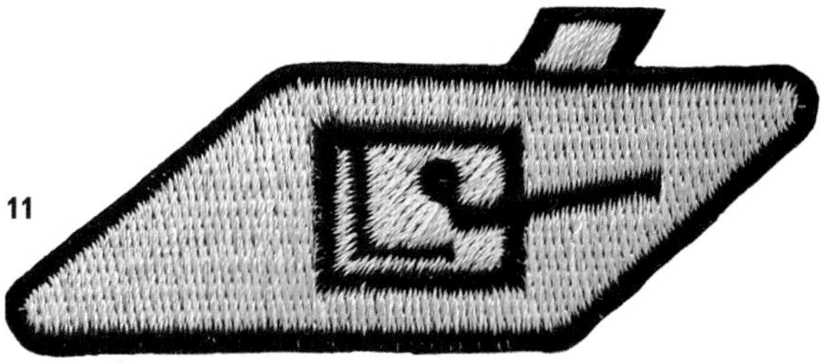

11

12

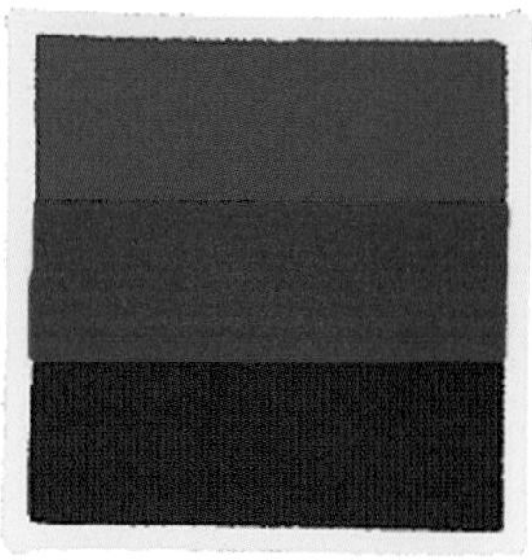

13

8

14

The Royal Tank Regiment colours are green, brown and red. On the creation of the Tank Corps in 1917, Major General Elles when looking for material to make up a flag found only a limited selection available in Flanders and settled on the three colours. Lieutenant Colonel John Fuller, Chief of Tank Staff coined the interpretation of the colours as 'From the mud, through the blood to the green fields beyond.'

opposite page

1 Royal Tank Regiment soldier's white metal cap badge 3.5 × 4.25 cm and anodised aluminium collar badges 2.5 × 3.25 cm.

2 Officer's silver and gilt No1 Dress collar badges 2.5 × 3.5 cm.

3 RTR Button.

4 Officers and Warrant Officers bronze Service Dress (No2 Dress) collar badges.

5 Sgt James Orr wearing No1 Dress with a silver wire-embroidered Tank badge on the right sleeve.

6 No1 Dress wire-embroidered Tank arm badge on a black backing 10 × 4.25 cm. The silver wire badge on a khaki backing is worn by The Westminster Dragoons (see p. 349).

7 Tank Arm badge worn on No2 Dress and working dress 9 × 4.25 cm.

this page

8 Captain David Pinkstone wearing Service Dress. His saffron lanyard indicates Service with 2 RTR.

9 Mess Dress Tank arm badge 7 × 3 cm.

10 The Tank arm badge is usually trimmed when worn on No1 Dress 8.5 × 3.75 cm.

11 Tank arm badge trimmed for No12 Dress, the black coveralls 7 × 3 cm.

12 Approved but unissued 1 RTR TRF.

13 Approved but unissued 2 RTR TRF.

14 Rare, possibly unique, RTR wire-embroidered beret badge 4.5 × 4.75 cm.

15

16

17

18

19

Lanyards are worn on the left shoulder of Number 2 Dress. Officers serving away from the regiment wear a black lanyard. All ranks of 1st Royal Tank Regiment wear a red lanyard and all ranks of 2nd Royal Tank Regiment wear a saffron lanyard. Soldiers serving away from the regiment wear the lanyard of whichever regiment with which they formerly served.

Lineage Tank Corps, Royal Tank Corps, Royal Tank Regiment (1917)

15 Captain Nigel Atkins wearing the silver wire-embroidered arm badge and silver and gilt collar badges.

16 WO2 Frankie Caldwell MBE wearing barrack dress with the regimental rank slide.

17 WO1 rank slide.

18 Soldier's waist belt clasp, anodised aluminium badge on the universal belt plate 7.25 × 5.5 cm.

19 Sgt Rab Dunlop and Cpl Jack Frost wearing the RTR distinctive black coveralls and Norwegian pullovers, their rank brassards indicate that they are serving with 1 RTR. The Tank arm badge in this order of dress indicates a Class 1 crewman.

Acknowledgement WO1 (RSM) GA Scott

Royal Tank Regiment Pipers

A pipe band was formed in the 4th Royal Tank Regiment, which recruited in Scotland, in 1971. It transferred to 1st Royal Tank Regiment in 1992. The pipers wear the Glengarry instead of the beret, and a feathered bonnet in Full Dress. There are two versions of the large piper's badge; the first produced by 4th Royal Tank Regiment and a later, better casting by 1st Royal Tank Regiment.

1

2

3

4

1 Original 4 RTR Glengarry badge 5.5 × 7.25 cm.
2 1 RTR Glengarry badge 5.5 × 8 cm.
3 Pipe Sergeant's plaid brooch 8.5 cm. The centre is the badge of the Machine Gun Corps, worn 1915–1922.
4 Piper's chrome plaid brooch 8.75 cm. The centre is the badge of the Tank Corps, worn 1916–1923.

Joint Nuclear, Biological and Chemical Defence Regiment

1st Royal Tank Regiment and 27 Squadron Royal Air Force Regiment together formed the Joint Nuclear, Biological and Chemical Defence Regiment in 2001. All personnel wear an olive green flash with black crossed retorts superimposed (necks down). Some Territorial Army units also wear the NBC badge.

The trial pattern NBC badge consisted of crossed yellow retorts on a diagonal Army, or 1st Royal Tank Regiment, red over RAF blue square and is reported to have been worn only by the Commanding Officer and Second in Command or senior RAF officer, and possibly by the Regimental Sergeant Major, in 2001–2002.

In 2003 a sand coloured badge was issued for the war in Iraq.

The Nuclear Biological and Chemical Defence badge is generally known within the regiment as the 'dog's bollocks' because of the distinctive design.

NBC defence arm badge 4.5 × 4.5 cm, 'The Dog's Bollocks'; the subdued pattern worn on combat kit, the sand coloured worn in the desert, and the first design which combined Army and RAF colours.

Royal Artillery

The Royal Artillery consists of Batteries with their own Battle Honour titles, history and traditions, which are grouped together as regiments.

The Royal Artillery, or RA, cap badge has been worn since 1903. The use of a Cannon as a design for badges was adopted in 1833 for use on various accoutrements. The cap badge sized badge was introduced with the leather pouch, which replaced the officer's Full Dress pouch in 1902. The following year the design was adopted as a cap badge when Service Dress was issued. The design is based upon the 9 pounder muzzle-loading gun issued to the Horse and Field Artillery in 1871. The Full Dress pouch is now only worn by The King's Troop, or sometimes at weddings, whilst the officer's leather pouch worn with Number 1 Dress has a gilt badge the same size as the Forage Cap badge, and that worn with Number 2 Dress has the same as the bronze Service Dress badge. The present cap badge surmounted by St Edward's (or Queen's) Crown was introduced in about 1955, with the soldier's badge produced in anodised aluminium being issued from 1958.

1

2

4

3

5

6

7

8

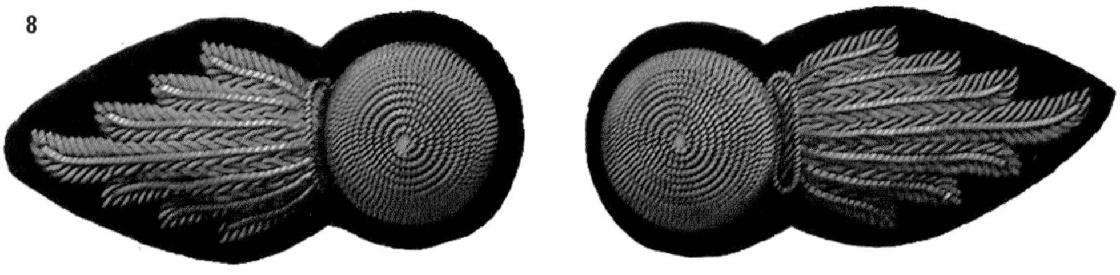

132 Battery (The Bengal Rocket Troop) has a silver model of a tiger standing over a rocket which was cast in 1924 from the Battery's silver badges which had been worn on the brow bands of the Troop's horses until mechanisation in 1924. Replicas of the model were also made as radiator mascots for the Troop's vehicles.

The badge is in two sizes. Large badges are worn on the Forage Cap and Service Dress cap and a reduced sized badge on the beret.

The mottos are *Everywhere*, (interpreted by the infantry as 'all over the place'), and *Where Right and Glory Lead* both of which were granted by William IV in 1832.

Because the design of the badge has remained unchanged since 1902, except for the Crown, some soldiers wear old or reproduction gilding metal badges in their berets. Officers wear a wire-embroidered beret badge. Towards the end of 2003 a contractor produced badges with a green field rather than the traditional gold. Although the badges are incorrect some were sold to officers and continue to be worn.

All Gunners wear the Gun badge, although those serving with the Royal Horse Artillery wear the cypher on the beret. Officers wear a wire-embroidered Grenade pattern badge on the side hat.

The Royal Artillery and Royal Engineers both wear collar badges consisting of a flaming grenade over a scroll embossed *Ubique*. As a general rule the Royal Artillery badges have seven flames, and Royal Engineers nine flames. Officer's wire-embroidered collar badges without a scroll, now worn on Number 1 Dress, were introduced in 1881. The present officers' bronze collar badges were introduced in 1902, and in 1953 gilt collar badges were introduced for Number 3 Dress.

9

10

11

12

13

14

15

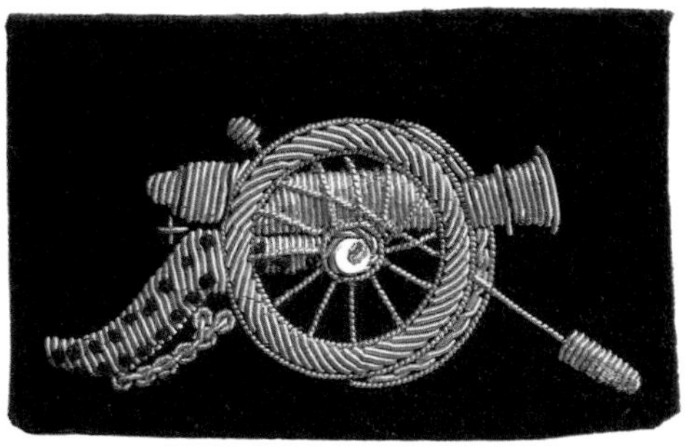

16

The grenade badge has been used since at least 1831, mainly as a collar badge but also as a cap badge on the Field Service Cap (a khaki Side Cap), which was worn from 1938 until the introduction of the beret during the Second World War. The grenade is retained as an officer's side hat badge.

Soldiers wore the universal brass Grenade collar badge without a scroll from 1880 until 1926 now worn only by The Royal Welch Fusiliers. It was replaced by the same nine flames Grenade with scroll as worn by the Royal Engineers until 1928 when the present seven flamed roped Grenade with scroll was adopted.

Soldiers serving with the Royal Horse Artillery wear the cypher as a collar badge.

In Number 2 Dress sergeants wear a cannon above their chevrons. The only order of dress in which rank is worn on both sleeves is Number 2 Dress and the pair of cloth badges are referred to in the Stores as 'Guns left and right'. A gun is crewed by a detachment usually commanded by a sergeant and therefore the badge is sometimes referred to by Gunners as the DC, or Detachment Commander's, badge

The Royal Artillery has two specialist Qualification badges. Crossed guns are awarded to soldiers who have completed a Gunnery Career Course and are carrying out the duties of Sergeant Major Instructor in Gunnery, abbreviated to SMIG. At present all are warrant officers and the crossed guns are worn below their rank badges. It is anticipated that some Staff Sergeants will be qualified as instructors in gunnery in 2005. The badge was introduced in 1877 as a prize badge for the most efficient gunners in each battery. Surmounted by a Crown, it became the appointment badge of an Assistant Instructor in Gunnery during the First World War and was discontinued as a prize badge in 1921.

17

18

Guns were first used in England during the 13th Century but English artillery did not became established until the 16th Century when 13 soldiers were recruited to maintain Henry VIII's artillery at the Tower of London.

Until 1715 Artillery Trains were formed as and when required. The failure to deploy artillery quickly at the outset of the Jacobite rebellion led to two companies of artillery being added to the Standing Army in 1716. In 1722 they were grouped with the Artillery Trains at Gibraltar and Minorca as the Royal Regiment of Artillery. Two Branches, Royal Field Artillery and Royal Horse Artillery, and Royal Garrison Artillery were formed in 1899. Separate Branches were abolished in 1924 although the Royal Horse Artillery title and precedence was retained.

19

20

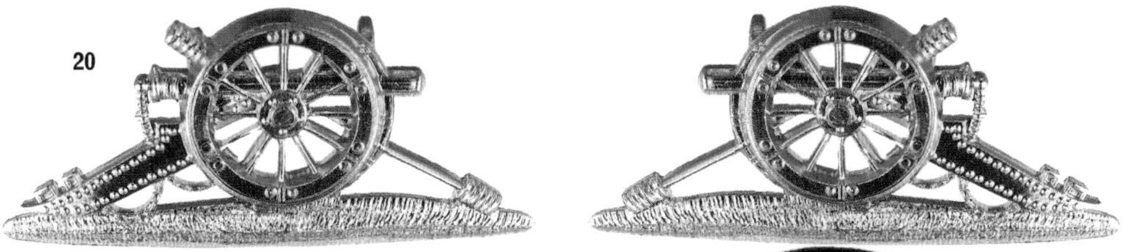

21

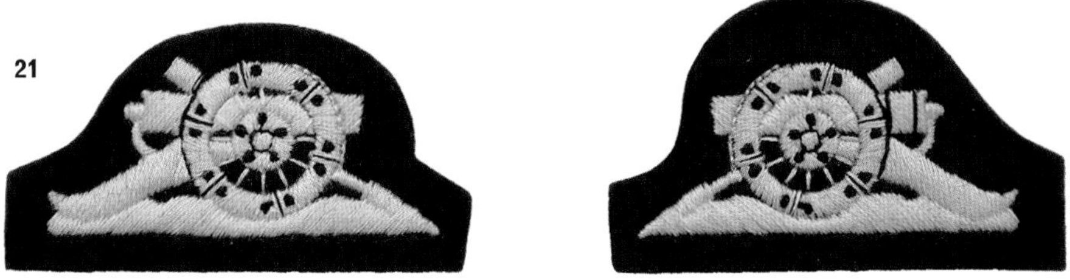

22

previous page

1 Royal Artillery soldier's anodised aluminium cap 6.5 × 4.75 cm and collar badges 2.5 × 3.75 cm. A smaller cap badge is worn on the beret.

2 RA button.

3 Anodised aluminium shoulder title 2 × 1 cm.

4 Officer's gilt Forage Cap badge 6.5 × 5 cm.

5 Officer's bronze Service Dress cap badge 6.5 × 5 cm.

6 Bdr Dan Warricker in No2 Dress. He wears the white lanyard worn by all Gunners below the rank of Warrant Officer. Above his stripes he has the crossed rifles badge of a Skill-at-Arms instructor.

7 Bdr Nick Tolley and Captain Trigger Buxton wearing the beret badges.

opposite page

8 Officers' No1 Dress collar badges 4.5 × 6 cm.

9 Officer's incorrect wire-embroidered beret badge with a green ground 6 × 4.75 cm.

10 Officer's correct wire-embroidered beret badge 6 × 5.25cm.

11 Officer's No3 Dress gilt collar badges 2.75 × 5 cm.

12 Officer's Service Dress bronze collar badges 2.75 × 5 cm.

13 Officer's wire-embroidered side-hat badge 3.25 × 4.75 cm.

14 Lt Col Jac Bazzard wearing the side cap.

15 No1 Dress wire-embroidered regimental rank badge 7 × 4.5 cm.

16 Mess Dress wire-embroidered regimental rank badge 6.5 × 4.25 cm.

this page

17 Soldier's anodised aluminium beret badge 3 × 4 cm.

18 Soldier's private purchase gilding metal beret badge 3.25 × 4 cm.

19 Soldier's waist belt clasp 7 × 5.75 cm.

20 Anodised aluminium 'Guns left and right' 6 × 3.5 cm.

21 Woven rank badges 6 × 3.5 cm.

22 SSgt Wayne Bullock wearing a private purchase gilding metal beret badge.

It has been the SMIG's badge since 1980.

The Gun Layer's qualification badge was introduced in 1892 as a prize badge awarded to 'The six most efficient in a 6 gun battery and each of the four most efficient in a 4 gun battery' and also 'For the most efficient in a Garrison Company.' The award attracted a prize of £1-10s-0d (£1.50), the equivalent of a month's pay. In 1901 the badge became an appointment badge worn on the upper right arm.

There are Employment badges authorised to be worn on the lower left arm for Range Taker, Fire Control Operator, Radar Operator, Surveyor and Regimental Surveyor, but they are no longer issued.

23

24

25

26

27

28

The *Ubique* honour was granted to the Royal Artillery in 1833 specifically in lieu of all other battle honours.

Lineage Royal Regiment of Artillery (1716).

29

30

31

33

opposite page

23 WO2 (SMIG) Blan Blanchette, his appointment identified by the crossed guns badge and white topped staff cap.

24 LBdr Mack MacKinnon wearing the Gun Layer's badge.

25 Instructor in Gunnery badge 5 × 5 cm.

26 Gun Layer's working dress cloth badge 5 × 6 cm.

27 Gun Layer's anodised aluminium badge 5.25 × 4.5 cm.

28 Officer's Full Dress cross belt tip decorated with a grenade, also worn by the Army Air Corps.

29 Lieutenant Colonel's rank slide.

30 Master Gunner Class 1 rank slide.

32 WO2 (Sergeant Major Instructor in Gunnery) rank slide.

this page

33 Private purchase Full Dress pouch – different in detail from the official pouch issued to The King's Troop RHA.

34 Officer's leather pouch decorated with gilt badge worn on a gold lace cross-belt with No1 Dress.

35 Officer's brown leather pouch decorated with a bronzed badge worn on leather cross-belt with Service Dress.

34

35

Acknowledgement
Major Bill Clarke, Sgt GJL Calder and Mr Paul Upton

The Royal Artillery Sergeant Major

1

5

6

1 WO1 (RASM) Tosh McIntosh wearing the No1 Dress rank badge.
2 Shirtsleeve order metal and enamel badge 4.5 × 5.5 cm worn on a wristband.
3 Mess Dress rank badge 9.5 × 10.75 cm (shown much reduced)
4 No2 Dress rank badge worn on both sleeves with the guns facing forwards 9.5 × 10.25 cm, two variations (shown much reduced).
5 Combat Dress rank slide.
6 No1 Dress rank badge, 9.5 × 10.5m.
7 Rank badge worn on the right sleeve of the Atholl Grey greatcoat 9.5 × 10 cm.

2

4

7

3

Helmet Rank Badges

1

2

6

7

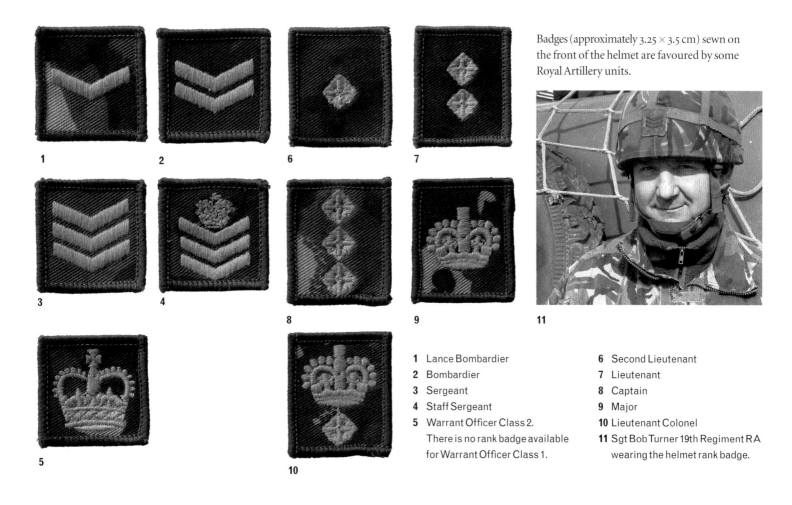

Badges (approximately 3.25 × 3.5 cm) sewn on the front of the helmet are favoured by some Royal Artillery units.

3

4

8

9

11

5

10

1 Lance Bombardier
2 Bombardier
3 Sergeant
4 Staff Sergeant
5 Warrant Officer Class 2. There is no rank badge available for Warrant Officer Class 1.
6 Second Lieutenant
7 Lieutenant
8 Captain
9 Major
10 Lieutenant Colonel
11 Sgt Bob Turner 19th Regiment RA wearing the helmet rank badge.

4th Regiment RA

1

2

1 4th Regiment RA arm badge 6 × 5 cm introduced in 2004.
2 Sgt P Cummins of 94 HQ Battery wearing the 4th Regiment RA arm badge.

Acknowledgement WO2 (RQMS) McAuley

5th Regiment RA

Soldiers who have completed the Special Observer (Basic) Course and are, or have served with 4/73 (Sphinx) Special OP Battery may wear the Special Observers Badge in perpetuity. The triangular badge is based upon the military map symbol for an artillery observation post. (An observation post is shown on a map by a triangle, the addition of a 'cannon ball' in the centre indicates an artillery observation post).

1 

2 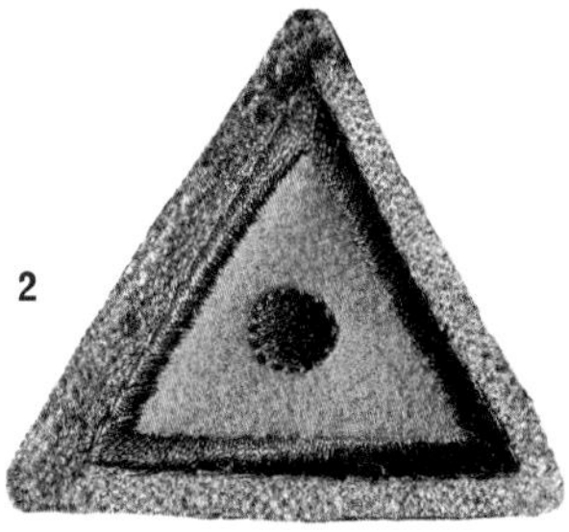

3 

4 

1 Bdr Kev Frances 12th Regiment RA, Allan Gilmour 7th Regiment RHA wearing the Pegasus badge on his left sleeve and David Greenland 5th Regiment RA wearing the Special OP badge on his left upper arm.
2 No2 Dress Special OP badge 4.5 × 4 cm.
3 Mess Dress Special OP badge 3.5 × 3.25 cm.
4 Sgt Jock Herrity of Q (Sannas Post) HQ Battery, 5th Regiment RA wearing the 1st Artillery Brigade flash below the Union Flag badge.

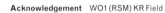

Acknowledgement WO1 (RSM) KR Field

12th Regiment RA

12th Regiment RA arm badge 6 × 5 cm adopted in 2004

14th Regiment RA

14th Regiment RA regimental police lance bombardier's rank slide.

14th Regiment RA is the training support and Depot regiment at the Royal School of Artillery.

16th Regiment RA

1 

2 

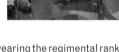

1 Sgt Lee Williams 16 Regt RA wearing the regimental rank badge above his chevrons.
2 SSgt Bruce Mann 16 Regt RA wearing the 7 AD Brigade arm badge.

Acknowledgement WO1 SJ Howe and WO2 (BSM) D Williams

19th Regiment Royal Artillery

'The Highland Gunners'

19th Regiment RA wear the Robinson Hunting Tartan. It is used for rank slides and the Orderly Sergeant's sash, is worn by the pipers and drummers and used to make officers' Mess Dress trews.

19th/5th (Gibraltar 1779–1783) Battery wears the ribbon of the French Croix de Guerre; it is worn on the beret immediately below the cap badge, on the right side of the Forage Cap and on both sleeves in Number 1 Dress and Mess Dress.

1

2

19th/5th (Gibraltar 1779–1783) Battery

The Croix de Guerre was awarded to 5th Battery for its actions in France on 27 May 1918.

> *Although, having suffered intense bombardment from HE and Gas throughout the night 26/27 May, the battery never slackened its fire on either SOS or counter preparations, with such guns which were still in action. At 0700 hours the enemy entered the position and the Battery Commander led a counter attack with the surviving officers and men. Eventually, only four gunners survived.*

The medal was stolen in 1960 but the replacement is accorded the same honours as the original.

1. Sgt Jimmy Frazer wearing the 5th Battery Croix de Guerre ribbon below the RA beret badge.
2. 19th Regiment RA Robinson Hunting tartan staff sergeant's rank slide.

26th Regiment RA

Lieutenant Colonel Julian Free MBE introduced the 26th Regiment RA arm badge when the regiment deployed to Iraq in 2003.

1

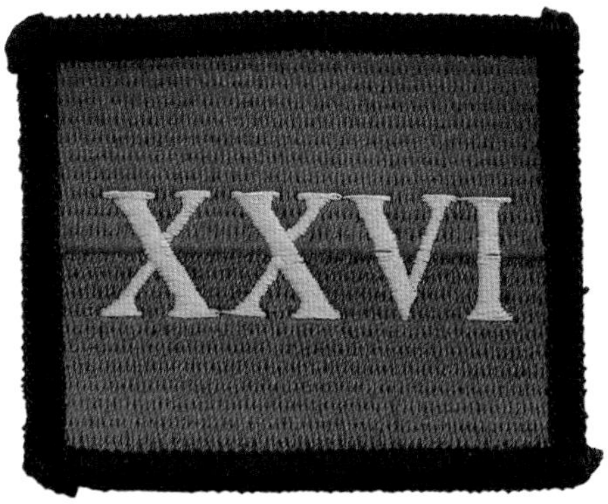

2

1. 26th Regiment RA arm badge 6 × 5 cm introduced in 2003.
2. Bdr Brendan Blatcher wearing the 26th Regiment arm badge and the United Nations cap badge and Blue Beret.

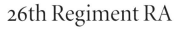

Acknowledgement WO1 (ASM) DI Wilson and Sgt D Smyth

29th Commando Regiment RA

Royal Artillery commandos wear the green beret, the officers with a wire-embroidered badge with a green backing.

148 (Meiktila) Commando Forward Observation Battery is a parachute unit and soldiers wear the Combined Operations badge as their Drop Zone flash. It was designed in 1942 by Lieutenant DA Grant RNVR serving on HMS Tormentor and approved by Lord Louis Mountbatten for wear by all British, American and allied forces connected with Combined Operations. The battery originally wore a square badge but in the 1990s it was changed to a circular badge worn on each sleeve of the combat smock.

4

5

1

2

3

1 29 Commando Regiment RA officer's wire-embroidered beret badge with the incorrect green ground 4 × 3.5 cm.
2 Gnr Tez Matthews 29 Commando Regiment RA.
3 WO2 Liam Kelly wearing the 148 Battery DZ flash. On his left breast is the parachute badge of the United States Marine Corps.
4 148 Battery combined operations DZ badges 7.5 cm worn with the Tommy Gun facing forward.
5 Obsolete 148 Battery DZ badges 7 × 7 cm.

40th Regiment Royal Artillery 'The Lowland Gunners'

40th Regiment RA wear Hume Tartan. It is used for rank slides, is worn by the pipers and drummers and used to make officers' Mess Dress trews.

From time to time RA Batteries wear special arm badges. 129 Battery (The Dragon Troop) has done so on at least three occasions since the 1980s, most recently in Iraq in 2004.

1

2

1 40th Regiment Hume Tartan Warrant Officer Class 2 rank slide.
2 The Dragon Troop arm badge 5 × 5 cm.

47th Regiment Royal Artillery

10 (Assaye) Battery wears the Syrena awarded by 2nd Polish Corps under General Wladyslaw Anders in Italy in recognition of the support provided during the fourth battle of Monte Casino, from 11 to 18 May 1944. At the time the Battery was known as 40th Medium Battery and its successor, 10 (Assaye) Battery, is the last remaining Royal Artillery battery to wear the honour.

21 Air Assault Battery wears the airborne forces maroon beret, and officer's the Royal Artillery badge wire-embroidered on a maroon backing.

The Battery wears the same Drop Zone flash as 7th (Parachute) Regiment Royal Horse Artillery but whilst 7 RHA wears the DZ Flash only on the smock, 21 Air Assault Battery wears it on the shirt as a Tactical Recognition Flash.

In April 1951 1st Battalion The Gloucestershire Regiment and C Troop 170th Independent Mortar Battery were granted the United States Distinguished Unit Citation, now known as the US Army Presidential Unit Citation, for outstanding gallantry during the Battle of Imjin 23–25 April 1951. The Battery's successor, 25/170 (Imjin) Battery, wears the ribbon of the award on the right sleeve of Number 1 Dress and Mess Dress and on both sleeves of Number 2 Dress. (See The Royal Gloucestershire, Berkshire and Wiltshire Regiment p.178).

1 Bdr Spence Jones wearing the 10 (Assaye) Battery Syrena below the crossed flags badge of a qualified signaller.
2 Incorrect officer's wire-embroidered airborne badge with a green ground 4.25 × 3.25 cm.
3 Correct officer's airborne beret badge 4 × 3.5 cm.
4 Bdr Matt Onn 21 Air Assault Battery wearing the maroon beret. On his right breast is the United States Army parachute badge.
5 Lt David Ferguson wearing the insignia of the US Army Presidential Unit Citation on both sleeves of his Service Dress having served with 25/170 (Imjin) Battery.
6 25/170 (Imjin) Battery US Army Presidential Unit Citation 3.75 × 2 cm.

1

2

3

4

5

6

Acknowledgement
WO1 (RSM) JA Howdon and WO2 Paul Jacques MBE

Royal Artillery Pipers

19th, 40th and 103rd Regiments RA

19th and 40th Regiments, along with 103rd Regiment, a TA unit, have volunteer pipe bands, each about 16 strong. Pipers wear the usual Royal Artillery insignia except their Glengarry has a distinctive badge, and on parade they wear a plaid brooch. The pipers wear a plain sporran except for the Drum Major 103rd Regiment who wears a collar badge on his sporran.

1

2

1 Bdr Spoot Berestord and LBdr Adam Fielding of 19th Regiment RA pipe band wearing the RA Glengarry badge and the Robertson Hunting tartan rank slide, with the 12th Mechanized Brigade badge on the left sleeve below the Union Flag badge.

2 PMaj Pipey Frazer and LBdr Gordon Cowle wearing 19th Regiment RA piper's Full Dress.

3 RA Glengarry badge 5.5 × 6.5 cm.

4 RA plaid brooch 9.5 cm.

3

4

Royal Engineers

The Corps of Royal Engineers was formed in 1856 tasked with enabling the Army to fight, move and survive.

The design of the Royal Engineers cap badge is thought to derive from a combination of earlier badges. The Royal cypher in the centre of the badge was worn on officers' cross belt plates in 1782 and also within a crowned Garter in 1823 by soldiers of the Royal Sappers and Miners. The laurel leaves were probably added to represent the honours gained in the 19th century.

The design was adopted in 1898 and the Crown and cypher altered for each monarch. The title, which had originally been on the Garter, was moved to below it when Edward VII's cypher was adopted in about 1902. The present badge, surmounted by St Edward's (or Queen's) Crown, was produced in bi-metal in about 1955 and issued in anodised aluminium from 1958.

1

2

3

4

5

6

The Royal Air Force, Royal Corps of Signals and elements of the Royal Electrical and Mechanical Engineers and the Royal Logistic Corps were formed from specialist Royal Engineers units.

7

8

9

The Royal Artillery and Royal Engineers both wear collar badges consisting of a flaming grenade over a scroll embossed Ubique. As a general rule the Royal Artillery badges have seven flames, and Royal Engineers nine flames. Officer's wire-embroidered collar badges without a scroll, now worn by Royal Artillery officers on Number 1 Dress, were introduced in 1881. They were also worn until recently by Royal Engineer officers although there are now nine flame Number 1 Dress badges available. The present officers' bronze collar badges were introduced in 1902. The badges are worn with the tip of the centre flame curling inwards. Soldiers had worn the universal brass Grenade collar badge without a scroll, now worn only by The Royal Welch Fusiliers, from 1880 until 1926 when the badge that is still worn replaced it; the nine flamed Grenade with scroll. The Royal Artillery also wore the badge for two years until 1928.

A cloth Royal Engineers shoulder title for Combat Dress was introduced in the British Army of the Rhine in the 1980s. The practice became widespread and eventually all Sappers were instructed to buy the badges (at £1.50 each) just before the Army Dress Committee ordered the titles removed in 2003. In order not to damage uniforms by cutting off the badges permission was given to wear the titles until the clothing required exchanging. A Tactical Recognition Flash was introduced in 2004.

Sergeants wear a nine flamed bomb as the regimental rank badge. It was the practice for Quartermaster Sergeant Instructors, or QMSI, who are identified by their appointment badge of a Crown within a wreath, to wear a small gilding

10

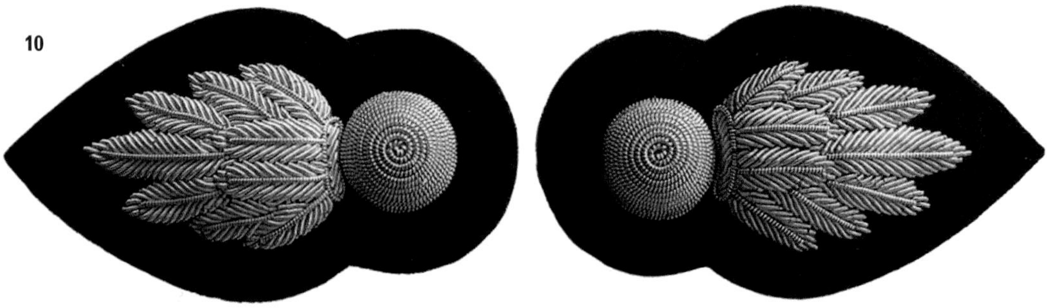

11

12

13

14

15

16

17

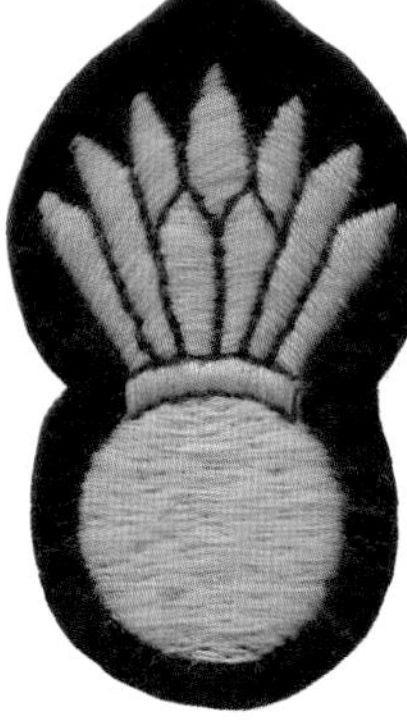

18

metal bomb below their rank on a wristband after they had passed the QMSI course. The practice has almost ceased now that Combat Dress has become the substitute for Barrack Dress and wristbands are rarely worn.

The classification of Qualified Instructor dates from 1882. The QI badge was introduced in 1914 for instructors below the rank of sergeant. In 1936 Warrant Officer instructors were authorised a Grenade badge which is still worn. During the 1960s Senior Non-Commissioned Officers who had gained an A Grade on the Field Engineering Course also wore the QI badge. In 1975 the QI and Grenade badges were authorised for instructors in Field Engineering who had gained a B grade on the course. The present size of badge was introduced in 1990 but the badge appears now to be obsolete.

The Royal Engineers deliver Explosive Ordnance Disposal, Infantry Pioneer, Diver and Carpenter and Joiner training for the Army.

EOD is an almost exclusive Royal Engineer employment, and the majority of divers are Royal Engineers. The majority of Infantry Pioneers are employed in Infantry Assault Pioneer platoons, although some Royal Armoured Corps soldiers and Royal Logistic Corps pioneers are also qualified Infantry Pioneers. The courses are conducted by the Royal Engineers.

19

Acknowledgement
WO1 (RSM) Bob Mather, WO1 (RSM) TJ Armstrong, Pat Patrick and Daz Rudd

The Infantry Pioneer's crossed hatchets badge is one of the earliest official badges, being listed in a Horse Guards Circular dated 1868.

The Carpenter and Joiner's wheel badge was also introduced by 1868. The King's Troop RHA wheelwrights wear an anodised aluminium version.

20

21

22

23

Lineage Corps of Royal Engineers (1717)

The first recorded military engineer in Britain was Bishop Gundulph, chief engineer to William the Conqueror, who built the White Tower. There was no permanent engineer staff until the 16th Century when the Ordnance Office formally employed officers. When required tradesmen were impressed, and then released at the cessation of hostilities. The growth of the far flung empire led in 1716 to the formation of the Corps of Engineers with qualified officers. A similar requirement led in 1787 to the formation of the Corps of Royal Military Artificer for soldiers. The two corps were amalgamated as the Corps of Royal Engineers in 1856.

previous page

1 Royal Engineer's soldier's anodised aluminium cap badge 3.75 × 4.5 and collar badges 2 × 3.25 cm.
2 Obsolete cloth shoulder title 12.25 × 3.5 cm.
3 Officer's silver and gilt Forage Cap badge 4 × 4.75 cm and bronzed Service Dress collar badges 3 × 5 cm.
4 Sgt Chris Coggins, identified as a RE Drill Instructor by his Service Dress cap and brown belt, and WO2 (SSM) Chris Vincent wearing the EOD badge on his left sleeve.
5 Soldier's private purchase bi-metal cap badge 3.75 × 4.5 cm.
6 RE button.
7 Officer's beret badge 4.5 × 6.25 cm.
8 Officer's airborne beret badge 4.25 × 6 cm.
9 Officer's commando beret badge 4.5 × 6 cm.

opposite page

10 Officer's No1 Dress collar badges 8.5 × 4.5 cm.
11 Sergeant's Mess Dress collar badges 3.5 × 2.5 cm.
12 Cpl Alan Richards wearing the TRF.
13 2Lt Andy Thorn wearing the wire-embroidered beret badge and the RE rank slide.
14 Officer's Mess Dress collar badges 4.5 × 6 cm.
15 TRF 5 × 4.75 cm.
16 Sergeant's No1 Dress rank badge 3.5 × 7 cm.
17 Sergeant's No2 rank badge 3 × 5 cm.
18 Warrant Officer Class 2 (Quartermaster Sergeant Instructor) locally made rank for shirtsleeve order, with 'Bomb' cut from a collar badge, worn by Combat Engineer instructors.

this page

19 Cpl Kev Daniels, 35 Engineer Regiment wearing the 20 Armoured Brigade arm badge.
20 Lieutenant Colonel and corporal's woven rank slides.
21 Qualified Instructor's badge 5 × 4 cm.
22 Carpenter and Joiner employment badge 4 cm.
23 Infantry Pioneer skill-at-arms badge 4.75 × 4.75 cm.

Divers

The Royal Engineers Diving Training Wing of the Defence Diving School trains military divers. Each Royal Engineers regiment and independent squadron has divers, as does each Royal Logistic Corps ship. There are also a few Royal Artillery commando divers. Divers are awarded one of three specialist badges based on the design of a diving helmet; similar badges are worn by Royal Navy divers. Two of the courses have been changed and the Army Compressed Air Diver, or Shallow Water badge is being phased out.

1
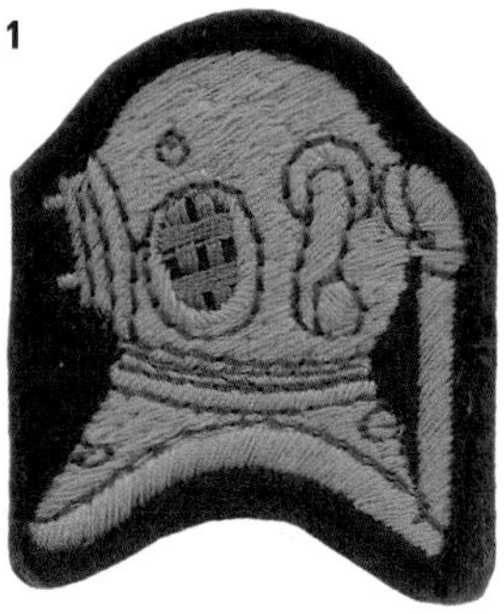

2

3

4
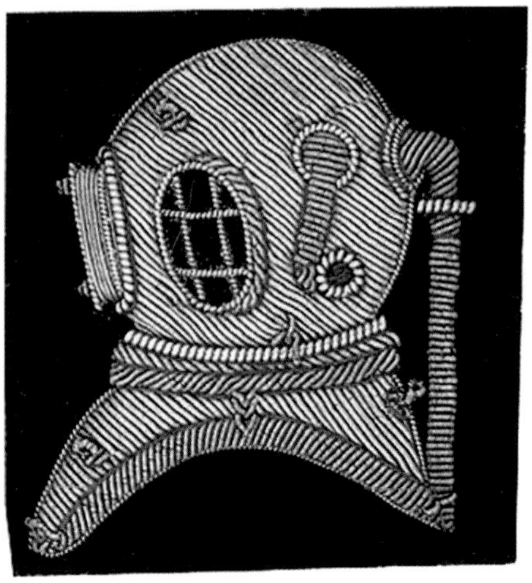

5
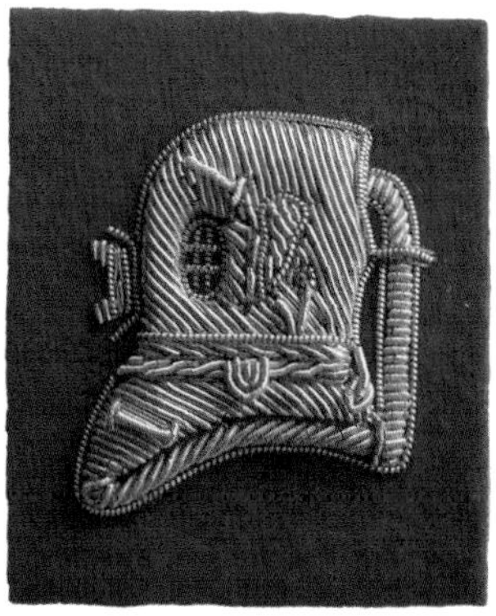

6
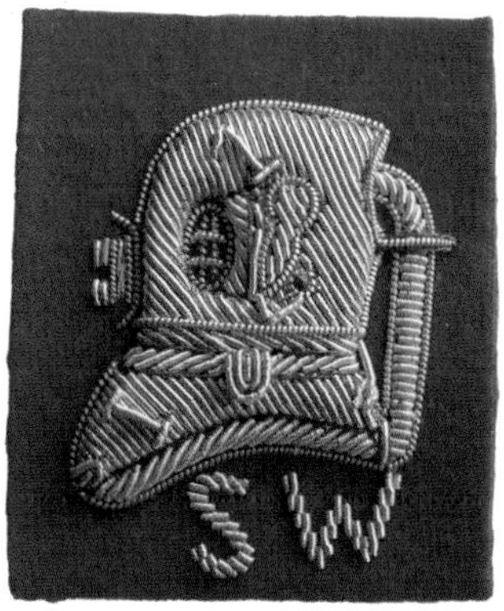

7

8

9

1 Army Diving Supervisor badge 3.5 × 3.75 cm.
2 Army Advanced Diver badge 4 × 4.75 cm.
3 Obsolete Army Compressed Air Diver badge 4.25 × 6.25 cm.
4 No1 Dress badge 6 × 6.5 cm.
5 Mess Dress badge 4 × 4.75 cm.
6 Obsolete Army Compressed Air Diver Mess Dress badge 4.5 × 5.5 cm.
7 Cpl Taff Davies wearing the Army Advanced Diver's badge. The style of wearing his maroon beret indicates service with 9 Parachute Squadron.
8 Obsolete unofficial subdued Army Compressed Air Diver badge 6.25 × 6.25 cm.
9 Unofficial subdued Army Advanced Diver badge 5 × 6 cm.

9 Parachute Squadron 23 Engineer Regiment (Air Assault) and 49 Field Squadron 33 Engineer Regiment (Explosive Ordnance Disposal) Royal Engineers

The maroon beret, until recently a distinction of 9 Parachute Squadron, is now worn by all ranks of 23 Engineer Regiment (Air Assault) and by troops of 49 Field Squadron (Explosive Ordnance Disposal), 33 Engineer Regiment who have passed pre-parachute selection or are qualified parachutists.

1

2

3
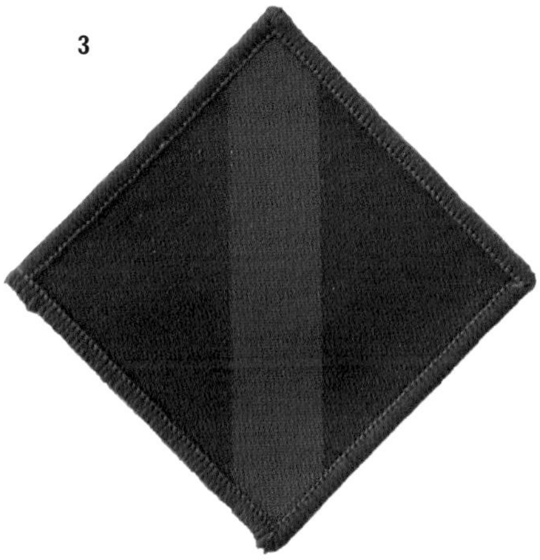

4

5

1 2Lt Rob Goût 9 Parachute Squadron wearing the DZ flash.
2 9 Parachute Squadron Drop Zone flash 7 × 7 cm.
3 1st Airborne Troop 49 Field Squadron Landing Zone flash 7 × 7 cm.
4 Mess Dress parachute badge on a red background for officers' 6.75 × 3 cm.
5 Mess Dress parachute badge on a black background for soldiers including Warrant Officers Class One 6.5 × 3 cm.

Acknowledgement WO1 (RSM) Darran Rudd

32 Engineer Regiment (The Assault Engineers)

32 Engineer Regiment is a descendent of the three engineer regiments of 1st Assault Brigade RE formed in 1943 to clear or bridge obstacles during the assault landings and subsequent operations in North West Europe. Soldiers wear berets, rather than Forage Caps with Number 2 Dress to reflect their service with specialist tanks.

The Regiment retains the distinctive Bull badge worn on the upper right sleeve introduced for the wartime 79th Armoured Division by Major General Sir PCS Hobart, the Crest of whose Arms was a bull passant. The inverted triangular shape represents V for victory.

1

2

26 Armoured Engineer Squadron continues to wear distinctive cloth titles. There are two explanations.

In the late 1980s it was recorded that the reason for the title was in honour of its history as the only armoured engineer squadron with an unbroken service since formation during the Second World War. The more recent explanation is that in 1916 King George V was given a smart salute by two Sappers whilst visiting the 1st Division in France. He is supposed to have said, 'I see you are from the Royal Engineers.'

'No Sir' was the reply, 'We're from 26.'

The King was delighted by the reply, which he said showed an excellent ésprit de corps and ordered that all those serving with what was then known as 26 Field Company should be identified with 26 on their uniform. The tradition has continued.

6

4

5

previous page

1 32 Engineer Regiment arm badge 6 × 5.5 cm
2 Captain Chris Axford MBE wearing the 32 Engineer Regiment arm badge.

this page

4 26 Armoured Engineers Squadron combat dress shoulder title 11.75 × 3.5 cm.
5 26 Armoured Engineers Squadron Barrack Dress and Coveralls shoulder title 11.75 × 3.5 cm.
6 Spr Jason Buckton wearing the 26 Armoured Engineer Squadron title above the 7th Armoured Brigade badge. He is also wearing the private purchase bimetal cap badge.

Acknowledgement
Major Ian Stanton, Capt DK Hunter and JR West

33 (Explosive Ordnance Disposal) Regiment Royal Engineers

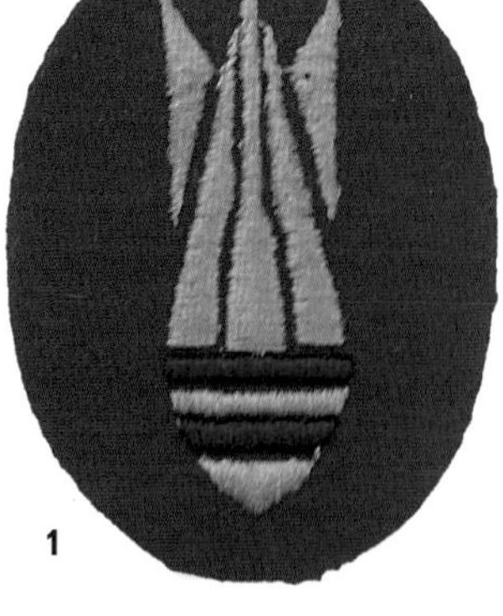
1

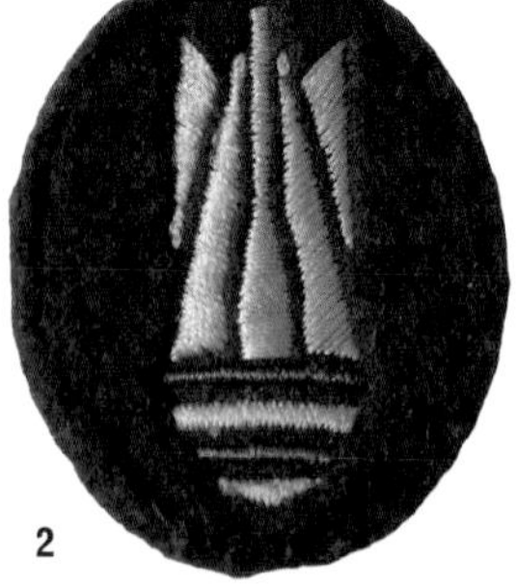
2

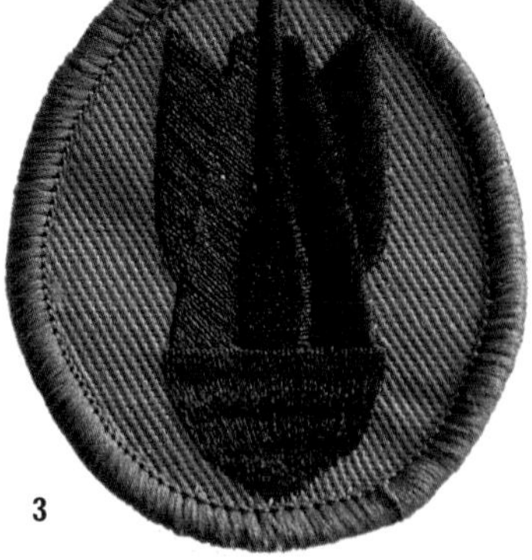
3

33 (Explosive Ordnance Disposal) Regiment is responsible for the disposal of bombs and mines. The task is extremely dangerous and since 1940 thirteen Royal Engineers have been awarded the George Cross for actions when carrying out Explosive Ordnance Disposal (EOD). In 1940 Queen Mary approved a badge to be worn by personnel serving in bomb disposal units. The Queen Mary Battle Honour badge continues to worn by all ranks serving in 33 (EOD) Regiment on the left forearm of Number 2 Dress.

Personnel serving in EOD units who have passed an EOD course appropriate to their rank wear a yellow bomb badge as a qualification badge on Combat Dress. Those no longer serving in an EOD unit and who have passed the Advanced EOD Course, usually only officers and senior NCOs, also wear the badge on all orders of dress as a qualification badge.

4

5

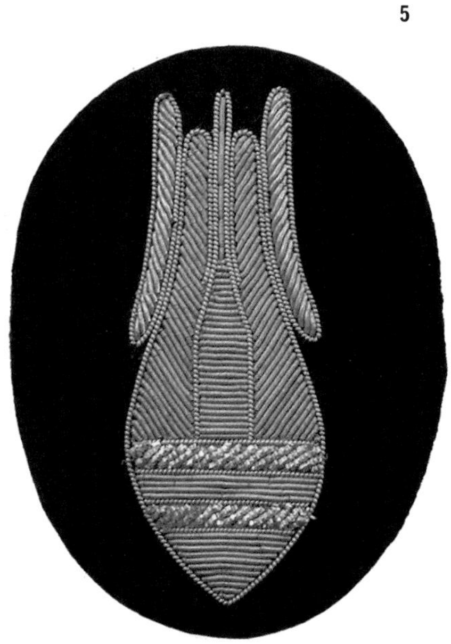

3

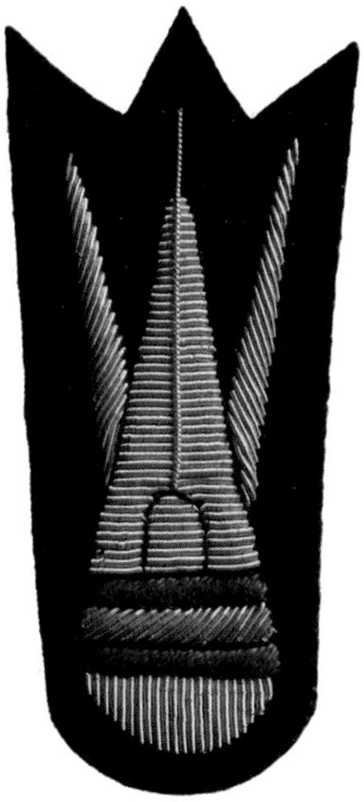

7

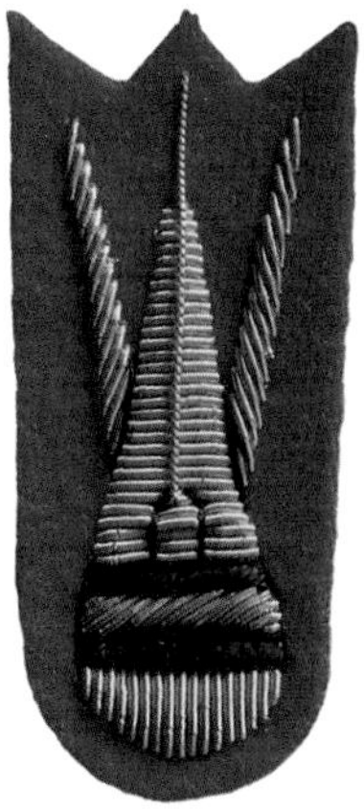

previous page
Explosive Ordnance Disposal wire-embroidered qualification badges.
1 Queen Mary Battle Honour Badge 4.25 × 5 cm.
2 EOD qualification badge 3.25 × 4 cm.
3 Unofficial subdued Combat Dress badge 4.5 × 5 cm.

this page
4 Cpl Abs Abel wearing the EOD qualification badge on his left sleeve.
5 Obsolete No1 Dress EOD badge 5.75 × 7.75 cm.
6 No1 Dress EOD badge 4 × 8.25 cm.
7 Mess Dress EOD badge 2.75 × 5.75 cm.

Acknowledgement Capt Henryk Pietrzak

Queen's Gurkha Engineers

The Queen's Gurkha Engineers was formed in 1955. The regiment is affiliated to the Royal Engineers and their badge is the Corps collar badge divided by two kukris in saltire. Brigade of Gurkhas uniform is worn in Number 1 and 2 Dress.

7

Lineage Gurkhas began training as Sappers in 1948. The numbers increased until in 1956 50 (Gurkha) Field Engineer Regiment was formed. The title Gurkha Engineers was authorised in 1955 and Queen's Gurkha Engineers in 1977.

1

2

3

4

5

6

8

9

10

11

previous page

1 Queen's Gurkha Engineers soldier's anodised aluminium cap badge and collar badges all 2.5 × 3 cm.
2 Anodised aluminium shoulder title worn in the Far East 2.75 × 1 cm.
3 Shoulder title 2.75 × 1 cm.
4 QGE button.
5 Officer's side cap badge 3 × 3 cm (badge 2.5 × 2.75 cm).
6 QGE officer's silver and gilt cap and collar badges all 2.5 × 3 cm.
7 Cpl Dil Rai and Gopal Rai and SSgt Nabin Gurung wearing the QGE cap badge and Brigade of Gurkhas TRF.

this page

8 Captain (QGO) Yog Thapa wearing Service Dress.
9 Officer's shoulder belt plate 7.25 × 10 cm.
10 Captain and Queen's Gurkha Officer rank slide. For the background to the ribbon worn by Gurkha officers see RGR p217.
11 Officer's pouch 16 × 9 cm, bright metal badge 2.5 × 3 cm.

59 Independent Commando Squadron RE

Almost all RE units have from time to time worn black painted cap badges. Sappers serving with 59 Independent Commando Squadron wear the blackened badge all the time, although on parade with other Sappers they wear the the anodised aluminium badge in the forage cap.

A key element of any reconnaisance is the 'Engineer Recce'. The Reconnaisance Troop, 59 Independent Commando Squadron is parachute trained in order to be able to operate with 3 Commando Brigade Patrol Troop. The Troop has an unofficial badge of the Fighting Knife superimposed on parachute wings. Usually confined to embroidery on sportswear or transfers on mugs, an example of the badge made by cutting down the two constituent badges does exist.

1

2

3

4

previous page

1 59 Commando Squadron black painted anodised aluminium cap badge 3.75 × 4.5 cm.

2 59 Commando Squadron unofficial Reconnaissance Troop badge 8.25 × 6.5 cm.

this page

3 Cpl Sharkey Bramhald, with the 3 Commando Brigade badge on his right sleeve, and Cpl Geth Jones, with the Commando Fighting Knife badge on his left sleeve, wearing the black cap badge on the distinctively shaped commando berets.

4 Lieutenant's Royal Marines style rank slide worn by officers serving with 59 Commando Squadron.

170 (Infrastructure Support) Engineer Group

The Military Works Force was renamed 170 (Infrastructure Support) Engineer Group in 2005.

Until 1959, the Corps of Royal Engineers was responsible for all works services for the Army throughout the world in peace and war. Peacetime responsibility was then passed to a civilian organisation, now known as Defence Estates. The Corps however, retained responsibility in areas where the operational situation warranted and specialist units were formed in order to plan and organise works. In 1978 these units were brought together as Military Works Force, or MWF, whose remit is now to deliver infrastructure engineering – permanent and temporary installations for the support and control of military operations.

MWF comprises Works Groups RE, Specialist Teams RE (STRE) and RE Specialist Advisory Team (RESAT). There is a Territorial Army element to the MWF.

The MWF badge features a Martello Tower built between 1804 and 1812 along the coast as defence against a French invasion.

1

2

1 Military Works Force arm badge 5 × 5 cm.

2 170 (Infrastructure Support) Engineer Group prototype arm badge 5 × 5 cm.

Royal Corps of Signals

The Royal Corps of Signals was formed as the Corps of Signals from the Royal Engineers Signal Service in 1920.

The Royal Signals adopted a figure of Mercury, Jove's messenger, with the caduceus, the ancient herald's wand, when it was formed in 1920 from the Royal Engineers Signal Service. The cap badge was redesigned in 1946 and the present badge, with the separate St Edward's (or Queen's) Crown, was adopted in 1954. The anodised aluminium version was issued from 1958.

The collar badges match the cap badges. Officers did until some years ago wear wire-embroidered Mess Dress collar badges. Wire-embroidered collar badges are now worn only by the Director of Music and Bandmaster of the Royal Signals Band.

Sergeants wear a badge similar in design to the cap badge and known as the 'Jimmy' above the rank chevrons. Jimmy was introduced in 1925 to distinguish sergeants from lance sergeants but was not formally approved until 1950. The lance sergeant rank is no longer used except by the Foot Guards.

1

2

3

4

5

6

7

The Commando Signallers
The design of the present cap badge is based upon the unofficial badge worn by Commando signallers serving with Special Service Brigade Signal Section sometime after 1940. The section's instrument mechanic altered his cap badge (3×5 cm) by removing the bronzed oval title and Crown to leave just the figure of Mercury (1.5×3 cm) to wear on his commando beret. The Officer Commanding approved the badge and it was worn by all Commando signallers until replaced by the present cap badge in 1947.

8

9

The Telegraph Battalion Royal Engineers first adopted Mercury, the messenger of the Roman Gods, as a letterhead badge. When the Corps of Signals was formed in 1920 the figure of Mercury by Giovanni da Bologna in the Pitti Palace in Florence was accepted as the model for the Corps badge.

10

11

12

13

14

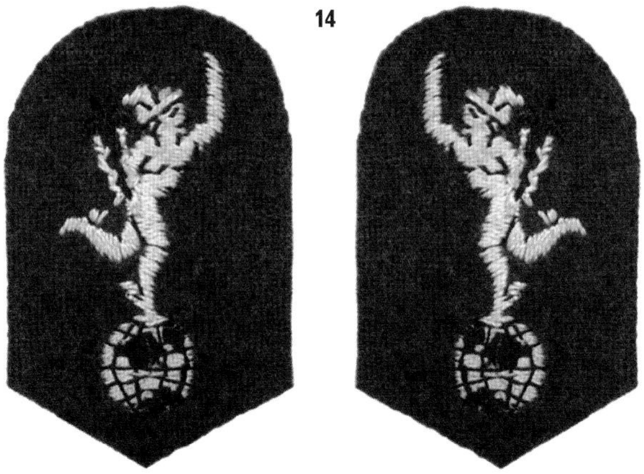

opposite page

1 Royal Signals soldier's anodised aluminium cap badge 2.75 × 5 cm and collar badges 2.5 × 3.5 cm.
2 Royal Signals officer's wire-embroidered beret badge 3.5 × 5.5 cm which appears to feature a pixie rather than Giovanni da Bologna's Mercury.
3 Royal Signals Button.
4 Royal Signals captain's rank slide.
5 Royal Signals officer's silver and gilt cap badge 2.75 × 5 cm and collar badges 2.5 × 3.5 cm.
6 WO2 John McNeill and SSgt David McCall with the Jimmy rank badge above his chevrons, wearing No2 Dress.
7 Original Royal Signals cap badge, 3 × 5 cm altered by Commando signallers during the Second World War.

this page

8 WO2 (SSM) Adrian Fadzilah with the blue sash worn by senior ranks serving with training regiments, WO1 (RSM) Steve Maclaren and Captain Alan Foote.
9 Badge for the blue sash worn by senior ranks serving in training units 6.5 × 10 cm.
10 Officer's obsolete wire-embroidered Mess Dress collar badges 3 × 3.5 cm.
11 Obsolete Telecommunications Technician badge 6 × 3.5 cm.
12 Soldier's waist belt clasp 7 × 5.75 cm.
13 Sergeant's No1 Dress wire-embroidered rank badge 4.25 × 7.5 cm
14 Sergeant's No2 Dress rank badge 3.5 × 5.5 cm worn on both sleeves.

15

19

Lineage Royal Corps of Signals (1920).

16

17

18

20

15 Segeant's Mess Dress wire-embroidered rank badge worn above the chevrons. The crossed rifles badge distinguishes a skill at arms instructor.
16 LCpl Charlie Brown wearing the TRF.
17 Royal Signals TRF 6 × 2 cm introduced in 2003 is similar in design to the Second World War arm-of-service stripe.
18 Sig James Watson wearing the 1st Signal Brigade arm badge.
19 LCpl Kenny Candler wearing the 2 Signal Brigade arm badge.
20 Sgt Al Hyland the Provost Sergeant at the Royal School of Signals, his appointment indicated by the blue sash with embroidered badge.

Acknowledgement Mr Peter Waring

1st (UK) Armoured Division Headquarters and Signal Regiment

The regiment is descended from the Telegraph Battalion RE formed in 1885, linked to 1st Division in 1907, and became 1 ADSR in 1993. The regiment wears the formation badge of 1st (UK) Armoured Division.

2nd Signal Regiment

The regiment is descended from the Telegraph Battalion RE formed in 1885, linked to 2nd Division in 1905, and became 2nd Signal Regiment in 1995. The regiment wears the formation badge of 2nd Division.

3rd (UK) Division Headquarters and Signal Regiment

The regiment is descended from the Telegraph Battalion RE formed in 1885, linked to 3rd Division in 1907 and became 3rd (UK) Division Headquarters and Signal Regiment in 1993. The regiment wears the formation badge of 3rd (UK) Division.

Joint Services Signal Unit (Ayios Nikolaos)

Formed by the amalgamation of 9 Signal Regiment and 33 Signal Unit RAF in 1999. 9th Signal Regiment had been formed in 1917 as Wireless Company, Egypt and Palestine.

The regiment wears an outline of Cyprus and the Electronic Warfare lightning flash superimposed on the Tri-Service colours.

1

3

2

1 Joint Services Signal Unit arm badge adopted in 2004.
2 Obsolete JSSU arm badge 5.75 × 4.5 cm replaced in 2004.
3 Cpl Linc Sims wearing the JSSU arm badge.

7th (ARRC) Signal Regiment

The regiment is descended from the Telegraph Battalion RE formed in 1885, linked to 1st Corps in 1914, and became 7th Signal Regiment in 1959. The regiment wears the badge of the former 1st (British) Corps superimposed on the Royal Signals colours.

1

2

1 Captain Harriet Cairns wearing the 7th Signal Regiment arm badge above the Royal Signals TRF.
2 7 Signal Regiment arm badge 6.5 × 6.5 cm.

11th Signal Regiment

The regiment is decended from the 2nd Training Battalion formed in 1920, becoming 11th Signal Regiment (Depot) in 1959 and is now part of the Royal School of Signals.

The regiment wore the arm badge of the Royal School of Signals from 1997 until it was ordered removed in 2003. The badge was based upon the design of that used by the Signal Training Brigade at Catterick. There is an aspiration by 11th Signal Regiment to readopt the badge.

1 Royal School of Signals obsolete arm badge 5.5 × 6.5 cm worn by 11 Signal Regiment.
2 WO1 (RSM) Si Hadley, the Corps RSM.

14th Signal (Electronic Warfare) Regiment

The regiment, decended from the Defence Telecommunications Network formed in 1937, became 14th Signal Regiment in 1959.

The regiment has worn the White Horse of Hanover badge since 1982, replacing the badge of the Coat of Arms of Gloucester which had been worn from 1966.

1 14th Signal (EW) Regiment coloured arm badge obsolete now that pullovers are no longer worn, 5 × 6.5 cm.
2 LCpl Dan Riches wearing the subdued14th Signal (EW) Regiment arm badge, 5 × 6.5 cm.
3 Subdued arm badge, 5 × 6.5 cm.

16th Signal Regiment

The regiment, descended from the Electrical Engineers formed in 1897, became 16th Signal Regiment in 1959.

The Regiment wore a badge of the Arms of Krefeld from 1962–1999 in recognition of its links with the German city. In 1999 it adopted the Crusader's Sword in recognition of its new role in 1st Signal Brigade.

1 16 Signal Regiment coloured arm badge obsolete now that pullovers are no longer worn, 4.5 × 5.5 cm.
2 LCpl Jason Giles wearing the subdued16th Signal Regiment arm badge, 4.5 × 5.5 cm.
3 Subdued arm badge, 4.5 × 5.5 cm

15th Signal Regiment

Formed in 1990 in Northern Ireland, the regiment traces a broken history to 8th Divisional Signals formed in 1938.

On reformation in Northern Ireland in 1990 the regiment chose as a badge an Egyptian cat, modelled on a bronze in the British Museum dated about 600 BC. The cat was chosen as it is effective against rats (in this case the terrorists in Northern Ireland). After the badge was ordered but before it could be worn, the Regiment was directed to wear the Headquarters Northern Ireland badge.

1 15 Signal Regiment obsolete arm badge 5 × 5 cm.

2 Sgt Sarah Staff wearing the HQNI arm badge.

Acknowledgement WO1 (RSM) D A Mitchell

21 Signal Regiment (Air Support)

The regiment is descended from 12th Air Formation Signals formed in 1943; the regiment became 21st Signal Regiment in 1959.

The red Beaufighter badge, introduced in 1948, was based on the design of the Second World War Indian Air Formation sign.

1 Capt Kate Hannaford wearing the 21 Signal Regiment arm badge, 6.5 × 6.5 cm.

2 Cpl Gaz Lea wearing the subdued 21 Signal Regiment arm badge, 6.5 × 6.5 cm.

Acknowledgement WO1 (RSM) RS Dyer

30 Signal Regiment

Formed as 5th Corps Signal Regiment in 1951, it became 30th Signal Regiment in 1959.

The swan badge is taken from the emblem of the Dyers Company with which the regiment was linked in 1960.

1

2

1 30 Signal Regiment arm badge 3.5 × 3.5 cm

2 Cpl Sid Reynolds wearing the 30th Signal Regiment arm badge.

Queen's Gurkha Signals

The Queen's Gurkha Signals was formed in 1955.

1

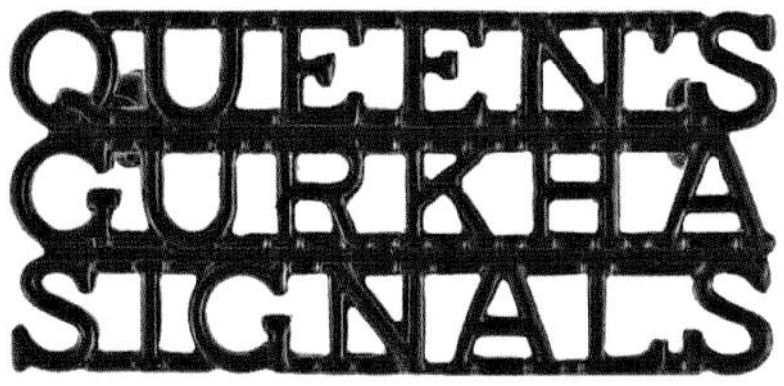

2

3

4

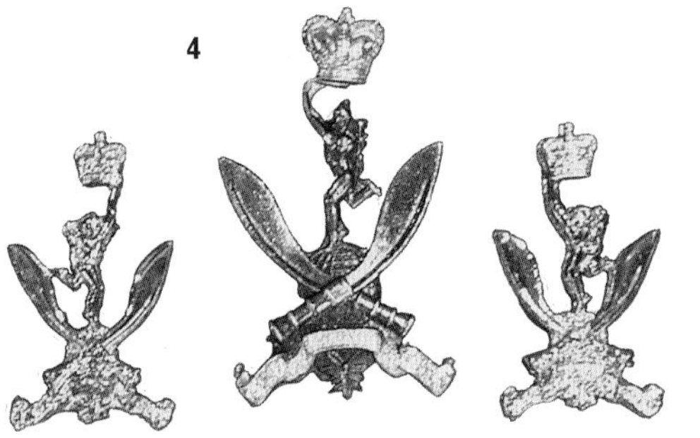

5

6

7

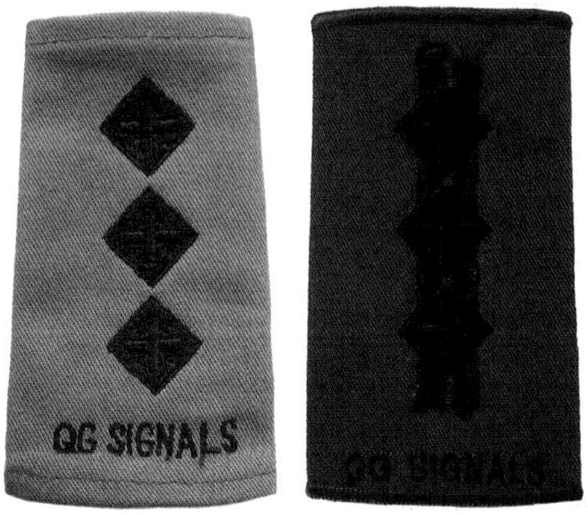

8

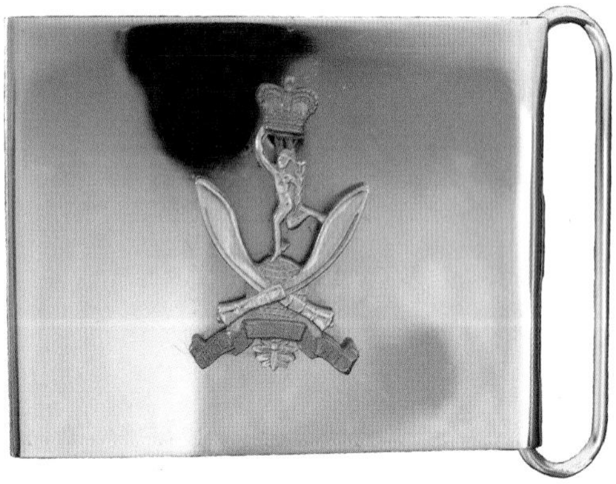

9

10

11

12

13

Lineage A cadre of Gurkha signallers served with Malaya District Signal Regiment from 1948. The numbers increased until in 1953 17 Gurkha Division Signal Regiment was formed. The title Gurkha Signals was authorised in 1955 and Queen's Gurkha Signals in 1977.

opposite page

1 Shoulder title 5.25 × 3 cm.
2 Queen's Gurkha Signals soldier's anodised aluminium cap badge 2.25 × 3.75 cm and collar badges 1.75 × 3 cm.
3 The cap badge worn on a Hunting Stewart backing on the Slouch Hat has a separate Crown.
4 Queen's Gurkhas Signals officer's silver and gilt cap and collar badges.
5 Officer's wire-embroidered beret badge 3.5 × 4.5 cm.
6 Sig Jeet Rana, wearing the Royal Signals TRF below the Brigade of Gurkhas TRF, and Sig Pradip Rai wearing the 30 Signal Regiment badge below the Union Flag badge.
7 Queen's Gurkha Signals captain's rank slide and QGO captain's rank slide. For the background to the ribbon worn by Gurkha officers see RGR p217.
8 QGS waist belt clasp 7 × 5.75 cm.
9 LCpl Lev Lever, Royal Signals serving with a Queen's Gurkha Signals Squadron and therefore wearing their badges.
10 Captain Luke Webber wearing the officer's beret badge and Brigade of Gurkhas and Royal Signals TRF.
11 Captain (QGO) Rajendra Gurung wearing the QGO rank slide.
12 Sgt Shudam Gurung.

this page

13 Shoulder belt plate 7.25 × 10 cm

ROYAL SIGNALS SQUADRONS

Royal Signals Squadrons provide the communications and 'life support' for brigade headquarters. Immediately following the parachute landings in Normandy in 1944 Lt Col Pygmy Smallman-Tew ordered his signallers to plait themselves lanyards from parachute rigging lines in order to have a length of strong cord if needed for escape and evasion. It became a tradition for all parachute trained signallers to wear the lanyard from 1944 and it was formally authorised in 1954.

200 Signal Squadron

20th Armoured Brigade Group Signal Squadron was formed from 4 Squadron 6th Armoured Divisional Signal Regiment in 1958, being numbered 200 Signal Squadron in 1959. The Squadron wears the arm badge of 20th Armoured Brigade.

Sig Mark Lowes wearing the 20 Armoured Brigade arm badge

201 Signal Squadron

Formed from 1st Guards Brigade Signal Squadron, being numbered 201 Signal Squadron in 1959 and 1 Squadron 1st Armoured Division Signal Regiment in 1993. The Squadron wears a white lanyard, rather than the usual blue Royal Signals lanyard, an honour granted in 1956 to all troops in 1st Guards Brigade.

203 Signal Squadron

203 Signal Squadron, numbered in 1959, having been disbanded twice was reformed as 3rd Infantry Brigade HQ and Signal Squadron in 1971 and disbanded for a third time in 2004.

204 Signal Squadron

4th Guards Brigade Signal Squadron was formed in 1947, being numbered 204 Signal Squadron in 1959. The Squadron wears the formation badge of 4th Armoured Brigade.

LCpls David Smart, Gillian Grant of 51 Signal Squadron (Volunteers); Cpl Adam Raison and Sig Emma Smith of HQ 4th Armoured Brigade in Iraq.

Acknowledgement WO1 (RSM) CD Lloyd

207 Signal Squadron

7th Armoured Brigade Group Signal Squadron was numbered 207 Signal Squadron in 1959. It was disbanded in 1993 and 201 Signal Squadron renumbered 207 Squadron the same day. The Squadron wears the formation badge of 7th Armoured Brigade.

WO1 (RSM) Martin Walsh wearing the 7th Armoured Brigade arm badge in Iraq.

209 Signal Squadron

19th Infantry Brigade Signal Squadron was formed in 1951, being numbered 209 Signal Squadron in 1959. The Squadron wears the formation badge of 19th Mechanized Brigade.

LCpl John Bromhead wearing the 19th Mechanised Brigade arm badge.

213 Signal Squadron

Formed as 213 Signal Squadron in 1959. The Squadron wears the formation badge of 39 Infantry Brigade.

Acknowledgement WO1 (RSM) P M Downie

215 Signal Squadron

Formed as 215 Signal Squadron in 1959 and later amalgamated the Squadron was reformed as 1st Infantry Brigade HQ and Signal Squadron in 1983. The squadron wears the formation badge of 1st Mechanized Brigade.

216 Signal Squadron

Formed as 16 Independent Parachute Brigade Signal Squadron in 1948, being numbered 216 Signal Squadron in 1959 and later disbanded, the Squadron was reformed in support of 5th Airborne Brigade in 1991 and transferred to 16 Air Assault Brigade in 1999. The Squadron wears the formation badge of 16 Air Assault Brigade. Parachute trained signallers wear a white over blue Drop Zone (DZ) badge. The officers' wire-embroidered badge is on a maroon backing to match the Brigade's maroon beret. The Squadron wears a khaki lanyard with Number 2 Dress.

1

2

1 216 Signal Squadron DZ Badge, 7 × 7 cm.

2 Major Rob Healey wearing the red airborne forces beret with wire embroidered badge.

218 Signal Squadron

Formed as 1 Army Group Royal Artillery Signal Squadron in 1955 and later disbanded, the Squadron was reformed in support of 8th Infantry Brigade in 1969, and wears the formation badge of 8th Infantry Brigade.

Sig Col Sutherland wearing the 8 Infantry Brigade arm badge.

228 Signal Squadron

Formed as SHAPE (British) Signal Squadron in 1951, being numbered 228 Signal Squadron in 1959 and later disbanded, the Squadron was reformed in support of 12th Mechanised Brigade in 1999, and wears the formation badge of 12th Mechanized Brigade.

Acknowledgement WO1 (RSM) K Marsh

252 Signal Squadron Defence Communication Services Agency (Germany)

The Defence Communication Services Agency was formed in 1998.
252 Signal Squadron joined DCSA(G) in 2003 and adopted the Agency's logo as an arm badge.

1 Defence Communication Services Agency arm badge 3.25 cm worn by personnel serving with 252 Signal Squadron.
2 LCpl Tanya Jordan wearing the DCSA arm badge.

Acknowledgement WO2 (SSM) G Steele

280 (UK) Signal Squadron

Formed as 28th Signal Regiment (Army Group) in 1952 and reduced in 1994 to one squadron in the multinational LANDCENT Signal Group

The LANDCENT shield was worn from 1996 until replaced in about 2003.

1 280 (UK) Signal Squadron obsolete arm badge 6 × 7 cm.
2 New arm badge 6 × 7 cm.

261 Signal Squadron

Formed as 261 Signal Squadron (Air Formation) in 1962, and later amalgamated, the Squadron was reformed in support of 101st Logistic Brigade in 2001 and wears the formation badge of 101st Logistic Brigade.

262 Signal Squadron

Formed as 262 Signal Squadron (District) in 1962, and later amalgamated, the Squadron was reformed in support of 102nd Logistic Brigade in 2001 and the wears the formation badge of 102nd Logistic Brigade.

264 (SAS) Signal Squadron

Formed as a troop to support the Malayan Border Scouts it was expanded into a squadron in 1966 to support 22 SAS.

Soldiers wear the SAS beret with Royal Signals cap badge.

1 Sgt Trev Tomkins having served with 264 Signal Squadron is permitted to wear the SAS beret whist serving in a recruit training unit.
2 264 Signal Squadron wear the SAS beret.
Photograph *R. Signals.*

Cyprus Communications Unit

The Cyprus Communications Unit was formed by the amalgamation of 259 Signal Squadron with elements of 12 Signal Unit Royal Air Force in 2002.

The Cyprus Communications Unit commands signals units from all the Services based on Cyprus which are not within the Joint Services Signal Unit.

2

3

1

1 Sig Laura Roberts wearing the CCU arm badge and a Joint Services stable belt.
2 Cyprus Communications Unit arm badge 6 × 4.5 cm featuring a Griffon Vulture on a lightening flash on the Joint Service tricolour.
3 259 Signal Squadron obsolete arm badge 3.75 × 5 cm featuring a statue of Aphrodite.

Acknowledgement WO2 (SSM) DJ Smith

The Royal Signals Motorcycle Display Team – The White Helmets

Formed in 1927 from Royal Signals Despatch Riders, the Team combined horses and motorcycles in displays until 1936, adopting the name The White Helmets in 1963.

The White Helmets have traditionally had the Royal Signals paper transfer badge on the front of their helmets. In 2004 the Commanding Officer introduced an arm badge, worn in Combat Dress and on the coveralls, known as Dunlop Skins after the sponsor that provides them.

1

2

1 Sgt Bob Sizeland wearing The White Helmets arm badge on his coveralls and the paper transfer badge on his helmet.
2 White Helmets arm badge 5.25 × 5.25 cm.

INFANTRY

The Infantry is organised into the Foot Guards and the Line, and consists of thirty two Regiments, almost all of which have been formed by amalgamations.

Regiments are grouped for administrative purposes into Divisions of Infantry; The Guards Division, The Scottish Division, The Queen's Division, The King's Division, The Prince of Wales's Division and The Light Division. The Royal Irish Regiment, The Parachute Regiment, and The Brigade of Gurkhas are outside of the Divisional groupings. Women are not allowed to serve as combat Infantrymen, although the restriction does not apply to the Territorial Army.

The Infantry badge is based upon the design of the bayonet. Until late 2003 the Infantry Recruiting Team wore a large bayonet badge on the right sleeve of the Field Jacket. The badges are thought to have been produced originally for the regimental police at the School of Infantry, Warminster.

The Infantry delivers much of the skill-at-arms training for the Army and is the authority for awarding the majority of Instructor and Skill-at-Arms and some Employment badges. Until the 1990s there were no badges to recognise basic or essential Infantry skills, as opposed to specialist skills. Four Infantry badges, which are still worn, were introduced with the Combat Infantry Course in about 1992, and are available in various individual regimental colours.

All Infantry and Brigade of Gurkhas recruits complete the Combat Infantry Course during recruit training and are awarded the Combat Infantry badge. After 18 months service privates and lance corporals who are Class 2 can take the annual Class 1 test and if successful are elevated to the higher pay band and awarded the Class 1 Infantry soldier badge.

The Section Commanders Battle Course, or SCBC, trains Infantry lance corporals in the operational duties of a corporal commanding a rifle section. A few non-Infantry junior non-commissioned officers also attend the course. Similarly the Platoon Sergeants Battle Course, or PSBC, trains Infantry corporals in the operational duties of a sergeant in a rifle platoon. A number of non-Infantry soldiers also attend the course. All who successfully complete the courses are awarded one of the Crossed Bayonets badges. Those gaining a distinction on PSBC wear a five pointed star badge above the Crossed Bayonets in Wreath badge. There is a slightly larger Star badge mounted with a rosette on the centre, which is worn as the driver's qualification badge. However when a Star is worn in combination with Crossed Bayonets within a Wreath, Crossed Flags or Crossed Swords it indicates a Distinction gained on a specific course.

Infantrymen must gain an appropriate infantry course qualification for promotion to the next rank. Those who do not attend the Battle Courses can train as a support weapon specialist.

Soldiers who achieve Class 2 standard are authorised a skill-at-arms badge worn on the left fore arm. Advanced skill-at-arms instructors are authorised a badge which is worn on the right

1

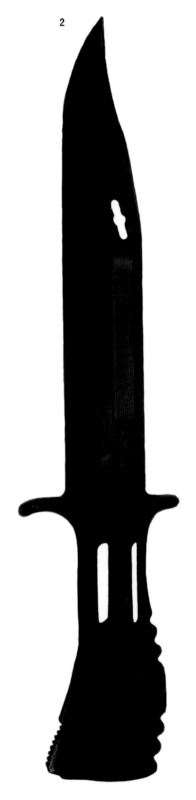

2

Acknowledgement Cpl Steve Murphy and Mr Bob Little

3

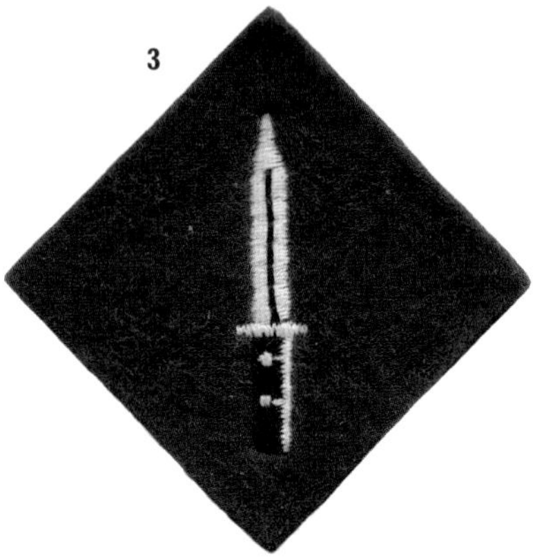

4

5

6

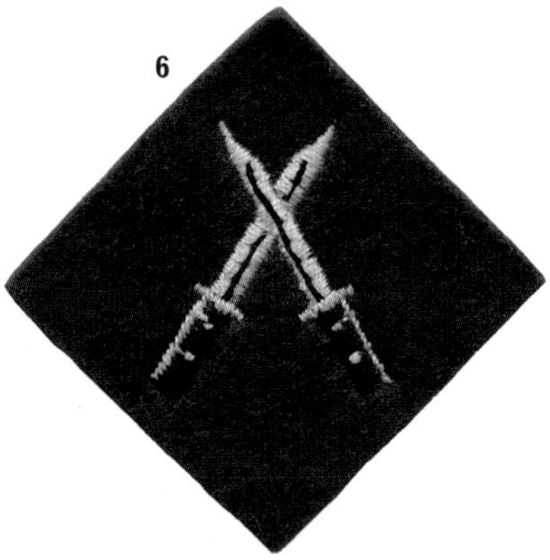

7

arm either above rank chevrons or below the rank by Warrant Officers. Some training is conducted in Battalions, some in Infantry training units and a few courses are delivered by other Arms and Services; Infantry Pioneers are trained by the Royal Engineers, Regimental Medical Assistants by the Defence Medical Education and Training Agency and Physical Training Instructors by the Army Physical Training Corps.

There are Infantry qualification badges for snipers, drummers (who also train as machine gunners), anti-tank guided weapon controllers, mortarmen and Rarden gunners. (The shooting badges are illustrated with the Small Arms School Corps p.334.)

8

9

10

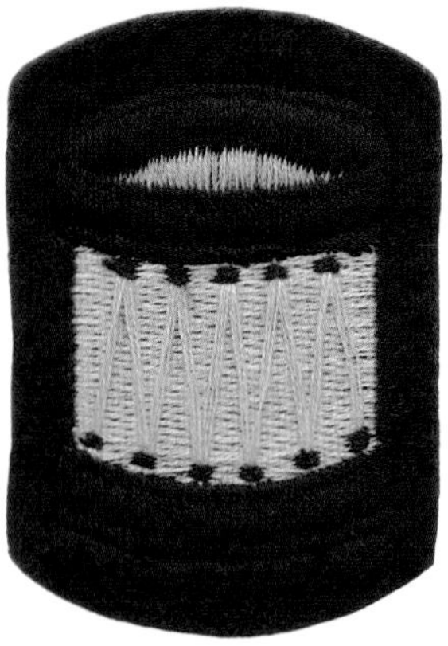

11

previous page

1 Obsolete Infantry Recruiting Team arm badge 6.5 × 9 cm worn until late 2003.

2 The SA 80 Bayonet, the model for the Infantry symbol 6 × 28.5 cm.

this page

3 Combat Infantryman employment badge 5.25 × 5.25 cm.

4 Five point star 3.25 cm, worn above Crossed Bayonets in Wreath, Crossed Flags and Crossed Swords to show a Distinction gained on certain courses.

5 Class 1 Infantry soldier employment badge 6.75 × 5.5 cm.

6 Section Commanders' Battle Course Intermediate skill-at-arms badge 5.25 × 5.25 cm.

7 Platoon Sergeants' Battle Course Advanced skill-at-arms badge 6.75 × 5.5 cm.

8 Anti-Tank Guided Weapons Controller badge 4.75 × 4 cm.

9 Mortarman badge 4.75 × 4 cm.

10 Drummer badge 3.75 × 5.25 cm.

11 Rarden Gunner badge 4.75 × 4 cm.

The Guards Division

'Blue-red-blue'

The soldiers of the regiments of the Guards Division are both a traditional part of the pageantry of Britain, and infantrymen. Battalions are expected to carry out both functions. The regiments are renowned for their unceasing pursuit of excellence, and the Guards have always been the Sovereign's personal troops.

In 1958 all Infantry regiments were grouped into administrative Brigades, which lasted until about 1970 when they were replaced by administrative Divisions. The Foot Guards continue to be grouped together as The Guards Division. Not to be confused, The Household Division is the unique grouping of The Household Cavalry and The Guards Division.

The Guards share a number of uniform distinctions whilst jealously guarding their individual traditions. The regiments of Foot Guards wore blue berets until 1971 or 1972 when the khaki beret, which had been worn during the Second World War, was readopted. In 1983 a number of other infantry regiments and The Royal Pioneer Corps adopted the khaki beret for tactical reasons.

It is said that the blue-red-blue badge backing was first worn by The Pretoria Regiment, a South African armoured regiment. In 1944 24 Infantry Brigade (Guards), was supported in Italy by tanks of The Pretoria Regiment. The Regiment's impressive ability to get their armoured vehicles up difficult slopes gained it the nickname The Mountain Goats. When the Order of Battle changed, and The Pretoria Regiment was due to leave the brigade, Brigadier AFC Clive DSO MC, the brigade commander, invited Lieutenant Colonel AM Johnstone DSO ED to incorporate The Household Division colours into his regiment's badge backing. Heraldic red and blue wings above the Royal Armoured Corps scarlet and gold arm of service stripe were chosen. The backing continues to be worn behind The Pretoria Regiment's cap badge.

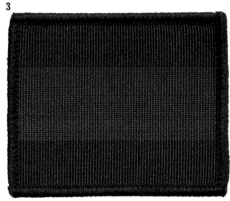

1

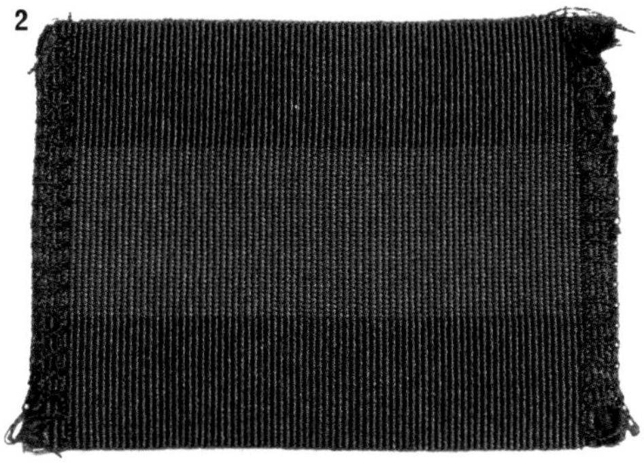

2

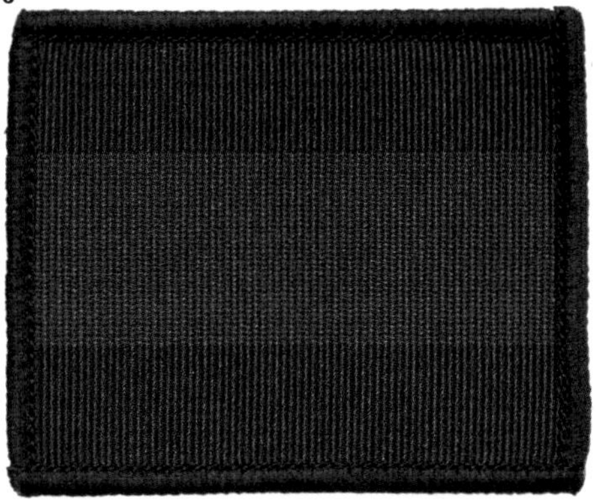

3

Foot Guards ranks are shown on the peaks of their Forage Caps

Five gold bands
Warrant Officer Class 1, The Academy Sergeant Major always wears a cap with a scarlet band as worn by the Officer Cadets.

Four gold bands
Warrant Officer Class 2, Grenadier Guards.

Three gold bands
Drum Major, Coldstream Guards.

Three brass bands
Colour Sergeant and Sergeant, Scots Guards.

Two brass bands
Lance Sergeant, Irish Guards.

One brass band
Lance Corporal and Guardsman, Welsh Guards.

Until they were disbanded in 1975 the Guards Independent Parachute Company wore a blue-red-blue cloth backing to their badges on the maroon beret. In 1988 a meeting of Household Division Warrant Officers Class 1 recommended that consideration be given to adopting the blue-red-blue badge backing for all Household Division units. The proposal was agreed by the Major General in consultation with the Colonels Commanding Regiments and was approved by the Army Dress Committee in 1989. The blue-red-blue silk ribbon is worn as a badge backing by all members of the Household Division and by attached troops on the strength of each of the regiments, with the exception of Scots Guards officers who continued to wear a square of Royal Stuart tartan.

With their beret badge backing and matching Tactical Recognition Flash it has become common shorthand to refer to The Guards as the 'blue-red-blue'.

The Sergeant Major's Badge

Regimental Sergeant Majors of Foot Guards battalions, as well as the Garrison Sergeant Major London District, Headquarters London District Superintendent Clerk and former Regimental Sergeant Majors of battalions, wear a rank badge quite different from those worn by almost all other Warrant Officers Class 1. The badge is a large Royal Arms badge worn on the upper arm. Those who wear the badge are sometimes known as members of The Big Badge Club. They are called Sir by non-commissioned ranks, but Sergeant Major by officers.

The badge is produced in coloured embroidery on khaki for Number 2 Dress, wire embroidery on red for the Full Dress tunic, and on blue for Number 1 Dress and Mess Dress. It is sometimes known by Guardsmen as the Big Dogs badge, and is known to those who embroider them, because of their size, as The Dinner Plate.

The Academy Serjeant Major, for many years a post held by a Foot Guards Warrant Officer, wears a unique version of the rank badge (see Royal Military Academy Sandhurst).

The Royal Artillery Sergeant Major, and the Drum Majors of the Royal Engineers Band and the Royal Signals Band also wear unique large rank and appointment badges. The Drum Major of the Royal Artillery Band will do so from 2005 (see The Royal Artillery, Royal Artillery Band, Royal Engineers Band and Royal Signals Band).

The rank of Guardsman replaced that of Private in all Guards regiments in 1919, an honour awarded by King George V in recognition of their Service during the First World War.

4

5

The Foot Guards have a unique rank structure. The Army rank of corporal is known in the Foot Guards as lance sergeant, and they have membership of the Sergeants Mess. In most orders of dress lance sergeants and sergeants wear identical rank badges, however on the Full Dress tunic lance sergeants are identified by three white chevrons; sergeants are identified by three gold chevrons. Sergeants also wear a red sash.

6

7

8

previous page

1 Beret badge backing 6 × 5.5 cm.
2 Obsolete arm badge 6.5 × 4.5 cm worn from about 1988.
3 TRF 6.25 × 5 cm introduced in 2002.

opposite page

4 Her Majesty's Ceremonial Warrant Officer, WO1 (GSM) Billy Mott wearing Summer Guard Order with Forage Cap.
5 Foot Guards RSM rank badge 14 × 16 cm for the Full Dress tunic.

this page

6 WO1 (RSM) John Mateer wearing the Sergeant Major's badge with Combat Dress.
7 Foot Guards RSM Number 2 Dress and working dress rank badge 14 × 15.75 cm.
8 Foot Guards RSM Number 1 Dress and Mess Dress rank badge 14 × 15.75 cm.

Guards Division Rank Badges

1

2

3

4

5

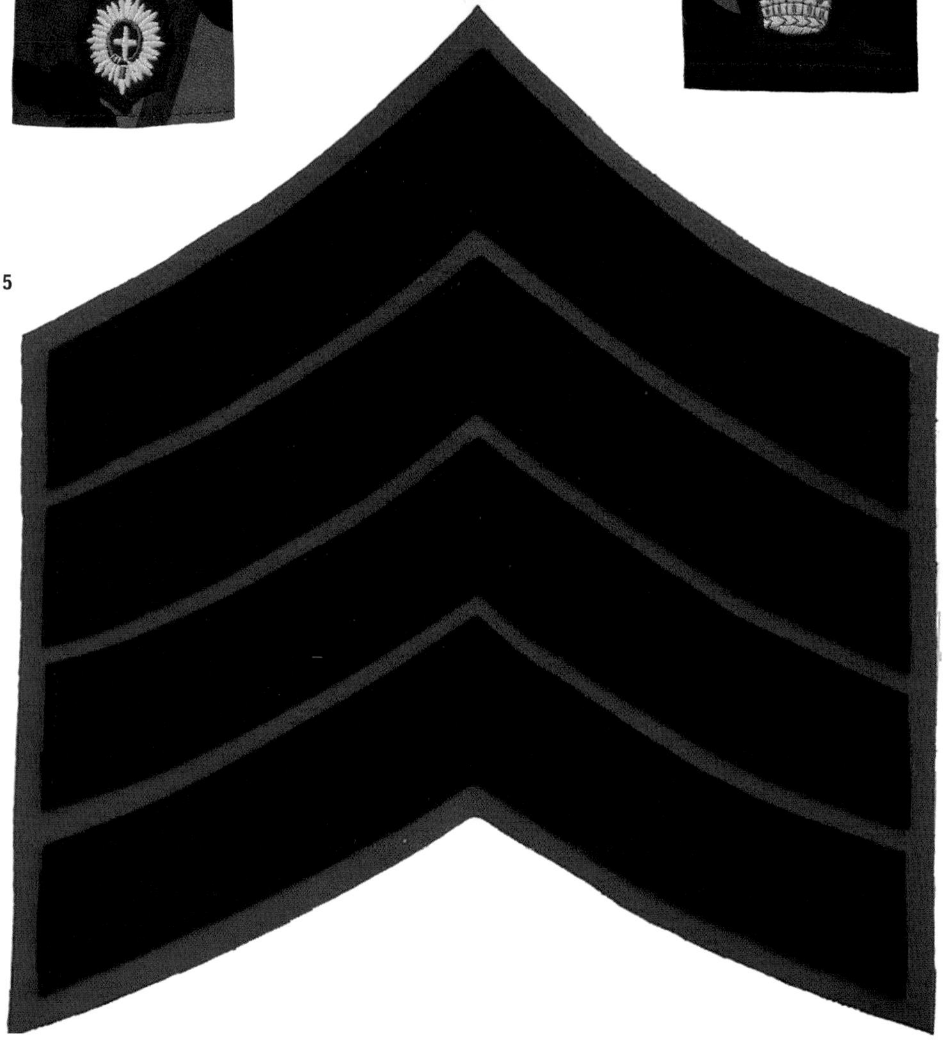

1 Full Dress wire-embroidered tunic rank star and No1 Dress rank star, and anodised aluminium Service Dress rank star worn by Grenadier, Coldstream and Welsh Guards officer's 3 × 4 cm. Some officers wear obsolete polished gilding metal rank stars on Service Dress.

2 Rank slide worn by captains of the Grenadier, Coldstream and Welsh Guards.

3 Major's rank slide with the large St Edward's (or Queen's) Crown worn by all Foot Guards Field officers.

4 Lieutenant Colonel's rank slide combining the Garter Star and St Edward's (or Queen's) Crown.

5 Troops on Public Duties during the winter wear the Athol Grey greatcoat with special large rank badges. This rank represents a Sergeant Drum Major. Drum Major's chevrons 19.5 × 21 cm and Drum appointment badge 5.5 × 7 cm.

Guards Division Appointment, Skill-at-Arms and Employment Badges

Guards Division Appointment, Skill-at-Arms and Employment badges are larger than the badges worn by the rest of the Army. The badges cover all of the extant qualifications except the four infantry 'Bayonet' badges.

3

1

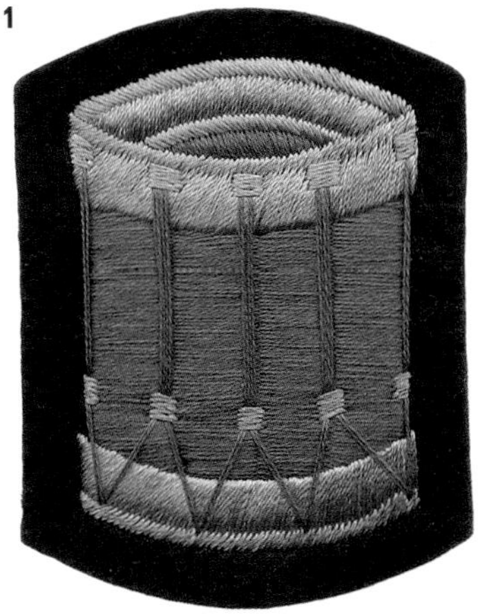

2

4

5

6

7

8

9

10

11

12

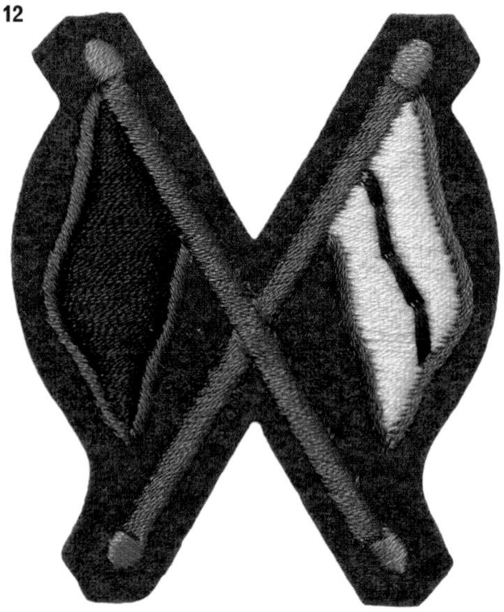

13

14

previous page

1 Drummer badge 4.75 × 6 cm, possibly introduced by the 1st Foot in 1849 and adopted universally by 1874.

2 All Arms Physical Training Instructor badge 7.5 × 4.75 cm, introduced in 1881. Also worn as a rank badge by Warrant Officers Class 2 of the Grenadier Guards.

3 Sgt Bush Bushby wearing No2 Dress with the AT badge of a Class 2 Guided Weapon Controller.

4 Guided Weapon Controller badge 6.5 × 5 cm (formerly Anti-Tank Gun Layer), introduced in 1957 when the recoilless 120mm BAT was issued to battalions to replace the 18 Pounder Anti-Tank Gun.

5 Infantry Pioneer badge 7 × 7 cm, introduced in 1868.

6 Rifle Marksman and also Skill-at-Arms Instructor badge 7.5 × 7 cm, introduced in 1856.

7 Sniper badge 6 × 8.5 cm, introduced in 1942 when it was awarded by Commanding Officers. It was replaced for the remainder of the Army in 1960 but the Foot Guards have retained the original badge.

8 Mortarman badge 6.5 × 5.25 cm, introduced in 1957.

9 Regimental Medical Assistant badge 5 cm, introduced in 1962.

this page

10 Driver or Driver Radio Operator badge 4.75 × 4.75 cm, introduced in 1950.

11 Group B Tradesman badge 6.5 × 5 cm, introduced for 107 trades in 1944 and now only worn in the Foot Guards by tailors.

12 Regimental Signaller badge 6.25 × 7.5 cm, introduced in 1881.

13 Household Division brooch 8 × 8 cm worn by the Senior Drum Major in State Dress.

14 DMaj Andy Grey wearing State Dress with the Senior Drum Major Household Division brooch on his sash.

Acknowledgement WO2 (Master Tailor) Barry Lawton

Grenadier Guards

'First' or 'Grenadier Regiment of Foot Guards'

The Grenadier Guards was raised in 1660.

The badge of the Grenadier Guards was the Royal Cypher and Crown until the Prince Regent authorised the regiment's change of title to First or Grenadier Regiment of Foot Guards in recognition of its actions during the Battle of Waterloo. At the same time the Regiment adopted the grenadiers' Bearskin Cap and the Grenade badge. A plain gilding metal grenade cap badge is worn by all Guardsmen up to and including the rank of Lance Sergeant. The present design of the grenade badge was produced for the funeral of King George VI in 1952 and worn at the coronation of Queen Elizabeth II in 1953. In 1958 when anodised aluminium badges were being introduced for the Army it was found impossible to stamp such a deep bowl as required for the grenade badge in aluminium and therefore the Grenadier Guards is the only regiment not to have been issued with an anodised aluminium cap badge. From time to time blackened badges and woven cloth beret badges have been worn in Northern Ireland.

The two badges, The Royal Cypher and Crown and the Grenade, are combined in the Sergeants' badge, consisting of the gilding metal grenade embossed with an interlaced and reversed Royal Cypher. Warrant Officers wear the grenade mounted with silver interlaced and reversed Royal Cypher. Badges are worn on a square of Household Division silk on the khaki beret.

1

2

3

4

5

6

7

8

9

10

Officers wear wire-embroidered badges on all caps and the beret. In 2004 Inkerman Company officers readopted the Side Cap with a wire-embroidered badge differing in detail from the badge worn on the beret, Forage and Service Dress caps.

The Bearskin Cap introduced in 1815 is worn in Full Dress. A white plume is worn on the left side – eagles' feathers for officers, cock feathers for senior ranks and horsehair for junior ranks.

Embroidered grenade collar badges are worn horizontally and in pairs on the Full Dress tunic; the ball of the grenade nearer the opening of the collar.

From the introduction of Number 2 Dress in 1956 until 1990 soldiers wore a metal shoulder title on Number 2 Dress. The introduction of the SA80 rifle, which is carried at the slope, resulted in damage to the titles and to the reintroduction of cloth shoulder titles.

On the Full Dress tunic the Royal Cypher, reversed and intertwined, is embroidered on soldiers' epaulettes; wire-embroidered for Senior Non-Commissioned Officers and woven in cotton for junior ranks.

Sergeants and lance corporals wear a seven flame Grenade above their chevrons. It differs from that worn by Royal Engineer sergeants, which has nine flames.

In Number 2 Dress Colour Sergeants and Warrant Officers Class 2 wear a crossed swords arm badge in addition to the Grenade badge. In Number 1 Dress, Full Dress tunic and Mess Dress they wear ornate 'Colour Badges', consisting of a regimental colour above crossed scimitars. The Regimental Sergeant Major wears a large coat of arms badge (see p.90).

Buttons on the Full Dress tunic and on all officers' uniforms are worn evenly spaced to denote the Regiment's place as the senior regiment of Foot Guards.

11

12

13

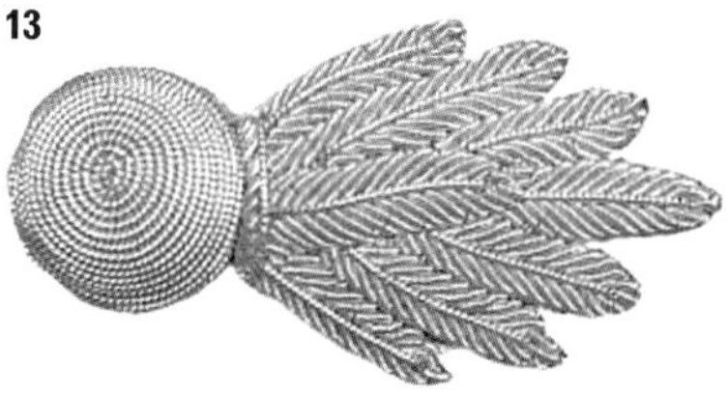

14

15

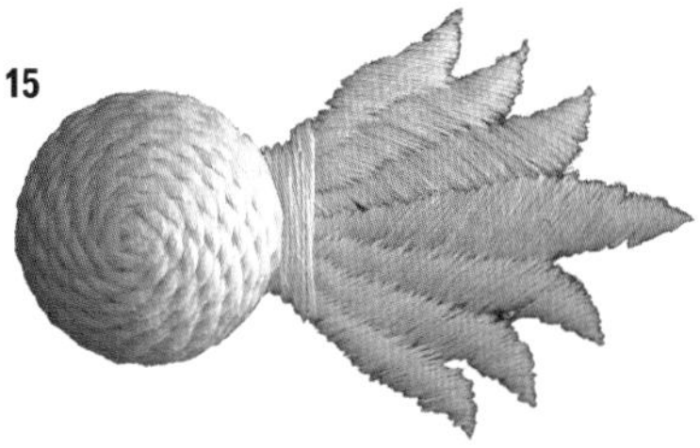

16

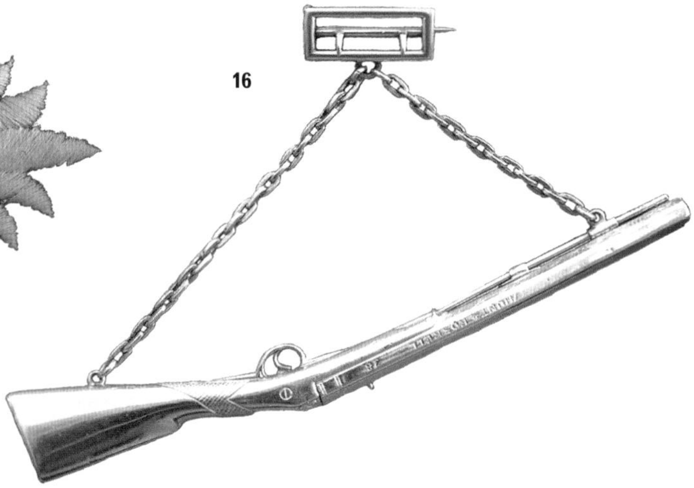

The regiment consists of the 1st Battalion, which includes two companies with special privileges. The Queen's Company is commanded by The Queen and has a Royal Standard. The Officer Commanding is in the usual way a major, but is known as The Captain. Inkerman Company retains the inherited privileges of the 3rd Battalion, which had served with distinction during the Crimean War. Nijmegen Company is separate from the Battalion and carries out Public Duties. It retains the inherited privileges and Colours of the 2nd Battalion.

17

18

19

20

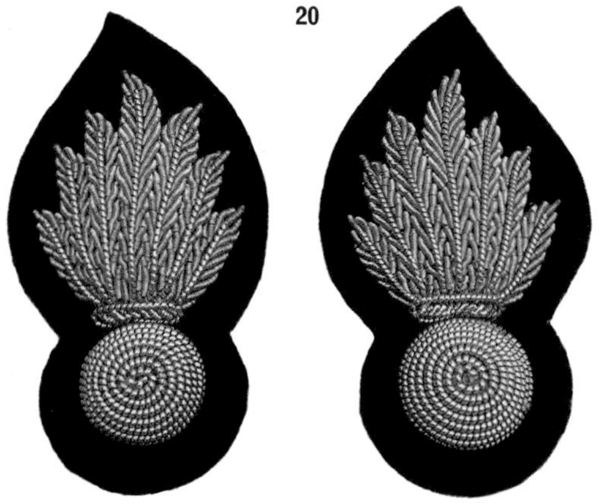

previous page

1 Officer's wire-embroidered cap badge 4 × 5 cm.
2 Officer's wire-embroidered side cap badge 3.25 × 5 cm.
3 Gdsm Tomo Thomas wearing No2 Dress with the cloth shoulder title, his rank in this view indicated by the single brass band on the peak of his Forage Cap.
4 Gilding metal cap badge 4 × 4.5 cm.
5 Sergeant's gilding metal cap badge 4 × 4.5 cm.
6 Warrant Officer's bi-metal cap badge 4 × 4.5 cm.
7 Grenadier Guards button.
8 LCpl Glen Cameron wearing the Guardsman's cap badge, Sgt Vandell McLean wearing the sergeant's cap badge and WO2 (CSM) Mark Hardwick wearing the Warrant Officer's badge. All worn on the Household Division blue/red/blue ribbon.
9 No2 Dress cloth shoulder title 12.5 × 4 cm.
10 Sand coloured cloth shoulder title. It is reported that samples were produced for all Household Division regiments in the 1990s but not issued although those for The Life Guards, Grenadier Guards and Welsh Guards are available.

opposite page

11 Lieutenant Colonel's rank badges for Shirt Sleeve Order.

Grenadier Guards tunic collar badges

12 Officer's wire-embroidered collar badge 11 × 5 cm.
13 Warrant Officer's wire-embroidered collar badge 5.5 × 2.75 cm sewn onto the gold lace collar.
14 Sergeant's gold wire badge 6 × 3.5 cm.
15 Junior ranks badge 5 × 3 cm both it and the sergeant's badge was originally embroidered directly onto the blue collar but because of damage from the rifle carried at the Slope is now available separately.
16 The 'Golden Gun' awarded to the best shot in the 1st Battalion and worn below any medals on the left breast in Summer Guard Order when on parade with the Commanding Officer. The miniature rifle was presented in 1856 by Lieutenant Colonel The Honourable J Lindsay 10.5 × 7.5 cm.

Grenadier Guards Full Dress tunic shoulder badges

17 Senior ranks' wire-embroidered shoulder badge 4.5 × 5.75 cm.
18 Drum Major's wire-embroidered badge 3 × 4.5 cm.
19 Junior ranks badge, woven directly onto the blue epaulet 4.5 × 5.75 cm.

20 Officer's Mess Dress collar badges 3 × 5.5 cm.

this page

21 Sgt Windy Miller wearing Summer Guard Order. His rank is shown by gold chevrons, by the gold wire-embroidered collar badges and by the red sash.
22 LSgt Tim Baker wearing No2 Dress with the regimental rank badge above his chevrons. The two brass bands on the peak of his Forage Cap show his lance rank.

Grenadier Guards No2 dress rank badges

23 Warrant Officer Class 2 and Company Quartermaster Sergeant's crossed swords 7 × 4.5 cm.
24 Sergeant and lance sergeant's grenade 3.5 × 6 cm.

Colour Sergeant's rank badges (shown much reduced)

25 Colour Sergeant No1 Dress rank badge.
26 Colour Sergeant Full Dress tunic rank badge. Sergeants wear Gold stripes, hence the name 'Gold Seregeant' – Lance Sergeants wear white stripes.

21

22

23

24

25

26

27

28

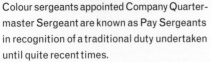

Colour sergeants appointed Company Quartermaster Sergeant are known as Pay Sergeants in recognition of a traditional duty undertaken until quite recent times.

29

In 1655 The Commonwealth entered into an alliance with France against Spain, and the exiled Charles II with James, Duke of York left Paris for Bruges. From his supporters Charles had six regiments raised for service with the Spanish, including the Royal Regiment of Guards. Although the regiment did not survive long, it was reformed to accompany the King to England in 1660. At the Restoration the King's Regiment of Guards was raised in England, and the two Guards regiments amalgamated in 1665. As the senior infantry regiment of the Army, the regiment was given the title The First Regiment of Foot Guards. In 1815 the regiment was in the front line of the Duke of Wellington's army and defeated the final assault by the Grenadiers of the French Imperial Guard, in honour of which the regiment was given the title of First or Grenadier Regiment of Foot Guards.

30

31

32

33

34

35

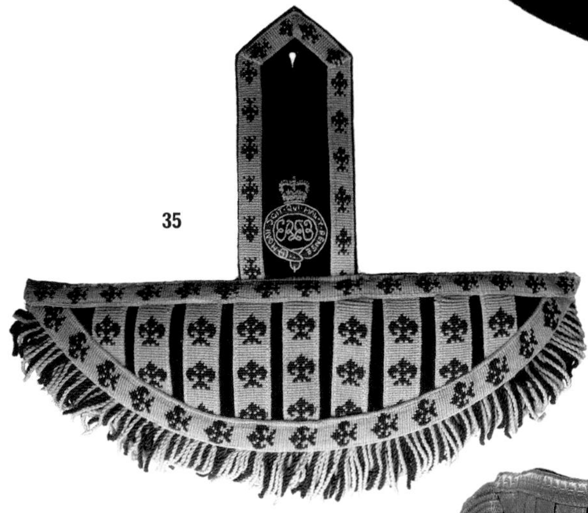

36

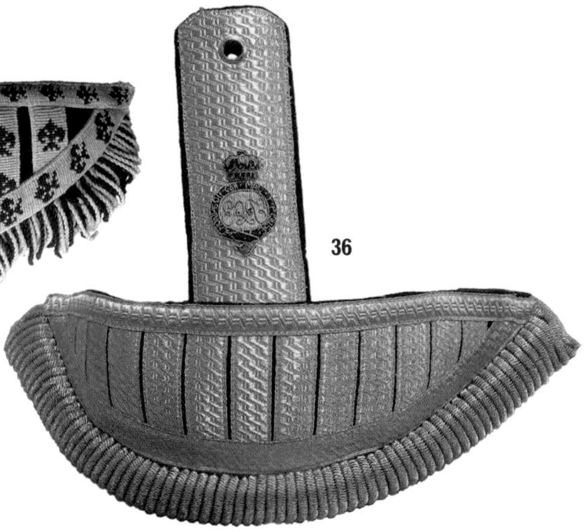

opposite page

27 Regimental rank badges, the Grenade and crossed swords as worn by a Colour Sergeant on the upper sleeve of No2 Dress. A Warrant Officer Class 2 wears the regimental badges below a large crown on the lower sleeve. Lance Sergeants and Sergeants wear only the Grenade above the chevrons.

28 'Colour badge' worn by Warrant Officers Class 2 on the upper right arm 9.5 × 13.25 cm and in a smaller size 5 × 7.75 cm by Colour Sergeant's on their Number 1 Dress chevrons.

29 Drum Major's brooch worn on the sash in State Dress 6.5 × 9 cm.

30 DMaj Tony Moors wearing Summer Guard Order with Drummer's Wings on his tunic. His silver wire collar badges show him to be a Warrant Officer and he wears a Staff waist belt clasp.

this page

31 Regimental Staff waist belt clasp 10 × 5.75 cm, worn by the RSM, RQMS, Drill Sergeants and the Master Tailor.

32 Soldier's waist belt clasp 10 × 6.5 cm.

33 Gilding metal 'Pugri Badge' 3.75 × 6.75 cm used by the 1st Battalion, and

34 Wire-embroidered blazer badge 8 × 10.5 cm used by Nijmegen Company on backpacks carried during parades in public places.

35 Drummer's Full Dress wing, and

36 Drum Major's wing 32 × 26.5 cm.

Acknowledgement
Lt Col Andrew Ford and WO2 Stitch Hawkins

Lineage Grenadier Guards (1656).

Coldstream Guards

'Nulli Secundus'

Raised in 1650.

The Regiment's first badge was the Crown and Cypher of King Charles II. The present badge is the Star of the Order of the Garter granted to the Regiment by William III in 1696, making it possibly the oldest badge worn in the Army. It has been suggested that the Garter Star was granted as the badge in honour of the first Colonel, General George Monk, 1st Duke of Albemarle KG who was the first non-royal member of the Order. The badge is known in the regiment as the Cap Star. There is a Guardsmen's myth that the number of holes by the buckle on the Garter represents the number of the Battalion.

Soldiers, up to the rank of Colour Sergeant, are encouraged to buy and to polish gilding metal badges. As a guide the badge should be well polished but St George's Cross should still be clearly visible.

The officers' wire-embroidered beret badge was introduced in 1951.

The Bearskin Cap introduced in 1831 is worn in Full Dress. A red plume is worn on the right side – eagles' feathers for officers, cock feathers for senior ranks and horsehair for junior ranks.

From thc introduction of Numbcr 2 Drcss in 1956 until 1990 soldiers wore a metal shoulder title on Number 2 Dress. The introduction of the SA80 rifle, which is carried at the slope, resulted in damage to the titles and to the reintroduction of cloth shoulder titles. In the Full Dress tunic a Rose, possibly taken from the Collar of the Order of the Garter, is embroidered on soldiers' epaulettes; wire-embroidered for Senior Non-Commissioned Officers and woven in white for junior ranks. Since the introduction of Number 2 Dress in 1962 soldiers of the 1st Battalion have worn a red Roman numeral I on the upper right sleeve in Number 2 Dress. Soldiers serving with Number 7 Company wear a Roman numeral II.

Buttons on the Full Dress tunic and on all officers' uniforms are worn in pairs to denote the Regiment's place as the second senior regiment of Foot Guards.

1

2

3

4

5

6

7

8

During the English Civil War white was the Parliamentary colour. The reason for the white band around the Coldstream Guards Forage Cap is obscure but may reflect the regiment's Parliamentary antecedents.

The regiment consists of the 1st Battalion and 7 Company, which is separate from the Battalion and carries out Public Duties. It retains the inherited privileges and Colours of the 2nd Battalion.

9

10

11

12

13

14

15

16

17

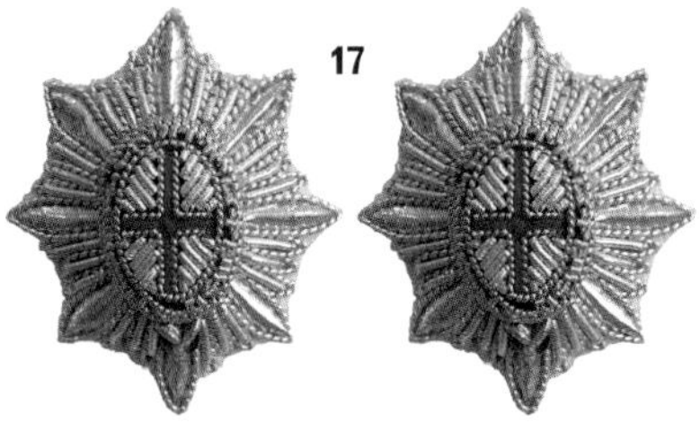

18

Some soldiers wear silver cap badges said to date to the lack of brass during the Second World War. However the examples seen appear to be much older and the small size of the Garter suggests that the silver cap star may well be 19th Century Warrant Officers badges.

opposite page

1 Officer's wire-embroidered beret badge 2.5 × 3.5 cm.

2 Officer's silver, gilt and enamel Service Dress badge 2.75 × 3.5 cm.

3 Officer's Forage Cap badge 4.25 × 5.5 cm.

4 Battalion Staff silver and enamel badge 4.25 × 4.25 cm.

5 Anodised aluminium badge 4.25 × 4.25 cm.

6 Soldier's private purchase gilding metal badge 4.25 × 4 cm.

7 Black painted anodised aluminium cap badge worn in the Field.

8 Old silver cap badge.

9 Soldier's No2 Dress cloth shoulder title 12.25 × 4 cm.

10 Coldstream Guards button.

this page

Coldstream Guards Full Dress tunic collar badges

11 Officer's wire-embroidered collar 11 × 5 cm.

12 Warrant Officer's badge 4 × 2.5 cm sewn onto gold lace collar.

13 Sergeant's badge 4 × 3.5 cm now embroidered directly onto the blue collar although older examples are still sewn on.

14 Junior ranks badge 3.5 × 3.5 cm embroidered directly onto the blue collar.

15 Captain Ian Lowther wearing the officer's wire-embroidered beret badge, WO2 Bruce Lee wearing the Staff cap star, and Gdsm Mark Dryden wearing the private purchase gilding metal cap star.

16 Lieutenant's rank slide.

17 Officer's Mess Dress collar badges 2.5 × 3.5 cm.

18 LSgt Scot Swalwell identified by his white chevrons, a Full Sergeant wears gold stripes, and WO2 (CSM) Mick Donohue in Summer Guard Order. Photograph *Coldstream Guards*

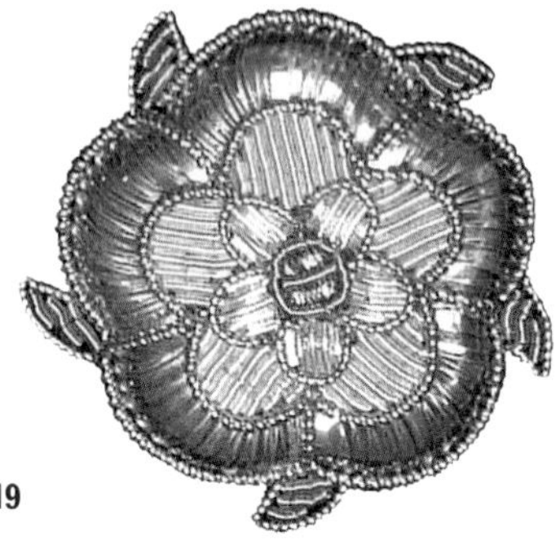

19

20

21

22

23

24

25

The regiment was raised in 1650 for Parliament and is the only regular Army regiment to be directly connected with the New Model Army of the Civil War. To prove their allegiance to Charles II at the Restoration the regiment laid down its arms on Tower Hill in 1661 and took 'them up again as entertained by His Majesty in service...' they were immediately advanced to His Majesty's service as an 'Extraordinary Guard to his Royal person.' Although raised before the Grenadier Guards, the regiment served Parliament during the Civil War and is ranked junior to the Grenadier Guards, which served the King.

26

27

28

29

opposite page

Coldstream Guards Full Dress tunic Shoulder Badges

19 Senior ranks badge 4 cm also worn as the Mess Dress collar badges.

20 Junior ranks badge woven directly onto the epaulet 3.5 cm.

21 CSgt Murph Murphy, a Drill Instructor, wearing the 1st Battalion numeral on No2 Dress.

22 Captain Tom Bailey wearing Service Dress with the large cap star on his Forage Cap and his buttons in pairs.

23 Drum Major's brooch 7.5 × 9 cm worn on the sash in State Dress.

24 'Colour badge' 8.5 × 15.25 cm worn by Warrant Officers Class 2 on the upper right arm in Full Dress tunic and the smaller size 3.75 × 6.75 cm worn on No1 Dress. Colour Sergeants wear the small badge on their chevrons in both orders of dress.

25 CSgt Badger Coupland wearing No1 Dress with the regimental 'Colour Badge' on sergeant's stripes

this page

26 Pugri badge 6.75 × 8.5 cm, used as decoration around the Regiment

27 Pouch badge 7 × 8.5 cm used on backpacks carried during parades in public places.

28 Regimental Staff waist belt clasp 10 × 6.25 cm, worn by warrant officers.

29 Soldier's waist belt clasp 10 × 6.5 cm.

Lineage Coldstream Guards (1650)

Acknowledgement Colonel Hugh Boscawen

Scots Guards

The Scots Guards was brought on to the English establishment in 1686.

The Scots Guards 'cap star' is the star of the Order of the Thistle. Recruits are issued the anodised aluminium cap star although trained soldiers buy and polish a gilding metal badge. Sergeants wear a white metal star with gilding metal centre, Warrant officers and Drum Majors wear a silver and gilt Staff cap star. Officers wear silver and gilt cap stars. In 1920 Scots Guards officers adopted as their rank badge the Star of the Order of the Thistle, later the rank star was adopted as the officers' beret badge.

In 1916 officers of the 1st Battalion began to wear a small patch of Royal Stuart tartan on each side of their Service Dress caps. The practice continues with patches of tartan 1 × 2 inches. Royal Stuart tartan badge backing was adopted for wear on berets in 1944.

Embroidered thistles are worn as collar badges on the Full Dress tunic and the star of the Order of the Thistle on Mess Dress. Until the late 1980s white metal collar badges were worn on the Sergeant's Mess Dress.

From the introduction of Number 2 Dress in 1956 until 1990 soldiers wore a metal shoulder title on Number 2 Dress. The introduction of the SA80 rifle, which is carried at the slope, resulted in damage to the titles and to the reintroduction of cloth shoulder titles. On the Full Dress tunic a star of the Order of the Thistle is embroidered on soldiers' epaulettes; wire-embroidered for Senior Non-Commissioned Officers and woven in white with a button in the centre for junior ranks.

Buttons on the Full Dress tunic and on all officers' uniforms are worn grouped in threes to denote the Regiment's place as the third senior regiment of Foot Guards.

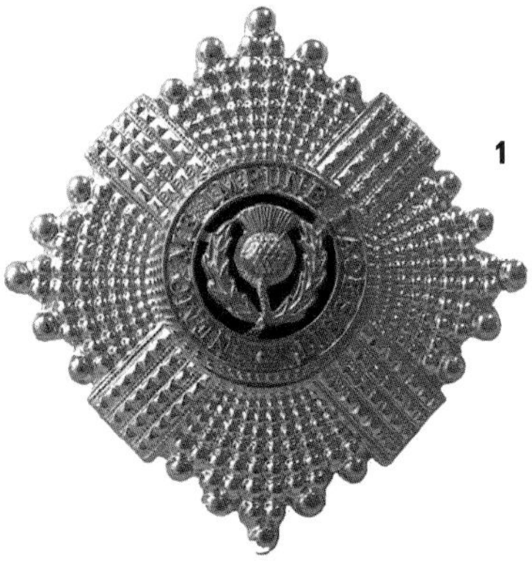
1

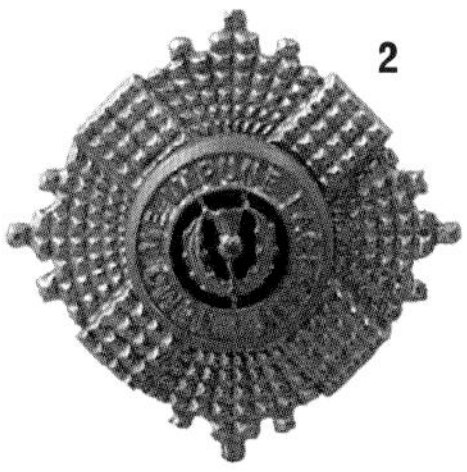
2

3

4

5

6

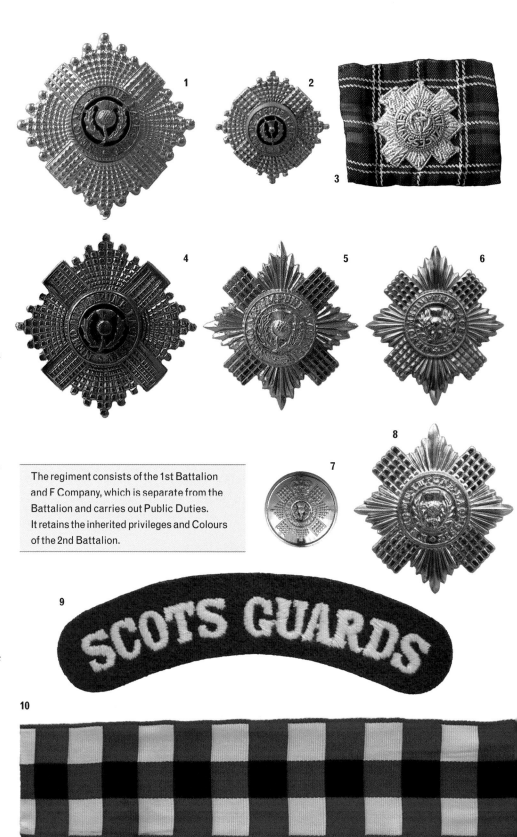

The regiment consists of the 1st Battalion and F Company, which is separate from the Battalion and carries out Public Duties. It retains the inherited privileges and Colours of the 2nd Battalion.

7

8

9

10

11

12

13

opposite page

1 Officer's silver, gilt and enamel Forage Cap star 5 × 5 cm.

2 Officer's Service Dress cap star 2.5 × 2.5 cm.

3 Officer's wire-embroidered beret star on tartan backing 4.5 × 3.5 cm.

4 Warrant Officer's and Battalion Staff silver and gilt cap star 5 × 5 cm.

5 Senior rank's silver and gilt cap star 4 × 4.25 cm.

6 Soldier's private purchase gilding metal cap star 4 × 4.5 cm, curved to fit the cap.

7 Scots Guards button.

8 Anodised aluminium cap star 4 × 4.25 cm.

9 No2 Dress cloth shoulder title 11.5 × 3.5 cm.

10 Forage Cap ribbon.

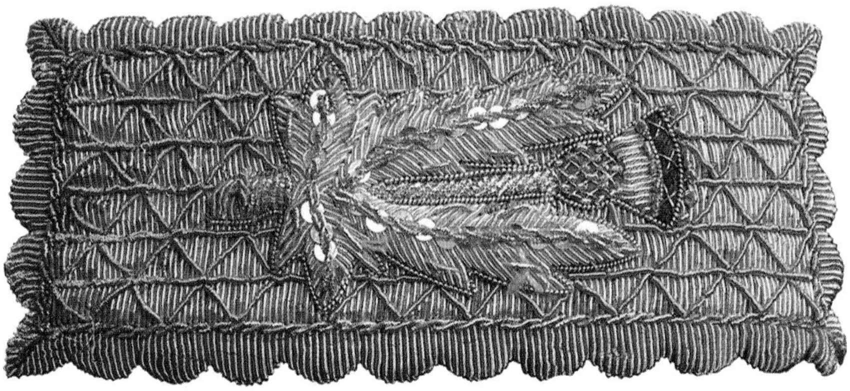

14

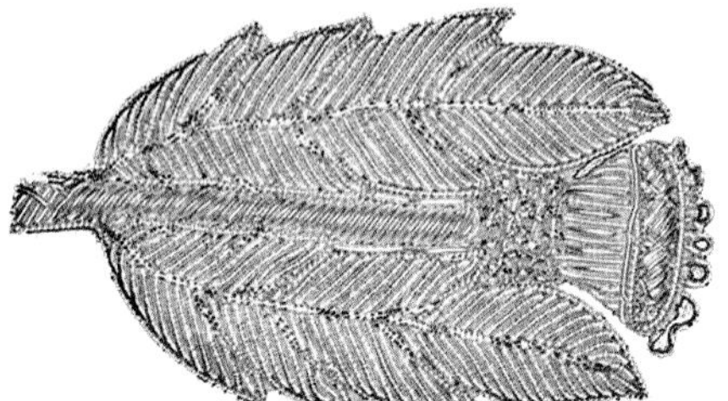

15

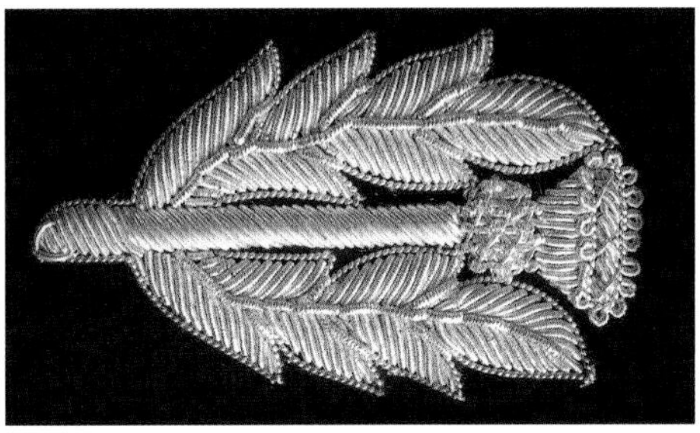

16

17

18

19

20

21

this page

11 Regimental Staff waist belt clasp 7 × 5.5 cm. The RSM has a unique clasp with a silver thistle.

12 WO1 (RSM) MA Cape wearing the Sergeant Major's rank badge.

13 LSgts Scotty Farr and Rab McGuire wearing Full Dress tunics with Forage Cap, their ranks as lance sergeants indicated by white chevrons, white collar badges and two brass bands on the peaks of their Forage Caps.

Scots Guards Full Dress tunic collar badges Worn in facing pairs; the difference is in the angle of the stem of the thistle and is only clearly seen on the collar badge worn by Lance Sergeants and below.

14 Officer's wire-embroidered collar 11 × 5 cm.

15 Warrant Officer's badge sewn onto the gold lace collar 6 × 3.5 cm.

16 Sergeant's badge 6 × 3.5 cm embroidered directly onto the blue collar.

17 Junior rank's left collar badge 4.25 × 7 cm embroidered directly onto blue collar.

18 Officer's Mess Dress wire-embroidered collar badges 3.75 × 3.75 cm.

19 Sergeant's Mess Dress wire-embroidered collar badges 3 × 3.25 cm.

20 Senior ranks full dress tunic shoulder badge 3 × 3 cm.

21 Junior ranks badge 3 × 3.25 cm woven directly onto the epaulet and fitted with a button.

22

23

24

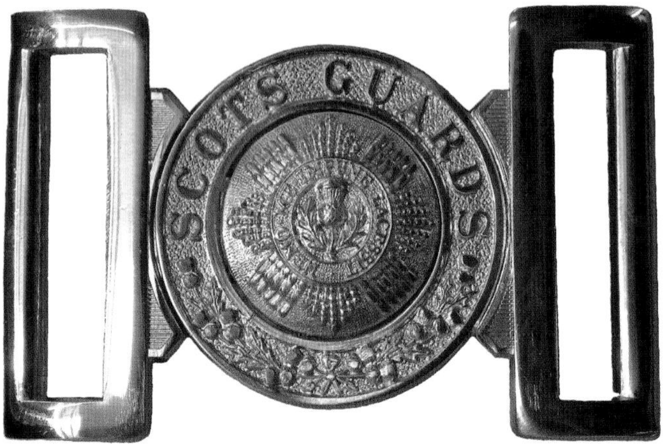

25

26

27

28

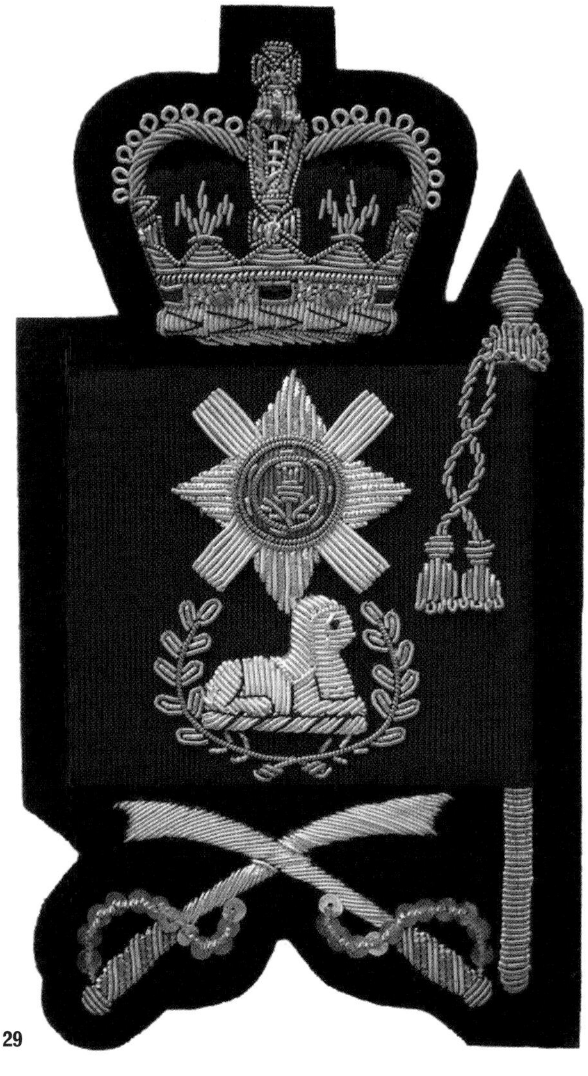

29

30

31

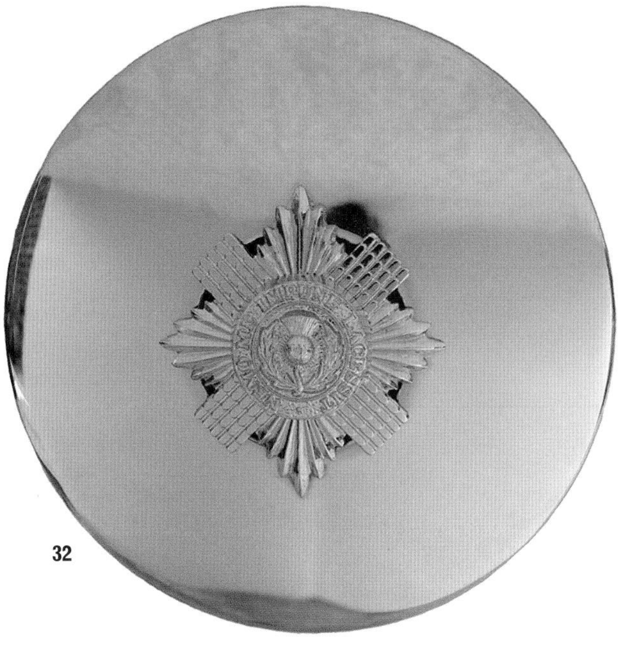

32

33

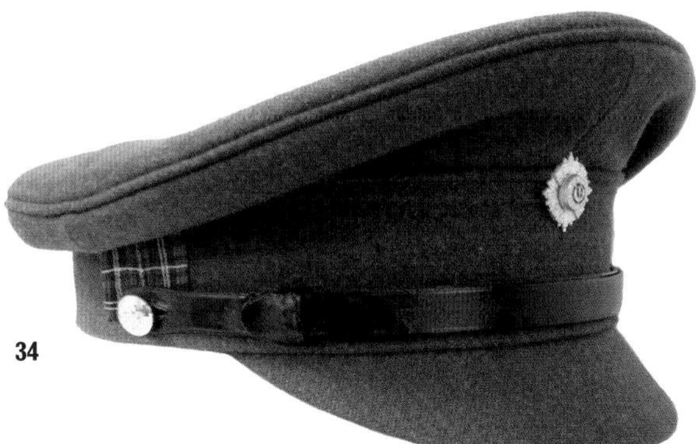

34

35

36

37

38

opposite page

22 Lt Col Andrew Foster wearing Service Dress. Officers wear their buttons grouped in threes whilst Non-Commissioned ranks wear the issue Number 2 Dress with evenly spaced buttons.
23 Captain Tim McEwan riding Vitez.
24 CSgt Billy Stewart wearing No1 Dress with the regimental Colour Badge mounted on sergeant's chevrons.
25 Soldier's waist belt clasp 9 × 5.5 cm.

Officers' rank stars display the regiment's unique thistle design.
26 Full Dress rank star 4 × 4 cm.
27 Number 1 Dress rank star 4 × 4 cm.
28 Service Dress rank star 3 × 3 cm.

29 'Colour badge' worn by Warrant Officer Class 2 on the upper right arm 8.5 × 15 cm.

this page

30 'Colour badge', 4 × 7.25 cm, worn by Colour Sergeants on their chevrons.
31 Dmr Tam McFeely, his Full Dress tunic decorated with Drummers Lace and Wings and Ppr John Mowatt.
32 Plaid brooch 9.25 cm.
33 Second Lieutenant's rank slide.
34 Officer's Service Dress cap with tartan patches.
35 DMaj Dean Colbert wearing State Dress.
36 Drum Major's brooch 6 × 7 cm worn on the sash in State Dress.
37 Piper's button.
38 Sporran badge, a sergeant's cap star 4 × 4 cm.

39

40

43

46

41

44

45

42

A 'Royal Regiment' of Scotsmen was raised for service with Charles 1 during the Irish rebellion in 1642 although, because of the outbreak of the Civil War, the King did not himself go to Ireland. The regiment, by then known as the Irish Companies, returned to Scotland and was reorganised into 'The Foote Regiment of His Majesties Life Guardes' for Charles II in 1650 but was dispersed the following year on the defeat of the King at Worcester. On the Restoration in 1660 the English garrisons in Edinburgh and Dumbarton were replaced by Scottish troops with four further companies being raised in 1662 to form the 'New Regiment of Foot Guards', which in 1686 was brought on to the English establishment as the Scotch Guards. Some of those granted commissions at the Restoration had served with the former regiment during the Civil War and claimed a continuation of the regiment's service from 1642.

39 Kilt pin.
40 Ppr Phil Stevenson wearing Combat Dress and the regimental Glengarry with piper's badge (**45**). On his sleeve is the 4th Armoured Brigade badge.
41 Piper's waist belt clasp.
42 WO2 (RQMS) Rab Carney and (CSM) Gary Dunning escorting Major James Kelly carrying the Queen's Colour of the 2nd Battalion. The Colour is usually carried by a Subaltern with an armed escort. Here the Colour is being escorted to Chapel.

Pipers' glengarry badges 7 × 6cm.
43 Pipe Major's silver and gilt.
44 Senior NCO silver.
45 Piper anodised aluminium.
46 PSgt Bruce Draper wearing Commanding Officer's Drill Order.

Acknowledgement WO1 (RSM) MA Cape

Irish Guards

Raised in 1900.

The Irish Guards, or IG, cap star is the Star of the Order of St Patrick, with the motto *Who shall separate us*, and the date 1783; the date that the Order was instituted rather than the raising of the regiment. Officers and Warrant Officers wear silver, gilt and enamel badges, and a wire-embroidered beret badge. The silver and gilt 'Centenary Star' was introduced for Colour Sergeants and Sergeants on the anniversary of the formation of the regiment in 2000, it is said at the instigation of Warrant Officer Class 2 Jimmy Duggan. Lance Sergeants and below are issued an anodised aluminium badge but buy and polish a gilding metal badge. The Regimental Sergeant Major wears the Kenny Star, one of the original silver badges made for the regiment in 1900 and which was presented to the regiment by the retired Regimental Sergeant Major John Kenny.

From the introduction of Number 2 Dress in 1956 until 1990 soldiers wore a metal shoulder title on Number 2 Dress. The introduction of the SA80 rifle, which is carried at the slope, resulted in damage to the titles and to the reintroduction of cloth shoulder titles.

1

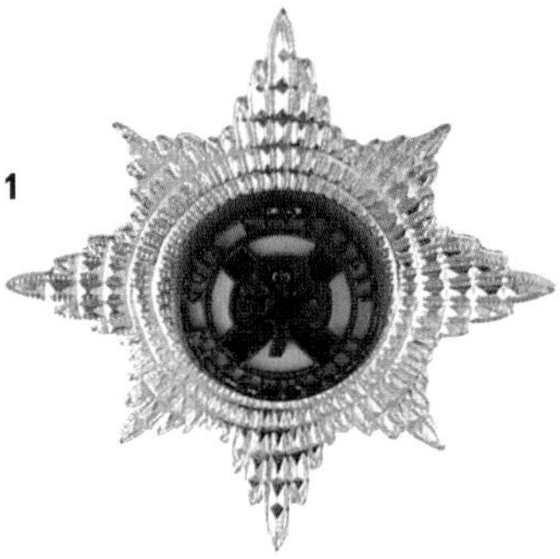

2

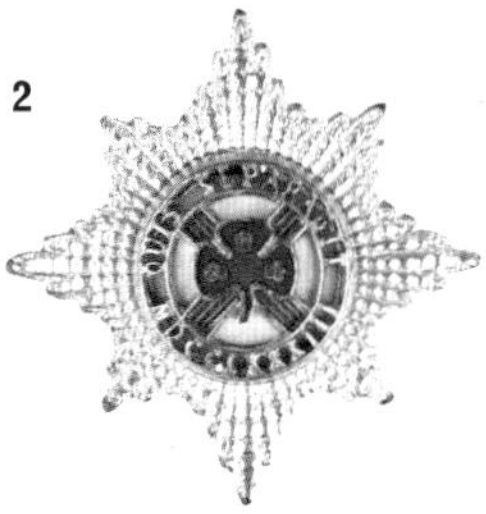

3

4

5

6

7

8

9

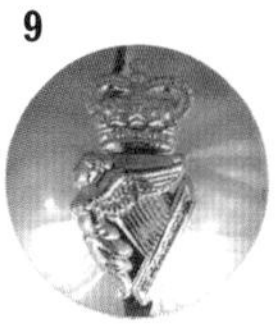

10

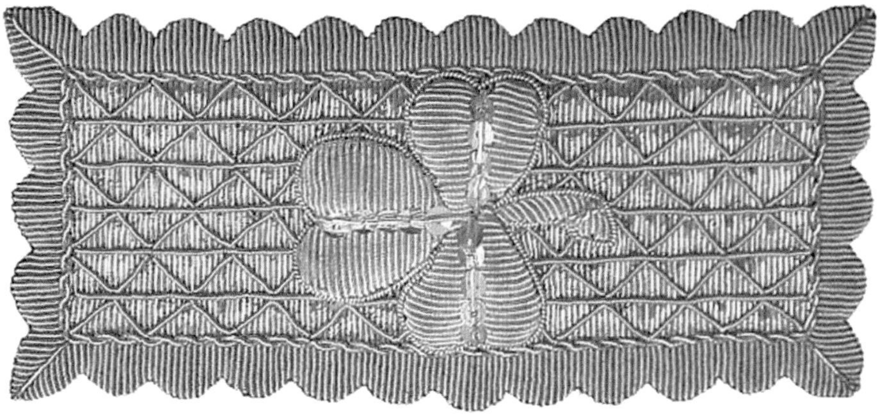

The Bearskin Cap is worn in Full Dress. A St Patrick's blue plume is worn on the right side – eagles' feathers for officers, cock feathers for senior ranks and horsehair for junior ranks.

Buttons on the Full Dress tunic and on all officers' uniforms are worn in fours to denote the Regiment's place as the fourth senior regiment of Foot Guards.

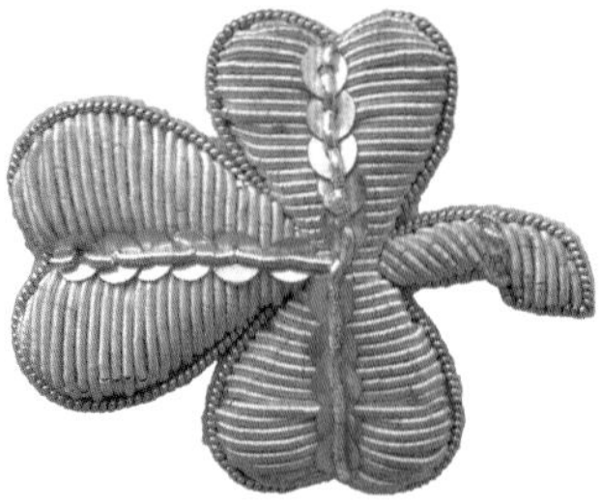

11

12

13

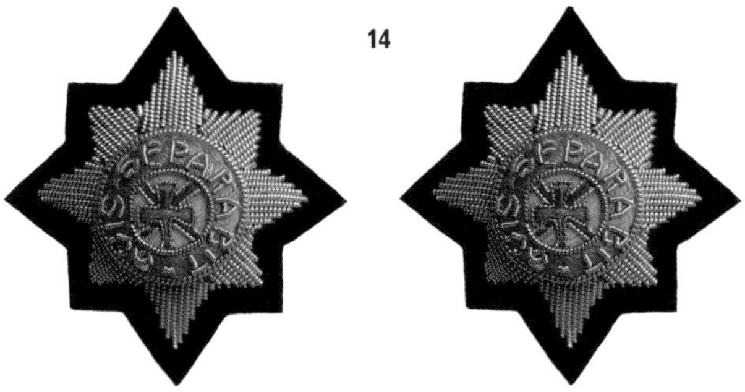

14

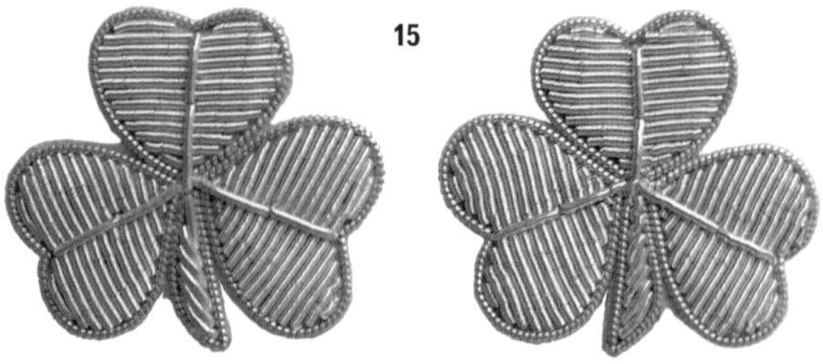

15

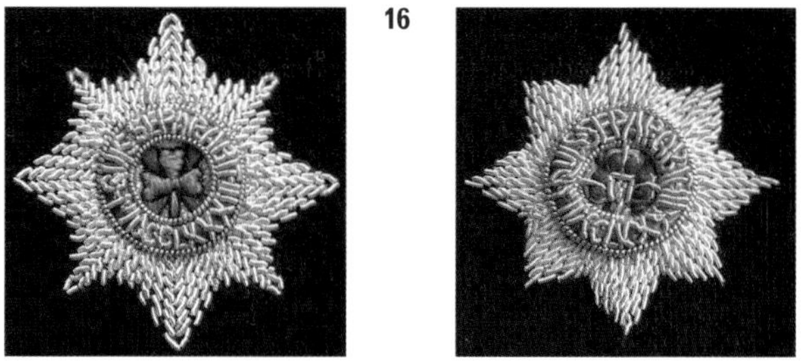

16

17

18

19

20

21

22

23

24

previous page

1 Officer and Warrant Officer's silver, gilt and enamel Forage Cap star 4.5 × 4.5 cm.

2 Officer's Service Dress Cap star 3.25 × 3.25 cm.

3 Officer's beret badge 4 4 cm, which is also worn as the Mess Dress collar badge.

4 Colour Sergeant and Sergeant's bimetal 'Centenary Star' 4.5 × 4.5 cm.

5 Anodised aluminium cap star 4.5 × 4.5 cm.

6 Private purchase gilding metal cap star 4.5 × 4.5 cm.

7 LCpl Gaz Byrne wearing combat dress with the anodised aluminium cap star.

8 No2 Dress cloth shoulder title 11.5 × 3.5 cm.

9 Irish Guards button.

Irish Guards Full Dress tunic collar badges worn in facing pairs with the difference being in the angle of the stem of the shamrock.

10 Officer's wire-embroidered collar. Badge 4.25 × 3.5 cm

opposite page

11 Warrant Officer's collar badge sewn onto gold lace collar 3.75 × 4cm.

12 Sergeant's collar badge 3.75 × 4cm.

13 Junior rank's left collar badge 3.75 × 3.5 cm embroidered directly onto the blue collar.

14 Officer's Mess Dress wire-embroidered collar badges 4 × 4 cm.

15 Sergeant's Mess Dress wire-embroidered collar badges 3 × 3.5 cm.

16 Senior ranks badge and junior ranks Full Dress badges 3 × 3 cm woven directly onto the epaulet.

17 Sgt Kev Fletcher wearing No2 Dress, his rank as a sergeant rather than a lance sergeant indicated by the red sash and the three brass bands on the peak of his Forage Cap.

18 Lance Sergeant Paul Mooney wearing Summer Guard Order.

19 Irish Guards Regimental Staff waist belt clasp 10.25 × 5.5 cm.

20 Irish Guards waist belt clasp 10 × 6.5 cm.

this page

21 Officers rank stars displaying the regiment's unique shamrock design. Full Dress tunic and No1 Dress rank stars, each 4 × 4 cm, and Service Dress rank star 3 × 3 cm.

22 Irish Guards 'Colour badge' worn by Warrant Officers Class 2 on the upper right arm 8.5 × 15 cm and in a smaller size 4 × 7 cm by Colour Sergeants on their chevrons

23 Irish Guards captain's rank slide.

24 Irish Guards piper's cloak chain. Clasps 4.25 × 4.25 cm.

25

26

27

28

29

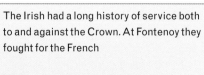

The Irish had a long history of service both to and against the Crown. At Fontenoy they fought for the French

'We're not so old in the Army,
But we're not so young at our trade,
For we had the honour at Fontenoy
Of meeting the Guards Brigade.'

Rudyard Kipling

It was not until 1900 that Queen Victoria gave authority to raise the Irish Guards 'to commemorate the bravery shown by the Irish regiments in the operations in South Africa'.

30

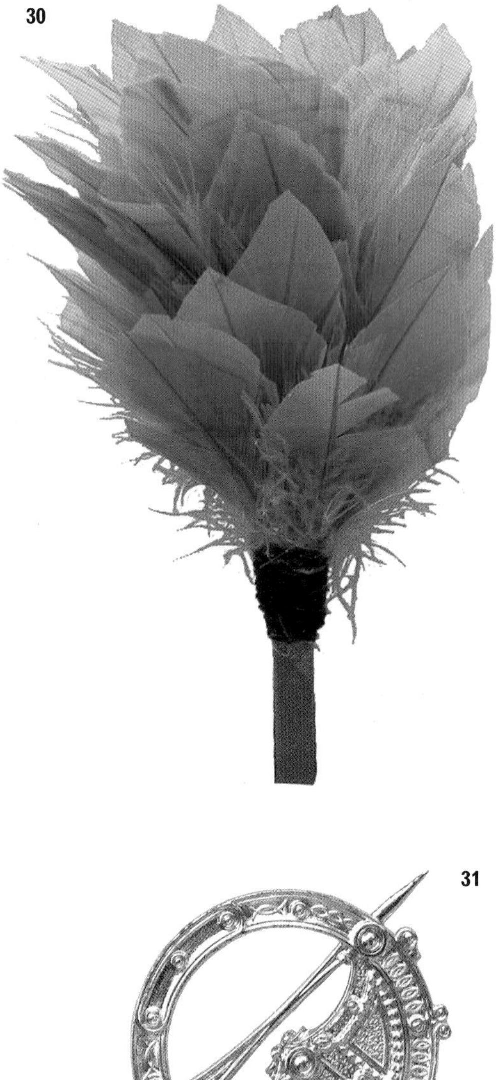

31

32

33

34

35

36

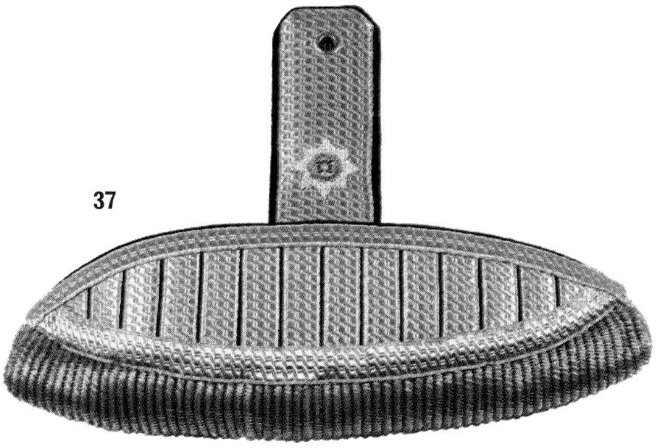

37

opposite page

25 Drum Major's brooch 8.5 × 8.5 cm worn in State Dress.

26 Pipe Major's silver, gilt and enamel caubeen star 8 × 8 cm.

27 Piper's chrome caubeen star, 8 × 8 cm.

28 CSgt Paul Teague wearing No2 Dress.

29 LSgt Smudge Smith wearing Full Dress tunic, his buttons grouped in fours.

30 Piper's hackle 5.5 × 10.5 cm.

31 Tara brooch 5.5 × 3.75 cm.

this page

32 Ppr Stevie McLaughlin wearing Full Dress.

33 WO1 (RSM) Ken Gannaway-Pitts MSM Irish Guards – the Army's Senior Drum Major – wearing No2 Dress. His rank is shown by the five gold bands on his Forage Cap and the Household Division Royal Arms rank badge. As he is not a battalion RSM he does not wear a Sergeant Major's badge.

34 Gdsm Dan Riley wearing a Poppy behind his cap star, and Ppr Will Pintar wearing the piper's caubeen.

35 Piper's kilt badge 8.5 × 9.25 cm.

36 Piper's chrome waist belt clasp.

37 Drum Major's Full Dress wing.

Acknowledgement
Lt Will Hawley and WO1 (RSM) SM Nichols

Welsh Guards

Raised in 1915.

The badge chosen for the Welsh Guards was the ancient Welsh device of the leek. Welshmen serving with the Black Prince in 1314 were identified by leeks in their hats and the device is mentioned in Shakespeare's Henry V. Recruits wear an anodised aluminium leek, and trained soldiers buy and polish gilding metal badges. There is a gilt Staff cap badge although it is hardly known about even in the Regiment as Warrant Officers invariably retain their polished gilding metal badges.

Soldiers wear a woven cloth badge on a square of Household Division silk on the khaki beret.

Officers wear wire-embroidered badges on all caps; a small size on the Service Dress cap and khaki beret, and a larger one on the Forage Cap.

The Bearskin Cap is worn in Full Dress. A green and white plume is worn on the left side – eagles' feathers for officers, cock feathers for senior ranks and horsehair for junior ranks.

Collar badges, a woven leek for Guardsmen and wire-embroidered for officers, are worn only in Full Dress tunic. Small wire-embroidered leeks are worn on Mess Dress, gold for officers and silver for senior ranks.

Buttons on the Full Dress tunic and on all officers' uniforms are worn grouped in fives to denote the Regiment's place as the fifth regiment of Foot Guards.

The metal cap badge was known in the days of National Service, which ended in 1962, by some soldiers but never by the Welsh Guards, as the NAAFI fork.

1

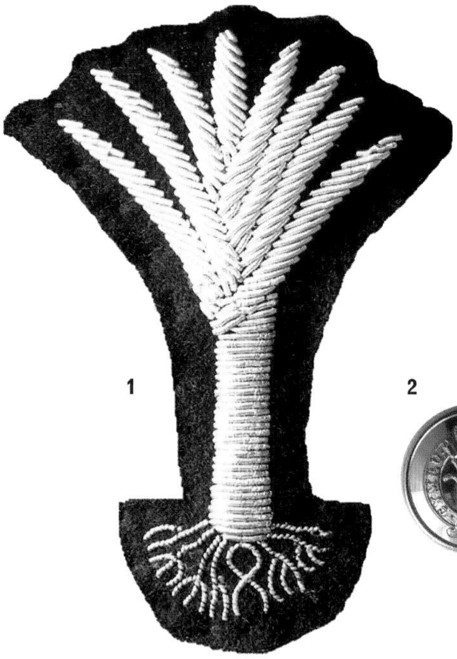

2

3

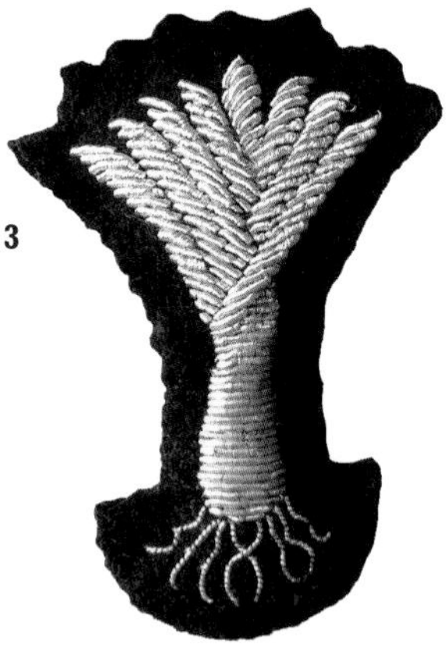

4

5

6

7

8

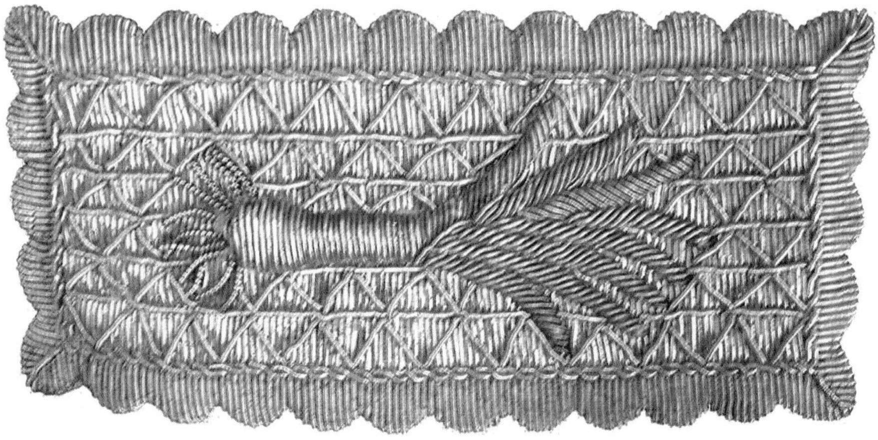

9

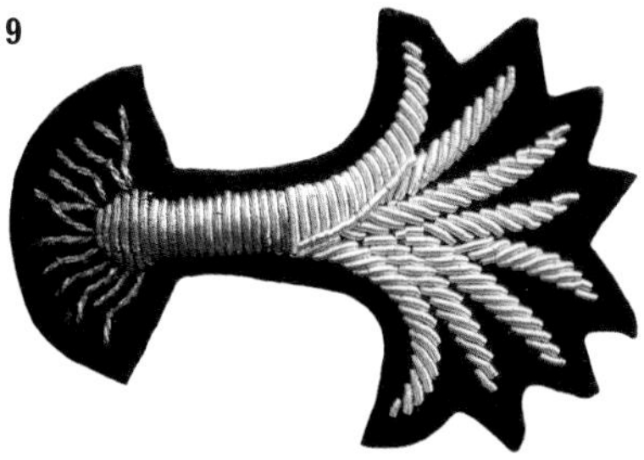

12

10

13

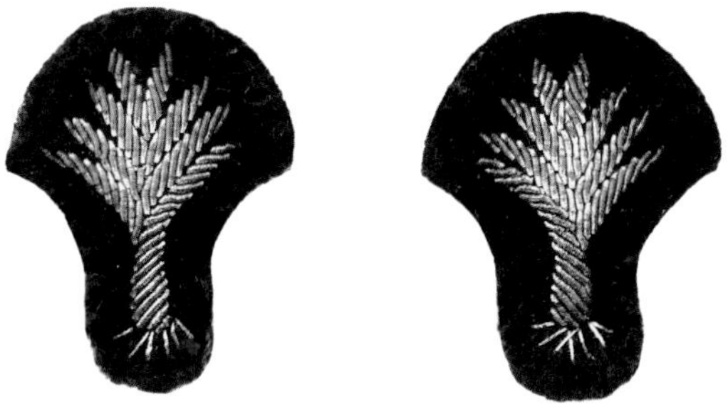

11

14

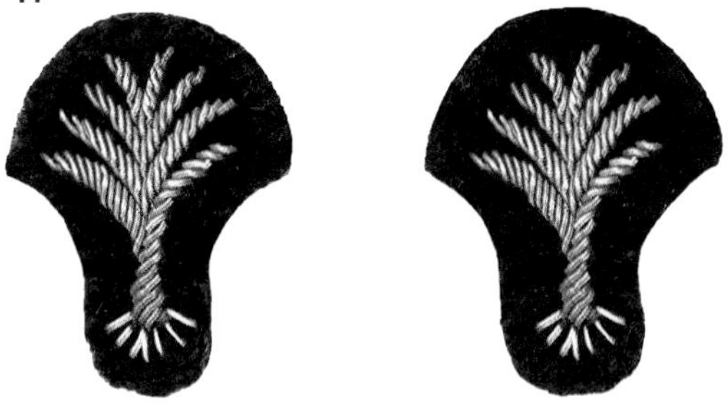

15

16

17

18

opposite page

1 Officer's wire-embroidered Forage Cap badge 6.5 × 8.75 cm.

2 Welsh Guards button.

3 Officer's wire-embroidered beret badge 4 × 5.5 cm.

4 Anodised aluminium cap badge 3.5 × 4.75 cm.

5 Private purchase gilding metal badge 3.5 × 4.75 cm.

6 Soldier's woven beret badge 3.75 × 4.75 cm.

7 LCpl Gareth Griffiths and Jamie Lorimer wearing cloth beret badges on Household Division silk backing.

Welsh Guards Full Dress tunic collar badges worn in pairs.

8 Officer's wire-embroidered collar 11.5 × 5 cm. Badge 7.5 × 3 cm.

this page

9 Warrant Officer's wire-embroidered badge sewn onto the gold lace collar 5 × 3.5 cm.

10 Sergeant's wire badge 4.5 × 3 cm embroidered directly onto the blue collar.

11 Junior ranks' cotton collar badge 5 × 3.5 cm woven directly onto the blue collar.

12 No2 Dress shoulder title 15 × 4.5 cm.

13 Officer's Mess Dress gold wire-embroidered collar badges 2.75 × 3.5 cm.

14 Sergeant's Mess Dress silver wire-embroidered collar badges 2.75 × 3.5 cm.

15 WO2 (Drill Sergeant) Conrad Price wearing No2 Dress, his rank indicated by the anodised aluminium Crown on his sleeve and by the gold lace on the peak of his Forage Cap. His appointment as Drill Sergeant is indicated by the Sam Brown belt which otherwise is worn by officers and Warrant Officers Class 1.

16 Senior ranks' wire-embroidered full dress shoulder badge 6 × 4 cm.

17 Junior ranks full dress shoulder badge 3.25 × 4.5 cm woven directly onto the epaulet.

18 Sand coloured cloth shoulder title. It is reported that samples were produced for all Household Division regiments in the 1990s but not issued although those for The Life Guards, Grenadier Guards and Welsh Guards are available.

19

20

21

22

Lineage Welsh Guards (1915).

23

The Welsh Guards was formed during the expansion of the Army in 1915. George V authorised the raising of the fifth regiment of Foot Guards to represent Wales on 26 February and three days later the Regiment mounted its first King's Guard at Buckingham Palace having recruited Welshmen from within the Army. The Commanding Officer wore the first Welsh Guards cap badge, all the others on King's Guard wearing the cap badges of the regiments from which they had transferred.

24

26

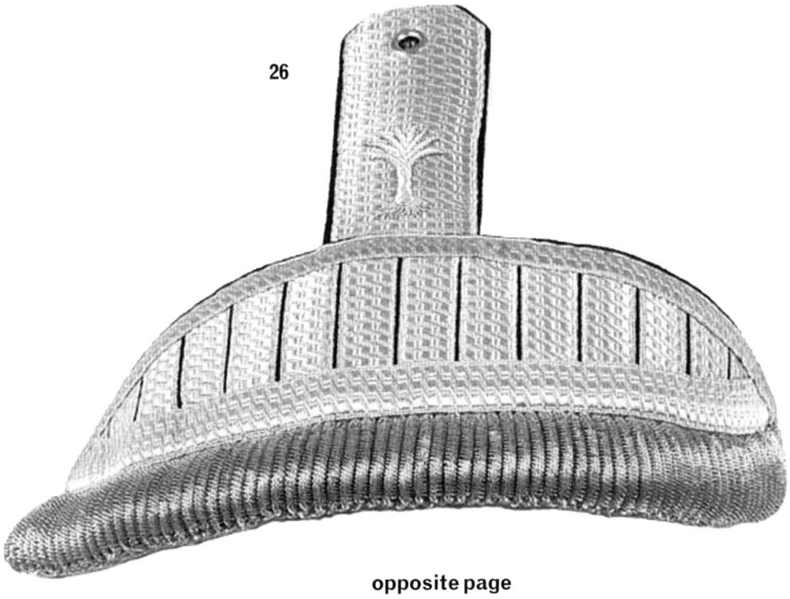

25

opposite page

19 Welsh Guards Regimental Staff waist belt clasp 7.75 × 5.5 cm. This is a pre-1953 buckle, which has been buffed down to an almost unacceptable level. As a guide the Crown, Leak and Motto should be clear and visible.

20 Welsh Guards waist belt clasp 8.75 × 5.5 cm.

21 Gdsm Rikki Johnson wearing No2 Dress.

22 W01 Evans 24, RSM All Arms Drill Wing wearing the Household Division WO1 rank badge.

23 Drum Major's brooch 6.25 × 8 cm worn in State Dress.

this page

24 Welsh Guards 'Colour badge' worn by Warrant Officer Class 2 on the upper right arm 8.25 × 15 cm.

25 Smaller 'Colour badge' worn by Colour Sergeant's on their chevrons, 3.75 × 6.75 cm.

26 Drum Major's Full Dress wing.

Acknowledgement Lt Col Andrew Ford.

In 1829 an order was issued that all soldiers were to be given a regimental number – the example given being 'Thomas Atkins. 5th Foot, No. 55.' The practice had been started by the 56th Foot (now The Royal Anglian Regiment) and noted during the regiment's annual inspection that year.

Because they were regimental numbers soldiers were given a new number if they transferred to another regiment, or to or from the Reserve. This caused considerable confusion during the First World War. There are examples of soldiers having six different numbers, receiving a new number each time they were posted from hospital to a different regiment.

In 1920 Army Numbers were introduced, the first, number 1 was allocated to the Royal Army Service Corps (now the Royal Logistic Corps). By 2005 soldiers were allocated 8 numbers beginning with 25000000, a very few numbers beginning with 23000000 dating from the 1960s remain in use.

In Welsh regiments in particular where there are a number of soldiers with the same surname, each is often identified by the last two numbers of their Army number, hence WO1 Evans 24 at the All Arms Drill Wing. In the Brigade of Gurkhas where three surnames predominate all soldiers are known by their 'last four'.

The Royal Scots
(The Royal Regiment)

The Royal Scots was raised by Royal Warrant for service with France in 1633.

The Royal Scots, or RS, cap badge, based on the Star of the Order of the Thistle, was introduced in 1896. For 12 years between 1958 and 1969 following the reorganisation of the infantry, the regiment wore the Lowland Brigade cap badge with regimental collar badges, after which the anodised aluminium regimental cap badge was introduced for junior ranks. Colour sergeants, warrant officers and officers wear the silver Staff badge. There are three distinct variations; the 1st Battalion Staff badge, the obsolete pre-1933 badge, known as the 2nd Battalion badge, which is worn by some senior Warrant Officers and Late Entry officers, and the private purchase silver badge sold at Edinburgh Castle.

The soldier's badge is worn with a red cloth backing behind the void centre; the 2nd Battalion was identified by a green backing. The badge is worn on a square Hunting Stewart tartan patch. When the Tam o'Shanter is worn in the field the badge is sometimes removed; soldiers are then identified by the tartan backing. In Full Dress black and white feathers of the Blackcock are worn above the cap badge.

Hunting Stewart tartan is also worn as the Tactical Recognition Flash, or TRF. A piece of the tartan has been worn as a regimental arm badge on combat dress since the Second World War. The present patch is not woven tartan but a durable machine made cloth fixed to a hessian backing. Pipers are distinguished by a Royal Stuart TRF and badge backing.

The difference between battalion Staff badges is apparently that the 2nd Battalion badges had 'wee bobbly bits on'.

To commemorate the 300th anniversary of The Royal Scots in 1933 George V approved that pipers of the regiment could wear the Royal Stuart tartan.

1

2

3

4

5

6

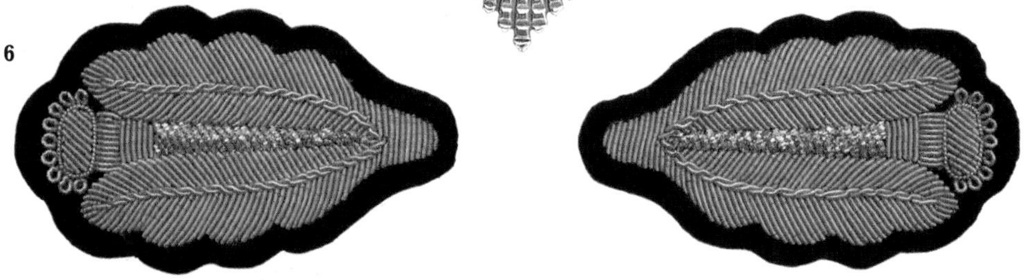

7

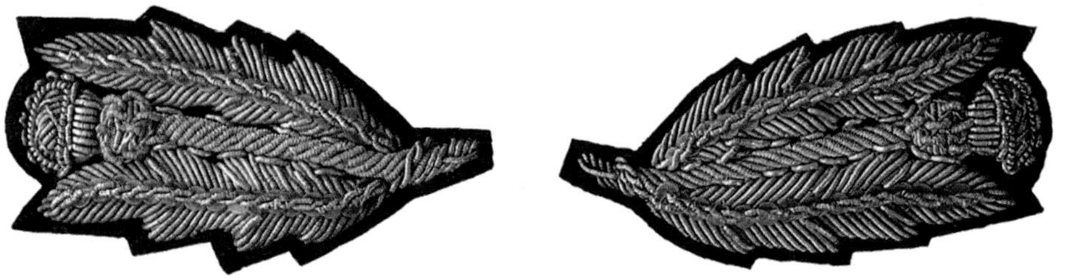

8

9

The Royal Scots, the oldest and therefore the senior Regiment of the Line, was raised by Royal Warrant for service in France in 1633. By 1635 the regiment was over 8,000 strong and included many Scottish mercenaries who had fought with the Swedish Green Brigade. It was by virtue of the Royal Warrant that the entire regiment was considered as British. In 1661, following the formation of the Army after the Restoration, the regiment was recalled by Charles II. Later, after returning from service in Tangiers in 1684, it was given the title The Royal Regiment. A second battalion was raised in 1686 and although the regiment was reduced to a single battalion in 1949 some 2nd Battalion badges are still in use.

10

11

12

13

opposite page

1 The Royal Scots soldier's anodised aluminium cap badge 5.75 × 5.75 cm and collar badges 3.75 × 2.5 cm.

2 The Royal Scots button.

3 Officers', Warrant Officers' and Colour Sergeants' Staff cap badge 5 × 5.5 cm.

4 2nd Battalion Staff badge with 'wee bobbly bits on' favoured by some senior Warrant Officers and Late Entry officers 5 × 5 cm.

5 Private purchase silver cap badge 5 × 5.5 cm.

6 Officer's No1 Dress collar badges 3.5 × 6 cm.

7 Old No1 Dress collar badges 3 × 6 cm.

opposite page

8 WO2 Dod McIntyre wearing a private purchase silver cap badge, regimental rank slide and the 52nd (Infantry) Brigade badge below the Union flag.

9 Captain Davy Henderson wearing a pre-1933 badge, known as the 2nd Battalion Staff cap badge.

10 Hunting Stewart tartan TRF 7 × 7, also worn as a badge backing.

11 LCpl Colin Forbes returning from the field wearing his Tam o'Shanter without the cap badge.

12 Officer's Star of the Order of the Thistle silver and gilt Mess Dress and bronze No2 Dress collar badges 2.75 × 3.25 cm.

13 Major's rank slide.

14

17

18

15

19

20

16

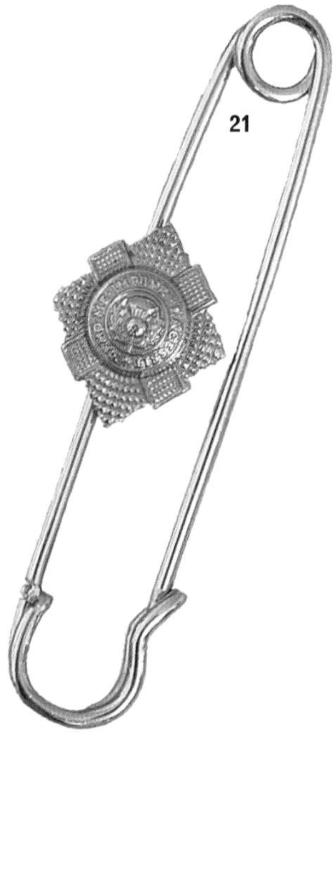
21

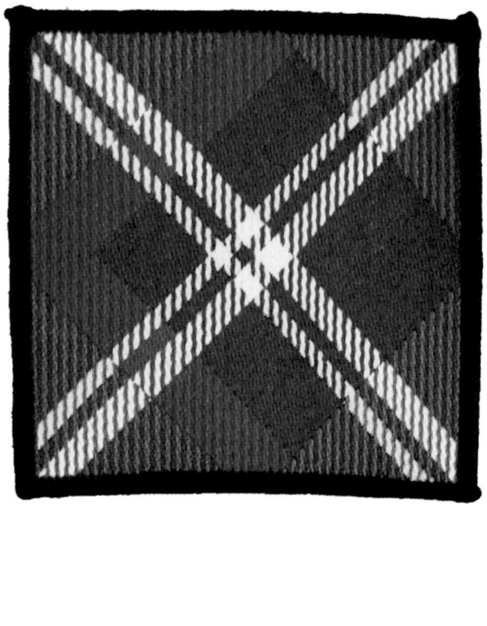
22

23

24

25

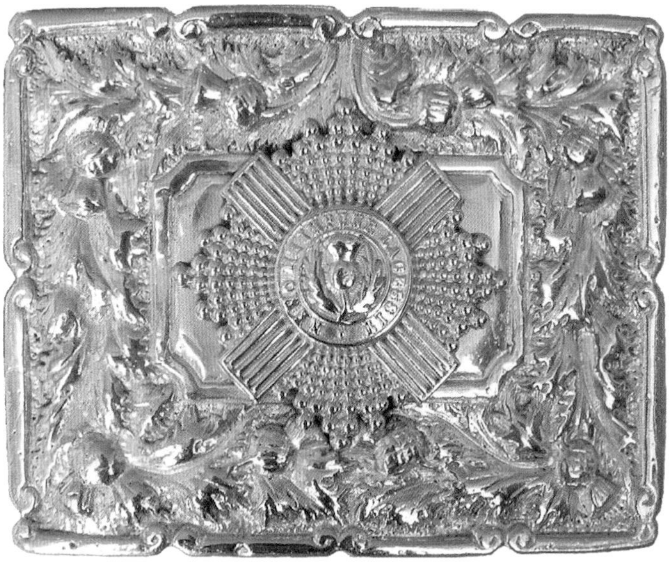

26

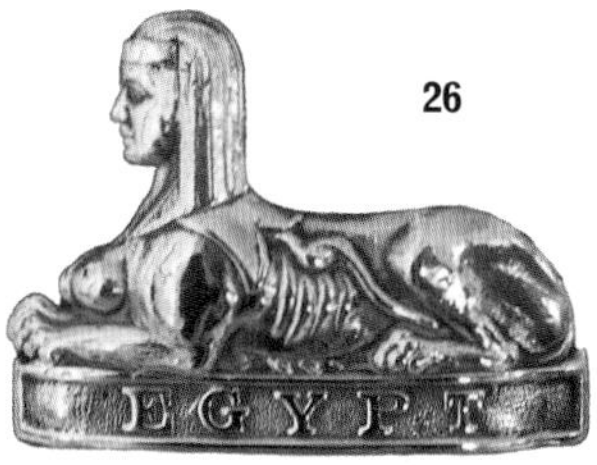

opposite page

14 Officer's shoulder belt plate 7.5 × 9.25 cm.

15 Officer's waist belt clap 5.5 × 5 cm.

16 CSgts Eddie Duff and Gary Erskine escorting the cased regimental colour carried by 2Lt Matty Hayton. Cased colours in their brass topped waterproof covers are traditionally known as 'rockets' because of their resemblance to 19th century artillery rockets.

17 Captain Graeme Wearmouth wearing No1 Dress.

18 Blackcock feathers worn behind the Glengarry badge on parade 14.5 × 23 cm shown much reduced.

19 Piper's cap badge 5 × 5.25 cm.

20 Pte Allan McIntyre wearing the piper's badge on its distinctive backing.

21 Kilt pin 3.25 × 10.25 - badge 2.5 × 3.25 cm.

22 Piper's TRF 7 × 7cm also worn as a badge backing.

this page

23 Dirk 4 × 22 cm.

24 Piper's waist belt clasp 7.75 × 10.

25 Pipe Major's waist belt clasp 9.5 × 7.75 cm.

26 Pipe Major's Sphinx badge mounted on the sheath of the dirk 4 × 3 cm.

The Royal Scots have had the nickname Pontius Pilate's Bodyguard. The nickname originated when the regiment was serving in the French army as Hepburn's Regiment. During a discussion with the Regiment de Picardie as to seniority an officer of that ancient regiment claimed that they were on duty on the night of Jesus' crucifixion, to which an officer of Hepburn's retorted, 'Had we been on duty we would not have been asleep.'

27

28

29

30

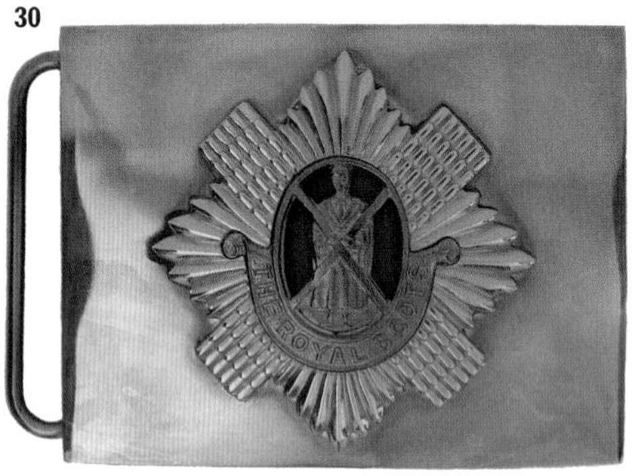

27 Pipe Major's sporran cantle.

28 Plaid brooch 11.25 cm still produced with the pre-1902 Queen Victoria's Crown.

29 DMaj Mark Morrison and PMaj Ally Cuthbertson wearing Full Dress.

30 Soldier's waist belt clasp 7 × 5.75 cm.

The Princess of Wales's Royal Regiment
(Queen's and Royal Hampshires)

The Princess of Wales's Royal Regiment was formed in 1992 by the amalgamation of The Queen's Regiment with The Royal Hampshire Regiment

The Princess of Wales's Royal Regiment, or PWRR, cap badge is based on that of The Queen's Regiment with the Hampshire Rose added below the Tudor Dragon, and the title changed. There was a delay in delivering the metal badges in 1992 and a cloth badge was worn by all ranks on the khaki beret, a few of which survive, worn on operations. A bright metal and enamel badge is worn by soldiers on the Forage Cap and a silver, gilt and enamel version with a red centre by officers. All ranks wear a bronze beret badge on a blue and yellow backing.

The Queen's Regiment collar badges are worn in facing pairs; bronze in Number 2 Dress and anodised aluminium in Full Dress, Number 1 Dress and Sergeants' Mess Dress.

1

2

3

4

5

6

7

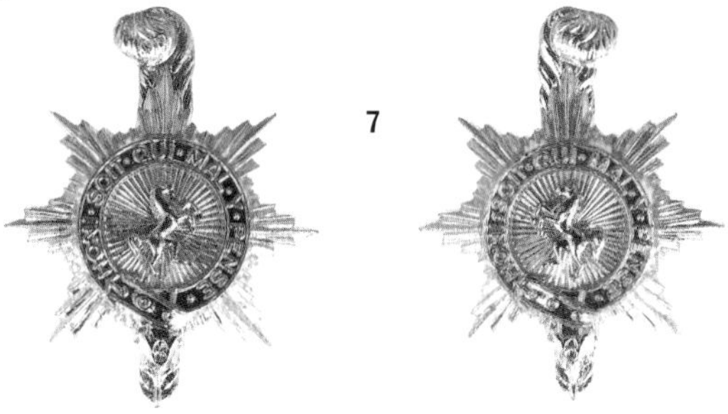

8

The centre of the regimental badge is the Elizabethan Dragon, awarded to The Buffs in recognition of their Tudor origin by Queen Anne, probably in 1707. The Hampshire Rose was worn by the Trained Bands of Hampshire who fought for Henry V at Agincourt in 1415 and later was the badge of The Royal Hampshire Regiment. The surrounding Garter was awarded to The Royal Sussex Regiment in 1832, and was also part of The Royal Hampshire Regiment officer's badge. The Prince of Wales's Coronet holds the ostrich plumes awarded to The Black Prince, taken from the helmet of the slain King John of Bohemia at the Battle of Crecy in 1346. The 15th Prince of Wales recommended to George III in 1810 that the plumes be awarded to the 77th Foot for its exploits in India.

The White Horse on the centre of the collar badges is the badge of Kent, dating from the 16th Century and ascribed to Horsa the Saxon. The Star and Plume were taken from The Royal Sussex Regiment, the Plume commemorating the defeat of the French Roussillon Regiment at the Battle of Quebec in 1759.

The regiment wears a cloth Tiger arm badge. The Tiger had been awarded to the 67th Foot by George IV in 1826 in recognition of 21 years service in India, from 1805 to 1826, much of it on active service. The badge is worn on the left sleeve in all orders of dress except Combat Dress when it is worn on the right sleeve.

Officers wear the Eversleigh Star rank star (pip). Soldiers wear rank badges and qualification badges on a blue backing on Number 2 Dress.

Three of the constituent regiments of The Princess of Wales's Royal Regiment fought at Albuhera in Spain in 1811. The defeated French Marshal Soult wrote of the British soldiers, 'There is no beating these troops. They were completely beaten, the day was mine and they did not know it and would not run.' After the battle the surviving officers and sergeants gathered at an Inn and swore to meet annually to commemorate the slaughter of their comrades.

A silent toast is drunk individually on 16 May from a silver Loving Cup reputably made from the accoutrements of the officers of the 57th Foot who had fought at Albuhera. The cup is adorned with the Military General Service medal awarded to Colour Sergeant Holloway, who had served during the battle as an 11 year old Drummer Boy, and was the longest living survivor of the battle.

9

10

11

12

13

14

15

16

At Sobraon in India in 1846 Sergeant Bernard McCabe picked up the Colour of the 31st Foot after most of the officers had become casualties. As he advanced, the regiment followed and turned the tide of the battle. Each year the best sergeant is appointed Sobraon Sergeant and carries the regimental colour on parade.

In 1992 two platoons were attached to 1st Battalion The King's Regiment. One platoon carried out Public Duties wearing The King's Regiment uniform and insignia but with a wire-embroidered Tiger badge worn on the left sleeve of the Number 1 Dress tunic. It therefore appeared at the time as though some Kingsmen were wearing the Tiger arm badge.

Lineage The Princess of Wales's Royal Regiment (Queen's and Royal Hampshires) (1992) from The Queen's Regiment (1966) and The Royal Hampshire Regiment (1881). The Queen's Regiment from The Queen's Royal Surrey Regiment (1959), The Queen's Own Buffs, The Royal Kent Regiment (1961), The Royal Sussex Regiment (1881) and The Middlesex Regiment (Duke of Cambridge's Own) (1881). The Queen's Royal Surrey Regiment from The Queen's Royal Regiment (West Surrey) (1881), formerly 2nd Foot (1661), and The East Surrey Regiment (1881), from 31st Foot (1702) and 70th Foot (1758). The Queen's Own Buffs from The Buffs (Royal East Kent Regiment) (1881), formerly 3rd Foot (1665) and The Queen's Own Royal West Kent Regiment (1881), from 50th Foot (1755) and 97th Foot (1824). The Royal Sussex Regiment from 35th Foot (1701) and 107th Foot (1853). The Middlesex Regiment from 57th Foot (1755) and 77th Foot (1787). The Royal Hampshire Regiment from 37th Foot (1702) and 67th Foot (1756).

17

18

Acknowledgement
WO1 (RSM) DS Sharrocks and SA Whyte

previous page

1 The Princess of Wales's Royal Regiment soldier's bright metal cap badge 3 × 4.75 cm and bronze collar badges 3 × 3.75 cm.
2 All ranks bronze badge worn on the beret on a square of blue, yellow, blue silk 3 × 4.75 cm.
3 Officer's silver, gilt and enamel badge 3 × 4.75 cm.
4 Bronze shoulder title 4.5 × 2.25 cm.
5 PWRR button.
6 Eversleigh Star rank star (pip).
7 Soldier's anodised aluminium collar badges worn in Full Dress, Number 1 Dress and on sergeants Mess Dress 3 × 3.75 cm.
8 Pte Lovell Cadet wearing No 2 Dress.

opposite page

Regimental Tiger arm badge
9 No1 and No2 Dress cotton embroidered badge 4.5 × 4 cm.
10 Combat Dress woven badge 4.75 × 4 cm.
11 Mess Dress wire-embroidered badge 4 × 3.5 cm.

12 Warrant Officer Class 2 (Regimental Quartermaster Sergeant)'s rank slide.
13 Lt Dan Power and Sgt Hugh Jordon wearing Mess Dress showing the officer's silver and gilt collar badges and the Sergeant's anodised aluminium collar badges, and the Tiger arm badge.
14 Cpl Bish Bishop and Pte Eric Butadroka wearing combat dress with the Tiger arm badge worn on the shirt. The TRF is worn on the jacket.
15 Sgts Kev Jordan, wearing the Platoon Sergeants' Battle Course badge, and Gaz Pullen wearing No2 Dress with the distinctive blue backed badges.
16 TRF 6.75 × 6.75 cm.

this page

17 Waist belt clasp 7 × 5.5 cm.
18 The Corps of Drums wear the Infantry Blue Cloth Helmet ornamented with a bright metal helmet plate 10.5 × 12.5 cm.

The King's Own Royal Border Regiment

The King's Own Royal Border Regiment was formed by the amalgamation of the King's Own Royal Regiment (Lancaster) with The Border Regiment in 1959.

The King's Own Royal Border Regiment, or KORBR, wears the Lion of England badge from The King's Own, surrounded by the wreath taken from the badge of The Border Regiment. For 11 years from its formation in 1959 until 1970 the regiment wore The Lancastrian Brigade cap badge with regimental collar badges, after which the regimental cap badge was introduced.

The diamond shaped red backing was originally worn by The King's Own on the sun helmet from about 1901 and readopted for the beret and Drummers helmet on amalgamation in 1959.

Officers wear a wire-embroidered side hat badge, and Warrant Officers a woven badge. Soldiers wear a left collar badge as the side hat badge.

In about 1990 the 1st Battalion reintroduced a small cloth badge, the Roman numerals IV, for wear in the Field. The style of badge originated with The King's Own in the 1950s when a larger version was worn on the front of the jungle hat. When reintroduced it was worn on the left side of the soft camouflage hats which when issued are known by soldiers as 'Hats, floppy, ridiculous'.

The regiment, along with The Staffordshire Regiment, wears a glider badge on the right shoulder. The Staffordshire Regiment's badge differs by being sewn on to a black patch, and is also worn as their Tactical Recognition Flash.

1

2

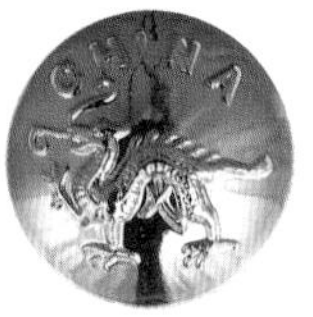

3

4

5

6

7

The King's Own had a tradition that William III bestowed the Lion of England badge on the regiment because it had been the first English regiment to join him after he landed at Torbay in 1688. It was noted as an 'ancient badge' in 1751 and first worn as a metal badge in about 1774.

The Border Regiment's laurel wreath had been awarded to the 34th Foot by the Duke of Cumberland for its courage and discipline in covering the withdrawal of the Army after the Battle of Fontenoy in 1745.

The China honour and Dragon on the button dates from the Opium War fought against China from 1839 to 1842. The Battle Honour was awarded to five British regiments but was of particular significance to the 55th Foot as Lieutenant Butler captured the only Imperial Dragon Banner to be taken during the war, at Chusan in 1841.

8

9

16

10

11

12

13

14

15

opposite page

1 King's Own Royal Border Regiment soldier's anodised aluminium cap badge 3.5 × 4.5 cm and collar badges 3.5 × 1.5 cm
2 KORBR button.
3 Officer's wire-embroidered beret badge, 6.5 × 6.5 cm
4 Soldier's woven beret badges 6.5 × 6.5 cm.
5 Officer's silver and gilt cap and silver collar badges.
6 Shoulder title 5.5 × 2.5 cm.
7 Cpl Nick Leeson wearing the woven beret badge

this page

8 Major Rich Cartwright wearing the wire embroidered beret badge
9 Major's rank slide.
10 Officer's wire-embroidered Side Hat badge 5.25 × 5 cm
11 Warrant Officer's woven Side Hat badge 5 × 5 cm.
12 Cpl Reidy Reid in No2 Dress, the regiment's Glider badge is on his right sleeve above the Section Commanders Battle Course crossed bayonets badge. He wears the regimental waist belt clasp.
13 Number 2 Dress Glider Battle Honour arm badge 6 × 4 cm.
14 Combat Dress Glider Battle Honour arm badge 6 × 3.5 cm.
15 Mess Dress Glider Battle Honour arm badge 4.25 × 2.75 cm. (For other variations see The Staffordshire Regiment, p. 191.)
16 Pte John Crowder wearing No2 Dress with the Glider battle honour badge on his right sleeve.

17

18

The King's Own Royal Border Regiment celebrates St George's Day, when all ranks wear a fresh red rose, officially in their hats but if wearing berets, in their lapel or top left buttonhole.

19

20

21

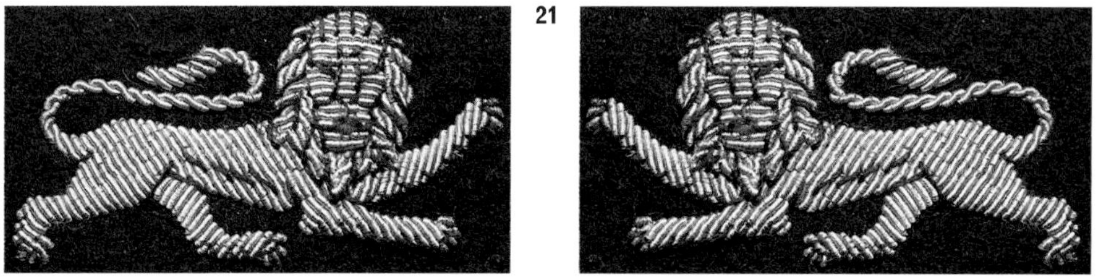

22

The Arroyo Drums

During a surprise attack on the village of Arroyo dos Molinos in the Peninsular in 1811 the 2nd Battalion 34th (Cumberland) Regiment 'Unaided, cut off, and made prisoners, many French officers of distinction – General Brune, the Prince d'Aremberg, and an immense suite, besides an entire battalion of the French 34th of the Line, the brass drums and drum-major's staff of which were long after used by the captors.' Tradition has Sergeant Moses Simpson taking the French drum major's staff. Annually on Arroyo Day the Corps of Drums dressed in period uniforms Troop the captured Drums. In 1811 the 34th Foot also took the red over white feathers worn by the French in their shakos. In time similar hackles or tufts were adopted by the whole Army at which time the 34th Foot were authorised to wear theirs reversed, white over red. With the introduction of helmets in 1879 the distinctive red and white tufts were dispensed with and to preserve the distinction, the centre of the officers' helmet plates and later badges were enamelled white over red. The distinction is maintained by the red diamond backing to beret badges and to the Drummers' helmet plates.

above
Drummers led by Sgt 'John Boy' Watson, wearing period uniforms of the 34th Foot, Troop The French Drums on Arroyo Day. Drummers' uniforms at the time were in 'reversed colours', yellow coats with red facings whilst the remainder of the regiment wore red coats with yellow facings.

23

24

opposite page

17 Lt Andrew Franklin wearing a cut down version of the jungle hat with the obsolete cloth badge.
18 Obsolete cloth badge, IV representing the 4th Foot, now replaced by the TRF.
19 DMaj Stax McLardie wearing No 2 Dress, his rank badges mounted on the distinctive red backing.
20 In Full Dress the Corps of Drums wear the Royal Marines white helmet ornamented with a bright metal helmet plate mounted with a detachable centre 10.5 × 12.5 cm.
21 Mess collar badges 5 × 2.5 cm.
22 Waist belt clasp 10 × 6.25 cm.
23 TRF 6 × 6 cm introduced in 2004. The colours represent William of Orange, the Royal blue and Kendal green.
24 CSgts John Foster and Jock Wildey escorting Captain Pete Higgins with the Queen's Colour.

The Border Regiment was awarded the glider badge in 1950 in recognition of the 1st Battalion's action in the first glider landing, against Sicily in 1943. During the war glider trained soldiers wore a blue Hotspur glider badge on the lower left sleeve. The present badge represents a Horsa, the first glider that was used for training from 1940. Walter Cronkite, the US journalist, described the particular dangers of a glider assault: 'If you've got to go into combat, don't go by glider. Walk, crawl, parachute, swim, float – anything. But don't go by glider!'

Lineage The King's Own Royal Border Regiment (1959) from The King's Own Royal Regiment (Lancaster) (1881), formerly 4th Foot (1680) and The Border Regiment (1881), from 34th Foot (1702) and 55th Foot (1755).

Acknowledgement
Captain Mark Graham, WO1 (RSM) Max Davison and Mr Peter Donnelly BA AMA

The Royal Regiment of Fusiliers

'That astonishing Infantry'

The Royal Regiment of Fusiliers was formed on St George's Day 1968 by the amalgamation of the Fusilier regiments of England which were serving together in The Fusilier Brigade; The Royal Northumberland Fusiliers, The Royal Warwickshire Fusiliers, The Royal Fusiliers (City of London Regiment) and The Lancashire Fusiliers.

1

2

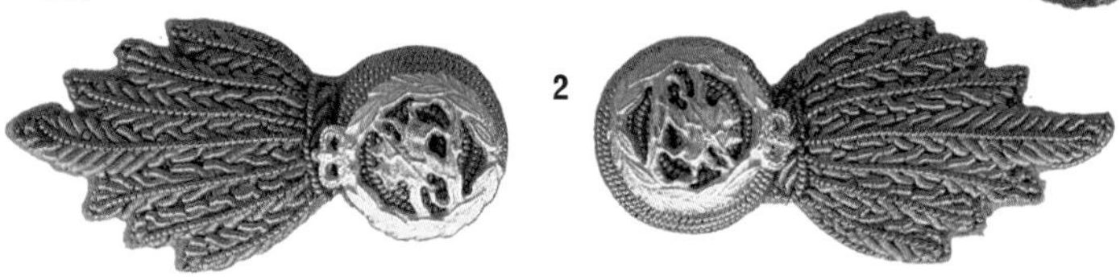

The Royal Regiment of Fusiliers, or RRF, cap badge, designed for the Fusilier Brigade in 1958, combines St George and the Dragon from The Royal Northumberland Fusiliers, the Crown from The Royal Fusiliers and the laurel wreath from The Lancashire Fusiliers. Many trained soldiers buy a bimetal badge to wear in place of the issue anodised aluminium badge.

The Royal Warwickshire Fusiliers are represented by the design on the button.

A red and white hackle adopted from The Royal Northumberland Fusiliers is worn above the beret badge.

3

5

6

4

7

8

After defeating a French attempt to take St Lucia in 1778 the 5th Foot took the white plumes from the French caps and began a custom for the next 51 years of wearing white plumes, by which time all Grenadiers in the Army were wearing white plumes. The 5th Foot were then authorised to wear their plumes tipped with red to perpetuate their distinction. The name hackle is used as the plumes are made from the hackle, or neck, feathers of a duck.

9

10

11

15

12

13

14

16

In 1988 the 1st Battalion was assigned to 5th Airborne Brigade and the lead element was parachute trained. The primrose over rose Drop Zone flash was introduced which was retained as the battalion Tactical Recognition Flash until 2004.

opposite page

1 Royal Regiment of Fusiliers all-ranks anodised aluminium beret badge 4 × 5 cm and soldier's collar badges 2.25 × 3.25 cm.
2 Officer's Mess Dress collar badges 4 × 2 cm.
3 RRF hackle adopted from The Royal Northumberland Fusiliers 15 × 6.5 cm.
4 WO1 (RSM) Joe Coleman wearing No1 Dress.
5 Officer's silver and gilt collar badges 2.25 × 3.5 cm.
6 Private purchase beret badge worn by all ranks 4 × 5.25 cm.
7 RRF button.
8 Shoulder title 2.75 × 1 cm.

this page

9 Soldier's waist belt clasp 7 × 5.25 cm.
10 1st Battalion TRF 4 × 4 cm worn on the right side of the helmet.
11 Lieutenant's rank slide.
12 Obsolete LZ Flash 7 × 7 cm which was worn on the right sleeve until 2004.
13 1st Battalion shoulder title worn in Combat Dress 7 × 3.5 cm.
14 2nd Battalion shoulder title worn in Combat Dress 6.5 × 3.5 cm.
15 Fus Mark Canham and Fish Fisher and LCpl Nick Abbott wearing No2 Dress with the distinctive red backing to the qualification badges.
16 Lt Tom Kibble wearing the 1st Battalion title above the Union Flag badge.

17

18

The red and white roses, symbols of England, date to the six Holland regiments recruited in Britain and from British mercenaries already serving the Dutch against France, in 1673. The regiments accompanied William of Orange to England in 1688 and two, The Royal Northumberland Fusiliers and The Royal Warwickshire Fusiliers remained permanently on the English establishment with English roses as badges on the Colours.

There is no clear indication of why the Antelope was chosen as a badge by The Royal Warwickshire Fusiliers. It was a Royal badge dating to Henry IV, 1367–1413, but possibly the badge was copied from a Colour captured by the Regiment from the Spanish at the Battle of Saragossa in 1710. St George and Dragon was authorised as a badge to be worn on the back of the fur cap by William IV in 1836 when the Regiment became Fusiliers. However in 1751 the badge was recorded as its 'ancient badge' to be borne on the Colours.

The Lancashire Fusiliers used the wreath surrounding St George and the Dragon and tradition suggests that it may record its action at the Battle of Minden in 1759.

19

21

20

22

Bobby, an antelope, is one of nine official mascots in the Army. Always named Bobby, the mascot was inherited from The Royal Warwickshire Fusiliers and leads Battalions on ceremonial occasions.

Battalions are also preceded by four corporals acting as ceremonial pioneers, a custom inherited from The Lancashire Fusiliers. The mascot handlers and ceremonial pioneers wear the same insignia as the Drummers.

Lineage The Royal Regiment of Fusiliers (1968) from The Royal Northumberland Fusiliers (1881), formerly 5th Foot (1674), The Royal Warwickshire Fusiliers (1963), formerly The Royal Warwickshire Regiment (1881) and 6th Foot (1673), The Royal Fusiliers (City of London Regiment), formerly 7th Foot (1685), and The Lancashire Fusiliers (1881) formerly 20th Foot (1688).

opposite page

17 Red and white roses 7 × 9.5 cm are worn on St George's Day, 23 April, a tradition retained from The Royal Northumberland Fusiliers.

18 Minden Roses 7 × 9 cm are worn on 1 August, a tradition retained from The Lancashire Fusiliers.

19 CSgt Thom Darkoh, 2nd Battalion wearing red and white roses on St George's Day.

20 Drummer's Full Dress Grenade badges gilding metal 4 × 9 cm and bimetal 4 × 9.25 cm.

21 Sgt Pete Green 2 RRF wearing No2 Dress training as a Drum Major.

this page

22 Bobby with handlers Fus Ash Ashton and Cpl Bob Skillen on parade with the 2nd Battalion, with the ceremonial pioneers, Cpl Pru Prudham and Adam Benfield, and the Corps of Drums led by DMaj Dave McKenna.

Acknowledgement
Lt Col Jolyon Willans, Capt Dan Taylor, Duncan Wilson, and WO2 (RQMS) A Whilton and Mr Chick Mackie

The King's Regiment

The King's Regiment was formed by the amalgamation of The King's Regiment (Liverpool) and The Manchester Regiment in 1958.

The King's Regiment, or KINGS, cap badge was designed in 1958. However for 12 years from the formation of the regiment in 1958 until 1969 the regiment wore the Lancastrian Brigade cap badge with regimental collar badges, after which the regimental cap badge was introduced. The small anodised aluminium badge lacked definition and from the late 1970s there had been an aspiration to increase the size of the badge and change the title from Gothic to English script. The present large bright metal badge was introduced in 2001, followed shortly afterwards by a black badge worn on the beret during training and operations. It is said that this reflects the practice of The Devonshire and Dorset Regiment; the 1st Battalion at the time being commanded by an officer from that regiment.

The first arm badge was adopted in 1992 by the 1st Battalion, which was serving in London and wanted a badge to complement the blue, red, blue that was being worn by the battalions of the Guards Division serving in the same brigade. The original silk ribbon was replaced by a 7 × 7 cm Tactical Recognition Flash in 2000 and approved in a slightly reduced size, 6 × 6 cm, in 2002.

1

2

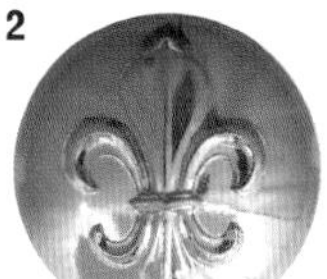

3

4

5

6

7

8

opposite page

1 The King's Regiment all-ranks bright metal cap badge 3.25 × 4.5 cm and collar badges 2.5 × 3.5 cm
2 The King's Regiment button.
3 Anodised aluminium shoulder title 4.25 × 1.5 cm.
4 Officer's wire-embroidered side hat badge 3.5 × 4.25 cm.
5 All-ranks black operational badge 3.25 × 4.5 cm.
6 Officer's Mess Dress wire-embroidered collar badges 3 × 4 cm.
7 Kgn Steven Judge, WO2 (CSM) John Jones and Cpl Dave Muldoon at the end of an exercise wearing the black cap badge.
8 TRF 6 × 6 cm.

this page

9 Major Nigel Smith wearing the regiment's distinctive blue shirt and Side Hat with wire-embroidered badge.
10 Sgt Dave Connor wearing No2 Dress.
11 The Corps of Drums wear the Infantry Blue Cloth Helmet ornamented with a bright metal helmet plate mounted with a detachable centre 10.5 × 12.5 cm.
15 Gold brooch 2.25 × 3 cm made in 1990 and therefore with gothic lettering, worn by attached female officers on the left breast in barrack dress.
12 Acting WO2 Paul Brady wearing Combat Dress.

9

10

11

15

12

13

14

13 Soldier's waist belt clasp 8 × 6.5 cm.
14 Corporal's rank slide.
15 Commanding Officer's Bugler gold wire-embroidered badge 10 × 8.5 cm
16 Adjutant's Bugler silver wire-embroidered badge 10 × 8.5 cm.

The best buglers selected by an annual competition are appointed Commanding Officer's and Adjutant's Buglers and wear a special badge on the right sleeve in Full Dress.

Lineage The King's Regiment (1958) from The King's Regiment (Liverpool) (1881), formerly 8th Foot (1685), and The Manchester Regiment (1881), from 63rd Foot (1757) and 96th Foot (1824).

15

16

Although not a 'Royal' regiment the 8th Foot, had since at least 1742 worn the blue facings of a Royal Regiment and it was always listed amongst the Royal Regiments in Orders. In 1868 the Army adopted a new shako and with it Royal Regiments were permitted to wear a red ball tuft above the badge. This distinction was lost in 1879 when the Prussian inspired helmet, which is still worn by Corps of Drums, was introduced. However, as the 8th Foot had worn the red ball tuft it was authorised to place a piece of red cloth behind the helmet plate. A red backing was also worn with the Glengarry badge. When cap badges were introduced in 1898 there was no red backing, The King's Regiment wore a red diamond backing behind the badge on the Wolsey helmet worn in South Africa in 1900 and the White Helmet worn in Egypt and India until the First World War. The red backing disappeared after the First World War, to reappear in Italy in 1944. The Commanding Officer of 2nd Battalion The King's Regiment insisted on cap badges being worn when the battalion was out of the line. Badges were a low priority for resupply but turnout was so important that the Pioneers even cast badges from cartridge cases. One morning the Mortar Officer, Lieutenant Trevor Cole-Rees, appeared wearing a square red patch behind the cap badge on his beret. His idea was adopted by the Battalion and in 1948 authorised for the whole Regiment.
Lieutenant Cole-Rees also wore a blue shirt with brass titles and rank stars on that morning in 1944 which although not adopted then, is now worn by officers of The King's. Such is the stuff of regimental tradition.

In 1715 The Queen's Regiment distinguished itself at the Battle of Dunblane fought against the Jacobites in Scotland. King George I was a German who spoke no English, and the greatest accolade he could give an English regiment was the right to wear his Hanoverian insignia. He renamed the regiment The King's Regiment and directed that the White Horse be borne on the Colours. The White Horse was painted on the Colours and probably first worn as a wire-embroidered sleeve badge by the Drummers.

The Royal Anglian Regiment

The Royal Anglian Regiment was formed in 1964 by the amalgamation of the 1st East Anglian Regiment (Royal Norfolk and Suffolk), the 2nd East Anglian Regiment (Duchess of Gloucester's Own Royal Lincolnshire and Northamptonshire), the 3rd East Anglian Regiment (16th/44th Foot) and The Royal Leicestershire Regiment.

The Royal Anglian Regiment, or R ANGLIAN, cap badge was adopted in 1964 and combines the star taken from The Bedfordshire and Hertfordshire Regiment's badge and Gibraltar castle, which had been part of the badges of The Suffolk Regiment, The Northamptonshire Regiment and The Essex Regiment. The badge is worn on a black square backing by officers and a black 'tombstone' backing by soldiers on the khaki beret.

The 1st Battalion collar badges represent the Royal Norfolk Regiment's figure of Britannia, which had been approved in 1799, and Gibraltar castle and key, which had been granted to the Suffolk Regiment after the siege of 1779–1783.

The 2nd Battalion collar badges represent The Royal Lincolnshire Regiment's Sphinx, which had been granted following the Egyptian campaign of 1801, and the Northamptonshire Regiment's 1809 battle honour Talavera.

The 1st Battalion The Royal Norfolk Regiment wore the yellow lanyard and yellow on black cloth shoulder titles, which had been introduced at the end of the Second World War. Ordered to change them to the white on red Infantry colours in 1947 by the Director of Infantry, Lieutenant Colonel FP Barclay DSO MC challenged the Director to a duel of High Cockalorum after a Mess dinner. Barclay won and the lanyard stayed. The following year George VI commented on how smart The Royal Norfolk Regiment looked and the lanyard was retained after cloth titles were discontinued.

1

2
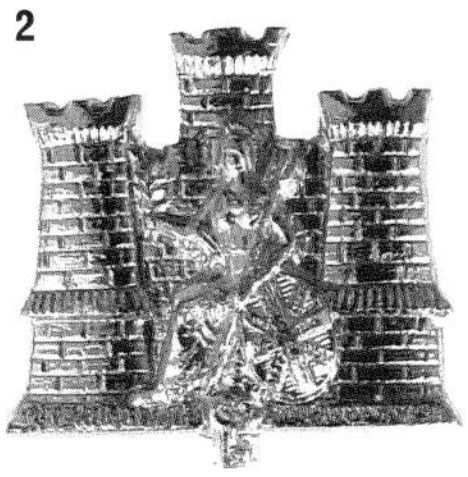

3

2
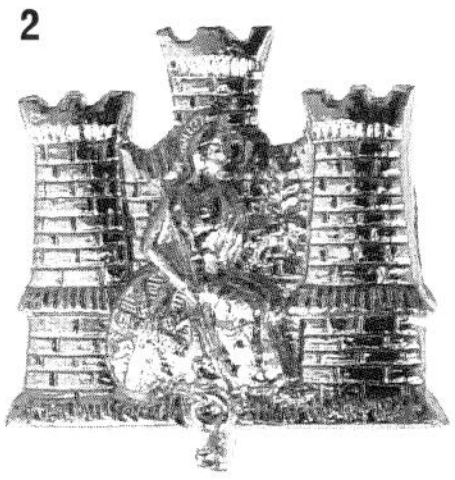

4

5
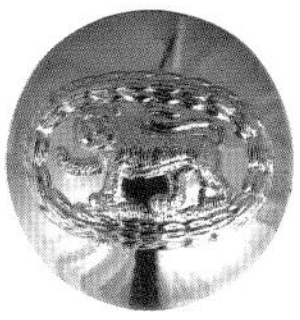

4

6

7
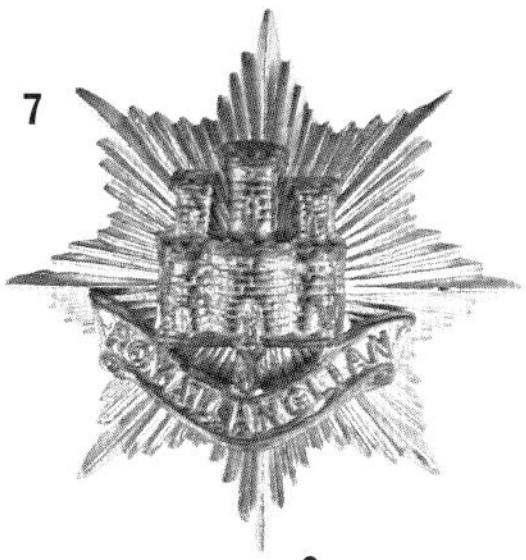

6

8

9

Although there is no longer a 3rd Battalion, some senior ranks who formerly served with the battalion wear their 3rd Battalion collar badges on the underside of the lapels on their Mess Dress. The collar badges consist of the Garter, which formed part of the Bedfordshire and Hertfordshire Regiment cap badge, enclosing the Essex Regiment's Imperial Eagle captured at the Battle of Salamanca in 1812.

During the Battle of Salamanca in 1812 Lieutenant Pearce of the 2nd Battalion 44th Foot captured the Eagle of the 62ème Régiment d'infanterie de ligne. The 44th Foot were granted the Eagle as a badge which was passed down to the 3rd Battalion The Royal Anglian Regiment. When the 3rd Battalion was disbanded in 1992 the badge was adopted by the whole Regiment worn on the left sleeve in Number 2 Dress.

In 1978 the 1st Battalion was posted from Allied Command Europe Mobile Force (AMF) where they wore a small Union flag badge on the sleeve, to a mechanised role in Celle, West Germany where the Union flags were removed. To cover the obvious mark on the sleeve left by removing the badge the Commanding Officer reintroduced the red and yellow Minden badge, which had previously been worn by The Suffolk Regiment. The Colonel of the Regiment, General Sir Timothy Creasey KCB OBE, approved its extension to other orders of dress.

The 2nd Battalion followed the lead of the 1st Battalion in adopting an arm badge, choosing The Bedfordshire and Hertfordshire Regiment yellow and black arm badge, which has been known from time to time as the Bumble Bee.

In the mid-1990s both battalions adopted cloth shoulder titles worn whilst on operations in Bosnia. The 1st Battalion's badge, THE VIKINGS appears to have completely disappeared, although the 2nd Battalion's THE POACHERS title survived until 2004 when replaced by new rank slides.

In 1942 1st Battalion The Royal Norfolk Regiment joined 24th Guards Independent Brigade Group and the officers adopted the Guards' khaki beret, but to assert their difference wore their cap badge on a black backing. Black was the regimental colour and is attributed to the regiment's presence at the funeral of Sir John Moore at Corunna in 1806. The khaki beret went out of use after the Second World War but was readopted in 1960, its wear extended to all Royal Anglian officers and warrant officers in 1970, and finally to all ranks in 1976.

10

11

12

13

14

15

16

17

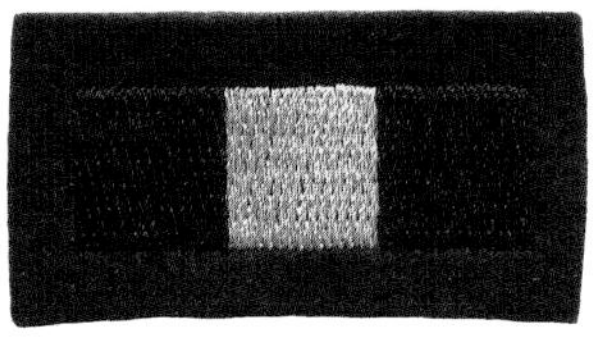

18

19

20

During the Battle of Minden, in Germany, on 1 August 1759 a badly written order resulted in six English infantry regiments advancing unsupported against the French cavalry. French officers are said to have laughed at this 'audacious proceeding'. The British, advancing through a storm of fire, picked wild roses for their caps before standing firm and defeating three cavalry charges. The French infantry, witnessing the destruction of their cavalry by British musketry, broke and ran. Five of the regiments celebrate the victory by wearing roses in their caps each anniversary;

12th Foot now 1st Battalion The Royal Anglian Regiment.
20th Foot now The Royal Regiment of Fusiliers.
25th Foot now The King's Own Scottish Borderers.
37th Foot now The Princess of Wales's Royal Regiment.
51st Foot now The Light Infantry.
The 23rd Foot now Royal Welch Fusiliers do not celebrate the victory.

21

22

24

23

previous page

1 Royal Anglian Regiment cap badge 3 × 3 cm,
2 Collar badges of the 1st Battalion 2.5 × 2.5 cm
3 Anodised aluminium shoulder title 5.5 × 2.25 cm.
4 Collar badges of the 2nd Battalion 3.5 × 3 cm.
5 The Royal Anglian Regiment button.
6 3rd Battalion collar badges worn unofficially by some former members of the battalion under the lapels of their Mess Dress 3 × 3.5 cm.
7 The Royal Anglian Regiment officer's bright metal cap badge 3 × 3 cm
8 WO2 Lee Jay holding the Salamanca Eagle.
9 Cpl Knighty Knight wearing No1 Dress with 2nd Battalion collar badges.

opposite page

10 Officer's 1st Battalion silver and gilt collar badges 2.5 × 2.5 cm
11 Officer's 2nd Battalion silver and gilt collar badges 3.5 × 3 cm.
12 The Royal Anglian Regiment arm badge 5.5 × 5.5 cm.
13 New arm badge embroidered on The Essex Regiment's purple facing colour.
14 Sgt Si Towe, training as a Drum Major, wearing 2nd Battalion collar badges and black lanyard, and the regimental arm badge.
15 1st Battalion, Minden arm badge 4.5 × 2.5cm
16 2nd Battalion, Bedfordshire and Hertfordshire Regiment 'Bumble Bee' arm badge 4 × 2 cm.
17 2nd Battalion arm badge introduced in 2004 4.5 × 2.5 cm.
18 Royal Anglian Regiment registered TRF 7 × 7 cm worn by some TA soldiers.

this page

19 Captain James Inch with the black cap badge backing worn on the beret. He is wearing the 2nd Battalion 'Bumble Bee' arm badge.
20 Minden Roses 7 × 8 cm worn by soldiers of the 1st Battalion on 1 August to commemorate the Battle of Minden, 1759. Officers and Warrant Officers wear fresh roses.
21 CSgts Tim Newton and Jimmy Self wearing No1 Dress with 1st Battalion collar badges.
22 Obsolete 2nd Battalion shoulder title worn on combat dress until 2004.
23 2nd Battalion captain's rank slide.
24 DMaj Paul Howlett leading the Corps of Drums of the 1st Battalion, The Royal Anglian Regiment.

25

26

27

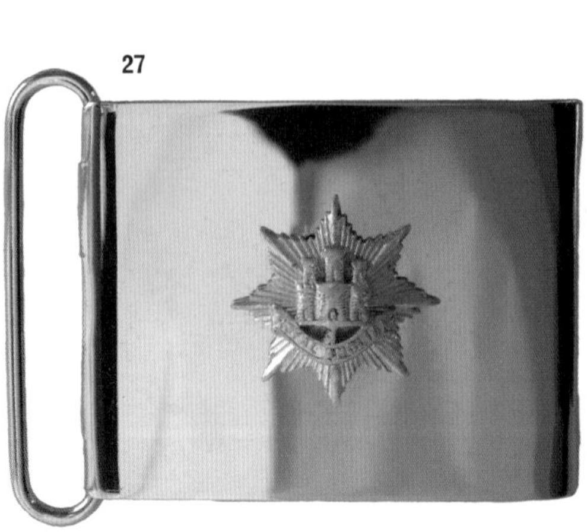

Lineage The Royal Anglian Regiment (1964) from 1st East Anglian Regiment (Royal Norfolk and Suffolk) (1959), 2nd East Anglian Regiment (Duchess of Gloucester's Own Royal Lincolnshire and Northamptonshire) (1960), 3rd East Anglian Regiment (16th/44th Foot) (1958), and The Royal Leicestershire Regiment (1881), formerly 17th Foot (1688). 1st East Anglian from The Royal Norfolk Regiment (1881), formerly 9th Foot (1685), and The Suffolk Regiment (1881), formerly 12th Foot (1685). 2nd East Anglian Regiment from The Royal Lincolnshire Regiment (1881), formerly 10th Foot (1685), and The Northamptonshire Regiment (1881), from 48th Foot (1741) and 58th Foot (1755). 3rd East Anglian Regiment from The Bedfordshire and Hertfordshire Regiment (1881), formerly 16th Foot (1688), and The Essex Regiment (1881), from 44th Foot (1741) and 56th Foot (1757).

Each battalion of the Royal Anglian Regiment is known by a nickname. It is said that the 1st Battalion did not have a traditional nickname and when serving in Cyprus organised a 'phone-in on BFBS – the British Forces Broadcasting Service – which produced the name The Vikings. The name was marked by a recruiting party which arrived in Norfolk sailing down the river dressed as Vikings.

The 2nd Battalion has always been known as The Poachers, handed down from The Royal Lincolnshire Regiment

25 The regiment's Corps of Drums wear the Infantry Blue Cloth Helmet ornamented with a bright metal helmet plate mounted with a replica of the Royal Anglian Regiment cap badge 10 × 12.5 cm. 1st Battalion with a blue backing to the badge. 2nd Battalion with a red backing to the badge

26 Obsolete 2 R ANGLIAN regimental police badge 5.5 cm.

27 Soldier's waist belt clasp 7 × 5.5 cm.

Acknowledgement
Lt Col Peter Dixon OBE, Major Steve Pallant, Captain D Mackness, WO1 (RSM) Rich Bredin and Chris Tate

The Devonshire and Dorset Regiment

The Devonshire and Dorset Regiment was formed in 1958 by the amalgamation of The Devonshire Regiment with The Dorset Regiment.

The design of The Devonshire and Dorset Regiment, or D and D, cap badge is taken from The Devonshire Regiment's badge and is based upon Exeter castle. The Devonshire Regiment also provided the motto, *Semper Fidelis*, or Ever Faithful. The Dorset Regiment provided the Sphinx awarded to the 54th Foot in 1801, as well as the unique Egyptian battle honour Marabout awarded in 1802. The motto *Primus in Indis* was awarded to the 39th Foot in 1757.

For 12 years from the regiment's formation in 1958 until 1969 the regiment wore the Wessex Brigade cap badge with regimental collar badges, after which the regimental cap badge was introduced. Soldiers' badges are produced in anodised aluminium, and are worn on a square grass green backing, with badges painted matt black for wear with Combat Dress.

Officers wear wire-embroidered badges on a green background on the beret and on a blue background on the Forage Cap.

The 1st Battalion holds an annual Duke of Kent's Competition which is conducted in three parts; a fitness competition, the Sarah Sands march and shoot competition and the H Jones military skills competition. The winning platoon, known as the Duke of Kent's Platoon, wears an identifying arm badge in working dress and The Devonshire Regiment's red and green Croix de Guerre lanyard with Number 2 Dress.

2nd Battalion The Dorsetshire Regiment (the title was changed to Dorset in 1951) wore a green pugri flash on the tropical helmet and jungle hat from 1942–1946. Officers of the regiment wore a green backing to the beret badge from 1945, which was adopted by all ranks in 1949 and authorised in 1951. It was retained on amalgamation.

1

2

3

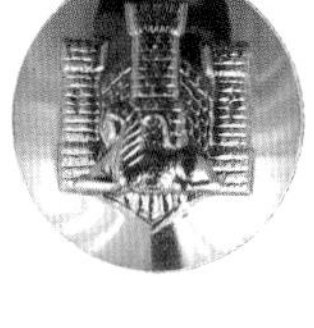

4

5

6

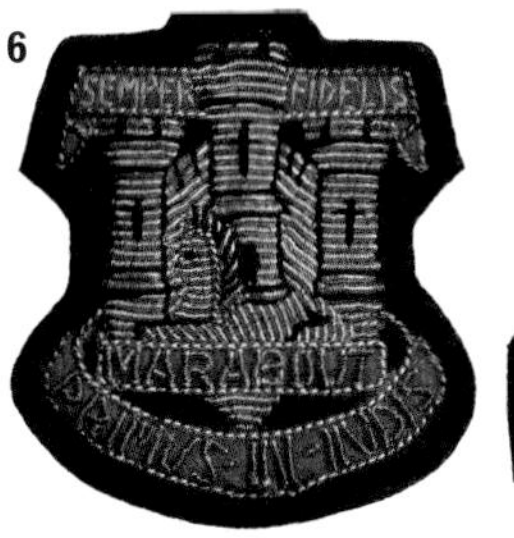

7

8

9

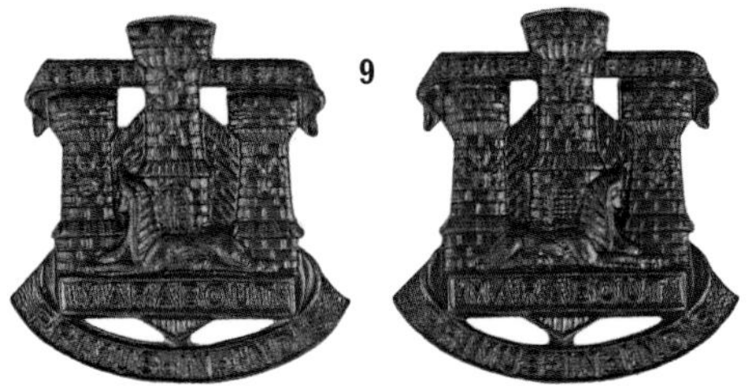

10

11

The motto *Primus in India* denotes that the 39th Foot were in 1754 the first King's, as opposed to Honourable East India Company, regiment to serve in India, and were the only King's infantry at the Battle of Plassey in 1757. The motto appeared first on a silver drum major's staff presented to the Regiment by the Nabob of Arcot after the battle.

13

14

12

The ribbon of the Croix de Guerre is worn in recognition of 2nd Battalion The Devonshire Regiment's heroic defence at Bois des Buttes, 27 May 1918, for which the regiment was awarded the French Croix de Guerre avec Palm. The anniversary of the battle in which the battalion lost 28 officers and 552 soldiers was marked annually until 1939 by a red and green cockade worn behind the cap badge on 27 May.

Duke of Kent's Platoon Competition

The regiment's close connection with the House of Kent began in 1802. On Christmas Eve, and again on Boxing Day, two regiments mutinied and marched on Government House in Gibraltar. The 54th Foot (later to become 2nd Battalion The Dorset Regiment) remained loyal to the Governor, HRH Prince Edward, Duke of Kent, and eventually opened fire to disperse the mutineers. In 1953 HRH Princess Marina, Duchess of Kent was appointed Colonel in Chief of The Dorset Regiment, continuing after amalgamation in 1958. After her death Field Marshal His Royal Highness The Duke of Kent was appointed Colonel in Chief.

In November 1857 the 54th Foot were on route for India in the troopship Sarah Sands, which caught fire and nearly foundered in the Indian Ocean. The heroic efforts and superb discipline of the troops brought the fire under control and the damaged ship was sailed safely to Mauritius. The conduct of the troops led to an amendment to the recently introduced Warrant for the Victoria Cross, which originally restricted bravery 'in the face of the enemy'. In 1858 the revised Warrant allowed the award for '...courage and bravery displayed under circumstances of extreme danger, such as the occurrence of a fire on board ship, or of the foundering of a vessel at sea'.

Lieutenant Colonel H Jones, a Devonshire and Dorset Regiment officer was selected to command 2nd Battalion The Parachute Regiment and was killed and awarded the Victoria Cross at the Battle of Goose Green in the Falkland Islands in 1982.

15

16

17

18

19

20

The Devonshires held this trench
The Devonshires hold it still
– A sign at Mansell Copse, The Somme, where the regiment's dead were buried in the trenches where they died.

Lineage The Devonshire and Dorset Regiment (1958) from The Devonshire Regiment (1881), formerly 11th Foot (1685), and The Dorset Regiment (1881), from 39th Foot (1702) and 54th Foot (1755).

previous page

1 Soldier's anodised aluminium cap and collar badges 3.25 × 4cm.
2 Anodised aluminium shoulder title 4.75 × 2.75 cm.
3 The Devonshire and Dorset Regiment button.
4 Soldier's anodised aluminium cap badge painted black for wear on the beret.
5 Officer's wire-embroidered beret badge 3.25 × 3.5 cm worn on a square green backing.
6 Officer's wire-embroidered Forage Cap badge 3.25 × 3.5 cm on a blue backing.
7 Officer's wire-embroidered Mess Dress collar badges 3.5 × 3.5 cm.
8 Officer's No1 Dress silver and gilt collar badges 3 × 3 cm.
9 Officer's bronze Service Dress collar badges 3 × 3 cm.
10 Major Tim House wearing the wire-embroidered beret badge with Combat Dress.

opposite page

11 Pte Stuart Blake wearing No2 Dress with the ribbon of the French Croix de Guerre on the sleeves and the Drummer's waist belt clasp.
12 Ribbon of the medal of the Croix de Guerre 2.5 × 1 cm worn on both arms of No1 and No2 Dress and Mess Dress.
13 Officer's Mess Dress wire-embroidered collar badges 3.5 × 3.5 cm.
14 Cpl Jason Betts wearing No2 Dress with a Drummer's badge on the right sleeve.
15 Duke of Kent's Platoon badge 6x6 cm worn on the upper right arm by members of the winning platoon of the 1st Battalion's annual inter-platoon competition.
16 TRF 4.5 × 4.5 cm.
17 Drummer's waist belt clasp 8 × 6.5 cm.

this page

18 Sergeant's rank slide.
19 Soldier's waist belt clasp 7 × 5 cm.
20 The Corps of Drums wear the Royal Marines white helmet ornamented with a bright metal helmet plate mounted with a detachable helmet plate centre 10.5 × 12 cm.

The Light Infantry

The Light Infantry was formed in 1968 by the amalgamation of The Somerset and Cornwall Light Infantry, The King's Own Yorkshire Light Infantry, The King's Shropshire Light Infantry and The Durham Light Infantry.

The Light Infantry, or LI, cap badge was introduced on the formation of the regiment in 1958 and the red cloth backing between the strings of the bugle horn was introduced in 1968. The red backing was originally worn by The Duke of Cornwall's Light Infantry, or DCLI, and symbolises the red feathers adopted by the Light Company of the 46th Foot, and subsequently by all companies, after the successful Light Infantry action at Paoli during the American War of Independence in 1777.

Between 1959 and 1968, whilst the regiments served together in the Light Infantry Brigade, the DCLI red backing was worn on the collar badges, as Dress Regulations forbade the wearing of cap badge distinctions unless worn by the whole Brigade.

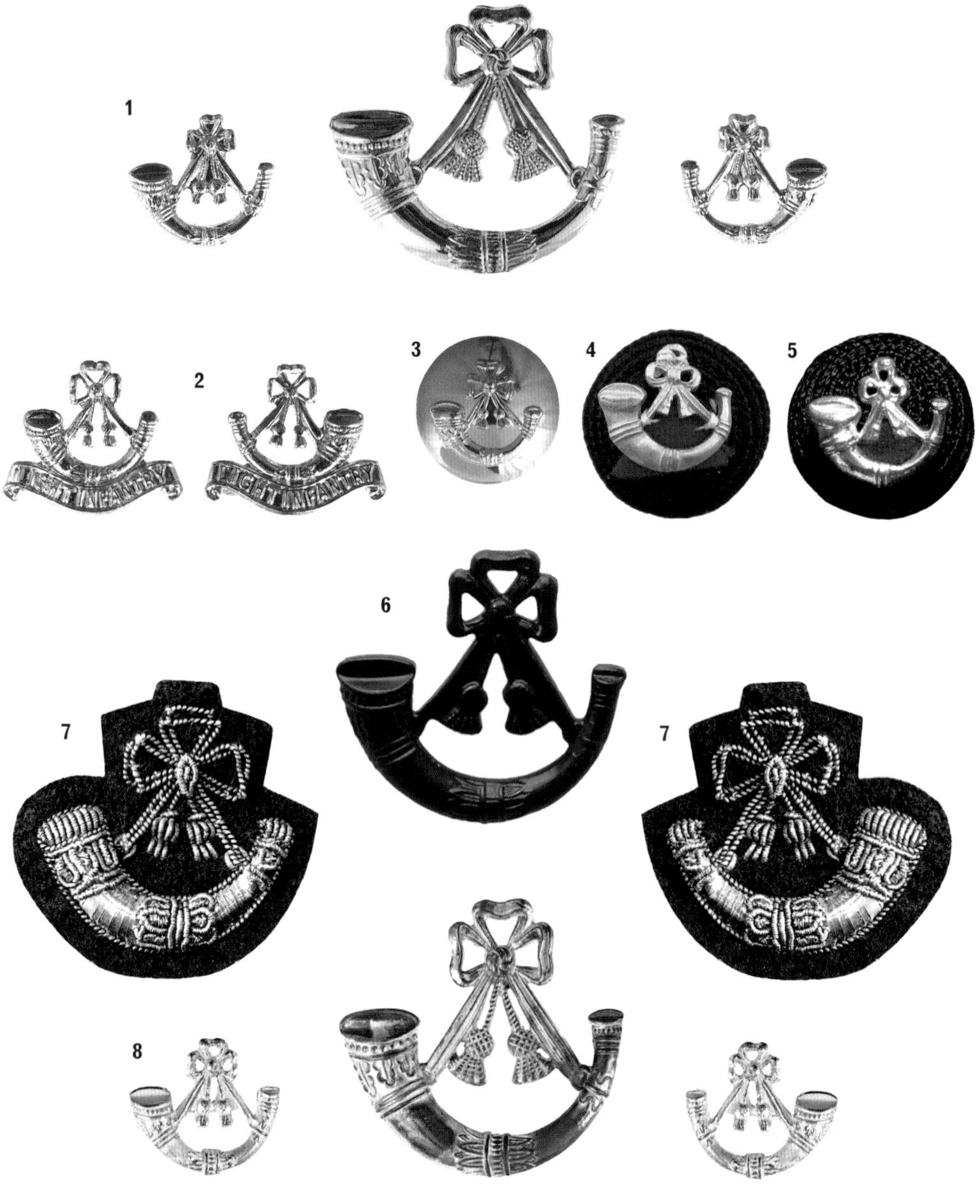

9

On the night of 20 September 1777 during the American War of Independence, the Light Companies of six regiments including the 46th Foot organised as a composite battalion, attacked and defeated a large American force in the forest at Paoli at what became known as the Battle of Brandywine. As a result the Americans vowed vengeance and declared 'The Light Battalion need never expect quarter'. The Light Infantry Battalion in its turn sent a message that they were 'Quite ready' and in a token of defiance stained their green feathers red. After the War only the 46th Foot retained the red feathers, which were adopted by the whole regiment. In the 19th Century feathers were replaced by 'Tufts' worn on the shako, which in turn were replaced by a red backing to the cap badge. In 1959 this distinction was lost when The Light Infantry was formed and the red backing was worn behind the collar badges. It was reintroduced as a cap badge backing in 1968.
The Royal Gloucestershire, Berkshire and Wiltshire Regiment wear a red Brandywine flash in commemoration of the same tradition.

10

11
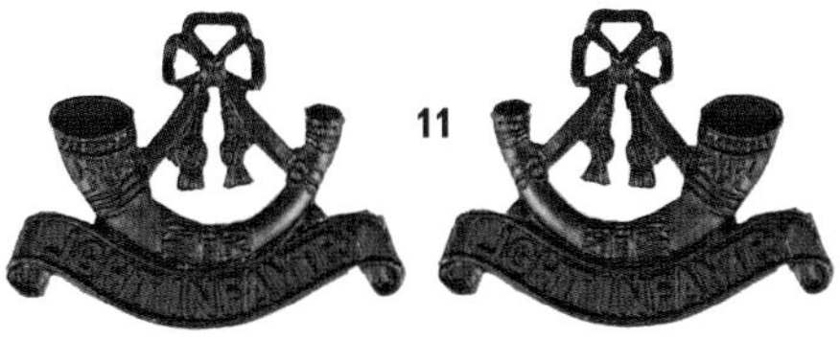

Serjeants, the rank is spelt in the traditional way with a 'j', wear their red sashes over the left rather than the right shoulder. The custom was officially recognised in 1865 but is said to date to the Battle of Culloden, 1746, when the sergeants took command after the officers became casualties. At that time serjeants wore their sashes over the right shoulder whilst officers wore sashes over the left. The Inkerman chain is worn on the red sash and is said to honour the serjeants who again took command after the officers became casualties during the Battle of Inkerman in 1854. Regimental mythology says that officers carried whistles used for signalling orders, secured to their cross belts by chains which were removed from officer casualties by the serjeants as they took command and were worn clipped to their sashes. In fact whistles had been authorised for officers and sergeants of Rifle and Light Infantry regiments by the first comprehensive Dress Regulations published 29 years before Inkerman, in 1825.

A white rose is worn by The Light Infantry on 1 August to commemorate the Battle of Minden, 1759. The white rose reflects the Yorkshire connection as the Battle Honour was awarded to the 51st Foot, which became The King's Own Yorkshire Light Infantry.

12

13

14

15

16

17

18

19

opposite page

1 The Light Infantry soldier's cap badge 4 × 3.75 cm and collar badges 1.75 × 2 cm.
2 Soldier's anodised aluminium shoulder titles 2.75 × 2.25 cm.
3 Light Infantry button.
4 Light Infantry officer's silver side hat and Full Dress Busby badge mounted on a cord boss 2.5 cm.
5 Soldier's anodised aluminium Full Dress Busby badge 2.5 cm worn by the buglers.
6 Blackened cap badge worn by the 2nd Battalion on deployments.
7 Officer's Mess Dress wire-embroidered collar badges 4 × 4 cm.
8 Officer's silver Forage Cap badge 3.75 × 3.5 cm and No1 Dress collar badges 2 × 1.75 cm.
9 Pte Dan Render wearing No2 Dress.

this page

10 Officer's No2 Dress bronze collar badges 1.75 × 2 cm.
11 Officers No2 Dress bronze shoulder titles 2.75 × 2.25 cm.
12 Officer's shoulder belt plate 6.25 × 8 cm.
13 Officer's cross belt Boss 5 cm.
14 Major's rank slide.
15 Colour Serjeant's rank slide with the distinctive green on maize colours.
16 Privates wear the Bugle on a slide as the TRF.
17 LCpl Wesley Bradley and Dean Oakley wearing Combat Dress with the distinctive green on maize coloured rank badges.
18 CSjt Rob Chapman wearing No1 Dress with the Inkerman Chain worn on the sash over the left shoulder. He is holding a pace stick. The Light Infantry does not carry pace sticks except when training recruits.
19 2Lt Tim Illingworth wearing Service Dress with the cross belt.

20

21

22

24

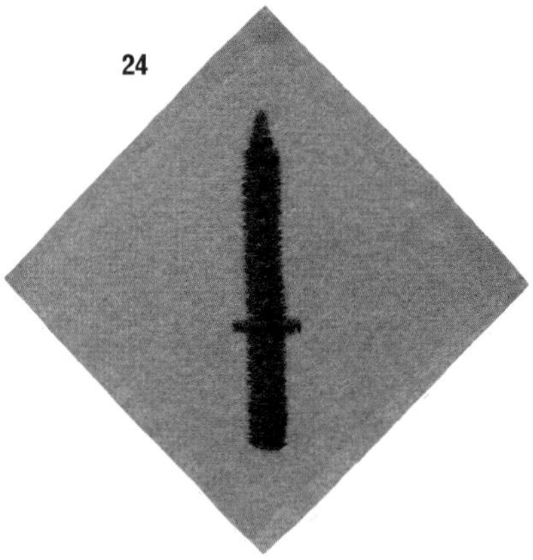

25

23

26

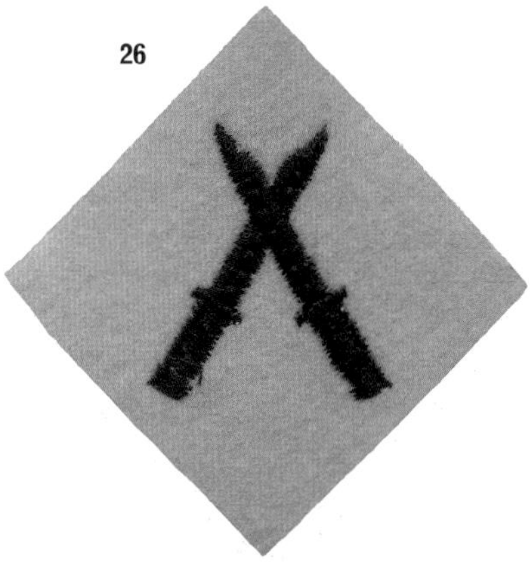

27

28

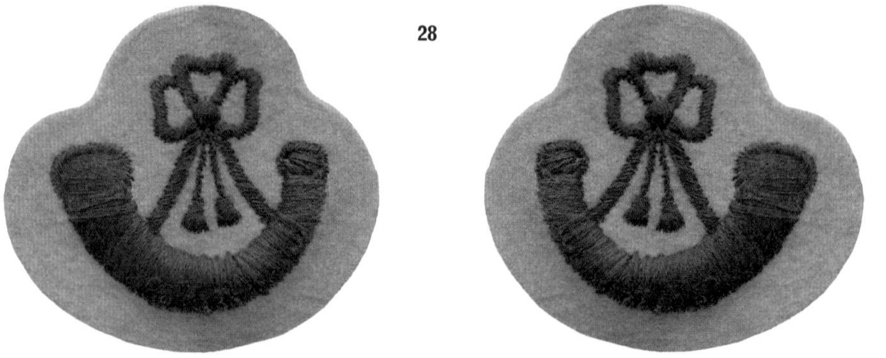

29

31

32

opposite page

20 Officer's pouch.

21 Serjeant's Inkerman Chain Boss 3 × 3.5 cm.

22 Soldier's waist belt clasp 7 × 5 cm.

23 WO2 Harry Kharikhou and CSgt John Dale escorting the 1 LI Queen's Colour carried by Lt Owen Jones.

Infantry qualification badges worn on Number 2 Dress.

24 Combat Infantryman 5.5 × 5.5 cm.

25 Class 1 Infantryman 7 × 5.75 cm.

26 Passed Infantry Section Commanders' Battle Course.

27 Passed Infantry Platoon Sergeants' Battle Course.

28 Bugler's No2 Dress left and right sleeves appointment badges 5 × 5.5 cm.

this page

29 Cpl Martin Wear wearing the crossed bayonets badge having passed the Section Commanders Battle Course, and the crossed rifles badge of a Skill at Arms instructor.

30 The Light Infantry white Minden Roses 4.5 × 7.75 cm worn annually on 1 August.

31 Bugler's No1 Dress appointment badge 6 × 5.5 cm.

32 BMaj John 'Boy' Morris leading the Band and Bugles of The Light Division.

33 Pte Ako Atkins and Roxy Hancox, and Cpl Shaun Held wearing No1 Dress 'Greens'.

30

The Light Infantry wear a white Rose in commemoration of the action of the 51st Foot at the Battle of Minden. The tradition is that the British infantry who fought at Minden in 1759 picked roses as they advanced to attack the French cavalry. In fact the troops moved off from their bivouac that Wednesday morning at 0330 in a gale of wind which followed a prolonged rainstorm, and were in action at 0400. The sun rose at 0430 and the battle was over by 0900. There is no evidence that roses were worn either during the battle or indeed before 1860. There are records that during the attack on Walcheren on 1 August 1809 and in the Peninsular on Minden Day 1813 troops wore sprigs of laurel and other greenery in their shakos, perhaps following the award of the Battle Honour for Minden in 1801.

Lineage The Light Infantry (1968) from The Somerset and Cornwall Light Infantry (1959), The King's Own Yorkshire Light Infantry (1881), The King's Shropshire Light Infantry (1881) and The Durham Light Infantry (1881). The Somerset and Cornwall Light Infantry from The Somerset Light Infantry (Prince Albert's) (1881), formerly 13th Foot (1685), and The Duke of Cornwall's Light Infantry (1881), from 32nd Foot (1702) and 46th Foot (1741). The King's Own Yorkshire Light Infantry from 51st Foot (1755) and 105th Foot (1839). The King's Shropshire Light Infantry from 53rd Foot (1755) and 85th Foot (1793). The Durham Light Infantry from 68th Foot (1756) and 106th Foot (1839).

33

Acknowledgement
WO1 (RSM) Jock Cameron and Cpl J Ward

The Prince of Wales's Own Regiment of Yorkshire

The Prince of Wales's Own Regiment of Yorkshire was formed in 1958 by the amalgamation of The West Yorkshire Regiment (The Prince of Wales's Own) with The East Yorkshire Regiment (Duke of York's Own)

1

2

3

4

5

The White Horse badge of The Prince of Wales's Own Regiment of Yorkshire, or PWO, had been the cap badge of The West Yorkshire Regiment whilst the White Rose of York on a star worn as the collar badge had been the badge of The East Yorkshire Regiment.

The 15th Foot fought at the capture of Quebec in 1759 and in memoriam of General Wolfe, who was killed during the battle, adopted a black line in the officers' gold lace which in time became a black backing to The East Yorkshire Regiment badges and is now represented by a black backing on the present officers' collar badges. The black line is repeated in the regiment's stable belt and represented by the black canes carried by senior ranks.

For 12 years from the regiment's formation in 1958 until 1969 the regiment wore the Yorkshire Brigade cap badge with regimental collar badges, after which the regimental cap badge was introduced.

6

7

8

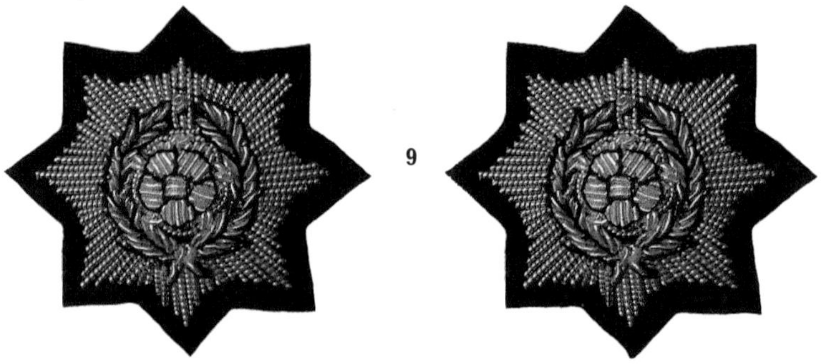
9

10

The White Horse had been granted to the 14th Foot in 1855, having previously been worn by the Regiment's Grenadiers since 1765.

The Prince of Wales's feathers on the button were granted to the 14th Foot in 1876.

The White Rose had been granted to the York Regiments of Militia in 1811 and had been worn by the 15th Foot, which had been styled York East Riding Regiment in 1782.

The 15th Foot was one of seven English regiments which had a black stripe in its officers' rose pattern lace.

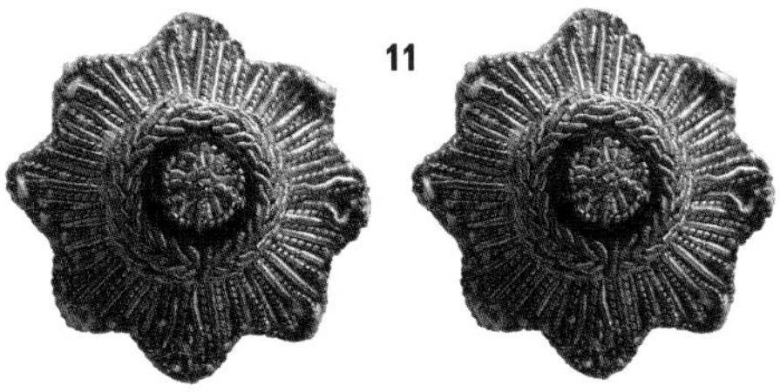

11

Lineage The Prince of Wales's Own Regiment of Yorkshire (1958) from The West Yorkshire Regiment (The Prince of Wales's Own) (1881) formerly 14th Foot (1685), and The East Yorkshire Regiment (Duke of York's Own) (1881), formerly 15th Foot (1685).

13

12

opposite page

1 The Prince of Wales's Own Regiment of Yorkshire soldier's anodised aluminium cap badge 4.5 × 3 cm and collar badges 2.75 × 2.75 cm.
2 Gilding metal shoulder title 5.5 × 3 cm.
3 Obsolete anodised aluminium shoulder title 3 × 1 cm.
4 PWO button.
5 Officer's silver cap badge 4.25 × 2.75 cm and gilt and enamel collar badges 2.75 × 2.75 cm.
6 Dmr Lee Ellis wearing Number 2 Dress.
7 Officer's wire-embroidered beret badge 5.75 × 4 cm.
8 Officer's wire-embroidered Side Hat badge 5.5 × 4 cm.
9 Sergeant's Mess Dress wire-embroidered collar badges 4.25 cm.

this page

10 TRF 7 × 7 cm.
11 Officer's Mess Dress wire-embroidered collar badges 2.75 cm.
12 CSgt Martin Field and Sgt John Handley escorting the Queen's Colour carried by 2Lt Gary England.
13 Pte Mike Butcher and Robert Sykes wearing combat dress with the regimental rank slide and TRF.
14 The Corps of Drums wear the Infantry Blue Cloth Helmet ornamented with a bright metal helmet plate mounted with a detachable centre 10.5 × 12.5 cm.
15 Sergeant's rank slide.
16 Soldier's waist belt clasp 8.5 × 5 cm.

14

15

16

Acknowledgement WO2 (RQMS(T)) SW Price.

The Green Howards

(Alexandra Princess of Wales's Own Yorkshire Regiment)

Formed from independent companies raised to support William of Orange during the Glorious Revolution in 1688, The Green Howards remains unamalgamated.

1

2

3

4

5

4

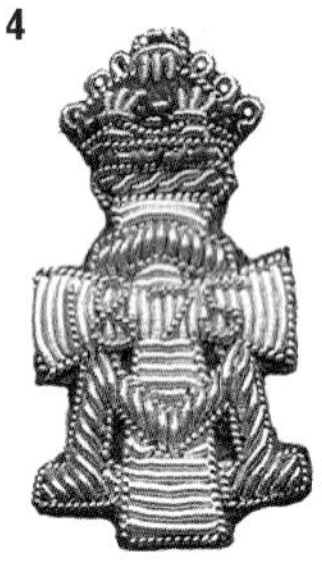

The Green Howards, or GH, cap badge represents the cross or Dannebrog of the Danish royal family and the cypher of Alexandra, Princess of Wales and daughter of Christian IX of Denmark, above XIX; reflecting the regiment's seniority as the 19th Foot. The date 1875 is the year in which Alexandra became Princess of Wales. It is also the year she became Colonel in Chief and presented Colours to the regiment. It has been suggested that Princess Alexandra designed the badge herself. The Danneborg is also worn by Queen Alexandra's Royal Army Nursing Corps.

For 12 years between 1958 and 1969 the regiment wore the Yorkshire Brigade cap badge with regimental collar badges, after which the regimental cap badge was restored.

In 1975, King Olav V of Norway, the regiment's Colonel in Chief, gave permission for the champion company to be known as King Olav's Company. He authorised the company to wear a copy of his Royal Bodyguards' badge as a sleeve badge. It was not worn from 1982, when badges had been ordered to be removed from combat dress, but was restored in 1987. On the accession of King Harald V His Majesty consented to the champion company being known as King Harald's Company and authorised his badge as the company's arm badge.

The Dannebrog – the Danish Cross – originated during the Battle of Lyndanisse fought in Estonia in 1219. The Danes were hard pressed when King Waldemar or, in another version, Archbishop Anders, prayed for victory. He saw a white cross in the sky against a red background, which inspired the Danes to victory and was adopted as their national emblem.

6

7

8

9

10

Lineage The Green Howards (Alexandra, Princess of Wales's Own Regiment of Yorkshire), formerly 19th Foot (1688).

opposite page

1 Soldier's anodised aluminium cap badge 3 × 4 cm and collar badges 2.5 × 3.5 cm.

2 The Green Howards button.

3 Anodised aluminium shoulder title 4.5 × 1.75 cm.

4 Officer's Mess Dress wire-embroidered collar badges 2 × 3.5 cm.

5 Officer's wire-embroidered beret badge 5.5 × 5.5 cm.

6 Pte Ryan Hanson wearing No2 Dress.

7 Captain Pat Ralph MM wearing the officer's wire-embroidered cap badge and the green and white TRF.

this page

8 TRF 7 × 7 cm.

9 Soldier's waist belt clasp 7.25 × 5.25 cm.

10 Sgt Noah Clayton wearing No2 Dress.

11 The Corps of Drums wear the Infantry Blue Cloth Helmet ornamented with a bright metal helmet plate mounted with a detachable helmet plate centre 10 × 12.5 cm.

12 King Harald's Company arm badge worn on the TRF by the champion company 3.25 × 4.5 cm.

13 Officer's waist belt clasp 6 × 5 cm.

11

12

13

The Royal Highland Fusiliers

(Princess Margaret's Own Glasgow and Ayrshire Regiment)

The Royal Highland Fusiliers was formed in 1959 by the amalgamation of the Royal Scots Fusiliers with the Highland Light Infantry (City of Glasgow Regiment).

The Royal Highland Fusiliers, or RHF, badge is based upon the gilding metal flaming grenade, which was the badge of The Royal Scots Fusiliers, and the white metal monogram HLI from the centre of The Highland Light Infantry badge. The cap badge is worn on the Glengarry whilst a white hackle is worn on a square of Mackenzie tartan on the Tam o'Shanter, known as the ToS.
The 21st Foot appears to have worn white feathers until 1838. They were restored in 1900 for wear on the right side of any suitable headdress; the regiment did not wear the Tam o'Shanter. The Royal Highland Fusiliers adopted the white hackle with the ToS on amalgamation in 1959 and in Aden in 1960 began to wear it without the cap badge.

1

2

3

5

4

6

7

8

9

opposite page

1 Royal Highland Fusiliers soldiers anodised aluminium cap badge 3.5 × 6.75 cm and collar badges 2 × 4 cm.
2 Shoulder title 2.5 × 1 cm.
3 RHF button.
4 Silver and gilt No1 Dress collar badges 2 × 4 cm.
5 Officer's silver and gilt cap badge 3.5 × 6.75 cm
6 Officer's bronze No2 Dress collar badges 2 × 4 cm.
7 Cpl Shawsie Shaw wearing the regiment's white hackle on a square of MacKenzie tartan.
8 MacKenzie tartan TRF 7 × 7 cm.
9 Cap badge backing 7.5 × 7 cm.

this page

10 Soldier's hackle 8 × 9.5 cm.
11 Cpl Ian Anderson
12 Lt Christopher Douring wearing the Glengarry with Barrack Dress.
13 Captain Nigel Jordan-Barber wearing Service Dress Mounted Order. He wears aiguillettes as he holds a representational post.
14 Sporran badge 2.75 × 4.25 cm.
15 Sgt Troowzers Trousdale wearing No2 Dress.

10

11

12

The distinguished conduct of the 74th Foot at the Battle of Assaye, 1803, was recognised by the presentation of an honorary third Colour by the Honourable East India Company. The third Colour is still carried by the regiment.

13

To commemorate the 250th anniversary of The Royal Scots Fusiliers in 1928 pipers were given permission to wear the Erskine tartan, the regiment having been raised by the Colonel Charles Erskine, 5th Earl of Mar in 1678.

14

15

16

17

18

19

20

21

22

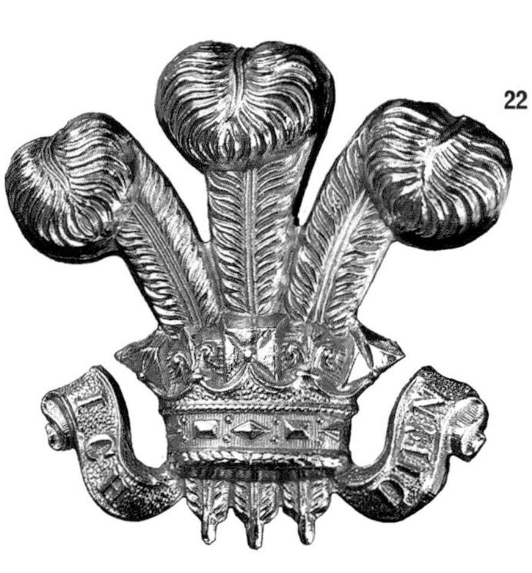

opposite page

16 Officer's old waist belt clasp 7 × 5.5 cm.
17 Officer's waist belt clasp 7 × 5.5 cm.
18 Officer's shoulder belt plate 9 × 10. 75 cm.
19 Piper's waist belt clasp 10 × 7.75 cm.
20 Pipe Major's bi-metal Glengarry badge 6.5 × 6.5 cm.
21 Piper's white metal badge 6.5 × 6.5 cm.
22 Piper's shoulder belt plate 6 × 5.75 cm.

this page

23 Pipe Major's plaid brooch 10 cm.
24 Officer's Full Dress shoulder badges 5.5 × 4.5 cm.
25 Piper's plaid brooch 10 cm.
26 Royal Highland Fusiliers Dirk.
27 Badge on Dirk scabbard.

23

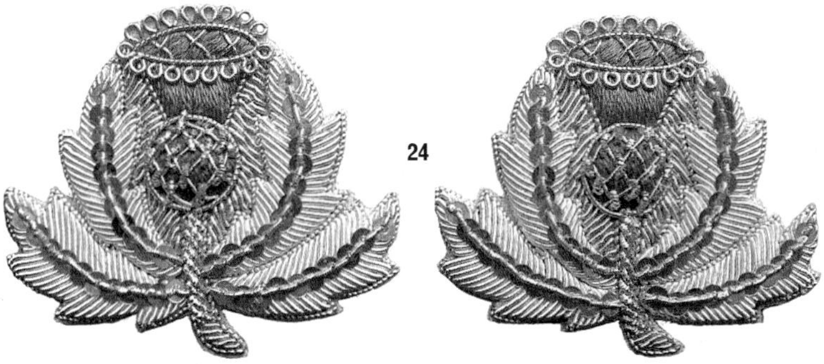

24

25

26

27

Lineage The Royal Scots Fusiliers (Princess Margaret's Own Glasgow and Ayrshire Regiment) (1959) from The Royal Scots Fusiliers (1881), formerly 21st Foot (1678), and The Highland Light Infantry (City of Glasgow Regiment) (1881), from 71st Foot (1771) and 74th Foot (1787).

28

29

30

28 Pipe Major's Full Dress sporran cantle.

29 Pipe Major's Full Dress appointment badge 10 × 10 cm.

30 PMaj Hugh Walker and Fus Steven Young wearing Full Dress.

The 22nd (Cheshire) Regiment

The Cheshire Regiment was raised in 1689 in Chester and remains unamalgamated.

The Cheshire Regiment, or CHESHIRE, cap badge was introduced in 1922, replacing the first pattern which had been worn since 1896. For 12 years between 1958 and 1969 following the reorganisation of the infantry the regiment wore the Mercian Brigade cap badge with regimental collar badges, after which the regimental cap badge was reintroduced.

The Cheshire's leaved acorn badge is claimed to commemorate the action by a Draft from the regiment, which saved King George II from capture during the battle of Dettingen. The King is said to have plucked an oak twig and handed it to them, desiring the regiment to wear the emblem in memory of their gallant conduct. In their present guise replica acorn leaves have been worn behind the cap badge on regimental days and in the presence of royalty since 1933.

A Draft is a detachment sent to reinforce a unit. The Cheshire Regiment was not present at the battle of Dettingen but it is quite possible that a Draft may have been.

1

2

3

4

5

6

7

8

9

The cerise and buff diamond regimental arm badge dates to 1916 when it was painted on steel helmets. During the Second World War it was produced as a cloth badge. Traditionally, when the arm badge was worn with the cerise half to the front it indicated a regular battalion, and when the buff to the front, a Territorial battalion. The arm badge was approved in 2002 as the Tactical Recognition Flash with the proviso that there would not be a separate inverted version for the Cheshire Company of The King's and Cheshire Regiment.

The Cheshire Regiment wears the largest waist belt clasp worn by any regiment in the Army, although some Scottish pipers wear larger waist belt plates. Soldiers sometimes buff the striations behind the numerals flat in order to make polishing easier.

In 1964 the 1st Battalion was in Munster, prior to moving to Cyprus at a time when Battle Dress was being phased out to be replaced by Number 2 Dress and Barrack Dress. The Cheshires decided to adopt a regimental pullover to be worn with pale khaki cavalry twill barrack dress trousers. The colour was chosen to be 'different'; whilst there may have been an intention to choose the regimental colour of cerise, practicality, cost and the weave available played a part. The pullover was originally worn by officers and the Regimental Sergeant Major, initially with no badges of rank, however very soon it was extended to all Warrant Officers and badges of rank adopted.

10

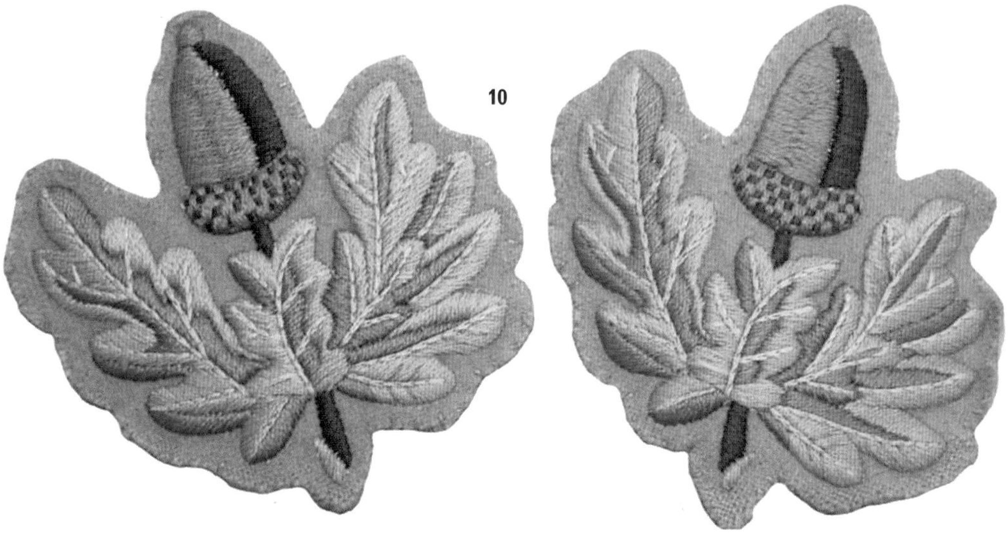

11

12

13

14

14

The first documentary link between the 22nd Foot and Dettingen dates from 1833, when new Colours were presented to the regiment in Jamaica by the Governor, The 2nd Earl of Mulgrave. In his address the Governor said that 'at the Battle of Dettingen, under George II the regiment peculiarly distinguished themselves and were in consequence permitted to wear oak leaves in their caps.' The Dictionary of National Biography describes the 2nd Earl of Mulgrave as 'the author in early life of a number of romantic tales, novels and sketches, avowedly founded on fact.' Regiments were known by the name of their Colonel at the time of Dettingen, 1743, and it is possible that the Earl of Mulgrave confused a kinsman. Major General Thomas Handasyde who was Colonel of the 22nd Foot from 1702–1712 and his son Lieutenant General Roger Handasyde, who was Colonel from 1712–1730. However at the time of the Battle of Dettingen, it was Brigadier General William Handasyde who was Colonel of the 31st Foot (1737–1745). Whilst the 22nd Foot were not at Dettingen, the 31st Foot were and were noticed by George II who famously gave them the nickname *The Young Buffs*.

Lineage The 22nd (Cheshire) Regiment (1881), formerly 22nd Foot (1689).

previous page

1 The Cheshire Regiment soldier's anodised aluminium cap badge 4.75 × 4.75 cm and collar badges 2.5 × 3 cm.
2 The Cheshire Regiment button.
3 Shoulder title 4.5 × 1.5 cm.
4 Officer's wire-embroidered side cap badge 3.5 × 3.5 cm.
5 Officer's silver, gilt and enamel cap badge 3 × 3 cm and silver and gilt collar badges 2.75 × 2.75 cm.
6 Cpl Sean Taylor wearing Combat Dress with the TRF on his right sleeve.
7 TRF, worn cerise to the front, 4 × 5.5 cm.
8 Captain's rank slide.
9 Sgt George Copeland, the Provost Sergeant, wearing Barrack Dress.

opposite page

10 Acorn badges embroidered on the officer's Mess Dress waistcoat 8 × 7 cm.
11 Waist belt clasp 10.75 × 7.5 cm.
12 Real oak leaves worn above the cap badge by officers and replica leaves 7 × 5.5 cm worn by soldiers on the regimental anniversary, Meeanee Day, 17 February.
13 Captain Nick Brown wearing the side hat worn by officers serving with the 1st Battalion.
14 Major Bede Etherington wearing the Regiment's Barrack Dress with unique pullover. The Service Dress cap is rarely worn except by the RSMaj and by some officers serving away from the 1st Battalion.

this page

15 The Corps of Drums wear the Infantry Blue Cloth Helmet ornamented with a bright metal helmet plate 10.5 × 12.5 cm.

Acknowledgement WO1 (RSM) Kev Fletcher

The Royal Welch Fusiliers

The Royal Welch Fusiliers was raised in 1689 and remains unamalgamated.

The Royal Welch Fusiliers, or RWF, was made a fuzileer regiment in 1702 and a Royal Regiment in 1713, both awards in honour of its fighting qualities. Almost since formation the regiment has combined the Bomb, the traditional badge of Fusiliers, with the Prince of Wales's feathers. In 1702 the regiment became The Royal Regiment of Welch Fusiliers, and officers began wearing white feathers to indicate that they were fusiliers in about 1709. The practice was sanctioned in 1789. White hackles have been worn in the beret since 1950.

The Bearskin Cap is worn by officers and senior ranks in Full Dress. A white plume is worn on the right side, the opposite side to the Grenadier Guards. Junior ranks wear the Fusilier Busby.

1

2

3

4

5

6

7

8

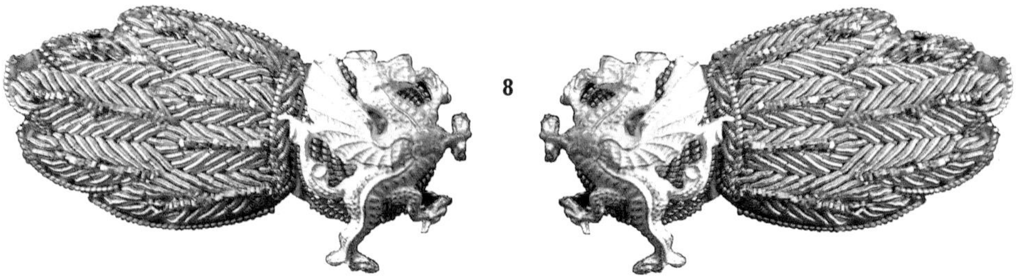

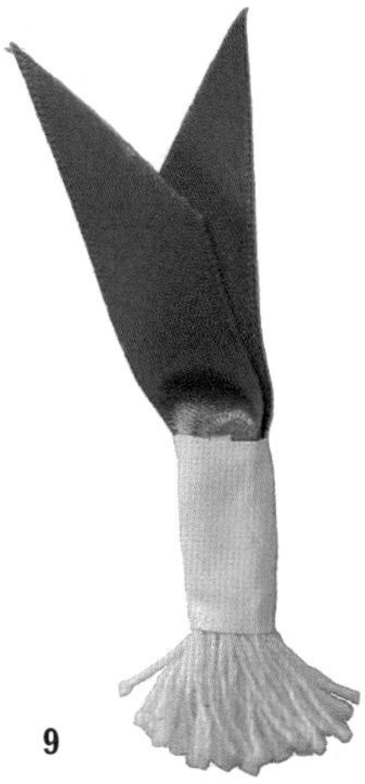

9

10

opposite page

1 RoyalWelch Fusiliers soldier's anodised aluminium cap badge 2.75 × 4.5 cm and collar badges 2 × 3.25 cm.
2 Anodised aluminium shoulder title 3.5 × 1 cm.
3 RWF button.
4 Officer's Service Dress bronze cap badge and collar badges 2 × 5.5 cm.
5 Fus Anthony Gossling wearing No2 Dress.
6 Officer's wire-embroidered beret badge on a red backing 4 × 5 cm.
7 Officers' wire-embroidered Forage Cap badge on a blue backing 4 × 5 cm.
8 Mess Dress wire-embroidered collar badges 2.5 × 6 cm.

this page

9 Silk leek worn on St David's Day.
10 Hackle 8 × 9.5cm.
11 Soldier's Flash 16 × 23 cm and officer's Flash 16 × 28 cm, each made up of five ribbon tails.
12 Cpl Scorch Suller wearing No2 Dress with the Flash showing on the collar.

Prior to 1808 soldiers wore long hair in a pigtail with a queue bag protecting the back of the uniform. In 1808 hair was cut short in the Army but the officers of the 23rd Foot, and later senior ranks retained the ribbons on the collar, which had formerly been worn by soldiers to secure the bag. The ribbons were referred to as the flash, a contemporary name for a wig. In 1834 King William VI approved the custom, 'as a peculiarity whereby to mark the dress of that distinguished Regiment'. The tradition was extended to all ranks in 1900.

The regiment celebrates St David's Day when a silk leek is worn on the cap. Leeks are also worn on the right collar of Mess Dress.

The RoyalWelch Fusiliers is the only one of the Minden regiments not to wear red roses on the anniversary of the battle.

11

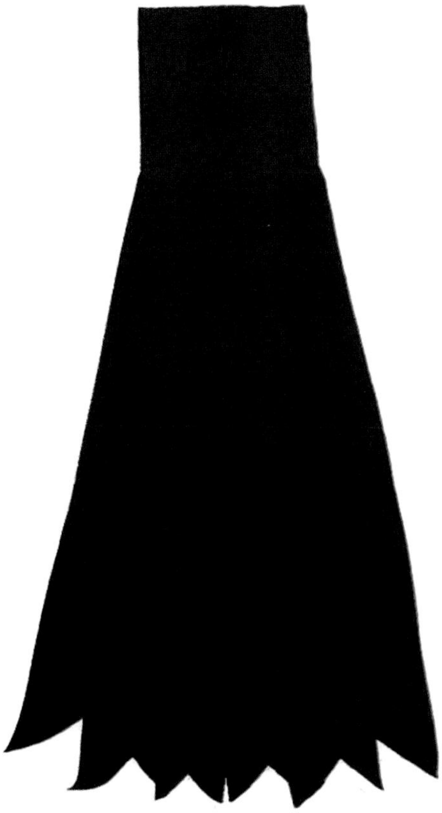

12

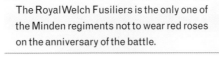

13

14

19

20

21

15

16

17

18

Lineage The Royal Welch Fusiliers (1921), formerly The Royal Welsh Fusiliers (1881) and 23rd Foot (1689).

13 Obsolete TRF 6 × 7.5 cm.
14 TRF 3.5 × 5 cm introduced before the deployment to Iraq in 2004 and known as the Desert Dragon.
15 WO1 (RSM) Shady Kent wearing the Desert Dragon in Iraq.
16 CSgt Vic Hughes and Sgt Rich Jones escorting the Queen's Colour carried by Lt Matthew Hughes, all wearing Full Dress.
17 Bi-metal cap badge 4 × 9 cm worn on the Fusilier Busby.
18 Captain Colin Jones MBE, Fus David Coate wearing a leek on his beret, and Goat Major LCpl Davies with Billy, the regimental goat.
19 Fus Bala Martin and Med Meadowcroft in Iraq.
20 Full Dress shoulder title, made up of the anodised aluminium title and collar badge worn together on the epaulette.
21 Waist belt clasp 7× 5 cm.

Acknowledgement WO1 (RSM) Shady Kent

The Royal Regiment of Wales

(24th/41st Foot)

The Royal Regiment of Wales was formed in 1969 by the amalgamation of The South Wales Borderers with The Welch Regiment.

The Royal Regiment of Wales, or RRW, was formed by the amalgamation of The South Wales Borders and The Welch Regiment whilst they were part of the Welch Brigade in 1969. The new regiment continued to wear the Welch Brigade cap badge. The present badge was introduced in 1975; it is said at the express wish of the Prince of Wales, Colonel in Chief of the regiment.

The design of the collar badge is based on that introduced for the South Wales Borderers in 1957; the Roman numerals XXIV, representing the 24th Foot, within a wreath of immortelles (everlasting flowers). In 1879 many of the 1st Battalion 24th Foot were killed at the Battle of Isandlwana whilst B Company 2nd Battalion won fame at the Battle of Rorke's Drift. In honour of the attempt to save the colours of the 1st Battalion and of the successful defence of Rorke's Drift Queen Victoria was 'graciously pleased to command that a silver wreath shall in future be borne around the staff of the Queen's Colour of both battalions of the 24th Regiment'.

The collar badges of The Royal Regiment of Wales consist of The Welch Regiment's dragon, which had been adopted as the design on their buttons in 1881, within The South Wales Borderers wreath of immortelles.

The Regiment wears a Dragon arm badge. The original design was ordered altered by the Army Dress Committee before being approved as the Tactical Recognition Flash because when worn on the right sleeve the Dragon faced to the rear. In the approved badge the Dragon faces to the left, or forward.

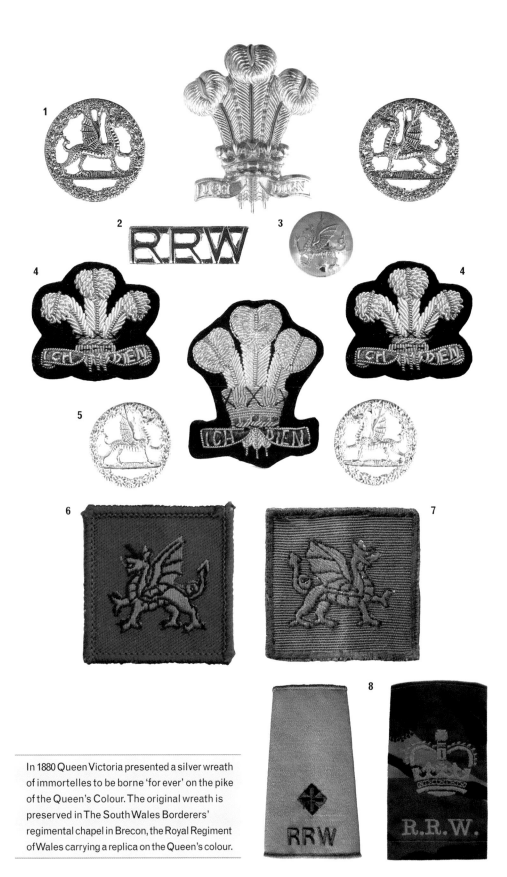

In 1880 Queen Victoria presented a silver wreath of immortelles to be borne 'for ever' on the pike of the Queen's Colour. The original wreath is preserved in The South Wales Borderers' regimental chapel in Brecon, the Royal Regiment of Wales carrying a replica on the Queen's colour.

9

10

14

11

12

15

13

Lineage The Royal Regiment of Wales (24th/41st Foot) (1969) from The South Wales Borderers (1881), formerly 24th Foot (1689), and The Welch Regiment (1921), formerly The Welsh Regiment 1881), from 41st Foot (1719) and 69th Foot (1758).

previous page

1. The Royal Regiment of Wales soldier's anodised aluminium cap badge 4 × 4.5 cm and collar badges 2.75 × 2.75 cm.
2. Anodised aluminium shoulder title 3 × 1 cm.
3. RRW button.
4. Officer's Mess Dress wire-embroidered collar badges 3.5 × 3.25 cm.
5. Officer's wire-embroidered cap badge and silver collar badges.
6. Obsolete arm badge introduced in 1998 but rejected as the TRF because the Dragon faces to the rear when worn on the right sleeve.
7. TRF 4 × 4 cm.
8. Second Lieutenant's and Warrant Officer Class 2 rank slides. Soldiers' slides have R.R.W. whilst the officers have RRW.

this page

9. CSgt Mark Kretzschmar wearing No1 Dress.
10. Captain Nigel Crewe-Read MBE wearing No1 Dress.
11. WO1 (RSM) IJ Osborne wearing Combat Dress with a soldier's rank badge. His cap badge is worn on a green square backing.
12. CSgt Craig Stockdale wearing No2 Dress with the Platoon Sergeants Battle Course qualification badge on his right sleeve.
13. CSgts Paul Cuff and Daryl Owen escorting the Queen's Colour carried by Lt Richard Arden.
14. The Corps of Drums wear the Infantry Blue Cloth Helmet ornamented with a bright metal helmet plate 10.5 × 12.75 cm.
15. Waist belt clasp 7 × 5 cm.

Acknowledgement WO1 (RSM) IJ Osborne

The King's Own Scottish Borderers

The King's Own Scottish Borderers was raised in 1689 for the defence of Edinburgh and within four hours was guarding the gates of the city.

The King's Own Scottish Borderers, or KOSB, cap badge features Edinburgh Castle over St Andrew's Cross. In 1802 the regiment was awarded the Sphinx for its service in Egypt but it did not become a key element of the regiment's insignia because in 1803 the regiment 'attracted the special notice of King George III, who changed its title to that of the 'King's Own Borderers,' and conferred on it the badge of the King's Crest, with an accompanying motto, chosen by himself.'

The Royal Crest continues to be worn on the Pipe Major's shoulder belt and is irreverently known as the 'dog and bonnet'.

The two mottos on the badges are *Everything without the Lord is in vain* and *I trust in the truth of religion.*

As the regiment has not been amalgamated and the design of the badges has remained unchanged except for the Crown for over 100 years, many soldiers wear old or reproduction cap badges. Badges with different Crowns and with both solid and void letters are worn by both officers and soldiers.

1

2

3

4

5

6

7

8

Edinburgh Castle was first mentioned in Queen's Regulations 1844 as a badge to be borne on the Colours but is known to have been used earlier in the design of one of the four versions of the ornate plate worn on the front of the Regency shako between 1816–1829.

In Full Dress black and white feathers of the Blackcock are worn above the cap badge.

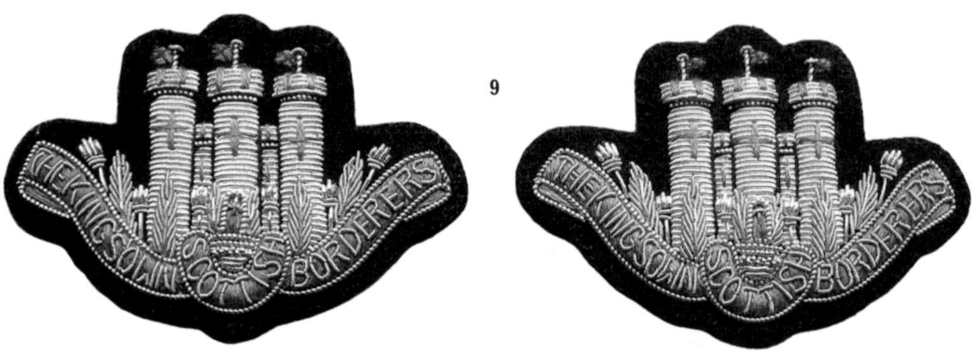

9

10

13

15

16

11

12

14

17

18

19

20

21

22

23

24

previous page

1 King's Own Scottish Borderers soldier's anodised aluminium cap badge 5 × 6.75 cm and collar badges 3.5 × 2.5 cm.

2 Anodised aluminium shoulder title 3.25 × 1 cm.

3 KOSB button.

4 Officer's silver cap badge 5 × 6.75 cm and bronze collar badges 3.5 × 2.5 cm.

5 Cpl James Haslam wearing the soldier's badge on the Tam o'Shanter.

6 WO1 (RSM) Tom Brass wearing No 1 Dress Ceremonial with silver cap badge and Blackcock feathers, and wire-embroidered collar badges.

7 WO1 Steven Hardcastle wearing Blue Patrols.

8 WO2 Fred Leith wearing Barrack Dress.

opposite page

9 Officer's No1 Dress and Mess Dress wire-embroidered collar badges 6.75 × 4.5 cm.

10 Officer's waist belt clasp 6.5 × 5 cm.

11 A square of Leslie tartan has been worn as a TRF since 1998 7 × 7 cm.

12 Leslie tartan cap badge backing.

13 Officer's shoulder belt plate 8 × 10.5 cm.

14 DMaj Thomas Gallagher and PMaj Steven Bell wearing No1 Dress Ceremonial.

15 1897 pattern white metal cap badge 5 × 6.75 cm still in use.

16 Officer's cap badge with void letters 5 × 6.75 cm.

17 Major's rank slide.

this page

18 Soldier's waist belt clasp 8.5 × 7.25 cm.

19 Pipe Major's shoulder belt plate 4 × 5 cm, known as the Dog and Bonnet. Originally worn by all 1st Battalion pipers but lost in 1948 when the Regiment was reduced to one battalion.

20 Purse badge 3 × 3.75 cm.

21 Piper's button.

22 Pipe Major's Full Dress appointment badge 8.5 × 11 cm.

23 Pipe Major Steven Bell wearing full dress.

24 Pipe Major's kilt pin, the badge with Queen Victoria's Crown dating it from *c.*1881–1901, 5 × 13 cm.

25

26

27

28

29

30

opposite page

25 Piper's and drummers chrome plaid brooch 11.25 cm.

26 Blackcock feathers worn in the glengarry

27 Piper's and drummers waist belt clasp, the Dog and Bonnet with Queen Victoria's Crown dating it from c.1881-1901, 9.5 × 7.5 cm.

28 Pipe Major's waist belt clasp, the badge with Queen Victoria's Crown dating it from *c*.1881–1901, 8 × 10.75 cm.

this page

29 Pipe Major's plaid brooch set with a Cairngorm stone with the Tudor (or King's) Crown dating it from *c*.1902–1952, 11.5 cm.

30 Drum Major's plaid brooch, the badge with the Tudor (or King's) Crown dating it from *c*.1902–1952, 11.5 cm.

31

33

Lineage The King's Own Scottish Borderers (1881), formerly 25th Foot (1689).

32

31 PMaj Steven Bell, Sgt Keith Harris, CSgt Ian Forsyth and Paul Wood, Sgt Alan Falconer, Martin Galagher, Ian Campbell, Duncan Lowe, David Robertson and Allan Harris. In front WO1 (RSM) Thomas Brass and Captain Leigh Drummond, all are wearing No1 Dress.

32 Pipe Major's sporran cantle ornamented with the 'Dog and Bonnet' with Queen Victoria's Crown dating it from *c.*1881–1901.

33 Pipe Major's shirtsleeve order rank badge 5.25 × 6.75 cm worn on a wristband.

Acknowledgement WO1 (RSM) Tom Brass

The Royal Irish Regiment

(27th (Inniskilling), 83rd and 87th and The Ulster Defence Regiment)

The Royal Irish Regiment was formed by the amalgamation of The Royal Irish Rangers with the Ulster Defence Regiment on 1 July 1992, the anniversary of the Battle of the Somme.

The Royal Irish Regiment, or R IRISH, adopted the cap badge of The Ulster Defence Regiment, or UDR, and the collar badges of The Royal Irish Rangers. A gold anodised aluminium badge is worn by Rangers in the green beret and a silver anodised aluminium badge in the Caubeen. Officers' wear a wire-embroidered beret badge and a silver caubeen badge. Pipers wear a larger caubeen badge, originally gold anodised aluminium when worn by the UDR, the badges were silvered for The Royal Irish Regiment.

For commercial reasons some manufacturers sell the same badge as The Royal Irish Regiment officer's beret badge and The Queen's Royal Lancers senior ranks arm badge.

The Harp and Crown are from the Order of St Patrick instituted by George III in 1783 and inherited from the 83rd County of Dublin Regiment of Foot, which was raised in 1793.

The collar badges worn on Number 1 and Number 2 Dress represent the Castle of Inniskilling with St George's banner, commemorating the gallant defence of the city in 1690 during the war between James II and William III.

1

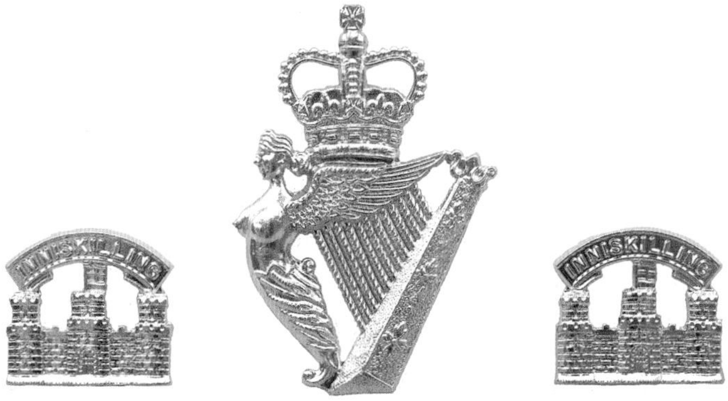

2

3

4

5

6

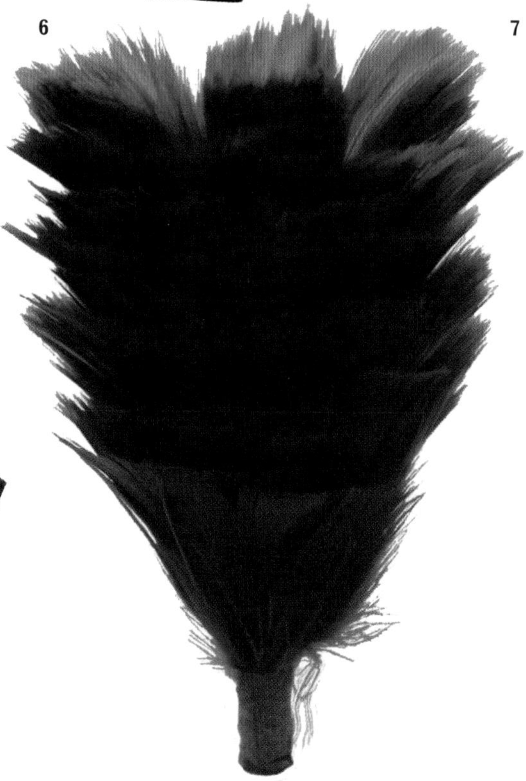

7

8

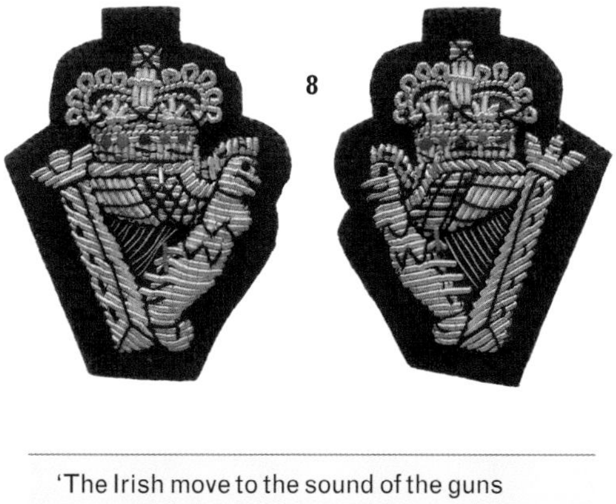

'The Irish move to the sound of the guns like salmon to the sea.' *Rudyard Kipling*

9

The 2nd Battalion 87th Foot was raised in 1804 by Sir Charles Doyle, son of the Commanding Officer of the 1st Battalion. At the Battle of Barrosa in 1811 the Battalion captured the first Imperial Eagle to be taken from the French. The Battalion charged with the shout of *Faugh-a-ballagh* (Clear the way). Ensign Keogh was killed trying to take the Eagle of the 8ème Régiment d'infanterie de ligne. Sergeant Patrick Masterson then killed the French Ensign and grabbed the Eagle, reportedly shouting, 'Be jabbers boys, oi have the cuckoo!' Sergeant Masterson was commissioned captain and the regiment honoured with the title The Prince of Wales's Own Irish Regiment and awarded the Imperial Eagle as a badge. In 1877 an application to adopt the motto *Faugh-a-ballagh* was refused but was finally approved in 1968. (It is said that the Mastersons were an Army family and that Major James Masterson, awarded the Victoria Cross in 1900, was a direct descendent).

10

11

12

The shamrock backing to the regimental badges on the kilt is also worn by other regiments with the saffron kilt, and in the case of The Royal Irish Regiment represents the shamrock backing worn by troops who served with 38 (Irish) Brigade in Italy in 1944.

14

The Royal Irish Regiment is the largest infantry regiment, with the 1st Battalion allocated to Land Command for operations worldwide, and the 2nd, 3rd and 4th Battalions, including both Part Time and Full Time soldiers recruited for Home Service in Northern Ireland.

13

15

16

17

18

19

20

21

22

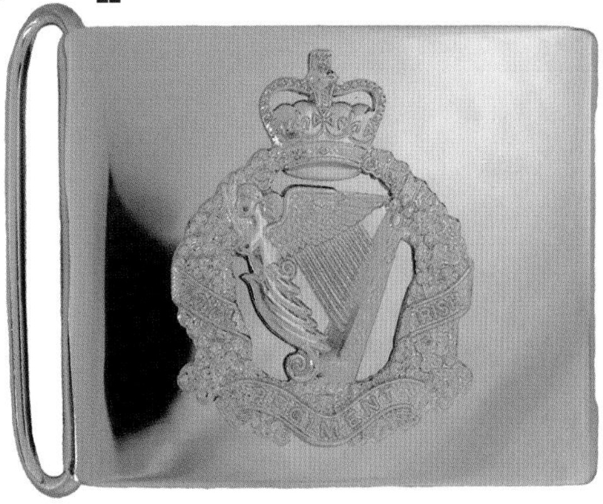

The Tactical Recognition Flash had originally been worn as a formation badge by 38th Infantry Brigade, 78th Division, composed of battalions of Northern Irish regiments during the Second World War. The North Irish Brigade adopted it in 1948.

previous page

1 The Royal Irish Regiment soldier's anodised aluminium caubeen badge 3.25 × 4.75 cm and collar badges 2.25 × 2 cm.

2 Officer's wire-embroidered beret badge 3.25 × 4.75 cm.

3 R IRISH button.

4 Shoulder title 4 × 2 cm.

5 Soldier's gold anodised aluminium beret badge 3.25 × 4.75 cm.

6 Hackle worn with the silver badge on the caubeen 7 × 10 cm.

7 Sgt John Cronin wearing No 2 Dress with caubeen and the distinctive dark green on black rank badges.

8 Officer's Mess Dress wire-embroidered collar badges 3 × 4 cm.

opposite page

9 Officer's silver caubeen badge 3.5 × 5 cm and collar badges 2 × 2 cm.

10 LCpls Jimmy Nesbitt and Strainer Strain wearing Combat Dress with the caubeen. Their rank slides with company colours show that they are serving with the 1st Battalion.

11 Lt Col Peter Harvey wearing shirtsleeve order.

12 Silver pouch badge 3.75 × 5 cm.

13 TRF 5.5 × 5.75cm.

14 Shoulder belt plate 7.75 × 9.5 cm.

15 Whistle chain boss 5 cm.

this page

16 Officer's plastic pouch 16 × 8.5 cm.

17 DMaj John Sherlock wearing Full Dress with the piper's large cap badge.

18 Major Andy Hart wearing No 1 Dress with the cross belt.

19 Home Service sergeant's rank slide.

20 Warrant Officer Class 2 Regimental Quartermaster Sergeant rank badge 8 × 6.5 cm worn on the forearms.

21 Guided Weapon Controller skill-at-arms badge 4.5 × 3.5 cm worn on the left forearm by corporals and below.

22 Soldier's waist belt clasp 7 × 5.75 cm, also worn by The London Irish. Pipers wear the same badge on a larger waist belt plate 9.5 × 7.5 cm.

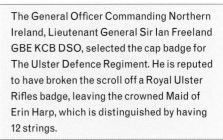

The General Officer Commanding Northern Ireland, Lieutenant General Sir Ian Freeland GBE KCB DSO, selected the cap badge for The Ulster Defence Regiment. He is reputed to have broken the scroll off a Royal Ulster Rifles badge, leaving the crowned Maid of Erin Harp, which is distinguished by having 12 strings.

23

24

25

The Royal Irish Regiment's green hackle is not connected with Ireland; rather it represents the regiment's antecedents as light infantry. In the 1770s infantry battalions added a Light Company, the equivalent of the present Recce Platoon, which was distinguished by a green plume on the soldiers' shakos, whilst the battalion companies wore white over red plumes. In about 1808, during the Peninsular War, Light Companies were brigaded together to form Rifle Regiments, all ranks wearing green plumes. The 87th Foot distinguished itself during the war and when Tactical Recognition Signs were introduced during the First World War their successors, The Royal Irish Fusiliers, adopted an inverted green triangle (the shape of a plume) as their sign. In the 1920s the Regiment adopted a green hackle, which was retained on amalgamation in 1968 and 1992.

29

28

26

27

opposite page

23 Qualified parachutist badge 10 × 4 cm worn by all ranks on the right shoulder in perpetuity. Whilst assigned to 16 Air Assault Brigade from 1999–2003 many 1 R IRISH soldiers qualified as parachutists.

24 All Arms Physical Training Instructor qualification badge.

25 Pipe Major's Full Dress appointment badge 11 cm.

26 Piper's large cap badge 5.25 × 7.75 cm.

27 Piper's Tara cloak brooch 6.5 × 5.5 cm.

28 Piper's button.

29 4 R IRISH Queen's Colour carried by Lt Steven Nixon, escorted by CSgts Colin Barrett and Lee Whiteside wearing the distinctive green on black rank and qualification badges.

this page

30 Obsolete Landing Zone badge worn by the 1st Battalion whilst in 16 Air Assault Brigade 7 × 7 cm.

The Royal Irish Regiment Kilt Ornaments, Shamrock 8.5 × 9.25 cm.

31 The Royal Ulster Rifles anodised aluminium cap badge.

32 The Royal Inniskilling Fusiliers anodised aluminium cap badge.

33 The Royal Irish Fusiliers anodised aluminium cap badge.

34 WO 2 Pipey Kidd wearing Full Dress with the cap badges of the constituent regiments as kilt ornaments, and the Tara brooch on his cape.

35 Piper's shoe buckle 11 × 11 cm.

30

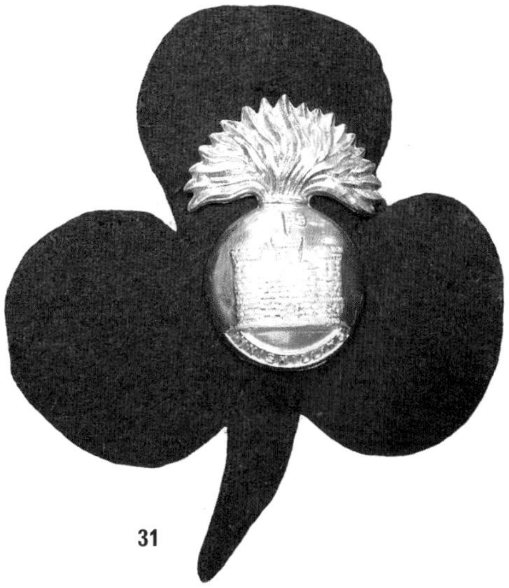

31

32

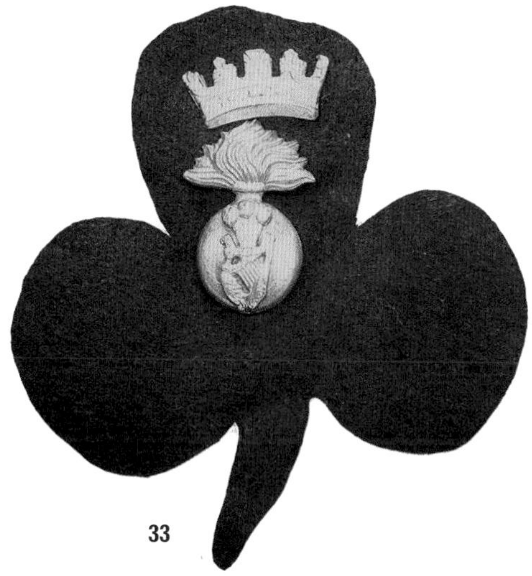

33

34

35

36

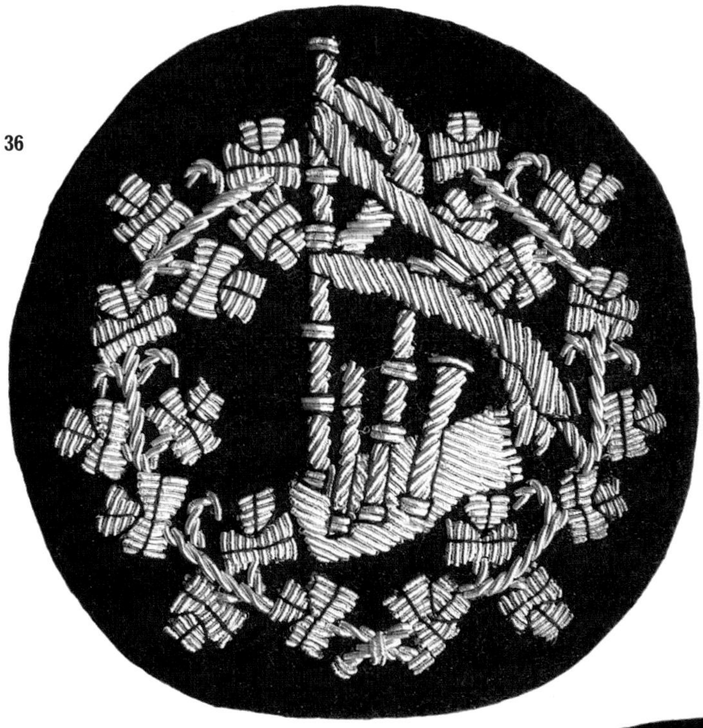

37

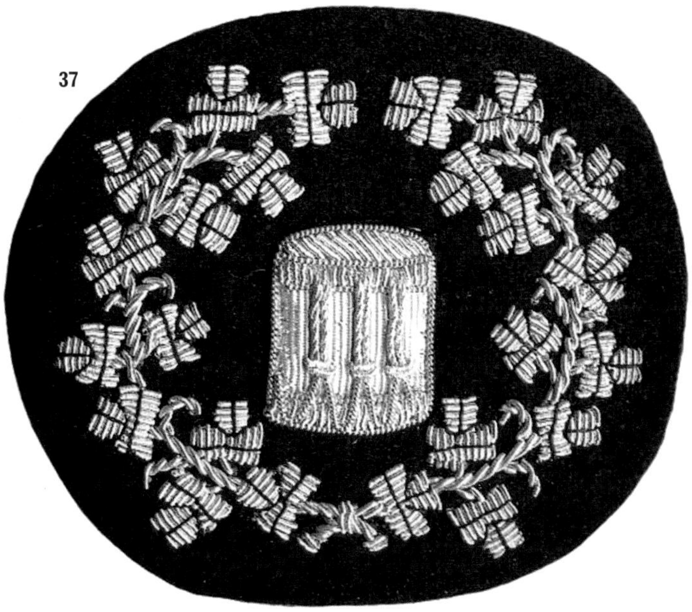

38

Lineage The Royal Irish Regiment (27th (Inniskilling), 83rd, 87th and UDR) (1992) from The Royal Irish Rangers (27th (Inniskilling), 83rd, 87th) (1968) and The Ulster Defence Regiment (1970). The Royal Irish Rangers from The Royal Inniskilling Fusiliers (1881), The Royal Ulster Rifles (1921), formerly The Royal Irish Rifles (1881), and The Royal Irish Fusiliers (Princess Victoria's). The Royal Inniskilling Fusiliers from 27th Foot (1689) and 108th Foot (1854). The Royal Irish Rifles from 83rd Foot (1793) and 86th Foot) (1793). The Royal Irish Fusiliers from 87th Foot (1793) and 89th Foot (1793).

36 Pipe Major's Mess Dress appointment badge 8 × 8 cm.

37 Drum Major's Mess Dress appointment badge 8 × 7 cm.

38 Bugle Major's Mess Dress appointment badge 8 × 7 cm.

Acknowledgement WO1 (RSM) CP Brown and E McDonnell

The Royal Gloucestershire, Berkshire and Wiltshire Regiment

The Royal Gloucestershire, Berkshire and Wiltshire Regiment was formed by the amalgamation of The Gloucestershire Regiment with The Duke of Edinburgh's Royal Regiment in 1994.

The cap badge of The Royal Gloucestershire, Berkshire and Wiltshire Regiment, or RGBW, combines elements from its three constituent regiments; the cross pattée of The Wiltshire Regiment combined with The Gloucestershire Regiment's Sphinx worn on The Royal Berkshire Regiment's triangular red Brandywine patch. The badge introduced in 1994 was very large and was replaced by a smaller version in 2003, with the larger badges being passed on to cadet detachments. The regiment also wears The Gloucestershire Regiment Sphinx badge on the back of the headdress to commemorate the action of the 28th Foot fighting back-to-back in Egypt in 1801.

The ribbon of the US Army Presidential Unit Citation, awarded to The Gloucestershire Regiment for its action at the Battle of Imjin River in Korea in 1951, is worn on both sleeves.

1

2

3

4

5

6

8

7

10

11

9

12

(Because of its shape and colour it has the nickname, the swimming pool). The regiment wear the blue ribbon surrounded by a wire-embroidered frame. Soldiers attached to 1 RGBW, principally RLC, RAMC, REME and AGC, wear a badge with a metal surround fitted with two pins to obviate the requirement to sew badges onto uniforms during what are often short attachments. When awarded to 1st Battalion The Gloucestershire Regiment and to C Troop 170th Independent Mortar Battery RA in 1951 the Citation was known as the United States Distinguished Unit Citation and was worn pinned above the right breast pocket. The title of the Citation was changed in 1965.

Metal Back Badges were worn by The Gloucestershire Regiment soldered to the back of steel helmets until the Second World War during which they were replaced by paper transfer badges. In 1989 Lieutenant Colonel Paul Arengo-Jones introduced a cloth Back Badge worn on the helmet cover in Berlin. The practice did not last long, however the cloth badge Back Badge was reintroduced as the Tactical Recognition Flash in 2003. The Brandywine flash had been worn as a Landing Zone flash from 1995 but was obsolete before the TRF was introduced.

13

14

15

US Army Presidential Unit Citation

In April 1951 the Chinese launched an offensive against the United Nations forces in Korea. The 29th British Brigade was deployed in the hills south of the Imjin River when the Chinese attacked. A platoon of 1st Battalion The Gloucestershire Regiment killed 100 Chinese as they made four attempts to cross the Imjin in front of its positions. The Chinese eventually forced a crossing and A Company took severe casualties while B Company killed 100 more Chinese. A counterattack by Lieutenant Philip Curtis' platoon failed to drive the Chinese off a dominating position, but the ferocity of Curtis' assaults prevented the enemy from exploiting their position. Curtis was killed and later awarded a posthumous Victoria Cross. Chinese attacks continued as the Glosters contracted their line from almost four miles to only 600 yards of frontage. As the rest of the 29th Brigade made good their withdrawal after fierce fighting, 1 Glosters had no way of withdrawing. On the third morning permission was given for the battalion to try and break out through the Chinese encirclement. Only two platoons made it back to safety. The battalion earned the nickname The Glorious Glosters. The Commanding Officer, Lt Col James Carne DSO was awarded the Victoria Cross for his inspirational leadership. A second platoon commander, Lt Terence Waters was awarded a posthumous George Cross for his courage and fortitude when taken prisoner.

When the front collapsed under the weight of Chinese assaults 2nd Battalion, Princess Patricia's Canadian Light Infantry and 3rd Battalion, The Royal Australian Regiment were ordered to hold the escape route of the withdrawing Allied forces. 3 RAR held out as long as possible before being ordered to withdraw. 2 PPCLI, in positions near the village of Kapyong, was next subjected to multiple assaults by a Chinese force nine times their number. The battalion held its position and eventually the Chinese offensive melted away.

8th US Army Headquarters, commanding the United Nations forces, placed great importance on the actions of the three Commonwealth brigades. They were credited with saving the entire situation in Korea, by providing withdrawing units the time to regroup and by standing fast had completely upset Chinese plans, stopping an advance that might have taken the capital Seoul. On its recommendation the United States Distinguished Unit Citation was awarded to 1 Glosters, 3 RAR, and 2 PPCLI.

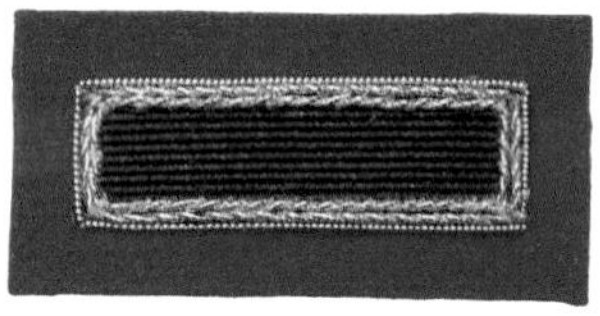

16

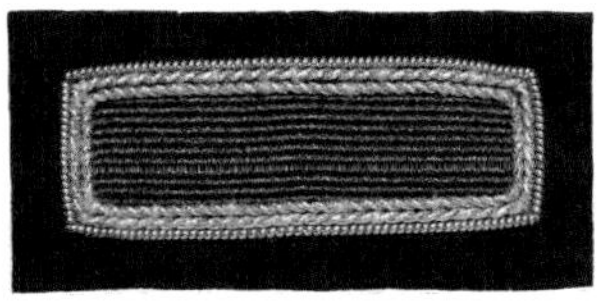

17

18

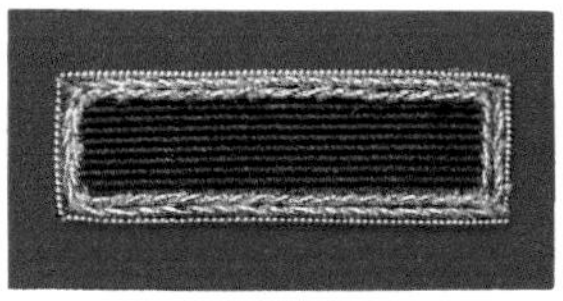

19

20

21

22

On 20 December 1845 during the First Sikh War the British attacked and were repulsed at the entrenched camp at Ferozeshah. The 62nd Foot lost 17 officers and 250 soldiers. When operations resumed the following morning, the 21 December, sergeants were filling most command appointments. Annually on Ferozeshah Day the Commanding Officer hands over the Colours to the Warrant Officers and Sergeants Mess for the day in commemoration of their predecessor's actions.

23

24

previous page

1 The Royal Gloucestershire, Berkshire and Wiltshire Regiment soldier's anodised aluminium cap badge 3.25 × 3.25 cm, back badge 2 × 2 cm and collar badges 2.5 × 2.5 cm.
2 Bright metal shoulder title 4 × 1 cm.
3 RGBW button.
4 Obsolete large cap badge replaced in 2003 4.25 × 4.25 cm.
5 Officer's wire-embroidered Forage Cap badge 4.25 × 4.25 cm.
6 Officer's silver and gilt Service Dress Cap 4 × 4 cm.
7 Officer's wire-embroidered beret badge 6 × 6 cm.
8 Pte AP McCarthy wearing the back badge
9 Officer's wire-embroidered Back Badge 3 × 3 cm.
10 Officer's silver, gilt and enamel No 1 Dress collar badges 2.5 × 2.5 cm.
11 Officer's silver and gilt No 2 Dress collar badges 2.5 × 2.5 cm.
12 Officer's wire-embroidered Mess Dress collar badges 3 × 3 cm.

opposite page

13 Soldier's waist belt clasp 10 × 6.5 cm.
14 Drummer's rank slide.
15 Pte AP McCarthy with the US Army Presidential Unit Citation on his left sleeve.

US Army Presidential Unit Citation

16 Full Dress 4.5 × 2.25 cm.
17 Number 1 Dress 4.5 × 2 cm.
18 Number 2 Dress 4.5 × 2 cm.
19 Mess Dress 3.75 × 1.75 cm.
20 Metal brooch worn by attached personnel 3.5 × 1.5 cm.

this page

21 WO2 Peter Jefferies wearing No 2 Dress with the US Army Presidential Citation on his upper arm.
22 The Back Badge is worn on the back of the helmet as the TRF 4.25 × 4.25.
23 The Corps of Drums wear the Infantry Blue Cloth Helmet ornamented with a bright metal helmet plate 10.5 × 12.75 cm
24 Bright metal Blue Cloth Helmet back badge 2.75 cm.

The Back Badge is worn in commemoration of the action of the 28th Foot during the Battle of Alexandra fought in Egypt in 1801. The Regiment was stood-to in a partly constructed redoubt on the sand dunes when the French Grenadiers, 'The Invincibles', made a dawn attack. A second column advanced from the rear. The rear rank of the 28th Foot faced about and the regiment fought back to back. Having defeated the attack the Regiment then went to the assistance of the 42nd Foot, The Royal Highland Regiment, later The Black Watch, which was also surrounded.

At that time the Army was adopting the Shako as the headdress, ornamented by a brass plate showing the regiment's number. In about 1802 the Regiment adopted a 'Back number' worn on the rear of the shako in commemoration of its action in Egypt. Officers wore a Sphinx and soldiers the number 28. By 1815 the Back Number was reported being worn on the Forage Cap, known at the time as the Low Cap – as opposed to the tall shako – at the Battle of Quatre Bras. The Duke of Wellington gave authority for the Back Badge in 1830. Up to then the Regiment had bought silver badges but there was a problem with the soldiers selling them and therefore from 1830 soldiers were issued a brass badge, only musicians retaining the silver badge. The Sphinx was adopted as the Back Badge for all ranks in 1881 on the formation of The Gloucestershire Regiment by the amalgamation of the 28th and 61st Foot although the 2nd Battalion, formerly the 61st Foot, delayed wearing the Back Badge until 1887. For over 50 years, until the Second World War, the annual Sergeants Mess Ball held on 21 March was known as the Back Number Ball.

In 1918 the 1st Battalion again fought back to back during the Battle of Festubert and a large Back Badge was adopted and worn until 1935 when the small badge was readopted.

25

27

26

28

29

30

Lineage The Royal Gloucestershire, Berkshire and Wiltshire Regiment (1994) from The Gloucestershire Regiment (1881) and The Duke of Edinburgh's Royal Regiment (Berkshire and Wiltshire) (1995). The Gloucestershire Regiment from 28th Foot (1694) and 61st Foot (1756). The Duke of Edinburgh's Royal Regiment from The Royal Berkshire Regiment (Princess Charlotte of Wales's) (1881) and The Wiltshire Regiment (Duke of Edinburgh's) (1881). The Royal Berkshire Regiment from 49th Foot (1743) and 66th Foot (1756). The Wiltshire Regiment from 62nd Foot (1756) and 99th Foot (1824).

31

32

'Our late commanding officer, Sir Charles Philip Belson, during the Peninsular war, instituted two badges of merit amongst the non-commissioned officers of the regiment. Whenever new clothing came out, there were always a number of embroidered crowns and stars. The crown he gave for gallantry in the field, and the star for steady good conduct in quarters. They were worn above the chevrons. The emulation it caused and the good it did were very great; it was considered a terrible disgrace if anything occurred to deprive any one of his badge of honour.'

Narrative of the Campaigns of the Twenty-Eighth Regiment by Lieut-Colonel Charles Cadell (London, Whittaker Co., 1835).

opposite page

25 WO 2 Leo Sayer wearing the wire-embroidered beret badge and Cpl John Lambert wearing the anodised aluminium badge with Pte Luke Mortimer displaying the Back Badge.

26 Cpl Shaun Emberson, WO2 Paul Pergrum and Sgt Steven Jewell wearing No 1 Dress.

27 The Duke of Edinburgh's Royal Regiment drummer's shoulder belt plate 6.5 × 6.5 cm retained but not worn by RGBW.

28 Obsolete Brandywine LZ Flash 7 × 7 cm.

this page

29 Embroidered badge worn on the back of packs carried on Public Duties 24 × 39 cm, regimental badge 17.75 × 17.75 cm and Back badge 12.25 cm.

30 Ferozeshah Colour Party. CSgt Anthony Rose and Rodney Poulter carrying the Colours escorted by Sgt Peter North, WO1 (RSM) Anthony Watkins, WO2 Neil Edwards and Sgt Gerry Caldwell.

31 Lt Col Nicholas Welch MBE wearing No1 Dress.

32 Sgt Steven Johnson and Rupert Guest wearing the Athol Grey Greatcoat with the large rank badges (see The Guards Division p. 92).

Acknowledgement Sgt PM Higgins and Cpl Charlie Drake

The Worcestershire and Sherwood Foresters Regiment

The Worcestershire and Sherwood Foresters Regiment was formed by the amalgamation of The Worcestershire Regiment with The Sherwood Foresters (Nottinghamshire and Derbyshire Regiment) in 1970.

The Worcestershire and Sherwood Foresters Regiment, or WFR, cap badge is based on the Garter Star, thought to have been chosen originally by the 29th Foot because the first and several later colonels had served in the Coldstream Guards. The motto 'Firm' came from the 36th Foot and was possibly awarded by Field Marshal Lord Stair, whose family motto it was and who commanded the Army in Flanders during the 1740s. Alternatively it may date to 1791 when Lord Cornwallis referred to the regiment's alacrity and firmness during the assault on the fortress of Bangalore.

The Maltese Cross, oak wreath and stag on the cap badge are from the 95th Foot, which amalgamated with the 45th Foot and the county militias in 1881. The Nottinghamshire Militia also had a wreath in their badge in allusion to Sherwood Forest, and two Royal Stags form the supporters to the Arms of the City of Nottingham. The Maltese Cross is said to have been adopted because many of those recruited into the 95th Foot on formation in 1823 had served in the former 95th Foot which became the Rifle Brigade in 1816 and had the same Cross as its badge.

The 29th Foot wore a Star badge on their ammunition pouch from sometime during the reign of King George III, 1760–1820. The badge was authorised in 1877 'as a special distinction for service in the field' and the regiment, which continues the privilege, is said to be the only one to have such a distinction.

1

2

3

4

5

6

2nd Volunteer Battalion The Sherwood Foresters originally wore a green diamond flash on the sun helmet in about 1900. In 1915 the flash was worn on the side of the khaki Service Dress cap and in 1916 worn on the back of the tunic. During the Second World War it was readopted worn on the back of the Battle Dress blouse. With the introduction of the beret the diamond shape was worn behind the cap badge until amalgamation when WFR adopted square backing. The diamond was readopted as a helmet flash in the 1990s.

7

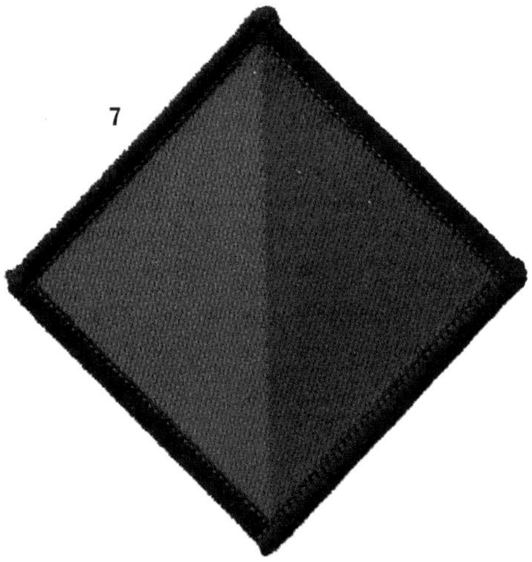

8

The Worcestershire Regiment maintained the custom of the Orderly Officer wearing his sword at dinner, the practice having begun in North America in 1746 when Indians thought to be loyal treacherously attacked the officers of the 29th Foot. Thereafter the officers always wore their swords. The WFR orderly officer continues the custom of being 'always sworded'.

opposite page

1 The Worcestershire and Sherwood Foresters Regiment soldier's bright metal cap badge 3.5 × 5 cm and anodised aluminium anodised collar badges 2 × 3 cm.
2 WFR button.
3 Anodised aluminium shoulder title 4.5 × 3 cm.
4 Silver collar badge worn polished as the officer's beret badge 2.25 × 3.25cm.
5 Officer's silver, gilt and enamel cap badge 3.25 × 5.25 cm and silver and gilt collar badges 2 × 3 cm.
6 Identification flash worn on the left side of the helmet 6 × 6 cm.

this page

7 TRF 7 × 7 cm worn green to the front.
8 Officers' wire emboidered mess dress collar badges 2.5 × 3.5cm.
9 Pte Paul Turner, LCpl Steven Hutton and Pte Mark Oscroft wearing Drummer's Full Dress.
10 Sgt Paul Yates and Major Andrew Wadland wearing Combat Dress. Officers have their uniforms altered to attach epaulettes.
11 Major's rank slide 6 × 10.5 cm.

9

10

A number of regiments claim to have fired their buttons on running out of musket balls. A detachment of the 62nd Foot at Carrickfergus fought off a French invasion of Ireland in 1758 and did fire their buttons before being reduced to throwing rocks and then closing with the bayonet.

11

12

14

Lineage The Worcestershire and Sherwood Foresters Regiment (29th/45th Foot) (1970) from The Worcestershire Regiment (1881) and The Sherwood Foresters (Nottinghamshire and Derbyshire Regiment) (1881). The Worcestershire Regiment from 29th Foot (1694) and 36th Foot (1701). The Sherwood Foresters from 45th Foot (1741) and 95th Foot (1823).

13

12 The Corps of Drums wear the Infantry Blue Cloth Helmet ornamented with a bright metal helmet plate 10.5 × 12.25 cm.

13 Valise star 7.5 × 10.5 cm worn by the Corps of Drums on the Prussian Box.

14 CSgts Baz Mitchell and Willy Wilson wearing No 2 Dress.

Acknowledgement
Capt Richard Blaney and DMaj Bryn Knowles

The Queen's Lancashire Regiment

The Queen's Lancashire Regiment was formed in 1970 by the amalgamation of The Lancashire Regiment (Prince of Wales's Volunteers) and The Loyal Regiment (North Lancashire).

1

2

3

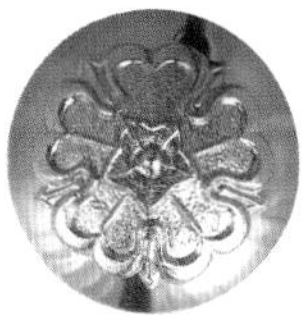

The Queen's Lancashire Regiment, or QLR, gilt and enamel cap badge was introduced in 2003 to replace the anodised aluminium design worn since 1968. The former cap badge was worn by soldiers on the beret backed by a yellow plastic diamond. The new badge is worn on a diamond of pale yellow flexible material, known commercially as 'Funky Fun Foam'.

The soldiers' Lancastrian rose collar badges are produced in anodised aluminium and soldiers are required to paint in the red petals when the badges are issued.

The Regiment's first arm badge was a narrow ribbon in regimental colours adopted in 1995 for wear in Bosnia. A Tactical Recognition Flash was proposed in 2000 and approved in a slightly reduced size in 2002. The first pattern was again a length of ribbon, which was replaced by a woven TRF in 2004.

4

5

The primrose diamond cap badge backing was derived initially from the facing colour of the 30th Foot worn from 1702 to 1881. In 1916 1st Battalion The East Lancashire Regiment adopted primrose recognition flashes on their sleeves and helmet for the Battle of the Somme. The diamond shape was chosen by 2nd Battalion The East Lancashire Regiment, nicknamed 'The Lilywhites' when it adopted a white flash on their sun helmets in India from 1902 to 1903.

The two traditions were combined at the end of the Second World War in 1945 when the 1st Battalion The East Lancashire Regiment adopted a primrose diamond cap badge backing. The tradition was continued on the amalgamation of The Queen's Lancashire Regiment in 1970.

6

7

Annually on 18 June the Queen's Lancashire Regiment celebrates the conduct of the 30th and 40th Foot at the Battle of Waterloo by wearing a natural laurel leaf in the cap. A laurel wreath is also placed on each Colour. The practice dates from the Duke of Wellington's authorisation that regiments which fought at Waterloo could bear laurels on their Colours.

8

10

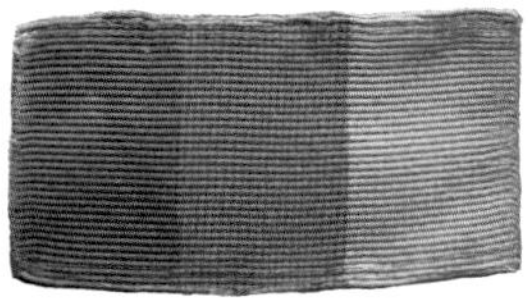

11

9

12

15

14

13

16

17

18

19

20

Lineage The Queen's Lancashire Regiment (1970) from The Lancashire Regiment (Prince of Wales's Volunteers) (1958) and The Loyal Regiment (North Lancashire) (1881), from 47th Foot (1741) and 81st Foot (1783). The Lancashire Regiment from The East Lancashire Regiment (1881) and The South Lancashire Regiment (Prince of Wales's Volunteers) (1881). The East Lancashire Regiment from 30th Foot (1702) and 59th Foot (1755). The South Lancashire Regiment from 40th Foot (1717) and 82nd Foot (1793).

previous page

1 Gilt and enamel cap badge 3.25 × 4.5 cm and anodised aluminium collar badges 3.25 × 2.75 cm the petals of which are painted red by recruits when first issued.
2 Anodised aluminium shoulder title 4.75 × 2 cm.
3 QLR button.
4 Officer's silver and enamel cap badge 3.25 × 4.5 cm and collar badges 3.25 × 2.75 cm. The collar badges are also worn by sergeants on Mess Dress.
5 Cpl Lee Calvy wearing No2 Dress with the crossed bayonets badge having successfully completed the Infantry Section Commanders Battle Course.
6 Officer's wire-embroidered beret badge 4 × 4.5 cm.
7 Officer's obsolete beret badge 4.5 × 3.75 cm worn during the transition in 2004.

opposite page

8 Officers and Warrant Officers Mess Dress wire-embroidered collar badge worn in pairs, 6 × 5 cm.
9 WO1 (RSM) Kevin Hayes wearing the wire-embroidered beret badge.
10 Obsolete arm badge 3.5 × 2 cm.
11 TRF worn 2003–2004 5.75 × 5.75 cm.
12 TRF introduced in 2004 5.5 × 4.5 cm.
13 Soldier's 'Funky Fun Foam' beret badge backing 5 × 6.5 cm.
14 Pte Dale Gouldsbrough and LCpl Dave Smith wearing Combat Dress with the cap badges on the yellow backing.
15 WO1 (RSM) Colin Howard wearing the officer's beret badge and the former TRF.

this page

16 Chrome waist belt clasp 10 × 6.25 cm.
17 LCpl Andrew Daw wearing a regimental police brassard.
18 The Corps of Drums wear the Infantry Blue Cloth Helmet ornamented with a bright metal helmet plate 10.5 × 13.5 cm.
19 Captain's rank slide.
20 Regimental police waist belt clasp 7 × 5.75 cm.

Acknowledgement
Lt Col John Downham MBE, Capt Alan Goodenough and WO1 (RSM) KM Hayes

The Duke of Wellington's Regiment (West Riding)

The Duke of Wellington's Regiment was formed by the amalgamation of the 33rd and the 76th Regiments of Foot in 1881 and is the only regiment named after a personage who was not a member of the Royal Family

The cap badge of The Duke of Wellington's Regiment, or DWR, is the crest and motto of the Duke of Wellington, which were adopted by the 33rd Foot and were retained when The Duke of Wellington's Regiment was formed in 1881.

The elephant, worn as the collar badge, derives from the 76th Foot, which was granted the badge of an elephant with howdah, along with the Battle Honour Hindoostan, for its service during General Lake's campaign of 1803–1805.

The Tactical Recognition Flash was adopted in 1995, although when approved in 2002 by the Army Dress Committee it was with a recommendation that the badge was increased in size. A larger version had been worn in Bosnia in 1994–1995.

1

2

3

4

4

5

6

The 76th Foot served with distinction in India from 1787–1807, particularly during the campaign from 1803–1805 after which the Governor General presented the regiment with a pair of Honoury Colours. The Duke of Wellington's Regiment retains the honour and is the only regiment to have four Colours.

The Duke of Wellington's Regiment scarlet badge backing was adopted in 1934 although square or rectangular scarlet patches had been worn on the sun helmet in India and elsewhere from about 1900. Soldiers wear a triangular scarlet patch, it is said in commemoration of the regimental square formed in battle during the Napoleonic War, culminating in the square formed during the Battle of Waterloo, 1815. The 33rd Foot suffered such casualties that only three sides could be manned and the square collapsed into a triangle. Officers wear a square scarlet patch; it is said in commemoration of the reorganisation of the regimental square at Waterloo when the Officers and Sergeant Major filled gaps in the ranks to reform the fourth side of the square.

7

The 1st Duke of Wellington was long associated with the 33rd Foot. As the Honourable Arthur Wellesley he purchased a major's commission in the regiment in 1793, and later the same year became the Commanding Officer. He was Colonel of the Regiment from 1806 to 1813 and after his death in 1853 Queen Victoria granted permission for the regiment to use the additional title 'Duke of Wellington's'. The Duke's Crest and Motto were used by the 33rd Foot and continued in use after the amalgamation with the 76th Foot in 1881 and were used as the cap badge introduced in 1897.

opposite page

1 Duke of Wellington's anodised aluminium cap badge 5.5 × 4.5 cm and collar badges 3 × 2.75 cm worn on a red felt outline.
2 DWR button.
3 Anodised aluminium shoulder title 3x1 cm.
4 Separate Mess Dress collar badges 3.75 × 3.5 cm used by some tailors.
5 Officer's silver and gilt cap 5.5 × 4.5 cm and collar badges 3 × 2.75 cm. On the Forage Cap the red backing is pre-cut to shape.
6 Officer's wire-embroidered beret badge 6 × 5.5 cm.
7 Major James Brydon wearing Service Dress, his Forage Cap badge on the red backing.

this page

8 Soldier's gilding metal waist belt clasp 10 × 6 cm.
9 Lieutenant's rank slide 3 × 10.5 cm.
10 Officer's Mess Dress collar badges embroidered directly onto the lapels. Collar badges 3.25 × 3.5 cm.
11 WO2 (CSM) Nat Cole wearing the officer's wire-embroidered beret badge on the square backing.
12 Sgt Gary Peacock wearing No 2 Dress with the rank and skill at arms badges on red background. He has the crossed bayonets and laurel wreath badge having successfully completed the Infantry Platoon Sergeants Battle Course.
13 TRF 3.5 × 2 cm.
14 The Corps of Drums wear the Infantry Blue Cloth Helmet ornamented with a bright metal helmet plate 11.5 × 13.5 cm.

Lineage The Duke of Wellington's Regiment (West Riding) (1881) from 33rd Foot (1702) and 76th Foot (1787).

8

9

10

14

11

12

13

Acknowledgement
Major Brian Thomas BEM and WO2 (RCMO) NS Wilson

The Staffordshire Regiment

(The Prince of Wales's)

The Staffordshire Regiment was formed by the amalgamation of The South Staffordshire Regiment with The North Staffordshire Regiment in 1959.

1

2

3

4

The Staffordshire Regiment, or STAFFORDS, adopted the Stafford knot, which had been worn before amalgamation as the cap badge by both The North Staffordshire Regiment and The South Staffordshire Regiment. The present badge includes Prince of Wales's Plumes from The North Staffordshire Regiment and is worn on an oval Buff Holland Patch backing from The South Staffordshire Regiment.

In 1984 the Regiment adopted a cloth beret badge for wear on operations in Northern Ireland. The badges survived into the 1990s. A cloth badge was reintroduced for the desert and jungle hat before deploying to Iraq in 2005.

The collar badges incorporate the Crown from The South Staffordshire Regiment and the Prince of Wales's Feathers from The North Staffordshire Regiment. The Prince of Wales's designation had been awarded to the 2nd Battalion, The North Staffordshire Regiment in 1876.

The South Staffordshire Regiment was authorised the Buff Holland Patch as a backing to the regimental badge in 1935 to commemorate the 57 years from 1707 spent by the 38th Foot in the West Indies during which time the Regiment wore uniforms made of Holland cloth. It has been said that Holland was a rough local sacking and that the 38th Foot were forced to wear it because they had been 'forgotten' by their agents. Research indicates that Holland was a fine cloth made and exported to the American colonies by William Clarke & Sons of Upperlands, County Londonderry for waistcoats and to line the red tunics. In the heat of the West Indies it was usual to wear the waistcoat without the tunic.

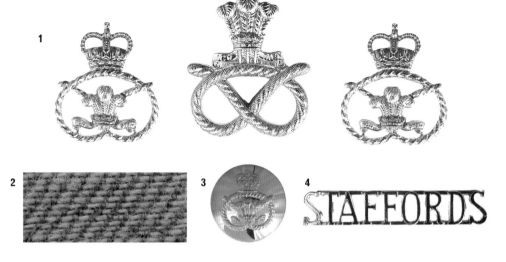

5

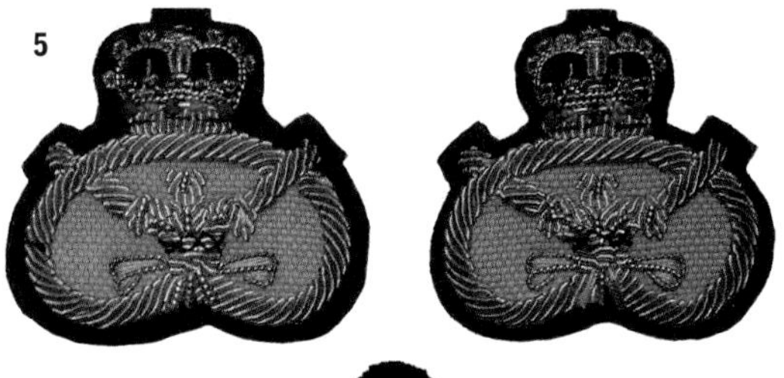

6

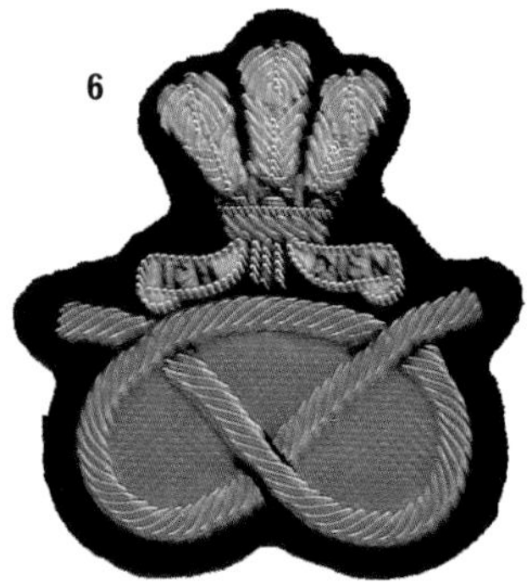

7

8

9

The regiment, along with The King's Own Royal Border Regiment, wears a gold glider Battle Honour badge. Wire-embroidered glider badges are worn by The Staffordshire Regiment on Number 1 Dress and Mess Dress and on officers' Service Dress. Badges for soldiers' Number 2 Dress are cloth embroidered on khaki backing sewn on to a black patch. The cloth embroidered badges do not survive the constant washing of Combat Dress and pullovers and a new badge of man-made fibres is proving much more robust. Officers and Warrant Officers wear a brass or anodised aluminium glider on the black regimental pullover, which had been introduced for the lightweight uniform in Gibraltar in 1981.

The regiment was authorised a Tactical Recognition Flash in 2003 consisting of a green on black Stafford Knot to perpetuate a tradition of battalions of The Staffordshire Regiment wearing various coloured Knots dating back to the Great War. The Army Dress Committee did suggest that the regiment reconsider the colour of the knot. Worn on the right sleeve of the field jacket, the TRF is similar to the 1984 cloth beret badge and the 2005 desert hat badge.

Glider Battle Honour Arm Badges

King George VI awarded the glider badge with the Battle Honour Landing in Sicily to 2nd Battalion The South Staffordshire Regiment in recognition of its part in the first major airborne landing, in Sicily in 1943. The assault achieved complete surprise, largely because it was mounted in bad weather. Unfortunately about a third of the gliders ended up in the sea and the remainder were widely scattered. Only one platoon of The South Staffords reached the objective, Ponte Grande, but the bridge was secured and reinforced by troops from the 1st Battalion The Border Regiment. Both regiments were awarded the Glider Battle Honour badge.

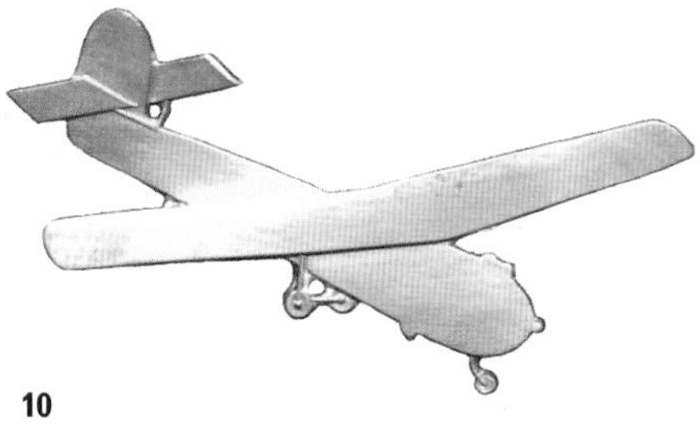

10

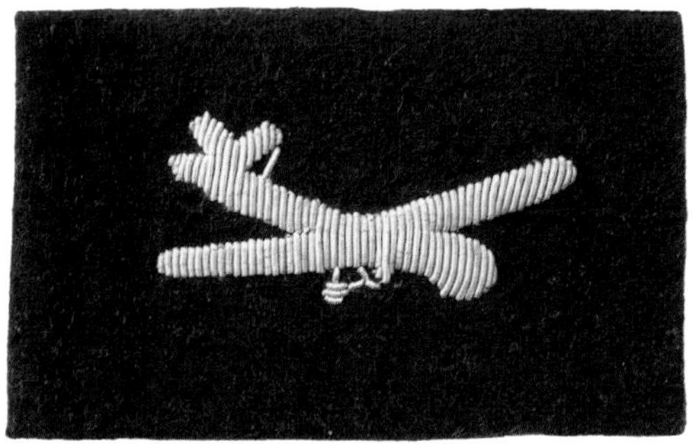

11

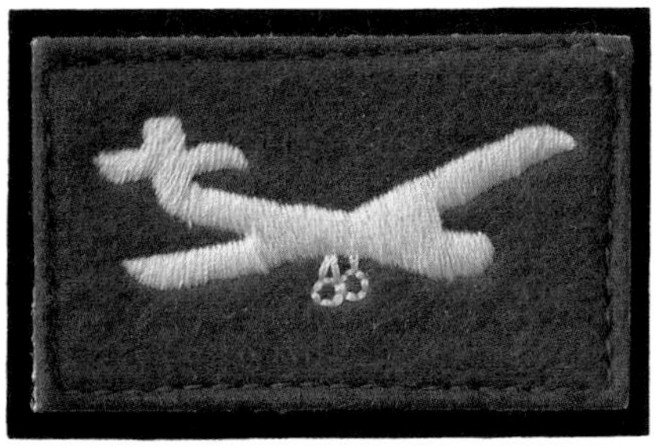

12

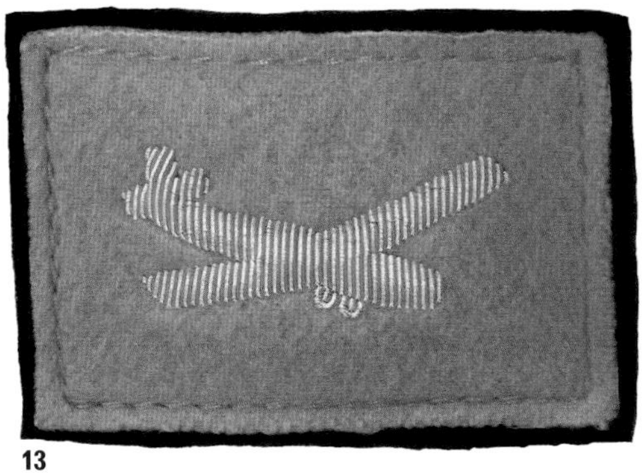

13

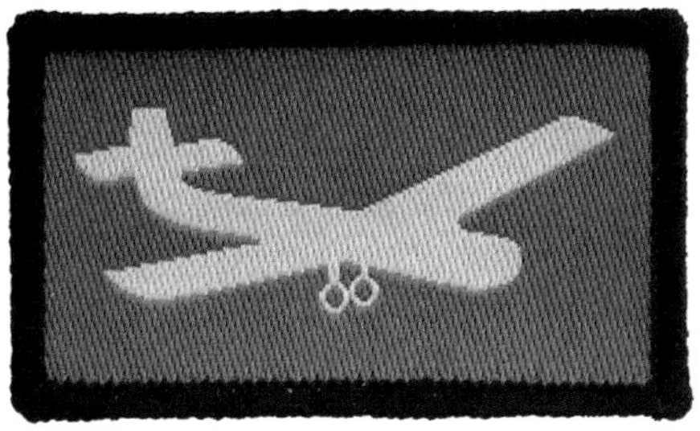

14

15

opposite page

1 The Staffordshire Regiment soldier's frosted bi-metal cap badge 3.25 × 3.75 cm, and collar badges 3 × 3.5 cm
2 Holland patch 3.25 × 2 cm worn behind the cap badge.
3 STAFFORDS button.
4 Soldier's anodised aluminium shoulder title 5.25 × 1 cm.
5 Officer's Mess Dress wire-embroidered collar badges.
6 Officer's wire and coloured embroidered beret badge on a Holland patch 4.25 × 4.5 cm.
7 Sgt Richie Watson wearing No 2 Dress with the anodised aluminium shoulder title and woven Glider badge. He is also wearing the crossed bayonets badge with laurel wreath having passed the Infantry Platoon Sergeants Battle Course.
8 Officer's silver and gilt cap badge 3.5 × 4 cm and collar badges 3 × 3.5 cm.
9 Officers and Warrant Officers gilding metal shoulder title for the regimental pullover 5 × 2.25 cm.

this page

Glider Battle Honour Arm Badges

10 Regimental pullover bright metal badge 6 × 3.5 cm.
11 No 1 Dress wire-embroidered badge 7 × 4.5 cm.
12 Soldier's No 2 Dress woven badge 6 × 4 cm.
13 Officer's Service Dress wire-embroidered badge, this example for No 4 Dress 7 × 4.75 cm.
14 Combat Dress printed badge 6 × 3.5 cm.
15 Mess Dress wire-embroidered badge 4 × 2.5 cm

16 Cloth badge 5 × 5 cm introduced for the desert and jungle hats in 2005.
17 TRF 4.5 × 3 cm.

16

17

18

19

There is a story that the Stafford Knot came to prominence when the Sheriff of Staffordshire had four men to hang and only one rope and that one of the men saved his life by showing the Sheriff how to hang three together from one rope by means of a special knot.

The earliest record of the Knot is on the seal of Joan, Lady of Wake, a descendent of Hereward the Wake, who died in 1443. Her beneficiary was Humphrey, Earl of Stafford. The Knot did not form part of the armorial bearings but was worn as a badge by his retainers in Stafford. It was eventually incorporated into the borough arms and its use spread throughout the county, although it remains the Stafford Knot, not the Staffordshire Knot.

20

21

22

Lineage The Staffordshire Regiment (The Prince of Wales's) (1959) from The South Staffordshire Regiment (1881) and The North Staffordshire Regiment (The Prince of Wales's) (1881). The South Staffordshire Regiment from 38th Foot (1705) and 80th Foot (1793). The North Staffordshire Regiment from 64th Foot (1756) and 98th Foot (1824).

23

opposite page

18 WO2 Karl Lester wearing the cloth desert hat badge and distinctive black rank badge and stable belt.

19 CSgt Mick Whillock, as an instructor at the Royal Military Academy Sandhurst he is permitted to wear the Warrant Officer's regimental pullover.

20 LCpl Clint Walker with the printed glider badge on his right sleeve. Cpl James Cook is wearing the regiment's black T-shirt, and the 12 Mechanized Brigade badge on his left sleeve.

21 Soldier's chrome waist belt clasp 7 × 5.25 cm.

22 Captain's rank slide.

this page

23 LCpl Jonah Jones wearing the Glider badge on his shirt and Cpl Flinty Flint wearing the TRF on his jacket.

24 The Corps of Drums wear the Infantry Blue Cloth Helmet ornamented with a bright metal helmet plate curved to fit the helmet 11.5 × 13.5 cm.

Acknowledgement
Capt Tony Canniford and WO1 (RSM) GJ Dawson

24

The Black Watch (Royal Highland Regiment)

'The ladies from hell'

Originating from independent companies raised in 1725 to police or 'watch' doubtful Highland clans, The Black Watch was formed in 1739. The title of the regiment is derived from the Gaelic *Am Freiceadan Dubh*, or Black Watch, used by the clansmen to distinguish the companies from the English 'Redcoats' or *Saighdearan Dearg*.

The Black Watch, or BW, has the unique distinction, dating from 1822, of wearing a red hackle in place of, rather than in addition to, a cap badge.

The regimental badge combines the Star of the Order of the Thistle and St Andrew and the saltire. The original 'modern' cap badge had two scrolls, 'The Royal' and 'Highlanders' flanking the Crown and two scrolls at the bottom, 'Black' and 'Watch'. In 1934 the regimental title was changed and the scrolls reversed to read 'The Black Watch' at the top and 'Royal Highland Regiment' at the bottom. It was found that the lower scrolls were too small to carry the longer title and it was decided to dispense with the titles altogether. The regimental badge is worn on the Glengarry, worn with Mess Dress and by pipers. The collar badges are worn only on Number 1 Dress.

Each regiment wearing the Tam o'Shanter, or ToS, evolved a distinctive style of wearing the headdress; one reason being apparently that the issue ToS looks like 'a joiner's nail bag'. The Black Watch has worn theirs in a 'pork pie' style. The style is actively discouraged and the ToS is required to be pulled well down on the right.

The practice of wearing the red hackle is said to date from the regiment's success at the Battle of Geldermalsen in Holland in 1795 when it recovered some lost guns. There is some evidence that red vulture feathers had been adopted earlier during its 13 years in North America from 1776. The hackles were first officially issued on parade at Royston in 1795.

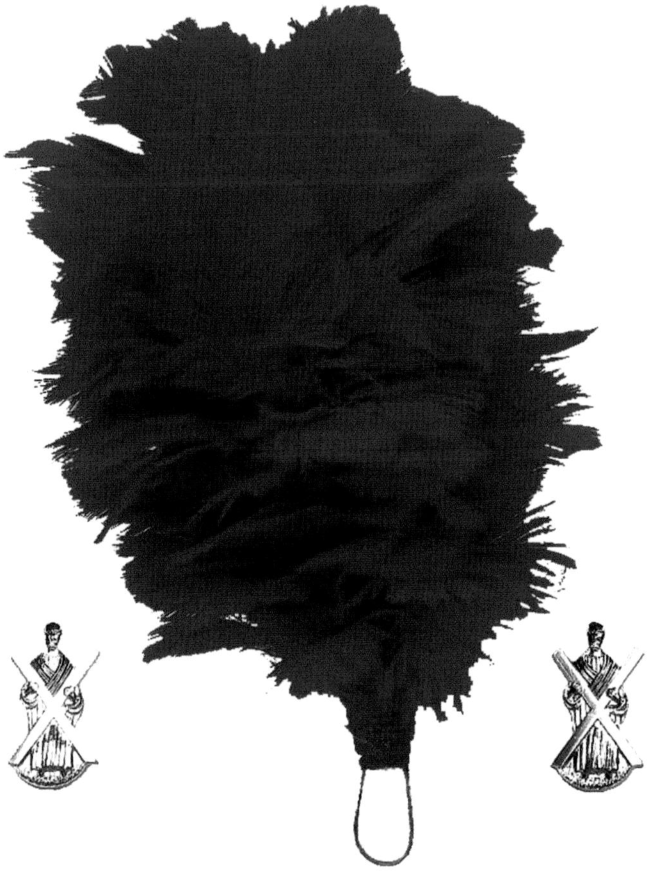

1

2

3

4

opposite page

1 Black Watch hackle 6.5 × 11.5 cm worn without a badge in the Tam o'Shanter, and soldier's anodised aluminium collar badges 1.5 × 2.5 cm worn only in No1 Dress.

2 Button.

3 Officer's silver and gilt Glengarry badge 8.5 × 6.5 cm.

4 Polished Glengarry badge 8.5 × 6.5 cm.

this page

5 Pte Jim Clark wearing the distinctive red hackle in a traditional but unapproved 'pork pie' shaped To'S.

6 Sgt Kev Wann wearing No2 Dress with the distinctive red hackle, no collar badges and the sporran with badge.

7 Officer's silver collar badges 2 × 3.5 cm.

8 Officer's silver and soldier's anodised aluminium sporran badges, known as 'Jimmy' 3 × 4.5 cm.

9 Officer's silver and gilt waist belt clasp 6.75 × 4.5 cm.

10 Officer's shoulder belt plate, known as the Chest Plate 7.75 × 10 cm.

11 Privates' rank slides are embroidered BW, all other ranks, in this case the Pipe Major, do not have the title.

12 Officer's Full Dress gilt bonnet badge 4.5 × 3 cm.

13 Drum Major's silver bonnet badge 4.5 × 3 cm.

5

6

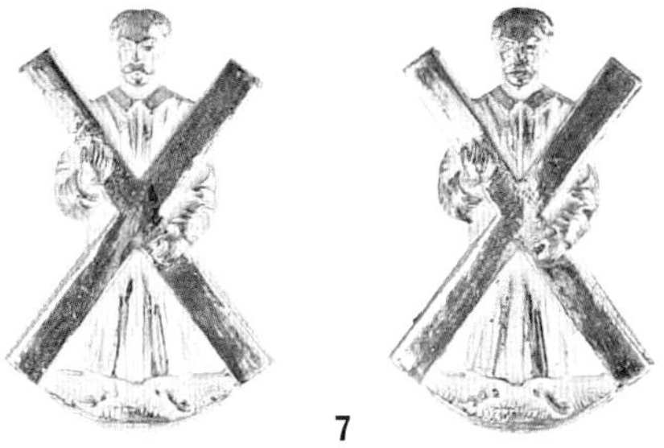

7

8

9

10

11

12

13

14

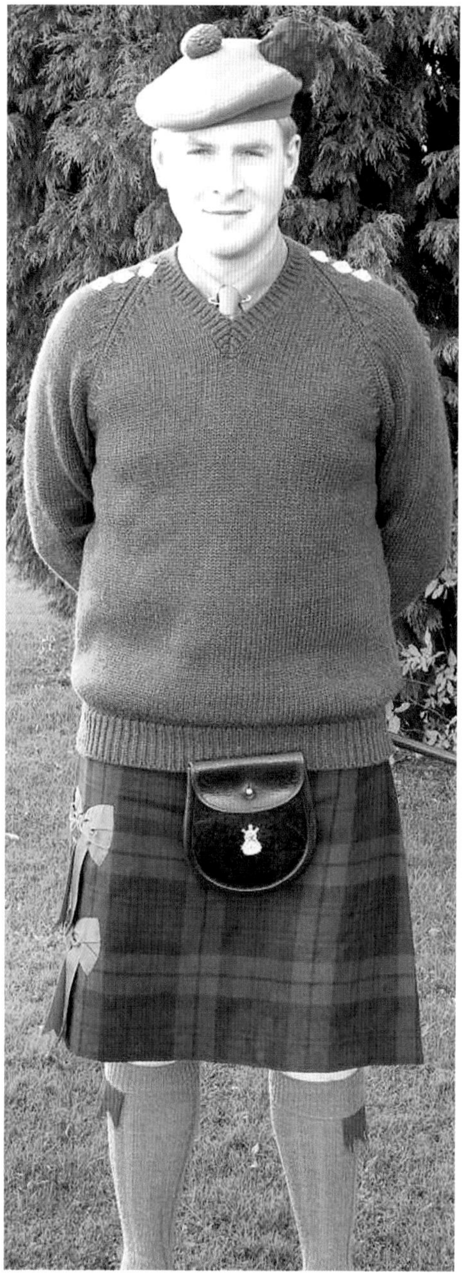

15

19

In 1939 the Black Watch were ordered to hand in their kilts and to wear Battledress instead. This, explained the War Office instruction, was to prevent the regiment being identified. 'But damn it,' (or words to that effect) protested a mortified company sergeant major, 'we want to be recognised.'

16

17

18

20 

21 

The Regiment adopted the sombre Black Watch tartan shortly after its formation from independent Companies. Being the first authorised military tartan it was known as 'Government Tartan'.

22 

23 

opposite page

14 Cpl Darren Leathley wearing No2 Dress ceremonial.

15 Captain James Riddell wearing Barrack Dress.

16 Reproduction 42nd Foot pre-1881 Glengarry badge 5.75 × 7.25 cm worn on the piper's cross belt.

17 Piper's cap badge 5.5 × 7.25 cm.

18 79th Foot pre-1881 officer's Glengarry badge 5.5 × 5.5 cm worn on the piper's cross belt.

19 Sgt Alistair Duthie wearing Full Dress.

this page

20 *Sgian Dubh* 3 × 18 cm.

21 42nd Foot silver belt tip 7.5 × 5.75 cm worn on the piper's cross belt.

22 Piper's plaid brooch 8.75 cm.

23 Pipe Major's waist belt clasp 10 × 8 cm.

24

26

25

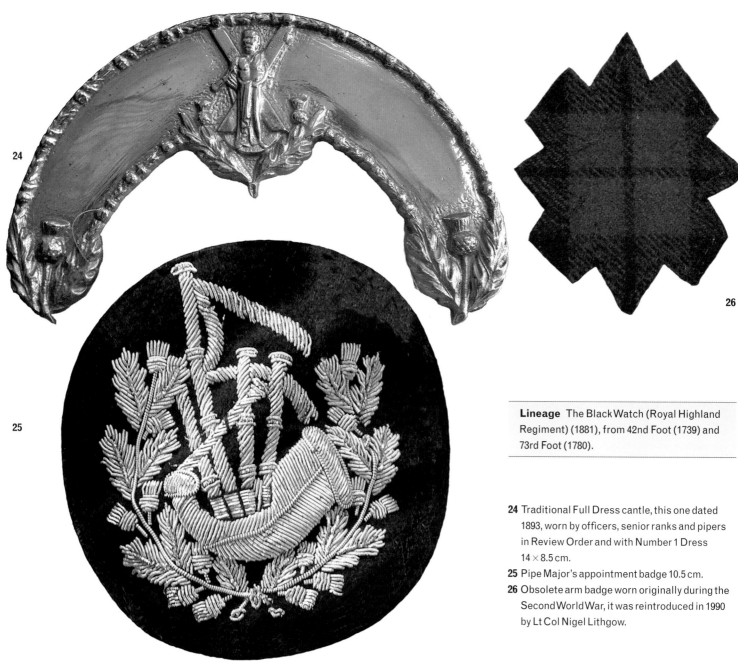

Lineage The Black Watch (Royal Highland Regiment) (1881), from 42nd Foot (1739) and 73rd Foot (1780).

24 Traditional Full Dress cantle, this one dated 1893, worn by officers, senior ranks and pipers in Review Order and with Number 1 Dress 14 × 8.5 cm.

25 Pipe Major's appointment badge 10.5 cm.

26 Obsolete arm badge worn originally during the Second World War, it was reintroduced in 1990 by Lt Col Nigel Lithgow.

Acknowledgement Captain Campbell Close

The Highlanders

(Seaforth, Gordons and Camerons)

The Highlanders was formed by the amalgamation of the Queen's Own Highlanders (Seaforth and Cameron) with The Gordon Highlanders in 1994.

On amalgamation, spoken of as a Union within the Regiment, The Highlanders adopted the cap badge of the Queen's Own Highlanders and the kilt of The Gordon Highlanders. It was decided that the soldiers would wear the officers' handsome three part cap badge with the three dimensional stag's head, but made in bright white metal rather than silver, which was to be worn by officers and Warrant Officers. The silver badge is also awarded as a prize badge to the soldier who passes out top of the Junior Non-Commissioned Officers Cadre. Principally for reasons of cost, a flat two part anodised aluminium badge is worn by junior ranks on the Tam o'Shanter, or ToS. The Highlanders badge is the only British Army badge with a Gaelic motto, *Cuidlich'n Righ*.

Pipers wear an eagle feather above the cap badge. In the presence of the Commanding Officer and royalty the Pipe Major wears two feathers.

1

2

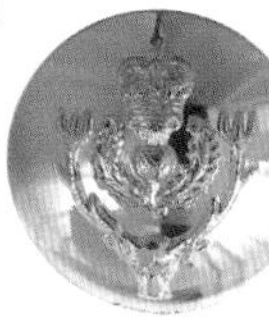

3

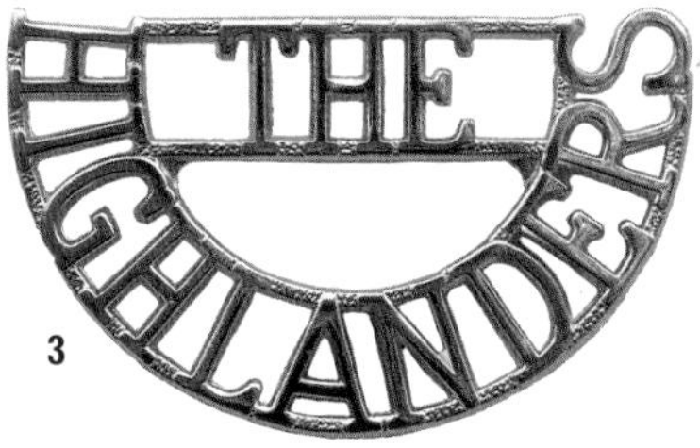

4

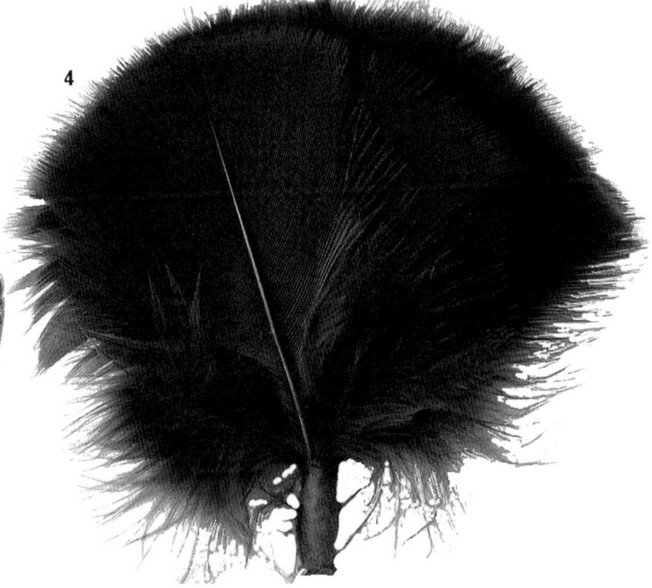

5

6

7

All ranks, except for Pipers and Drummers, wear the Cameron of Erracht tartan as a badge backing on the Tam o'Shanter. Pipers and Drummers wear The Gordon Highlanders tartan badge backing.

The cap badge is large and those serving with commando, airborne and Army Air Corps units and therefore required to wear a beret have worn the top part of the badge or the almost identical sporran badge, the Thistle and Crown Royal Badge of Scotland, as a beret badge.

The tiger collar badge of The Gordon Highlanders, known as the Hindoostan tiger, is worn by officers on Number 1 Dress Ceremonial and by Drummers on Full Dress. The Battle Honour *India* and the *Royal Tiger* had been awarded to the 75th Highlanders, later The Gordon Highlanders, in 1807. The Battle Honour *Hindoostan* had been awarded to the 72nd Foot, later Seaforth Highlanders, in 1806.

Soldiers in Number 1 Dress wear the Queen's Own Highlanders Elephant and Assaye collar badge. The Battle Honour *Assaye* and the *Elephant* had been awarded to the 78th Highlanders in 1807 for the battle fought during the Second Mahratta War in India in 1803.

In a tradition passed down from The Seaforth Highlanders, soldiers do not wear collar badges in other Orders of Dress. In Service Dress officers wear The Gordon Highlanders Sphinx over Egypt collar badge. The Battle Honour *Egypt* and the *Sphinx* had been awarded to the 92nd Highlanders following the campaign against the French in Egypt in 1801. The badge had been worn as a cap badge from 1805 to 1872.

The Pipe Major wears The Seaforth Highlanders elephant collar badges in Full Dress. The Seaforth Highlanders had worn two collar badges. The Elephant was worn in facing pairs alongside a separate cypher F over the motto *Caber Feidh*, translated as *Antlers of the Deer*. The cypher was that of Frederick Duke of York and Albany, Commander in Chief when the 72nd Foot was given the title Duke of Albany's Own Highlanders in 1832.

All ranks, except for Pipers and Drummers, wear The Gordon Highlanders kilt, which was handed down from the 92nd Highlanders. Pipers

In 1837 the 78th Highlanders left Ceylon for Scotland after 11 years taking with them a young elephant, which had been presented by an officer of the 58th Foot and was trained to march at the head of the Band as a living embodiment of the badge. The elephant was presented to the Zoological Gardens, Edinburgh in 1840 but died soon afterwards.

The stag's head badge had been worn by both 72nd and 78th Highlanders, later The Seaforth Highlanders, since they were raised in 1777 and 1793. Traditional has it that in 1266 Alexander III of Scotland was unhorsed whilst hunting in the Forest of Mar and was attacked by a stag. Colin Fitzgerald of Kintail rushed to his Sovereign's aid with a shout of *Cuidich'n Righ*, translated as *Help the King*, and with such a blow severed the stag's head immediately behind its antlers. As a reward Fitzgerald was granted a stag's head with motto *Cuidich'n Righ* as his crest. A descendent of Fitzgerald became the first Earl of Seaforth in 1623. Later Lieutenant Colonel Kenneth MacKenzie, Earl of Seaforth, raised the 72nd Foot. The Regiment's stag's head badge therefore comes from the Arms of the Mackenzies of Seaforth.

The Thistle and Crown, the Royal Badge of Scotland, was conferred on the 79th Foot when it was made The Queen's Own Cameron Highlanders in 1873.

8

9

10

11

12

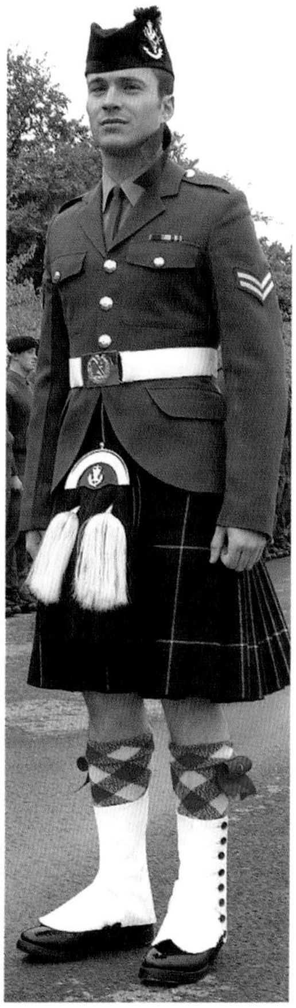

and Drummers wear the Cameron of Erracht tartan kilt handed down from the 79th Highlanders. The reverse to the badge backings worn on the Tam o'Shanter. The Cameron of Erracht tartan is said to be the only surviving military tartan not based on the Black Watch, or Government tartan.

Trews rather than kilts are worn on Fridays. The reason is unclear although it has been suggested that it is because the kilts are laundered on a Friday.

The Highlanders wear black spat buttons, the only regiment to do so, in perpetual mourning for Sir Thomas Moore killed at the Battle of Corunna fought against the French in Spain in 1809.

The Regiment wears 'Bellied Flashes' on the stockings worn with the kilt. The looped flashes commemorate the action by 1st Battalion 92nd Highlanders which charged with the Royal Scots Greys during the Battle of Waterloo in 1815. The Highlanders are said to have held on to the cavalry's stirrups whilst charging with cries of 'Scotland Forever'.

previous page

1 The Highlanders soldier's bright metal three part Glengarry badge 5.75 × 7.5 cm and No1 Dress anodised aluminium collar badges 2.25 × 2.5 cm.
2 The Highlanders button.
3 Bright Metal shoulder title 5 × 3 cm.
4 The Highlanders hackle 9 × 8.5 cm.
5 Lt Nick Charteris wearing the three part cap badge and hackle.
6 Junior ranks two part anodised aluminium ToS badge 5.75 × 7 cm.
7 Cap badge backing.

opposite page

8 Officer's silver cap badge 6 × 8 cm and bronze Service Dress collar badges 3 × 2 cm.
9 Officer's wire-embroidered No 1 Dress Ceremonial collar badges 4 × 3 cm.
10 Pipe Major's gilding metal Full Dress collar badges 3.5 × 2.25 cm.
11 Drummer's anodised aluminium Full Dress collar badges 4 × 2.75 cm.
12 Cpl Ian Cadger wearing No2A Dress with the three part cap badge.

this page

13 Officer's Full Dress cantle.
14 Lieutenant colonel's rank slide.
15 WO1 Joe Darroch BEM wearing Mess Dress with Mackenzie Trews which are worn on Fridays.
16 Officer's silver and soldier's anodised aluminium sporran badges 2.75 × 4 cm.
17 Soldier's shoulder title worn on the pullover 6 × 3.5cm.
18 TRF 3.5 × 3.5cm.

13

14

15

For gallantry at the Battle of Assaye in 1803 the Honourable East India Company awarded the 78th Highlanders an honorary Colour, known as the Assaye Colour.

16

17

18

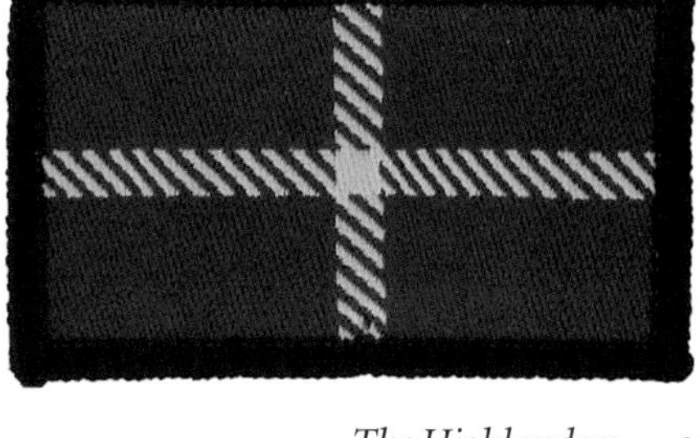

There is a stag's head in the Officers Mess, similar to that used as the design of the cap badge, known as Hector. The cap badge is also referred to by some as Hector. The Gordon Highlanders also had a stag's head in the Officers Mess, which was known as Angus.

19

20

21

22

23

24

25

26

27

28

29

30

31

32

opposite page

19 Officer's waist belt clasp 8.75 × 6 cm.
20 Soldier's waist belt clasp 9 × 6.5 cm.
21 Officer's shoulder belt plate 8 × 10 cm.
22 Capt Barry Macmaster wearing No1A Dress Ceremonial.
23 Lt Tom Walker wearing No2A Service Dress.
24 Lt Tom Hawkins wearing No1B Dress.
25 WO2 Lance Darling wearing No1A Dress.
26 Sgt Colin McCart wearing No1A Dress.
27 Sgt Danny Williamson wearing No1B Dress.
28 DMaj Drummy Clarke wearing Full Dress.

this page

29 Hldr Brian Taylor wearing Full Dress.
30 PMaj Olly Gray MBE wearing Full Dress.
31 LCpl Richard Grisdale wearing No1A Dress.
32 LCpl Andrew Stainthorpe No2A Dress.
33 Piper's plaid brooch 9 cm.
34 Piper's waist belt clasp 9 × 7.5 cm.

33

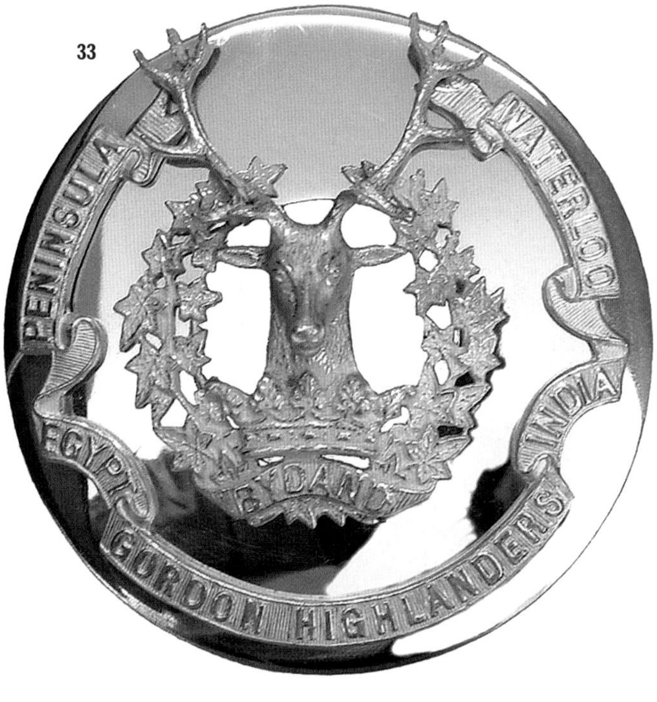

34

The Royal blue hackle was adopted in France in 1940 by 1st Battalion The Queen's Own Cameron Highlanders with the approval of the Colonel-in-Chief, King George VI. Shortly after kilted regiments had been ordered to wear Battle Dress trousers, the Commanding Officer ordered that in order to maintain a distinction the white hackle normally worn with the tropical helmet was to be worn on the balmoral. King George V inspected the battalion in December 1939 and approved the hackle but suggested that Royal Blue was more appropriate. Eight hundred hackles were made up and the battalion wore them at Arras for the first time in February 1940. The battalion also continued to wear the kilt, and was the last to wear it in action, memorably during the famous counter-attack against General Rommel at the River Escaut in May 1940. The hackle was eventually authorised in 1951, retained by The Queen's Own Highlanders on amalgamation in 1961 and again by The Highlanders on amalgamation in 1994. It is worn with the glengarry and the balmoral, except for pipers in Full Dress who wear an eagle feather in lieu of the hackle. The hackle is also worn by The Liverpool Scottish (see The King's and Cheshire Regiment) and The Queen's Own Cameron Highlanders of Canada.

35

36

37

38

39

40

41

Lineage The Highlanders (1994) from The Queen's Own Highlanders (Seaforth and Camerons) (1961) and The Gordon Highlanders (1881). The Queen's Own Highlanders from The Seaforth Highlanders (Ross-shire Buffs, The Duke of Albany's) (1881), formerly 72nd Foot (1777) and 78th Foot (1793), and The Queen's Own Cameron Highlanders (1881), formerly 79th Foot (1793). The Gordon Highlanders from 75th Foot (1787) and 92nd Foot (1793).

opposite page

Piper's Shoulder Belt badges

35 Top badge 6.5 × 7.5 cm.
36 Middle badge 5.25 × 5.25 cm.
37 Slide 7.5 × 3 cm.
38 Pipe Major's waist belt clasp. 9 × 7.25 cm.
39 Drum Major and Pipe Major's regimental appointment badge 10.5 × 11 cm
40 Pipe Major's Full Dress cantle.

this page

41 Drum Major and Pipe Major's rank and appointment badges.
42 Drummer's waist belt clasp 9.5 × 7 cm.

42

Acknowledgement
Maj Cameron Humphires, Capt Matt Munro and Jonnie Williams, WO1 (RSM) RG Christie and DMaj Drew Caldwell

Pipers

Pipers' badges were authorised in 1949, having been adopted in about 1940 during the widespread adoption of badges of all kinds during the build up of the Army after Dunkirk. Pipers have served with the Army since at least 1684, although they were not authorised as part of the establishment until 1854 when some Highland regiments were authorised pipers. All Highland regiments were allowed pipers on their establishment in 1881 and this was extended to Lowland regiments in 1918.

The badges now worn have three drones and the ribbon appears to represent tartan. From 1949–1977 the badge issued to pipers in Irish Regiments had two drones and plain ribbons.

'Macleod, the regimental piper, who was amongst the first to force his way through at the front breach, and then began to play his bagpipes, and continued to do so throughout the fighting, in places perfectly exposed, and, as Captain Burgoyne remarks, 'doubtless to the astonishment of the Sepoys.'

(From the records of the 93rd Sutherland Highlanders. The assault of the Begum's Palace, Lucknow 11 March 1858.)

1

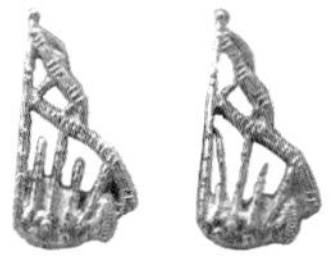

2

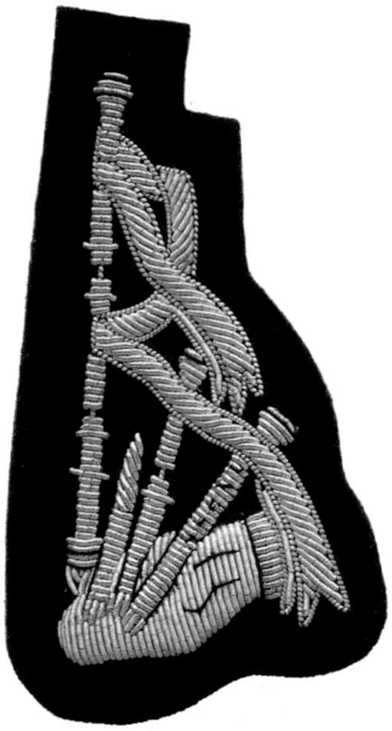

3

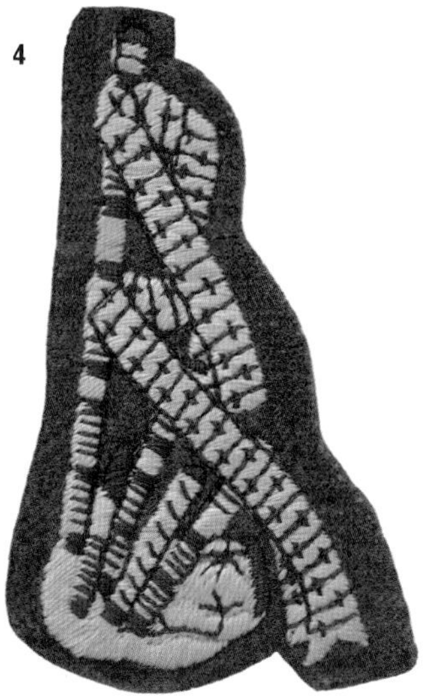

4

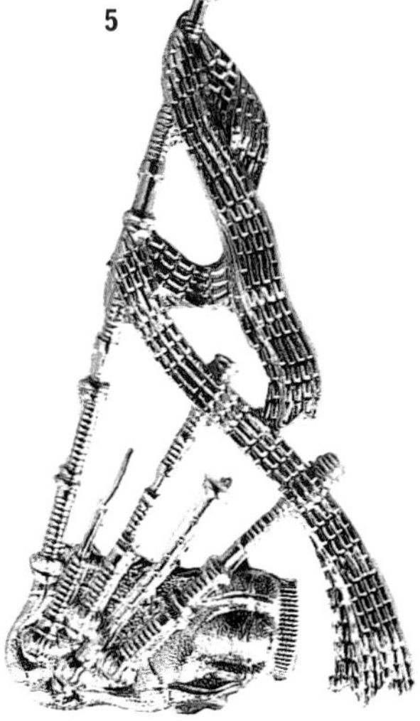

5

6

7

The origins of the bagpipe are lost although there is a strong possibility that the pipes are part of a culture inherited from the Celts, as various forms of Celtic pipes survive throughout Europe. However it was in the Scottish glens that the *Piob-mhòr*, or Great Highland Pipe was developed and pipers have always accompanied Scottish warriors. At Culloden in 1746 the Duke of Cumberland watched the loyal Regiments of Munro, Campbell and Sutherland march past with their pipers and is reported to have asked, 'What are these men going to do with such bundles of sticks? I can supply them with better weapons of war.' A Scottish officer assured him, 'Your Highness cannot do so. These are the bagpipes, the Highlanders' music in peace and war. Wanting these, all other instruments are of no avail.'

After the suppression of the rebellion the Courts of Justice declared the playing of the pipes to be a treasonable act. At his trial in York, Piper James Reid pleaded that he did not carry a weapon during the rebellion. The judge decided that as a Highland regiment never marched without a piper, bagpipes were a weapon. Reid was hanged as a traitor.

opposite page

1 Pipe Major's Full Dress wire-embroidered appointment badge 10 × 9.25 cm (also made on green and red backings)

2 Piper's anodised aluminium miniature wristlet badges in both gold and silver anodised aluminium 0.75 × 1.5 cm.

3 Piper's No1 Dress badge 4.5 × 7.75 cm.

4 Piper's No2 Dress appointment badge 4.5 × 7 cm.

5 Anodised aluminium appointment badge 3.75 × 6.75 cm.

6 Anodised aluminium Irish piper's badge 3.5 × 7 cm.

this page

7 Highland drummer Drum Major's Full Dress wire-embroidered appointment badges 10 × 9.5 cm (also made on green backings).

The Argyll and Sutherland Highlanders

(Princess Louise's)

The Argyll and Sutherland Highlanders, the immortal 'Thin Red Line' was formed by the amalgamation of the 91st Princess Louise's Argyllshire Highlanders and 93rd Sutherland Highlanders in 1881.

The Argyll and Sutherland Highlanders, or A&SH, has the largest and possibly the oldest metal cap badge in the Army. The badge was adopted in 1881 on the amalgamation of the 91st and 93rd Foot and was based closely upon that previously worn by the 93rd Foot since about 1820. There have been subtle differences in the badge since 1881, principally in the position of the cat's tail, and whether the centre is void or solid, and in the material.

Officers wear a silver badge, whilst soldiers wear both old and reproduced white metal badges, although the issued badge is produced in anodised aluminium.

The collar badge introduced in about 1884 is a complicated heraldic mix. The Boar's head over a scroll inscribed *Ne obliviscaris* within a wreath of myrtle intertwined with a wreath of butcher's broom enclosing a wildcat upon a scroll bearing *Sans peur*, represent the Sutherland clan. The cadency mark of Princess Louise is an heraldic label with three points, the middle one bearing a rose, and the other two a billet.

1

2

3

4

5

6

7

8

9

The regiment has a sporran decorated with a badge of two reversed and intertwined letters L surmounted by a coronet, for Princess Louise, with a boar's head at the left and a wildcat at the right.

In ceremonial dress officers and sergeants wear a sporran decorated with a badger's head which was introduced by Lieutenant Colonel Sir Charles Gordon, Commanding Officer 93rd Foot from 1823 to 1826.

The red and white diced arm badge, which had been in use since at least the Second World War, was superseded by a Tactical Recognition Flash in 2003. The Glengarry bonnet with regimental diced border had been authorised for the 93rd Sutherland Highlanders in 1851.

The 1st Battalion was placed under command of 16 Air Assault Brigade in 2003 and required to adopt a Landing Zone flash. The regiment adopted a square of Government Tartan worn on its point, mounted with the regiment's traditional red and white diced strip. Worn correctly, there is a red square at each end of the top row. The obsolete arm badge worn in 1995 during an operational deployment to Northern Ireland inspired The King's Royal Hussars in the adjoining Tactical Area of Responsibility to adopt its own arm badge.

The Plaid Brooch is a solid cast silver quoit decorated with regimental devices.

Unlike many regiments The Argyll and Sutherland Highlanders have a waist belt plate with a badge differing from the cap badge. The design is based on the collar badge with the addition of title scrolls.

In Number 1 Dress officers wear a cross belt which supports the Scottish Broadsword. The cross belt plate is decorated with a design similar to that of the waist belt plate but with greater detail, including 15 battle honours.

10

At Balaclava in the Crimea on 25 October 1854 a Russian assault overran in succession three redoubts manned by Turkish troops. The 93rd Sutherland Highlanders were drawn up in two ranks facing the advancing Russian army. William Russell reported for *The Times*:

> The Russians in one grand line dashed at the Highlanders. The ground flies beneath their horses' feet: gathering speed at every stride, they dash on towards that thin red streak tipped with a line of steel. As the Russians come within six hundred yards, down goes that line of steel in front, and out rings a rolling volley of Minié musketry. The distance is too great; the Russians are not checked but still sweep onwards through the smoke. With breathless suspense every one awaits the bursting of the wave upon the line of Gaelic rock; but ere they come within a hundred and fifty yards, another deadly volley flashes from the levelled rifle, and carries death and terror into the Russians. They wheel about, open files right and left, and fly back faster than they come. "Bravo, Highlanders! Well Done!"'

11

opposite page

1 The Argyll and Sutherland Highlanders soldier's anodised aluminium cap badge 6 × 8 cm and collar badges 4.75 × 2.75 cm.
2 Anodised aluminium shoulder title 3.75 × 1 cm.
3 No1 Dress officer's silver and gilt collar badges 4.75 × 2.75 cm.
4 A and SH button.
5 No2 Dress officer's bronze collar badges 4.75 × 2.75 cm.
6 WO2 Mac McKenzie wearing a private purchase Tam o'Shanter with Combat Dress.
7 Sgt William Gilmour wearing Barrack Dress.
8 LCpl Andrew Marshall wearing Combat Dress with the distinctive rank brassard which is shared with the Black Watch.
9 WO2 Colin McFarlane wearing the TRF.

this page

10 Cap badge backing.
11 Cpl Kenny Brown wearing No2 Dress.
12 The Queen's Colour carried by Lt Johnny MacKley, escorted by CSgts Scott MacKenzie and Davie Laird.

12

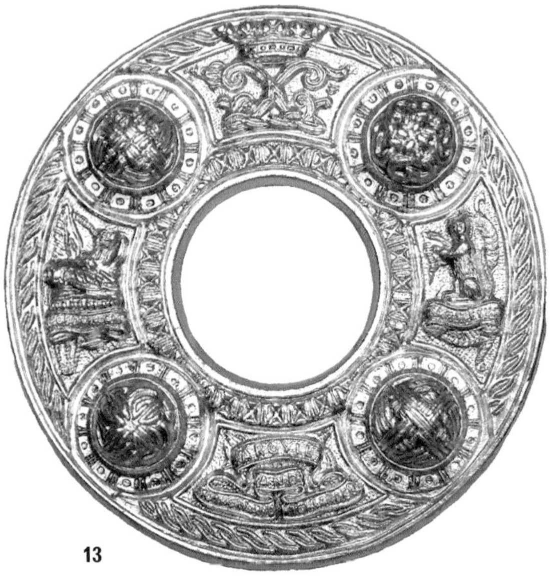

13

16

17

18

14

Lineage The Argyll and Sutherland Highlanders (Princess Louise's) (1881) from 91st Foot (1794) and 93rd Foot (1799).

15

19

13 Silver Plaid Brooch 7.75 cm.

14 Officer's silver on gilt waist belt clasp 7 × 5.5 cm.

15 Officer's silver on gilt shoulder belt plate 7.5 × 9.5 cm.

16 Obsolete arm badge 7.5 × 3.5 cm.

17 Sporran badge 2.25 × 3 cm.

18 Landing Zone Flash 9 × 9 cm adopted by the 1st Battalion in 2003.

19 Officer's cap badge 5.75 × 7.75 cm, this example hallmarked 1943.

Acknowledgement WO1 (RSM) J Howe

The Parachute Regiment

The Parachute Regiment was formed in 1942 from existing parachute units.

The Parachute Regiment, or PARA, cap badge has remained unchanged in design from that introduced in 1943 with the exception of the change to St Edward's (or Queen's) Crown in about 1955.

The anodised aluminium badge was introduced in about 1958 and service in Northern Ireland in the 1970s led to the introduction of a black cap badge. The black badge is no longer worn in the battalions but is worn by some soldiers serving in training units. Silver badges are authorised for officers and the issue badges are now manufactured in white metal and worn by all ranks.

In 1990, to mark the 50th anniversary of The Parachute Regiment and Airborne Forces, Prince Charles presented the first Prince of Wales's Badge to an outstanding recruit. The badge, worn on the left upper arm in all forms of dress was not awarded to a recruit from every intake but only to a recruit considered by the training staff to be outstanding, and to possess qualities and potential not normally expected of a recruit. In this respect it differs from the Royal Marines' King's Badge, presented to the best recruit from each intake. The Prince of Wales's badge was awarded to sixteen soldiers between 1990 and 1992 when the awards were stopped on the closure of the Depot The Parachute Regiment. It is believed that only one of those soldiers awarded the badge, Colour Sergeant Arny Armstrong, is still serving.

Until 1953 The Parachute Regiment was manned by volunteers from across the Army, in that year direct enlistment for soldiers was authorised. The direct commissioning of officers into the Regiment was authorised in 1958. The Parachute Regiment continues to accept volunteers from other regiments and corps; two years for officers and three for soldiers. All wear The Parachute Regiment insignia whilst with the Regiment.

1

2

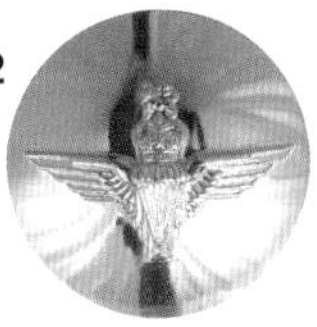

3

4

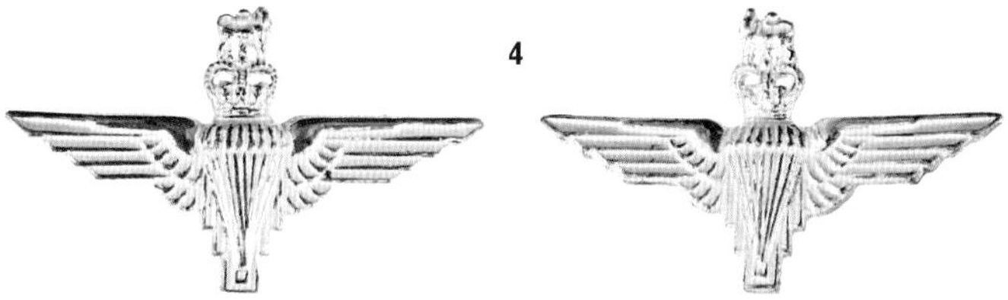

5

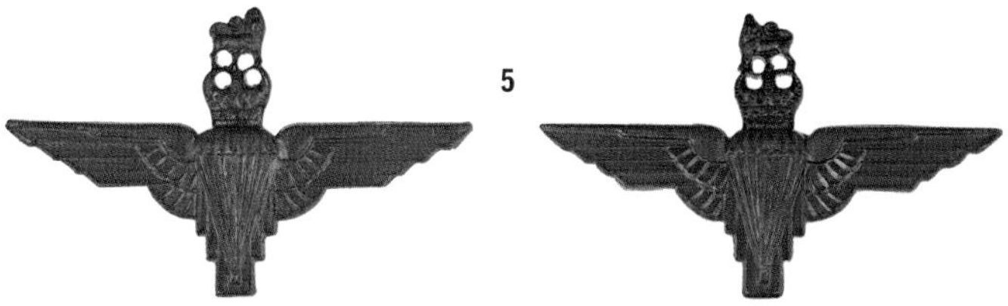

6

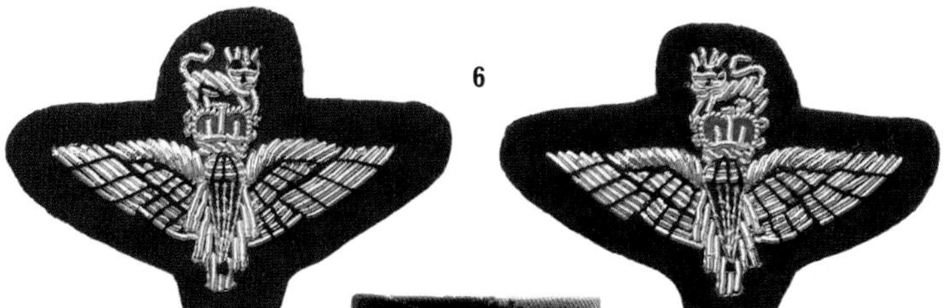

7

8

9

The Parachute Regiment retains Drop Zone, or DZ, flashes for each unit of the regiment rather than wearing a single Tactical Recognition Flash. All four battalions have separate coloured DZ flashes, and as a unique distinction regimental headquarters of the Parachute Regiment is also authorised a DZ flash in order that those no longer serving or eligible to serve with a parachute battalion, in particular officers over the age of 44, can wear a regimental distinction.

Officers over the age of 44 are no longer considered for command, and the category also includes those who have been promoted to the rank of colonel or above. However it has become the practice for officers promoted from lieutenant colonel to wear the DZ flash of their last battalion, or indeed none.

In common with all regiments, The Parachute Regiment no longer has a Depot although the Depot PARA DZ flash has been retained for those serving with recruit training units.

Minute from Prime Minister
To Chiefs of Staff
22 June 1940

We ought to have a Corps of at least 5,000 parachute troops. I hear something is being done already to form such a Corps but only, I believe, on a very small scale. Advantage must be taken of the summer to train these forces who can none the less play their part meanwhile as shock troops in home defence. Pray let me have a note from the War Office on the subject.

Winston S Churchill

A Parachute Training School was formed in 1940 and Number 2 Commando selected for training as 11th Special Air Service Battalion, renamed in 1941 1st Parachute Battalion. The Parachute Regiment was formally established in 1942.

10

11

13

12

14

15

16

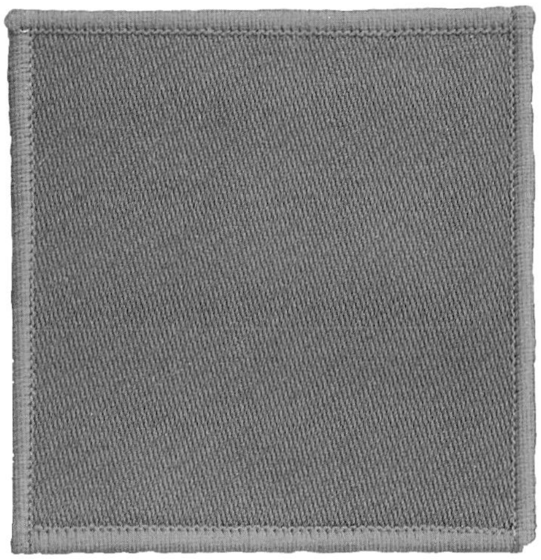

17

18

19

previous page

1 The Parachute Regiment white metal cap badge 7 × 4.5 cm and soldier's anodised aluminium collar badges 4 × 2.25 cm.
2 PARA button.
3 Black cap badge 7 × 6.5 cm.
4 Silver No 1 Dress officer's collar badges 4 × 2.5 cm.
5 Bronze Service Dress officer's collar badges 4 × 2.5 cm.
6 Mess Dress wire-embroidered officer's collar badges 4.75 × 3.5 cm.
7 Prince of Wales's Combat Dress badge 3.5 cm.
8 Captain's rank slide.
9 Prince of Wales's No 2 Dress badge 4 cm.

opposite page

10 CSgt Tony Hobbins wearing No1 Dress with the Royal Military Academy Sandhurst waist belt plate.
11 Parachute Regiment Drop Zone Flashes. Sgt Joey Madden 1 PARA, Cpl Geordie Redden 2 PARA, LCpl Mark Mills 3 PARA and Cpl Frankie Vaughn Depot PARA.
12 WO2 Smudge Smith, WO1 (RSM) Andy Stone, HRH The Duke of York in the uniform of Colonel in Chief The Staffordshire Regiment, WO1 Paul Mort and Sgt Rocky Rowlands all served during the Falkland War 1982.
13 Cpl Simpson and Sgt Ackroyd in No2 Dress. The pale blue and maroon lanyards, the same colours as their Depot PARA DZ flashes, indicate they are serving with a recruit training unit.
14 Major Dave Robson wearing the 1 PARA DZ flash.

this page

15 RHQ PARA DZ flash 7 × 7 cm.
16 Depot PARA DZ flash 7 × 7 cm.
17 1 PARA DZ flash 7 × 7 cm.
18 2 PARA DZ flash 7 × 7 cm.
19 3 PARA DZ flash 7 × 7 cm.

Lineage The Parachute Regiment (1942)

Acknowledgement
Maj AV Clark, Capt CJ Humm and Ollie Kingsbury, WO1 (RSM) JR Chetty and Paul Raison

Airborne Forces

British Airborne Forces began parachute training in 1940. There are now parachute troops from almost every Arm and Service, principally serving with Special Forces, 3 Commando Brigade and 16 Air Assault Brigade.

The Special Air Service, or SAS, wears a different parachute qualification badge (see SAS p.226). During the Second World War SAS troops who had been engaged on a 'conspicuous service operation' or completed an operational parachute descent transferred their parachute wings from the right sleeve to the left breast above any medal ribbons. The background to this might be in the original 1940 proposal for qualification badges for parachutists and commandos 'comparable to the 'wings' of the Royal Air Force'. The SAS parachute badge, although approved in theatre by Major General Neil Richie had not received approval from the Army Dress Committee and was not finally recognised until 1948. At the end of the war the ADC directed that those who had gained SOE wings or SAS 'Sabre' wings were to transfer them from the left breast to the upper right sleeve, the only qualification badge allowed on the left breast was the Army Flying Badge. During the Second World War the parachute course involved four training descents, this taken together with the SOE and SAS traditions has led to a continuing belief amongst some that parachute wings may be worn on the left breast after completing three operational parachute descents. No serving soldier has completed more than two operational parachute jumps to date.

Assistant Parachute Jump Instructors wear a special qualification badge. The APJI assist in preparing soldiers for parachuting and the qualification is said to be more likely to be gained by those serving with the Territorial Army in than with Regular units.

Qualified parachutists who were neither regular parachute troops nor instructors wear a parachute badge on the left forearm. The badge, which is almost obsolete, was one of the prototype designs for the qualified parachutist badge and was worn by some early instructors before parachute 'wings' were authorised in 1940. In recent years the badge, known as the 'Light Bulb' was in the majority of cases awarded to Officer Cadets and their instructors who completed the discontinued 'Edward Bear' course from the Royal Military Academy Sandhurst.

To qualify as a parachutist all ranks must complete a parachute course and complete a minimum of eight descents. It is generally understood that in accordance with the instruction published in ACI 395 in 1948 the parachute qualification badge may also be worn after an operational jump, although this assertion is not covered by The Queen's Regulations which states:

- **a** Parachute descents, other than forced descents, are to be made only by:
- **1** Trained parachutists whose duties require it.
- **2** Service personnel on authorised training courses...

During the Second World War Special Operation Executive, or SOE, operatives wore their parachute badge above any medal ribbons on the left breast after competing an operational parachute descent into enemy held territory and successfully returning to the UK or other friendly territory.

1

2

3

4

5

6

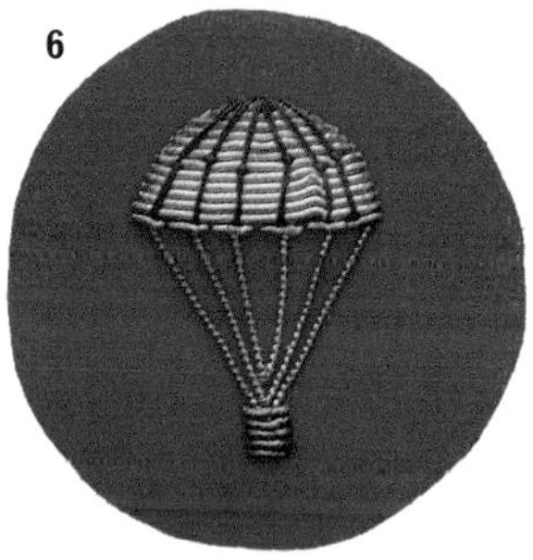

7

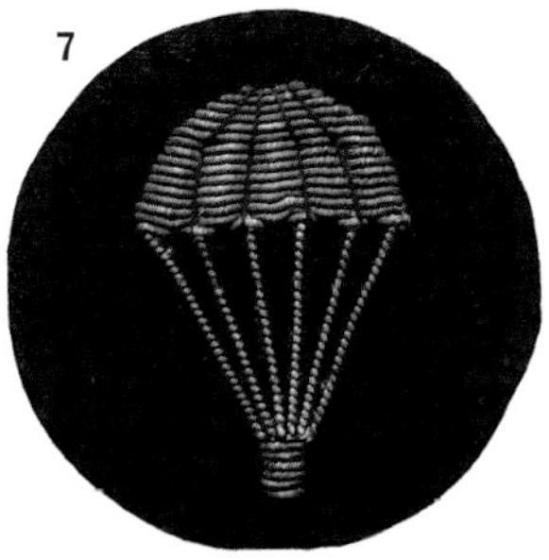

10

8

9

11

opposite page

1 Parachute badge introduced in 1940 10.5 × 4 cm.
2 Assistant Parachute Jump Instructor badge introduced in 1955 7.75 × 4 cm.
3 Private purchase subdued parachute badge 9.75 × 4 cm.

this page

4 Full Dress wire-embroidered parachute badge 9 × 4 cm.
5 No 1 Dress wire-embroidered parachute badge 9 × 4 cm.
6 Mess Dress wire-embroidered parachute badge worn on the left forearm 4 cm.
7 No1 Dress wire-embroidered parachute badge worn on the left forearm 4 cm.
8 The principle airborne units are the battalions of The Parachute Regiment. Major Dan Jarvis wears the green DZ flash of 3 PARA below his parachute badge.
9 OCdt Gerald Hennigan wearing the parachute badge whilst at the Royal Military Academy Sandhurst having spent 12 years as a chef with parachute and commando units before being selected for officer training.
10 Lt Col Niall MacGregor-Smith wearing Service Dress with the parachute badge on his lower left sleeve.
11 Woven No2 Dress parachute badge worn on the left forearm 5 × 5 cm.

The Brigade of Gurkhas

Kaphar Hunnu Bhanda Mornu Ramro Chhaa

The Brigade of Gurkhas was formed in 1948 from The Gurkha Regiment which had been formed earlier in the year to administer the Gurkha regiments which were transferring from the Indian Army to the British Army.

The Brigade of Gurkhas, or BG, consists of The Royal Gurkha Rifles, The Queen's Gurkha Engineers, The Queen's Gurkha Signals, Queen's Own Gurkha Logistic Regiment, The Band of the Brigade of Gurkhas, Gurkha Company, 3rd Battalion, Infantry Training Centre Catterick, Gurkha Company (Sitang), Royal Military Academy Sandhurst, Gurkha Company (Mandalay), Infantry Battle School Brecon, Brigade of Gurkhas Training Team, and the Gurkha Language Wing, Catterick.

The design of the Brigade of Gurkhas, or BG, badge and indeed the individual regimental badges is based upon crossed kukris, the traditional Gurkha fighting knife. The plain crossed kukri badge is issued on enlistment in Nepal and worn during recruit training.

The British Gurkha camp in Pokhara is the focal point for all recruiting activities in Nepal. In December each year the culmination of procedures sees 370 young men being selected, 230 for the British Army and 140 for the Gurkha Contingent of the Singapore Police Force.

On enlistment the Gurkha recruits are given their Army numbers, eight numbers as for all British soldiers. As there are really only three surnames amongst the Gurkhas they are immediately known by their last four numbers and even those who are commissioned as Queen's Gurkha Officers usually retain their 'last four'.

In retirement many Gurkhas enlist in the Gurkha Reserve Unit in Brunei.

1

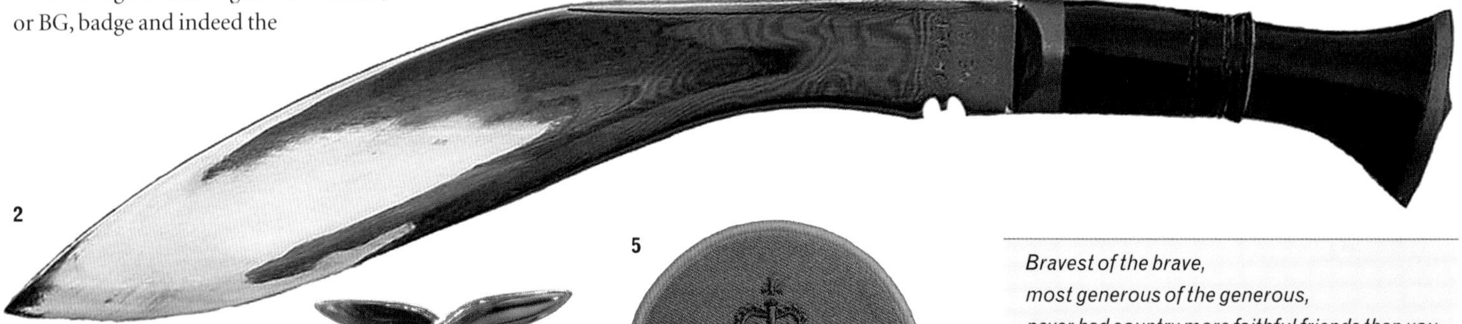

2

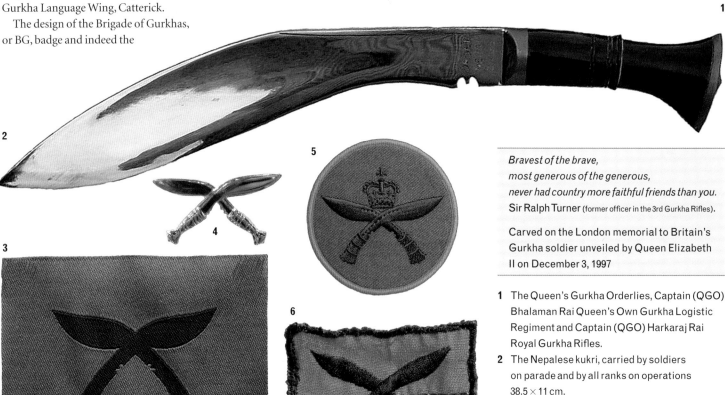

Bravest of the brave,
most generous of the generous,
never had country more faithful friends than you.
Sir Ralph Turner (former officer in the 3rd Gurkha Rifles).

Carved on the London memorial to Britain's Gurkha soldier unveiled by Queen Elizabeth II on December 3, 1997

4

5

3

6

1 The Queen's Gurkha Orderlies, Captain (QGO) Bhalaman Rai Queen's Own Gurkha Logistic Regiment and Captain (QGO) Harkaraj Rai Royal Gurkha Rifles.
2 The Nepalese kukri, carried by soldiers on parade and by all ranks on operations 38.5 × 11 cm.
3 Brigade of Gurkhas TRF 7.75 × 5.75 cm.
4 Gurkha recruit cap badge 3.5 × 2 cm.
5 Gurkha tracksuit badge 7.75cm.
6 British Gurkhas Pokhara arm badge 5.5 × 4 cm.

Royal Gurkha Rifles

The Royal Gurkha Rifles was formed by the amalgamation of The 2nd King Edward VII's Own Gurkha Rifles (The Sirmoor Rifles), The 6th Queen Elizabeth's Own Gurkha Rifles, The 7th Duke of Edinburgh's Own Gurkha Rifles, and The 10th Princess Mary's Own Gurkha Rifles in 1994.

The Royal Gurkha Rifles, or RGR, badge of crossed kukris surmounted by a Crown is produced in silver for officers and nickel for soldiers although all ranks usually wear the nickel badge on the beret. A small badge mounted on a black cord boss is worn by officers on the side hat.

Gurkhas are issued the Hat Felt Gurkha, its official designation in the stores, for wear with Number 2 Dress. The cap badge is worn on the right side on a square of Royal Hunting Stuart tartan.

Collar badges are worn only by Queen's Gurkha Officers and by senior ranks on Number 10 Dress, the Warm Weather Mess Dress.

1

2

3

4

5

6
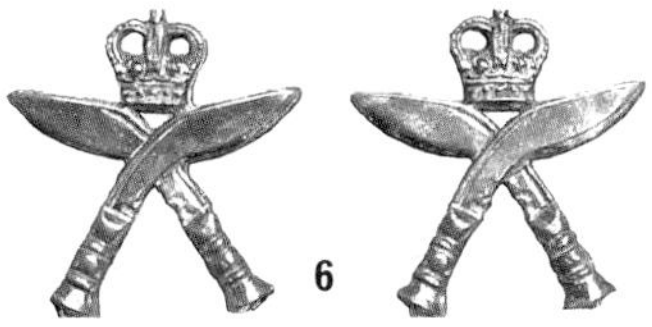
7

8

9

10

11
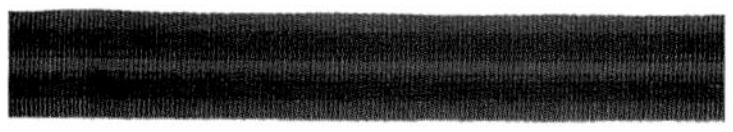
12

13

14

15

16

17

18

20

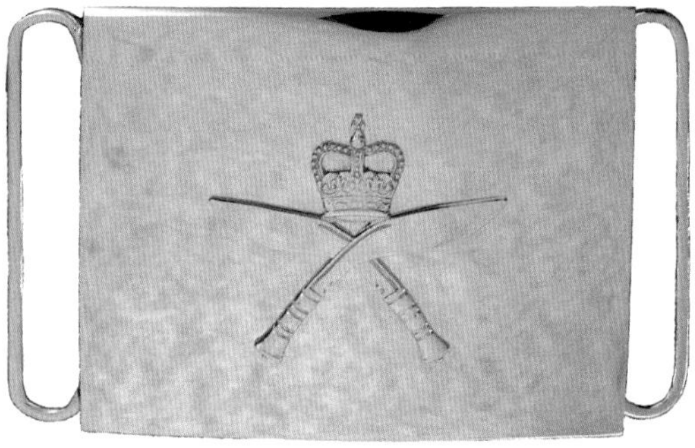

21

Lineage Royal Gurkha Rifles (1994) from 2nd King Edward VII's Own Goorka Rifles (The Sirmoor Rifles) (1815), 6th Queen Elizabeth's Own Gurkha Rifles (1817), 7th Duke of Edinburgh's Own Gurkha Rifles (1902) and 10th Princess Mary's Own Gurkha Rifles (1887).

22

19

23

During the Indian Mutiny, 1857–1858, the 2nd Goorkhas showed striking proof of their loyalty at Delhi where, together with the 60th Rifles (now Royal Green Jackets), they held Hindu Rao's house, the key to the British position which was under continuous fire from the mutineers for over three months. During this period the 2nd Goorkhas suffered 327 casualties, including 8 of their 9 British Officers, out of a total strength of 490. In recognition of the close relationship between the two regiments Queen's Gurkha Officers wear a piece of Royal Green Jackets regimental ribbon under their badges of rank.

24

25

26

At the end of the Nepalese War in 1816 it was agreed that Nepalese could be enlisted into the armies of the Honourable East India Company. After the abolition of the Company following the Indian Mutiny in 1858 the Gurkha regiments were transferred to the British Indian Army. In 1947, on Indian independence, under a tripartite agreement between India, Nepal and the United Kingdom four regiments transferred to the British Army and six remained with the Indian Army. The British later raised additional specialist Gurkha units.

All Gurkha recruits are trained together as infantry before some undertake special to arm training.

previous page

1 Royal Gurkha Rifles officer's silver cap badge3.5 × 3.25 cm.
2 All ranks nickel cap badge 3.5 × 3 cm.
3 Black operational badge 3.5 × 3 cm.
4 Shoulder title 3 × 1 cm.
5 RGR button.
6 Queen's Gurkha Officers and senior ranks warm weather Mess Dress collar badges 2 × 2 cm.
7 Officer's side cap badge 3 × 3 cm (badge 2 × 1.75 cm).
8 Captain's rank slide.
9 Royal Hunting Stuart tartan backing for the Hat Felt Gurkha.
10 Queen's Gurkha Officer captain's rank slide.
11 RGJ regimental ribbon worn by Queen's Gurkha Officers under their rank badges.
12 Major Surya Upadhya wearing Service Dress.
13 Captain Campbell Lyle wearing Combat Dress with the brigade of Gurkhas TRF on his right sleeve. Until 2004 the regiment provided a reinforcement company to The Parachute Regiment and parachute 'Wings' are not uncommon.
14 1 RGR printed jungle hat badge 6.75 × 8.25 cm.

opposite page

15 LCpls Nabin Gurung and Buddhi Sunuwar 1 RGR with the Brigade of Gurkhas TRF on their right shoulders, and LCpls Basanta Rai and Chola Limbu 2 RGR with the Brunei Garrison badge on their left sleeves.
16 Ppr Bhim Pun, Dmr Gun Thapa, Ppr Nirmal Thapa, Dmr Min Thapa and Ppr Tik Gurung 1 RGR wearing the large cap badges and waist belt plates. The pipers wear the cross belts and plaid brooches.
17 Piper's cap badge 5 × 4.5 cm.
18 Officer's whistle boss 5 cm.
19 Pipe major's plaid brooch
20 Officer's cross belt plate 7.5 × 9 cm.
21 RGR soldier's waist belt clasp 7 × 5.5 cm.
22 Pipers plaid brooch 8.5 cm.

this page

23 Officer's leather pouch with silver The King's Royal Hussars badge.
24 Pouch badge 2.75 × 3.5 cm.
25 Pipers waist belt clasp 9.5 × 7 cm.
26 Queen's Truncheon of the 1st Battalion carried by Lt (QGO) Dilip Thapa, escorted by Sgts Moti Sunwar and Rohit Gurung.

Acknowledgement
Major Claude Davidson, Capt Charlie Timmis and John Meredith

The Royal Green Jackets

The Royal Green Jackets was formed by the amalgamation of the 1st, 2nd and 3rd Green Jackets in 1966.

The centre of The Royal Green Jackets, or RGJ, badge is a bugle horn, the traditional badge of rifle and light infantry regiments, mounted on a Maltese cross derived from the former badges of both The King's Royal Rifle Corps and The Rifle Brigade. Battle honours are listed on the four arms of the cross, as the regiment does not carry Colours on which to display the Honours. The naval crown at the base of the Cross commemorates The Rifle Brigade's action at the Battle of Copenhagen, 1801. The issue anodised aluminium badge is not popular; it has been likened to recycled milk bottle tops, and many officers and soldiers buy a nickel badge from the PRI. Officers may buy a silver cap badge on commissioning but usually wear a nickel badge. The 3rd Battalion was identified by blackened beret badges. Originally painted, in 1989 black plastic badges were sold through battalion PRI shops.

Officers wear a miniature bugle badge on a cord boss (sometimes referred to as a worm cast) on the front of the side hat.

6

10

The Regiment has two waist belt clasps. Instructors and Staff such as the regimental police wear the universal pattern plate mounted with a cap badge. The Snake clasp is the usual order of dress on parade and dates from the formation of the Regiment.

Riflemen in the 2nd Battalion wear a regimental slide without a rank. In the 1st Battalion slides are worn only by lance corporals and above. 1 RGJ wore an arm badge until 1999 and 2 RGJ considered a variation. Both were superseded by a regimental TRF in 2004 although it is only worn by the RGJ TA companies.

Officers wear a cross belt and pouch. King's Royal Rifle Corps and Rifle Brigade cross belts are widely worn by officers, whilst those Warrant Officers issued a cross belt wear the Royal Green Jackets pattern.

In recognition of its distinguished service during the Napoleonic War, culminating in the Battle of Waterloo the 95th Foot was removed from the numbered regiments of the line in 1816 and constituted as a separate corps as The Rifle Brigade. It ranked as 'Left of the Line', a distinction inherited by The Royal Green Jackets.

11

12

13

14

15

opposite page

1 Royal Green Jackets soldier's anodised aluminium cap badge 4 × 5 cm and black collar badges 2 × 1.5 cm.
2 Officer's side hat badge 2.5 cm.
3 Shoulder title 2.5 × 2.5 cm.
4 RGJ Warrant Officer's ball button.
5 RGJ soldier's button.
6 WO2 Andy Spalding wearing the nickel cap badge and regimental rank slide.
7 Officer's silver cap badge 4 × 5 cm and blackened collar badges 2 × 1.5 cm.
8 Private purchase nickel cap badge 4 × 5 cm.
9 Black plastic cap badge 4 × 5 cm.

this page

10 CSgts Lee Rider and Tony Weeks wearing pullover order with ranks on brassards and shoulder titles on the epaulettes.
11 Lt Col Roddy Winser wearing the TRF.
12 Obsolete arm badge 5 × 3 cm worn 1997–1999.
13 2 RGJ proposed and now obsolete arm badge 6 × 3 cm.
14 TRF 7 × 6 cm.
15 Cpl Sean Martin wearing No1 Dress.
16 Corporal's rank slide.
17 2 RGJ Rifleman's rank slide.
18 Snake waist belt clasp 6 × 4 cm.

The bugle horn was granted as a badge to Rifle Regiments and Light Infantry in 1814. The Maltese Cross was also used as a badge by the Light Dragoons and represented light troops.

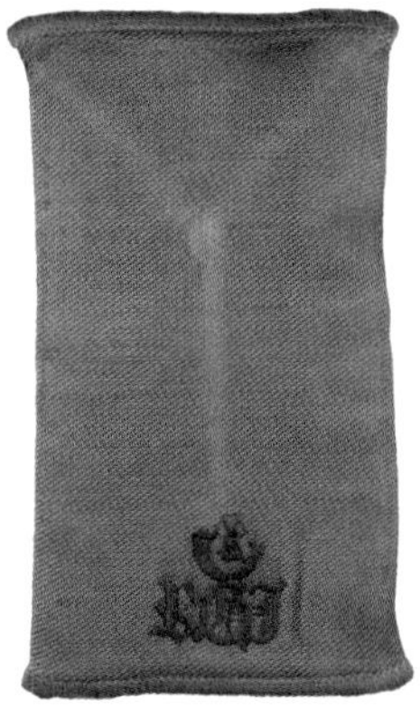

16

17

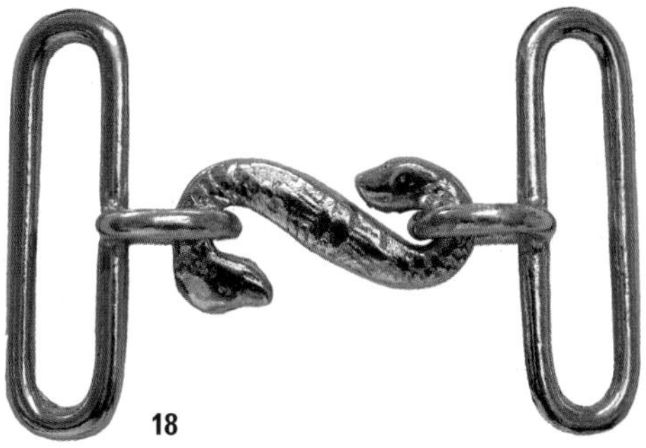

18

19

20

21

22

23

24

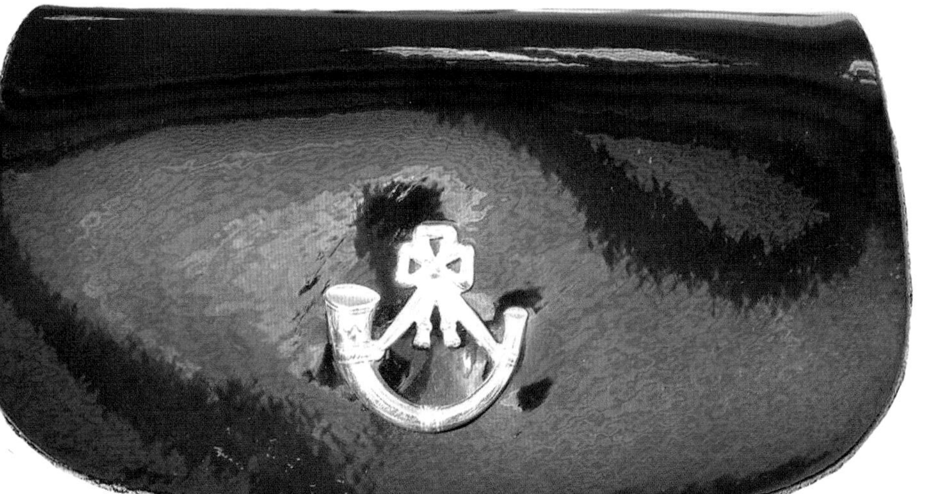

25

26

27

28

29

30

31

opposite page

19 Waist belt clasp 7 × 5.5 cm.

20 Bugler's arm badge 5 × 4.5 cm.

21 Cpl Mike Lines wearing No1 Dress and Cpl Dell Raper wearing No2 Dress.

22 Cpl Stuart Rankin wearing bugler's No1 Dress with the Bugle badge on his right sleeve worn above the chevrons.

23 BMaj Mac Macleod wearing the RGJ cross belt.

24 RGJ patent leather pouch.

25 RGJ shoulder belt plate 6.25 × 8 cm.

this page

26 King's Royal Rifle Corps officer's plastic pouch.

27 King's Royal Rifle Corps shoulder belt plate 6.25 × 9.25 cm.

28 King's Royal Rifle Corps whistle chain boss 5 cm.

29 Rifle Brigade officer's plastic pouch.

30 Rifle Brigade officer's shoulder belt plate 6.25 × 8.25 cm.

31 Rifle Brigade officer's whistle chain boss 5 cm.

32

33

Lineage The Royal Green Jackets (1966) from The Oxfordshire and Buckinghamshire Light Infantry (1908), formerly The Oxfordshire Light Infantry (1881), The King's Royal Rifle Corps (1755), formerly 60th Foot, and The Rifle Brigade (Prince Consort's Own) (1800), formerly 95th Foot. The Oxfordshire and Buckinghamshire Light Infantry from 43rd Foot (1741) and 52nd Foot (1755).

34

36

37

38

39

32 Captain Henry Powell-Jones wearing a Rifle Brigade cross belt.

33 Lt Col Richard Carrow wearing the private purchase nickel cap badge.

34 Lt Col Harry Emck MBE and WO1 (RSM) Rob Cutler wearing the different patterns of officer's and senior ranks Mess Dress.

Examples of RGJ Qualification Badges

36 All Arms Physical Training Instructor 5.5 × 3.75 cm.

37 Parachutist 10.5 × 4 cm.

38 Anti-Tank Guided Weapon Controller 4.75 × 4 cm.

39 Mortarman 4.75 × 4 cm.

Acknowledgement WO1 (RSM) RP Cutler

Special Air Service Regiment

Special Forces formed in 1952.

The SAS was originally raised in 1941 and the Second World War badges were readopted when the SAS was reformed in 1952. The cap badge, worn on the distinctive sand coloured beret, represents King Arthur's Sword Excalibur surmounted by flames and was designed by Serjeant Bob Tait MM in 1941. The shape of Excalibur is said to have been based on the issue Sykes Fairburn fighting knife carried by commandos as the North African tailors who embroidered the original badges knew nothing of the legendary sword but were able to copy the knives carried by the soldiers. The Regiment's founder, Lt Col David Stirling OBE DSO, reportedly chose the famous motto. He was reported as saying in 1985, 'I put down a £10 bet on anyone improving it. Randolph Churchill insisted *Who Dares Wins* was totally rotten and that he had a much better one coming up. He never came up with it. But he had to come up with his ten quid.'

The colours of the flames and scroll, light blue and dark blue, are said to represent the rowing colours of Oxford and Cambridge Universities.

The original beret introduced in 1941 was white, then (after an interval when the khaki side cap was worn) changed to beige, then to maroon, and eventually in 1957 back to beige.

1

2

3

4

5

6

SAS soldiers wear unique parachute 'wings' awarded in perpetuity after specialist training. Wings are not worn by the Regiment on Combat Dress as they identify the wearer as being a Special Forces soldier; however, those who are no longer serving with the Regiment sometimes wear them. The only wings worn in the Regiment are the coloured cloth embroidered badge worn on the pullover and Number 2 Dress.

Wire-embroidered badges, silver parachute and gold wings, are available for Number 1 Dress.

Mess Dress is rarely, if ever, worn in the Regiment by those badged SAS. Those soldiers serving back with their parent regiment or corps, and who therefore wear Mess Dress, wear full sized wire-embroidered wings in reversed colours, gold parachute with silver wings, whilst officers wear smaller wings having a silver parachute and gold wings. The usual backing is red, although the manufacturers are able to embroider the wings onto any colour backing to match the Mess Dress.

Lineage Special Air Service (1952).

The title Special Air Service was first used in 1940 when Number 2 Commando was selected for parachute training as 11th Special Air Service Battalion, renamed in 1941 1st Parachute Battalion. Brigadier Dudley Clark who ran a deception operation to convince the Axis that the allies had an airborne brigade in the Middle East also used the title for his imaginary formation. His parachutists were small dummies, which from the distorting perspective of the desert looked like men at a greater distance. He agreed to assist Lt Col David Stirling if he also adopted the SAS title as some real parachutists could only help the deception. The new unit was formed as L Detachment SAS.

The SAS was disbanded at the end of the Second World War. The title was assumed in 1947 by the Territorial Army 21st SAS (Artists) Regiment; 21 being chosen as it preserved the numbers of the wartime 1st and 2nd SAS. 22 SAS was formed as a regular regiment from The Malayan Scouts in 1952. A second TA regiment, 23 SAS was added later.

previous page

1 Special Air Service soldier's cotton embroidered beret badge 3.5 × 5.75 cm and anodised aluminium collar badges 2 × 3.5 cm.
2 RSM's beret with officer's wire-embroidered badge.
3 Obsolete shoulder title 2.5 × 1 cm.
4 SAS button.
5 Regular Army staff sergeant's rank slide.
6 Officer's wire and cotton embroidered beret badge 3.5 × 5.5 cm and silver and gilt collar badges 1.75 × 3.5 cm.

this page

7 No1 Dress wire-embroidered parachute badge 7.25 × 3.5 cm.
8 Padded cloth parachute badge for No2 Dress and working dress 7.75 × 3.25 cm.
9 Officer's Mess Dress wire-embroidered parachute badge 6.75 × 3 cm.
10 Sergeant's Mess Dress wire-embroidered parachute badge 7.5 × 3.75 cm.
11 Older style of parachute badge embroidered without any padding 7.5 × 2.75 cm.
12 Those serving with the Regiment do not wear SAS parachute wings on combat dress.

7

12

8

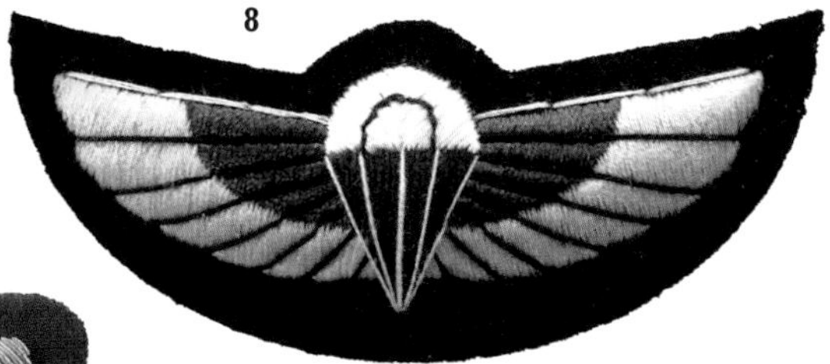

9

10

11

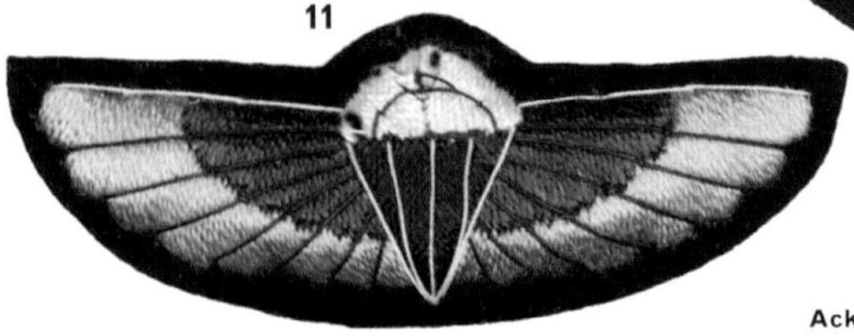

Acknowledgement Major Mick Bohanan and SSgt Harry Clare

Special Reconnaissance Regiment

Special Forces formed in 2005.

The Special Reconnaissance Regiment, or SRR, was formed in April 2005. The nature of its duties led newspapers to comment that the beret badge 'underlines the clandestine nature of the regiment – a dagger with a face mask.' In common with the SAS and SBS the design is based upon the sword Excalibur 'ensuring conformity within the Special Forces Group. The Corinthian style helmet was favoured by the ancient Greeks from the early 7th to 4th centuries BC. The helmet faces forward and suggests the viewer is being watched while the wearer behind the mask is anonymous.'

The Army Dress Committee directed that the final version of the badge was to be a brown helmet on a dark blue background.

A qualification badge for the SRR is under consideration with the favoured design being the Commando style Fighting Knife, point uppermost, dividing the letters S and R. As with other specialist qualification badges it is expected that authority will be given for it to be worn by all ranks in perpetuity.

Special Reconnaissance Regiment prototype beret badge 3.5 × 5 cm.

Special Boat Service

Royal Marines Special Forces.

The wartime Army Special Boat Squadron, when they wore badges at all, wore a shield shaped beret badge consisting of Excalibur being held up from the water surrounded by the letters SBS. When the Royal Marines SBS was formed after the Second World War, Royal Marines badges were worn. The wire-embroidered SBS beret badge was introduced in 2004.

The Royal Marines wear the Army parachute badge but to complement the new beret badge a set of special parachute badges, similar to the special badges worn by the SAS was approved.

Special Boat Service beret badge 3.75 × 5.25 cm.

In November 1940 No 8 Commando formed a Folboat Section which, when deployed, became Middle East Folboat Section. In 1942 it was renamed D Squadron Special Air Service, and later that year amalgamated with Commando Special Boat Sections to form the Special Boat Squadron. It was disbanded in 1945. Its ethos lives on in the Royal Marines Special Boat Service.

1 Number 1 Dress Parachute Badge 8.25 × 3.25 cm.
2 Lovat Dress Parachute Badge 8.25 × 3.25 cm.
3 Mess Dress Parachute Badge 6 × 2.25cm.
4 Tropical Dress Parachute Badge 8.25 × 3.25 cm.
5 Combat Dress Parachute Badge 8.25 × 3.25 cm.

1

4

3

2

5

Acknowledgement Lt Cmdr Alec Parry RN

Army Air Corps

The Army Air Corps was formed in 1957 from the RAF Air Observation Post Squadrons and Glider Pilot Regiment Light Liaison Flights.

The Army Air Corps, or AAC, cap badge reflects the insignia of both the previous Army Air Corps and of the Glider Pilot Regiment. The badge was authorised in 1957 and produced in anodised aluminium for soldiers in 1958 just after the Glider Pilot Regiment badge had been produced with a St Edward's (or Queen's) Crown. When worn on the Cambridge Blue beret the Army Air Corps cap badge is backed by a square of dark blue felt. Officers wear a wire-embroidered badge on the beret. Personnel attached to the Army Air Corps wear their regimental badge, plus any appropriate backing, on the Army Air Corps beret. In about 1985 the Army Air Corps Dress Committee authorised dark blue berets with a pale blue cap badge backing for wear in the field, on the grounds that the pale blue beret would show up on air photographs and possibly give away an otherwise camouflaged position. The practice has died out.

1

2

3

4

2

5

6

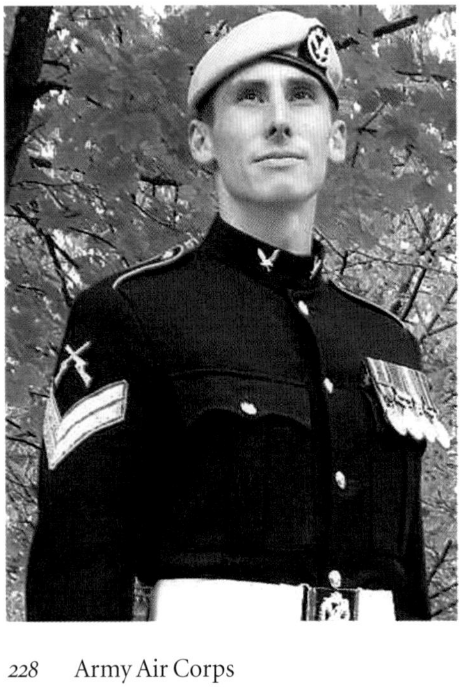

7

8

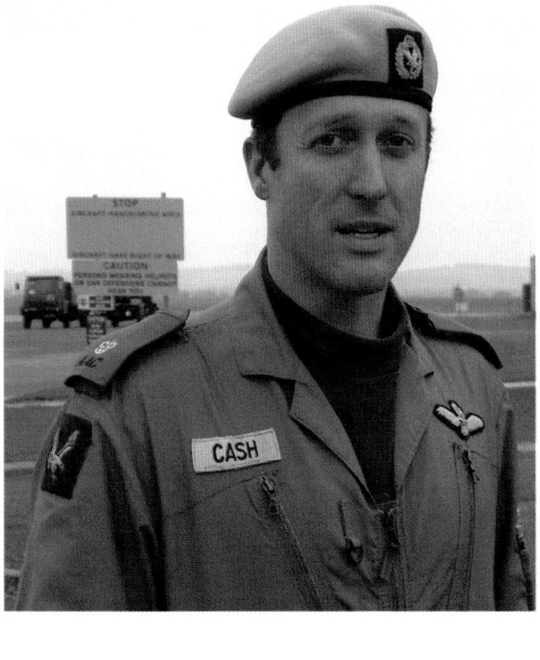

Eagle collar badges are worn on all tunics except for the officers' Mess Dress. A swooping eagle on a square background is worn by all ranks on the right shoulder of the flying suit. The badge had originally been worn on Battle Dress, and although not approved for wear on Number 2 Dress, introduced in the early 1960s, it survived on tropical dress until approved for flying clothes in 1969.

Pilots, usually between the ranks of corporal and lieutenant colonel, wear the Army Flying Badge or 'wings'. The badge may be worn in perpetuity. Introduced for 1st Glider Pilots in 1942, the badge with the St Edward's (or Queen's) Crown has been worn since 1953 on the left breast, initially by Glider Pilot Regiment pilots and since 1957 by all Army pilots. (However mistakes do happen and in 1975 AAC units in Northern Ireland were issued Royal Flying Corps badges embroidered RFC. Some of which were worn proudly until quite recently).

Some RAF personnel wear their names woven below their flying badges, or brevets. Director Army Aviation actively discourages the practice amongst AAC aircrew; although members of the display teams and some TA pilots do so.

The pressures placed on pilots operating during training in West Germany led in 1960 to the introduction of a crewman seated next to the pilot in the cockpit who was qualified as an observer and awarded a 'half-wing'; the Army Observer Badge. Later missile controllers were also qualified.

Originally known as the Series 500 course, observers were trained in their units and wore the Observer badge on the lower right sleeve; some are still to be seen in that position. From 1976 to 1992 courses were run at the Army Air Corps Centre. Army Observer badges awarded there

9

10

11

12

13

14

opposite page

1 Army Air Corps soldier's anodised aluminium cap badge 4 × 5 cm and collar badges 2.5 × 2 cm.

2 Sergeant's wire embroidered Mess Dress collar badges 2.5 × 2.5 cm. Officers do not wear collar badges on their Mess Dress.

3 AAC button.

4 Anodised aluminium shoulder title 3 × 1 cm.

5 Officer's wire embroidered beret badge 4.25 × 5 cm and silver collar badges 2.5 × 2.5 cm.

6 Cpl Tim Couzens wearing No1 Dress with the crossed rifles badge of a Skill at Arms instructor on his right sleeve.

7 Lt Col Dan Nicholas wearing the AAC distinctive light coloured Service Dress. He wears the Syrena badge awarded to 651 and 654 Squadrons on his left sleeve.

8 Major Andy Cash wearing a flying suit with the Army Flying Badge on the left breast and the AAC Eagle badge on the right sleeve.

this page

9 No1 Dress wire embroidered Army Flying Badge 9.25 × 4.25 cm.

10 No2 Dress wire and cotton embroidered Army Flying Badge 10 × 4 cm.

11 Working Dress cotton embroidered Army Flying Badge 10.5 × 4.5 cm.

12 Officer's wire embroidered Mess Dress Army Flying Badge 6.5 × 2.75 cm.

13 AAC NCO's wire embroidered Mess Dress Army Flying Badge 6 × 3 cm.

14 Non-AAC NCO's wire embroidered Mess Dress Army Flying Badge 6 × 2.75 cm. The badges are unofficially woven on different coloured backings to match the Mess Dress.

were authorised to be worn on the left breast.

Similarly, in 1969 the arming of helicopters with SS11 missiles required missile controllers who, when qualified, wore the Army Air Gunner Badge. Gunners did the observers course with an additional three weeks missile controllers training. Both badges were usually awarded to junior NCOs. Neither badge has been awarded since 1992 but some are still worn by qualified personnel.

Operations in Northern Ireland led in about 1979 to helicopters being routinely fitted with machine guns mounted in the doors. Those personnel qualified as 'Door Gunners' wear an unofficial DG badge on the lower left sleeve of their flying clothing. With the demise of both Observer and Air Gunner courses and pressure for an official badge for the door gunners, the increased complexity of army aviation has led the Director Army Aviation to recommend a new 'half-wing' for all qualified crewmen.

Senior ranks wear the swooping eagle rank badge. The badge was authorised for sergeants to be worn above the chevrons in 1970, and in 1974 for warrant officers to wear below the rank badge on the right sleeve only. The rank badges are also

The Army began using tethered balloons for observation in 1878; followed by tethered kites in 1906 and the first airship in 1907. Army Aeroplane No1 flew 400 yards in 1908, but such had been the pace of development that in 1911 the Air Battalion was formed, which became the Royal Flying Corps in 1912. The Royal Air Force was formed in 1918 and direct support to the Army was vested in Army Co-operation Squadrons with a mixture of RAF and Royal Artillery pilots. The Second World War showed the limitations of the squadrons, which operated from RAF airfields, and in 1941 Air Observation Post Squadrons with Army pilots were formed to provide real time artillery fire control. The direction by Winston Churchill in 1940 to form a parachute force was not achievable because of the RAF's limited troop carrying capacity and therefore gliders were procured and piloted by soldiers whose task was to land the gliders and then to fight as infantry. In 1942 the Glider Pilot Regiment, or GPR, was formed and eventually 1,500 RAF aircrew also retrained as glider pilots and infantrymen. The Army Air Corps was formed in 1942 to administer The Parachute Regiment, the Gilder Pilot Regiment and from 1944 the SAS. The Army Air Corps disbanded in 1950 but the Air OP Squadrons survived and the much reduced GPR took on liaison flying for the Army until disbanded in 1957 when the Army Air Corps was formed.

16

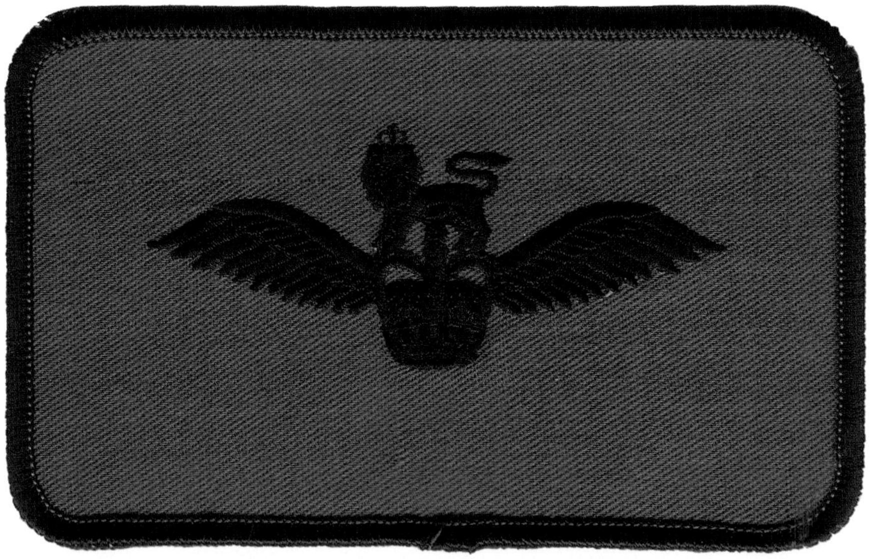

17

15

18

authorised informally for all non-commissioned ranks wearing Number 1 Dress to a wedding.

The Colonel-in-Chief's Trophy has been awarded annually since 1995 to the aircraft commander who achieves the best results in the aviation standards test. The recipient is presented with an engraved silver box by Prince Charles and a cloth Prince of Wales badge that may be worn in perpetuity on the upper left arm of the flying overall and cold weather jacket. Whilst investigating the existence of the Prince of Wales's badge two officers were asked if there was a discrete version worn on Number 2 Dress. 'Pilots don't do discrete' was the response.

The Director Army Air Corps did not wish to wear a Corps Tactical Recognition Flash but was required to register a design. 3rd, 4th and 9th Regiments AAC assigned to 16th Air Assault Brigade wear distinctive Landing Zone (LZ) flashes. Subsequently the Army Dress Committee did not approve these as Tactical Recognition Flashes.

The 4th Regiment Army Air Corps rank slide with red and green edge was introduced by Lieutenant Colonel Michael Volkers OBE in about 1976 to differentiate his soldiers from those of two other Army Air Corps units in Detmold, West Germany. The red is taken from the 654 Squadron Syrena Honour Badge and the green from the Lincoln Green of 664 Squadron.

opposite page

15 Eagle badge worn on the right sleeve of the flying suit 6.25 $\times$ 7 cm.

16 An example of an unofficial subdued Army Flying Badge with room for a name to be woven 12.25 $\times$ 7.5 cm.

17 Display team 'wings' and name badge 12.5 $\times$ 7.5 cm.

18 AAC approved subdued 'Combat wings' 9.5 $\times$ 4.25 cm.

this page

19 No1 Dress wire embroidered Army Observer badge 6 $\times$ 4 cm.

20 No2 Dress wire and cotton embroidered Army Observer badge 6.75 $\times$ 3.75 cm.

21 Working Dress cotton embroidered Army Observer badge 7 $\times$ 3.75 cm.

22 Mess Dress wire embroidered Army Observer badge 5.5 $\times$ 3.25 cm.

23 No2 Dress wire and cotton embroidered Army Air Gunner badge 6.75 $\times$ 3.75 cm.

24 Working Dress cotton embroidered Army Air Gunner badge 6.75 $\times$ 4 cm.

25 Mess Dress wire embroidered Army Air Gunner badge 5.5 $\times$ 3.25 cm.

26 Door Gunner badge worn on the lower left sleeve 8 $\times$ 4 cm.

27 Sgt Nelly Grannell wearing the Door Gunner qualification badge and the 657 Squadron badge on his flying suit.

19

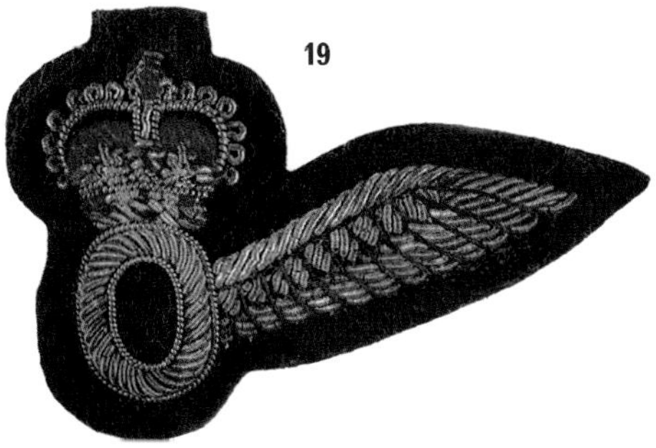

20

21

22

23

24

26

25

27

28

29

30

31

32

33

35

36

34

37

38

39

Lineage Army Air Corps (1957)

40

41

opposite page

28 No1 Dress wire embroidered rank badge 7.75 × 7 cm.

29 Mess Dress wire embroidered rank badge 3.75 × 4.25 cm.

30 Silver embroidered major's slide worn by the display teams.

31 4 Regiment AAC captain's rank slide

32 Second lieutenant's rank slide.

33 AAC rank badges worn by sergeants on both sleeves and by warrant officers on the right sleeve only of No2 Dress 5.5 × 6 cm.

34 Prince of Wales Badge 9 cm.

35 WO2 (SSM) Cappy Capstick and SSgt Jamz Cunningham wearing No2 Dress with the Eagle rank badge. A poppy is worn behind their cap badges for Remembrance Day.

36 Major Bob Blair wearing the Prince of Wales's badge on his flying suit.

37 WO2 Tim Trott wearing the AAC aircrew Eagle badge. WO2 Tom O'Malley is also wearing the Attack Helicopter instructor's badge.

38 3rd Regiment AAC LZ flash 7 × 6.5 cm.

39 5th Regiment AAC souvenir badge 9 cm.

this page

40 9th Regiment AAC LZ flash 7.25 × 7.25 cm.

41 4th Regiment AAC LZ flash 7 × 7 cm.

Acknowledgement
Maj James Anderson, Jim Donovan, Charlie Moores and Brendan Shaw, Capt Mike Denton, Alasdair Mack, Martin McGrath, Andrew Stirling and Alistair Stocker, WO1 (RSM) M Allison and MA Hart, WO2 (SSM) Matt Barlow, SSgt Steve Anthony, SSgt Ian Chapman, Graham Wayman, SSgt (SQMS) Flynn and Terry Rumble of Terrane Ltd the manufacturers of almost all the embroidered badges.

SQUADRON BADGES

Squadron numbers 651 to 673 were originally allocated to RAF units directly supporting the Army, and since 1957 the numbers have been dedicated to Army Air Corps units. Squadrons numbered 651 to 666 were Air Observation Post units, of which 663 Squadron was Polish and Squadrons 664, 665 and 666 were Canadian. Squadrons 668 to 673 were glider units formed in India. Squadron numbers 674 to 699 are RAF allocation although numbers 674 to 679 have not been allocated.

651 Squadron AAC

'Direct'

651 Squadron was formed as the first Air Observation Post squadron in 1941 from D Flight Air OP, which had been formed in 1940. Disbanded in 1955, its title was given to 657 Squadron the same day, and the renumbered 651 Squadron was transferred to the Army Air Corps in 1957. The Squadron badge, representing a flaming torch (actually a seashell), is a simple representation combining the torch of learning and the Royal Artillery flaming grenade.

The squadron was awarded the Syrena, or Maid of Warsaw, badge for service in Italy in support of 2nd Polish Corps during the Second World War (see The Queen's Royal Hussars p. 30).

651 Squadron badge 9.5 × 11.75 cm.

652 Squadron AAC

'In the Air and In the Field'

652 Squadron was formed as an Air Observation Post squadron in 1942 and transferred to the Army Air Corps in 1957. The Squadron badge represents a gun barrel supported by wings in the Royal Artillery colours.

In 1967 an aircraft of 652 Squadron unwittingly transported a frog from Luneberg Heath back to Bunde, both in West Germany. The frog, now 'Sergeant Fred', has completed over 800 flying hours and frog shaped flourescent 'zaps' appear wherever the Squadron serves, resulting in the nickname 'Frog Squadron'.

652 Squadron badge 8.25 × 11.25 cm.

Flourescent self adhesive frog which appears wherever 652 Squadron serves.

653 Squadron AAC

'Watching Everywhere'

653 Squadron was reformed in 1971, having previously served from 1958 to 1967. The squadron number was originally allocated in 1942 to an Air Observation Post squadron disbanded in 1945. The Squadron badge combines an eagle's head with gun barrels, representing artillery controlled from the air

A pink panther soft toy has been the squadron mascot since the early 1980s. Known as Air Trooper Panther 'he will promote immediately as he has shown significant potential.' The badge is worn on cold weather jackets, and the central motif is embroidered on helmet visor covers.

653 Squadron badge 9.5 × 12.25.

653 Squadron helmet badge 10 cm.

654 Squadron AAC

'Progressive'

654 Squadron was formed in 1958. The squadron number was originally allocated in 1942 to an Air Observation Post squadron disbanded in 1947. The Squadron badge combines an aircraft propeller with a gun barrel, representing the combination of flying and artillery.

The squadron was awarded the Syrena, or Maid of Warsaw, badge for service in Italy in support of 2nd Polish Corps during the Second World War. (See 651 Squadron).

654 Squadron badge 9.5 × 11.75 cm.

Unlike previous marks of the aircraft the Lynx Mark 9 Light Battlefield Helicopter is fitted with wheels rather than skids 9cm.

655 (The Scottish Horse) Squadron AAC 'Anzio'

655 Squadron was formed in 1962. The number was originally allocated in 1942 to an Air Observation Post squadron many of the pilots of which were from an artillery regiment, The Scottish Horse, which disbanded in 1945. The motto records the Squadron's first battle during which it flew in direct support of The Scottish Horse. The badge with the Scottish Horse crest was authorised by the Duke of Atholl in 1962. A request to wear a tartan backing to the beret badge at the same time was refused by the AAC Dress Committee, however the squadron badge is worn on a tartan backing on the flying suit.

654 Squadron badge 9.5 × 11.75 cm.

656 Squadron AAC

'Flying and Seeing'

656 Squadron was formed in 1942 as an Air Observation Post squadron, reduced to 1914 Flight in 1946, and reformed as a squadron in 1977. The Squadron's Chinthe badge representing the Squadron's first theatre of operations, Burma, and the guns, the squadron's role controlling artillery.

654 Squadron badge 9.5 × 11.75 cm.

The 656 Chinthe badge

The *Chinthe* (pronounced 'chin-thay'), the mythical leo-gryph of Burma, guardian of the temples, goes far back into Buddhist and Burmese mythology. The Mahavamsa, the Great Pall Chronicle of Ceylon (*c.*500 AD), tells the story somewhat like this.

A princess had a son through her marriage to a lion, but forsook the lion, which then became the terror of the land. The son set out to slay the lion. When he found the lion he shot an arrow at him, but so great was the lion's unshaken love for his son that the arrow rebounded from the lion's brow and fell to earth at the youth's feet. Three times this happened. But then the lion grew wrathful; and when the youth let fly the fourth arrow, it pierced the lion's body and killed him. Thus the lion lost his life because he had lost his self-possession and allowed wrath to pervade his heart.

Legend goes on to say that the son later erected a statue of the lion as guardian of the temple, to atone for this murder. The Chinthe is revered as a protector, which can pounce on the enemies of religion (i.e. the State), from nine different directions. It was used symbolically on the royal thrones of Burma and became famous as the formation sign of the Chindits who fought in Burma in 1943 and 1944.

657 Squadron AAC

'By land and Sky'

657 Squadron was formed in 1969. The squadron number was originally allocated in 1943 to an Air Observation Post squadron which was reduced to two Flights in 1945 and which were numbered 651 Squadron in 1955. The Squadron badge represents the control of artillery.

657 Squadron badge 8.5 × 11.25 cm.

659 Squadron AAC

'By land and Sky'

659 Squadron was formed in 1969. The squadron number was originally allocated in 1943 to an Air Observation Post squadron which disbanded on the partition of India in 1947 with the aircraft forming 659 Indian Army Air OP Squadron. The Squadron badge represents an artillery shell being controlled from the air although due to a misunderstanding an earlier batch of badges, some of which remain in use, was woven to the RAF design with an RAF single laurel wreath and the Eagle clutching a missile. The squadron uses the unofficial title 'Night Hawks'

659 Squadron incorrect badge 8.75 × 11 cm made with RAF single laurel wreath and Eagle clutching missile.

659 Squadron replacement badge 9.5 × 11.75 cm made with Army triple laurel wreath and Eagle clutching artillery shell.

660 Squadron AAC

'Assistance from the skies'

660 Squadron was formed in 2000; the squadron number had originally been allocated in 1943 to an Air Observation Post squadron, which disbanded in 1946. The Squadron badge represents the sword and key from 6 Armoured Brigade's formation sign, the unit which the squadron supported in battle. The Eagle is taken from the Arms of Andover and Salisbury where the squadron originally served. The V shape of the barrels represents long range artillery as the squadron spotted for guns at Dover firing across the Channel. A modification to include crossed kukris to record the Squadron's post-war service in Hong Kong has been suggested and rejected at various times.

660 Squadron badge 9 × 11.5 cm.

661 Squadron AAC

'With my eyes I designate [the victim] for slaughter'

661 Squadron was formed in 1969. The squadron number was originally allocated in 1943 to an Air Observation Post squadron, which disbanded in 1945. The number was later allocated in 1949 to a Royal Auxiliary Air Force squadron, which disbanded in 1957. The Squadron badge is the flaming grenade, representing artillery, surrounded with a compass ring, representing accuracy.

The squadron wears the Red Patch emblem of 1st Canadian Infantry Division awarded as an honour badge in 1945 by Major General C Volkes. The squadron was known then as C Flight 657 Squadron (Air Observation Post) and supported the 1st Canadian Army in Italy and North West Europe.

1

2

1 661 Squadron badge 9.5 × 11.75 cm.
2 1st Canadian Infantry Division badge 3 × 1.75 cm.

662 Squadron AAC

'Death dealing eye'

662 Squadron was formed in 1971. The squadron number was originally allocated in 1943 to an Air Observation Post squadron, which disbanded in 1945. The number was later allocated to a Royal Auxiliary Air Force squadron in 1949, which disbanded in 1957. The Squadron badge combines an eagle's head with gun barrels, representing artillery controlled from the air.

662 Squadron badge 9 × 11.5 cm.

663 Squadron AAC

'We fly for the guns'

663 Squadron was reformed in 1977, having previously served from 1969 to 1977, when 660 Squadron was renumbered as 663. The squadron number was originally allocated to an Air Observation Post squadron formed from Polish troops to support 2nd Polish Corps in 1944, and disbanded in 1947. The squadron number was allocated to a Royal Auxiliary Air Force squadron in 1949, which disbanded in 1957. The Polish eagle badge represents 663 Squadron's wartime affiliation and the snaffle bit represents control.

663 Squadron badge 9.25 × 12 cm.

664 Squadron AAC

'Woe to which is seen' or 'I've spied it, woe betide it'

664 Squadron was formed in 1969. The squadron number was originally allocated in 1944 to an Air Observation Post squadron manned by Canadian troops supporting 1st Canadian Army, which disbanded in 1946. The squadron number was later allocated to a Royal Auxiliary Air Force squadron in 1949, which disbanded in 1957. The archer represents Hucknell in Nottinghamshire 664 Squadron's first station. Archery was also a popular artillery symbol during the Second World War.

1

2

1 664 Squadron badge 9.25 × 11 cm.
2 Lynx Flight badge 9.75 × 12.25 cm.

665 Squadron AAC

'Providence'

665 Squadron was formed in 1986 having previously served from 1971 until amalgamated with 657 Squadron in 1978. The squadron number was originally allocated in 1945 to an Air Observation Post squadron with Canadian troops to support 1st Canadian Army, which disbanded in the same year. The badge with the harp and maple leaf was approved in 1988, linking service in Northern Ireland with 665 Squadron's service with the Canadians during the Second World War.

The Squadron is particularly known for the selection of unofficial badges worn by the aircrew. The bat used in most of the designs represents the Squadron's expertise at operational night flying. The squadron has a history of producing unofficial badges, the most famous being 'Paddy don't surf'. Although a variety is sold as souvenirs, the 'bat' is said to be the only one worn at present.

'Paddy Don't Surf' and 'Saddam Don't Surf' refer to the most famous military helicopter flying scene in a film; the assault by Lieutenant Colonel Kilgore's air cavalry battalion to the accompaniment of Wagner's Ride of the Valkyries in the 1979 film about the war in Vietnam, *Apocalypse Now*. The actor Robert Duvall, playing the surfing enthusiast Commanding Officer, in answering a question as to why he is attacking a Viet Cong controlled village on the Mekong Delta which has good surfing waves, explains that 'Charlie don't surf'. The Lynx Flight 665 Squadron adopted the motto because some of the squadron were keen surfers – and possibly because it's a great line from a film with spectacular flying scenes.

1

2

1 665 Squadron badge, 9.25 × 11 cm.
2 665 Squadron badge, 7.75 cm.

660 Squadron badges Paddy Don't Surf badge worn in Northern Ireland and Sadam Don't Surf badge worn during the war in Iraq 2003, 7.75 cm.

667 (Development and Trials) Squadron AAC

667 Squadron was formed in 1989 having previously served from 1957 until converted into 7 Regiment AAC in 1973. The squadron number had previously been allocated in 1943 to an Army and Royal Navy co-operation squadron, disbanded in 1945.

667 Squadron badge 9.25 × 12 cm.

668 (Training) Squadron AAC

668 Squadron was formed in 2001. The squadron number was originally allocated to an RAF Air OP squadron formed at Calcutta, India in 1944 and disbanded in 1945. The khumjahs on the badge represent Sharjah where the Squadron reformed, with the propeller distinguishing the badge from that of local forces.

668 Squadron badge 9.5 × 11.75 cm.

669 Squadron AAC

'We will do it'

669 Squadron was formed in 2001. The squadron number was originally allocated to an RAF glider squadron at Bikham, India in 1944 but renumbered 671 Squadron when it was realised that it had been formed at the wrong airfield. It reformed at Basal, India in 1945 and disbanded in the same year. The Squadron badge is from the arms of the Duchy of Limburg where the Squadron was stationed when the badge was authorised.

669 Squadron badge 8.5 × 11 cm.

670 Squadron AAC

670 Squadron was formed in 1986. The squadron number was originally allocated to an RAF glider squadron at Fatehjang, India in 1944 and disbanded in 1946. The badge, approved in 1988, of a winged cobra ready to strike, combines the images of flying and India, where the Squadron was originally formed.

670 Squadron badge 9.5 × 12 cm.

671 Squadron AAC

'Cunning and stealth'

671 Squadron was formed in 1986. The squadron number was originally allocated to 669 Squadron, an RAF glider squadron at Bikham, India in 1944 but renumbered 671 Squadron when it was realised that it had been formed at the wrong airfield. Disbanded in 1945. The badge links the Army's swords with the tiger representing India, where the Squadron was originally formed.

671 Squadron badge 9.5 × 12 cm.

672 Squadron AAC

'Wrathful and merciful'

672 Squadron was formed in 2002. The squadron number was originally allocated to an RAF glider squadron at Bikham, India in 1944 and disbanded in 1946. The badge is the Hindu God Shiva representing India, where the Squadron was originally formed.

672 Squadron badge 8.5 × 11 cm.

673 Squadron AAC

'Beware nightfall'

673 Squadron was formed in 2003. The squadron number had originally been allocated to an RAF glider squadron at Bikham, India in 1944, which disbanded in 1946. The badge represents the Taj Mahal and a melamistic leopard, which hunts at night, together representing both India, where the Squadron was originally formed, and the squadron's night fighting capability. The College of Heralds did not approve the inclusion of the Taj Mahal and the new batch of badges does not have it in the design.

1. 673 Squadron obsolete badge including the Taj Mahal 9.25 × 12 cm.
2. 673 Squadron badge new design without the Taj Mahal 9.25 × 11.75 cm.
3. Attack Helicopter Instructor's badge 9 cm.

1

2

3

674 Squadron AAC

674 Squadron was formed in 2003.

674 Squadron badge 9.5 × 11.75 cm.

HQ Squadrons

Prepared in mind and resources

The Headquarter Squadron of each regiment has the same badge, the regiment being identified by its number in Roman numerals. As yet no badges for uniforms are known.

School of Army Aviation

The badge of the School of Army Aviation was that of the former 227 Officer Cadet Unit and the Light Aircraft School.

1 Flight AAC

1 Flight AAC badge illustrates the history of the Flight which was originally equipped with Beaver aircraft, now superseded by Island aircraft. The background represents the sky and the sea around an outline map of Northern Ireland.

1 Flight badge 9 × 11 cm.

7 Flight AAC

Based in Brunei, the design of 7 Flight's badge features a Bell 212 helicopter and mimics the image used to advertise the musical 'Miss Saigon' which culminates in a dramatic helicopter evacuation scene during the Viet Nam War. The circular badges feature the Bell 212 helicopter above an outline of Brunei.

1

2

3

1 7 Flight badge 9 × 11.5 cm.
2 7 Flight patch with Brigade of Gurkhas crossed kukris badge 9 cm.
3 7 Flight patch 9 cm.

G Flight AAC

G Flight shares the image of the night flying bat with 665 Squadron AAC. The G is said to stand for the Gazelle helicopter, and 8 to represent the number of pilots in the Flight.

1

2

1 G Flight 7.75 cm patch
2 G Flight 9 cm patch

12 Flight AAC

The central motif of the badge is a Gazelle, representing the Gazelle aircraft flown by 12 Flight.

12 Flight badge 8 × 10.5 cm.

25 Flight AAC

25 Flight is based in Belize. Its obsolete badge featuring a Gazelle helicopter was introduced in 1983 when the Flight was given the number originally allocated to the Flight which had operated in British Guiana. The badge was altered when Bell 212 helicopters replaced the Gazelles.

25 Flight obsolete badge 10 cm and new badge 9 cm.

29 (BATUS) Flight AAC

29 Flight badge represents a Gazelle helicopter which supports training at the British Army Training Unit Suffield in Canada.

29 Flight badge 12.5 × 9.5 cm.

Central Flying School

Central Flying School badge 10.25 × 13.5 cm.

Blue Eagles Display Team

'Joined in skill we fly'

Blue Eagles badge 9.25 × 11.75 cm.

The AAC display team was formed in 1962 and established as the semi-permanent Blue Eagles in 1968. Disbanded in 1976, ad hoc teams such as the Silver Eagles were formed for special occasions. The Blue Eagles Display Team has been reformed and their badge designed by Major Penny Kitson in 2004. She has also designed the Army Historic Aircraft Flight crest, which has not yet been produced as a badge.

Following a number of accidents with aging Lynx, a Dutch pilot in about 2002 had the 'crash test' symbol produced as a badge. SSgt Martin Darlington refined the design to the WASTELAND'S LYNX, a play on the manufacturer's name.

Royal Army Chaplains' Department

Chaplains have ministered to the forces since at least 430 AD. The Army Chaplains' Department was established in 1796. Until 1827 only Church of England clergy were accepted, but in that year Presbyterians were authorised, followed by Roman Catholics in 1836, Wesleyans in 1881 and the first Jewish chaplain was appointed in 1892. There are about 150 chaplains, known to soldiers as padres, divided into four classes, Class 4 rank as captains, Class 3 as majors, Class 2 as lieutenant colonels and Class 1 as colonels. In addition the Principal Roman Catholic Chaplain is ranked as a colonel, the Assistant Chaplain General ranks as a brigadier, and the Chaplain General ranks as a major general.

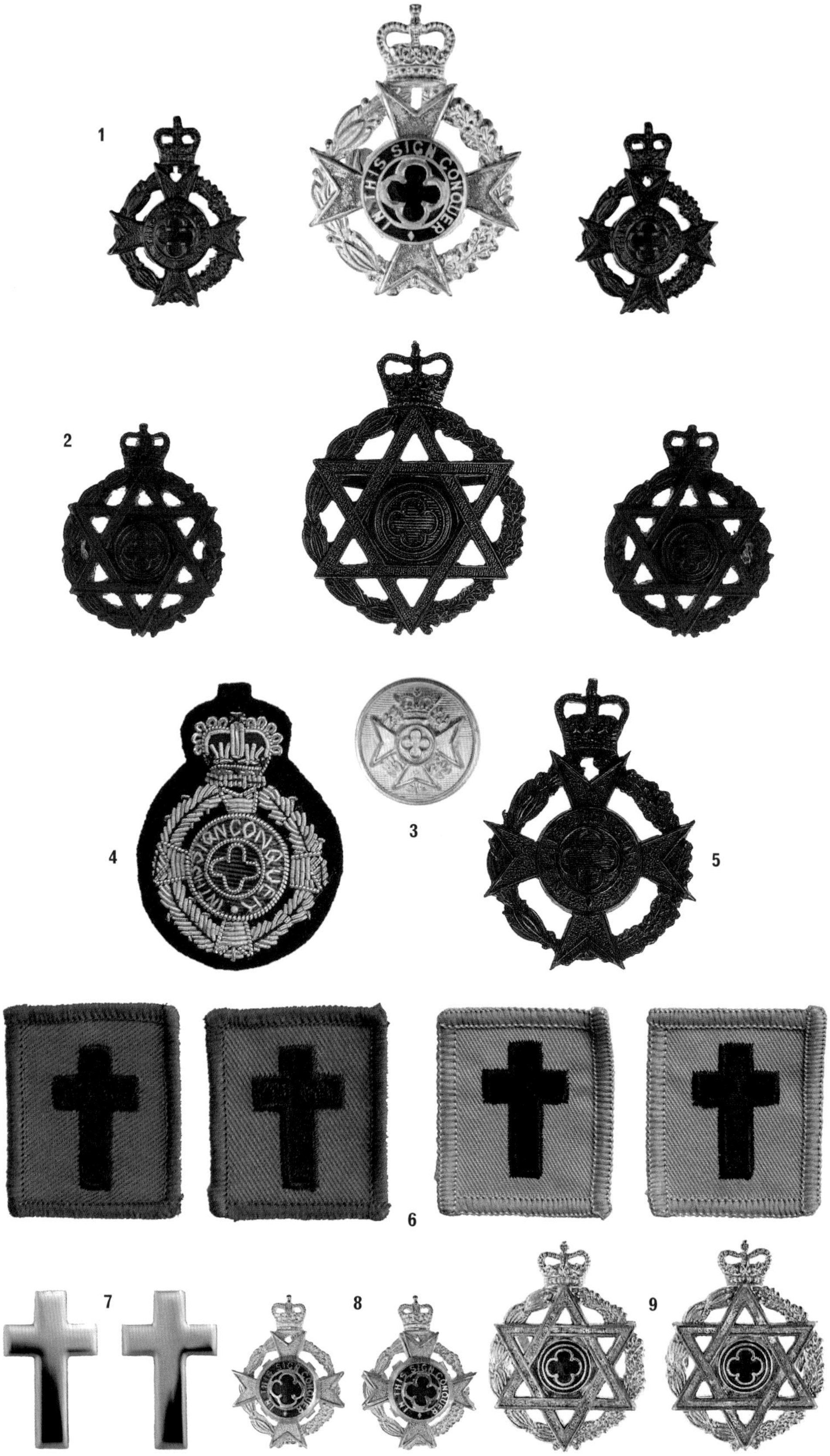

There are two cap badges for the Royal Army Chaplains Department, or RAChD, both introduced in 1940, one for Christian Denominations and one for Jewish Chaplains, although there are no Jewish padres serving at present. The centrepiece of each badge is a quatrefoil within a wreath representing the laurel of victory and the olive of peace. A wire-embroidered badge is worn on the beret, a black badge on the Service Dress cap and Christian chaplains wear a silver, gilt and enamel badge on the Forage Cap.

The Jewish Chaplain's badge is often referred to as the rarest in the Army. In fact, because chaplains rank as officers and have to buy their own badges, there is a stock of the badges available.

Collar badges are reduced sized replicas of the cap badges; black badges on Number 2 Dress and silver and gilt badges on Number 1 Dress and Mess Dress. In combat dress woven black cloth crosses are worn on the collars. For many years black metal crosses were worn but the pins used to secure them to the collars were considered to be a health and safety hazard and had to be replaced. Chrome crosses remain in use for Barrack Dress although they are now bought from the United States PX (the equivalent to the NAAFI). On operations padres also wear the Red Cross armband authorised for non-combatant personnel. Chaplains wear nametapes on Combat Dress embroidered 'Padre' followed by their surname.

Miniature badges are authorised for wear on 'civilian coats' although the stock of official badges appears to be exhausted.

Senior Chaplains 'red tabs' are purple and rank slides have the rank badges edged in ecclesiastic purple. However older rank slides with black badges remain common.

Two or three senior chaplains may be appointed Honorary Chaplain to the Queen, up to a total of six for the three Services. They are identified by a gilt and enamel brooch worn on the Preaching Scarf below any medals. Former Honorary Chaplains who are appointed Dean or Bishop retain the brooch, those who are not so elevated wear a smaller brooch.

Chaplains wear a Preaching Scarf ornamented with an embroidered badge. Styles vary according to what tailors have supplied in the past, some have the design woven directly onto the Preaching Scarf others have separate badges sewn on. In 2000 a stock of new standardised Preaching Scarves was procured for the RAChD. Christian denominations other than Roman Catholics have a square end to the cross, whilst the Roman Catholic Scarf has a Maltese Cross. Officiating Chaplains, that is civilian priests who act as chaplain to a Garrison, wore a silver, gilt and enamel brooch on their Preaching Scarf. The stock of brooches is now exhausted and Officiating Chaplains to the Forces now wear wire-embroidered letters OCF on the Preaching Scarf. Territorial Army chaplains wear a woven yellow T on their Preaching Scarf.

opposite page

1 Christian chaplain's No2 Dress silver, gilt and enamel cap 3 × 4.5 cm and black collar badges 2 × 2.5 cm.
2 Jewish Chaplain's No2 Dress black cap 3.5 × 4.5 cm and collar badges 2.5 × 3.25 cm.
3 RAChD button.
4 Christian chaplain's wire-embroidered beret badge 3.5 × 4.5 cm.
5 Service Dress cap badge 3 × 4.5 cm.
6 Subdued cloth collar badges worn on Combat Dress 3.5 × 4 cm.
7 Chrome pin back collar badges worn in barrack dress 1.5 × 2.5 cm.
8 Christian chaplain's No1 Dress and Mess Dress silver, gilt and enamel collar badges 2 × 2.5 cm.
9 Jewish Chaplain's No1 Dress and Mess Dress silver, gilt and enamel collar badges 2.5 × 3.25 cm.

this page

10 RAChD Staff gorgets, 2 inches or 3 inches long.
11 The Reverend Norman McDowell, as a CF3 he wears major's rank.
12 Silver shoulder belt plate 5 × 4.5 cm.
13 Silver pouch badge 3 × 4 cm.
14 New and old pattern Class 4 Chaplains rank slides.
15 Preaching Scarf badge worn by civilian officiating chaplains 4.75 × 7 cm.

10

11

12

13

14

15

16

17

18

19

23

20

21

22

Live with the men. Go everywhere they go...... Pray with them sometimes, but pray for them always.

The Reverend GA Studdert-Kennedy
CF 1883–1929 'Woodbine Willy'

24

Uniform was authorised for the Army Chaplains Department in 1860, with an embroidered black silk Maltese X edged gold noted as the first badge in 1890. Black metal badges were introduced in 1902 for 'active service'. The gilt Forage Cap badge was authorised in 1911. The Chaplain General was authorised a black and gold version of the generals' badge in 1915, and the Deputy Chaplain General, the Staff cap badge in 1931. The present badges were introduced in 1930, and changed to St Edward's (or Queen's) Crown in 1956.

25

16 Old Preaching Scarves with different styles of embroidered badges remain in use 7.5 × 13 cm.

17 Preaching Scarf badge 7 × 12.5 cm for Christian denominations other than Roman Catholics embroidered onto the Scarf.

18 Padre Mark Christian with the embroidered RAChD badge on his Preaching Scarf.

19 Monsignor Phelim Rowland, Principal Roman Catholic Chaplain wearing the badge of an Honorary Chaplain to the Queen.

20 Badge of an Honorary Chaplain to the Queen 3.5 × 4 cm.

21 Badge of a former Honorary Chaplain to the Queen 2.5 × 2.75 cm.

22 Obsolete badges for wear on 'civilian coats', Christian 2 × 3 cm, and Jewish 2.5 × 3 cm.

23 Preaching Scarf badge 8 × 10 cm for Roman Catholics.

24 Father Mark Okeeffe conducting a Service in the Field for Australian, British and Canadian troops. The Red Cross armband shows his non-combatant status. He wears a purple Preaching Scarf as the only item of his vestments.

25 New style Preaching Scarf badge for Officiating Chaplains to the Forces 11.5 × 5.5 cm (letters 8.5 × 2.5 cm).

The RAChD badges introduced in 1930 had the new motto 'In this Sign Conquer'. It was noted in the press at the time that this broke Army tradition by adopting an English rather than Latin motto. It was said that King George V believed that the Latin motto, attributed to Constantine the Great, *In hoc signa vinces* would not be understood by soldiers and asked for the Anglicised version on the new badge.

Lineage Royal Army Chaplains' Department (1919) formerly Army Chaplains' Department (1796).

Acknowledgement Mr David Blake

Chaplains' Assistant

Chaplains' Assistants undertake the same functions as Lay Readers in a Parish. They wear uniform appropriate to the Service of the chaplains they were supporting. There is only one chaplain's Assistant serving at present. Cap and collar badges and shoulder titles were issued and the Chaplain's Assistants apparently embroidered their own slip on titles for wear in Barrack Dress and therefore they are all different. The gilt cap badge remains available but unissued whilst the Chaplain General has a small stock of the silver badges and titles.

1

2

3

1 Chaplain's Assistant silver and gilt cap badges 2.75 × 3.75 cm.

2 No2 Dress shoulder title 12 × 3.25 cm.

3 Hand embroidered slip on title 5.25 × 4 cm.

4 Padre Keith Barry leads LCpl Bracks Brackenbury on his final journey, the coffin carried by Sgt Dunny Dunn, SSgt Tiffy Pascoe, Sgt Taff Allen and Sgt Godders Godfrey, and Sgt Stevie Branick past the 1 STAFFORDS Battle Group in Al Amara.

4

Royal Logistic Corps

The Royal Logistic Corps was formed in 1993 by the amalgamation of the Royal Corps of Transport, Royal Army Ordnance Corps, Royal Pioneer Corps, Army Catering Corps and the Royal Engineers Postal and Courier Service. The RLC supplies the Army with everything necessary to fight and to handle a wide range of worldwide emergencies.

Sergeant RR MacNeilage RAOC designed the Royal Logistic Corps, or RLC, cap badge. His design combines the Garter from the Royal Engineers, the star and wreath from the Royal Corps of Transport, the crossed axes from the Royal Pioneer Corps, the Arms of the Board of Ordnance from the Royal Army Ordnance Corps, and the motto of the Army Catering Corps. The basic design has remained constant, although the detail has been altered, most recently in 2003 when the soldiers badges with coloured centres were replaced by uncoloured gold and silver anodised aluminium badges. The RLC is the largest single cap badge Corps in the Army, with over 1,700 officers and 14,000 soldiers wearing its badge.

Most RLC soldiers serve in the Field Army but logistic support for the Army, and indeed of all three Services, requires a very large organisation and there are also 13,000 civilians under the management of RLC officers.

Logistics is one of the four main elements of combat power and the RLC makes a key contribution to operations by providing both specialist services and materiel at the right time, in the right place and in the right quantity and condition. The RLC includes 13 trade skills, a number of which are unique to the Corps.

The Royal Logistic Corps registered the blue over yellow diagonal, square Tactical Recognition Flash, the original design being 7 × 7 cm in common with many of the designs submitted to the Army Dress Committee. The design represents a mounted corps and is similar to a pattern originally worn by the Royal Army Service Corps.

1

2

3

4

5

6

7

8

It was not adopted in its large form and possibly only two manufacturer's samples were worn. Issues of a much smaller version began in late 2004 with an instruction that it was to be worn by all ranks RLC from April 2005 and was to replace all other recognition badges.

Different arm badges continue to be worn by specialist units. 13 Air Assault Support Regiment supports 16 Air Assault Brigade and the soldiers wear a different colour Landing Zone Flash to the RLC TRF on the combat jacket. The Cyprus Service Support Unit, or CSSU, is a Tri-Service unit which includes the RLC General Support Squadron. All ranks wear the CSSU arm badge.

The RLC has the unique appointment of Conductor. A Group 1 Warrant Officer Class 1, a Conductor acts in place of a subaltern officer when required. On all parades he takes post as an officer but does not salute. The earliest known record of the appointment of Conductor is in the Statute of Westminster dated 1327 which refers to what seems to be an established post responsible for conducting, or guiding, soldiers from the Shires to the Army's place of assembly. In 1879 a class of Warrant Officer was nominated Conductor of Supplies and Conductor of Stores. The Army Service Corps appointment, Conductor of Supplies was abolished in 1892 and replaced by Staff Sergeant Major 1st Class, now a Group 4 Warrant Officer Class 1. The Conductor of Stores continued in the Royal Army Ordnance Corps until the formation of the Royal Logistic Corps. The appointments of Conductor and of Staff Sergeant Major continue in the Royal Logistic Corps. (See Warrant Officer Class 1 rank badges).

9

10

11

12

13

14

15

Lineage The Royal Logistic Corps (1993), from the Royal Corps of Transport (1965), Royal Army Ordnance Corps (1918), Royal Pioneer Corps (1940), Army Catering Corps (1941) and the Royal Engineers Postal and Courier Service. Royal Corps of Transport from the Royal Army Service Corps (1918) and Royal Engineers Transport and Movement Control Service. Royal Army Service Corps from the Commissariat and Transport Staff (1858) and Corps (1856).

16

17

18

19

20

21

previous page

1 Soldier's bright metal cap badge 4 × 4.5 cm and collar badges 2.75 × 3 cm.
2 Officer's wire-embroidered beret badge 5 × 5 cm.
3 RLC button.
4 Anodised aluminium shoulder title 2.5 × 1 cm.
5 Sgt Steve Murray wearing No 2 Dress with the crossed rifles badge of a skill at arms instructor on his right sleeve.
6 Officer's silver, gilt and enamel cap badge 4 × 4.5 cm and collar badges 2.75 × 3 cm.
7 Sgt Spud Murphy wearing No2 Dress. Soldiers wear berets rather than Forage Caps.
8 Cpl Dippy Diprose wearing No2 Dress.

opposite page

9 RLC prototype TRF 7 × 7 cm.
10 WO2 (SQMS) Andrew Wilmot wearing the bright metal cap badge and WO1 (SSM) Geoff Nuzum wearing the wire-embroidered beret badge. Both are wearing the RLC TRF below Parachute wings.
11 The restriction on trade and employment badges being worn on combat dress has led to some being worn on the rank slide, in this case the slide is that of a staff sergeant skill at arms instructor.
12 Conductor's rank slide.
13 RQMS are differentiated from other RLC Warrant Officers Class 2 by a red backing to their rank badge 6.5 × 5.25 cm.
14 Capt Davie Chambers wearing No 2 Dress with the silver, gilt and enamel badges.
15 RLC TRF 4 × 4 cm.

this page

16 Captain Elaine Caufield wearing the wire-embroidered beret badge. She is also wearing the Army Flying Badge although the RLC blue beret indicates that she is not serving with the Army Air Corps.
17 Lt Col David Wicks wearing the 13 Air Assault Support Regiment LZ flash.
18 13 Air Assault Support Regiment LZ Flash 7 × 7 cm.
19 Cyprus Service Support Unit arm badge 5.75 × 5.5 cm.
20 WO1 (RSM) Mark Lappin wearing the 16 Air Assault Brigade badge below the Union flag.
21 Woven title worn on the pullover by units in Germany.

Acknowledgement
Major Mitch Pegg and Pete Williams, WO1 (GSM) Anthony Topping, WO1 (RSM) DM Lappin and WO2 (TQMS) Tony Brankin

Air Despatch

Air Despatch is handled by 47 Air Despatch Squadron, 13 Air Assault Support Regiment. The squadron works with the Royal Air Force and is responsible for ensuring that supplies carried by air are carried and delivered safely.

The Air Despatch Drop Zone flash is a yellow Dakota aircraft on a blue background. The badge was awarded or possibly adopted as a Battle Honour badge by the Air Despatch Group following their service during the Battle of Arnhem, 1944. Each soldier now has a facing pair of badges which are worn 'flying towards the heart'. One is worn as a DZ flash on the right sleeve of the combat smock, and the other over the left breast of the flying overalls. The present badges are woven whilst in the recent past printed badges were worn.

In 1965 Air Despatch skill at arms badges were authorised for all ranks who had completed 40 flights as air despatch crewmen. Air Despatchers also qualify for additional pay. Senior non-commissioned officers who are Category A Air Despatchers with over three years experience can qualify as Qualified Air Despatch Instructors. There are also an average of six warrant officer Air Despatchers in various appointments who wear the unofficial Master Air Despatcher badge.

1

4

2

5

3

6

opposite page

1 Air Dispatch badge 6.5 × 4.5 cm.

2 Qualified Air Despatch Instructor badge 7 × 4.75 cm.

3 Unofficial Warrant Officer's Master Air Dispatcher badge 7 × 4.5 cm.

4 Cpl Scott Rees wearing the Dakota badge on his flying suit along with the Air Dispatcher Skill at Arms badge and 16 Air Assault Brigade badge on his left sleeve.

5 Sgt Phil Jones wearing the Air Despatch badge, SSgt Russ Wood wearing the Qualified Air Despatch Instructor badge, and WO2 Andy Johnson wearing the Master Air Despatch badge.

this page

6 Air Despatch DZ flash 8 × 6.5 cm worn 'flying towards the heart', one on the combat smock and the other on the flying overalls.

Driver

Qualified Class 2 drivers are authorised a star badge. The badge was introduced in 1950 to replace the various badges, both official and unofficial, which had proliferated for drivers during the Second World War. The badge is based on that authorised for Class 1 drivers of The Tank Corps which had been introduced in 1923 and later became the much prized qualification badge for corporal driver mechanics of The Royal Tank Regiment. The original badge was a Mullet, a five pointed star with black rays. The present driver's badge is a five pointed star with a rosette on the centre. A similar but much smaller badge is worn by the Infantry to indicate a Distinction gained on specialist courses (see Infantry p.88). In the RLC the badge is sometimes referred to as the Staff Car driver's badge and there is a wire-embroidered version for wear on Number 1 Dress which is very similar to the star introduced in 1881 for a volunteer who was 'Returned as efficient in rifle drill and practice for five years.' The first regulations for the Territorial Force in 1908 state that 'a man who has been returned efficient four times may wear the star.' A star badge, either woven in black or in gilding metal for soldiers and silver for officers, was proposed in 1940 as the qualification badge for commando volunteers but at that time no qualification badge was adopted as the first raids were carried out by Infantry battalions and therefore raiding was seen as an Infantry skill. The TA star badge was discontinued in 1952 and it is possible that surviving stocks were used as the Driver's Number 1 Dress badge.

1

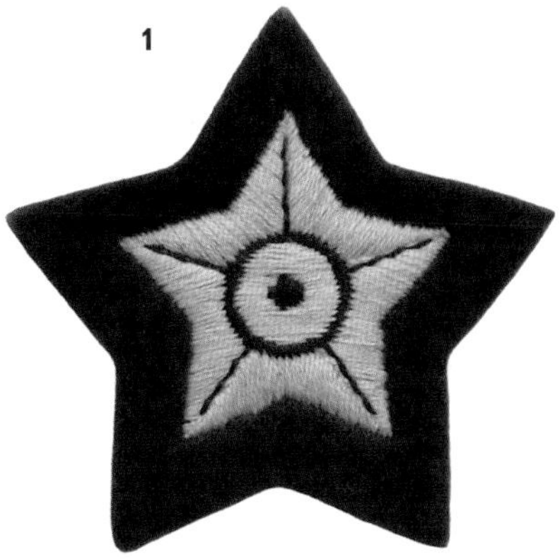

2

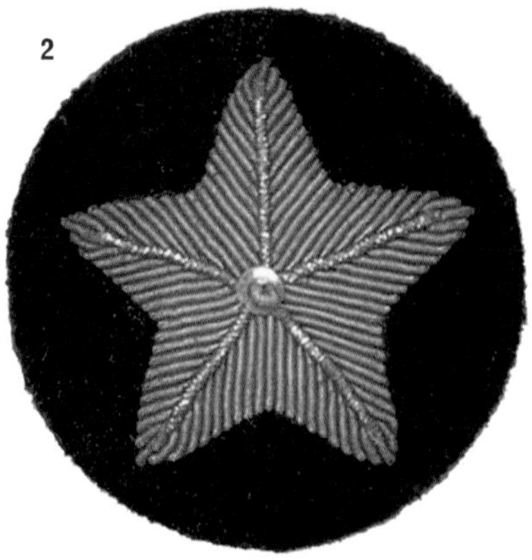

1 Driver's No2 Dress badge 5 cm.

2 Driver's wire-embroidered No1 Dress badge 5 cm.

7 Transport Regiment RLC

7 Transport Regiment has been based in Germany for many years, originally as a tank transporter regiment manned in part by civilians from the Mixed Services Organisation, or MSO. Many of the MSO were Polish, principally Displaced Persons from the Second World War, many with considerable wartime service, who maintained their own Mess. As a particular honour British officers and Warrant Officers who had been invited to the MSO Mess and said the grace in Polish were awarded a silver Polish Eagle badge by the Superintendent which was worn on left collar of Number 2 Dress and Mess Dress. With the disbandment of the MSO the Polish badge was adopted by 7 Transport Regiment, worn on the right collar in Mess Dress.

Polish tank transporter badge 1.25 × 1.5 cm.

Tank Transporter Driver

In 1982 a badge to be worn on the lower left sleeve was authorised for tank transporter drivers who had more than one year's experience. The badges, representing the Thornicroft Antar transporter and Chieftain tank, were issued in 1984 and were eventually also worn above the left breast pocket on Combat Dress and coveralls. They have been ordered removed from those orders of dress and the tank transporter squadrons have found alternative means of identifying the drivers. 3 Squadron had a pewter badge representing the Commander transporter carrying a Challenger 2 tank produced in Catterick in 1998 for an operational tour in Bosnia. A much smaller metal and enamel badge was produced for wear on the lapel in mufti but was also worn on the rank slide on combat dress before the introduction in mid-2004 of rank slides with a woven Tank Transporter design.

The present transporter is the Oshkosh HET M107OF which may be identified by the large number of wheels all along the trailer. As yet it has not inspired the design of a badge.

1

2

3

4

1 3 Tank Transporter Squadron private purchase pewter badge 8.5 × 2.5 cm.
2 3 Tank Transporter Squadron discrete metal badge 3 × 1 cm.
3 Tank Transporter rank slide introduced in 2004.
4 WO1 (GSM) Tony McMullan wearing the Tank Transporter badge.
5 LCpl David Crampton wearing the tank transporter driver qualification badge on his combat jacket.
6 No2 Dress Tank Transporter Driver badge 8.5 × 2.75 cm.
7 No1 Dress wire-embroidered Tank Transporter driver badge 8.5 × 3.25 cm.

5

6

7

8 Transport Regiment

When formed in Germany as part of the British Army of the Rhine, or BAOR, in 1964 8 Transport Column Royal Army Service Corps was responsible for the delivery of special weapons to 570th US Army Artillery Group and chose the scorpion insignia because it is an American insect with a sting in its tail. In 1981 13 Squadron commanded by Major Roy Ratazzi introdued a European style pocket fob. Others squadrons followed suit until in 1986 all had fobs. In 1989 Lt Col Ratazzi, then the Commanding Officer, introduced the regimental pattern fob to replace the squadron fobs. The regiment also adopted a cloth scorpion arm badge. As with other 'regimental' badges it was to be replaced by the RLC TRF by April 2005.

1

2

1 8 Regiment RLC pocket fob 4 × 8.5 cm (badge 3 × 3.5 cm).
2 8 Regiment RLC arm badge 7.25 × 5 cm.

10 Transport Regiment

10 Transport Regiment retained the Roman numeral X as the regimental emblem when transferred from the RCT to the RLC. Senior ranks wear a small silver X on the left collar of their Mess Dress

10 Transport Regiment sergeant's Mess Dress regimental collar badge 1 × 1 cm.

Acknowledgement
Major Blackie Widdows, WO1 (RSM) AR Relph, WO2 (SSM) Baz Parker and Edge Wilton

Movement Controller

The spoked wheel is the Employment badge of qualified Movement Controllers.

Movement Controllers, both Army and RAF are identified at airfields, ports and railheads by a large version of the badge sewn to a red brassard. Known as the 'Wagon wheel' the large badge is worn, by some detachments, on a disruptive pattern material, or DPM, brassard.

3

1

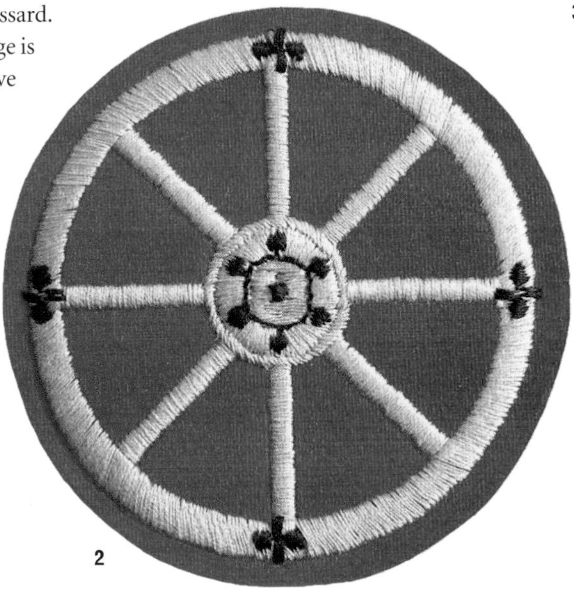

2

5

4

1 WO1 (SSM) Abe Swaby wearing the 'Wagon wheel' badge on a brassard and Sgt Lisa Bean wearing the Movement Control armband.
2 'Wagon wheel' Movement Control badge 8 cm.
3 Movement Control armband.
4 Cpl Tomo Thompson wearing the Movement Controllers armband.
5 Movement Control employment badge 3.5 cm.

Acknowledgement WO1 (RSM) A Hunt

Pioneer

Pioneers are responsible for labour support. 23 Pioneer Regiment wears a red and green arm badge on the left sleeve of the combat shirt and the pullover, red to the front; the soldiers remember the correct way round by 'Red close to the heart' or by 'Blood on the grass'. The colours are those of the former Royal Pioneer Corps and similar badges have been worn by Pioneers serving in other units (see Royal Logistic Corps Territorial Army). As with other 'regimental' badges it was to be replaced by the RLC TRF by April 2005.

1

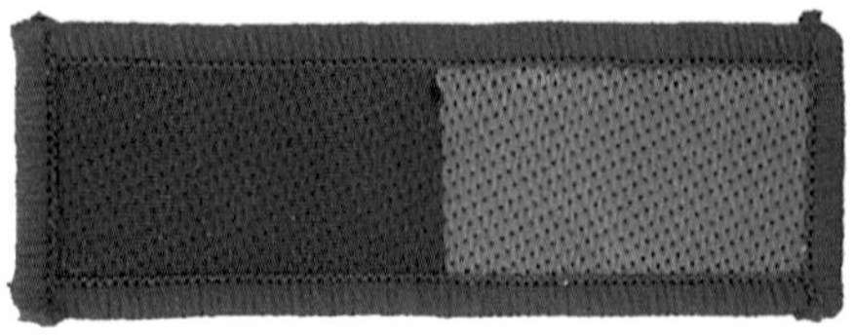

2

1 LCpl Dean Martin wearing the 23 Pioneer Regiment arm badge.
2 23 Pioneer Regiment arm badge 5.5 × 2 cm.

Port Operator

The Army operates the Military Port at Marchwood and with the expeditionary nature of operations is frequently required to arrange the receipt of supplies and equipment into a theatre of operations through a foreign port, which may have been damaged. 17 Port and Maritime Regiment RLC includes Port Operators and also Seamen, Navigators and Marine Engineers who operate Army vessels ranging from landing craft to work boats.

Introduced in about 1942 the Blue Ensign with crossed swords cloth arm badge was worn by Watermen and Seamen serving with the Waterborne Fleet Royal Army Service Corps. The badge was then adopted by all ranks of the Maritime Regiment Royal Corps of Transport and is now worn by personnel of 17 Port and Maritime Regiment RLC. As with other 'regimental' badges it was to be replaced by the RLC TRF by April 2005 except for those serving afloat.

Ocean Watchkeepers and Chief Engineers have, since 1967, worn a crown and anchor Skill at Arms badge on the lower left sleeve, both of which may be worn in perpetuity

The Union Flag was introduced in 1801 as a result of the Act of Union. The Royal Navy flew three coloured ensigns with the Union Flag in the upper quarter of the hoist, identifying the senior admirals; Admirals of the White, Red and Blue. In 1864 the Royal Navy was reorganised and henceforth the coloured ensigns were to identify types of ships. The Royal Navy kept the White Ensign (it is said because Lord Nelson as Admiral of the White, flew the White Ensign at the Battle of Trafalgar), the Merchant Marine took the Red Ensign and other military vessels took the Blue Ensign; this included vessels of the Ordnance Board Fleet which traced its formation to 1414, the year before the Battle of Agincourt.

The crossed swords had been authorised as the Army's badge in 1938 and were included on the Army flag. In 1942 the Ordnance Board vessels became the War Department Fleet and the Royal Army Service Corps soldiers who crewed them adopted the Army's Blue Ensign as an arm badge. Army vessels are now designated the Royal Logistic Corps Fleet and are operated by 17 Port and Maritime Regiment.

1

2

3

4

opposite page

1 Ocean Watchkeeper, ultra-marine, and Marine Engineer, purple, Skill at Arms badges 3.5 × 6.5 cm.

2 Captain Andy Rockall wearing the 17 Port and Maritime Regiment arm badge below a QADI badge.

this page

3 Ocean Watchkeeper and Marine Engineer wire-embroidered Mess Dress badge 2.75 × 5 cm.

4 17 Port and Maritime Regiment arm badges, worn with the Union Flag to the front 7 × 4 cm.

Acknowledgement SSgt Dutch Holland

Railway Operator

Originally a Railway Engine Driver was a Class A Trade and Railway Engine Driver (Diesel) was a Class B Trade. Qualified soldiers wore the A or B within a wreath badge (see Army). Qualified railwaymen are now identified by an Employment badge representing a cross section of a railway line, which is worn on the upper right arm.

Railwayman employment badge 6.5 × 5.5 cm.

Ammunition Technician

'That's a cool badge, what do you do?' Unknown chef to WO2 (SQMS) Martin Hook RLC in the cookhouse in Pristina, Kosovo.

Ammunition is a key component of combat capability. Ammunition Technicians are responsible for the inspection, repair, proof, testing, modifications and disposal of all ammunition. Ammunition technical personnel are also responsible for Explosive Ordnace Disposal, including terrorist bomb disposal. The 'troubles' in Northern Ireland, which began in 1969, led to a constant conflict between terrorist bombers and the Army's Ammunition Technical Officers, or ATO. They are responsible for making safe the bombs, known to the Army as Improvised Explosive Devices, or IED. In recognition of the very specialist nature of their duties, in 1975 ATO were authorised an employment badge to be worn in perpetuity.

The ATO badge followed the design of the badge worn by Ammunition Technicians, or AT, who replaced Ammunition Examiners in 1950. The original badge was produced in gilding metal and the present cloth badge was introduced in 1960. As with the ATO badge it also may be worn in perpetuity.

1

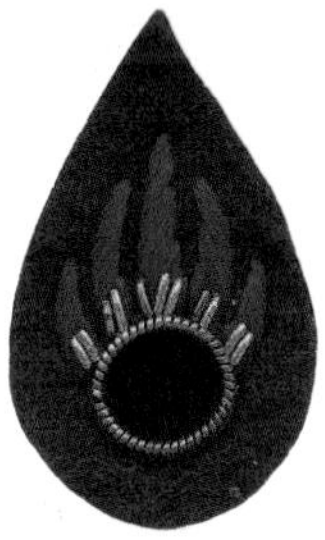

2

3

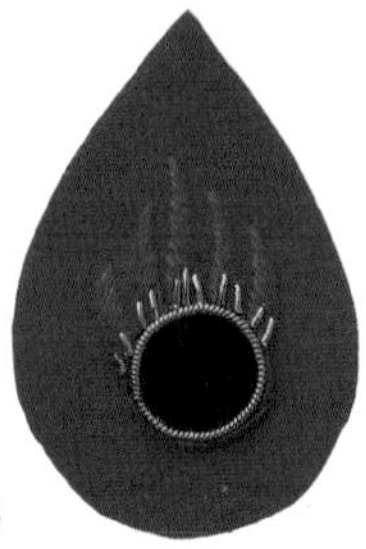

4

5

6

The trade of Ammunition Examiner gained prominence during the Second World War and an employment badge was authorised in 1942. There was no metal version of the badge provided for wear in khaki drill, the uniform worn in warm climates. The RAOC overcame the deficiency, producing an AE badge, by altering the Warrant Officer II badge (then a Crown surrounded by a wreath). The Crown was removed to be replaced by an A from the RA shoulder title, and E from the RE title. The locally made badges survived until about 1950 when the gilding metal Ammunition Technician badge was introduced.

7

8

previous page

1 No1 Dress wire-embroidered ATO badge 2.25 × 3.25 cm.
2 No2 Dress wire-embroidered ATO badge 2.25 × 3.5 cm.
3 Woven working dress ATO badge 3 × 4 cm.
4 Mess Dress wire-embroidered ATO badge 2.5 × 3.5 cm.

this page

5 Sgt Ritchie Cunningham wearing the 321Squadron 'Felix' badge above her AT badge and Captain Simon Bratcher wearing the ATO badge.
6 WO2 John Ridgeway wearing the AT badge.
7 No1 Dress wire-embroidered AT badge 4 × 5 cm.
8 No2 Dress Woven AT badge 4 × 5 cm.

Acknowledgement Major P Sutterby

321 (Explosive Ordnance Disposal) Squadron

321 EOD Unit RAOC was formed as a shadow unit in 1968 to be activated as required. It was first deployed to Anguilla in 1969 and then in 1970 to Northern Ireland where it has remained.

In 1970 the radio appointment title for the Royal Army Ordnance Corps, or RAOC, was Rickshaw with connotations of the delivery of stores. The appointment title was considered inappropriate for RAOC EOD teams who adopted the alternative appointment title Felix after the cartoon character – not only because a cat has nine lives but also because of his ability on the silver screen to survive all sorts of mayhem.

In 1974 Staff Sergeant Bryan Shepherd 'sketched a slightly scruffy and surprised Felix wearing a helmet', which was reproduced as the Squadron's emblem. Felix appeared on vehicles, notice boards and letterheads and was produced as an arm badge in 2002.

321 EOD Squadron is the only agency in Northern Ireland permitted to investigate and render safe suspected IED. During the 'Troubles' the Army's bomb disposal experts dealt with some 54,326 emergency calls – an average of about 40 a week – of which almost 5,500 were actual terrorist devices. ATO have recovered well over 200 tonnes of explosives, much of it in an unstable condition.

321 EOD Squadron 'Felix' arm badge 4 × 6 cm

Acknowledgement
WO1 (SSM) Neil Reede and Sgt AP Gatty AGC (SPS)

Joint Force Explosive Ordnance Disposal Group

JFEOD Group was formed for the Iraq War in 2003.

In 2003 831 EOD Squadron RLC deployed to the Middle East for the Iraq War. The Squadron adopted the nickname the Desert Cats, following on the theme of Felix from Northern Ireland. WO2 Georgie Dunville designed the Desert Cat arm badge which is now worn by the JFEOD Group, which includes RE and RLC, both regular and TA, RAF and New Zealand and Norweigan troops.

1

2

1 JFEOD Group 'Desert Cat' arm badge 4 × 6 cm.
2 SSgt Si De Gruchy wearing the AT badge on his right sleeve and the Desert Cat badge on his left.

Acknowledgement WO1 Mike Warden

Chefs

The RLC concentrates on the provision of chefs to deployable units, most catering for non-deployable units now being provided by contractors.

The chefs wear miniature chrome rank badges on the breast pocket of their white jackets. The miniature chevrons are also worn in certain orders of dress by Royal Military Police, Royal Army Dental Corps and Queen Alexandra's Royal Army Nursing Corps non-commmissioned officers.

1

2

1 Sergeant's miniature chrome rank badge worn by chefs on the white jacket 5 × 4 cm.
2 LCpl Tony Beckett with his miniature chrome rank badge on a maroon backing as he is serving with The King's Royal Hussars.

Queen's Own Gurkha Logistic Regiment

The Queen's Own Gurkha Logistic Regiment was formed in 2001 by redesignating The Queen's Own Gurkha Transport Regiment, which had originally been formed as the Gurkha Army Service Corps in 1958.

The Queen's Own Gurkha Logistic Regiment, or QOGLR, badges follow the pattern of those designed for The Gurkha Army Service Corps and later The Gurkha Transport Regiment and The Queen's Own Gurkha Transport Regiment; crossed kukris mounted on a star plate similar to that of the sponsoring Corps.

The soldier's anodised alluminium cap badge is also used as the officer's pouch badge. Officers wear a small badge, the same size as the soldiers' collar badges, as both cap and collar badges.

1

2

3

4

5

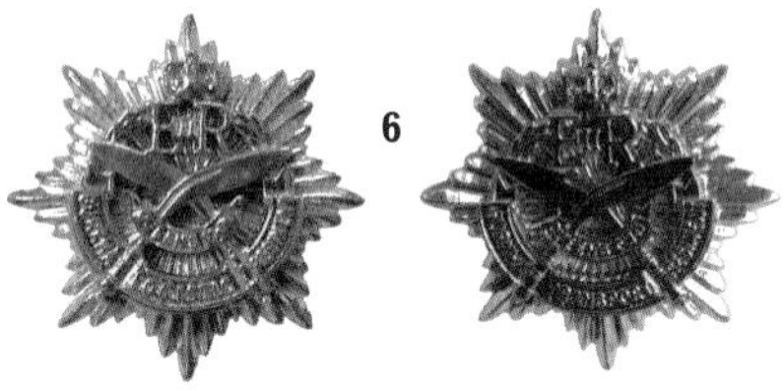

6

7

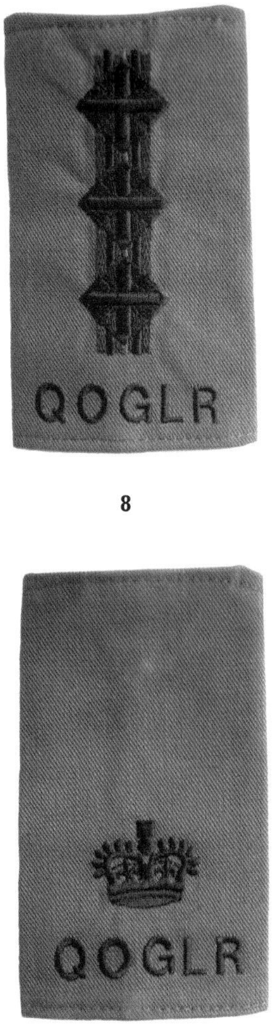

8

9

opposite page

1 Queen's Own Gurkha Logistic Regiment soldier's anodised aluminium cap badge 4.25 × 4.25 cm and collar badges 2.5 × 2.5 cm.

2 Shoulder title 4 × 1 cm.

3 Queen's Own Gurkha Logistic Regiment button.

4 Pte Bishal Limbu wearing the Brigade of Gurkhas TRF above the Cross Swords badge of an All Arms Physical Training Instructor, and WO2 (SSM) Laxmiprasad Chongbang wearing the 101 Logistic Brigade badge below the Union Flag badge. The silver bands on his cane are each engraved with the name of his predecessors.

this page

5 Queen's Own Gurkha Logistic Regiment plastic pouch mounted with a Queen's Own Gurkha Transport Regiment anodised aluminium cap badge.

6 Queen's Own Gurkha Logistic Regiment and Queen's Own Gurkha Transport Regiment silver and gilt badges, both 2.5 × 2.5 cm worn as both cap and collar badges. The obsolete Queen's Own Gurkha Transport Regiment badges are still worn.

7 Silver crossed kukris badge 2.5 × 1.75 cm made by the unit's goldsmith and worn on the sleeve of officer's Mess Dress.

8 Major's rank slide and Captain (Queen's Gurkha Officer) rank slide identified by the regimental ribbon (for the background to the ribbon see Royal Gurkha Rifles, p. 217).

9 Bright metal shoulder belt badge 7.5 × 7.75 cm, also worn as the plaid brooch by pipers.

Acknowledgement WO2 Chhatra Rai

Army Commandos

Army commandos were formed after the retreat from Dunkirk in 1940 when the Prime Minister, Winston Churchill, called for 'specially trained troops of the hunter class, who can develop a reign of terror down these (enemy occupied) coasts.'

The Green Beret is the distinctive hallmark of commando troops, indicating that those who wear it have attended and passed a gruelling and physically demanding test of endurance, by displaying the commando qualities of unselfishness, cheerfulness under adversity, courage, determination and high professional standards. Army Commandos wear a Fighting Knife badge on the left sleeve in pertetuity.

The Army formed ten commandos in 1940 followed in 1942 by the first Royal Marines Commando. In 1943 the Commandos were grouped into brigades, including 102 Royal Marines Brigade which was later renamed 3 Commando Brigade Royal Marines. Although the Army Commandos were disbanded at the end of the Second World War soldiers have continued to provide specialist support to 3 Commando Brigade.

The Army commando units are 29 Commando Regiment RA, 20 Commando Air Defence Battery RA; 59 Independent Commando Squadron RE, 131 (Volunteer) Independent Commando Squadron RE and 2 Commando Troop (EOD) 33 Engineer Regiment RE; plus a large proportion of the personnel in Commando Logistic Regiment RM.

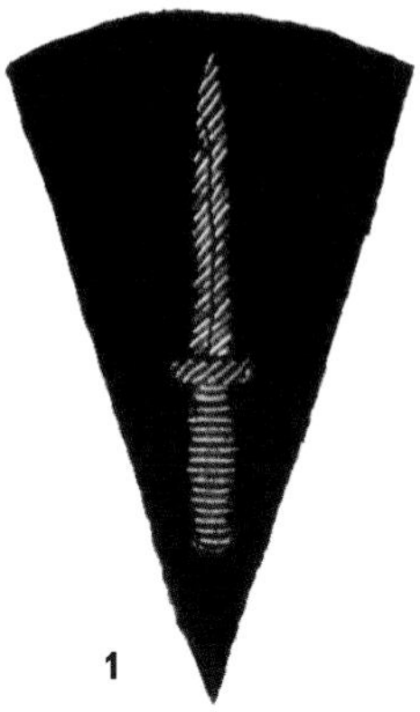
1

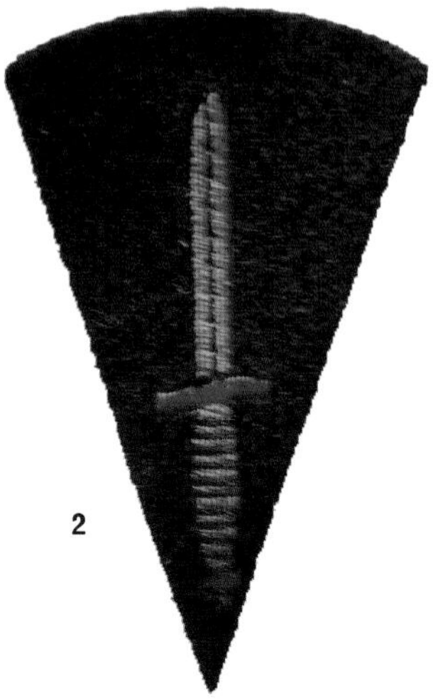
2

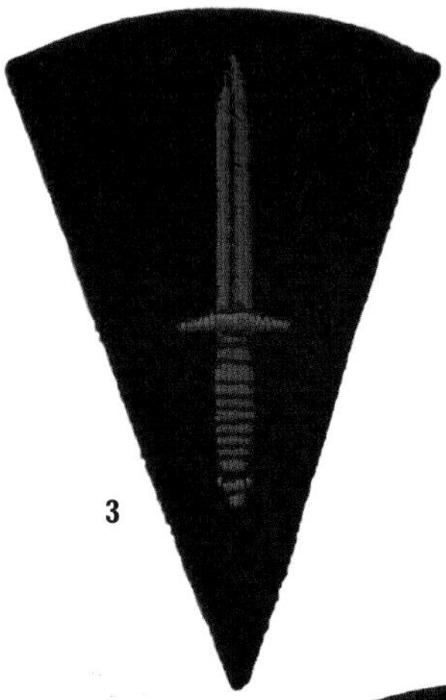
3

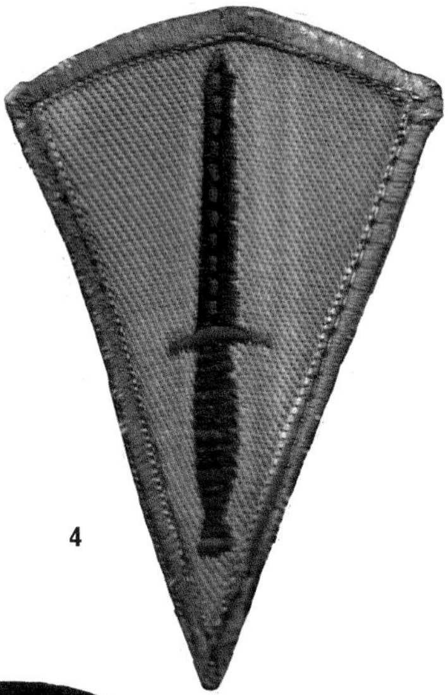
4

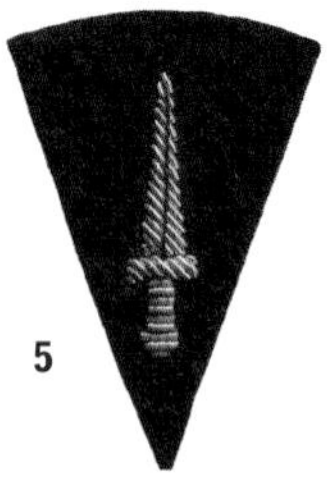
5

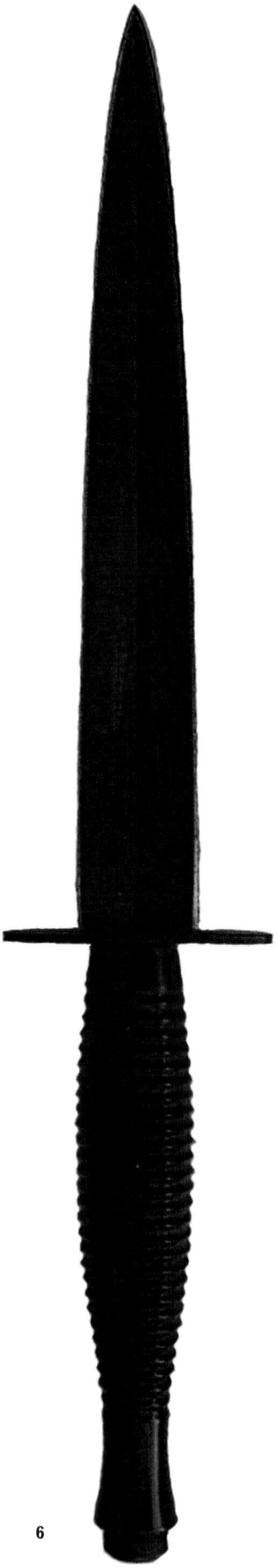
6

1 No1 Dress wire-embroidered Commando badge 3.25 × 5.25.
2 Woven Commando badge 4.25 × 6.75 cm with S-shaped guard.
3 Woven Commando badge with straight Guard 4.25 × 6.5 cm.
4 Unofficial Combat Dress subdued Commando badge 4.75 × 7 cm.
5 Mess Dress wire-embroidered Commando badge 2 × 3 cm.
6 Fairburn Sykes Fighting Knife 5 × 29.5 cm developed by two officers who had served in the Shanghai Municipal Police, and introduced in about 1940. Originally with an S-shaped guard.

Commando Logistic Regiment RM

The Commando Logistic Regiment is manned by personnel from the Royal Navy, Royal Marines and Army. All ranks are qualified commandos and wear the green beret with their own cap badge.

1

2

3

1 Cpl Steve Gaze RLC wearing the green beret with RLC cap badge and the Fighting Knife arm badge.

2 Lt Tim Turner wearing the green beret with REME cap badge.

3 Lt Cliff Green RLC and Captain Pip Tattersall AGC (ETS) wearing the green beret with their own cap badges, Fighting Knife arm badge on the left sleeve and 3 Commando Brigade badge on the right.

Royal Army Medical Corps

The Royal Army Medical Corps, or RAMC, adopted the traditional medical symbol of the rod of Æsculapius, the Greek God of medicine, with a serpent entwined round it as its badge when formed in 1898. The cap badge was authorised in 1902 and the scroll altered to the motto, which is commonly translated as *Steadfast in Adversity*, in 1948. A dull cherry ovoid beret badge backing was introduced in 1956 following a suggestion by Colonel HC Benson, Commandant RAMC Depot.

Class 2 soldiers in the rank of corporal and below wear a bar of worsted tubular braid on the outside of the right sleeve on the Number 2 Dress jacket. Class 1 soldiers wear two bars. The practice dates to 1886 when orderlies of the Medical Staff Corps wore bars of scarlet braid on the right sleeve of the tunic. The practice was stopped at some time but reintroduced in 1956.

The Royal Army Medical Corps colours, Blue for the colour of the uniform in 1898, Old Gold for the Royal title, and Dull Cherry for the uniform facings are reproduced on the stable belt and on the Landing Zone flash.

Warrant Officers Class 2, irrespective of appointment, wear the Crown within the laurel wreath as the badge of rank as recognition that until the 1960s all were appointed Quartermaster Sergeant.

The Royal Army Medical Corps delivers medical training for the Army. Royal Armoured Corps and Infantry Regimental Medical Assistants wear the rod of Æsculapius and entwined serpent skill at arms badge.

1

2

3

4

5

6

7

8

9

10

The earliest known record of an Army surgeon is 1223, 'One, Master Thomas, an army surgeon, who knew how to cure wounds, a science particularly useful in the siege of castles.' Surgeons from then on are regularly mentioned in reports and returns until in 1541, by an Act of Parliament, their status as non-combatants was acknowledged when they were 'exempted from bearing armour'. In 1794 the Surgeon's mate became a commissioned rank styled Assistant Surgeon. The following year five Royal Military Hospitals were opened, at Chelsea, Deal, Gosport, Portsmouth and Plymouth. Hospital Sergeants were added to regimental establishments in 1824 and the first Army Medical School opened at Chatham in 1858.

11

12

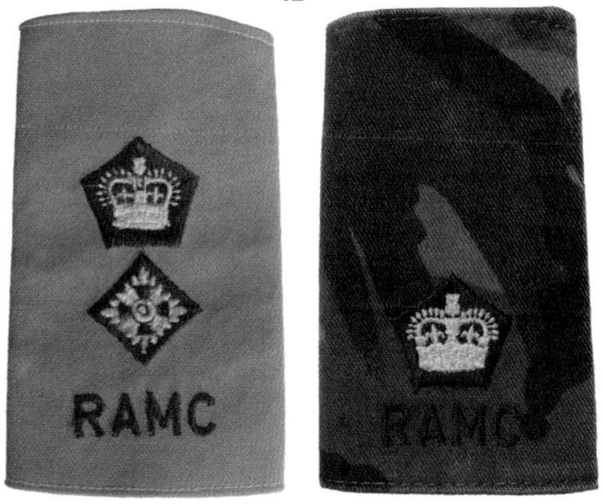

13

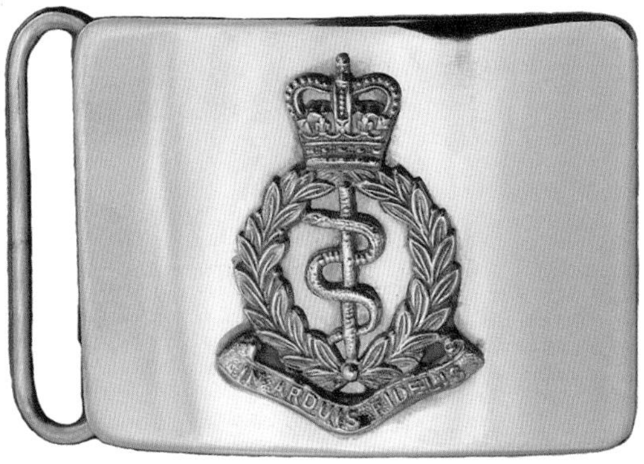

14

opposite page

1 Royal Army Medical Corps soldier's anodised aluminium cap badge 3 × 4.5 cm and collar badges 2.5 × 3.5 cm.

2 RAMC button.

3 Officer's silver and gilt cap badge 3.25 × 4.5 cm and collar badges 2.5 × 3.5 cm.

4 RAMC Class 1 Tradesman qualification tubular braid bars worn on the lower right sleeve of Number 2 Dress.

5 LZ flash 7 × 6 cm introduced for 23 Parachute Field Ambulance and now worn by all RAMC units in 16 Air Assault Brigade.

6 Officer's wire-embroidered beret badge 4.5 × 4.75 cm.

7 Officer's wire-embroidered beret badge on a maroon backing for airborne forces 4.5 × 4.75 cm.

8 Officer's wire-embroidered badge originally worn as a sash badge on female officers' Mess Dress 5 × 4.75 cm and still seen as a beret badge.

this page

9 Lt James Salt wearing No1 Dress.

10 Cpl Taff Thorne an airborne Class 1 Combat Medical Technician wears the pale blue and maroon lanyard from 23 Parachute Field Ambulance.

11 Cpl Jenny Willis wearing No1 Dress with the crossed rifles badge of a skill-at-arms instructor on her right sleeve.

12 Lieutenant colonel's and major's rank slides.

13 Soldier's waist belt clasp 7 × 5.5 cm. Unusually, the bimetal badge is fitted to the backing plate by the manufacturer rather than being a cap badge fitted to the universal plate.

14 Cpl Anne Nicholl with the RAMC backing to her cap badge.

15

16

17

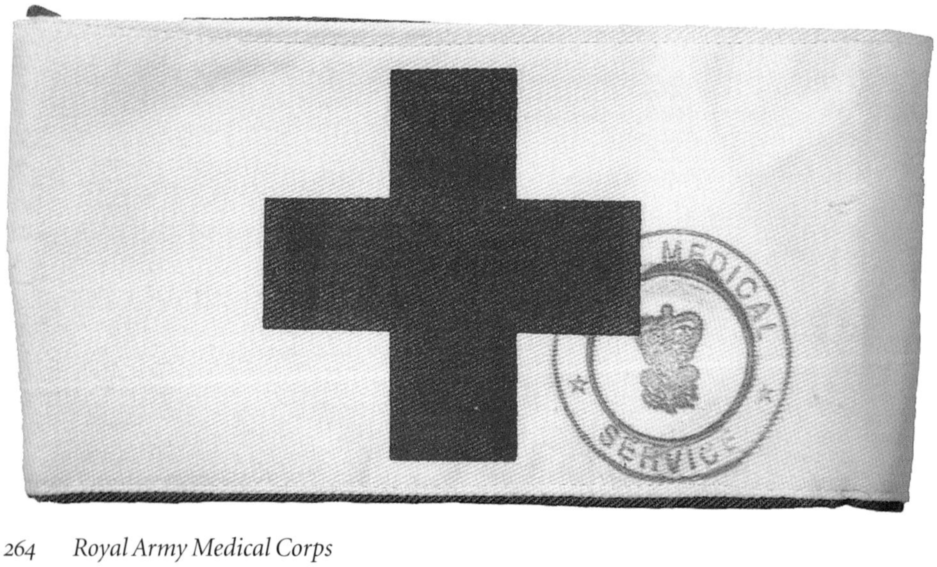

R3 MIMU arm badge 6 × 6 cm worn at the hospital at Sipovo in Bosnia Herzegovina. R3 MIMU is the multi-national field hospital based at Sipovo in Bosnia Herzognia, which supports Multi-National Brigade (North). Originally organised to support Multi-National Division (South West) it included medical personnel from Canada, Czech Republic, Netherlands, Iceland and the UK.

18

19

20

opposite page

15 RAMC General and Staff No1 Dress gorgets.

16 Lt Jo Willcock, Capt Charity Cooper and Nicola Wiseman wearing embroidered beret badges.

17 The Geneva Red Cross arm badge worn by all personnel working with medical units. Under international law the badge should be authenticated, in this case by an Army Medical Service ink stamp.

this page

18 RAMC helmet plate 10.5 × 12.5 cm. The RAMC has a number of Full Dress uniforms for wear on Corps parades.

19 Regimental Medical Assistant No1 Dress wire-embroidered skill-at-arms badge 5.5 cm.

20 Regimental Medical Assistant No2 Dress woven skill-at-arms badge 5.5 cm.

Acknowledgement
Lt Col MJ Lindley and WO1 (RSM) RS Parkes

Army Aviation Medicine

The Army Aviation Medicine badge is worn by Army Specialists in Aviation Medicine on the left sleeve of the flying suit; all are doctors and pilots. It was designed in 1983 by Major Malcolm Braithwaite and the original embroidered by Mrs Libby Braithwaite. The design combines the colours of the Royal Army Medical Corps around those of the Army Air Corps and the AAC eagle above the medical rod of Aesculapius. 'Whether the eagle is about to stoop, or the snake to strike, is open to interpretation.'

1

2

1 Army Aviation Medicine badge 8 cm.

2 Col Malcolm Braithwaite OBE wearing the Army Aviation Medicine badge he designed.

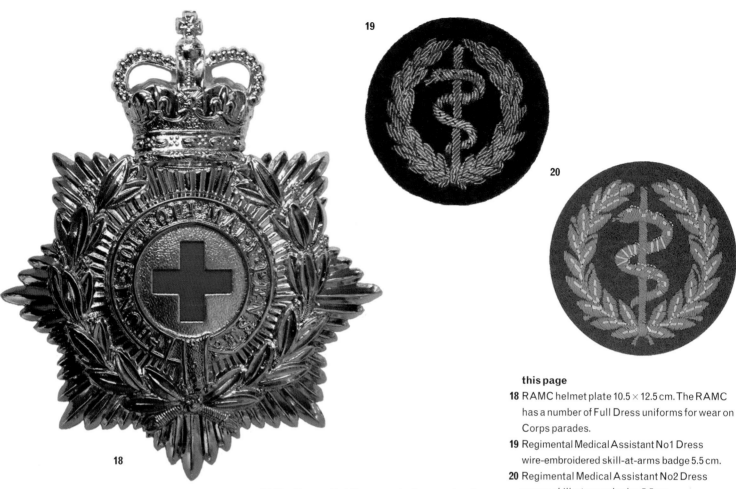

Royal Electrical and Mechanical Engineers

REME was formed in 1942 by transferring technical soldiers from the Royal Army Ordnance Corps, Royal Engineers and the Royal Army Service Corps. The original establishment of REME was 'approximately 5,000 officers and 97,000 Other Ranks. This information is not to be broadcast since it might give a clue to the size of the Army.'

The first REME badge, introduced in 1942, was functional, easy to mass-produce and considered 'attractive and most suitable', but as early as 1943 there was discussion about adopting a more heraldically pleasing design. In 1949 both the Corps' badge and title were changed. The renamed Corps of Royal Electrical and Mechanical Engineers adopted the white horse suggesting horsepower, chained to emphasis that it was under control, poised above a globe indicating the worldwide deployment of the Corps, and backed by a lightening flash to illustrate the electrical function of the Corps. The badge was designed by Major General Colin Campbell, Inspector REME and Mr Geoffrey Bell working with Mr Brandham of JR Gaunt & Son. (It did not take long for soldiers to suggest rather unkindly that the new badge actually shows a horse dropping a bollock). There is a known variation where an enterprising craftsman has removed the horse from the badge, and replaced it with a

1

2

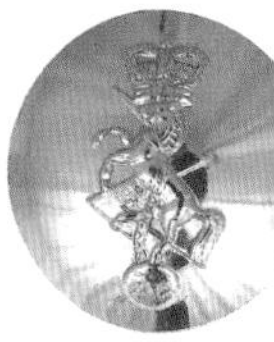

3

4

5

6

7

8

9

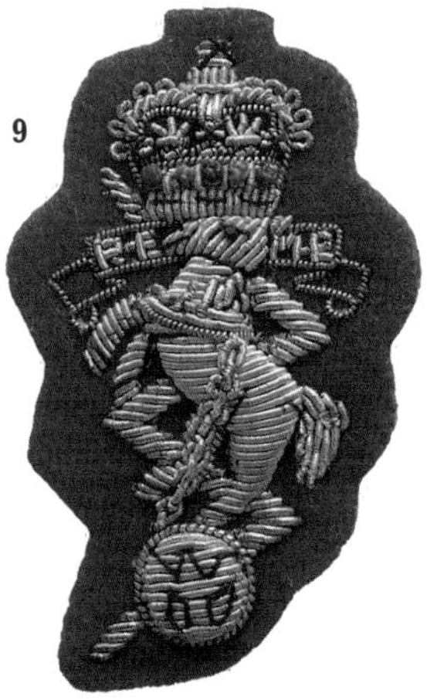

neatly cut out silhouette of Andy Capp, the Daily Mirror newspaper cartoon character, complete with beer mug, cigarette and billiard cue.

The new badge was surmounted by the Tudor (or King's) Crown, which was changed to the St Edward's (or Queen's) Crown in about 1955 and produced in anodised aluminium from about 1958. On the wire-embroidered badge the crown has each element picked out with the pearl and ermine base in silver, the cushion in crimson and the jewels in colours representing ruby, emerald, sapphire, emerald and ruby.

The collar badges were also altered to St Edward's (or Queen's) Crown in about 1955. As with the cap badge officers' badges are produced in silver and gilt, and soldiers in anodised aluminium. In Mess Dress officers' wear wire-embroidered collar badges, those for male officers on a black backing and those for female officers on a scarlet backing.

REME sponsor two employment badges. The crossed hammer and pincers employment badge is worn on the right sleeve by REME tradesmen and Royal Engineers metal smiths

The value of badges on operations is that they easily identify particular qualifications. However some badges are unfamiliar to the majority of soldiers. It is told that during a winter exercise in Norway an Air Despatcher was walking through a hanger when a REME Air Technician misidentifying his AD badge for an AT badge asked for the air despatcher's opinion on the air worthiness of a helicopter's rotor gear. 'Yeah, it looks fine to me' said the AD as he wandered off never having seen a rotor gear before, and having no idea what it did.

10

11

12

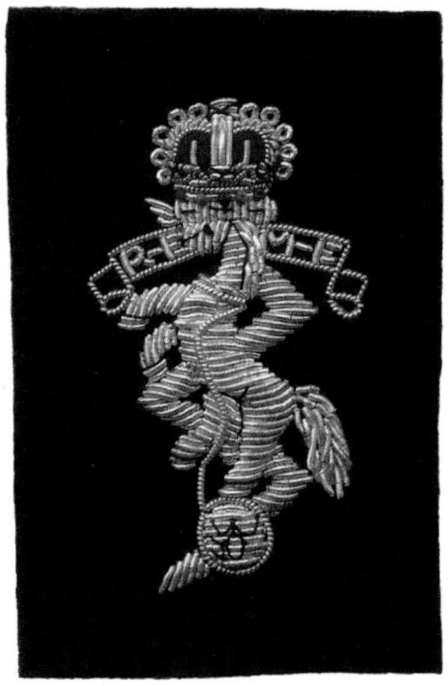

13

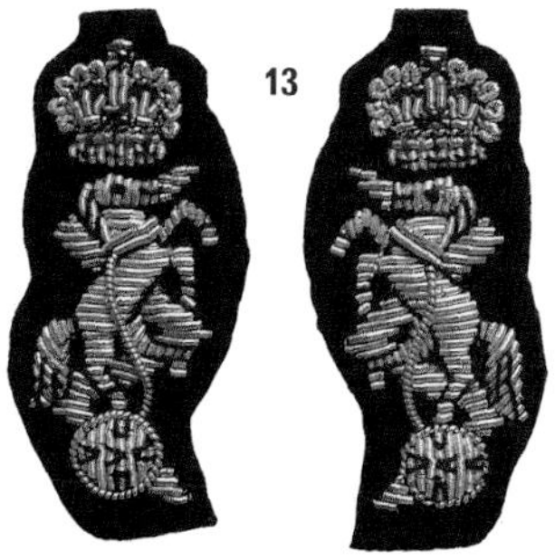

14

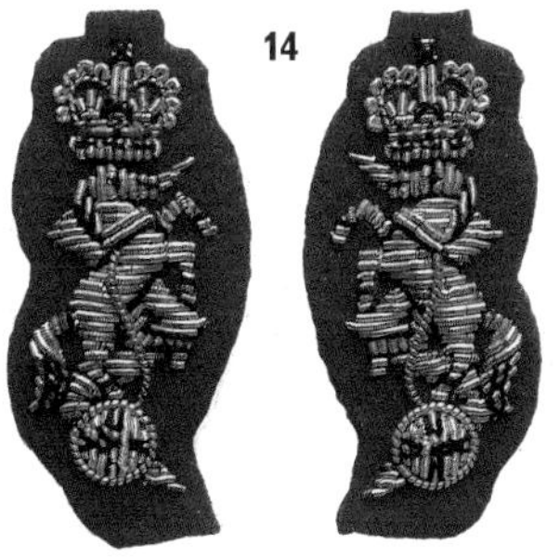

15

opposite page

1 REME soldier's anodised aluminium cap 3 × 5 cm and collar badges 1.75 × 3 cm.

2 REME button.

3 REME shoulder title

4 Private purchase bi-metal cap badge 3.25 × 4.75 cm.

5 REME officer's silver and gilt cap badge 3 × 5 cm and collar badges 1.75 × 3 cm.

6 Officer's wire-embroidered beret badge, blue backing 3.75 × 5cm.

7 Officer's wire-embroidered beret badge, maroon backing for airborne forces 4 × 5.5 cm.

8 Officer's wire-embroidered beret badge, green backing for Commando forces 3.5 × 5.5 cm.

9 Officer's wire-embroidered Side Hat badge 3.5 × 6 cm.

this page

10 Sgt Glyn Painter wearing No2 Dress.

11 WO2 (CSM) Sandy Mack wearing No2 Dress with red sash and sword belt as he is serving at an Army Training Regiment.

12 Officer's wire-embroidered beret badge on black backing 4.5 × 7 cm for wear on the Army Air Corps beret.

13 REME male officers' Mess Dress collar badge on black background 1.75 × 4 cm.

14 REME female officers' Mess Dress collar badge on red background 2 × 4 cm.

15 Old pattern Mess Dress collar badges 3.25 × 4.75 cm.

below the rank of sergeant. The badge is also worn as an appointment badge by REME artificers. It is said that the badge represents St Eligus, the Roman swordmaker, and patron saint of REME. Variations of the wire-embroidered Mess Dress badge are produced on red and black backing. It is understood that the black badges are worn by Artificer Sergeant Majors. The hammer and pincers badge is known to have been worn above the wheel badge by wheelwrights of the Corps of Ordnance Artificers *c.*1886.

Amongst the specialisations within the REME are the trades connected with maintaining aircraft. REME personnel wear the AAC pale blue beret with the REME cap badge. Qualified Air Technicians, Class 1 and Class 2, of the rank of corporal and below wear the Air Technician badge which was introduced in 1959, on the right arm.

In common with several Corps the REME encourages pipers. The Princess Marina College, the REME apprentice college, offered piping as a hobby. The young pipers wore REME badges on Highland dress. In 1989 the college had a REME chromed plaid brooch produced which is still available although the College has closed.

16

17

18

19

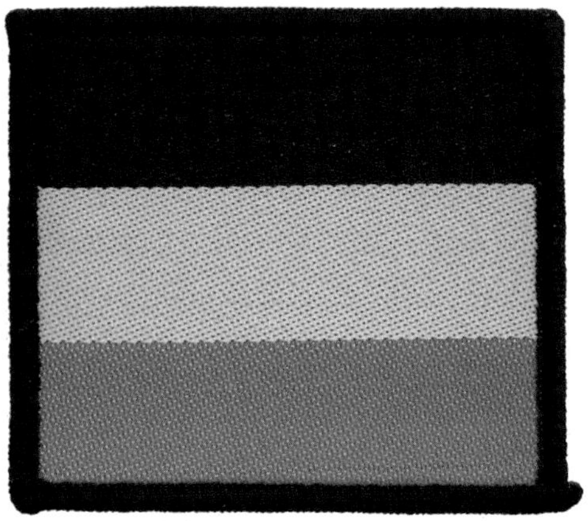
20

21

22

23

24

25

26

27

opposite page

16 No2 Dress woven Artificer badge 5.5 × 4.25 cm.
17 Mess Dress wire-embroidered Artificer badge 5.5 × 4.25 cm.
18 Sergeant Major's Mess Dress wire-embroidered Artificer badge 5.5 × 4.25 cm.
19 Air Technician badge 7 × 5 cm.
20 Proposed REME TRF 7 × 7 cm.
21 REME major's rank slide.
22 WO2 (AQMS) Tony Redfern serving in an aircraft workshop and therefore wearing the AAC beret, and a poppy for Remembrance Day.
23 LCpl Col Smith, a regimental policeman wearing No1 Dress.
24 Obsolete Control Equipment Technician badge 6 × 3.75 cm.
25 Obsolete Radar Technician badge 6 × 3.75 cm.

this page

26 Captain Matt Davis wearing the wire-embroidered beret badge and Sgt Richie Bennett wearing the anodised aluminium cap badge.
27 REME piper's plaid brooch produced for Princess Marina College 9.25 cm.

Acknowledgement
WO1 (RSM) RG Carr and AM Mack and Mr Brian Baxter

Adjutant General's Corps

The AGC was formed in 1992 to pay, administer, educate, discipline and where necessary detain soldiers.

The Adjutant General's Corps, or AGC, is organised into three functions: Staff and Personnel Support, or SPS; Provost, Educational and Training Services, or ETS; and Army Legal Services, or ALS. Provost consists of the Royal Military Police, Military Provost Staff and Military Provost Guard Service.

The AGC badge, introduced on its formation in 1992, is unique in featuring three crowns (the third is on the lion's head). All ranks of the SPS and officers of the ETS wear the cap badge. Officers' badges are produced in silver and gilt, and soldiers in anodised aluminium. Officers wear wire-embroidered beret badges which are produced on different colour backings to match headdress colours.

The AGC does not wear a Tactical Recognition Flash but has registered the design of red over black divided diagonally. It asked to identify each branch by lettering ALS, ETS, MPGS, MPS and SPS across the centre.

1

2

3

4

6

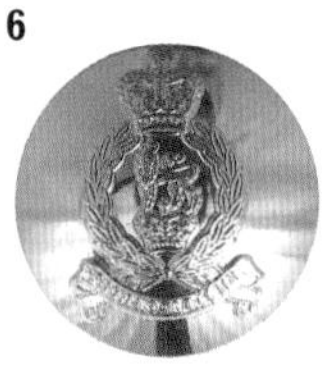

5

7

8

9

10

11

12

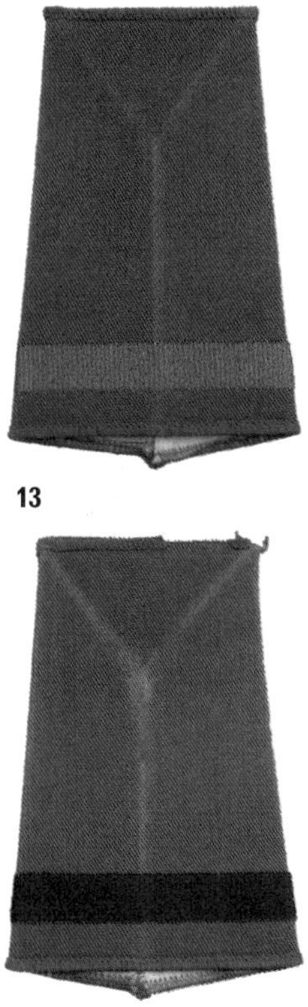

13

14

opposite page

1 Adjutant General's Corps Staff and Personnel Support soldier's anodised aluminium cap badge 4 × 5 cm and collar badges 2.5 × 2 cm.

Officer's wire-embroidered beret badges

2 Green backing for the Corps beret 4.25 × 5.5 cm.
3 Black backing for non-AGC headdress 4.25 × 5.5 cm.
4 Maroon backing for airborne forces beret 4.25 × 5.5 cm.
5 Khaki backing for the khaki beret 4.25 × 5.5 cm.
6 AGC button.
7 Sgt Angela Barber wearing No2 Dress. She is wearing The King's Regiment beret as she is serving with 1 KINGS.
8 AGC SPS officer's silver and gilt cap badge 4 × 5 cm and collar badges 2.5 × 2 cm.

this page

9 WO1 Laura York wearing the officer's wire-embroidered badge and Sgt Lesley Huddleston wearing the soldier's badge.
10 AGC Second Lieutenant's rank slide for shirtsleeve order and sergeant's rank slide for combat dress.
11 Officer's Mess Dress wire-embroidered collar badges for wear on a jacket with a waistcoat 3 × 3.5 cm, and for wear with a dress 1.75 × 2.25 cm.
12 Cpl Andy McSkimming wearing Barrack Dress, with the crossed rifles badge of a skill at arms instructor.
13 Potential Officer Development Course, red, and Pre-RMA Sandhurst Course, blue, appointment slides worn by soldiers at the Army School of Education 7 × 10.5 cm.
14 AGC waist belt clasp worn by recruit instructors.

Lineage Adjutant General's Corps (1992) from the Royal Army Education Corps (1845), Royal Army Pay Corps (1875), Military Provost Staff Corps (1901) Royal Military Police (1926), Army Legal Corps (1948), Women's Royal Army Corps (1949) and Royal Army Ordnance Corps Staff Clerks.

Royal Military Police

The Corps of Military Police was formed in 1926 by the amalgamation of the Military Mounted Police with the Military Foot Police.

The Military Police cap badge was introduced in 1908, the cypher changing with each monarch. The title was altered to Royal Military Police, or RMP, in 1948 and the badge was changed to the Queen's Crown and EIIR cypher in 1955. The soldiers' badges have been produced in anodised aluminium since about 1958. Officers' badges are produced in silver, except for the beret badge, which is embroidered.

The Royal Military Police are identified by the red top to their Forage Caps, hence the nickname Red Caps, or by their red berets. On duty an MP arm badge is worn, which has also been adopted as the Tactical Recognition Flash. Some military police companies have worn the previous MP arm badge on the helmet. It has been suggested that this practice may have been restricted in recent years to parachute troops, certainly it is not widespread. Royal Air Force police also wear the MP badges. RMP serving with 16 Air Assault Brigade are permitted to wear a private purchase black on green subdued pattern MP arm badge.

A Provost Marshal, or PM, commands Military Police; the senior is PM (Army). Provost Marshals wear the initials PM rather MP on their sleeve under certain circumstances.

The Cyprus Joint Police Unit, made up of RMP and RAF police, is considering introducing a unit arm badge similar to that worn by joint communications and logistic units based in the Sovereign Base Areas (see Royal Signals and Royal Logistic Corps).

The RMP detachment at BATUS has since 1996 attempted to gain funding for an arm badge based on the design of the badge worn by the Medicine Hat Police with whom they conduct joint patrols. In the meantime the BATUS arm badge is worn on the brassard with the MP Tactical Recognition Flash (see BATUS).

1

2

3

4

5

6

7

8

9

10

11

12

13

opposite page

1 Corps of Royal Military Police soldier's anodised aluminium cap badge 4.75 × 4.5 cm and collar badges 3.25 × 3 cm.

2 Anodised aluminium shoulder title 3 × 1 cm.

3 RMP button.

4 Officer's wire-embroidered beret badge 4.25 × 3.75 cm.

5 Officer and sergeant's Mess Dress wire-embroidered collar badges 3.5 × 3.5 cm.

6 Officer's silver cap badge 4.75 × 4.5 cm and collar badges 3.25 × 3 cm.

7 RMP and RAF police TRF 7 × 6 cm.

8 Military Police helmet badge and obsolete arm badge 7.5 × 5.5 cm.

this page

9 SSgt Shane Boulton wearing No 1 Dress.

10 Cpl James Baxter wearing No1 Dress. As well as the crossed rifles badge of a skill at arms instructor he also has the traditional police whistle.

11 Cpl Lizzie Brandon wearing Combat Dress with the MP TRF and Corporal Paul Glowienko wearing Barrack Dress with the MP brassard.

12 Cpl Mel Mountford RMP and Cpl Steve McCann RAF police wearing the MP TRF on joint patrol. Photograph PM (Army)

13 Military Police brassard worn when on duty on the right sleeve of No 1 and No 2 Dress and Barrack Dress 35 × 9 cm.

14 LCpl Catrin Emily Evans wearing the RMP LZ flash above a subdued MP TRF on her right sleeve, with the 16 Air Assault Brigade badge on her left sleeve.

14

15

16

17

18

19

21

20

22

23

24

opposite page

15 Cpl Emma Morris wearing the LZ flash.
16 LZ flash worn by RMP serving with 16 Air Assault Brigade 7 × 7 cm.
17 Unofficial subdued TRF worn by some RMP serving in 16 Air Assault Brigade.
18 Provost Marshal TRF 7 × 6 cm.
19 Brig Colin Findlay MBE, PM (Army), speaking to Cpl Lee Ashton wearing KRH No1 Dress. In the background are WO1 (RSM) Tony Price 9/12 L and Lt Col Stuart Barnard AAC.
20 PM (Army) brassard.
21 Lt Col Paul Watton OBE wearing the Provost Marshal brassard with Service Dress.

this page

22 Lieutenant Colonel PM brassard.
23 Colonel's rank slide.
24 RMP BATUS proposed Canadian style badge 8 × 9 cm.

Close Protection

Corporals qualified and employed on close protection duties, body guard in common parlance, may wear the Close Protection badge. However the NCOs generally wear either combat dress or civilian clothes and therefore they have little opportunity to wear the highly prized badge.

1

2

3

1 No1 Dress wire-embroidered Close Protection badge 4 × 3.25 cm.
2 No2 Dress worsted Close Protection badge 4.5 × 3.75 cm
3 Cpl Marcus Turnbull wearing the Close Protection skill at arms badge on his lower left sleeve.

Special Investigation Branch

The Special Investigation Branch, or SIB, has for many years routinely worked in civilian clothes. Deployments to the Balkans, which began in 1992, required all troops to wear uniform. The RMP is recognised by wearing the MP Tactical Recognition Flash but operational experience highlighted the need to differentiate SIB investigators from soldiers assigned to General Police Duties. WO1 Martin Lark designed the SIB 'lozenge' combat dress badge. The badge was first worn by Major Peter Attridge in Bosnia in 1996 above the MP arm badge. The badge was approved by the Corps Dress Committee in 2003 but not approved by the Army Dress Committee. It continued to be worn in some operational theatres with the approval of local Commanding Officers until approved in 2005 as an operational embellishment.

The Special Investigation Branch emblem has 19 small branches representing the original 19 detectives who formed the SIB. Investigators wear a small bright metal badge in civilian clothes (often known in the Army by the Indian word *mufti*).

Acknowledgement
Lt Col JT Green OBE, WO1 (RSM) SJ Flack, GR Keighley, GN Laing, MJ Larkin, Stuart Reilly, WO1 (SA) DE Evans, SSgt SA Tickner and Sgt S Giddins

1

2

3

In November 1939 the Army asked the Metropolitan Police for detectives to investigate the large scale theft of stores in France. By February 1940 nineteen detectives had been drafted into The Corps of Military Police to form a Special Investigation Branch and were working amongst the British Expeditionary Force with spectacular results. As the Germans advanced into France the Special Investigation Branch suffered their first casualty when the Officer Commanding, Major Clarence Campion, was killed during an air raid on a hospital where he was being treated for wounds received the previous day.

1 Special Investigation Branch operational embellishment 3.5 × 2 cm.

2 SIB mufti badge 1.25 × 1.5 cm – 19 branches representing the original nineteen detectives.

next page

3 The actress Tamsin Outhwaite wearing the SIB badge and obsolete arm badge when acting in the television series Redcaps, with SSgt Morven Sayer, advisor to the film company. Photograph *PM (Army)*.

REGIMENTAL POLICE

The regimental police are described as being 'the backbone of the Battalion, essential for maintaining discipline and high standards. On operations they may be called upon to control traffic, co-ordinate the defence of Battalion Headquarters and oversee the control of prisoners of war. A regimental policeman is expected to be impartial, well turned out and have high standards of personal behaviour.'

Most units have had Regimental Police since at least the First World War and it is usual to see them identified by a brassard ornamented with brass or gilding metal letters; PS for the Provost Sergeant, PC for the Provost Corporal and RP for other regimental police. The origin of the Provost Sergeant is understood to date from the Regimental Provost Marshals of the New Model Army formed in about 1645. The term regimental police is now considered to be an inappropriate use of nomenclature as the RPs have no police training or powers and more appropriate terms are being considered. It has been said that consideration is being given to the new names being compatible with the existing brass letters many of which were procured in India in the early 20th Century.

Military Provost Staff

The Military Prison Staff Corps was formed in 1901, becoming the Military Provost Staff Corps in 1906, and Military Provost Staff in 1993.

The Military Provost Staff, or MPS, Crown and Cypher has been the cap badge since the formation of the Military Prison Staff Corps in 1901. The cypher has been changed with each monarch and the title scroll was added in about 1955 and the badge produced in anodised aluminium from about 1958.

The Military Provost Staff run the Military Corrective Training Centre at Colchester and also have an operational role handling prisoners, most recently in Kosovo, Sierra Leone, Afghanistan and Iraq.

1

2

3

6

5

4

7

1 Military Provost Staff soldier's anodised aluminium cap badge 4.25 × 4.25 cm, and collar badges 3.5 × 3.5 cm.
2 Anodised aluminium shoulder title 3 × 1 cm.
3 MPS button.
4 SSgt Dave Sneddon wearing Combat Dress.
5 Officer's Mess Dress wire-embroidered collar badges 3 × 3 cm.
6 Officer's wire-embroidered beret badge 4 × 4 cm.
7 Staff sergeant's rank slide.

Acknowledgement WO1 (RSM) MW Smith

Military Provost Guard Service

The Military Provost Guard Service was formed in 1997

The Military Provost Guard Service, or MPGS, badge was introduced on formation in 1997 and combines the Army's Lion and Crown with crossed keys representing security. The initial issue was a cloth badge, soon replaced by a bright metal badge. Wire-embroidered badges have been authorised for Mess Dress. In the AGC there are smaller sizes Mess Dress badges produced for females, but as there are no female sergeants in the MPGS only the larger size is available. There are no MPGS officers and therefore no officers' badges, although the Colonel Commandant does wear an MPGS rank slide when representing the Service.

The Military Provost Guard Service provides an overt armed and unarmed security guard service for barracks, replacing Ministry of Defence Police. MPGS soldiers are enlisted into the Service as privates, many of them have held Warrant Officer or senior non-commissioned officer rank in their former service. The Military Local Service Engagement provides for a term of three years service restricted to a particular area in the UK.

1

2

3

4

5

6

1 Military Provost Guard Service metal cap badge 4.5 × 4.5 cm.
2 Mess Dress wire-embroidered collar badges 3.5 × 3.5 cm.
3 Anodised aluminium shoulder title 3.75 × 1 cm.
4 Obsolete cloth beret badge 5 × 5 cm.
5 Lance corporal's rank slide and Colonel Commandant's rank slide.
6 Pte Naomi Borrows wearing the MPGS badge in the AGC beret.

Acknowledgement WO1 (SA) LJ Holden

Educational and Training Services

The Army Education Corps was formed in 1920 on the disbandment of The Corps of Army Schoolmasters being renamed the Education and Training Services in 1992.

The Education and Training Services, or ETS, wear the AGC cap badge and Royal Army Education Corps, or RAEC, collar badges. The RAEC badges were introduced in 1950 based upon a fluted flambeau of five flames, the emblem of learning. A system of Army education began in the 18th century followed by Sergeant-Schoolmasters being appointed to regiments in 1811. The non-commissioned officer Corps of Army Schoolmasters was formed in 1846, and replaced by the Army Education Corps, or AEC, in 1920, which also included officers. The first badge was both interesting and attractive with an open book upon crossed lances and rifles. When the corps was granted the Royal prefix for its work during the Second World War the torch of learning was adopted as the badge. The RAEC became an officer only corps in 1962.

1

3

2

4

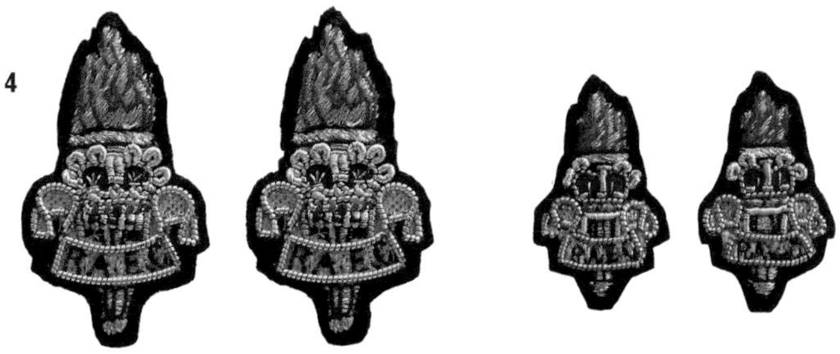

5

1 Officers of the Educational and Training Services wear the Adjutant General's Corps silver and gilt cap badge 4 × 5 cm and Royal Army Education Corps collar badges 2.5 × 1.75 cm.

2 Lt Col David Cartwright MBE wearing AGC ETS No1 Dress.

3 2Lt John Ward and Alex Wright wearing the AGC wire-embroidered cap badge.

4 Educational and Training Services Mess Dress wire-embroidered collar badges. For wear on a jacket with a waistcoat 2 × 3.5 cm, and for wear with a dress 1.25 × 2.5 cm.

5 Lieutenant colonel's rank slide.

Army Legal Services

The Army Legal Services was formed in 1948

The Army Legal Services, or ALS, adopted its present badges in 1978 having been formed in 1948 as the Army Legal Service. Previously officers had been appointed to the Military Department of the Office of The Judge Advocate General. At that time they wore the insignia of the Extra-Regimentally Employed List, now worn only by colonels and brigadiers as the Staff badge (and by officers of the Westminster Dragoons). The ALS badge was introduced in 1958. The title was changed to Army Legal Corps, or ALC, in 1978, and the words on the badge also changed to reflect the new title. It became the ALS again in 1992 as one of the branches of the AGC, retaining the ALC insignia. The original badges continue to be worn by the New Zealand Army Legal Corps who adopted them in 1965.

1

2

3

4

6

7

5

9

1 Army Legal Services silver and enamel cap badge 3 × 4.25 cm and collar badges 2.5 × 3 cm.
2 ALS button.
3 Lt Col Emma Peters wearing the silver and enamel cap badge in her Service Dress hat and Major Jo Bowen with a wire-embroidered badge in her beret.
4 ALS wire-embroidered beret badge 3 × 4.25 cm on a blue backing.
5 ALS wire-embroidered side hat badge 3 × 4.25 cm on a red backing.
6 Capt Patrick Larkin wearing No1 Dress.
7 Director Army Legal Services Major General's rank slide.
8 ALS officers' Mess Dress wire-embroidered collar badges; for wear on a jacket with a waistcoat (not produced as a facing pair) 2.5 × 3.25 cm and for wear with a dress (produced as a facing pair) 2 × 2.5 cm.

Acknowledgement Lt Col Susan Ridge

Royal Army Veterinary Corps

The Army Veterinary Corps was formed in 1903.

The Royal Army Veterinary Corps, or RAVC, was formed in 1903 and adopted as a badge the initials AVC within a crowned laurel wreath. In 1918 the Corps received the Royal title as a result of its work during the First World War and adopted the centaur figure of Chiron, half man and half horse from Greek mythology, as the central feature of the new badge. A bi-metal version of the present badge with St Edward's (or Queen's) Crown was introduced in about 1957, shortly afterwards replaced by the present anodised aluminium version. Officers' badges are produced in silver and gilt, with a wire-embroidered badge on a dark blue background worn on the beret. A Tactical Recognition Flash in the same colours as the Corps stable belt has been issued in 2005.

The Royal Army Veterinary Corps was formed in 1903 as the Army Veterinary Corps to administer soldiers. In 1906 it absorbed the Army Veterinary Department, which had been formed in 1858 to administer veterinary officers.

1

2

3

4

5

6

7

8

9

10

11

previous page

1 Royal Army Veterinary Corps soldier's anodised aluminium cap badge 3 × 4.5 cm and collar badges 2.75 × 3.75 cm.
2 Anodised aluminium shoulder title 4.5 × 1 cm.
3 RAVC button.
4 Cpl Doddsy Dodds wearing No2 Dress with the crossed rifles badge of a skill at arms instructor.
5 Pte Gareth Hitchin wearing combat dress.
6 Lt Richard Meeks and Cees Bennett wearing the RAVC wire-embroidered beret badge.
7 TRF 6 × 4.5 cm.
8 Officer's wire-embroidered beret badge 3.75 × 5 cm.

this page

9 Officer's silver and gilt cap badge 3 × 4.5 cm and collar badges 2.75 × 3.75 cm.
10 Waist belt clasp 7 × 5.75 cm worn only by recruit instructors.
11 RAVC rank slide.

Army Dog Unit (Northern Ireland)

Army dog handlers in Northern Ireland have been identified since 1971 by a small red enamel and gilt paw badge worn above and to the left of their cap badge. This, the smallest badge in the Army, was authorised by Major General Peter Leng who was at the time Commander Land Forces Northern Ireland and also Colonel Commandant Royal Army Veterinary Corps. The red was chosen both because it is a martial colour and because it represents the bloodied paws of the Army dogs injured when working in the rubble of destroyed buildings.

With the wider use of helmets on operations the unit was given permission in 1998 to wear an identifying badge on the upper right arm in place of the small cap badge, although the red paw beret badge continues to be worn.

1

2

The ADU(NI) is responsible for approximately 170 Army dogs in Northern Ireland, each trained for a specific role; Guard Dog, Arms Explosive Search Dog, Vehicle Search Dog, and Tracker Dog and all are handled by volunteers from across the Army. There are currently 27 different cap badges represented in the Army Dog Unit (Northern Ireland).

1 ADU (NI) arm badge 6.5 × 4 cm.
2 ADU (NI) beret badge 0.5 × 0.5 cm.

Small Arms School Corps

The Small Arms School Corps was formed in 1929 by renaming the Corps of Small Arms and Machine Gun Schools, which had been formed in 1923.

The Small Arms School Corps, or SASC, badge was introduced in 1930, featuring a Vickers medium machine gun and crossed Number 1 Mark 3 rifles, together representing the infantry's principal weapons at the time. The detail was altered by the change from Tudor (or King's) Crown to St Edward's (or Queen's) Crown in 1956 following the accession of Elizabeth II. The original King's Crown badges were produced in gilding metal and the first Queen's Crown badges in chrome. The present anodised aluminium badges were introduced in about 1958 to replace the chrome badges.

All ranks of the Small Arms School Corps usually wear a green beret except in Number 1 Dress when a Forage Cap is authorised. Instructors at the Royal Military Academy Sandhurst are issued Number 1 Dress which they wear with their berets, as Forage Caps are not actually obtainable although the appropriate silver cap badges are available.

Officers wear a wire-embroidered beret badge. Formerly officers and Warrant Officers Class 1 had different sized badges but the larger badges replaced the officers small badges in order to bring the SASC into line with Infantry regiments which have the same embroidered badges for officers and Warrant Officers Class 1.

The arm badge worn red to the front on combat dress is in the same colours as the Corps's stable belt. Green and yellow were the colours of the Small Arms School Hythe, scarlet and dark blue the colours of the Small Arms School Netheravon, and Cambridge blue was chosen as the Corps facing colour in 1952.

The SASC is a small corps manned by volunteers who usually transfer in the rank of sergeant and serve throughout the Army, often in individual posts. SASC soldiers from the rank of sergeant to Warrant Officer Class 1 wear the crossed rifles badge as a Specialist Instructional badge.

1

2

3

4

6

7

8

5

A clean, well made smooth bore musket whether of 1700 or 1850, when loaded with a well cast tight fitting ball and a carefully measured powder charge, might hit a man fairly regularly at 80 or 90 yards. The effects of battle reduced the effective range to little more than 30 yards therefore the infantry fired in volleys in order to optimise the effect. Musketry was a question of drills and therefore a matter for drill sergeants.

Rifles were specialist weapons until 1851 when the Minie rifle was introduced and proved such a success, it even outranged some of the smooth bore artillery, that it was on general issue to the Infantry in 1854. Lord Hardinge, Master General of the Ordnance, believed that the new rifle was so revolutionary that an establishment was needed to study the scientific use of the rifle, to evolve a doctrine and to develop a uniform system of instruction by which such doctrine could be passed on to individual soldiers as needed. Lt Col Charles Crawford Hay 19th Foot was appointed to conduct the trials and the following year became the first Commandant of the School of Musketry.

9

10

previouspage

1 Small Arms School Corps soldier's anodised aluminium cap badge 4 × 4 cm and collar badges 2.25 × 2.5 cm.
2 SASC button.
3 Obsolete anodised aluminium shoulder title 4 × 1.75 cm.
4 Officers' wire-embroidered beret badge 4 cm.
5 Officer's frosted silver forage cap badge 4 × 4 cm and silver collar badges 2.5 × 2.5 cm.
6 WO2 (QMSI) Mark Murray wearing No2 Dress with the crossed rifles Specialist Instructional badge below his badge of rank.
7 Capt Rick Shaw wearing Service Dress.
8 SASC TRF 4.25 × 2.25 cm.

this page

9 WO2 (QMSI) Andy Shorrock wearing the NCO's cap badge and Corps arm badge on his right sleeve and WO1 (SMI) CZ Ciereszko wearing the officer's embroidered beret badge.
10 SASC captain's rank slide.

Acknowledgement Major John Conway

Shooting

Shooting became an infantry skill from 1854 following the issue of the Minie rifle. The crossed rifles badge was introduced by Royal Warrant in 1856. It was originally awarded in gold for the best shot in each company of an Infantry regiment or Depot and in worsted for each qualified marksman. By 1881 the award had been extended to the cavalry and Royal Engineers. In 1909 the present regulations were introduced and the badge was awarded to all soldiers qualified as marksmen with the Service rifle, and was worn on the left forearm. The present badge was introduced in 1960 and represents the Lee Enfield Number 4 Rifle, which had then been replaced by the Self Loading Rifle (SLR). It is the only qualification badge regularly awarded to Officer Cadets at the Royal Military Academy Sandhurst.

The crossed rifles badge is also awarded as an Advanced Skill-at-Arms and Instructors Badge, worn on the right arm, by tactics and weapon training instructors who have passed the regimental NCOs Skill-at-Arms Instructors, Anti-Tank Section or Detachment Commander, Sniper Instructor, Driving Instructor or Counter Surveillance Unit Instructor course.

Snipers were used during the English Civil War from about 1644 but the skill was only widely developed during the First World War. The Qualified Sniper badge was introduced for the infantry in 1942, and in some cases replaced unofficial regimental badges. The present badge has been worn since 1960 although the Household Division continues to wear the 1942 design (See Household Division).

The Queen's Medal

The Army Best Shot Medal was instituted in 1869 as an annual reward for the best shots in the Army. The competition ended in 1882 and was revived in 1923 when it was known as The King's Medal. It was renamed The Queen's Medal on the accession of Queen Elizabeth II. The same reverse has been used throughout. One medal is held by the Army Rifle Association to be presented to the champion shot at the end of the Regular Army Skill-at-Arms Meeting (RASAAM) and at the end of the Territorial Army Skill-at-Arms Meeting (TASAAM); the recipient then receives either a medal or a bar noting subsequent success from the Army Medal Office. There are similar awards to the Royal Navy, Royal Air Force and to some Commonwealth forces.

1

2

3

1 Marksman or Advanced Skill-at-Arms and Instructor Badge 5.5 × 5 cm.
2 Qualified Sniper Badge 5.25 × 5.5 cm.
3 Sergeant's Mess Dress wire-embroidered crossed rifles badge 5 × 4.5 cm, also available on a dark blue backing but it can be produced on any backing colour.
4 Woven Army 100 No2 Dress badge 6 × 6.25 cm.
5 Mess Dress wire-embroidered Army 100 badge 5 × 4.5 cm.
6 No1 Dress wire-embroidered unofficial Army 100 badge 5 × 5.25 cm.
7 Woven TA 50 No2 Dress badge 5.5 × 6.5 cm.
8 Mess Dress wire-embroidered TA 50 badge 3.75 × 4.5 cm.
9 Major Ian Thompson QRL wearing the Army 100 badge on the left forearm in No1 Dress.
10 SSgt John Chapman REME attached to 3 PWRR wearing the TA 50 badge on the left forearm of Combat Dress, the only uniform issued to the TA.

Army 100 and Territorial Army 50

Competitors who reach the final 100 in the Army Service Rifle Championship at the Regular Army Skill At Arms meeting, or Territorial Army personnel who are placed in the top 50 in the Queen's Medal Competition at the annual TA Skill at Arms meeting are authorised to wear an advanced skill at arms badge. The Army 100 badge for Number 2 Dress is issued; other patterns are private purchase from the Army Rifle Association, available on khaki, fawn, red and green backing. The Mess Dress badges are also worn on Number 1 Dress and available on green, red and blue backing, although any backing colour could be provided. Inevitably there is an unofficial version of the badge.

4

7

8

5

6

9

10

Acknowledgement Lt Col Richard Hoole

Royal Army Dental Corps

The Army Dental Corps was formed in 1921.

The Royal Army Dental Corps, or RADC, was formed in 1921 and copied the Army Veterinary Corps' simple badge design of initials within a crowned laurel wreath. In 1946 the Corps received the Royal title as a result of its work during the Second World War and adopted the Chinese dragon symbol of dentistry as the central feature of the new badge. A bi-metal version of the present badge with St Edward's (or Queen's) Crown was introduced in about 1957, followed in 1958 by the present anodised aluminium version. Cap badges are worn on a green backing on the beret. There are three specialisations for soldiers within the RADC, Dental Support Specialist (Dental Nurse), Dental Technician and Dental Hygienist. Qualification badges are worn on indoor dress. The RADC became part of the Defence Dental Agency, or DDA, in 1997 and training is in line with National Certification. Dental Support Specialists are awarded the national chrome and enamel brooch, whilst Dental Hygienists wear either the silver plated Army hygienist badge or, if qualified since 1997, the DDA enamel version.

1

2

3

4

9

8

5

7

10

6

11

12

13

14

15

16

opposite page

1 Royal Army Dental Corps soldier's anodised aluminium cap badge 5 × 3.5 cm and collar badges 3.5 × 2.5 cm.
2 RADC button.
3 Anodised aluminium shoulder title 4.5 × 1 cm.
4 Officer's wire-embroidered beret badge 4.25 × 5 cm.
5 Officer's Mess Dress wire-embroidered collar badges 3.5 × 3 cm.
6 Capt Steve Davis wearing Combat Dress with the wire-embroidered beret badge.
7 Cpl Lisa Light wearing indoor dress with the DDA dental hygienist badge and rank badge correctly on the right sleeve.
8 Defence Dental Agency dental hygienist badge 3.25 × 3.25 cm.
9 Army dental hygienist badge 4 × 4 cm.
10 SSgt Kirsty Grant wearing indoor dress with the Army dental hygienist badge and chrome rank badge.

this page

11 Cpl Japie Van Wyk, a Dental Technician, wearing Combat Dress.
12 Officer's silver and gilt cap badge 3.75 × 5 cm and collar badges 2.5 × 3.25 cm.
13 Cpl Louise Mowatt wearing No 2 Dress. On her right sleeve are the crossed rifles badge of a skill at arms instructor and the two green bars of a Class 1 dental specialist (**14**).
14 RADC Class 1 Tradesman qualification tubular braid bars worn on the lower right sleeve of Number 2 Dress.
15 Captain's rank slide.
16 Cpl Rachel Hendry a Dental Support Specialist wearing Class 1 braid bars on her right sleeve.
17 LCpl Elle Daley a dental nurse.
18 Dental Nurse badge 3 cm.
19 RADC Staff gorgets.

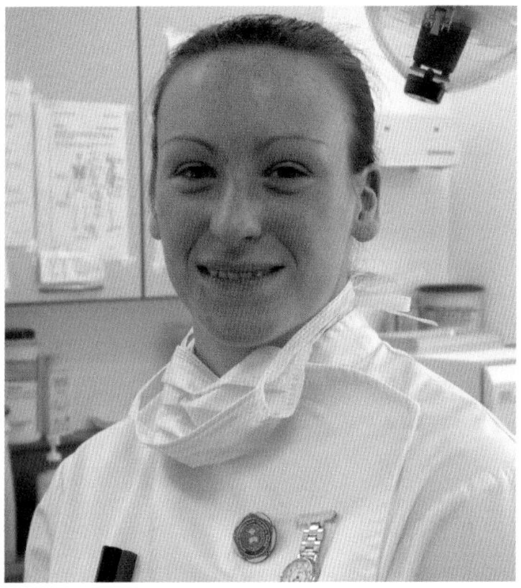

17

The dragon is the Chinese emblem of dentistry. In Greek mythology Cadmus, son of Agenor, King of Phoenicia, slew a dragon that had killed his companions. On instructions from Athena he sowed the dragon's teeth and a race of fierce men grew, called Sparti (meaning 'Sown'). In Greek mythology Jason also sowed dragon's teeth which grew into warriors.

Formed in 1921 to overcome the problems experienced as a result of untreated dental disease during the First World War, the Army Dental Corps was granted the Royal title in 1946 in recognition of its service during the Second World War. Dental care is now administered by the Defence Dental Agency, co-ordinating dental staff of all three Services.

18

19

Acknowledgement WO1 (RSM) PA Wiles

Intelligence Corps

The Intelligence Corps was formed in 1940.

The Intelligence Corps badge was introduced in 1940, featuring the rose, the flower of secrecy, surrounded by laurel leaves, rather unkindly identified by the rest of the Army as a pansy resting on its laurels.

There have always been intelligence staff but the nature of their duties usually led them to operate incognito. Until the First World War, the Staff wore the insignia of their own regiment or corps. During the First World War the Intelligence Corps had been hidden behind the title of the 20th Battalion The Royal Fusiliers, wearing the Royal Fusiliers regimental badge. During the Second World War the insignia of the General Service Corps was often worn.

1

2

3

4

5

6

1 Intelligence Corps soldier's anodised aluminium cap badge 3.5 × 4.5 cm and collar badges 2.5 × 3.5 cm.
2 Intelligence Corps button.
3 Anodised aluminium shoulder title 6 × 2 cm.
4 Officer's wire-embroidered beret badge 4 × 5 cm and silver collar badges 3.75 × 3.5 cm.
5 WO1 David Bellringer wearing No1 Dress. The green beret is worn in all orders of dress. He wears the officer's wire-embroidered beret badge, silver collar badges and green-edged rank badge.
6 Intelligence Corps major's rank slide.

Army Physical Training Corps

The Army Physical Training Corps was formed in 1940 from the Army Physical Training Staff.

The Army Physical Training Corps, or APTC, badge was introduced for the Army Gymnastic Staff in about 1902 with the cypher and crown altered by the change from Tudor (or King's) Crown to St Edward's (or Queen's) Crown after the accession of Queen Elizabeth II in 1953. Soldiers wear the badge on a red and black backing on the beret which reflects the red and black jersey worn for many years by PT instructors. The red and black stripes are also used on the Tactical Recognition Flash and the stable belt.

The crossed swords badge had been introduced in 1881 as a gold wire prize badge worn by the best swordsman in each cavalry troop, and in worsted by each qualified swordsman. It was also worn by instructors at the School of Gymnastics and by Infantry Sergeant Instructors of Gymnastics. In 1894 it was extended to sergeant and corporal Instructors of Fencing and Gymnastics. In 1909 it was further extended to Warrant Officers. Crossed swords continue to be worn by All Arms Physical Training Instructors whilst the crossed swords with Crown remains the badge of the Army Physical Training Corps.

1

2

3

4

5

6

NCOs on transferring into the APTC are issued and wear anodised aluminium cap and collar badges. On promotion to Warrant Officer Class 1 soldiers are expected to wear officers' silver and gilt badges. However because officers wear a wire-embroidered badge in the beret, the usual form of dress, and the expectation is that Number 2 Dress with Forage Cap will be worn no more than once a year for the Remembrance Parade most WO1s adapt their soldier's badges by painting the crowns gold. If selected for a commission they then obtain the correct badges with the officer's Service Dress uniform and Forage Cap.

The crossed swords skill at arms badge is worn by All Arms Physical Training Instructors as a qualification badge and by all APTC soldiers as an Specialist Instructional badge.

A key task for the APTC is remedial training of soldiers recovering from injury. Remedial Instructors are principally based at Hedley Court and at recruit training units. They wear a special qualification badge and usually a distinctive white Tri-Service tracksuit top.

The Tactical Recognition Flash is based upon the ribbon worn on the beret behind the cap badge by soldiers. It is known as the 'bar code'. (RAF officers' rank badges are also known as bar codes and it has become a rather tired joke at the Defence Academy for some RN and Army officers when passing an RAF officer to imitate the 'beep' heard at shop checkouts).

All Arms Physical Training Instructors, usually junior non-commissioned officers from every regiment and corps in the Army, are qualified following courses run at the Army School of Physical Training. They are identified by a crossed swords badge. The badges are worn in all orders of dress and a version for the PT vest is unit produced by removing or covering the crown on the APTC badge. (Only members of the APTC wear the crossed swords with a Crown badge.).

7

One reform following the Crimean War was the formation in 1861 of the Army Gymnastic Staff with instructors drawn from across the Army. The success of the appointment of Major Hemmersley and the 'Twelve Apostles' led the following year to an order to provide a gymnasium with its own staff in every garrison. In the 1890s the Staff became responsible for bayonet fighting and Sergeant Major MB Betts was commissioned and granted the distinction, Master at Arms, an appointment that has been handed down to all APTC officers. On the outbreak of war in 1914 most of the instructors returned to their regiments. The Army Physical Training and Bayonet Staff was formed in France in 1916. In 1918 responsibility for bayonet fighting was passed to the Musketry Schools and the Army Physical Training Staff served on until the vast expansion of the Army led in 1940 to the Staff being granted Combatant Corps status as the Army Physical Training Corps.

8

9

10

11

13

12

14

15

16

17

18

19

21

22

20

previous page

1 Army Physical Training Corps soldier's anodised aluminium cap badge 4 × 3.5 cm and collar badges 2.75 × 2.5 cm.
2 Obsolete anodised aluminium shoulder title 4 × 1 cm.
3 APTC button.
4 Officer's silver and gilt cap badge 4 × 3.75 cm and collar badges 2.75 × 2.75 cm.
5 Sgt Bob Dillon wearing the APTC badge on its distinctive red and black backing.
6 Major Brian Dupree and Captain Sheff Appleby wearing No 1 Dress with the APTC silver and gilt badges. As a Field Officer, Major Dupree has a gold peak to his Forage Cap.

opposite page

7 Soldier's anodised aluminium badges with the crowns painted gold by a WO1.
8 Captain Sulle Alhaji wearing the officer's wire-embroidered badge, the APTC TRF and rank slide.
9 Officer's wire-embroidered beret badge 5 × 4.5cm.
10 Captain's rank slide.
11 Physical Training Instructor's No1 Dress wire-embroidered badge 7.5 × 4.75 cm.
12 Physical Training Instructor's No2 Dress woven badge 5.5 × 3.75 cm.
13 Physical Training Instructor's Mess Dress wire-embroidered badge7.5 × 4.75 cm.
14 TRF 5 × 3cm.

this page

15 Vest badge 7 × 7 cm.
16 Sgt Keith Norval wearing the APTC vest badge and holding a tracksuit with the soldier's badge.
17 SSI Paul Hudson, a remedial instructor, wearing the distinctive Tri-Service tracksuit top with both the APTC vest badge and the Remedial Instructor's brooch.
18 Remedial Instructor brooch 3 cm.
19 Officer's tracksuit badge 7 × 8.5 cm.
20 Soldier's tracksuit badge 7 × 8.5 cm.
21 LCoH Scott Hodgson, Blues and Royals. As an All Arms Physical Training Instructor he wears the crossed swords badge without crown on his vest.
22 Cpl Wooly Wooldridge RGJ and LCpl Richard Duffy LI wear regimental ranks on the All Arms Physical Training Instructors blue tracksuit tops.

Acknowledgement
WO1 (RSM) S Horridge and WO1 (SMI) Ian Lester

General Service Corps

Formed in 1942 as a 'Reception Corps' administering recruits before allocation to field force units. It remains an administrative office for the very few officers awaiting allocation to a regiment or corps.

There are only officers' badges available for the General Service Corps, or GSC; a gilt Royal Arms badge for the beret and forage cap and bronze cap and collar badges for Number 2 Dress. The badges were introduced in 1942 and changed to St Edward's (or Queen's) Crown and EIIR arms in about 1955. There is what appears to be a soldier's anodised aluminium badge which is issued as a Warrant Officer Class 1 rank badge for wear on the wristband and on Number 2 Dress by the 9th/12th Royal Lancers.

1

2

3

4

1 General Service Corps bronze cap badge 4.75 × 4 cm and collar badges 3.5 × 3 cm.
2 Gilt cap badge 4.75 × 4 cm.
3 GSC button
4 Anodised aluminium Warrant Officer Class 1 rank badge that appears to be a soldier's cap badge 4 × 3.75 cm

Queen Alexandra's Royal Army Nursing Corps

Formed in 1949, Queen Alexandra's Royal Army Nursing Corps established regular and Territorial Army nurses in the Army. The existing Queen Alexandra's Imperial Military Nursing Service and the Territorial Army Nursing Service were not replaced by the QARANC but gradually wasted out as their nurses retired

The Queen Alexandra's Royal Army Nursing Corps, or QARANC, took the existing cap badge of Queen Alexandra's Imperial Military Nursing Service, or QAIMNS, with a revised title. The badge is based upon the Dannebrog cross with a laurel wreath and motto *Under the White Cross.* Queen Alexandra was a Danish princess who married the Prince of Wales, later Edward VII in 1863.

Until 1949 military nursing had been done by Royal Army Medical Corps male orderlies and by State Registered Nurses of the QAIMNS. The Army first employed female nurses in 1866 and the Army Nursing Service was formed in 1881. State Registered Nurses were granted officer status in 1904 but did not receive regular commissions until QARANC was formed in 1949. A year later other ranks were recruited.

The scarlet band on the QARANC forage cap and the backing to the beret badge was handed down from the scarlet ribbon worn on their straw boaters by nursing sisters of the Army Nursing Service and the Princes Christian's Army Nursing Service Reserve during the Boer War, 1899–1902.

In Ward Dress nurses wear qualification badges, the officer's version is known by them as the Commissioning Medal. Army nurses who qualify as a State Registered Nurse wear a blue brooch on the left side of Ward dress. State Enrolled Nurses used to be recruited and they wore a green brooch.

There is a badge for psychiatric nurses although there is no history readily available and the badge now appears to be obsolete.

1

2

3

4

5

6

The Dannebrog – the Danish Cross – originated during the Battle of Lyndanisse, Estonia in 1219. The Danes were hard pressed when King Waldemar or, in another version, Archbishop Anders, prayed for victory. He saw a white cross in the sky against a red background, which inspired the Danes to victory and became their national emblem.

7

8

9

10

11

The length of the short cape, known as a tippet, worn by the officers, was, according to a lady who served at the formation of the Corps, designed to be long enough to conceal the ladies' breasts from the soldiers whilst leaving their arms unrestricted for their duties.

12

13

14

15

previous page

1. Queen Alexandra's Royal Army Nursing Corps soldier's anodised aluminium cap badge 2.5 × 4 cm and collar badges 2 × 3.5 cm.
2. Captain Anita Combes wearing the wire-embroidered beret badge.
3. QARANC button
4. Officer's wire-embroidered beret badge 4.5 ×4.5 cm.
5. Officer's silver and gilt cap badge 2.5 × 4.25 cm and collar badges 2.25 × 3.5 cm.
6. QARANC Staff gorget.
7. Name badges introduced with a new Ward Dress in 2004.

this page

8. QARANC 'Commissioning Medal' 3.5 × 9 cm, each is hallmarked silver and serial numbered.
9. Cpl Dan Cook, Lt Lynda Ricketts and Cpl Patricia Haeley wearing Ward Dress.
10. Psychiatric Nurse brooch 2.5 × 4 cm.
11. State Registered Nurse brooch 2.5 cm.
12. Capt Lou Wylie wearing Service Dress.
13. QARANC nurse's Ward Badge worn on the left breast.
14. Warrant Officer Class 1 Ward Dress rank badge worn on the right sleeve.
15. Lieutenant's Ward Dress rank slide and Major's Combat Dress rank slide.

Corps of Army Music

Formed in 1994, the Corps of Army Music is one of the largest single employers of musicians in the world; over 1,100 musicians in thirty bands of the Regular Army ranging in rank from Musician through to Lieutenant Colonel. Each band is affiliated to a Regiment, a group of Regiments or to a Corps.

The Crimean War identified a number of critical deficiencies in the Army, amongst the less obvious, military music. In 1854 twenty regimental bands at Scutari in Turkey were to play the National Anthem in honour of Queen Victoria's birthday. This was the first time the Army had used a massed band and it was a failure, the various bands could not even play the National Anthem at the same tempo, in the same key or at the same pitch. The result was a cacophony of sound, it was deeply shaming to those concerned and worse, carried the implication that regiments which could not even make music together would be hard put to fight together. Amongst those present was The Duke of Cambridge commanding the 1st Division. In 1856 he became Commander in Chief and set about improving the standard of military music. Kneller Hall was acquired as the Military School of Music.

Permanent staff and recruits at the Royal Military School of Music, or RMSM, wear the Corps of Army Music, or CAMUS, badges. In

1

2

3

4

5

6

7

8

9

2004 the Army Dress Committee approved a change to the cap badge with 'THE' being delcted from the title scroll. The badges will be replaced on a maintenance basis, not as a new issue, over three years.

Musicians, usually sergeants, attending the Student Bandmasters Course wear the RMSM cap badge, which had been introduced in 1907 and changed to St Edward's (or Queen's) Crown in about 1955 and produced in anodised aluminium from about 1958.

Musicians not in training wear the badges of the Band with which they are serving.

Qualified Musicians and Bandsmen wear a crowned Lyre on the right sleeve in most orders of dress. The badge was introduced before 1890.

The Corps of Army Music adopted a Tactical Recognition Flash in 2004 designed by Lt Col Charles Webb and based upon the original design of the Corps cap badge, a golden lyre on a blue background. The argument for a single TRF for all bands is that they will never deploy with their peacetime affiliated cap badge units but with Army Medical Services, or AMS, units. Traditionally musicians have been trained as stretcher-bearers and latterly medical assistants. Clinical governance ethos determined that musicians are no longer employed in any specific medical role, but, as they are employed within AMS units, they must be easily distinguished from medical personnel.

Long before telephone and radio communication the Army musician could reach the ears of men well beyond the human voice. With a pattern of drumbeats or bugle calls it was possible for commanders to move large bodies of men around the battlefield.

The drum gave them the time and kept them together, the trumpet and bugle sounded the clarion call to arms. Drummers have been on official establishments since at least 1680. Before that time there were drummers but not necessarily officially funded. Drummers were traditionally issued a better quality of uniform and paid at a higher rate than the rank and file soldiers. In due course cavalry regiments replaced their drums with trumpets, which tended to be used in barracks, and bugles used in the field. Light Infantry in their turn also used bugles. Musicians were authorised about 1749 but it was not until about 1875 that they were all enlisted soldiers when a soldier replaced the last of the civilian Bandmasters. Bands were administered by an officer appointed by the Commanding Officer to be the Band President, an appointment which continues even though all bands now have a commissioned Director of Music as well as a Bandmaster.

Today's musicians are the public face of the Army. They represent the illustrious traditions associated with our country's military history. Their musicianship, precision, bearing and the splendour of their uniforms encapsulate the epitome of the Army.

13

10

11

12

14
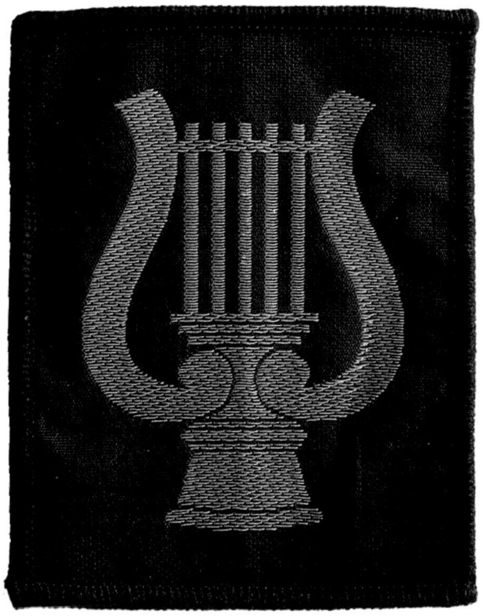

15

16

17

A Military Music Class was first established to train boys as Musicians and soldiers as Trumpet Majors and Bugle Majors at Kneller Hall in 1857. Having been named the Military School of Music it was granted the Royal title in 1887.

previous page

1 Corps of Army Music gilding metal cap badge 3.5 × 4 cm and collar badges 2.25 × 3 cm worn by recruits before posting to their first band.
2 Corps of Army Music button.
3 New cap badge 3.5 × 4 cm, minus 'THE' in the title.
4 Officer's wire-embroidered beret badge 5 × 5 cm.
5 Musician's Number 1 Dress wire-embroidered arm badge 5.25 × 6 cm.
6 Musician's Number 2 Dress woven arm badge 4 × 4.75 cm.
7 Musician's anodised aluminium arm badge 4.25 × 5.25 cm.
8 LCpl Froggy Stephens wearing Band of the Royal Lancers Full Dress with the wire-embroidered Musician's badge on his right sleeve.
9 Student Bandmaster Caroline Constantine wearing the RMSM anodised aluminium cap badge, WO1 (BSM) Graham Janes wearing the wire-embroidered beret badge and Musn Michael Sherriff wearing the gilding metal CAMUS badge.

opposite page

10 Sgt Robert Howitt AGC Band wearing No2 Dress with the Musician's badge on his right sleeve.
11 WO1 rank slide.
12 Student Bandmaster appointment slide introduced in 2003.
13 Student Bandmaster Colin Hales wearing the RMSM appointment slide.

this page

14 TRF 5 × 6.25 cm.
15 Royal Military School of Music anodised aluminium cap badge 4.5 × 4.25 cm worn by student bandmasters.
16 Royal Military School of Music button.
17 Student Bandmaster's appointment badge 5 × 8 cm introduced in 1951.

Acknowledgement WO1 (BSM) Gary Janes

Household Cavalry Bands

The Bands of The Life Guards and of The Blues and Royals wear the same uniforms as the regiments, with variations. In Review Order the musicians do not wear the cuirass, and the pouch is a different shape from the cartouche. The Bands have an additional uniform; State Dress consisting of a 'Gold' coat and blue jockey cap. It is said that the Lord Mayor of London originally provided Gold Coats in 1760 in order to improve the appearance of the Band. State Dress is worn on State occasions in the presence of the Queen, and in the presence of the Lord Mayor of London. Until 1832 State Dress was also worn by the Bands of the three regiments of Foot Guards, at that time the Grenadier, Coldstream and Scots Guards, but is now worn only by the Drum Majors.

1

In Review Order Corporals of Horse (equivalent to sergeant) wear Warrant Officers' aiguillettes, in other orders of dress Corporals of Horse and above wear officers' cap badges.

Traditionally the Bands of The Life Guards and The Blues and Royals when dismounted are led by the Band Corporal Major, with the Bandmaster taking his place in the ranks as a musician. The custom appears to date from the time when the senior bandsman acted as Bandmaster.

2

3

5

4

6

1 The Life Guards State Trumpeters, TMaj Gilbert Wheeler, CoH Martin Whybrow, LCpl Victor Hinchcliffe and LCoH Tim West wearing State Dress. Photograph *LG Band*

2 WO2 (BCM) Steve Kitching wearing Mounted Review Order leading The Band of The Blues and Royals. LCpl Matthew Spate, WO2 (ABCM) Dick Howe and WO1 (BM) Jason Griffiths in the front rank, and TMaj Robert Gough behind, wearing State Dress. Photograph *Band of The Blues and Royals*

3 State Coat button.

4 Crown 16 × 16 cm and Royal Cypher 24 × 15 cm worn on the chest of the State Coat.

5 Household Cavalry Bands' pouch worn in place of the cartouche worn by the regiments, this example with the Life Guards red backing to the badge.

6 Household Cavalry Mounted Bands wearing Mounted Review Order parading on Horse Guards with Directors of Music Major David Cresswell and Douglas Robertson. Photograph *CAMUS*

The Band of The Life Guards

The Band of The Life Guards dates from the entry of King Charles II into London at his restoration on 29 May 1660; Kettle Drummers and Trumpeters, followed by the King's Troop of Life Guards, led his triumphal procession.

The Trumpet Major is the only musician to wear an appointment or qualification badge in Review Order. The crossed trumpets are worn on the lower right sleeve.

> The practice of the cavalry carrying trumpets appears to date from 1764. In 1778 Captain Robert Hinde wrote in *The Discipline of the Light Horse*:
>
> *In the year 1764, his Majesty thought proper to forbid the use of brass side drums by the Light Cavalry, and in their room to introduce brass trumpets, so that each troop has one trumpet[er], who when they are dismounted form a band of music, consisting of two French horns, two clarinet, and two bassoons and also one fife to a regiment: but when mounted the trumpets only sound.*

1

2

3

1 WO2 (BCM) Richard Allen with one of the silver Kettledrums presented to the Band by King William IV in 1831.

2 Major David Cresswell the Director of Music wearing Review Order.

3 Trumpet Major's rank and appointment badges worn in Review Order.

The Band of The Blues and Royals

The Band of The Blues and Royals dates from the drummers and trumpeters of 1661. The first Bandmaster was appointed in 1805.

Formed in 1661 from members of the disbanded cavalry of the New Model Army, particularly Colonel Unton Crook's Regiment, the Regiment that was to become the Royal Horse Guards was early on given the nickname of the Oxford Blues, in reference to the first Colonel, Audrey de Vere, twentieth and last Earl of Oxford, and to their blue uniforms.

1

2

It is recorded that from the outset the Regiment had kettledrummers and trumpeters. They wore heavily embroidered and gold-laced frockcoats very similar to the present day State Dress. The main difference was the hat, then a black broad-brimmed affair adorned with a feather, in keeping with the normal full dress of the remainder of the Army. The present black velvet 'jockey cap' was not introduced until Queen Victoria's reign.

The Band appeared in Zoltan Korda's 1938 film 'The Drum' about the Army in India, which was made in UK and in which for the first and last time the Band wore the kilt.

The regimental quick march is the Grand March from Act II of Verdi's opera Aida. One explanation put forward for its adoption is that it was to commemorate the participation of the Regiment in the cavalry 'Moonlight Charge' at Tel-el-Kebir during the Egyptian campaign of 1882.

3

4

1 Band of The Blues and Royals led by WO2 (BSM) Dick Howe, wearing gauntlets, and conducted by the Director of Music Major Douglas Robertson.
2 LCpl Phil Bishop wearing Dismounted Review Order.

3 Blues and Royals officer's helmet.
4 CoH Stuart Marsh on Spartacus.
Photograph *The Band of The Blues and Royals*

Acknowledgement
Capt (DoM) Jason Griffiths and WO2 (BSM) Dick Howe

The Band of The Dragoon Guards

The Band of the Dragoon Guards was formed in 1994 by the amalgamation of the regimental bands of 1st The Queen's Dragoon Guards, The Royal Scots Dragoon Guards and The Royal Dragoon Guards

1

2

3

The Band of The Dragoon Guards wears scarlet Dragoon Guard tunics with blue facings. Bearskins with red plumes are worn by the percussion row with the remaining musicians wearing helmets with white plumes. The Director of Music and the Bandmaster wear red plumes.

The Band badges were introduced in 1996. Although of new design, the star shape of the helmet plate, collar badges and rank badge had been worn previously as collar badges by the 22nd Dragoons. The war-raised regiment, formed in 1940 and disbanded in 1948, had been formed from drafts of the 4th/7th Royal Dragoon Guards and the 5th Inniskilling Dragoon Guards, two of the regiments whose Bands were amalgamated into The Band of the Dragoon Guards.

Following the Cavalry custom, non-commissioned officers wear a regimental rank badge. The wire-embroidered rank badge, based upon the design of the helmet plate is worn on Full Dress, Number 1 Dress and Mess Dress by all warrant officers and NCOs except the Bandmaster. A metal version on blue felt backing is worn on Number 2 Dress and mounted on the officer's waist belt plate. Musicians wear a gilt snake clasp.

4

9

5

10

6

7

11

8

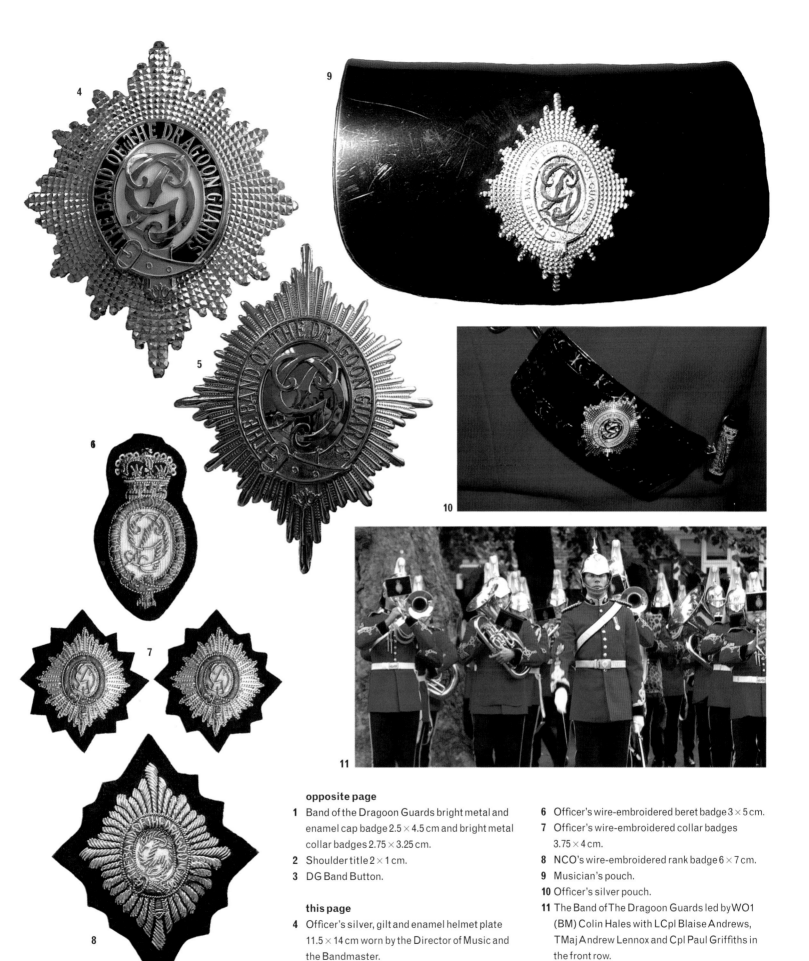

opposite page

1 Band of the Dragoon Guards bright metal and enamel cap badge 2.5 × 4.5 cm and bright metal collar badges 2.75 × 3.25 cm.

2 Shoulder title 2 × 1 cm.

3 DG Band Button.

this page

4 Officer's silver, gilt and enamel helmet plate 11.5 × 14 cm worn by the Director of Music and the Bandmaster.

5 Musician's bimetal helmet plate 11.5 × 14 cm.

6 Officer's wire-embroidered beret badge 3 × 5 cm.

7 Officer's wire-embroidered collar badges 3.75 × 4 cm.

8 NCO's wire-embroidered rank badge 6 × 7 cm.

9 Musician's pouch.

10 Officer's silver pouch.

11 The Band of The Dragoon Guards led by WO1 (BM) Colin Hales with LCpl Blaise Andrews, TMaj Andrew Lennox and Cpl Paul Griffiths in the front row.

Acknowledgement WO2 (BSM) R Stacey

The Band of The Hussars and Light Dragoons

The Band of The Hussars and Light Dragoons was formed in 1994 by the amalgamation of the regimental bands of The Queen's Royal Hussars, The King's Royal Hussars and The Light Dragoons

The Band of The Hussars and Light Dragoons bright metal and enamel cap badge, based upon that formerly worn by The Queen's Own Hussars, is worn by all ranks. In Full Dress the Band wear a Busby mounted with a yellow cord boss.

The collar badges are gilt versions of the anodised aluminium collar badges formerly worn by the 14th/20th King's Hussars.

Non-commissioned officers of the Band wear what is known as The King's Cypher, the regimental rank badge of The Light Dragoons but having a Tudor (or King's) Crown as worn by the 15th/19th The King's Royal Hussars between about 1950 and 1985, rather than the St Edward's (or Queen's) Crown as worn by The Light Dragoons. The wire-embroidered badge is worn on Full Dress and Number 1 Dress.

1

2

3

4

5

6

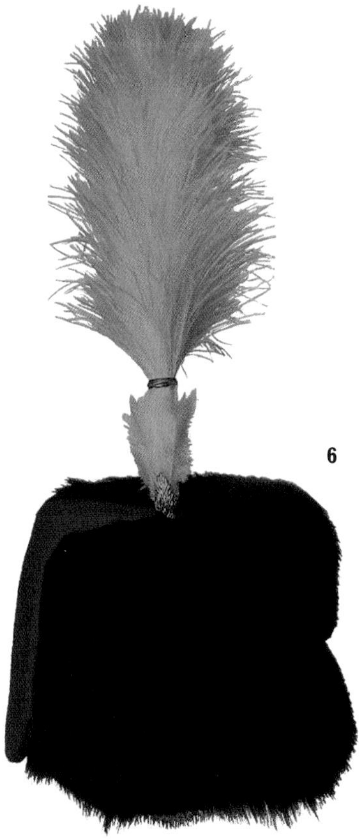

7

8

9

10

11

opposite page

1 The Band of The Hussars and Light Dragoons bright metal and enamel cap badge 4.5 × 2.5 cm and gilt collar badges 3 × 3.5 cm.

2 Busby boss 4 × 5.25 cm.

3 Full Dress and Number 1 Dress King's Cypher rank badge 4.25 × 6.25 cm.

4 10th Royal Hussars officer's cross belt worn by the Director of Music and the Bandmaster.

5 Officer's shoulder belt plate 5.75 × 9 cm and chain boss 5 cm.

6 Hussar Busby

this page

7 Director of Music and Bandmaster's silver pouch badge 4.5 × 3.25 cm.

8 Musician's anodised aluminium pouch badge 4.5 × 3 cm, and scroll 4.5 × 1.25 cm.

9 Director of Music and Bandmaster's patent leather pouch with silver badge 4.5 × 3.25 cm and scroll 4.5 × 1.25 cm.

10 Musician's plastic pouch 16 × 10.5 cm with anodised aluminium badge 4.5 × 3 cm and scroll 4.5 × 1.25 cm.

11 WO1 (BM) Glen Jones wearing Full Dress.

The Band of The Royal Lancers

The Band of The Royal Lancers was formed in 1994 by the amalgamation of the regimental bands of the 9th/12th Royal Lancers (Prince of Wales's) and The Queen's Royal Lancers.

The Band of The Royal Lancers adopted a traditional lancer uniform combining elements of the uniforms of the 9th/12th Royal Lancers and The Queen's Royal Lancers. The cap badge is the QRL motto; collar badges and the regimental rank badge are not worn.

Full Dress uniform is based upon that of the 9/12L. The Band's lance cap, or czapka plate, is understood to be the first new plate to have been designed since before the First World War. The officer's czapka, worn by the Director of Music and Bandmaster, is topped with feathers, whilst the musicians wear a horsehair plume. Until 2004 the plume was red but was changed to black in order to distinguish the Band from the Full Dress of the 9/12L.

1

2

3

4

1 Musician's czapka plate 17 × 12 cm curved to fit the cap.
2 WO1 (BM) Justin Matthews wearing Full Dress with the officer's czapka.
3 TMaj Andy Smart, Musn Ryan Heyward and LCpl Phil Seaman wearing Band of the Royal Lancers Full Dress.
4 Band of The Royal Lancers officer's silver and gilt czapka plate 17 × 12 cm curved to fit the cap.

Acknowledgement
Captain (DoM) Vernon Yates, WO2 (BSM) Phil Kershaw and Sgt Doc Ballard

The Royal Tank Regiment Cambrai Band

The Royal Tank Regiment Cambrai Band was formed in 1922 as The Tank Corps Band.

The Band wears RTR badges with the addition that in Full Dress a plume of feathers is worn behind the badges on the Full Dress beret. The feathers were worn from 1965 to 1977 by all ranks of RTR on the parade beret; the officer's type is a hackle whilst the soldier's is a plume with the feathers mounted on a stiffened backing.

Before the introduction of the RTR ceremonial Dress Beret in 1962 it had been the practice, possibly since 1934, for officers to wear a hackle in their berets on parade.

The soldier's Dress Beret was similar to the caubeen, and ornamented with 'Feathers, Plume' whilst the officers' beret was of astrakhan wool. The officer's Dress Beret was discontinued in 1971 and the soldiers' later in the 1970s, the plume was thereafter worn only by the regimental band, and retained by the band on the formation of the Corps of Army Music. The Band now wears a Dress Beret with two gold bands on the sweatband.

2

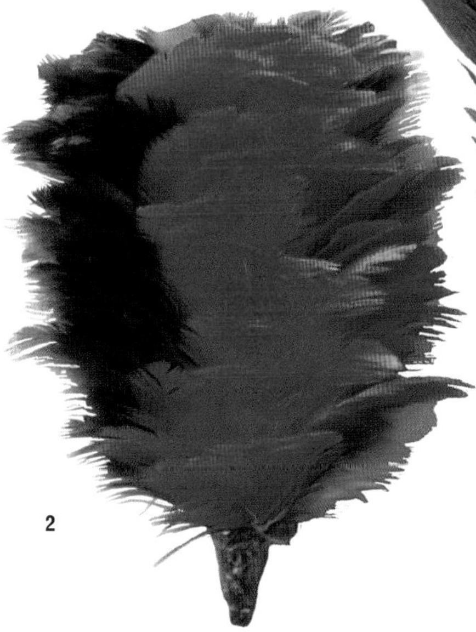

3

1

4

In France at dawn on 20 November 1917, some 300 British Mark IV tanks of The Tank Corps, led by Brigadier Hugh Elles, created a major break in the German Hindenburg Line and almost reached Cambrai itself. The Battle of Cambrai was so successful that the church bells were rung throughout Great Britain. Each year their first great battle is commemorated by The Royal Tank Regiment as 'Cambrai Day'.

1 Captain DJ Milgate the Director of Music wearing the frock coat with the distinctive RTR sash.
2 Officer's hackle 6.5 × 8.25 cm.
3 Musician's feathers, plume 11 × 12.5 cm.
4 The Cambrai Band led by WO1 (BM) WR Fitzpatrick and Captain (DoM) DJ Milgate.

Acknowledgement Cpl Alan Bacon

Royal Artillery Band

The Royal Artillery Band was formed in 1869 from the Royal Artillery Bugle Band, which dated its formation to the drummers of the first artillery companies in 1716.

The Band wears Royal Artillery badges. In Full Dress the musicians wear a Busby with a Grenade badge surmounted by a 37 cm red brush. The Director of Music and Bandmaster wear the officer's Busby which is topped with a white plume.

An ornate rank badge, based in design upon that worn by the Royal Artillery Bandmaster until 1884, when Cavaliere Zavertal was given permission to dispense with it, is to be reintroduced for the Drum Major in 2005.

In Full Dress the Royal Artillery musicians wear a Lyre badge without a wreath or Crown in place of the Musicians and Bandsmen's badge. The RA Band Lyre badge was introduced in 1856, worn on both sleeves but was replaced by the Musicians and Bandsmen's badge in 1931. The RA badge was reintroduced in 1950, worn on the lower right sleeve.

1

2

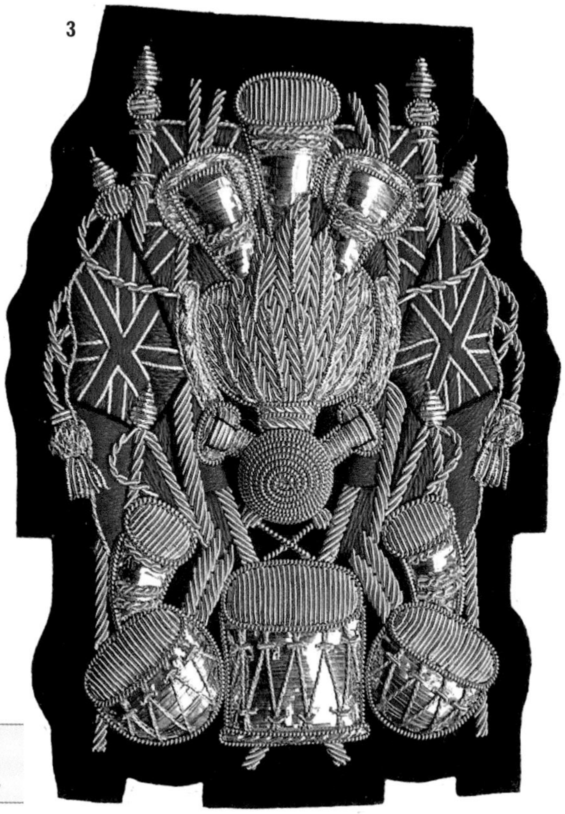
3

In 1762 The Royal Artillery Band formed the first symphony orchestra in England.

4

5

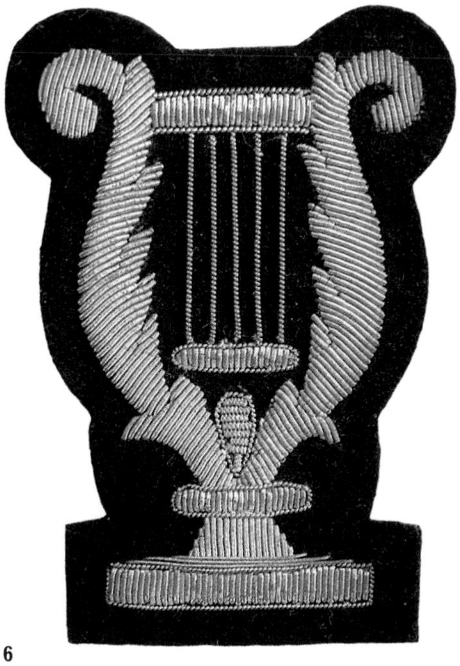

6

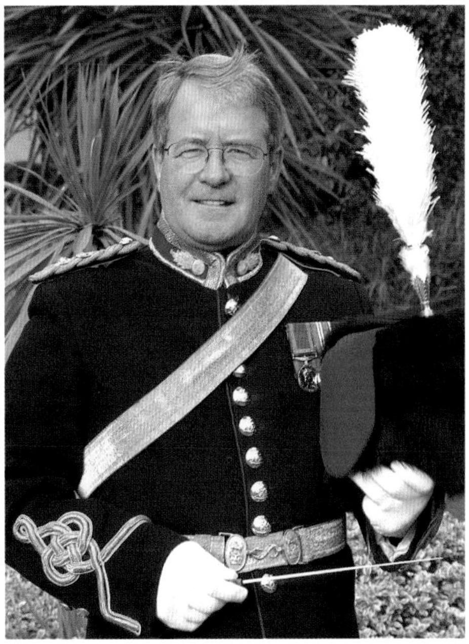

7

opposite page

1 The Royal Artillery Band led by DMaj Richard Pantrey, with the Director of Music Lt Col Malcolm Torrent and WO1 (BM) Pete Bede.

2 Full Dress badge 5 × 9.5 cm worn on the front of the Busby with a red plume.

3 Royal Artillery Band Drum Major's appointment badge 9 × 11.5 cm reintroduced in 2005.

4 DMaj Richard Pantrey wearing Full Dress before the reintroduction of the new rank badge.

5 Officer's waist belt clasp 11 × 5 cm worn by all ranks.

this page

6 Royal Artillery musician's Full Dress badge 6 × 8.5 cm.

7 Lt Col Malcolm Torrent, Director of Music wearing Royal Artillery Full Dress.

Acknowledgement DMaj Richard Pantrey

Royal Engineers Band

The Royal Engineers Band was formed in 1856 from the Royal Sappers and Miners Bugle Band

The Band wears Royal Engineers badges. In Full Dress the musicians wear a Busby with a Grenade badge surmounted by a 37 cm white brush. Until the funeral of King George V in 1936 the Band wore Bearskins; Busbies were introduced for the subsequent coronation of King George VI. The Drum Major wears an ornate rank badge on Number 1 Dress, Number 2 Dress and Full Dress. It is one of the oldest and most elaborate badges, which dates from at least 1855 and has changed little in design in 150 years.

The Band wears a black cross-belt with a standard sized patent leather pouch. The officers' pouches are ornamented with the traditional Coat of Arms badge. The badges have a Tudor (or King's) crown and have been handed down since before 1953. The musician's pouch is ornamented with the RE anodised aluminium cap badge.

1

2

4

3

5

8

9

6

7

previous page

1 Royal Engineers Band led by DMaj Colin Anderson with LCpl Michael Holt and LCpl Lee Fones.
2 Full Dress Busby grenade 5 × 8.75 cm worn with a white brush.
3 Officer's cross belt tip 5 × 4.5 cm.
4 DMaj Colin Anderson, WO2 (BSM) Kevin Spencer and WO1 (BM) Guy Booth wearing Full Dress.

this page

5 Drum Major's rank badge 9 × 11.5 cm.
6 Officer's patent leather pouch 16 × 9.5 cm and badge 5.5 × 5.5 cm.
7 Musician's patent leather pouch 16 × 8 cm mounted with a soldier's anodised aluminium cap badge.
8 Royal Engineers Band Busby.
9 SSgt Stephen Lenton and Terry Kallend wearing the Royal Engineers distinctive dark blue Greatcoat.

Royal Signals Band

The Royal Signals Band was formed in 1921 from the Royal Engineers Depot Band

The Band wears Royal Signals badges. Full Dress was approved for the Band in 1978, including the Busby with grenade badge and scarlet plume, which had been authorised as the officers Full Dress headdress in 1930.

The Drum Major wears an ornate appointment badge in Full Dress based upon that worn by the Drum Major of the Royal Engineers Band since at least 1855, the Royal Signals having been formed from the Royal Engineers.

In 1921 former Royal Engineers formed a volunteer Royal Signals Band. It was given official status in 1939, becoming a Staff Band in 1947.

1

5

4

2

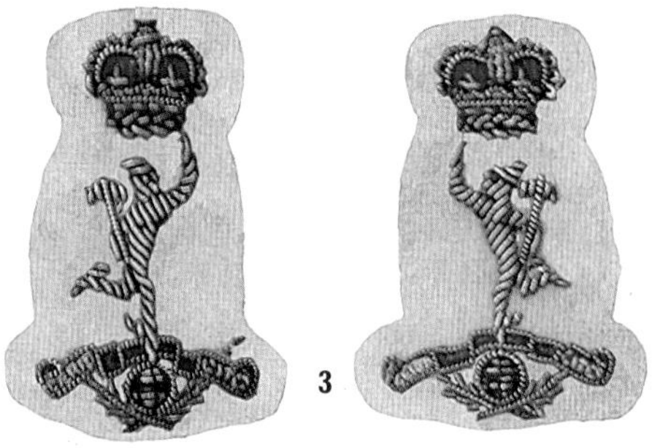

3

6

7

previous page

1 WO1 (BM) Paul Wilman wearing Full Dress.

2 Royal Signals Full Dress Busby badge worn with a scarlet plume 6 × 8.5 cm.

3 Full Dress wire-embroidered collar badges 3.25 × 4.5 cm.

4 Royal Signals Band Drum Major's appointment badge 9 × 11 cm.

5 Sgt (DMaj) Nigel Hind wearing the special Royal Signals Band rank badge.

this page

6 Officer's patent leather pouch 16 × 7.5 cm with general pattern gilt badge 3.5 × 3.75 cm.

7 Soldier's leather pouch 16 × 7.75 cm mounted with a gilding metal badge.

Acknowledgement Major PL Murrell

Bands of Her Majesty's Foot Guards

The bands of the five regiments of Foot Guards are stationed in London where they provide musical support for State occasions and Public Duties

Junior ranks of the Foot Guards Bands wear the senior ranks cap badges of their affiliated regiments, and senior ranks wear Staff cap badges. The remainder of their badges and uniforms are the same as the regiments but with the addition of 'Wings' in place of the epaulettes in Full Dress. By the end of the nineteenth century Queen Victoria decreed that all members of Household Division Bands would be known by the title of 'Musician,' as opposed to 'Bandsmen' used by the remainder of the Army's Bands. The distinction is maintained in some official regulations, for instance *Material Regulations For The Army*, although the term musician is now general throughout the Corps of Army Music.

The Foot Guards Bands do not usually provide their own drum majors; drum majors from the two Foot Guards Public Duties battalions in London, along with the Senior Drum Major Household Division and the incremental drum major, carry out duties with the five bands. For major state occasions other Foot Guards drum majors may be drafted in.

Band of the Grenadier Guards

In 1685 King Charles II authorised the First Regiment of Foot Guards the maintenance of 12 Hautbois, an early wind instrument although in this context it refers to the musicians who played the instruments. 1685 is therefore is considered to be the date of the formation of the Band. So significant was the King to the musicians that from his death in the same year until the Second World War, the bass drummer of the band wore a black mourning armband.

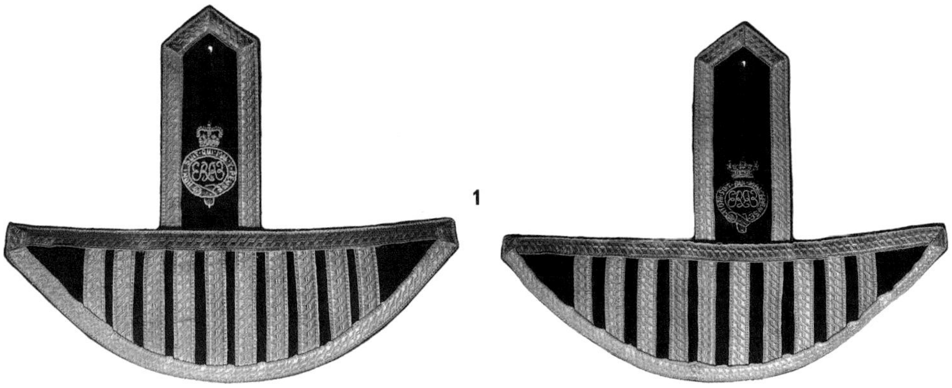

1

2

3

1 Senior ranks' wire-embroidered badge and junior ranks' woven badge of the Grenadier Guards on musicians' wings.
2 CSgt Arron Travis Grenadier Guards Band wearing Concert Order, his uniform protected from the euphonium by an apron.
3 DMaj Steve Staite Grenadier Guards wearing State Dress with the Welsh Guards Drum Major's sash.

Band of the Coldstream Guards

The Coldstream Regiment of Foot Guards had a 'Band of Music' from 1742 consisting of eight civilian musicians who were hired by the month by officers of the Regiment to provide music for the Changing of the Guard at St James' Palace. When, in 1785, the musicians were asked to perform at an aquatic excursion to Greenwich, they declined on the grounds that the performance was 'incompatible with their several respectable and private engagements.' This was too much for the officers who asked the Duke of York, Colonel of the Regiment, for a regular attested band. He agreed and from Hanover in Germany sent twelve musicians under the Director of Music Major CF Eley.

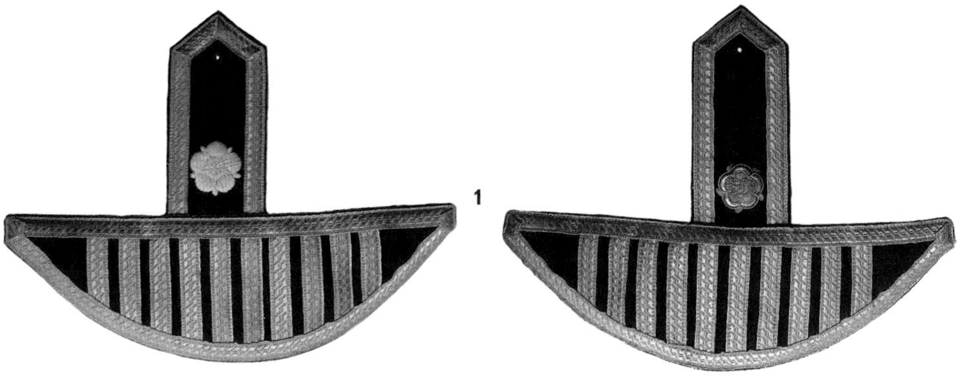

1

2

3

4

1 Senior ranks' wire-embroidered badge and junior ranks' woven badge of the Coldstream Guards on musicians' wings
2 LCpl Darren Hardy, Musn Rachel Smith and CSgt Tim Rampley, Band of the Coldstream Guards in concert.
3 Band of the Coldstream Guards at Buckingham Palace.
4 LSgt Martin Newsome Coldstream Guards Band.

Band of the Scots Guards

The Royal Warrant of 1685 authorizing the maintenance of Hautbois in the Foot Guards in London did not apply to the Scots Regiment of Guards, which was at the time on the Scottish Establishment. Soon after, however, the Scots Guards moved to London, becoming part of the Household troops in 1707, and by 1716 they too had six Hautbois together with three drummers. These drummers were employed as musicians, as distinct from the regimental drummers who had a military role, and were sometimes referred to as drum majors.

The uniform of the Hautbois and Drums on State occasions comprised elaborate gold braided coats with plush caps, similar to those now worn by the Household Cavalry and by Foot Guards drum majors. How effective this band was is not known, but the *Morning Advertiser* of 29 March 1749 reported that The Scots Guards now had German musicians.

Following the defeat of Napoleon in 1815, the three Foot Guards bands travelled to Paris. On their return to London from Paris, the hired professional musicians then serving were dismissed and replaced by enlisted men. The new band continued to wear the State uniform on special occasions; though this custom was discontinued in 1832 for all save the drum major.

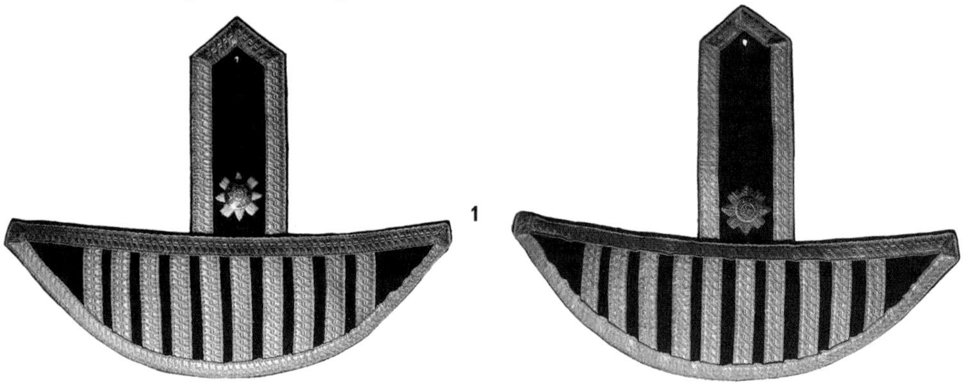

1

2

3

1 Senior ranks' wire-embroidered badge and junior ranks' woven badge with a Scots Guards button on the centre on musicians' wings.
2 CSgt Mark Newitt Scots Guards Band.
3 DMaj Deano Colbert Scots Guards wearing Summer Guard Order.

Band of the Irish Guards

The Irish Guards was formed on 1st April 1900 by Queen Victoria to commemorate the bravery shown by Irish Regiments during the South African campaigns. The Irish Guards Band was formed shortly afterwards.

3

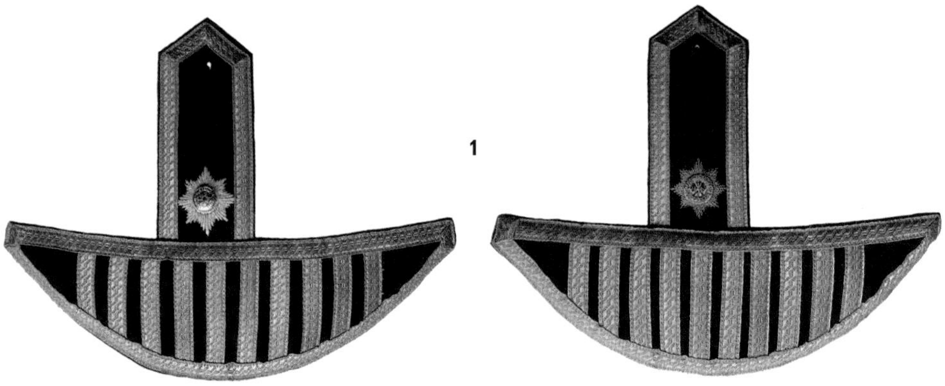

1

1 Senior ranks' wire-embroidered badge and junior ranks' woven badge with a Irish Guards button on the centre on musicians' wings,
2 Band of The Irish Guards.
3 Major Andrew Chatburn, Director of Music, Band of the Irish Guards.

Band of the Welsh Guards

The Band of the Welsh Guards was formed in 1915, the same year as the Regiment. The first set of instruments was presented by the City of Cardiff, which enabled the Band to carry out the first King's Guard Mounting on St. David's Day 1916. On the same day it gave its first concert on the stage of the London Opera House.

1 Senior ranks' wire-embroidered badge and junior ranks' woven badge of the Welsh Guards on musicians' wings.
2 Musn Andy Mercer Welsh Guards Band.

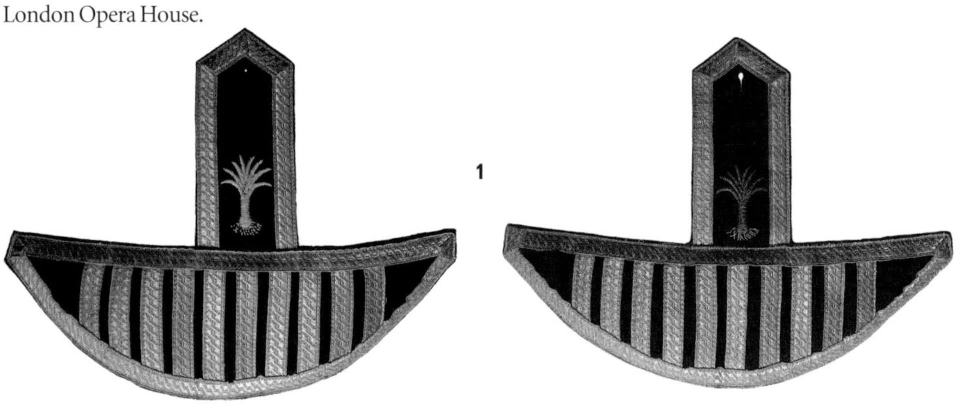

1

2

Acknowledgement Major Philip Shannon MBE, WO2 (BSM) Kevin Bird and Sgt Steve Gatfield

The Lowland Band of The Scottish Division

The Lowland Band was formed in 1994 from the regimental bands of The Royal Scots, The Royal Highland Fusiliers, and The King's Own Scottish Borderers.

1

The Lowland Band of the Scottish Division wears the Lowland Brigade badge, which had been worn between 1959 and 1968. The badge has some similarity to the badge of the Lowland Regiment, a Young Soldiers Battalion which existed from 1942 to 1943, although there is no direct link. The Director of Music and the Bandmaster wear silver badges and the musicians anodised aluminium badges. The badges were at some time produced in two sizes, the larger, 5.25 × 5.25 cm, worn on the Glengarry, and the smaller, 4.5 × 4.5 cm, worn on the Kilmarnock bonnet and the Tam o'Shanter. This is no longer the case and badges are now all of the larger size.

The collar badges were originally designed for The London Scottish, a volunteer unit raised as the 15th Middlesex Rifle Volunteer Corps in 1859, and now a company of The London Regiment.

2

3

4

5

6

previous page

1 Lowland Band musician's anodised aluminium cap badge 5.25 × 5.25 cm and collar badges 2.75 × 3 cm.

2 Musn Gary Newlands and Anthony Watson wearing Full Dress.

3 Bright metal plaid brooch 9 cm.

this page

4 Officer's silver Plaid Brooch 9 cm.

5 Director of Music and Bandmaster's waist belt clasp 7 × 6.25 cm.

6 Director of Music and Bandmaster's shoulder belt plate 7.5 × 10 cm.

Acknowledgement WO2 (BSM) M T Wilson

The Highland Band of The Scottish Division

The Highland Band was formed in 1994 from the regimental bands of The Black Watch, The Queen's Own Highlanders, The Gordon Highlanders and The Argyll and Sutherland Highlanders.

The Highland Band adopted the cap badge of The Highland Brigade which had been worn during an earlier reorganisation of the Infantry by The Black Watch, the Seaforth Highlanders (Ross-shire Buffs, The Duke of Albany's) and The Queen's Own Cameron Highlanders which amalgamated as the Queen's Own Highlanders (Seaforth and Camerons) in 1961, The Gordon Highlanders and The Argyll and Sutherland Highlanders between 1958 and 1969. The badge combines St Andrew's Cross, taken from The Queen's Own Cameraon Highlanders badge, the stag's head from the Crest of the Marquis of Huntley worn by The Gordon Highlanders and the motto which translates as *Help the King*, from the Seaforth Highlanders badge.

The Band wears The Black Watch collar badges and sporran badge.

1

2

3

1 On the Full Dress feather bonnet an anodised aluminium cap badge 4.5 × 5.5 cm is worn whilst on the Glengarry the badge is a very attractive three-dimensional white metal design 4.25 × 5.25 cm.

2 The Highland Band with DMaj Dougy Twycross, Major (DoM) George Rodger and WO1 (BM) Jon Milne.

3 The Highland Band plaid brooch 10.25 cm.

Acknowledgement WO2 (BSM) C Meldrum

Minden Band and Normandy Band of The Queen's Division

The Bands of The Queen's Division were formed in 1994. The Minden Band from the regimental bands of The Princess of Wales's Royal Regiment and The Royal Anglian Regiment, and the Normandy Band from the bands of The Royal Regiment of Fusiliers.

The Minden Band wears the Home Service pattern helmet in Full Dress.

The Normandy Band wears the Fusilier Busby in Full Dress. The Normandy Band also has two Northumberland Pipers who wear the Royal Regiment of Fusiliers beret and hackle, Percy Plaid and Brooch (Bomlet).

Each Division of Infantry is represented by a lieutenant colonel serving on the staff of the Director of Infantry. The Queen's Division representative wears a Queen's Division rank slide of the same style as those worn by the Bands, rather than a regimental rank slide.

1

2

3

4

5

6

7

The titles Minden Band and Normandy Band were chosen as they represent battle honours shared by the three regiments of The Queen's Division, The Princess of Wales's Royal Regiment and The Royal Anglian Regiment and The Royal Regiment of Fusiliers.

The Battle of Minden was fought in 1759 in north Germany during the Seven Years War when the British, Hanoverians, Hessians and Prussians defeated the French and Saxons. The Normandy Landing was the successful assault landing by allied troops against the French coast in 1944.

8

9

10

11

12

opposite page

1 Queen's Division Bands bi-metal and enamel cap badge 2.5 × 4.25 cm and collar badges 2 × 3.5 cm.
2 Shoulder title 4.25 × 2 cm.
3 Normandy Band in Full Dress led by DMaj Ian Patterson and WO1 (BM) Tony Adams.
4 LCpl Fraser Hurman wearing Minden Band Full Dress.
5 The Normandy Band in Cyprus with WO2 (BSM) Ian Cobb, WO1 (BM) Sean Riley and Captain (DoM) Kevin Roberts.
6 Wire-embroidered collar badges 2 × 3 cm worn by the Directors of Music and Bandmasters and by all musicians on Concert Dress.
7 Normandy Band Busby Grenade 4 × 9 cm.

this page

8 Minden Band helmet plate 11.5 × 13.5 cm.
9 Minden Band officer's helmet with silver, gilt and enamel plate.
10 Captain Kevin Roberts Director of Music of The Normandy Band.
11 Captain Jim Taylor former Director of Music of The Normandy Band.
12 DMaj Simon Stafford wearing the Atholl Grey greatcoat, his dress diffentiated from the Grenadier Guards by the white plume on the right side of the Bearskin.

13

14

13 Musn Jack Williams wearing the TRF on his right sleeve, DMaj Simon Stafford, LCpl Smudge Smith and Matt Simons wearing the 2nd Division arm badge on his left sleeve.
14 WO2 rank badge.

Acknowledgement
Major TD Arnold, Cpl John Nicholas and LCpl Alistair Smith

Waterloo Band and Normandy Band of The King's Division

The Bands of The King's Division were formed in 1994. The Normandy Band from the regimental bands of The King's Own Royal Border Regiment, The King's Regiment and The Queen's Lancashire Regiment, and The Waterloo Band from the regimental bands of The Prince of Wales's Own Regiment of Yorkshire, The Green Howards and The Duke of Wellington's Regiment.

The titles Waterloo Band and Normandy Band were chosen as they represent battle honours shared by most of the regiments of The King's Division.

The Battle of Waterloo was fought in 1815 in Belgium when the British, Germans, Belgians, Dutch and Prussians finally after 26 years of war defeated the French Grande Armée led by Napoleon. Captain Kincaid, a veteran of the Peninsular War, said 'I had never thought there would be a battle where everyone was killed. This seemed to be it.'

The Normandy Landing was the successful assault landing by allied troops against the French coast in 1944.

1

2

3

4

5

6

7

10

13

8

11

9

12

opposite page

1 King's Division Band gilt and enamel cap badge 3.75 × 4.5 cm and collar badges 2.5 × 3.5 cm.
2 Shoulder title 4.5 × 2 cm.
3 Button.
4 Officer's Full Dress collar badges 2.5 × 4 cm.
5 Captain Gary Clegg, Musn James Bullivant, DMaj Richard Dunning, CSgt John Drury, WO2 (BSM) Colin Pinington and CSgt Andy Firth wearing Full Dress.
6 Captain Wayne Hopla, Director of Music of The Waterloo Band.

this page

7 LCpl Nick Southorn wearing the musician's helmet and collar badges.
8 Officer's beret badge 4 × 4.5 cm worn on the khaki beret.
9 Bandmaster's and Musician's rank slides.
10 DMaj Keith Mowbray wearing Full Dress.
11 Officer's helmet plate worn by the Director of Music and the Bandmaster 11.5 × 14 cm (shown ⅔ actual size).
12 Musician's helmet plate 11.5 × 14 cm (shown ⅔ actual size).
13 WO1 (BM) Ian Johnson wearing the officer's helmet plate and collar badges.

Acknowledgement
WO2 (BSM) MC Pinington, Sgt MC Thompson and LCpl LC Whitworth

Lucknow Band and Clive Band of The Prince of Wales's Division

The Bands of The Prince of Wales's Division were formed in 1994 from the regimental bands of The Devonshire and Dorset Regiment, The 22nd (Cheshire) Regiment, The Royal Welch Fusiliers, The Royal Regiment of Wales, The Royal Gloucestershire, Berkshire and Wiltshire Regiment, The Worcester-shire and Sherwood Foresters Regiment and The Staffordshire Regiment.

In representing the Prince of Wales's Division, the Bands' badges display the Prince of Wales's feathers. Rather than design new badges, the cap badge of the Royal Regiment of Wales and the collar badges of the Royal Wiltshire Yeomanry are worn. The Clive Band wears a red backing to the centre of the helmet plate.

1

2

3

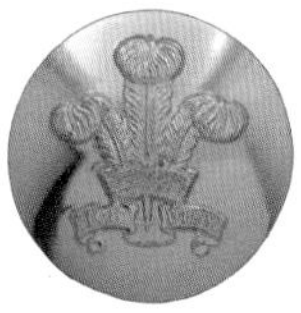

4

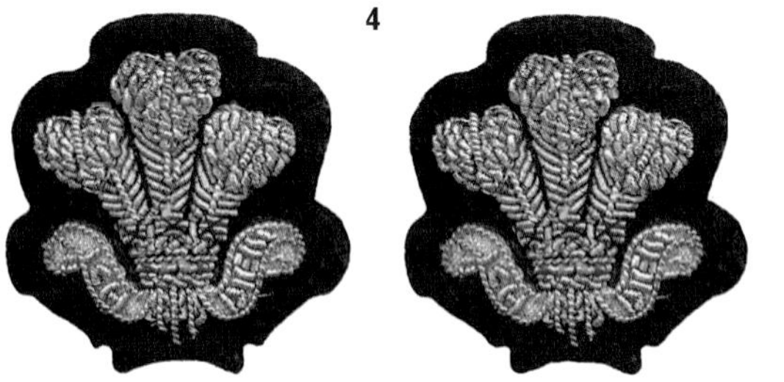

5

6

7

The Clive Band is also a Male Voice Choir and sings in the Welsh language.

The Bands are named after the barracks in which they were based on formation. Clive Barracks, opened in 1976 at the former RAF Ternhill, was named after Lord Robert Clive of India, a national figure who was born in 1725 and resided in the nearby town of Market Drayton, Shropshire.

Lucknow Barracks, built in Tidworth in 1905, is named after the heroic 87 day defence of the Lucknow Residency during the Indian Mutiny in 1857.

8

opposite page

1 The Prince of Wales's Division Band wears the cap badge of the Royal Regiment of Wales 4 × 4.5 cm and the collar badges of the Royal Wiltshire Yeomanry 2.5 × 2.5 cm.

2 Shoulder title 4 × 3 cm.

3 The Prince of Wales's Division Band button.

4 Officer's Full Dress wire-embroidered collar badges.

5 DMaj Chris Hould of The Clive Band.

6 Officer's helmet plate 11.5 × 13.5 cm worn by Directors of Music and Bandmasters.

7 Musician's helmet plate 11.5 × 13.5 cm.

this page

8 Captain (DoM) Tim Cooper and WO 2 (BSM) Bob Goodridge of the Lucknow Band wearing Full Dress with Forage Cap.

Acknowledgement
WO2 (BSM) Ian Allan, PD Aplin and RA Goodridge

Light Division Band and Bugles

The Light Division Band was formed in 1994 from the Corunna and Salamanca Bands of The Light Infantry and the Normandy and Peninsula Bands of The Royal Green Jackets. The Buglers are attached from battalions of The Light Infantry and The Royal Green Jackets for up to two years' musical training

The Light Division Band wears the beret badge of The Oxfordshire and Buckinghamshire Light Infantry in both the beret and the Forage Cap. The beret badge was adopted by The Oxfordshire and Buckinghamshire Light Infantry sometime after 1945 and is slightly smaller than the cap badge which had been worn by the regiment since 1897. The Oxfordshire and Buckinghamshire Light Infantry lost the badge in 1958 when the Green Jackets Brigade cap badge was introduced. The badge was reintroduced for the Light Division Band but produced with a new die, as the original was no longer available.

In Full Dress the Rifle Cap is worn, known as such by The Royal Green Jackets but as the Shako by The Light Infantry. It is ornamented on the front by a miniature badge sewn onto an oval cord boss – sometimes referred to as a 'worm cast'.

1

2

3

4

5

6

7

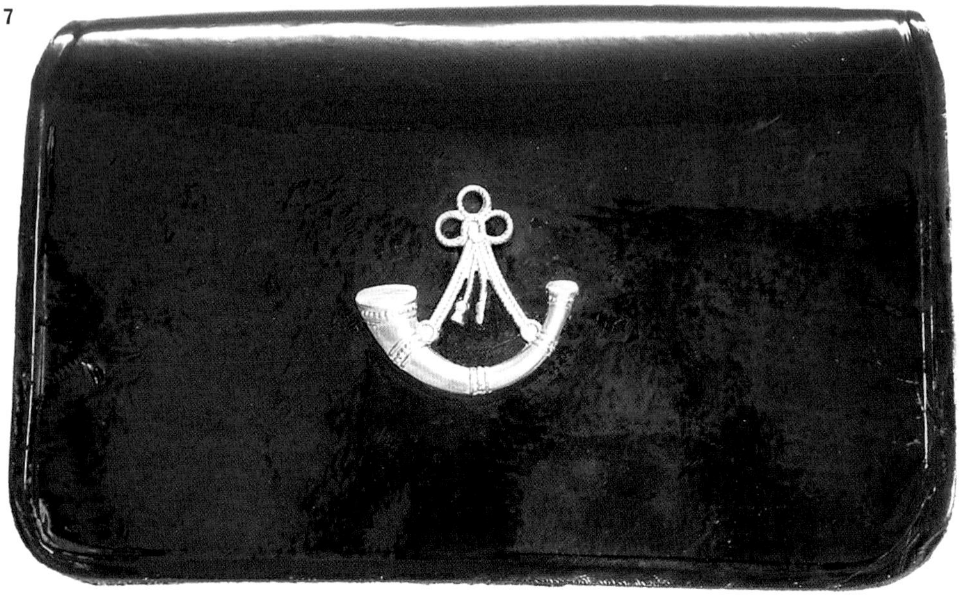

The Band wears the miniature black Royal Green Jackets collar badges, known as lapel badges, on Number 2 Dress.

The Band wears the gold wire-embroidered Musician's Lyre arm badge of the former RGJ Band.

The black plastic waist belt is fitted with the traditional Light Division snake fastener but is only worn with Number 2 Dress. Number 2 Dress is not worn by the Band on parade.

11

8

9

10

previous page

1 Light Division Band Oxfordshire and Buckinghamshire Light Infantry metal cap badge 3.5 × 3 cm and Royal Green Jackets anodised aluminium lapel badges 2 × 1.5 cm.

2 Light Division Band and Bugles. Photograph *CAMUS*.

3 Musician's Full Dress arm badge 5.25 × 6.5 cm.

4 Band snake clasp, Snake 4 × 2 cm.

5 Rifle Cap badge. Cord boss 3.25 × 4.5 cm, badge 1.75 × 1.75 cm.

6 Sgt Mark Wells, wearing a cross-belt ornamented with a Rifles whistle and chain, and Musn William Redpath, both wearing Ceremonial Dress.

this page

7 Senior rank's pouch, worn by sergeants, warrant officers and officers ornamented with a cap badge 15 × 9 cm.

8 Musician's pouch ornamented with a cap badge 16 × 7.5 cm.

9 Royal Green Jackets cross belt plate worn by the Director of Music and the Band Sergeant Major 6 × 7.5 cm.

10 Light Infantry cross belt plate worn by the Bandmaster 6 × 8 cm.

11 Rfn Scott Barnes RGJ and Pte Daniel Render LI, buglers serving with the Light Division Band.

Acknowledgement WO2 (BSM) Martin Shone

Royal Irish Regiment Band

The Band of The Royal Irish Regiment was formed in 1994 from the regimental bands of the 1st and 2nd Battalions, The Royal Irish Rangers.

The Band wears Royal Irish Regiment badges, with the musicians wearing the large Piper's cap badge, except for the Director of Music and Bandmaster who wear officer's badges.

The Band wears a badge of the 86th Foot on the music case. This badge consists of the Sphinx over Egypt above a Light Infantry bugle. The Sphinx was granted as a battle honour in 1802 in recognition of the 90 mile march across the desert by 2nd Battalion 86th Foot from Suez to Cairo in 1801 to enter the citadel on the surrender of the French. The bugle was added below the sphinx in 1881.

1

2

3

1 The Royal Irish Regiment Band led by DMaj John Sherlock, with Sgt Chris Betts Trombone, CSgt Davie Johnson Cornet, Cpl Colin Blackwood Trombone, Musn Mark Rae Euphonium and LCpl Dominic Campbell Trombone.
2 WO2 (BSM) Chalky White Full Dress.
3 Royal Irish Regiment Band music case 21 × 16.5 cm, badge 3.5 × 4.25 cm.

Acknowledgement Major Beattie Ferguson

Parachute Regiment Band

The Band of The Parachute Regiment was formed in 1994 from the Falklands and Pegasus Bands of The Parachute Regiment.

The Band of the Parachute Regiment wears the regiment's uniform. Two members of the Band are qualified parachutists and have the unusual distinction of wearing the Musician's Lyre badge below parachute wings.

1

The Parachute Regiment was formed on 1st August 1942 but did not have any musical support until 1947. At this time the 1st and 2nd Battalion bands were formed in Aldershot with Bandsmen from Infantry regiments whose battalions were being put into suspended animation after the end of the Second World War. A 3rd Battalion band was formed a year later from newly recruited musicians, each being directed by a Warrant Officer Class I Bandmaster. All three regimental bands accompanied their respective battalions providing musical and medical support.

As a result of the Defence Review in 1985 the Battalion bands were disbanded and reformed to produce two larger regimental bands – The Falklands and Pegasus Bands; which collectively supported the three Parachute Battalions and additional Airborne Forces. Further reductions in 1993 culminated in the formation of The Corps of Army Music and consequently the amalgamation of both bands to form The Band of the Parachute Regiment under the command of a commissioned Director of Music.

2

3

4

previous page

1 Musn Barry Ryall wearing No1 Dress.

this page

2 The Parachute Regiment Band led by DMaj Andy Rowe.

3 Captain Ian McEligott the Director of Music wearing the Frock Coat with silver collar badges.

4 Cpl Paul Lucas wearing Concert Dress.

Acknowledgement
WO1 (BM) S Goodwin and WO2 (BSM) Keith Mico

Brigade of Gurkhas Band

The Band of the Brigade of Gurkhas was formed in 1970 by the amalgamation of the regimental band 2nd Gurkha Rifles with the Brigade of Gurkhas Staff Band.

The Band wears Brigade of Gurkha badges.
The Band traces its history to 1859 when a Band was formed by the Sirmoor Rifle Regiment, later named the 2nd Gurkha Rifles but always known as the 2nd Goorkhas. In 1947 four Gurkha regiments were chosen to transfer to the British Army, including the 2nd Goorkhas, the only regiment with a Band, the others having Pipes and Drums. 2nd Goorkhas were selected for transfer 'owing to their close relationship with the 60th Rifles.' The Bandsmen however elected to stay in India and the new band did not form up and begin training until 1949.

1

2

3

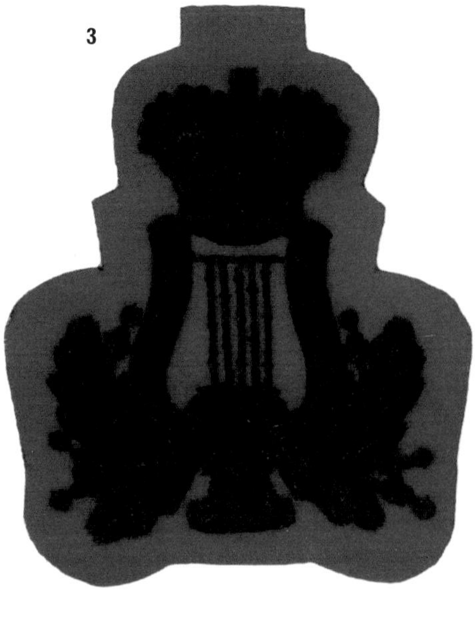

4

5

6

7

8

opposite page

1 Gurkha Band bright metal cap badge 3 × 3.5 cm.
2 Shoulder title 4.5 × 2.5 cm.
3 Gurkha Band musician's badge 5.5 × 7.5 cm.

this page

4 The Gurkha Band led by the Acting Bugle Major, Acting Sergeant Basudev Gurung at the Royal Military Academy Sandhurst.
5 Musn Shyambahadur Gurung.
6 Gurkha Band Music Case mounted with the Brigade of Gurkhas badge.
7 Lt (QGO) Tirtharaj Gurung, Assistant Director of Music.
8 Officer's shoulder belt plate 7.5 × 9.5 cm

Acknowledgement WO2 Popiraj Rai

Army Air Corps Band

The Band of the Army Air Corps was formed from the Royal Artillery Alanbrooke Band in 1993.

The Band wears Army Air Corps badges, and, in Full Dress a cross belt and pouch which is rarely seen elsewhere.

The Band wears Royal Artillery pattern cross belts identifiable for officers and Warrant Officers by the Royal Artillery Grenade on the tip of the belt. The Director of Music wears a wire-embroidered pouch, and the musicians a black plastic pouch mounted with a soldier's anodised aluminium cap badge. The Bandmaster wears the same pouch as the musicians but distinguished by a pale blue backing to his badge.

2

1

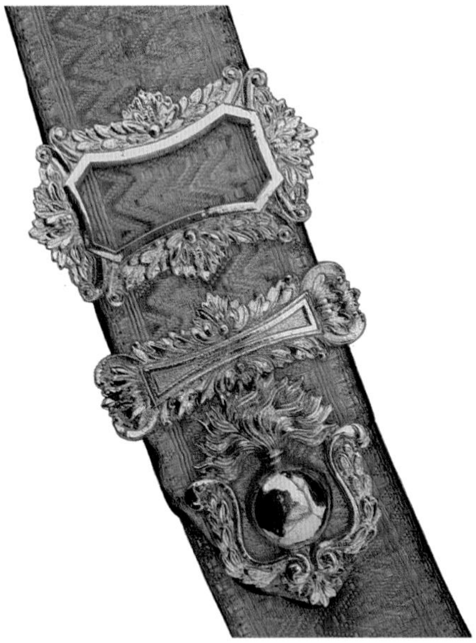

3

4

1 Director of Music's Royal Artillery pattern cross belt tip.
2 Director of Music's pouch.
3 Bandmaster's pouch mounted with an anodised aluminium cap badge.
4 Musician's pouch mounted with a soldier's private purchase white metal cap badge.

Acknowledgement SSgt Stephen Armstrong-Watkins

Royal Logistic Corps Band

The Royal Logistic Corps Band was formed in 1994 from the Bands of The Royal Corps of Transport and The Royal Army Ordnance Corps

The Royal Logistic Corps Band wears RLC badges and in Full Dress a helmet mounted with a universal pattern helmet plate.

The musicians' helmet plates were produced from a new die, whilst the officer's plates had to be hand made. Colonel Peter Walton on behalf of the Regimental Colonel bought six original pre-1914 officers' Helmet Plates (the antecedents were irrelevant); the Crowns, central badges and regimental title scrolls were removed. Six musicians plates were cut up to provide the correct St Edward's (or Queen's) Crown, the crossed axes and the Royal Logistic Corps motto, which were then fixed to the original star plates. The Ordnance Arms originally made for the Band of the Royal Army Ordnance Corps in 1986 was added to the centre and finally the Helmet Plates were gold and silver-plated.

After a couple of changes in the detail of the design over the years, the correct form of the Band's Full Dress uniform was eventually agreed in 2005. It represents a compromise between tradition and modern materials.

The RLC has a Corps of Drums, which supports the Band. The Drums date to 1799 when a drummer was appointed from amongst the trumpeters from each of the five original companies of the Royal Wagon Train. In their turn the RCT had a very successful Corps of Drums until 1993 and after some fallow years up to a dozen RLC soldiers now spend two years as drummers before returning to their trades, which include drivers, supply specialists, pioneers and chefs. Their military skills are said to contribute significantly to the Band's operational capability, and ability to live comfortably in the field.

1

2

3

4

5

6

previous page

1 Royal Logistic Corps officer's helmet plate 11.5 × 13.5 cm.
2 Musician's helmet plate 11.5 × 13.5 cm.
3 WO1 (BM) Kevin Duffy wearing Full Dress.
4 Officer's plastic pouch 16 × 8 cm, badge 3.25 × 3.5 cm.

this page

5 RLC Band officer's cross belt tip, upper slide 6.5 × 7.5 cm, tip 5 × 3.5 cm.
6 Drum Major Alfie Garner wearing Full Dress.

Acknowledgement Major Jim Taylor and SSgt Lee Dawson

Corps of Royal Electrical and Mechanical Engineers Band

A fife and drum corps was raised when The Corps of Royal Electrical and Mechanical Engineers was formed in 1942, the range of instruments increased until in 1947 the Corps Staff Band was authorised.

The Band wears REME badges and in Full Dress a helmet mounted with a universal pattern helmet plate.

In Full Dress the Director of Music and Bandmaster wear the female officers' wire-embroidered Mess Dress collar badges with a red background to match the colour of their collars.

The Band wears a white cross-belt with a standard sized white plastic pouch. The officer's pouch is wire-embroidered. The musician's pouch is ornamented with a metal REME badge, which is larger than the cap badge.

1

2

3

4

5

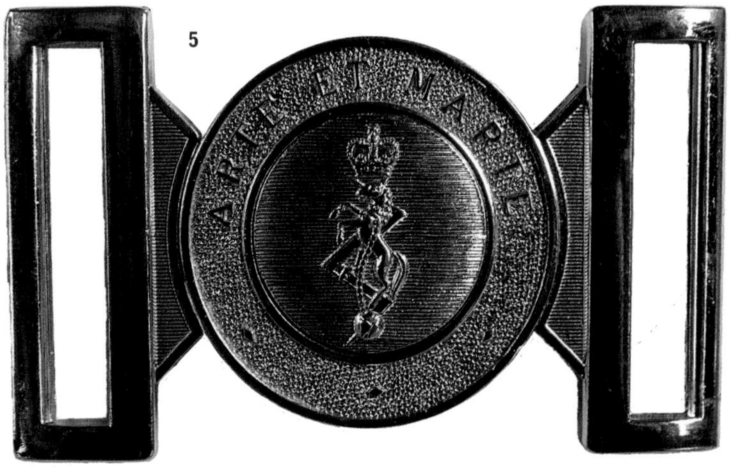

6

7

opposite page

1 REME Band officer's gilt and silver helmet plate worn by the Director of Music and the Bandmaster 11.5 × 13.5 cm.

2 Musician's bright metal helmet plate curved to fit against the body of the helmet 11.5 × 13.5 cm.

3 DMaj Julian Culverwell and Musn Shonagh Reid wearing Full Dress.

4 Officer's all gilt helmet plate 11.5 × 13.5 cm, which was replaced in 2004.

5 Waist belt clasp10 × 6.25 cm. The motto, reflecting the practical nature of REME, is said to read, 'Twist to open'.

6 Musician's white plastic pouch 16 × 8 cm mounted with a bi-metal badge 3 × 4.75 cm (larger than the cap badge).

7 Director of Music's pouch.

Acknowledgement WO2 (BSM) MW Richardson

Adjutant General's Corps Band

The Adjutant General's Corps Band was formed in 1994 from the Band of The Women's Royal Army Corps.

The Adjutant General's Corps Band wears AGC's badges except in Full Dress for which new insignia was designed.

The design of the helmet plate was introduced in 1898 for the Royal Army Medical Corps. The AGC helmet plate differs from that first pattern only in the use of St Edward's (or Queen's) Crown and the change of title. The musicians' helmet plate is finished in bright gilding metal and the officers' in gilt.

The musicians white plastic Music Case, known irreverently by them as the 'hand bag', is fastened to a cross belt. (On its formation the Adjutant General's Corps absorbed a sizable proportion of the Women's Royal Army Corps and therefore was immediately nicknamed the 'All Girlie Corps'). The nickname has faded but reference to the handbag continues.

1

2

3

4

5

opposite page

1 Officer's pouch 21.5 × 10.5 cm.

2 Musician's helmet plate 9 × 9.5 cm.

3 Officer's helmet plate 9 × 10 cm.

this page

4 Music case 21 × 17 cm, bright metal badge 4.5 × 7.5 cm.

5 DMaj Dave Stones and WO2 (BSM) Phil Greenwood wearing Full Dress.

TERRITORIAL ARMY

The Territorial Army, or TA, forms one quarter of the British Army, playing the vital role of reinforcing the Regular Army with paid voluntary part-time personnel. Trained TA soldiers are liable for call-out under the Reserve Forces Act 1996 – the TA is, therefore, not a hobby.

As a fully integrated and integral part of the British Army, the TA is divided into the same complex arrangement of regiments and corps as the Regular Army. However, the defining characteristic of the TA's structure is its units; local Independent Units and national Specialist Units.

The majority of TA personnel join their local TA centre, which is home to an Independent Unit. The units' roles vary, depending on the region, but are likely to be combat, communications, medical, engineering or logistics.

Specialist Units recruit people who are already professionally qualified and wish to use those qualifications within the TA in areas such as logistics, IT and communications, medicine, engineering and media.

TA soldiers are issued only Number 8 Dress, Combat Dress, which is worn with berets. Officers and senior NCOs also wear Mess Dress. Units hold some Number 1, Number 2 and a few Full Dress uniforms for special occasions. The only badges known to most of the soldiers are the beret badges.

Colonel Robert Sutcliffe OBE TD wearing The Royal Wiltshire Yeomanry No 1 Dress with the Staff cap badge and The King's Royal Hussars crossed kukris badge above the Fern Leaf badge.

Caldwell's Localisation of 1872 created geographic affiliations between Infantry regiments, the Militia and the Volunteer Corps. In 1881 the reforms were taken further when the Militia and Volunteer Corps became battalions of local regiments. Haldane's reforms, the Territorial Reserve Forces Act of 1908, created a much larger, and more closely integrated regimental structure with two reserve armies. The Militia provided a reserve for the Army while the Volunteer and Yeomanry units were assigned to home defence. The largest Arm, the Infantry, was to consist of regular battalions, Special Reserve battalions and a number of territorial battalions. This organisation provided the foundation for the armies raised to fight the First World War. In 1920 all reserve forces were again reorganised into the Territorial Army and from then on many infantry battalions were transferred to other arms. Generally infantry units became artillery, engineer or, during the Second World War, units of the Royal Armoured Corps, whilst the Yeomanry transferred to artillery and signals. Since the end of the Second World War the Territorial Army has been constantly reorganised and steadily reduced in size leaving a multitude of combined titles and traditions.

Royal Monmouthshire Royal Engineers (Militia)

The Royal Monmouthshire Royal Engineers (Militia), the 'Senior Regiment of the Reserve Army', was raised as a Trained Band in 1539 and converted to Militia Engineers in 1872

The Royal Monmouthshire Royal Engineers (Militia), or R MON RE, is a RE TA regiment with a unique cap badge. The design of the badge is based upon the Prince of Wales's feathers worn by the Royal Monmouthshire Militia prior to 1877. Soldiers are issued an anodised aluminium cap badge but it is reported that the majority buy a bi-metal badge. Officers wear a wire embroidered beret badge. The regiment has for sale a small stock of Hall Marked gold badges which were designed for wear on the officer's Forage Cap.

A wovern Militia Flash is worn on the left sleeve in all orders of dress. The green oblong badge is refered to in the regiment as the snooker table. A finer quality badge with a wire embroidered border is worn on the Mess Dress jacket.

The Royal Monmouthshire Royal Engineers (Militia) claims its seniority having served the Crown continuously since being mustered in 1539. The regiment adopted its present title in 1896.

The Honourable Artillery Company, although older, fought for Parliament during the Civil War and therefore lost its seniority. Similarily, the Royal Jersey Militia was also formed earlier but was disbanded in 1946 before being reformed as an Engineer squadron in 1992.

In 1914 the Colours of the East Monmouth Militia were presented to the Royal Monmouth Royal Engineers. The regiment is the only Royal Engineers unit to carry Colours.

1

2

3

4

5

6

7

1 Royal Monmouthshire Royal Engineers (Militia) soldier's anodised aluminium cap badge 4 × 4.5 cm.
2 Private purchase bi-metal cap badge 4 × 5 cm.
3 Officer's wire embroidered beret badge 4.5 × 5 cm.
4 Officer's hallmarked gold Forage Cap badge 4.5 × 5 cm.
5 Woven working dress Militia Flash 5.75 × 2 cm.
6 Wire embroidered Mess Dress Militia Flash 6 × 2 cm.
7 Spr Sally Derrick wearing the R MON RE anodised aluminium cap badge.

The Honourable Artillery Company

Formed in 1537, The Company has a unique organisation; in part Territorial Army regiment and in part a club which includes the ceremonial Company of Pikemen and Musketeers, and the Light Cavalry Squadron.

The Honourable Artillery Company, or HAC, is a Royal Artillery TA regiment which also has ceremonial roles in the City of London. It is responsible for firing salutes at Her Majesty's Tower of London and for providing Guards of Honour in the City. The HAC wears three different patterns of cap badge reflecting its traditions as a volunteer unit in the City of London, its close links with the Grenadier Guards and its artillery role. The regiment follows The Guards Division practice of wearing a khaki beret. The Arms of the HAC is worn as the cap badge, except by the Band and Corps of Drums. The beret badge is amongst the oldest badges in the Army, an example is embroidered on the front of a surviving Grenadier's Mitre Cap dated about 1710. The soldier's badge is worn on a black backing. The officer's wire-embroidered badge includes the motto, which translates as *Arms, the mainstay of peace.*

The Corps of Drums wear the Grenade badge on the Household Division blue/red/blue silk backing.

As with the remainder of the Territorial Army, combat dress is the usual Order of Dress. When firing Gun Salutes Number 1 Dress of the former Artillery Division, known as No 1 Dress (Gunner), is worn. Cavalry shoulder chains are worn in place of epaulettes. Number 1 Dress of the former Infantry Division, known as No 1 Dress (Infantry), is worn on other ceremonial occasions. Grenadier Guards pattern scarlet Full Dress is worn by the Band and Corps of Drums, and there are sufficient additional uniforms to furnish a small guard. The Company does not have Officer's and Sergeant's Messes, all ranks Mess together and all have Mess Dress.

Number 2 Dress is worn only by those undertaking specialist duties, such as attendance at the

1

2

3

4

5

6

7

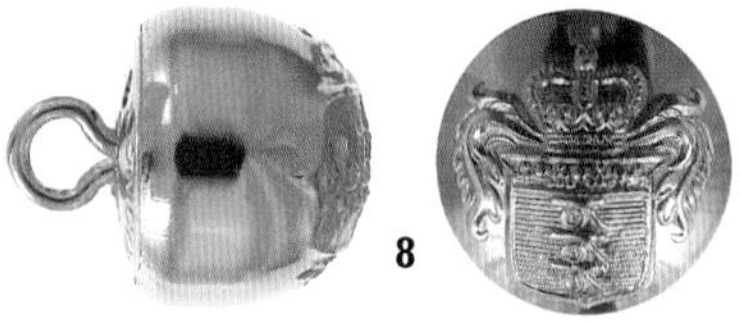
8

9

In 1537 the Overseers of the Fraternity or Guild of St George received a Charter of Incorporation from Henry VIII. The Guild became known as The Gentlemen of the Artillery Garden, after its practice ground in Spitalfields, and in time simply The Artillery Company. The courtesy prefix Honourable was first used in 1685 and officially confirmed by Queen Victoria in 1860.

Territorial Army Commissioning Course at the Royal Military Academy Sandhurst.

For normal duties the Artillery Division cap badge was worn only by the Troop Sergeant Major of the Gun Troop; now renamed Liaison Troop.

Collar badges are worn in Full Dress and No 1 Dress (Gunner). Full Dress collar badges are those of the Grenadier Guards in reversed metals. Officers and Warrant Officers wear gold Grenades, Sergeants wear silver Grenades and junior ranks wear the white woven Grenades.

In No 1 Dress (Gunner) officers and Warrant Officers wear wire-embroidered Royal Artillery collar badges. Soldiers wear Royal Artillery style anodised aluminium collar badges with HAC scrolls, worn horizontally.

In No 1 Dress (Gunner) officers wear a cross belt and pouch. Field officers wear the Royal Artillery Full Dress pouch whilst battery officers wear a 'leather' pouch, actually black plastic, mounted with a pre-1953 HAC gun badge, having a Tudor (or King's) Crown.

Each year since 1864, and at the recommendation of the Commanding Officer, the Captain General has awarded a prize to the officer or soldier who has made an outstanding contribution to the regiment. As the present Captain General is The Queen the award is known as The Queen's Prize. Recipients wear a badge incorporating the Captain General's cypher and the year of the award on Number 1 and Number 2 Dress and Mess Dress.

In 1906 King Edward VII gave The Company the distinction of a special ribbon for the Volunteer Decoration and Volunteer Long Service Medal. The ribbon, based on the King's racing colours, is red and blue edged with narrow yellow stripes. The ribbon is now worn on the Territorial Efficiency Decoration, Territorial Efficiency Medal and Volunteer Reserves Service Medal.

10

11

12

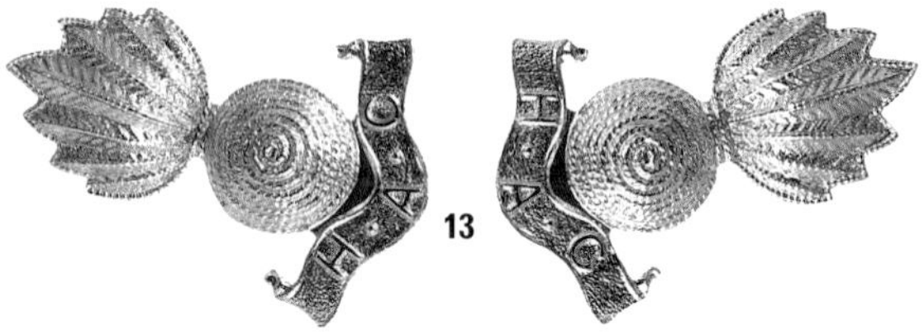

13

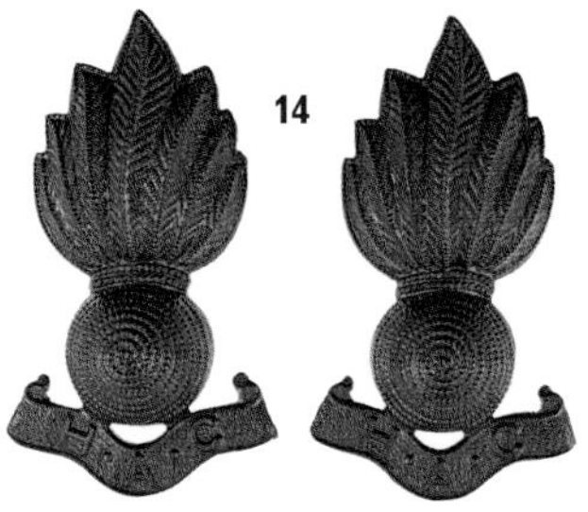

14

15

16

opposite page

1 Officer's gilt and wire-embroidered Forage Cap badge 3.5 × 4.25 cm.

2 Bimetal cap badge 4.25 × 5.5 cm worn by lance sergeants and above in the Forage Cap and by senior ranks of the Band and Corps of Drums as the beret badge.

3 White metal badge 4.25 × 5.5 cm worn by junior ranks in the Forage Cap and by junior ranks of the Band and Corps of Drums as the beret badge.

4 Arms of the HAC with the crest used as a beret badge.

5 Officer and Warrant Officer's wire-embroidered beret badge 6 × 5 cm.

6 Soldier's beret badge 3.25 × 2.5 cm.

7 Cloth shoulder title worn on No 2 Dress 15.5 × 4.25 cm.

8 HAC ball button.

9 Capt Adrian Small, Lt John Samuels and Ben Symes, and WO2 Tony Browne wearing the wire-embroidered beret badge.

this page

10 Officer's Artillery Division gilt Forage Cap badge 6.5 × 5 cm.

11 Soldier's anodised aluminium Forage Cap badge 6.5 × 5 cm.

12 Soldier's private purchase gilding metal cap badge 6.5 × 4.75 cm.

13 Soldier's anodised aluminium collar badges 2.5 × 3.75 cm.

14 Officer's obsolete Service Dress bronze collar badges 3 × 5 cm.

15 Dmr Woody Wooderson wearing the black beret badge on the Household Division backing.

16 Drummer's black painted beret badge 4.25 × 5.5 cm.

In Number 2 Dress soldiers wear Household Division style woven cloth shoulder titles. In Full Dress, Senior NCOs and Warrant Officers have HAC embroidered in silver wire on the epaulette; soldiers have the title woven.

Warrant Officers Class 2 wear a large Colour Badge of the same pattern as worn by the Grenadier Guards but embroidered in silver rather than gold wire. Colour Sergeants wear

17

18

19

20

21

22

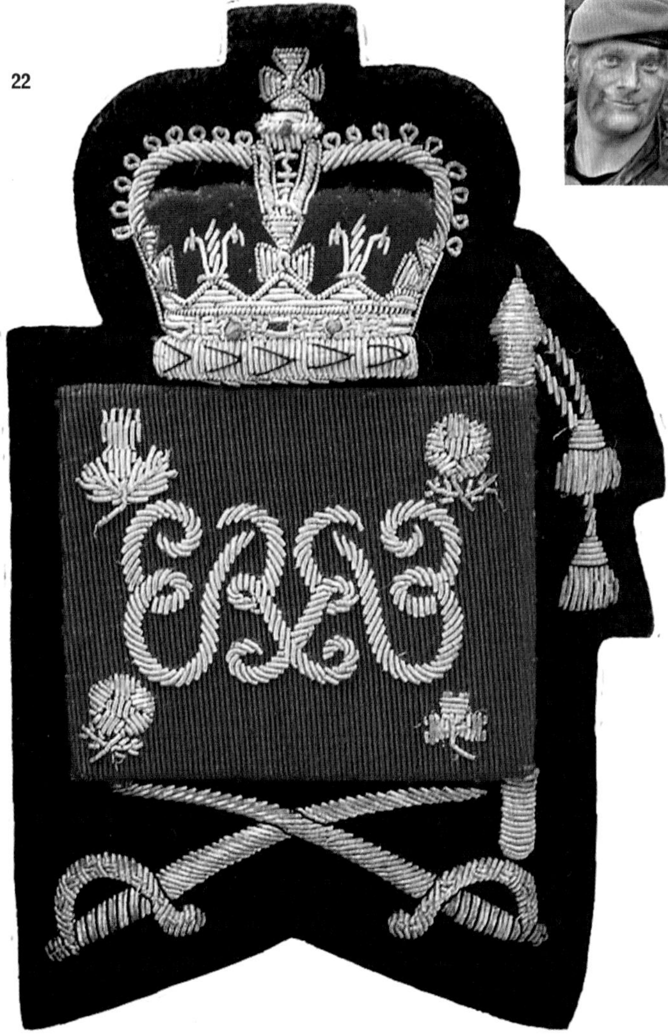

The Colours of the HAC are unique in including Battle Honours of the Artillery Division, an honour granted after the Great War. There is a story that The Company in the recent past unsuccessfully applied for the Battle Honour Armada having served in the army formed to counter the anticipated Spanish invasion in 1588.

23

the same size badge mounted on the silver lace chevrons in Full Dress, but a smaller version on No 1 Dress (Infantry). In No 1 Dress (Gunner) Royal Horse Artillery rank badges are worn.

In Number 2 Dress colour sergeants wear large Crowns above their chevrons, the same size as those worn on the forearm by Warrant Officers Class 2.

The Corps of Drums wear the Household Division blue/red/blue Tactical Recognition Flash.

The Honourable Artillery Company was organised in a fairly haphazard basis until after the Gordon Riots of 1780 when it was roled as an infantry battalion. Links with the Grenadier Guards date to at least 1770 when the Drill Serjeant of The First Regiment of Guards was engaged to drill the Company three times a week. In 1830 King William IV recognised the close links by authorising a uniform similar to that worn by the Grenadier Guards but with silver rather than gold lace.

In 1780 the Company received two 3-Pounder Field Guns, the infantry-support weapon of the time, and formed an Artillery Division which became operational Batteries. The Infantry and Artillery Divisions continued until 1973.

A Horse Artillery Troop was formed for a short period in the mid-19th Century. There was also a Light Cavalry Troop, which converted to Horse Artillery in 1891.

B Battery HAC supported The 10th Hussars during the Second World War and in 1972 The Queen approved the Battery wearing a 10th Hussar button as the top button on Number 1 and 2 Dress. The privilege passed to II Squadron when the HAC was reorganised in 1973.

24

25

26

27

28

opposite page

17 HAC Mess Dress old infantry pattern wire-embroidered collar badges 3.5 × 5.5 cm.

18 Mess Dress wire-embroidered collar badges 3.5 × 5.5 cm.

19 Warrant Officer's Full Dress wire-embroidered title 3.75 × 1.25 cm.

20 Soldier's Full Dress woven title 4 × 1.5 cm.

21 Tpr Melissa Shepherd, Venn King, Nadeem Aulzar, Dan Richardson, Nick Ross, Cpl Christopher Gerskowitch, Tpr Helen Johnson, Oliver Bingham, Henry Farrow, Tpr Ben Cresswell and Tracy Verga wearing the soldier's cap badge.

22 Warrant Officer Class 2 and Colour Sergeant's Colour Badge worn on Number 1 Dress and Full Dress 9.5 × 14 cm.

23 Staff waist belt clasp 10 × 6.5 cm.

this page

24 Officer's black plastic pouch 16 × 7.5 cm, referred to as leather, mounted with a pre-1953 badge with a Tudor (or King's) Crown.

25 Soldier's waist belt clasp 10 × 6.5 cm.

26 HAC ribbon worn on Territorial Efficiency Medal.

27 No1 and No2 Dress Queen's Prize Badge 6 × 7 cm.

28 Mess Dress Queen's Prize Badge 4.25 × 5 cm.

Acknowledgement
WO1 (RSM) KM Finney, WO2 Rick Keeson and CSgt Keith Hingle

Band of The Honourable Artillery Company

The Honourable Artillery Company Band wears Grenadier Guards Full Dress uniform. The Forage Cap worn in Concert Dress has a distinctive dark blue band dividing the scarlet band. The Bearskin cap is worn without a plume.

1

2

1 LCpl Budgie Brett-Hogan, identified by two stripes in The Guards Division style, and Sgt Steve Paine, both wearing Concert Dress.

2 HAC Band under the Director of Music Lt Col Stuart Watts OBE. CSgt John Joynson and WO2 Chas Bruton at the right in the front row both wear the distinctive Colour badge on the right sleeve.

Acknowledgement WO2 (BSM) AP Teague

Honourable Artillery Company Light Cavalry Squadron

The Honourable Artillery Company Light Cavalry Squadron is part of The Company, not the Territorial Army regiment, although the badges are closely modelled on the official insignia.

1

2

4

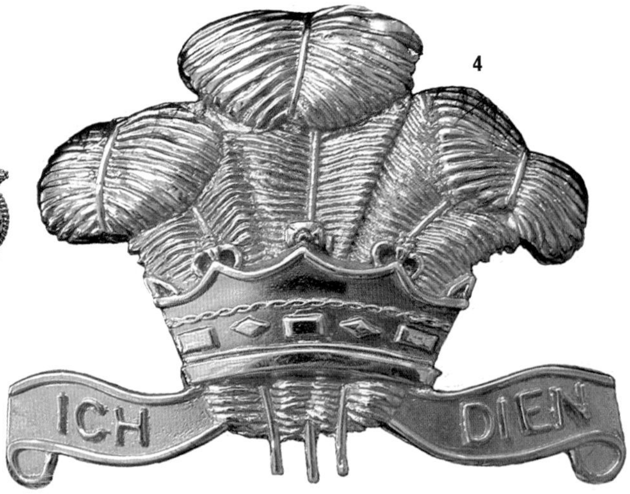

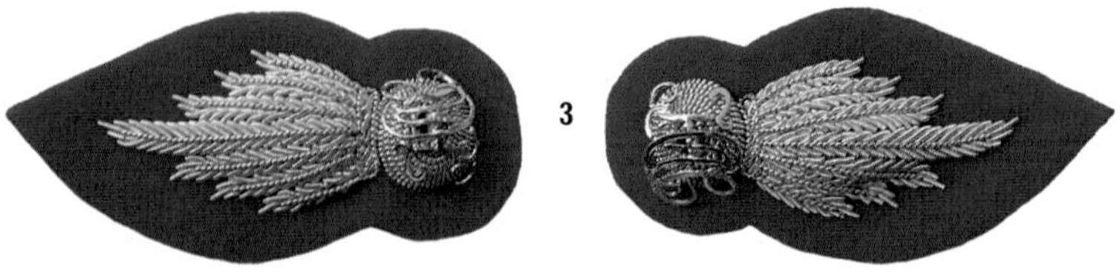

3

1 Light Cavalry beret badge 2.5 × 4 cm.

2 Officer's rank badge 2 cm with the Arms of the City of London in the centre. Cornets wear one star, two indicate the Second in Command and three the Captain.

3 Wire-embroidered collar badges 5.5 × 2.5 cm.

4 Tarleton helmet badge curved to fit helmet 8.5 × 6.5 cm worn on the right size of the Full Dress helmet.

Acknowledgement Mr Bob Lamble

The Yeomanry

The four Yeomanry regiments preserve the traditions of the volunteer cavalry. A number of Territorial Army Royal Artillery, Royal Engineers and Royal Signals units also preserve former yeomanry titles and traditions.

Women are not allowed to enlist in the Household Cavalry or Royal Armoured Corps. However the restrictions do not apply to the Territorial Army and there are women serving in the Yeomanry.

2Lt Emma Colquhoun, reconnaissance troop commander in The Dorset Yeomanry Squadron of The Royal Wessex Yeomanry

The Royal Yeomanry

The Royal Yeomanry was formed in 1967.

The Royal Yeomanry, or RY, has been subject to continual reorganisation since it was formed and this led to the decision to allow each squadron to retain its own cap badge. Regimental titles are worn, and a RY Tactical Recognition Flash was approved in 2002. This is known to the Regiment's regular Army permanent staff as the *Sinn Fein* badge because of its colours, which are very evident in republican areas of Northern Ireland. The colours are also those of the King's South Africa War Medal 1902, the first medal generally awarded to the yeomanry.

The King's South Africa War medal, sanctioned in 1902, was awarded for 18 months service during the Boer War, 1899–1902. The medal commemorated the nearly two years of fighting during the guerrilla war which followed the Boer surrender in 1900 during which the Imperial Yeomanry was widely employed.

1 

2

5

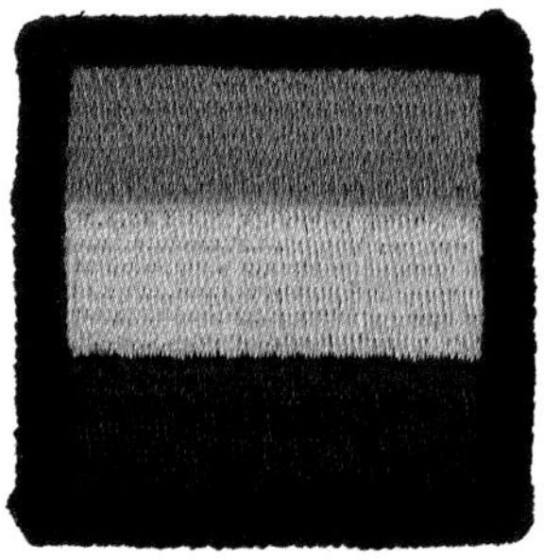

3

4

The Royal Yeomanry was formed in 1967 with squadrons of the Berkshire and Westminster Dragoons, Royal Wiltshire Yeomanry, Sherwood Rangers Yeomanry, Kent and County of London (Yeomanry) and the North Irish Horse. In 1992 the Sherwood Rangers transferred to The Queen's Own Yeomanry, the North Irish Horse became independent and the Leicestershire and Derbyshire Yeomanry Squadron was formed from the 3rd (V) Battalion The Worcestershire and Sherwood Foresters Regiment. In 1995 the Berkshire Yeomanry Squadron was formed from 2nd Battalion The Wessex Regiment. In 1999 the Berkshire Yeomanry transferred to the Royal Signals, leaving the renamed Westminster Dragoons Squadron. In the same year the Sherwood Rangers Yeomanry returned to the regiment.

1 Anodised aluminium shoulder title 4.75 × 1.5 cm.
2 OCdt Jim Graham wearing the RY TRF and The Leicestershire and Derbyshire Yeomanry beret badge.
3 RY TRF 4 × 4 cm.
4 Title woven onto the pullover epaulette.
5 Rank slides displaying a pragmatic TA solution to the problem of differentiating between the Crowns worn by majors and Warrant Officer Class 2.

Acknowledgement WO1 (RSM) Pete Surrage

A (Royal Wiltshire Yeomanry (Prince of Wales's Own)) Squadron

There are two Royal Wiltshire Yeomanry squadrons; A Squadron The Royal Yeomanry and B Squadron The Royal Wessex Yeomanry.

The Royal Wiltshire Yeomanry Prince of Wales's badge dates from 1863 when the regiment provided an escort to the Prince of Wales and was granted the honorary title 'Prince of Wales's Own'. There remains a small stock of bi-metal badges held by the squadron, and soldiers are encouraged to wear the metal badge. The majority however wear the issue anodised aluminium badge on a tombstone shaped red felt backing. Officers wear a wire-embroidered badge on a red outline backing; lance corporals and corporals also wear the wire-embroidered badge as a regimental rank badge in Number 1 Dress.

The collar badges are reduced sized replicas of the cap badge. They are not as rare as other Territorial Army collar badges as they are also worn by the Prince of Wales Division Bands.

All ranks of A Squadron wear a white metal fern leaf on the upper left sleeve in Number 2 Dress and Mess Dress, and a large wire-embroidered fern badge on Number 1 Dress. Lieutenant General Sir Bernard Freyberg VC presented the fern leaf in recognition of the support given by the regiment to 2nd New Zealand Division at the Battle of El Alamein in 1942.

All Warrant Officers and Non-Commissioned Officers wear a replica of the cap badge as a regimental arm badge. In Number 2 Dress a large bi-metal badge is worn on a red outline felt backing above the rank badges. In Number 1 Dress and Mess Dress corporals and lance corporals wear the officer's wire-embroidered beret badge. Sergeants and Warrant Officers wear a larger wire-embroidered badge.

In Number 1 Dress a cross belt is worn. Officers wear a hall marked silver Victorian pouch mounted with a gilt VR cypher and the regimental badge. Soldiers wear a black leather cartouche, dated 1900, mounted with the metal regimental rank badge on a red felt outline.

1

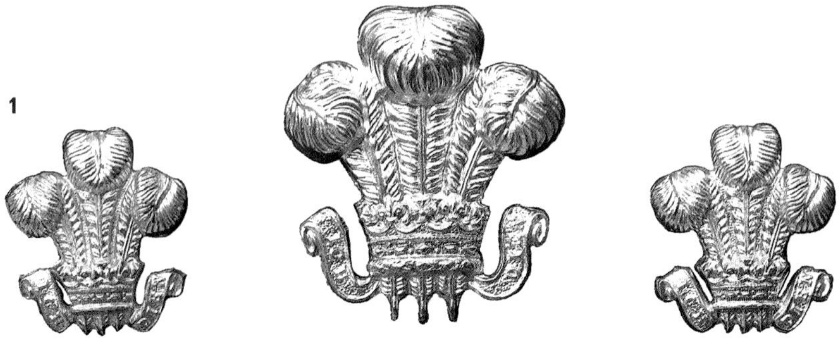

2

3

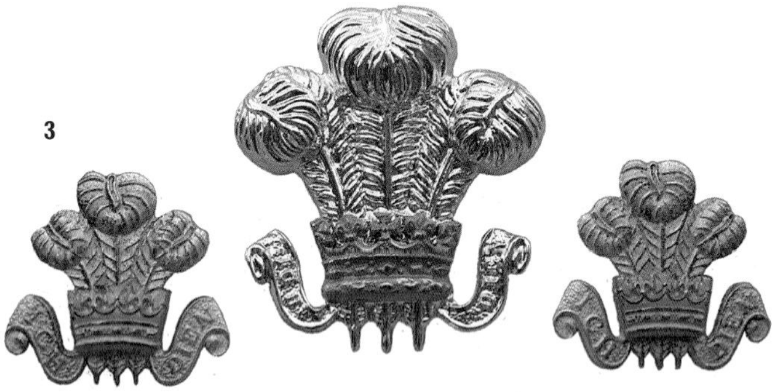

4

5

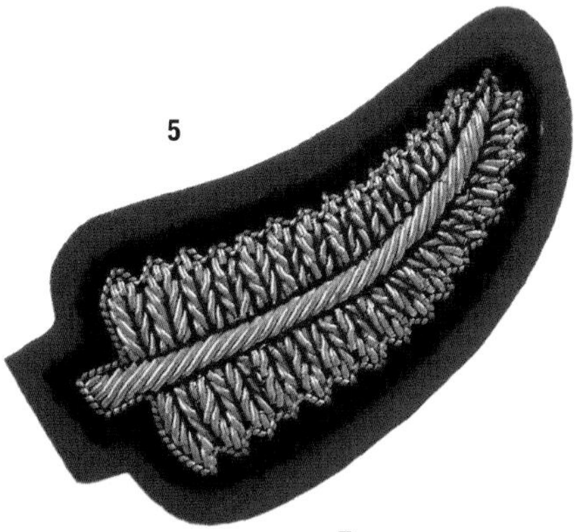

6

7

8

11

9

12

10

opposite page

1 Royal Wiltshire Yeomanry soldier's anodised aluminium cap badge 3.5 × 4 cm and collar badges 2.25 × 2.5 cm.

2 Old bi-metal badge 4 × 3.5 cm which soldiers are encouraged to wear.

3 Officer's silver and gilt cap badge and collar badges.

4 Number 2 Dress metal fern 2.5 × 1.25 cm.

5 Number 1 Dress and Mess Dress wire-embroidered fern 5.75 × 3.25 cm.

6 LCpl Andy Hyde wearing the NBC badge above the RY TRF, Tpr Colin Horne wearing the anodised aluminium cap badge and Capt Simon Keyes wearing the wire-embroidered cap badge.

7 SSgt Woody Wood wearing an old bi-metal cap badge.

this page

8 Number 2 Dress regimental rank badge 5 × 5.5 cm.

9 Junior NCO's Number 1 Dress regimental rank badge (also worn as the officers' beret badge) 5 × 5 cm.

10 Senior NCO's Number 1 regimental rank badge Dress 6 × 6 cm.

11 Officer's Victorian Hall-marked silver pouch 18.5 × 6.5 cm, badge 3.5 × 2.25 cm.

12 Soldier's cartouche (dated 1900 on the inside) 15 × 13 cm, badge 6 × 5.5 cm.

The first yeomanry Troop in Wiltshire was raised at Bishops Canning, in 1794, and was known as the Devizes Troop. Three years later Troops in surrounding towns were regimented as the Wiltshire Yeomanry Cavalry. The regiment was renamed the Royal Wiltshire Yeomanry in 1830 for its services during the Machine Riots; the first honoury and distinctive title conferred on a Yeomanry regiment. The regiment furnished an escort to the Prince of Wales on his visit to Savernake in 1863, the first Yeomanry escort he had been given and he gave the regiment permission to be titled The Prince of Wales's Own Royal Regiment of Wiltshire Yeomanry Cavalry. The regiment also adopted the Prince of Wales's badge. The regiment was disbanded in 1967. A Squadron Royal Yeomanry Regiment and B Company The Royal Wiltshire Territorials were concurrently formed in 1967 and preserved the traditions of the regiment.

S (Sherwood Rangers Yeomanry) Squadron

'... had seen more action than any other armoured regiment in the British Army'

GENERAL SIR BRIAN HORROCKS

Sherwood Rangers Yeomanry cap badges are not available from the Army and therefore gilding metal badges are bought from Squadron funds and issued to all soldiers. Officers wear a silver cap badge in the Forage Cap. The officers wear a wire-embroidered beret badge, which differs from the metal badges in not having a buckle in the design. The bugle horn in the centre of the badge is traditionally associated with Forest Rangers.

Soldiers wear anodised aluminium collar badges, also bought with Squadron funds. The only badges available from the Army are officers' collar badges. They have the incorrect wording on the circlet, NOTTS SHERWOOD RANGERS YEOMANRY but are worn because they are available.

NCOs from the rank of corporal to Warrant Officer wear the regimental rank badge. The silver badge on a Lincoln green backing is worn on Number 2 Dress. The wire-embroidered badge is worn on Number 1 Dress and Mess Dress.

In Number 1 Dress a cross belt is worn. Officers wear a pouch with the wire-embroidered badge on green velvet, and soldiers wear a black leather cartouche mounted with the metal regimental rank badge.

The Nottinghamshire Yeomanry dates from 1794 when four independent troops were formed; all except the Nottingham Troop were disbanded in 1802. The Newark Troop was re-formed in 1828 and together the Nottingham and Newark Troops formed the Nottinghamshire Yeomanry Cavalry (Sherwood Rangers). Reduced to B (Sherwood Rangers Yeomanry) Squadron, The Royal Yeomanry Regiment in 1971, the squadron transferred to The Queen's Own Yeomanry in 1992, and back to The Royal Yeomanry as S (Sherwood Rangers Yeomanry) Squadron in 1999.

1

2

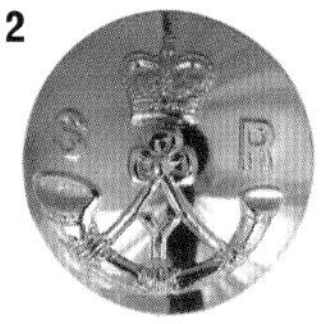

3

4

5

6

7

8

9

opposite page

1 Sherwood Rangers Yeomanry soldier's brass cap badge 2.5 × 4 cm and anodised aluminium collar badges 2 × 3.25.

2 Sherwood Rangers button.

3 Officer's silver cap badge 2.5 × 4 cm and collar badges with the incorrect wording on the circlet 2 × 3.25 cm.

4 2Lt James Harris wearing the wire-embroidered beret badge and Tpr Olli Hann wearing the gilding metal cap badge.

this page

5 Officer's bullion beret badge 2.5 × 4.5 cm.

6 No2 Dress white metal regimental rank badge 4 × 4 cm.

7 No1 Dress and Mess Dress wire-embroidered rank badge 5 × 5.5 cm, both worn on the chevrons.

8 Officer's wire-embroidered pouch 15.5 × 11 cm, badge 6.5 × 5.5 cm.

9 Soldier's cartouche 16.5 × 12 cm, badge 4 × 4 cm.

B (Leicestershire and Derbyshire Yeomanry (Prince Albert's Own)) Squadron

There are two Leicestershire and Derbyshire Yeomanry squadrons; B Squadron The Royal Yeomanry and 203 Squadron 158 (Royal Anglian) Regiment RLC.

1

The Leicestershire and Derbyshire Yeomanry cap badge consists of the rose from the badge of The Derbyshire Yeomanry, and the crest of the Prince Consort, which was granted to The Leicestershire Yeomanry in 1844. The only badges normally worn by the Squadron are the wire-embroidered badges worn by officers on their beret and the equivalent printed cloth badge worn by soldiers.

The squadrons initially wore replicas of their former cap badges in a reduced size as collar badges, but by 1968 had adopted the present badges; a replica of the cap badge without the title scroll. Officers' badges are produced in silver and gilt and soldiers in anodised aluminium.

NCOs and Warrant Officers wear a modern aluminium Rank Badge on Number 1 and 2 Dress. A wire-embroidered rank badge is worn on Mess Dress. The badges are based on The Leicestershire Imperial Yeomanry cap badge worn before the Prince Consort's crest was adopted as a cap badge in 1915. The embroidered badge is a direct copy of the pre-1915 badge, but with the letters LDY in place of the original LIY, and consequently has a Tudor (or King's) rather than St Edward's (or Queen's) Crown.

2

3

4

5

The Leicestershire and Derbyshire (Prince Albert's Own) Yeomanry was formed in 1957 by the amalgamation of The Leicestershire Yeomanry (Prince Albert's Own), and The Derbyshire Yeomanry. In 1975 The Leicestershire and Derbyshire (Prince Albert's Own) Yeomanry Squadron, 7th (Volunteer) Battalion, The Royal Anglian Regiment was formed and transferred as B (Leicestershire and Derbyshire Yeomanry) Company, 3rd (Volunteer) Battalion, The Worcestershire and Sherwood Foresters Regiment in 1978 and finally re-roled as B (Leicestershire and Derbyshire Yeomanry) Squadron, The Royal Yeomanry in 1992.

The Leicestershire Yeomanry was raised in 1803 from Troops raised during the Revolutionary Wars in 1794 and disbanded following the Peace of Amiens in 1802. The regiment was granted the title 'The Prince Albert's Own' in 1844 and adopted the crest of the Prince Consort as their badge. It gained its first battle honour for service in the South African War and the battle honour 'South Africa 1900–1902' continues to be displayed on the regimental rank badge.

The Derbyshire Fencible Cavalry was also raised in 1794, disbanded in 1802 and re-formed as Yeomanry in 1803. It was ordered to disband in 1828 but the Radbourne Troop continued to serve without pay until 1830 when it was augmented and accepted for service. The Derbyshire Yeomanry was finally regimented in 1864. The Derbyshire Yeomanry also displayed its first battle honour, South Africa 1900–1902 on its badge.

6

7

8

9

opposite page

1 Leicestershire and Derbyshire Yeomanry soldier's anodised aluminium cap badge 4 × 4 cm and collar badges 2.25 × 4 cm.

2 Lt Richard Legh-Smith wearing the wire-embroidered beret badge and LCpl Andy Kennedy wearing the printed badge.

3 Officer's wire-embroidered beret badges 4.5 × 4.5 cm.

4 Soldier's printed beret badge 4.5 × 4.5 cm.

5 2Lt Julian Harris wearing the officer's wire-embroidered beret badge.

this page

6 LDY aluminium regimental rank badge 4.5 × 4 cm.

7 Mess Dress wire-embroidered rank badge with the old Tudor (or King's) Crown 5.25 × 5 cm.

8 WO2 (SSM) Nick Barron wearing the wire-embroidered beret badge and QRH rank slide whilst serving with The Queen's Royal Hussars in Iraq.

9 Tpr Leon Griffin and Claire Deamer wearing the LDY printed beret badge.

Acknowledgement
Captain Mike Underhill MBE and WO2 (SSM) Nick Barron

C (Kent and Sharpshooters Yeomanry) Squadron

There are three Kent and Sharpshooters Yeomanry squadrons; C Squadron The Royal Yeomanry and Headquarters and 265 Squadrons (Kent and County of London Yeomanry), 71st (Yeomanry) Signal Regiment.

The Kent and Sharpshooters Yeomanry cap badge is a copy of the badge of The Sharpshooters with the White Horse of Kent superimposed on the centre in place of the previous numerals.

Warrant Officers and Non-Commissioned Officers wear a bi-metal rank badge based on the right collar badge so that the Horse faces to the front when worn on the right sleeve of Number 1 and 2 Dress. A larger wire-embroidered rank badge is worn on Mess Dress.

1

2

3

4

5

6

7

8

The Kent and Sharpshooters Yeomanry was formed as the Kent and County of London Yeomanry (Sharpshooters) in 1961 by the amalgamation of 3rd/4th County of London Yeomanry (Sharpshooters) with 297 (Kent Yeomanry) LAA Regiment, RA which subsequently went through a number of changes of role and affiliation. C (Kent and County of London Yeomanry) Squadron, The Royal Yeomanry Regiment was formed in 1967, and renamed C (Kent and Sharpshooters Yeomanry) Squadron, The Royal Yeomanry in 1973.

The Kent Yeomanry traced its history to the Royal East Kent Mounted Rifles and Queen's Own West Kent Yeomanry.

The East Kent Yeomanry began as independent Troops in 1794, which were stood down in 1802, partly formed as a regiment in 1803, and fully regimented in 1813. Disbanded in 1828, the regiment was reformed in 1830.

The West Kent Yeomanry also formed as independent Troops in 1794, being regimented in 1797. Disbanded in 1827, it was reformed in 1831. In 1915 the two Kent yeomanry regiments served together as 10th Battalion The Buffs, being amalgamated as 97th (Kent Yeomanry) Brigade RFA in 1920.

The Sharpshooters, known in London as 'The Sharps', were raised in 1900 as companies of the Imperial Yeomanry and regimented as the 3rd County of London Yeomanry (Sharpshooters) in 1901. In 1939 the 4th County of London Yeomanry (Sharpshooters) was raised, the two regiments amalgamating as 3rd/4th County of London Yeomanry (Sharpshooters) in 1944.

9

10

11

opposite page

1 The Kent and Sharpshooters Yeomanry soldier's anodised aluminium cap badge 3 × 4.5 cm and collar badges 2 × 3.5 cm.
2 Shoulder title 4 × 1 cm.
3 Officer's wire-embroidered beret badge (green backing) 3.5 × 4.5 cm.
4 Officer's wire-embroidered side hat badge (blue backing) 3.75 × 4.75 cm.
5 Officer's wire-embroidered Forage Cap badge (red backing) 3.75 × 4.75 cm.
6 No2 Dress metal regimental rank badge 3.25 × 4.5 cm.
7 Mess Dress wire-embroidered rank badge 5.25 × 6.5 cm.
8 WO2 (SSM) Chris Elgy wearing the anodised aluminium cap badge and Major David Turner wearing the green backed wire-embroidered beret badge.

this page

9 Obsolete arm badge 5 × 6 cm.
10 OCdt Andrew Carnwath wearing No2 Dress.
11 Tpr Adam Duvian, James Bellamy and James Cooper wearing combat dress with the anodised aluminium cap badge.

W (Westminster Dragoons) Squadron

Soldiers of The Westminster Dragoons wear the Arms of the City of Westminster produced in silver as the cap badge. The officer's badge is the wire-embroidered Staff cap badge on a black ground, the colour usually worn only by Staff who are promoted from The Royal Tank Regiment.

NCOs wear a wire-embroidered collar badge as the regimental rank badge above the chevrons on the black Number 1 Dress. A silver cap badge is worn on the chevrons on Number 2 Dress. The Squadron wears The Royal Tank Regiment's Tank arm badge. The wire-embroidered badges have been produced on a khaki background even though worn on black Number 1 Dress. It was a mistake made in 2001 when the present badges were made in Pakistan but accepted into use because they had been bought from squadron funds.

1

2

3

> The London and Westminster Light Horse served in 1779, and the Westminster Volunteer Cavalry served from 1797 until 1802. The Westminster Dragoons, raised in 1901, claim a tenuous link with the former yeoman. The regiment amalgamated with The Berkshire Yeomanry in 1961 as The Berkshire and Westminster Dragoons, which became a squadron of The Royal Yeomanry on formation in 1967. In 1969 The Berkshire Yeomanry reformed as a separate Royal Signals squadron, leaving The Westminster Dragoons as a squadron of the Royal Yeomanry. The Westminster Dragoons title was readopted in 1984.

4

5

opposite page

1 Westminster Dragoon's soldier's frosted silver cap badge 4 × 3.25 cm and collar badges 3.25 × 2.5 cm.

2 Westminster Dragoons button.

3 Soldier's No1 Dress collar badges 4.25 × 4 cm.

4 Major Richard Nall wearing the officer's wire-embroidered 'Staff' cap badge and Sgt Brooke Bowater wearing the silver cap badge.

5 Officer's polished gilt collar badges 2.75 × 2.5 cm.

this page

6 Tpr Richard Miller wearing the Squadron's RTR black coveralls.

7 Captain JB Burr wearing the distinctive Staff cap badge unique to The Westminster Dragoons.

8 Wire-embroidered collar badge 4.25 × 45 cm worn as a No1 Dress regimental rank badge.

9 Silver collar badge 3.25 × 2.5 cm worn as a No2 Dress regimental rank badge.

10 Westminster Dragoons No1 Dress wire-embroidered arm badge on khaki backing 8 × 4.5 cm.

11 Officer's plastic pouch 16 × 10 cm, gilt badge 3.5 × 3 cm.

6

7

8

9

10

11

In 1940 Major Geoffrey Bell, the Editor of Dress Regulations, recorded that in 1901 the Prince of Wales had dined with the officers of the recently formed Westminster Dragoons and left wearing the Commanding Officer's cap, leaving his with the Crown and Lion cap badge behind. When next day the Commanding Officer called on the Prince to effect an exchange he was told to keep the Prince's cap and to wear it as a memento of a 'damned good evening!'

Royal Yeomanry Band (Inns of Court and City Yeomanry)

The Royal Yeomanry Band wears the Inns of Court and City Yeomanry cap badge, produced in anodised aluminium for musicians and silver and gilt for the Director of Music.

The cap badge consists of the Arms of Lincoln's Inn, the Inner Temple, the Middle Temple and Gray's Inn overlayed with the Arms of the City of London.

The collar badge represent the winged devil Enfield with a spur bendwise, rowel upwards, worn with the devils facing outwards, or 'watching out behind'.

The Inns of Court Volunteers were inspected by George III in 1803 who, when told that the regiment was formed of members of the legal profession, is reputed to have exclaimed 'What, what! Call 'em The Devil's Own!'

In Full Dress the Band wears a Lance Cap mounted with a reproduction Czapka plate of The City of London Imperial Yeomanry (The Rough Riders) originally worn between 1901 and about 1914.

1

The Inns of Court and City Yeomanry Band was formed in 1961 on the amalgamation of The Inns of Court Regiment, which had been raised in 1803, and the City of London Yeomanry, which was raised for the South African War in 1900. The Band traces its history to the Bloomsbury and Inns of Court Volunteers who raised a Corps of Drums in 1771.

1 Inns of Court and City Yeomanry musician's anodised aluminium cap badge 3.5 × 4.25 cm and collar badges 3 × 3.25 cm.

2 Lt Col Rodney Parker, the Director of Music and the only one to wear officer's uniform, with Cpl Viv Davis. Photo *RY Band*

3 Lance Cap plate 23.5 × 12.25 cm.

2

3

Royal Wessex Yeomanry

The Royal Wessex Yeomanry was formed in 1971.

There is no Royal Wessex Yeomanry, or RWxY, regimental cap badge, neither is there a Guidon or March; squadrons wear their historic badges and maintain their own traditions.

The shoulder title is the only item of regimental insignia worn apart from the rank slide.

In 2003 His Royal Highness Prince Edward, Earl of Wessex KCVO was appointed Royal Honorary Colonel. As there is no regimental uniform he wears the uniform of the senior constituent regiment, The Royal Wiltshire Yeomanry.

The Royal Wessex Yeomanry asked in 2000 for a 5 × 3 cm Tactical Recognition Flash consisting of three equal horizontal bands in regimental colours, crimson divided by black. It was rejected by the Army Dress Committee as being too similar to that registered by the Adjutant General's Corps.

The Wessex Yeomanry was formed as a Home Defence Infantry Battalion in 1971 from a squadron of The Royal Wiltshire Yeomanry, and cadres of The Royal Gloucestershire Yeomanry and The Royal Devon Yeomanry/1st Rifle Volunteers. The regiment became The Royal Wessex Yeomanry in 1979 and absorbed The Dorset Yeomanry in 1998.

1

2

3

1 Major's rank slide, Captain's obsolete shirt-sleeve order rank slide, and present lieutenant colonel's shirt-sleeve order rank slide.
2 Anodised aluminium shoulder title 4.75 × 2 cm.
3 Embroidered title used on the officer's shirt-sleeve order rank slide 6.5 × 2.75 cm.

Acknowledgement WO1 (RSM) JD Page

A (The Dorset Yeomanry) Armoured Replacement Squadron

Major Colin Hepburn and Captain Colin Parr both of whom were involved in raising The Dorset Yeomanry in 1996 designed the cap and collar badges.

Class 1 tradesmen wear a wire-embroidered ram's head badge on the right sleeve in Number 1 and 2 Dress although in practice there are only a few of the badges sewn on Number 1 jackets held by the squadron.

In Number 1 Dress a cross belt is worn. Officers wear a hall marked silver Victorian pouch mounted with a gilt VR cypher. Soldiers wear a Royal Armoured Corps pattern pouch mounted with the cast metal Class 1 tradesman's badge on a green felt outline.

The Dorset Yeomanry is the first yeomanry regiment to have been raised for many years and in searching for a county identity the first Commanding Officer, Lieutenant Colonel JGY Radcliffe approached a relative, the Chairman of Young's Brewery. Mr John Young offered a Dorset Horn ram as the regimental mascot. The ram was enlisted shortly afterwards as Trooper Ramrod D'Arcy and the ram's head was adopted as the regimental badge.

1

2

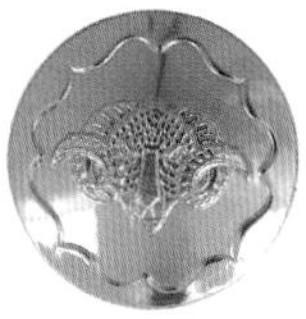

3

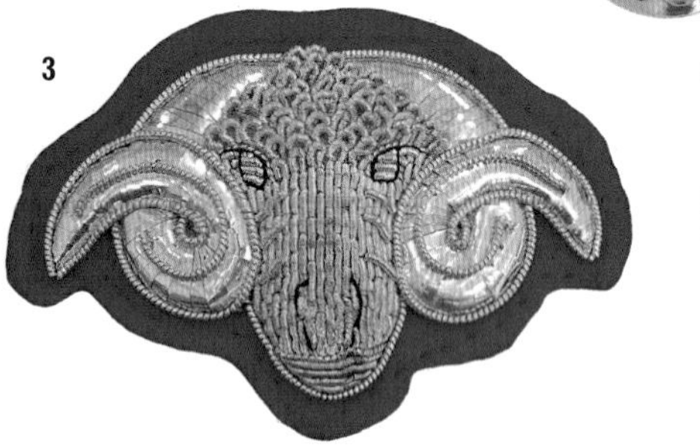

4

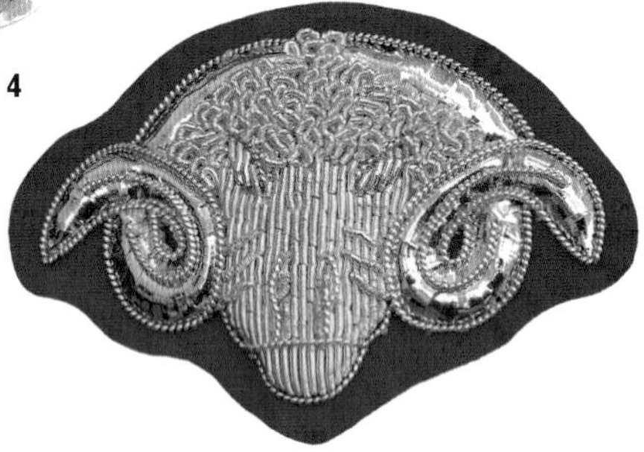

5

6

8

7

The motto *Tu ne cede Malis* was adopted as it was the motto of the Dawson-Damer family who, as the Earls of Dorchester, were closely connected with the raising of the Yeomanry in 1794.

11

12

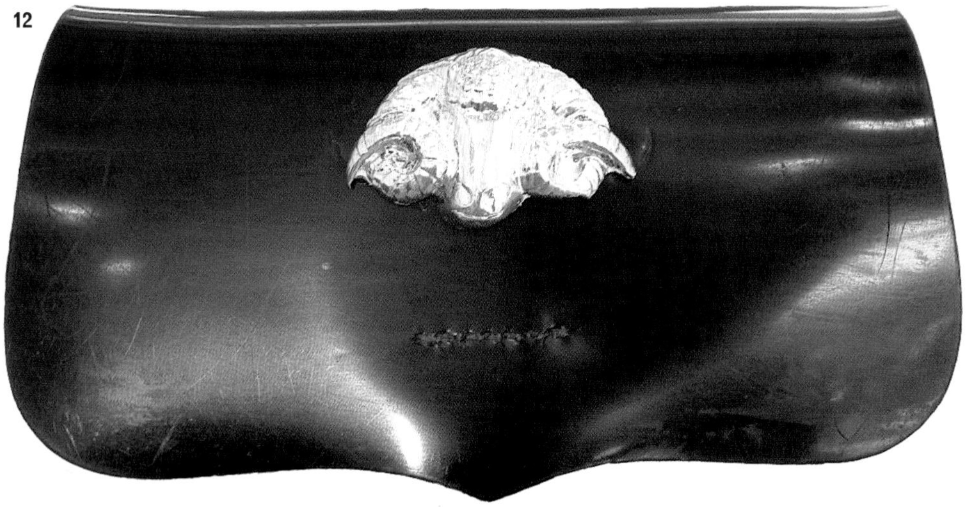

9

10

13

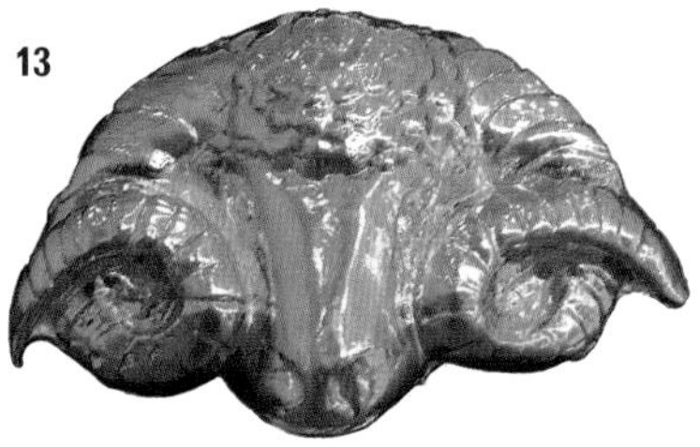

The Dorset Yeomanry served under various titles from 1794 until disbanded for the third time in 1992 when the D (Queen's Own Dorset Yeomanry) Company 1st Battalion The Wessex Regiment (Volunteers) was transferred to 4th (Volunteer) Battalion The Devonshire and Dorsetshire Regiment.

The present Dorset Yeomanry was formed as a TA Armour Replacement Regiment in 1997 but did not inherit the lineage and battle honours of The Queen's Own Dorset Yeomanry. The Dorset Yeomanry was reduced to a squadron of The Royal Wessex Yeomanry in 1999.

opposite page

1 The Dorset Yeomanry all-ranks metal and enamel cap badge 3.75 × 4.5 and collar badges 2.75 × 3.5.

2 The Dorset Yeomanry button.

3 Original wire-embroidered Class 1 tradesman's badge 6 × 4 cm, which has tarnished.

4 Bright silver version to replace **3**, 6 × 4.25 cm.

5 Major Will Curtis wearing the wire-embroidered beret badge.

6 No2 Dress Class 1 tradesman's badge 7 × 5 cm.

7 Mess Dress Class 1 tradesman's badge 5 × 3 cm.

8 Officer's wire-embroidered beret badge.

this page

9 Tpr Kev Anderson wearing a corporal's Dorset Yeomanry Full Dress.

10 Sgt Phil Morrish, the Ram Major, with Tpr Ramrod D'Arcy.

11 Officer's hallmarked silver Yeomanry pouch.

12 Soldier's plastic pouch mounted with a silver Ram's Head.

13 The Dorset Yeomanry silver pouch badge 5 × 3 cm.

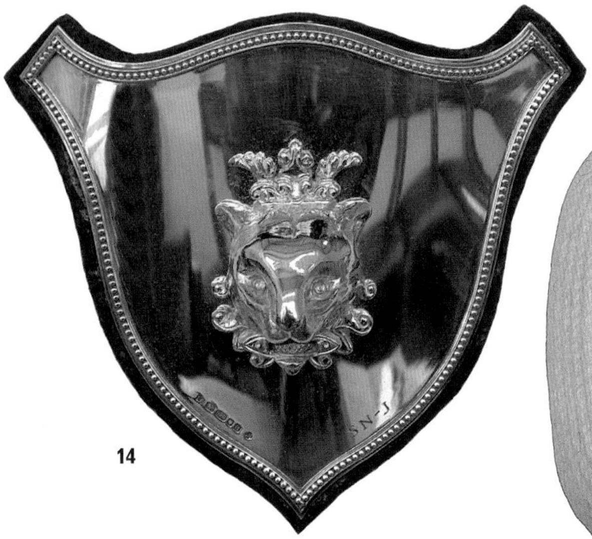

14

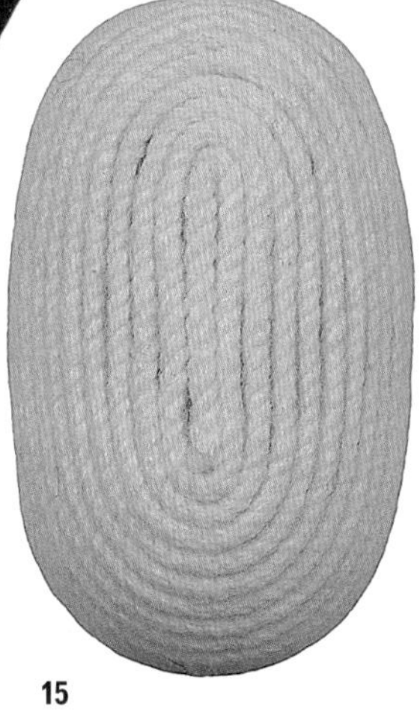

15

16

17

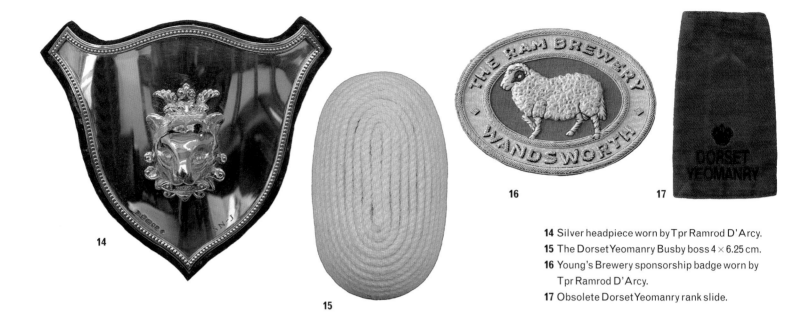

14 Silver headpiece worn by Tpr Ramrod D'Arcy.
15 The Dorset Yeomanry Busby boss 4 × 6.25 cm.
16 Young's Brewery sponsorship badge worn by Tpr Ramrod D'Arcy.
17 Obsolete Dorset Yeomanry rank slide.

B (Royal Wiltshire Yeomanry (Prince of Wales's Own)) Squadron

(See A Squadron The Royal Yeomanry)

The cap and collar badges worn by B Squadron are the same as worn by A Squadron The Royal Yeomanry. As with A Squadron, B Squadron wears the New Zealand fern badge, however in B Squadron the small metal fern badge is worn only as a lapel badge in civilian dress, not in uniform.

Warrant Officers and non-commissioned officers of B Squadron wear the Prince of Wales feathers rank badge. However unlike A Squadron, which has three variations of the badge, B Squadron wears the officer's beret badge on Number 2 Dress and a few old examples of the larger badge are worn on Number 1 Dress.

B Squadron shares Royal Wiltshire Yeomanry cross belts with A Squadron

1

2

3

4

1 SSgt Lee Trust wearing the Royal Wessex Yeomanry distinctive brown beret inherited from the 11th Hussars. On his left sleeve is the 43 (Wessex) Brigade badge below the Union flag.
2 LCpl Kim Houghton wearing Royal Wiltshire Yeomanry Full Dress.
3 Lt Col Tim Cherry wearing the officer's silver and gilt cap badge in the Service Dress cap and in combat dress with the wire-embroidered beret badge.
4 Old Royal Wiltshire Yeomanry wire-embroidered rank badge 6 × 6 cm worn on No1 Dress.

Acknowledgement Sgt David Cross

C (Royal Gloucestershire Hussars) Squadron

Formed in 1971 as a squadron preserving the title of the regiment disbanded in 1967.

The design of The Royal Gloucestershire Hussars, or RGH, cap and collar badges is taken from the crest of the Arms of the Dukes of Beaufort. All ranks wear the anodised aluminium badges, except on the beret where officers wear a wire-embroidered badge.

Sergeants wear a cast nickel regimental rank badge whilst corporals wear a Crown, the same as worn by staff sergeants, above their rank chevrons. Lance corporals wear two chevrons.

1

Independent Troops had served in Gloucestershire during the Revolutionary War and the subsequent civil unrest between 1795 and 1827. Troops were again formed in 1830 and regimented in 1834, becoming the Royal Gloucestershire Yeomanry in 1841 and the Royal Gloucestershire Hussars in 1848. Disbanded in 1967, the name was preserved as an infantry battalion. The title was passed to two squadrons of The Wessex Yeomanry in 1971, which finally reduced to one squadron of The Royal Wessex Yeomanry in 1999.

2

3

4

5

6

7

8

9

10

previous page

1 Royal Gloucestershire Hussars anodised aluminium cap badge 4.75 × 4 cm and collar badges 3 × 3 cm.
2 Officer's beret badge 4.75 × 4.5 cm.
3 Sergeant's regimental rank badge 4.75 × 5.5 cm.
4 Corporal's regimental rank badge 2.25 × 2.25 cm.
5 RGH button.
6 OCdt Michael Whitehead.
7 Major Philip Crook wearing the wire-embroidered beret badge.
8 Tpr Luke McShane wearing Royal Gloucestershire Hussars Full Dress.

this page

9 LCpl Jason Palmer wearing two chevrons, Cpl Doug Neaves's rank is distinguished by a Crown above his chevrons. LCpl Rob Cornish wears an old gilding metal cap badge.
10 Royal Gloucestershire Hussars officer's silver pouch.

In 1834 independent Yeomanry Troops in Gloucestershire were regimented under the command of Henry Marquis of Worcester and son of the sixth Duke of Beaufort. Henry became the seven Duke and in 1854 the eighth Duke succeeded as colonel.

D (Royal Devon Yeomanry) Squadron

1

The Royal Devon Yeomanry, or RDY, cap badge was introduced in 1924 after The Royal North Devonshire Hussars amalgamated with the Royal First Devonshire Yeomanry. Lord Rolle had raised both regiments and his crest, a hand grasping a parchment roll with a coronet above, was chosen as the central design. In 1976 the present inscription was authorised. Soldiers wear the badge on a red backing on the beret.

Previous badges, of the same design, had been inscribed 'Royal Devon Yeomanry Artillery' and 'Royal Devon Yeomanry RHA', and the first version produced with St Edward's (or Queen's) Crown in about 1955 had Yeomanry spelt without the letter 'n'. Those who acquire examples occasionally wear old badges.

Officers' badges are produced in silver, soldiers' badges in anodised aluminium, and officers' beret badges are wire-embroidered. Both cap and collar badges have the same split-pin style of fixing; cap badges do not have the traditional slider. The first batch of wire-embroidered beret badges was worked in silver rather than the correct gold and is not worn. The replacement badges made in gold wire were produced with the Tudor (or King's) Crown.

Cadets of the Devon ACF detachment in Barnstaple who train with the squadron wear a Royal Devon Yeomanry cap badge on their right sleeve.

The collar badges are replicas of the cap badges, produced in facing pairs. Officers wear bronze badges on Service Dress; in all other orders of dress all ranks wear anodised aluminium collar badges.

The squadron has a mix of hallmarked silver Royal North Devon Yeomanry and general Yeomanry pattern pouches for ceremonial wear.

2

3

4

5

6

7

8

The Royal 1st Devon Yeomanry dated from Troops raised in 1794, which were regimented in 1803, whilst the Royal North Devon Yeomanry (Hussars) dated from Troops raised in 1798. The two regiments amalgamated as the 11th (Devon) Army Brigade RFA in 1920. In 1967 the regiment was reduced to an infantry company in The Devonshire Territorials. A squadron was reformed for The Wessex Yeomanry in 1971.

9

10

opposite page

1 Royal Devon Yeomanry soldier's anodised aluminium cap and collar badges 2.25 × 4.25 cm.

this page

2 SSgt Pete Leach wearing Royal Devon Yeomanry Full Dress.

3 Officer's wire-embroidered beret badge 3 × 4.5 cm.

4 Officer's bronze Service Dress cap badge 2.25 × 4 cm.

5 Incorrect silver wire-embroidered badge 2.75 × 4.75 cm.

6 Officer's silver cap badge and Service Dress collar badges, all 2.25 × 4 cm.

7 Cpl Steve Owen wearing Combat Dress.

8 Royal Devon Yeomanry Sergeants and Warrant Officer's rank badge worn on No1 Dress, No2 Dress, and Mess Dress 4.75 × 6.5 cm.

9 Royal North Devon Yeomanry officer's hall marked silver pouch.

10 Yeomanry general pattern hall marked silver pouch worn originally by officers of the Royal 1st Devon Yeomanry.

The Royal Mercian and Lancastrian Yeomanry

The Royal Mercian and Lancastrian Yeomanry was formed by the amalgamation of The Royal Mercian Yeomanry with The Duke of Lancaster's Own Yeomanry in 1992.

All ranks of The Royal Mercian and Lancastrian Yeomanry, or RMLY, wear a bright metal and enamel cap badge which combines the Mercian's Imperial Eagle with the Duke of Lancaster's rose and coronet. A cloth beret badge was issued before the metal badges were produced and are now worn by the ACF detachment at Telford. Officers wear a wire-embroidered beret badge.

Regimental collar badges, embroidered versions of the cap badge, are worn on Mess Dress by those newly joining the Mess; existing Mess members are permitted to continue wearing their squadron badges. In other forms of dress squadron collar badges are worn.

In 2003 The Royal Mercian and Lancastrian Yeomanry proposed a 5 × 3 cm TRF consisting of red over Royal blue divided by a diagonal yellow stripe. The design was not approved by the Army Dress Committee as being too similar to the Royal Artillery TRF.

1

2

3

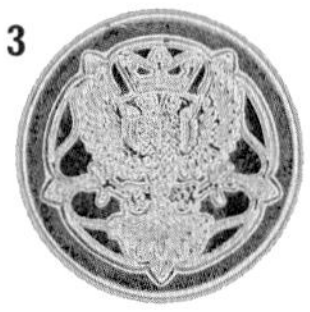

4

5

6

7

1 Anodised aluminium shoulder title 4 × 1 cm.
2 Royal Mercian and Lancastrian Yeomanry all ranks enamel and bright metal cap badge 3.25 × 4 cm.
3 RMLY button.
4 Sergeant's Mess Dress wire-embroidered collar badges 3 × 3.5 cm.
5 Officer's wire-embroidered beret badge 3.75 × 4 cm.
6 Tpr William McGovern and Chris Willdigg wearing the RMLY cap badge.
7 Captain's rank slide.

Acknowledgement WO1 (RSM) AM Sudlow

A (Staffordshire, Warwickshire and Worcestershire Yeomanry) Squadron

The Squadron wears Warwickshire Yeomanry collar badges. There has been discussion since 1999 about adopting a new badge with a design incorporating the Warwickshire Bear and Ragged Staff – although the Bear is to have a foot raised because the Lord Lieutenant reserves the Bear with both feet on the ground for his own badge – above the Staffordshire Knot and surrounded by a wreath of pear blossom. The new design was proposed by Major Charlie Miles and Captain Steve Hutchings.

The Warwickshire Yeomanry was awarded the New Zealand fern badge after the Battle of El Alamein in 1942 but the Staffordshire, Warwickshire and Worcestershire Yeomanry does not wear the badge at present.

Officers wear old hall marked silver Yeomanry pouches in Number 1 Dress. Soldiers wear a white cross belt and white pouch mounted with a Yeomanry badge.

1

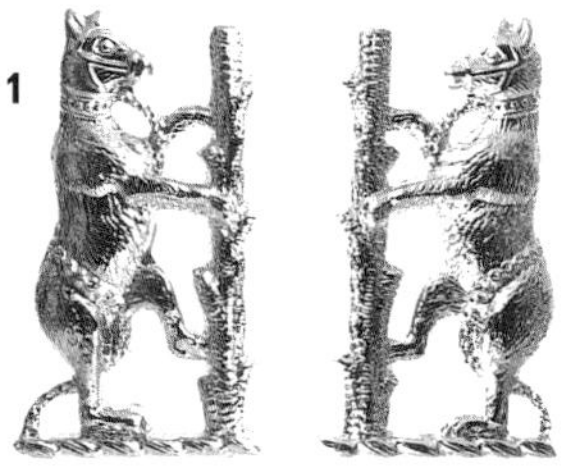

2

3

The crests of the Bear and ragged staff were first used by the Earl of Warwick in 1268 and were combined into a single crest in about 1369. In 1760 the crest was registered to the Earls of Warwick. The Bear is said by William Dugdale writing in the 1650s, to date from Arthgal, in legend the Earl of Warwick at the time of King Arthur, who claimed his name derived from artos, the Welsh for Bear. The ragged staff is said to date from Mordivus, another legendary Earl of Warwick who killed a giant with an ash staff.

A (Staffordshire, Warwickshire and Worcestershire Yeomanry) Squadron, The Royal Mercian and Lancastrian Yeomanry was formed in 1999 by amalgamation of A (Warwickshire and Worcestershire Yeomanry) Squadron, and B (Staffordshire Yeomanry) Squadron, The Royal Mercian and Lancastrian Yeomanry.

The Warwickshire Yeomanry was formed in 1794 and amalgamated with the Queen's Own Worcestershire Hussars in 1956.

The Worcestershire Yeomanry was raised in 1831. In 1922 it amalgamated with the Oxfordshire Yeomanry as the Worcestershire and Oxfordshire Yeomanry. In 1950 it became The Queen's Own Worcestershire Hussars and in 1956 amalgamated with The Warwickshire Yeomanry.

The Staffordshire Yeomanry was formed in 1794 and reduced to a cadre in 1969. It was reconstituted as a squadron of the Mercian Yeomanry in 1971.

The Queen's Own Warwickshire and Worcestershire Yeomanry, formed in 1956, became a squadron of The Mercian Yeomanry in 1971.

1 Warwickshire Yeomanry collar badges 1.5 × 3 cm worn by the Staffordshire, Warwickshire and Worcestershire Yeomanry Squadron.
2 Design for proposed Staffordshire, Warwickshire and Worcestershire Yeomanry collar badge.
3 Officer's silver Yeomanry pouch used by the Squadron.

Acknowledgement Captain Steve Hutchings

B (Shropshire Yeomanry) Squadron

There are two Shropshire Yeomanry squadrons; B (Shropshire Yeomanry) Squadron The Royal Mercian and Lancastrian Yeomanry, and 95 (Shropshire Yeomanry) Signal Squadron 35th (South Midlands) Signal Regiment.

The Shropshire Yeomanry badge incorporates three loggerheads, or leopard's faces, which have been part of the Arms of Shrewsbury since the 15th Century, and remains the design of the collar badges. Although the cap badge was superseded in 1992 officers of the Shropshire Yeomanry Squadron have readopted a side hat with a wire-embroidered Shropshire Yeomanry cap badge.

The Squadron Sergeant Major wears a silver Logger Head badge above his rank badge in Number 1 and Number 2 Dress, and a wire-embroidered badge in Mess Dress.

Until 2002 the Squadron wore the New Zealand fern badge. This had been awarded to 76th (Shropshire Yeomanry) Medium Regiment RA (TA) in 1945 by Lieutenant General Sir Bernard Freyberg VC commanding the Second New Zealand Expeditionary Force (2nd NZ Division) for the support the regiment provided during the battles from Cassino to the River Po. The tradition is continued by 95 (Shropshire Yeomanry) Signal Squadron, 35th (South Midlands) Signal Regiment. The Signal Squadron also wears Shropshire Yeomanry collar badges.

The Shropshire Yeomanry was formed in 1872 by amalgamation of North Salopian Yeomanry Cavalry, and South Salopian Yeomanry Cavalry. In 1971 it formed C (Shropshire Yeomanry) Squadron, Mercian Yeomanry, and 95 (Shropshire Yeomanry) Signal Squadron, 35th (South Midlands) Signal Regiment, Royal Signals. In 1999 C Squadron was re-titled B (Shropshire Yeomanry) Squadron, The Royal Mercian and Lancastrian Yeomanry.

1

2

3

4

5

1 Shropshire Yeomanry soldier's anodised aluminium collar badges 2.5 × 3 cm.
2 OCdt Nick Landon wearing No 2 Dress with the distinctive RMLY enamelled cap badge, Shropshire Yeomanry collar badges and the regiment's shoulder title.
3 Officer's wire-embroidered side hat badge 4.25 × 6.5 cm.
4 Squadron Sergeant Major's Number 1 and Number 2 Dress silver 'Logger Head' regimental rank badge 3 × 3.25 cm.
5 Squadron Sergeant Major's Mess Dress wire-embroidered rank badge 2.25 × 2.5 cm.

Acknowledgement SSgt Arnie Cowans

C (Cheshire Yeomanry) (Earl of Chester's) Squadron

There are two Cheshire Yeomanry squadrons; C Squadron (Cheshire Yeomanry) (Earl of Chester's) The Royal Mercian and Lancastrian Yeomanry and 80 (Cheshire Yeomanry) (Earl of Chester's) Signal Squadron 33rd (Lancashire and Cheshire) Signal Regiment

1

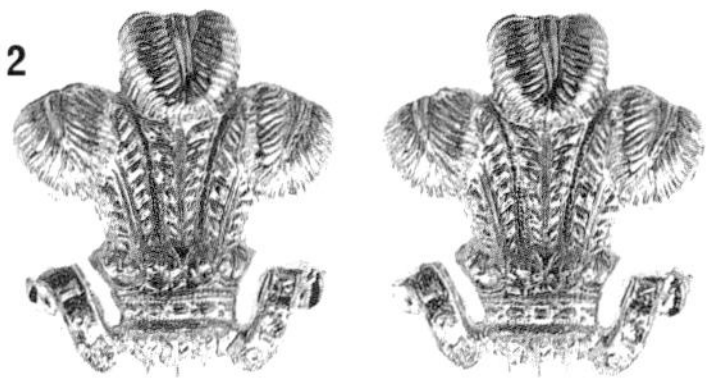
2

3

The Cheshire Yeomanry badge is the Prince of Wales's badge, which was granted in 1803. The Earl of Chester is one of the titles of the Prince of Wales. All ranks except recruits, wear the regimental cap badge on a blue and yellow backing. Cheshire Yeomanry collar badges are worn. Officer's wire-embroidered Mess Dress collar badges on a blue backing. Officers of 80 Signal Squadron wear the badges on a red backing

Non-commissioned officers wear what they know as the 'Feather Badge'; the Prince of Wales's feathers. In Number 1 Dress, the 9th/12th Royal Lancers white metal badge is worn; in Number 2 Dress the Royal Scots Dragoon Guards khaki badge; and in Mess Dress the 9th/12th Royal Lancers wire-embroidered badge.

The Guidon belt is ornamented with the universal pattern gilt cavalry shoulder belt plate on which is mounted a silver and gilt Cheshire Yeomanry badge.

4

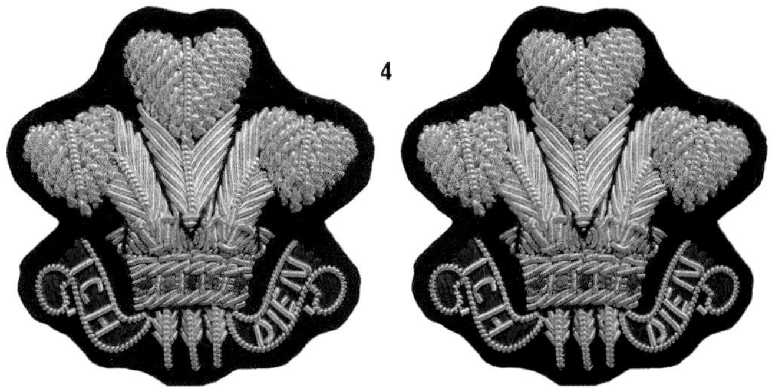

Six troops of yeomanry were raised in 1797 and formed into the Western Cheshire Yeomanry in 1803. It went through several different changes of name, including Prince Regent's Corps of Cheshire Yeomanry in 1819, the King's Cheshire Volunteer Legion in 1821, and the Earl of Chester's Regiment of Yeomanry in 1849. It became the Cheshire Yeomanry (Earl of Chester's) in 1908. Reduced to a cadre and 80 Signal Squadron in 1969. The cadre was formed into a yeomanry squadron in 1971.

5

6

7

8

previous page

1. Officer's wire-embroidered beret badge worn on the Cheshire Yeomanry backing 5.75 × 4.5 cm.
2. Cheshire Yeomanry soldier's anodised aluminium collar badges 2.25 × 2.5 cm.
3. OCdts Philip Morris and Giles Roberts wearing No2 Dress with the distinctive enamelled cap badge, Cheshire Yeomanry collar badges and the regiment's shoulder title and white lanyard.
4. Officer's Mess Dress wire-embroidered collar badges 3.5 × 4.5 cm.
5. No 1 Dress metal regimental rank badge 5.75 × 5.5 cm.
6. No 2 Dress cloth regimental rank badge 5 × 4.5 cm.
7. Mess Dress wire-embroidered regimental rank badge 4.25 × 4.25 cm.

this page

8. Cheshire Yeomanry Guidon belt plate 8.5 × 10.5 cm.

Acknowledgement Captain Jim McBride

D (Duke of Lancaster's) Squadron

Formed in 1992 the squadron preserves the traditions and history of The Duke of Lancaster's Own Yeomanry.

1

2

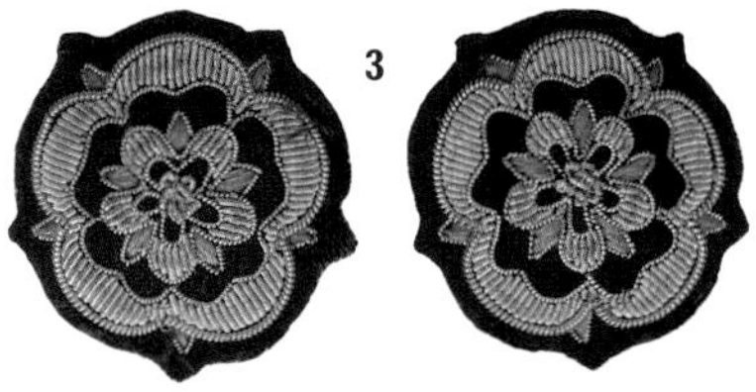

3

The Duke of Lancaster's squadron wears RMLY cap badges except in the officer's Side Cap when a wire-embroidered Tudor Rose badge is worn. The same wire-embroidered badges are worn as the officer's collar badges on Number 1 Dress and Mess Dress. Soldiers wear Royal Mercian and Lancastrian Yeomanry wire-embroidered collar badges on Number 1 Dress and Mess Dress.

The squadron wears the Duke of Lancaster's coronet as the rank badge; the Queen being the Duke of Lancaster. An anodised aluminium Coronet is worn on Number 2 Dress by NCOs above the rank of lance corporal. The Ducal Coronets were originally silver or white metal and a few remain in the squadron. Wire-embroidered coronets are worn on a red background on Number 1 Dress and on a blue background on Full Dress and Mess Dress.

The squadron has the singular distinction of wearing shoulder chains on its Number 2 Dress. During the First World War the squadrons were detached to different Divisions. A Squadron served with 42nd East Lancashire Division in Egypt and Palestine but, as a detached squadron was not entitled to the two battle honours awarded to regiments serving in the Division for the Battles of Rumain 1916 and Rafah 1917. C and D Squadrons serving in France and Flanders gained Battle Honours serving in III Corps Cavalry Regiment.

Shoulder chains had been worn on Full Dress until 1914. The only uniform available after the war was Service Dress and shoulder chains were retained on the uniform as a distinction to compensate for A Squadron's lack of formal Battle Honours.

DLOY has several sets of Full Dress, consisting of scarlet tunics and Dragoon Guards helmets mounted with old regimental gilding metal helmet plates. Officers wear hallmarked silver Yeomanry pouches and soldiers' old cavalry pouches mounted with a collar badge on red felt backing.

> Yeomanry troops were raised in Lancashire in 1798, being formed into the Lancashire Regiment of Yeomanry in 1828 and becoming the Duke of Lancaster's Own Yeomanry in 1834. In 1969 the regiment was reduced to a cadre with one squadron re-roling as 238 Squadron 156 Regiment RCT. The cadre was formed into an infantry battalion in 1971, back to yeomanry in 1983, and reduced to a squadron in 1992.

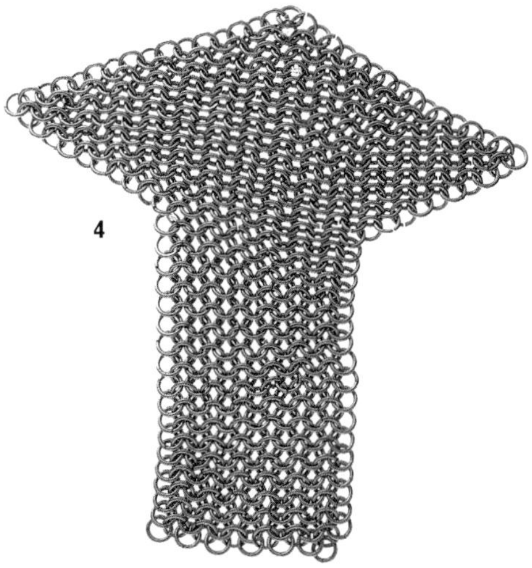
4

5

6

7

8

9

10

11

opposite page

1 Soldier's No 2 Dress anodised aluminium collar badges 2.75 × 2.75 cm.
2 Officer's Service Dress bronze collar badge 2.5 × 4 cm.
3 Officer's No 1 Dress and Mess Dress wire-embroidered collar badges 2.5 × 2.5 cm also worn as the officer's Side Cap badge.

this page

4 Cavalry shoulder chains 16 × 15.5 cm worn by many regiments on No 1 Dress but worn also on No 2 Dress by the Duke of Lancaster's Own Yeomanry.
5 SSgt John Burns wearing the RMLY cap badge.
6 No 1 Dress NCO's regimental rank badge wire-embroidered regimental rank badge 5.5 × 3.75 cm.
7 No 2 Dress NCO's anodised aluminium regimental rank badge 4 × 2 cm.
8 Obsolete No 2 Dress NCO's silver regimental rank badge 4.75 × 2.75 cm.
9 NCO's Mess Dress wire-embroidered regimental rank badge 6.25 × 3.75 cm.
10 NCO's new Mess Dress wire-embroidered regimental rank badge 5.5 × 3.5 cm.
11 Officer's silver Yeomanry pouch used by the Squadron.

12

13

14

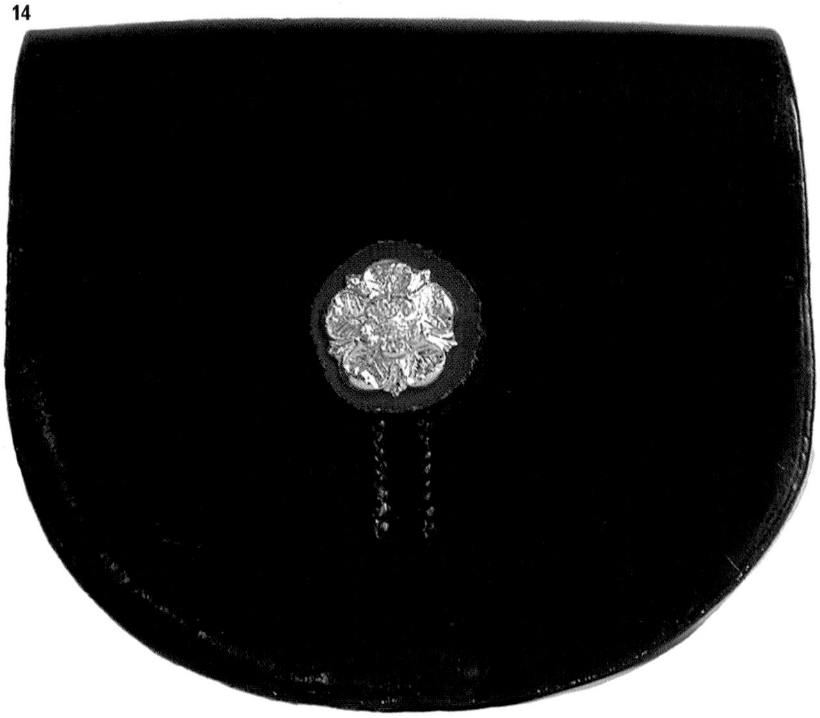

15

12 Duke of Lancaster's Own Yeomanry Guidon belt plate 8.5 × 10.5 cm.

13 Last pattern of officer's silver pouch introduced before the First World War in 1914.

14 Soldier's old cavalry pouch mounted with an anodised aluminium collar badge 15.5 × 13.5 cm.

15 Duke of Lancaster's Own Yeomanry curved helmet plate worn on the Dragoon Guards helmet in Full Dress 9 × 12.5 cm.

The Queen's Own Yeomanry

The Queen's Own Yeomanry was formed in 1971.

The Queen's Own Yeomanry cap badge is based upon the running fox design worn by the East Riding of Yorkshire Yeomanry. The soldier's badge is produced in anodised aluminium, and the officers in silver and gilt. Officers wear a wire-embroidered beret badge.

Until 2004 the Scottish squadrons wore the Royal Scots Dragoon Guards grey beret and the English and Northern Irish squadrons the blue beret. All the squadrons have been ordered to adopt the blue beret.

1

2

3

4

5

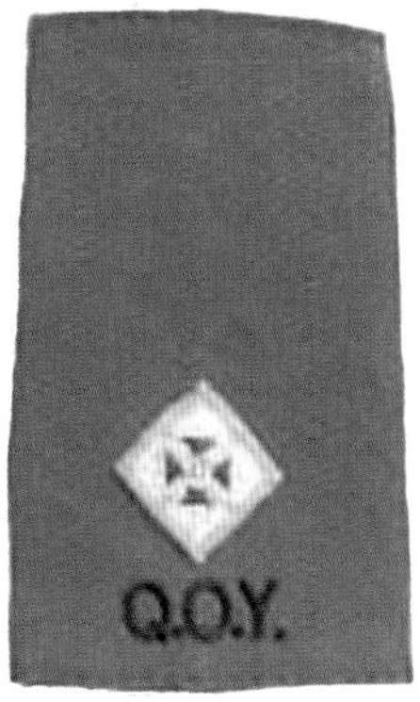

6

1 Queen's Own Yeomanry soldier's anodised aluminium cap badge 5.75 × 2.75 cm.
2 Officer's wire-embroidered beret badge 6.5 × 4 cm.
3 Shoulder title 2.75 × 1 cm.
4 Tpr Mark Hawke and Dominic Martinez. The Scottish squadrons wore the Royal Scots Dragoon Guards grey beret until 2004; all squadrons now wear the blue beret
5 2Lt Matt Greenwell wearing the wire embroidered beret badge.
6 Queen's Own Yeomanry second lieutenant's rank slide.

Y (Yorkshire) Squadron

The Yorkshire Squadron's collar badges are the same design as The Queen's Own Yorkshire Yeomanry badge introduced in 1956. The White Rose was central to the design of the badges of both The Yorkshire Dragoons and The Yorkshire Hussars. The East Riding Yeomanry was formed in 1903 from the foxhunting landowners and farmers and the motto *Forward* is from the hunting term *Hark Forward.*

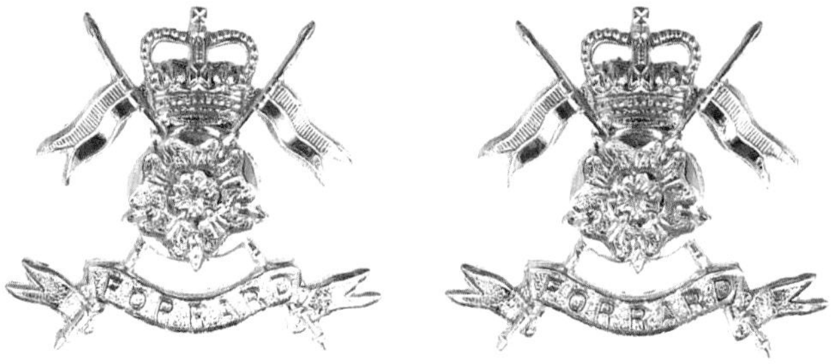

Yorkshire Yeomanry Squadron collar badges 3.75 × 3.5 cm.

The Yorkshire Squadron was formed in 1971 from The Queen's Own Yorkshire Yeomanry, which had been formed in 1956 by the amalgamation of The Yorkshire Hussars, The Queen's Own Yorkshire Dragoons and The East Riding Yeomanry all of which had been raised in 1794.

A (Ayrshire (Earl of Carrick's Own) Yeomanry) Squadron

The Ayrshire Yeomanry is the senior yeomanry unit in Scotland

The Ayrshire Yeomanry has the badge of the Earl of Carrick, a lion's head and neck, winged. The title has been a Royal one since 1328 when it descended to David de Bruce who ruled as King David II from 1324 to 1371, and since 1469 has been the hereditary title of the male heir to the throne of Scotland. HRH The Prince of Wales has held it since 1952.

1

2

3

4

The Ayrshire Yeomanry was raised in 1803, gaining the subsidiary title of Earl of Carrick's Own in 1897. It was reduced to a cadre in 1969 and reconstituted in 1971 as B Squadron, The Queen's Own Yeomanry and as 251 Squadron 154 Regiment RCT(V). B Squadron was transferred to the short-lived Scottish Yeomanry from 1992 to 1999 before returning to The Queen's Own Yeomanry.

1 Ayrshire Yeomanry anodised aluminium collar badges 3 × 2.5 cm.
2 Officer's Mess Dress wire-embroidered collar badge 4.75 × 4.25 cm worn as a pair facing the same way.
3 Officer's old pattern Mess Dress wire-embroidered collar badges in facing pairs 5.5 × 4.5 cm.
4 OCdt Alex Siddell wearing the QOY cap badge and shoulder title and the Ayrshire Yeomanry collar badges.

Acknowledgement Captain David Dickson

B (North Irish Horse) Squadron

There are two North Irish Horse squadrons; 69 (North Irish Horse) Squadron, 32nd (Scottish) Signal Regiment, Royal Signals and B (North Irish Horse) Squadron, The Queen's Own Yeomanry

The Irish contribution to the South African War was marked by the raising of The Irish Guards, the North Irish Horse and the South Irish Horse. The North Irish Horse, or NIH, badge has remained unaltered except for the Crown, which was altered from the Tudor (or King's) Crown to St Edward's (or Queen's) Crown in about 1955.

In 1944 the North Irish Horse fought with 1st Canadian Division during the frontal assault on the Hitler Line in Italy. In appreciation of their support the regiment was authorised to have the Maple Leaf emblem painted on their tanks. The honour is perpetuated by a silver Maple Leaf worn on the right arm in Number 1 and Number 2 Dress.

In the 1990s the Squadron was equipped with the Fox combat vehicle reconnaissance, wheeled, or CVR(W). The Squadron wore an arm badge on combat dress illustrating the Fox a very few of these, although obsolete (both vehicle and badge), survive.

1

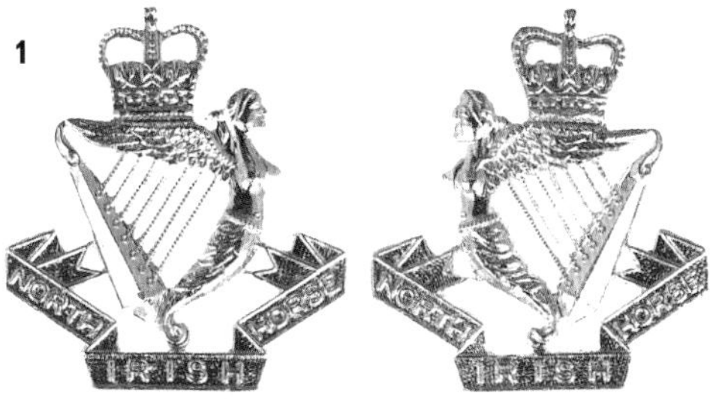

2

3

4

5

Acknowledgement SSgt (SQMS) Steve Pooley

The North Irish Horse, and the South Irish Horse, were raised in 1902 from many volunteers who had served in the Imperial Yeomanry during the Boer War. Following the First World War the South Irish Horse was disbanded and the North Irish Horse reduced to only one regimental officer named in the Army List. The regiment gained the nickname 'The One Man Regiment'. The North Irish Horse was reconstituted in 1939 and after serving throughout the Second World War was reduced in 1969 to D (North Irish Horse) Squadron, The Royal Yeomanry Regiment and to 69 (North Irish Horse) Squadron, 32nd (Scottish) Signal Regiment Royal Signals. The D Squadron was re-titled B (North Irish Horse) Squadron, The Queen's Own Yeomanry in 1999.

B Squadron is under operational control of the Royal Irish Rangers. The units have not merged but key appointments are filled by officers of either cap badge with the result that an unusual combination of badges may be seen.

1 North Irish Horse soldier's collar badges 3.5 × 3.75 cm.
2 North Irish Horse button.
3 Officer's silver collar badges 3.5 × 3.5 cm.
4 Obsolete arm badge 5 × 4 cm.
5 NIH Canadian Battle Honour badge 0.75 × 0.75 cm.

C (Fife and Forfar Yeomanry/Scottish Horse) Squadron

There are two Fife and Forfar Yeomanry/Scottish Horse squadrons; C Squadron The Queen's Own Yeomanry formed in 1992 and 239 (Highland Yeomanry) Squadron 153 (Highland) Regiment RLC.

The Fife and Forfar Yeomanry/Scottish Horse badge was adopted in 1956 and combines The Fife and Forfar Yeomanry mounted knight in armour and St Andrew's Cross from The Scottish Horse. The mounted knight is the county badge of Fife. The Scottish Horse badge was surrounded by a sprig of juniper on the left arm and bay leaves on the right arm. The sprigs were moved onto the Cross of the present badge.

Fife and Forfar Yeomanry/Scottish Horse collar badges 3.5 × 2.25 cm.

The Fife and Forfar Yeomanry/Scottish Horse was formed by amalgamation of The Fife and Forfar Yeomanry, and The Scottish Horse in 1956. It was reduced to C (Fife and Forfar Yeomanry/Scottish Horse) Squadron, The Scottish Yeomanry in 1992, and transferred to The Queen's Own Yeomanry in 1999.

D and HQ (Northumberland Hussars) Squadrons

The Northumberland Hussars wears the Norman castle from the Arms of Newcastle-upon-Tyne as its badge. The Battle Honour South Africa 1900–02 was gained for the service of the 14th and 15th Companies 5th Battalion Imperial Yeomanry during the South African War.

The Northumberland Hussars was formed as the Northumberland and Newcastle Yeomanry Cavalry in 1819. Transferred to the Royal Artillery in 1940, it was eventually reduced to D (Northumberland Hussars) Squadron, The Queen's Own Yeomanry in 1999.

1 Northumberland Hussars button.
2 Northumberland Hussars collar badges 2.25 × 3.5 cm.
3 Northumberland Hussars shoulder title 1.5 × 2.75 cm.
4 No1 Dress and Mess Dress wire-embroidered regimental rank badge 5.75 × 5 cm.
5 No2 Dress woven regimental rank badge 5.75 × 5.5 cm.

1

2

3

4

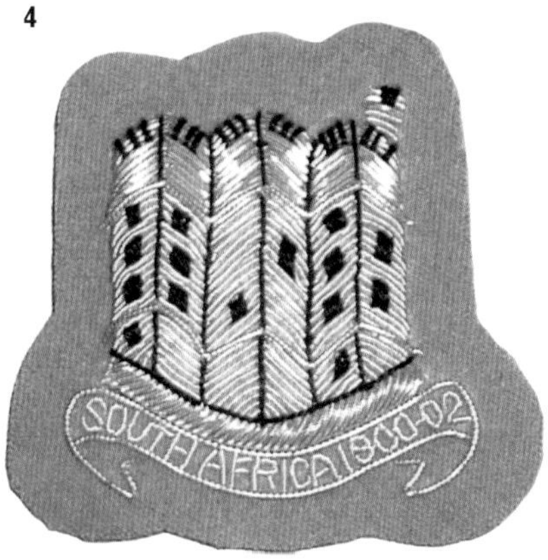

5

Acknowledgement WO2 (SSM) James Armstrong

Royal Artillery (Volunteers)

Royal Artillery Volunteers wear the same badges as the regular Army except for special embellishments which are authorised to perpetuate either battle honours or historical antecedents.

100th (Yeomanry) Regiment Royal Artillery (Volunteers)

100th (Yeomanry) Regiment Royal Artillery (Volunteers) was formed in 1967 from regiments which had been raised as Yeomanry. 201 (The Hertfordshire and Bedfordshire Yeomanry) Battery and 307 (South Nottinghamshire Hussars Yeomanry Royal Horse Artillery) Battery wear Yeomanry collar badges. 266 (Gloucestershire) Parachute Battery wore Gloucestershire Volunteer Artillery cloth shoulder titles until 1994 when it converted to a parachute Battery serving with 7th Regiment Royal Horse Artillery. As the Gunners qualified as parachutists the cloth shoulder title was discarded to be replaced by the parachute 'wings' on the right shoulder.

201 (The Hertfordshire and Bedfordshire Yeomanry) Battery

The Hertfordshire and Bedfordshire Yeomanry was formed in 1961 by the amalgamation of The Hertfordshire Yeomanry raised in 1794 and The Bedfordshire Yeomanry raised in 1797.

201 Battery wears the Hertfordshire and Bedfordshire Yeomanry collar badges. The badges, introduced in 1967, combine the cap badges of the Hertfordshire Yeomanry and Bedfordshire Yeomanry. The Hertfordshire Yeomanry wore the hart lodged in water, and The Bedfordshire Yeomanry what is said to be Bedford castle, which once stood on the banks of the River Ouse, on the eagle taken from the Arms of the Beauchamp family.

201 Battery wears a Pegasus badge on the lower right sleeve of Number 1 and Number 2 Dress and the pullover. It may be identified from other similar badges by having a khaki border. It also faces in the opposite direction to the Pegasus worn by 7th (Parachute) Regiment Royal Horse Artillery.

The Pegasus arm badge was awarded to 419 Battery, 52nd (Bedfordshire Yeomanry) Heavy Regiment RA in 1968 in recognition of the 'devastating and accurate' artillery support provided to airborne forces, particularly during their withdrawal, during the Battle of Arnhem fought in Holland in 1944.

1

2

307 (South Nottinghamshire Hussars Yeomanry Royal Horse Artillery) Battery

The South Nottinghamshire Hussars Yeomanry dates its formation to a Troop raised in Nottingham in 1794.

The South Nottinghamshire Hussars badge is emblematic of the oak forests of Nottinghamshire. The first yeomanry raised in the county in 1795 had an oak tree with golden acorns on its Standard. The present badges were taken into use in 1898. The South Nottinghamshire Hussars cap badge has been known to be worn from time to time by battery members.

The South Nottinghamshire Hussars served throughout the Second World War as a regiment of the Royal Horse Artillery and in 1955 was granted the honoury RHA title.

3

previous page

1 201 Battery soldier's anodised aluminium collar badges 2.5 × 3.5 cm.

2 201 Battery arm badge 6 × 6 cm.

this page

3 307 Battery anodised aluminium cap badge 5.25 × 4.5 cm and collar badges 4 × 3 cm.

101st (Northumbrian) Regiment RA (V)
The Geordie Gunners

101st (Northumbrian) Regiment was formed in 1967 by the amalgamation of 272nd and 274th Field Regiments, 439 and 463 Light Air Defence Regiments and 324 Heavy Air Defence Regiment.

101 (Northumbrian) Regiment RA has since 1996 worn a Tactical Recognition Flash, or TRF, with a design taken from the Arms of Newcastle.

1

2

204 *(Tyneside Scottish) Battery*

204 Battery traces its history to the four Durham Light Infantry 'Pals' battalions of the Tyneside Scottish, raised in 1914 and disbanded in 1918. The Tyneside Scottish was reformed in 1939 as 1st Battalion, The Tyneside Scottish, The Black Watch. After the war the regiment was retained as a TA gunner regiment

The Tyneside Scottish badge had been re-adopted prior to 1951 by 670 LAA Regiment RA (TA) and was retained when the regiment was reduced to S Battery, 439th Light Air Defence Regiment RA in 1961. The badge appears to have become defunct on the formation of 101 Regiment in 1967 but was reintroduced in 1985.

3

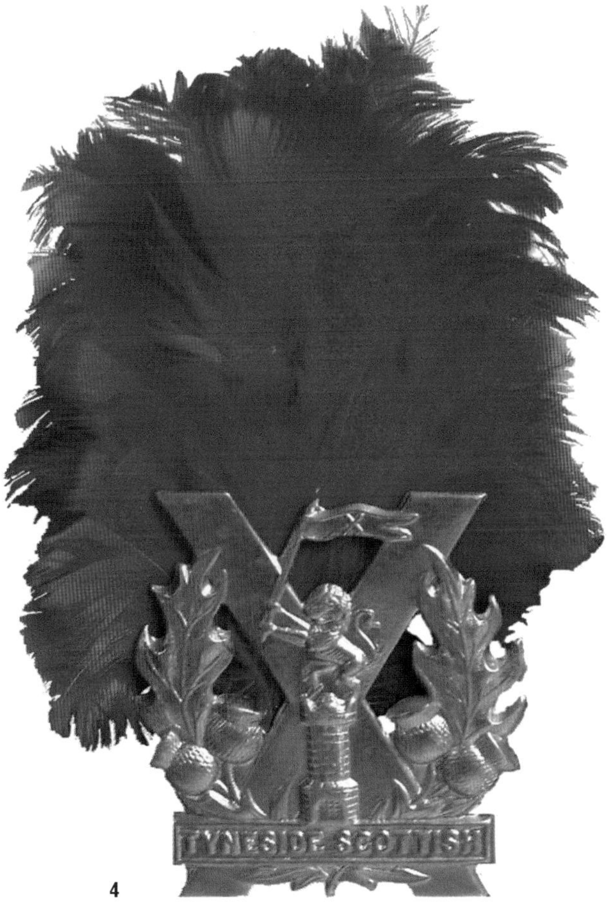

4

The present badge is a reproduction of the First World War badge worn with the Black Watch's red hackle on the Tam o'Shanter.

The Battery wears a square of Government Tartan behind the regimental TRF on the right sleeve.

opposite page

1 101st (Northumbrian) Regiment RA(V) wears the Arms of Newcastle as the TRF 5 × 5.75 cm.

2 WO2 (BSM) David Fail wearing the 101st (Northumbrian) Regiment RA(V) TRF.

3 Bdr Jo Boyle, Sgt Dave Hawthorne, WO2 Phil Guy and Geoff Blackborough wearing the Tyneside Scottish cap badge and hackle and 101st Regiment TRF on the Battery square of Government Tartan. The Sergeant Majors are displaying the 1st Artillery Brigade badge on their left sleeves.

this page

4 204 Battery cap badge 5 × 5.5 cm and hackle.

Acknowledgement WO1 (RSM) M McEvoy

103rd (Lancashire Artillery Volunteers) Regiment RA(V)

103rd (Lancashire Artillery Volunteers) Regiment RA(V) was formed in 1967.

A Troop (Liverpool Irish) 208 (3rd West Lancashire) Battery is the successor unit to The Liverpool Irish which was originally formed as a Rifle Volunteer Corps in 1860. It later became a battalion of The King's (Liverpool Regiment) and finally an artillery regiment after the Second World War. When The Liverpool Irish converted to Gunners the green over red hackle, which had been worn during the Second World War, was altered to the present blue over red hackle. All ranks retain the caubeen, which is pulled down to the left and worn with the Royal Artillery cap badge and hackle worn over the right eye.

Hackle worn by The Liverpool Irish Troop 208 Battery RA 9 × 10 cm.

Band of The Lancashire Artillery Volunteers

The Band of The Lancashire Artillery Volunteers wears similar uniform and insignia as the Royal Artillery Band. The only difference being the emblazoning on the drums.

Acknowledgement Bdr Philip Mather

105th Regiment RA(V)

105th Regiment RA(V) was formed in 1993 from Scottish and Ulster Gunner regiments.

206 (Ulster) Battery, formed on the disbandment of 102nd (Ulster) Air Defence Regiment RA(V) in 1993 retains the 'Red Hand' arm badge which had originally been introduced for 8th (Belfast) Heavy Anti-Aircraft Regiment in 1939. The arm badge lapsed sometime after the Second World War and was reintroduced in 1986. The Battery has a ceremonial role firing Royal Salutes at Stormont and is issued Number 1 Dress.

206 Ulster Battery arm badge 4 × 4.25 cm.

Acknowledgement Captain Alan Smith RA

106th (Yeomanry) Regiment RA(V)

202 *(Suffolk and Norfolk Yeomanry) Battery*

The Suffolk Yeomanry and Norfolk Yeomanry were amalgamated as a Gunner regiment in 1923 and disbanded in 1971. Reformed as the present battery in 1976, 202 Battery wears the Suffolk and Norfolk Yeomanry collar badges. The badges, introduced in 1976, combine the cap badges of the Loyal Suffolk Hussars and The King's Own Norfolk Yeomanry. The Loyal Suffolk Hussars wore the Castle emblematic of defence, and The King's Own Norfolk Yeomanry the Royal Cypher which had been worn since 1901.

1

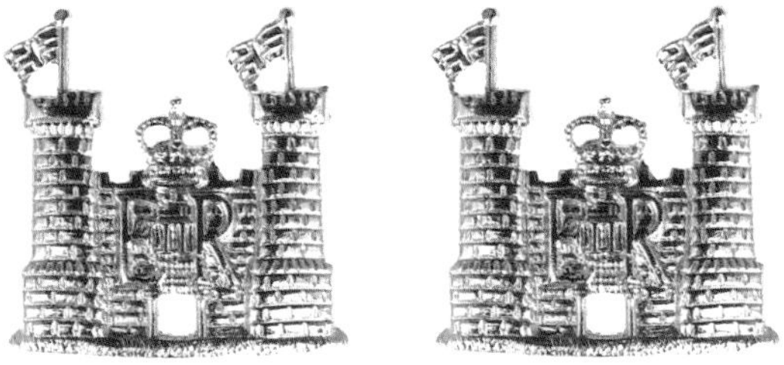

457 *(Hampshire Yeomanry) Battery*

The Hampshire Yeomanry was raised in 1831 and disbanded in 1955. The name was readopted in 1963 by the Royal Artillery and again discontinued in 1969. The title was readopted in 1992 by a Royal Engineers squadron, which was converted to artillery in 1999.

The Battery has worn a regimental arm badge on working dress and Mess Dress since about 1994. Hampshire Yeomanry RE rank slides are still worn by at least one officer who was extra regimentally employed in 1999.

2

3

4

opposite page

1 202 (Suffolk and Norfolk) Yeomanry soldier's anodised aluminium collar badges 3 × 3 cm.

this page

2 Hampshire Yeomanry working dress arm badge 5 × 3 cm.

3 Hampshire Yeomanry Mess Dress badge 4.25 × 2.5 cm.

4 Hampshire Yeomanry RE rank slide worn 1992–1999.

Acknowledgement SSgt Dave Pratt

Royal Engineers (Volunteers)

Royal Engineers Volunteers wear the same badges as the Regular Army except for special embellishments which are authorised to perpetuate historical antecedents.

71 Engineer Regiment RE(V)

71 Engineer Regiment was formed in 1999 as a result of TA restructuring.

In 1992 the former 71 (Scottish) Engineer Regiment adopted a piece of MacDonald of Keppoch tartan as an arm badge. In 1993 a spearhead was woven onto the tartan reflecting the regiment's role supporting the Allied Rapid Reaction Corps, or ARRC. The badge became obsolete when the regiment was amalgamated as 71 Engineer Regiment.

1

72 *(Tyne Electrical Engineers) Field Squadron (Air Support) RE(V)*

72 Field Squadron traces its formation to the Submarine Miners of 1st Newcastle Volunteer Engineer Company which was raised in 1862. Its badge was the Arms of the Master General of Ordnance, or MGO, 'Issuant out of a Mural Crown or, a dexter Cubit Arm Grasping a Winged Arrow Enflamed Proper.' The unit was re-titled Tyne Electrical Engineers in 1911. A cloth version of the MGO's badge was authorised for 'The Tynes', worn on the left arm, during the Second World War when there was a general encouragement of distinguishing marks to promote unit identity. Some members of 102 Battalion REME, which has been connected with The Tynes since 1947, wear the arm badge on Mess Dress.

In 1902 the Tyne Division Submarine Miners recruited a small Pipe Band which served until 1919. The Pipes reformed in 1932 and in 1957 transferred to the 105 Corps Engineer Regiment where they were known as The Tynes. In 1967 The Tynes transferred to the new 72 (Tyne Electrical Engineers) Engineer Regiment RE(V) which in 1999 was reduced to a squadron in 71 Engineer Regiment RE(V). The regiment already had a Pipe Band and The Tynes pipers, searching for a new home, were transferred to 102 Battalion REME(V).

2

3

4

5

previous page

1 71st (Scottish) Engineer Regiment arm badge 6 × 4.75 cm, now obsolete.

this page

2 Tyne Electrical Engineers soldier's anodised aluminium collar badges 2 × 3.25 cm.

3 Tyne Electrical Engineers officer's wire embroidered beret badge 4.5 × 6 cm.

4 Tyne Electrical Engineers officer's wire embroidered Mess Dress collar badges 4.5 × 6 cm.

5 Tyne Electrical Engineers arm badge 4 × 3.5 cm worn on the left sleeve.

73 Engineer Regiment RE(V)

73 Engineer Regiment was formed in 1999. Its origins are from the country infantry regiments of Nottingham, Derbyshire and Yorkshire. Only the Jersey Field Squadron wears items of non-RE uniform and insignia.

Jersey Field Squadron

Formed in 1987, the Jersey Field Squadron adopted the traditions of The Royal Militia of the Island of Jersey. The cap badge was introduced in 1991.

The arm badge represents the Arms of Jersey and Guernsey. Three lions on a red field were part of the Arms of King Richard I, who was also Duke of Normandy. It was also worn as a formation sign by Force 135, the Channel Islands Liberation Force in 1945. It is reported that the Squadron intend to produce examples of the badges in subdued black on green, and black on sand for combat dress.

The Squadron is investigating whether as a Militia unit they are entitled to wear the green Militia Flash worn by the Royal Monmouth Royal Engineers (Militia).

1

2

3

4

6

7

8

9

5

10

opposite page

1 Jersey Field Squadron anodised aluminium cap badge 3 × 4.5 cm.

2 Officer's beret badge 5 × 6 cm.

this page

3 Sgt Paul Davey wearing No 2 Dress with the Jersey Field Squadron cap badge and waist belt clasp and Royal Engineers collar badges.

4 2Lt Nick Spratley wearing Jersey Field Squadron Full Dress.

5 Jersey Field Squadron arm badge 4.25 × 4.75 cm.

6 Jersey Field Squadron gilding metal shoulder title 5 × 3.5 cm worn on Full Dress.

7 Jersey Field Squadron button.

8 Jersey Field Squadron waist belt clasp 7.5 × 7 cm.

9 Jersey Field Squadron officer's Full Dress pouch.

10 Jersey Field Squadron Full Dress helmet plate 6 × 9.5 cm.

Acknowledgement
Captain Allen Hawkins and SSgt (SQMS) A K Bruce

75 Engineer Regiment

75th Engineer Regiment was formed in 1967 with squadrons as successors to former regiments.

107 (Lancashire and Cheshire) Field Squadron

107 (Lancashire and Cheshire) Field Squadron was formed in 1967. There were discussions about adopting a Wirral Horn, Cheshire Wheatsheaf or Lancashire Rose as a badge, but in 1998 the decision was made to wear a Liver Bird arm badge.

In 1207 when King John needed a naval port to support operations in Ireland. He selected Liverpool which he proclaimed a borough and a port. The insignificant fishing community was granted a corporation seal which bore the representation of a bird with a twig in its beak, thought to be the eagle of St John the Divine carrying a sprig of broom. In 1797 a Coat of Arms was granted to Liverpool and a sea bird was considered a more appropriate emblem for a port. A cormorant was chosen holding laver, or seaweed , in its beak. As the symbol of Liverpool the Liver Bird was chosen as the cap badge for the six battalions of the Liverpool Pals raised as part of the New Army in 1914 and finally disbanded in 1920. A Liver Bird badge, on a trianglular backing, was also worn by A Company 5th/8th Volunteer Battalion The King's Regiment from 1993 on the back of the helmet cover. The 107 Field Squadron Liver Bird badge is now obsolete.

1

125 (Staffordshire) Field Squadron

125 (Staffordshire) Field Squadron was regimented with 75th Engineer Regiment in 1993 and retained the Stafford Knot which had been adopted in about 1990 as its arm badge.

2

3

4

143 Plant Squadron

143 Plant Squadron replaced 202 Field Squadron in the regiment in 1999. In 1981 the squadron acquired a stuffed Horned Hare whilst on annual camp at Munchenghausen. The fictitous animal had been featured in Baron Hieronymus von Munchenghasuen's tall tales in the mid-1700s. The Horned Hare became the squadron's emblem and the badge was introduced in 1998.

5

6

201 *HQ Squadron*

201 HQ Squadron traces its history to 1914; in 1943 it was reorganised as 617 Assault Squadron. In 1947 it was reformed as 201 Field Squadron. Disbanded in 1967 the squadron number was taken into use again in 1995 when the Assault Engineers Bull badge worn by 32 Armoured Engineer Regiment was readopted by the squadron in honour of its wartime service as Assault Engineers (see p. 71).

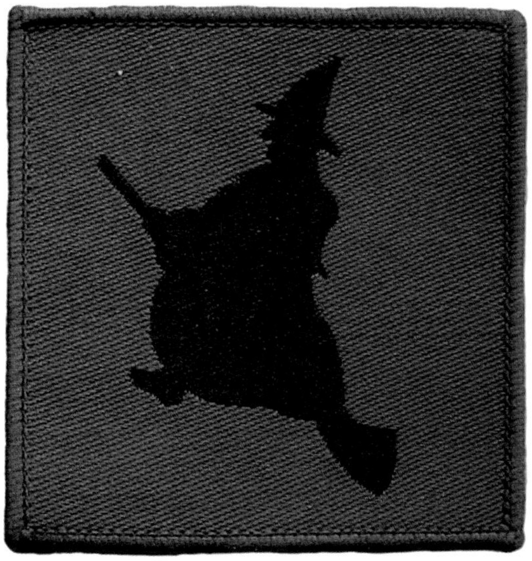

7

8

202 *Field Squadron*

202 Field Squadron was formed in 1967 and disbanded in 1999. The squadron was distinguished by the sign of the Witch of Pendle which was used as the design of an arm badge, examples of this survived until the introducion of the Royal Engineers Tactical Recognition Flash in 2004.

opposite page

1 107 Field Squadron arm badge 4 × 5 cm.
2 125 (Staffordshire) Field Support Squadron No2 Dress arm badge 4.5 × 4 cm.
3 125 (Staffordshire) Field Support Squadron Combat Dress arm badge 4.5 × 3 cm.
4 125 (Staffordshire) Field Support Squadron Mess Dress wire-embroidered badge 3.5 × 2.5 cm.
5 143 Plant Squadron No2 Dress arm badge 5 × 3 cm.
6 143 Plant Squadron Combat Dress arm badge 5 × 3 cm.

this page

7 202 Field Squadron arm badge 7 × 7 cm, now obsolete.
8 3 Troop 202 Field Squadron arm badge 5 × 5.75 cm.

Acknowledgement
Captain Vic Parsons and WO1 (RSM) AE Austin

101 (City of London) Engineer Regiment (Explosive Ordnance Disposal) (Volunteers)

All ranks of 101 Engineer Regiment wear the Queen Mary Battle Honour badge on the left forearm of Number 2 Dress. Personnel who have passed an EOD course appropriate to their rank wear the EOD badge on a khaki backing as a qualification badge on the upper right sleeve in Combat Dress (see p. 33 (EOD) Regiment RE p. 72). In the past a regimental arm badge consisting of a bomb on Dick Whittington's cat was worn but for many years has only appeared as a logo.

101 Engineer Regiment logo which was formerly worn as an arm badge.

Acknowledgement WO1 (RSM) R Fyvie RE

131 (V) Independent Commando Squadron

In the 1960s 131 Parachute Engineer Regiment (TA) adopted a small Drop Zone flash; a 5 × 2.5 cm red flash with two vertical blue lines. In 1978 131 Independent Commando Squadron was formed and the DZ flash fell into disuse. The new diamond shaped DZ flash was adopted after 2000 for wear on the smock.

1 131 (V) Independent Commando Squadron DZ Flash 7 × 7 cm.
2 Captain Karl Parfitt a TA officer with 131 Independent Commando Squadron wearing the traditional green beret with officer's RE beret badge, black rank badges, parachute wings and 3 Commando Brigade arm badge.

1

2

Joint CIMIC Group

The Joint Civil Military Cooperation Group is a specialist unit, formed as the Civil Affairs Group following the Strategic Defence Review it became tri-service in 2004. It operates with a small core of regular officers and senior NCOs supported by TA personnel. On operations the Joint CIMIC Group deploys a field team of between four and eight specialists who are tasked to liaise with civil government officials, non-governmental organisations (NGO) and civilians in order to ascertain what is happening in the operational area that may affect the force commander's mission. Tactical Support Teams can oversee projects designed to help local communities (often funded by the Department for International Development (DfID)), or run Civil Military Cooperation Centres (CIMIC Centres).

The colours chosen for the arm badge are understood to have been those of the Second World War Civil Military Government insignia. The Group has discounted an alternative suggestion that the colours were inspired by those of the Jamaican Bobsleigh Team, brought to prominence by the film 'Cool Running' which was on general release when the Civil Affairs Group was being formed.

1

2

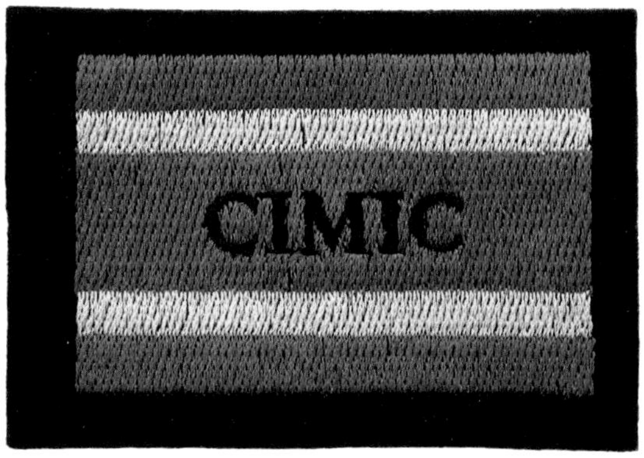

3

4

5

opposite page

1 Civil Affairs Group arm badge 7.25 × 5.25 cm.
2 Major Adam Wills IG wearing the new Joint CIMIC Group arm badge.
3 Joint CIMIC Group arm badge 7.25 × 5.25 cm introduced in 2005.

this page

4 Major Graeme Olley AGC(ETS) wearing the Civil Affairs Group arm badge.
5 CIMIC field team, Major Andrew Whelan RRF and Graeme Olley AGC(ETS) with CSgt David Ibbotson IG and Major Mike Dejamette US Army.

Acknowledgement Lt Col Richard Dickinson

The Engineer and Logistic Staff Corps RE (V)

The Engineer and Logistic Staff Corps is a corps of 60 civilian experts who hold TA commissions but do not wear uniform and are not paid. They deploy to advise on restoring infrastructure after a conflict. At present there is no special badge for the Staff Corps.

Formed as the Engineer and Railway Staff Corps from railway managers and civil engineers to plan and coordinate the movement of troops for the defence of the UK. Expanded in 1972 to include experts in airport design and construction, electrical and mechanical services, petrol and oil engineering, geology and soil mechanics, water and sewerage. Renamed the Engineer and Transport Staff Corps RE(V) in 1982 and the Engineer and Logistic Staff Corps RE(V) in 1993.

Royal Signals (Volunteers)

Royal Signals Volunteers wear the same badges as the Regular Army except for special embellishments which are authorised to perpetuate historical antecedents.

31st (City of London) Signal Regiment

31st (City of London) Signal Regiment was formed in 1967 by the amalgamation of 41 (Princess Louise's Kensington) Signal Regiment, 47 (Middlesex Yeomanry) Signal Regiment and 56 (City of London) Signal Regiment. The regiment carries the Colours presented to The Kensington Regiment by King Edward VII in 1909, the only Territorial Army signal regiment with Colours.

Three of the squadrons of 31st Signal Regiments are identified by historical badges. The regiment is united by the badge, the Sword of St Paul on a shield. This badge was introduced in 1966 in its present form and is worn by a number of London recruited TA units.

1

41 (Princess Louise's Kensington) Signal Squadron (V)

The squadron is decended from 13th County of London (Kensington) Battalion which became Princess Louise's Kensington Regiment in 1937. The regiment became famous during the Second World War as the General Headquarters Signal Regiment, known as 'Phantom'. The regiment lost its identity in 1967 and reformed later as 41 Signal Squadron.

The Kensington's dress regulations have been complicated by history. In 1947, on transfer to the Royal Signals, Kensington Regiment badges were retained. Royal Signals insignia was adopted in 1967 with the exception of Number 2 Dress collar badges. The Kensington Regiment Side Hat was never withdrawn although they appear not to have been worn for almost half a century. Technically therefore officers have retained a wire-embroidered Kensington Regiment badge on the Side Hat although none are thought to be worn. The squadron pool of Forage Caps was said to have The Kensignton Regiment cap badges, silver for officers and gilding metal for soldiers. It is also reported that The Kensington Regiment red and grey lanyard is worn .

2

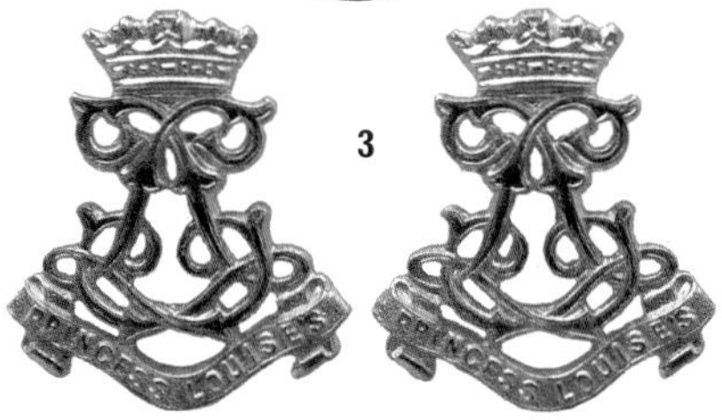

3

83 (London) Signal Squadron (V)

The Squadron wears the 'dutch tile' arm badge adopted by 47 (2nd London) Division during the First World War. The design is said to have been on a floor tile found by the GOC in Flanders and adopted by him as the Division badge. The right to wear the badge was passed down through 23 (Southern) Corps Signal Regiment. The badge, worn on a point, was presented to 83 Signal Squadron in 1985.

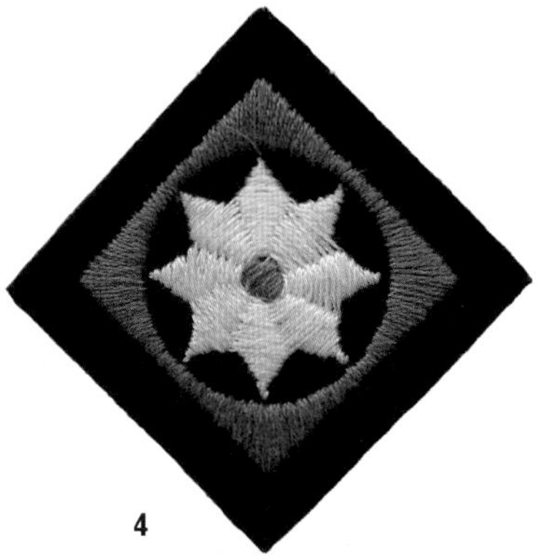

4

94 (Berkshire Yeomanry) Signal Squadron.

Formed in 1795 as a number of independent Troops the Berkshire Yeomanry was reduced to a Royal Signals squadron in 1969.

Officers and soldiers wear Royal Signals beret badges on a powder blue backing. Officers wear Berkshire Yeomanry 'Hungerford Star' collar badges, and soldiers the 'Berkshire (or Uffington) Horse' collar badges, a larger version of which is also worn as the regimental rank badge by non-commissioned officers.

5

6

7

8

9

12

11

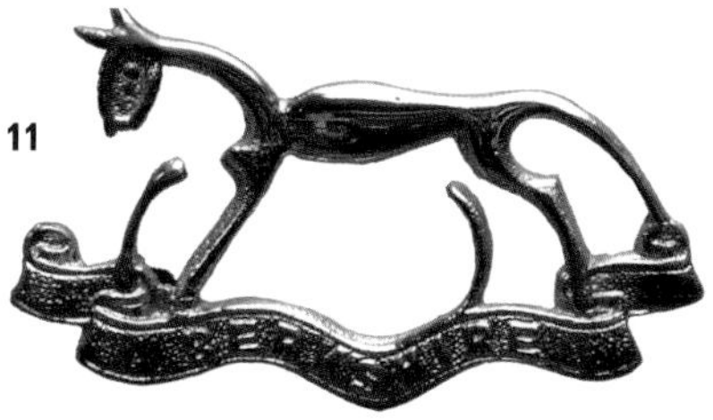

10

13

14

opposite page

1 OCdt Sam Osei-Agyemang wearing the City of London arm badge.

2 Princess Louise's Kensington button.

3 Princess Louise's Kensington soldier's anodised aluminium collar badges 2.75 × 3 cm.

4 83 (London) Signal Squadron 'Dutch Tile' arm badge 5 × 5 cm.

5 Berkshire Yeomanry officer's 3.5 × 5.5 cm and soldier's 2.75 × 5 cm cap badges.

6 Berkshire Yeomanry button.

7 SSgt Matthew Allan wearing the Berkshire Yeomanry cap badge backing and rank slide.

this page

8 Officer's Number 1 Dress and Number 2 Dress cast collar badges 2 × 3 cm.

9 Soldier's Number 1 Dress collar badges 3.25 × 1.75 cm.

10 Number 2 Dress cast collar badges 3.25 × 1.75 cm.

11 Berkshire Yeomanry senior NCOs rank badge 5.25 × 3 cm also worn as a pouch badge.

12 Berkshire Yeomanry cast brass shoulder title 5.5 × 1 cm.

13 Berkshire Yeomanry lieutenant and sergeant's rank slides.

14 Berkshire Yeomanry arm badge 7.25 × 4 cm worn on the right sleeve below the Royal Signals TRF.

Acknowledgement
Major Steve Smoothy, Capt SM Jones, WO1 (RSM) JJ Johnston and Mr Mark Barraclough

32nd (Scottish) Signal Regiment (Volunteers)

Formed in 1967, the regiment sponsors the Royal Signals volunteer pipe band.

All ranks of 32nd Signal Regiment wear a backing of Grant tartan behind the beret badge, authorised by Colonel Sir A Grant. All ranks of 51 Signal Squadron wear the Tam o'Shanter in place of the beret. All officers and senior ranks wear the Glegarry with a special Royal Signals badge.

1

2

3

previous page

1 Sig Stephen Flynn 52 Signal Squadron, wearing the Grant tartan backing to his Royal Signals badge.

this page

2 32nd Scottish Signal Regiment officer's cast brass and chrome Glengarry badge 5 × 6 cm.

3 Lt Beverley Gill wearing the Royal Signals wire-embroidered badge on the Grant tartan backing and the 2nd (National Communications) Signal Brigade arm badge.

Acknowledgement WO2 (RQMS) A Gemmell

Royal Signals Pipers

The Royal Signals have a volunteer pipe band which is sponsored by 32nd Signal Regiment. As with other volunteer bands there are a both Regular and TA soldiers, retired soldiers and civilians. Whilst the uniform and cap badges are common to all some non-military waist belt clasps, sporran cantles and plaid brooches are worn. The pipers of the Queen's Gurkha Signals are supported by the Pipe Band and wear some common insignia (see *Queen's Gurkha Signals* p. 82).

Royal Signals pipers wear a cast bi-metal Glengarry badge, of a different pattern to the badge worn by officers and senior non-commissioned officers of 32nd Signal Regiment. Above the badge the pipers wear a hackle in Corps colours; blue, green and pale blue. The hackle is also worn by officers and senior non-commissioned officers of 69 (North Irish Horse) Signal Squadron (V) (see 40th (Ulster) Signal Regiment p. 390).

3

1

2

4

5

6

7

opposite page

1 Royal Signals blue, green, pale blue hackle 5 × 9 cm.
2 Royal Signals plaid brooch 9.5 cm.
3 Royal Signals piper's cast Glengarry badge 5 × 6.75 cm.
4 Royal Signals piper's shoulder belt badge 3.5 × 6 cm.

this badge

5 Civilian chrome plaid brooch worn by some Royal Signals pipers and Queen's Gurkha Signals pipers 8.5 cm.
6 Civilian chrome waist belt clasp worn by Royal Signals and Queen's Gurkha Signals pipers 9.5 × 7.25 cm.
7 Civilian chrome sporran cantle worn by Royal Signals pipers.

Acknowledgement Colonel Tom Monkreith

33rd (Lancashire and Cheshire) Signal Regiment

33rd Signal Regiment was formed in 1967, with squadrons as successor units to TA regiments. There are two Cheshire Yeomanry squadrons; C Squadron The Royal Mercian and Lancastrian Yeomanry formed in 1971 and 80 Signal Squadron 33rd (Lancashire and Cheshire) Signal Regiment formed in 1973.

The regiment introduced an arm badge in 1998 featuring the Lancastrian Rose and Cheshire wheat sheaf which was worn until replaced by the Royal Signals TRF.

1

2

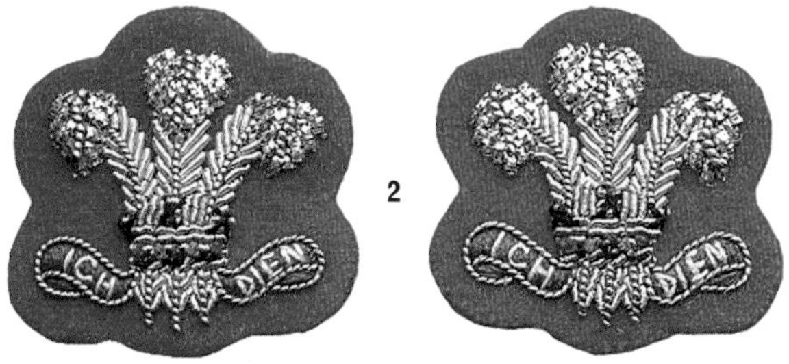

1 33 Signal Regiment arm badge 5 × 5 cm, now obsolete.
2 Cheshire Yeomanry officer's Mess Dress collar badges 3.5 × 4.5 cm worn by 80 Signal Squadron.

34th (Northern) Signal Regiment

34th (Northern) Signal Regiment was formed in 1967 by the amalgamation of 49th (West Riding) and 50th (Northumbrian) Signal Regiments.

90th (North Riding) Squadron included a contingent from The Yorkshire Yeomanry and those individuals were given permission to retain the Running Fox shoulder badges. Regimental arm badges were introduced in 1998 until replaced by the Royal Signals Tactical Recognition Flash.

1

2

1. Arm badge 3 × 3.75 cm, now obsolete.
2. WO1 PV McGarry taking over as RSM from WO1 D Newton, the Royal Signals TRF having replaced the regimental arm badge.

Acknowledgement Captain Harriet Hebblethwaite

Royal Signals (Northern) Band

The Royal Signals (Northern) Band wears similar uniform and insignia as the Royal Signals Band.

1

2
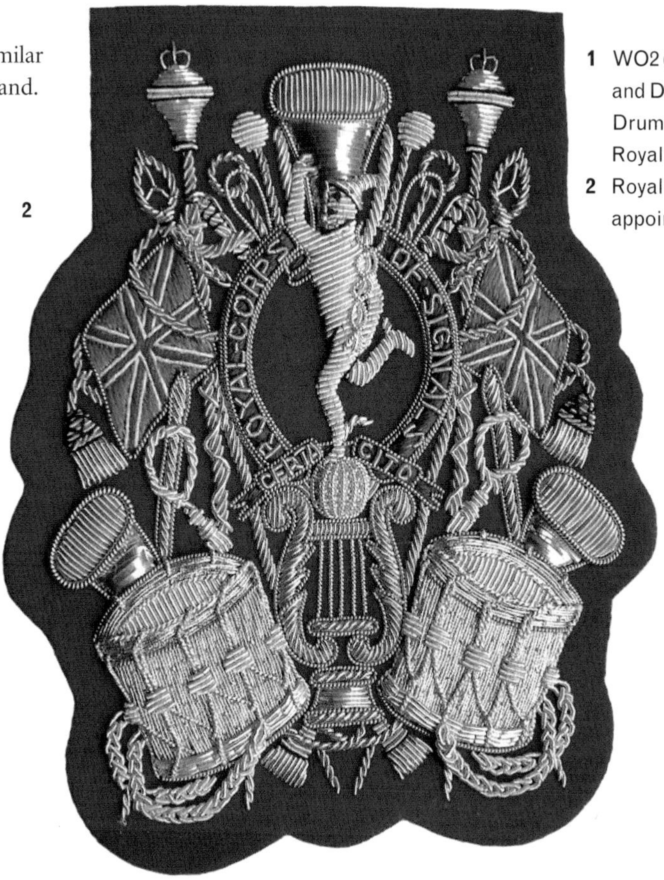

1. WO2 (BSM) Nigel Williams Royal Signals Band and DMaj Steve Ward, formerly the Senior Drum Major Household Division, now with the Royal Signals Northern TA Band.
2. Royal Signals (Northern) Band Drum Major's appointment badge 10.25 × 12.75 cm.

35th (South Midland) Signal Regiment

35th Signal Regiment was formed in 1967, with squadrons as successor units to TA regiments. The squadrons of 35th Signal Regiment are each identified by a squadron arm badge adopted in 1999 worn on the left sleeve in Combat Dress.

95 (Shropshire Yeomanry) Signal Squadron

95 (Shropshire Yeomanry) Signal Squadron has since 1999 worn a New Zealand fern leaf arm badge on the pullover and Number 2 Dress. The honour was granted to 76th (Shropshire Yeomanry) Medium Regiment RA (TA) in 1945 by Lieutenant General Sir Bernard Freyberg VC KCB KBE CMG DSO commanding the Second New Zealand Expeditionary Force (2nd NZ Division) for the support the regiment provided during the battles from Cassino to the River Po in Italy. This metal fern badge differs from that worn by The Royal Wiltshire Yeomanry in having NZ embossed on the design. This style is that worn by New Zealanders as a national lapel badge (see The Royal Wiltshire Yeomanry p. 340).

The Squadron also wears Shropshire Yeomanry collar badges.

1

2

3

4

6

5

7

8

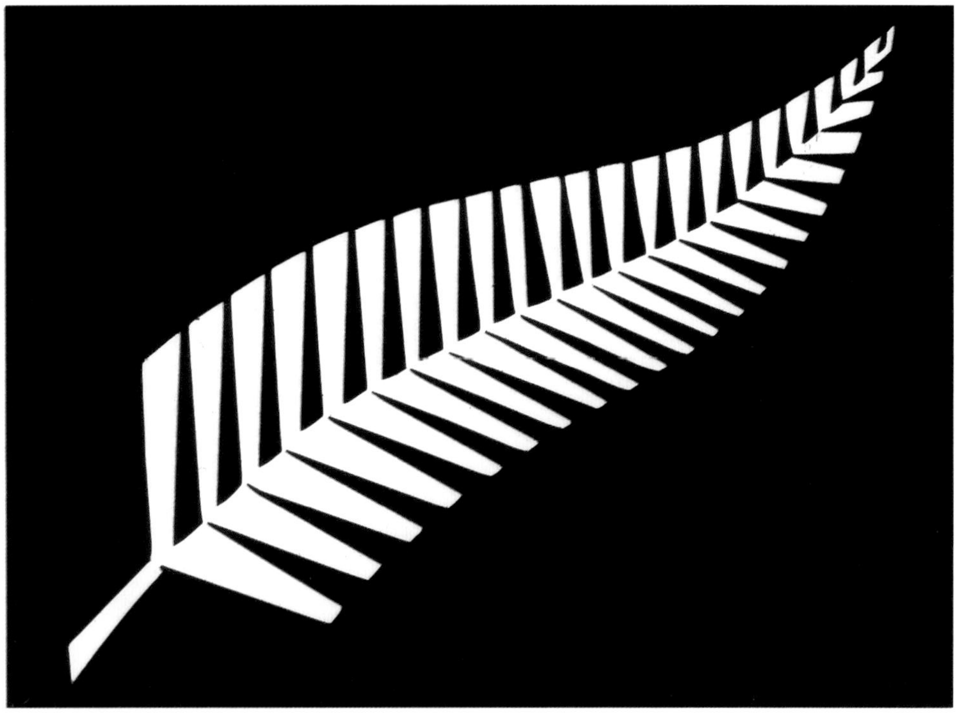

9

10

previous page

1 Regimental headquarters and HQ Squadron arm badge 8 × 5.5 cm.

2 48th (City of Birmingham) Signal Squadron arm badge 8 × 5.5 cm.

3 58th (Staffordshire) Signal Squadron arm badge 8 × 5.5 cm.

4 89th (Warwickshire) Signal Squadron 8 × 5.5 cm.

this page

5 95th (Shropshire Yeomanry) Signal Squadron arm badge 8 × 5.5 cm.

6 Shropshire Yeomanry No2 Dress New Zealand honour arm badge 3 × 1 cm.

7 Shropshire Yeomanry pullover New Zealand honour arm badge 4.75 × 3.5 cm.

8 Shropshire Yeomanry New Zealand fern paper transfer used as a vehicle badge 14 × 10.25 cm.

9 OCdt Sam Blackburn wearing Shropshire Yeomanry collar badges.

10 Shropshire Yeomanry officer's silver collar 2.5 × 3 cm.

Acknowledgement
Captain Glynn Ireland, Alex Rdgers and Dave Tarrant, WO1 (RSM) R Dalton and SSgt D MacKenzie

36th (Eastern) Signal Regiment

36th Signal Regiment was formed in 1967, with squadrons as successor units to TA regiments.

An arm badge was introduced in 1998 for soldiers who had successfully completed the recruits course but is now obsolete with the introduction of the Royal Signals Tactical Recognition Flash.

36 Signal Regiment arm badge 3 × 3.75 cm, now obsolete.

37 Signal Regiment (Volunteers)

37th (Wales and Western) Signal Regiment was formed in 1967 and reorganised as 37 Signal Regiment in 1992.

The squadrons wear Royal Signals insignia with the exception of 67 Signal Squadron which wears Queen's Own Warwickshire Yeomanry and Worcestershire Yeomanry insignia.

67 (Queen's Own Warwickshire and Worcestershire Yeomanry) Signal Squadron (V)

67 Signal Squadron wears Warwickshire Yeomanry collar badges. The Warwickshire Yeomanry Bear and Ragged Staff emblem was also used on the arm badge which was first worn in 1994 at the time of the Royal Review to celebrate the 200th Anniversary of the Yeomanry.

Senior NCOs and Warrant Officers wear the Queen's Own Worcestershire Hussars silver regimental rank badge.

2

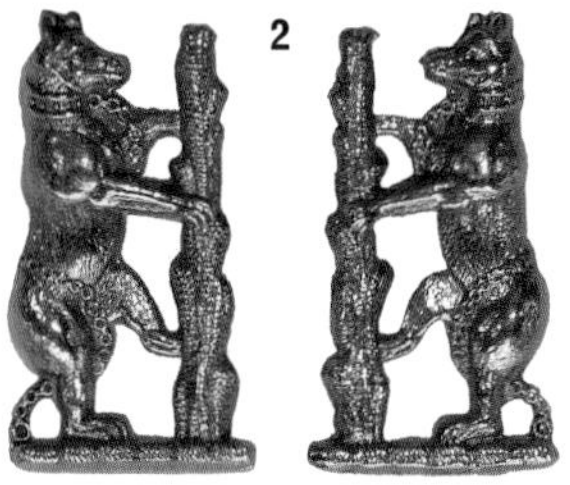

5

3

1

4

1 Worcestershire Yeomanry regimental rank badge 4.5 × 6 cm.
2 67 (Queen's Own Warwickshire and Worcestershire Yeomanry) Signal Squadron collar badges 1.5 × 3 cm.
3 67 Signal Squadron shoulder title 3.5 × 1 cm.
4 67 Signal Squadron major's rank slide.
5 67 Signal Squadron arm badge 5 × 5 cm.

Acknowledgement WO1 (RSM) MPE Angove

38 Signal Regiment (Volunteers)

The 38th Signal Regiment was formed in 1967 from 46th (North Midland) Signal Regiment TA, 64th Signal Regiment TA and 337th Brigade Signal Squadron. The senior of the new Regiment's forebears traced its lineage to the North Midland Telegraph Company Royal Engineers, raised in 1908.

The Regiment has been particularly successful in fostering close ties with the local communities in which it is based, and each squadron is named after its recruiting area. In 1995, the Regiment was re-titled 38th (City of Sheffield) Signal Regiment (Volunteers). In 1996 46 Squadron was re-titled 46th (City of Derby) Signal Squadron (Volunteers) and in 1998 87 Squadron was re-titled 87th (City of Nottingham) Signal Squadron (Volunteers). In 2001 64 Squadron became 64th (City of Sheffield) Signal Squadron (Volunteers) and the Regiment reverted to the title of 38th Signal Regiment (Volunteers).

The regiment has worn the 2 (National Communications) Brigade arm badge since 2003. A few of the squadron arm badges, now obsolete, survive.

46th (City of Derby) Signal Squadron (V) wore a version of the 49th (East Midlands) Brigade Polar Bear arm badge.

64th (Sheffield) Signal Squadron (V) wore a version of the 15th (North East) Brigade Merlin arm badge from 1993.

87th (City of Nottingham) Signal Squadron (V) wore an arm badge depicting an archer, representing the city of Nottingham from 1993.

Since 1993 Headquarters Squadron have worn an anvil representing Sheffield's steel industry .

1

2

3

4

1 HQ Squadron arm badge 6.5 × 5 cm.
2 46th (City of Derby) Signal Squadron arm badge 6.75 × 5 cm.
3 64th (City of Sheffield) Signal Squadron arm badge 5 × 7 cm.
4 87th (City of Nottingham) Signal Squadron arm badge 4.5 × 5.75 cm.

Acknowledgement WO1 (RSM) KP Innes

39 (Skinners) Signal Regiment

39th (City of London) Signal Regiment was formed by the amalgamation of 65 Signal Regiment and 92 Signal Regiment (AER) in 1967. In 1995 the regiment moved from London and adopted the title 'Skinners'.

In 1954 the Worshipful Company of Skinners adopted Number 1 Special Communications Regiment as part of a revived system of linking City of London based units of the Auxiliary Forces with Livery Companies. The Regiment adopted the emblem of the Company, the Lynx, as its own and all ranks wore the Lynx badge on each arm of their uniform until 1966. The association was reaffirmed in April 1995 when 'Skinners' was added to the regimental title on its relocation to Bristol and the Regiment readopted the Lynx badge. The badges are sometimes trimmed to leave the outline rather than the square backing sewn to the sleeve.

1

5 (Queen's Own Oxford Hussars) Squadron

5 Squadron was formed in 1971 and revived the disbanded yeomanry title in 1975.

Officers wear rank slides with QOOH woven in white; soldiers have QOOH woven in black.

47th (Middlesex Yeomanry) Signal Squadron.

The squadron is decended from The Middlesex Yeomanry formed in 1830 and reduced to a Royal Signals squadron in 1967.

Middlesex Yeomanry collar badges are worn. The motto reproduced on the badges and buttons is *For Heart and Home*, and MDCH stands for *Middlesex Yeomanry Duke of Cambridge's Hussars*.

The squadron wears a dull green and gold 'parachute rigging' lanyard in honour of its service as airborne signals from 1947 to 1961. The Squadron Quartermaster Sergeant wears four chevrons (see *The Queen's Dragoon Guards* p. 20).

2

The Middlesex Yeomanry Association Band

Formed in 1843 and disbanded in 1968, the Middlesex Yeomanry Band continues as a civilian band wearing Number 1 Dress uniform with Middlesex Yeomanry badges.

3

Acknowledgement Capt RJ Sheldon and WO2 TG Morrisey

1 Lynx badge worn on the left sleeve, woven on a blue backing in Number 1 and 2 Dress and woven with some wire on a red backing for Mess Dress 6 × 6 cm.
2 Middlesex Yeomanry anodised aluminium collar badges 3 × 3.5 cm.
3 Middlesex Yeomanry button.

40th (Ulster) Signal Regiment

40th Signal Regiment was formed in 1967, with squadrons as successor units to TA regiments. Officers, Warrant Officers and Staff Sergeants of 40 Signal Regiment wear a blue caubeen with a Royal Signals hackle above the cap badge (see Royal Signals Pipers p. 382). Officers also carry a Blackthorn cane. 69 Signal Squadron preserves the North Irish Horse traditions and badges.

Major Tom Dick wearing the Royal Signals hackle above the officer's wire embroidered cap badge on the caubeen.

69 (North Irish Horse) Signal Squadron (V)

The Squadron wears North Irish Horse collar badges.

The Squadron wears a silver maple leaf (see The Queen's Own Yeomanry p. 367) on the left sleeve of Number 2 Dress and an embroidered leaf on Combat Dress in recognition of the North Irish Horse's actions in support of 1st Canadian Infantry Division during the Battle of the Hitler Line on 23 May 1944. 25th Tank Brigade, with NIH, 51st Royal Tank Regiment and 142nd Regiment Royal Armoured Corps, provided close support to the Canadian Infantry. On 24 May 1944 a Special Order of the Day was issued:

> *General GC Vokes DSO Commanding 1st Canadian Infantry Division has intimated that he would be pleased if all ranks 25th Tank Brigade would wear the Maple Leaf emblem in token of the part played by the Brigade assisting 1st Canadian Infantry Division to breach the Adolf Hitler Line.*

Acknowledgement
Captain Oli Dinnis and K-B Kirkham-Brown

North Irish Horse Signal Squadron arm badge 7 × 7 cm.

71st (Yeomanry) Signal Regiment

71st Signal Regiment was formed in 1969.

68 (Inns of Court and City Yeomanry) Signal Squadron

Officers wear a wire-embroidered Royal Signals badge on a green triangular backing on the beret. Soldiers wear a cloth woven version. Officers posted away from the Squadron are reported to wear a wire embroidered 'Devil on Spur' beret badge. Officers wear the Inns of Court and City Yeomanry badge on the forage cap.

The Squadron wears Inns of Court and City Yeomanry collar badges (see The Royal Yeomanry p. 350).

The Inns of Court and City Yeomanry regimental rank badge is worn by NCOs and Warrant Officers; produced in chrome for Number 2 Dress and wire embroidered for Number 1 Dress.

The Squadron wears a white lanyard instead of the blue Royal Signals lanyard.

1

2

3

The Inns of Court and City Yeomanry was formed in 1961 by the amalgamation of The Inns of Court Regiment, and The City of London Yeomanry (Rough Riders), The Rifle Brigade. In 1969 it was reduced to form 68 (Inns of Court and City Yeomanry) Squadron, 71 (Yeomanry) Signal Regiment, Royal Signals.

4

5

6

7

70 (Essex Yeomanry) Signal Squadron

But here's to the horses and here's to the men,
Who stuck to the task that was given to them then,
Who proved themselves Yeomen and true Essex men,
When they charged on Monchy-le-Preux.

The squadron was formed in 1969, but traces its history to 1798.

8

9

10

The Squadron wears the dark green light infantry beret in all order of dress except Number 1 Dress, and in 1984 adopted the Royal Signals cap badge embroidered on a red backing, wire-embroidered for officers and woven for soldiers. In 1994 soldiers adopted the standard Royal Signals cap badge.

The Squadron wear Essex Yeomanry collar badges. The motto on the badges, *Decus et Tutamen*, Shield and Protection, is also used on the English £1 coin. Shoulder titles are EY produced in anodised aluminium.

Since 1955 officers have worn the Royal Horse Artillery cypher on their shoulder chains in Number 1 Dress in recognition of The Essex Yeomanry service as a RHA regiment from 1921 to 1947.

Senior ranks wear The Essex Yeomanry cypher on the right sleeve in Number 1, Number 2 and Mess Dress. The Squadron wears a white lanyard instead of the blue Royal Signals lanyard.

11

12

13

14

265 *(Kent and County of London Yeomanry) Signal Squadron*

The Squadron wear Kent and County of London Yeomanry collar badges, shoulder titles and rank slides. The Sharpshooters Rank Badge is worn by corporals and above in Number 1 Dress. In Number 2 Dress the KCLY Rank Badge, known as The Monkey, is worn.

A cross belt is worn with Number 1 Dress. A green and yellow lanyard is worn instead of the blue Royal Signals lanyard.

The Kent and Sharpshooters Yeomanry was formed as the Kent and County of London Yeomanry (Sharpshooters) in 1961 by the amalgamation of 3rd/4th County of London Yeomanry (Sharpshooters), and 297 (Kent Yeomanry) LAA Regiment, RA and went through a number of changes of role and affiliation. HQ (265 London & Kent) Squadron, 71st (Yeomanry) Signal Regiment, Royal Signals was formed in 1969 and renamed 265 (Kent and Sharpshooters Yeomanry) Squadron, 71st (Yeomanry) Signal Regiment, Royal Signals in 1973.

previous page

1 Inns of Court and City Yeomanry Signal Squadron officer's wire-embroidered cap badge 3.5 × 5 cm.
2 Soldier's woven cap badge 3.25 × 4.75 cm.
3 Officer's forage cap badge 4 × 5 cm.
4 OCdt Karen Woodhouse wearing No2 Dress with Inns of Court and City Yeomanry collar badges.
5 Sig Camille Rebelo wearing the distinctive Inns of Court and City Yeomanry Signal Squadron woven cap badge.
6 Inns of Court and City Yeomanry shoulder title 4 × 1 cm.
7 Inns of Court and City Yeomanry regimental rank badge 5 cm.
8 Essex Yeomanry Signal Squadron Officer's wire-embroidered cap badge 3.5 × 4.5 cm and soldier's woven cap badge 4 × 5.75 cm, now obsolete.
9 Essex Yeomanry anodised aluminium shoulder title 3 × 1.75 cm.
10 Essex Yeomanry officer's gilt and soldier's anodised aluminium collar badges 3 × 3.5 cm.

this page

11 Essex Yeomanry second lieutenant's rank slide.

Essex Signal Squadron rank badges

12 No1 Dress 4 × 6 cm.
13 No2 Dress 3.75 × 5.5 cm.
14 Mess Dress 3.5 × 5 cm.

Acknowledgement
Major Michael Wood, Captain Al Garrett, Steve Slaney and WO1 (RSM) PR Curtis

63th (SAS) Signal Squadron (V)

The SAS Signal Squadron was formed in 1951 and numbered 63 Signal Squadron in 1967. The officers wear an unofficial wire-embroidered Royal Signals beret badge on a sand coloured backing.

OCdt Peter Mapledoram 63 (SAS) Signal Squadron.

Land Information Assurance Group (Volunteers)

LIAG is a specialist TA unit responsible for Information Assurance.

The LIAG(V) badge is a sword representing a LAND capability crossed with the Electronic Warfare lightning flash; the symbol also used by the US Land Information Warfare Agency, which carries out a similar function for the US Army. The gold and black badge was to have been complemented by a subdued black on olive green version for combat jackets but this version has not been adopted. The Strategic Defence Review established a 40 strong IT Specialist Pool (Volunteers) under Royal Signals sponsorship in 1998, which became LIAG(V) in 1999. When serving officers join LIAG(V) they retain their cap badge but officers commissioned into the unit are badged Royal Signals.

LIAG arm badge 5 × 5 cm.

Acknowledgement Maj John Pringle and SSgt L M Camm

Infantry

52nd Lowland Regiment

The 52nd Lowland Regiment was formed in 1999 by the amalgamation of The 3rd (Volunteer) Battalion, The Royal Highland Fusiliers and The Lowland Volunteers both of which were renamed in 1995 from battalions of the 52nd Lowland Volunteers, which had been formed in 1967. The name commemorated that of the 52nd Lowland Division, which fought during the First and Second World Wars.

52nd Lowland Regiment infantry companies wear the cap badges of their affiliated regiments; Royal Scots, Royal Highland Fusiliers and King's Own Scottish Borderers. The Lowland Regiment badge is worn only within the Regiment by the Commanding Officer and by the Regimental Sergeant Major. It is also worn by the Director of Music of The Lowland Band; the remainder of the Band wear a bright metal version of the badge. Number 2 Dress is rarely worn but if required collar badges of the former regiments are also worn.

1

2

3

1 OCdt Calum MacFarlane A Company 52nd Lowland Regiment wearing his Royal Scots Tam o'Shanter. He has the badge of the 51 (Scottish) Brigade on his left sleeve.

2 Lowland Regiment silver badge 5.25 × 5.25 cm worn only by the Commanding Officer and the Regimental Sergeant Major.

3 52nd Lowland Regiment rank slide.

The Band of 52 Lowland Brigade

The Band of 52 Lowland Brigade was formed in 1958 as the Band of 7th/9th (Highlanders) Battalion, The Royal Scots (The Royal Regiment). With reductions to the TA the Band had different sponsor units until it received its present title in 1999. The Band has always worn Royal Scots cap badges but originally also wore the kilt of Hunting Stewart tartan. As a Lowland Band trews were adopted in about 1970.

1

2

1 SSgt David Nelson wearing Full Dress.
1 Musn Robert Fraser wearing Full Dress.

3rd (Volunteer) Battalion The Princess of Wales's Royal Regiment (Queen's and Royal Hampshire)

3rd (Volunteer) Battalion, The Princess of Wales's Royal Regiment, 'The TA Tigers', was formed by the amalgamation of the 5th (Volunteer) Battalion and part of the 6th/7th (Volunteer) Battalion

The Princess of Wales's Royal Regiment is one of only two Infantry regiments with TA battalions. 3 PWRR celebrates the same regimental traditions as the regular battalions and has the same dress regulations.

Following the custom handed down from the 31st Foot, each year the best sergeant is nominated as the Sobraon Sergeant and has the honour of carrying the Regimental Colour on the anniversary of the Battle of Sobraon fought in India in 1846.

1

2

3

opposite page

1 Pte Bill Westley and Mike Maddams wearing Combat Dress.
2 OCdt Jamie Gordon wearing Number 2 Dress.
3 Sgt Dale Holly, the 2005 Sobraon Sergeant.

The Royal Rifle Volunteers

The Royal Rifle Volunteers was formed in 1999 by the amalgamation of part of 6th/7th (Volunteer) Battalion The Princess of Wales's Royal Regiment, part of 2nd (Volunteer) Battalion The Royal Gloucestershire, Berkshire and Wiltshire Regiment and the 5th (Volunteer) Battalion The Royal Green Jackets.

The Royal Rifle Volunteers, or RRV, companies wear the cap badges of their affiliated regiments; Princess of Wales's Royal Regiment, Royal Gloucestershire, Berkshire and Wiltshire Regiment and Royal Green Jackets. Number 2 Dress is rarely worn but if required collar badges of the former regiments are also worn.
The Regiment wore a Tactical Recognition Flash consisting of the 145 Brigade badge superimposed on colours representing the RGJ, PWRR and RGBW until early 2005.

Between 1999–2000, when the subsidiary titles were dropped, the regiment is reputed to have included a sub-unit with the longest unit title in the Army; 9 (Princess Beatrice's Isle of Wight Rifles) Platoon, C (Princess of Wales's Royal Regiment (Queen's and Royal Hampshires)) Company, The Royal Rifle Volunteers.

Acknowledgement WO1 (RSM) Reg Hollis

1

2

3

1 WO2 Colin Chatfield, Cpl Cookie Cook, LCpl Tim Lindsell and Sgt Timothy Neate displaying different cap badges worn by the RRV.
2 OCdt Bryn Monnery wearing the RRV TRF above his PWRR company TRF.
3 RRV TRF 5 × 3 cm, now obsolete.

Waterloo Band Royal Green Jackets (Volunteers)

The Waterloo Band RGJ(V) is based with the RRV.

1 Cpl Derek Webb, as the Commanding Officer's Bugler he wears a double bugle badge on his right sleeve (see The King's Regiment p136).
2 BMaj Patrick Mannion leading The Waterloo Band.

Acknowledgement LCpl Mike Carter

1

2

The London Regiment

The London Regiment was formed in 1993 by the amalgamation of 8th Battalion, The Queen's Fusiliers, D Company 4th Battalion The Royal Irish Rangers and G Company 1st Battalion 51st Highland Volunteers

The London Regiment companies wear the cap badges of their former or affiliated regiments; Princess of Wales's Royal Regiment, Royal Regiment of Fusiliers, Royal Green Jackets, London Scottish and London Irish. Number 2 Dress is rarely worn but if required collar badges of the former regiments are also worn.

1

2

3

4

The London Scottish

The London Scottish was raised in 1859, becoming the 14th (County of London) Battalion, The London Regiment (London Scottish) in 1908. It was eventually reduced to a company attached at various times to The Gordon Highlanders, the 51st Highland Volunteers, The London Yeomanry and Territorials, the 1st Battalion, 51st Highland Volunteers and finally in 1993 to The London Regiment.

1

2

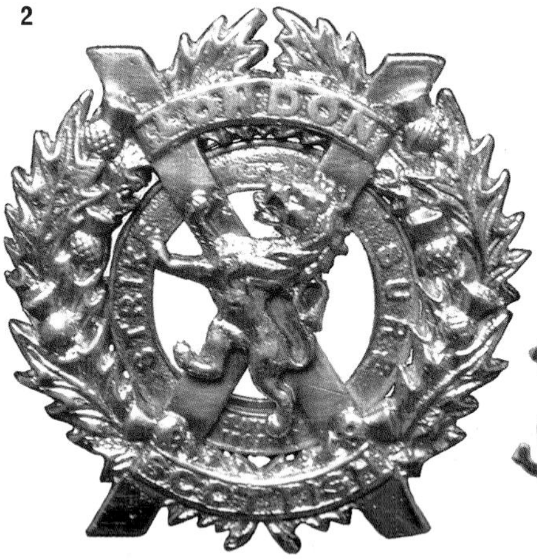

3

4

5

6

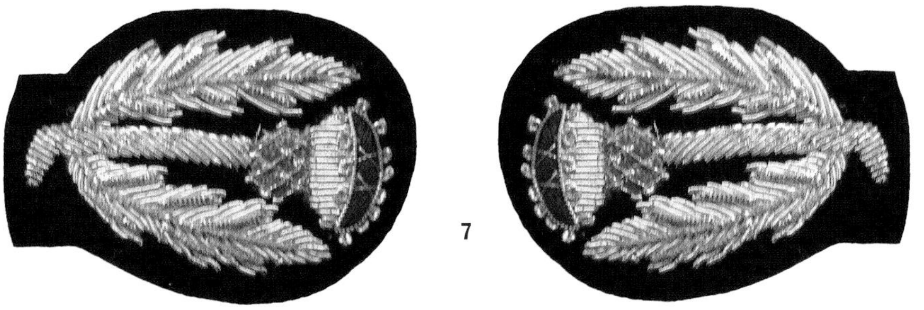

7

8

9

opposite page

1 LCpl Phillip Vergottini, Rng Mark Brown, LCpl Adam Chapman, Sgt Ricky Francis and Pte Paul Glover displaying different cap badges worn by The London Regiment.

2 No1 Dress and No2 Dress London arm badges 4 × 5.25 cm.

3 Officer's 3.5 × 1.5 cm and soldier's 4.5 × 2.25 cm shoulder titles, now obsolete.

4 London Regiment TRF 6.75 × 6.75 cm worn in Iraq.

this page

1 The London Scottish white metal cap badge 5.5 cm and anodised aluminium collar badges 2.5 × 3 cm.

2 The London Scottish officer's silver cap badge 5.5 cm.

3 London Scottish button.

4 Shoulder title 4.5 × 2.5 cm.

5 The London Scottish TRF 5 × 5 cm introduced in 1999.

6 The London Scottish purse badge 4.75 × 4.25 cm.

7 The London Scottish officer's Full Dress collar badges 5.5 × 3.75 cm.

8 The London Scottish kilt pin 2.75 cm.

9 The London Scottish Drum Major's waist belt clasp 9 × 4.5 cm sewn onto the belt.

this page

10 The London Scottish Colour Sergeant's rank badge 8 × 14.25 cm.

11 WO2 Tom Hallett QVSM wearing No2 Dress.

12 Queen Elizabeth's badge 2 × 2.5 cm worn on the officer's Sgian dhub. The Pipe Major wears a larger badge as a plaid brooch.

13 The London Scottish officer's sporran cantle 17.5 × 11.5 cm.

14 The London Scottish piper's sporran cantle 17 × 9.5 cm.

15 Drummer's waist belt clasp 8.5 × 6.5 cm.

opposite page

16 Piper's waist belt clasp 9.5 × 8 cm.

17 Piper's sword belt ornaments 7.5cm.

18 Pipe Major and Drum Major's appointment badges 11 cm.

10

11

12

13

14

15

16

17

18

The London Irish Rifles

The London Irish was raised in 1860, becoming the 18th (County of London) Battalion, The London Regiment (London Irish Rifles) in 1908. It was eventually reduced to a company attached at various times to The Royal Ulster Rifles, the North Irish Militia, The Royal Irish Rangers, The Queen's Fusiliers (City of London) and finally in 1993 to The London Regiment.

19

20

21

22

23

24

25

26

27

28

29

30

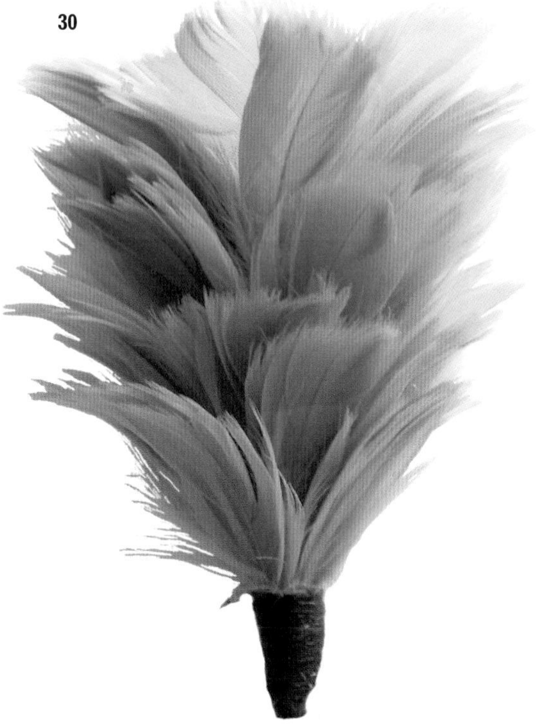

31

32

opposite page

19 The London Irish soldier's anodised aluminium cap badge 3.75 × 6.25 cm and collar badges 1.75 × 2.75 cm.

20 Pipe Major Dominic Murphy wearing Full Dress.

21 The London Irish soldier's hackle 6.5 × 12 cm.

22 Officer's anodised aluminium cap badge. 3.75 × 6.25 cm and black collar badges 2.5 × 2.5 cm.

23 Rank slide.

24 Rng Badger Bajracharya wearing the caubeen pulled down to the left.

25 The London Irish TRF 6.75 × 6.75 cm

26 Rng H Sebukima and CSgt Sammy Kilpatrick wearing combat dress with the caubeen pulled down to the left.

this page

27 The London Irish piper's anodised aluminium cap badge 6 × 8 cm and collar badges 2.5 × 2.5 cm.

28 Piper's Full Dress arm badge 4.5 × 4.5 cm.

29 Bugler's Busby badge. Boss 3.25 × 4.5 cm, badge 2.75 × 3.75 cm.

30 Officer and piper's hackle 7 × 9 cm.

31 The London Irish officer's shoulder belt ornaments. Plate 6 × 8 cm, Battle honours 2 × 3 cm.

32 Officer's pouch badge 2 × 4 cm.

Acknowledgement Captain Bob Keating

The Lancastrian and Cumbrian Volunteers

The Lancastrian and Cumbrian Volunteers was formed in 1999 by the amalgamation of 4th (Volunteer) Battalion The King's Own Royal Border Regiment and 4th (Volunteer) Battalion The Queen's Lancashire Regiment.

The Lancastrian and Cumbrian Volunteers companies wear the cap badges of their affiliated regiments; The King's Own Royal Border Regiment and The Queen's Lancashire Regiment. The Machine Gun Platoon in B Company is badged Royal Regiment of Fusiliers as a link with the former Lancashire Fusiliers. Number 2 Dress is rarely worn but if required collar badges of the former regiments are also worn.

The Tactical Recognition Flash, or TRF, combines the Kendal green of the King's Own Royal Border Regiment, the primrose of the Royal Regiment of Fusiliers and the Cardinal red of the Queen's Lancashire Regiment.

1

2

3

1 LCV TRF 6 × 6 cm.
2 SSgt Ron Campbell REME attached, Capt Andy Derby and 2Lt Andrew Metcalfe displaying different cap badges worn by The Lancastrian and Cumbrian Volunteers.
3 The Queen's Colour of 4 QLR carried by Capt Martin Smith, escorted by WO2 Tommo Thompson and CSgt Steve Cooney.

Acknowledgement WO2 (RQMS) P Wainman MBE

The Tyne Tees Regiment

The Tyne-Tees Regiment was formed in 1999 by the amalgamation of 6th Bn The Royal Regiment of Fusiliers (Volunteers), 4th/5th Bn The Green Howards (Yorkshire Volunteers), and 7th Bn The Light Infantry (Volunteers).

Tyne Tees Regiment companies wear cap badges of their affiliated regiments; Royal Regiment of Fusiliers, Light Infantry, and Green Howards. Number 2 Dress is rarely worn but if required collar badges of former regiments are also worn.

The Tyne Tees Regiment TRF was originally designed as the Divisional badge of 50th (Motor) Division by Colonel JM Grant DSO OBE when serving as Staff Captain in 1938–1939. The capital Ts represent the rivers Tyne and Tees whilst, when viewed sideways, the Ts form an H representing the river Humber.

1

2

1 Tyne Tees Regiment TRF 6 × 6 cm.
2 Colours of 6 RRF decorated with wreaths of red and white roses on St George's Day carried by Lts Will Henwood and Dale Smith and escorted by WO2 Ian Cowie, and CSgt Bob Davison and Sgt Gaz Gannon of Z Company.

The Northumbria Band

The Northumbria Band of The Tyne-Tees Regiment was formed in 1999 with musicians from the former 6th Battalion The Royal Regiment of Fusiliers and the Burma Light Infantry Band.

1 The Northumbria Band wears the uniform of The Royal Regiment of Fusiliers.
2 DMaj Peter Elcoat wearing Full Dress

Acknowledgement WO2 (BI) R B Creasey

The West Midlands Regiment

The West Midlands Regiment was formed in 1999 with the amalgamation of 5th (Warwickshire) Battalion The Royal Regiment of Fusiliers (Volunteers), 5th (Shropshire and Herefordshire) Battalion The Light Infantry (Volunteers) and 3rd (Volunteer) Battalion The Staffordshire Regiment.

The West Midland Regiment, or WMR, companies wear the cap badges of their affiliated regiments; Royal Regiment of Fusiliers, Light Infantry, Worcestershire and Sherwood Foresters Regiment and Staffordshire Regiment. Number 2 Dress is rarely worn but if required collar badges of the affiliated regiments are also worn.

A regimental TRF consisting of the Cross of St Chad was adopted in 1999.

1

2

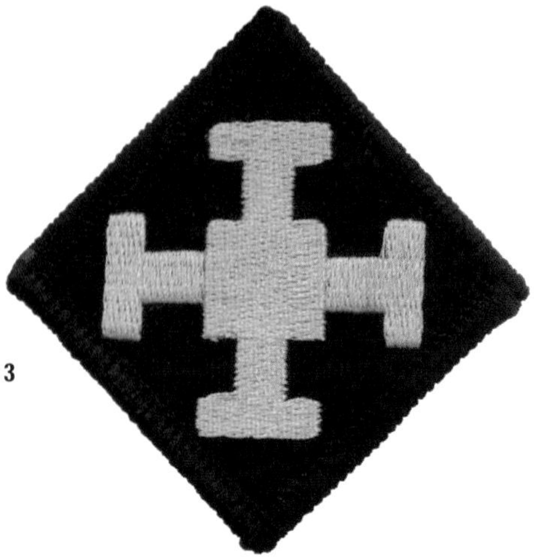

3

4

5

previous page

1 Captain Ted Wibberley wearing the regimental TRF, the Cross of St Chad, on his right sleeve, and Pte Fitz Fitzpatrick, LCpl Dean Caffery REME attached to A (Fusilier) Company, Pte James Andrew and Pte Luke Cole, wearing the 143 Brigade arm badge below the Union Flag badge on his left sleeve, displaying different cap badges worn by The West Midlands Regiment.

2 Major Jerry Richardson, badged WFR, and Richard Jones, badged LI.

this page

3 West Midlands Regiment TRF 6.5 × 6.5 cm.

4 Cpl Lisa Birch AGC (SPS) of A (Fusilier) Company, a finance clerk who retrained as a Guard Dog handler in Iraq, wearing the Fusilier hackle with the AGC cap badge.

5 Pte Tom Corns, badged WFR.

Acknowledgement Capt DC Forrest MBE and Ben McGuire

The King's and Cheshire Regiment

The King's and Cheshire Regiment was formed in 1999 by the amalgamation of 5th/8th (Volunteer) Battalion, The King's Regiment and 3rd (Volunteer) Battalion, The Cheshire Regiment.

The King's and Cheshire Regiment, or KCR, companies wear the cap badges of their affiliated regiments; The King's Regiment and The Cheshire Regiment. 2 Platoon A Company, wears the insignia of the Liverpool Scottish. Number 2 Dress is rarely worn but if required collar badges of the former regiments may be worn.

The Cheshire Company had continued the Militia practice of wearing the Cheshire Regiment Tactical Recognition Flash reversed. In 2002 the Army Dress Committee ordered that this practice should cease.

1

2

3

The Liverpool Scottish

The Liverpool Scottish Platoon wears the Forbes Tartan. The Glengarry badge is the original badge of the Liverpool Scottish introduced in 1908 and worn until 1937. It was reintroduced in 1992, worn with the Queen's Own Highlanders blue hackle to commemorate service as a battalion of the Cameron Highlanders. The Queen's Own Highlanders sporran is also retained.

The Liverpool Scottish was raised in 1900 as the 8th (Scottish) Volunteer Battalion, The King's (Liverpool Regiment), becoming The Liverpool Scottish, The Queen's Own Cameron Highlanders in 1937. In 1971 it was reduced to V Company (Liverpool Scottish), and in 1999 to the Liverpool Scottish Platoon, A (King's) Company, The King's and Cheshire Regiment.

Acknowledgement WO1 (RSM) Colin Deegan

1

2

3

opposite page

1 OCdt Colin Koke wearing The King's Regiment cap badge and TRF.

2 Kgn Mike Davison MC wearing The King's Regiment TRF on Combat Dress in Iraq.

3 WO1 (RSM) Colin Deegan KINGS taking over from WO1 (RSM) Kevin Fletcher CHESHIRE

this page

1 Liverpool Scottish cap badge 6 × 6 cm.

2 Highlanders sporran badge worn by The Liverpool Scottish.

3 OCdt Richard Mulcaster wearing Liverpool Scottish No2 Dress.

The East of England Regiment

The East of England Regiment was formed in 1999 by the amalgamation of 6th and 7th (Volunteer) Battalions The Royal Anglian Regiment and 3rd (Volunteer) Battalion The Worcestershire and Sherwood Foresters Regiment).

The East of England Regiment companies wear the cap badges of their affiliated regiments; Royal Anglian Regiment and Worcestershire and Sherwood Foresters Regiment. Number 2 Dress is rarely worn but if required collar badges of the former regiments are also worn.

Two companies wear distinctive arm badges in place of the regimental Tactical Recognition Flash. A (Norfolk and Suffolk) Company wear a yellow badge, known affectionately as the Kohima Flash. The badge was adopted *circa* 1990 by A (Norfolk and Suffolk) Company 6th Battalion The Royal Anglian Regiment. The colour represents the facing colours (that is, the colour of the collar and cuffs – hence, in a slightly different context, the military observation that 'the collar and cuffs don't match!') on The Norfolk Regiment's Full Dress uniform which was worn from 1881–1914.

E Company wear a badge combining the regimental colours of the Essex Regiment and the Bedfordshire and Hertfordshire Regiment. The badge was adopted circa 1990 by C (Essex) Company 6 R ANGLIAN.

The Siege of Kohima was fought between the British and Indian Army against the attacking Japanese in Burma in 1944 at the same time as the Battle of Imphal. The battle around Imphal resulted in the greatest defeat on land ever suffered by the Japanese army. 2nd Battalion The Royal Norfolk Regiment fought at Kohima, the savage nature of the battle illustrated in the painting *Battle of the Tennis Court* by Terence Cuneo.

1

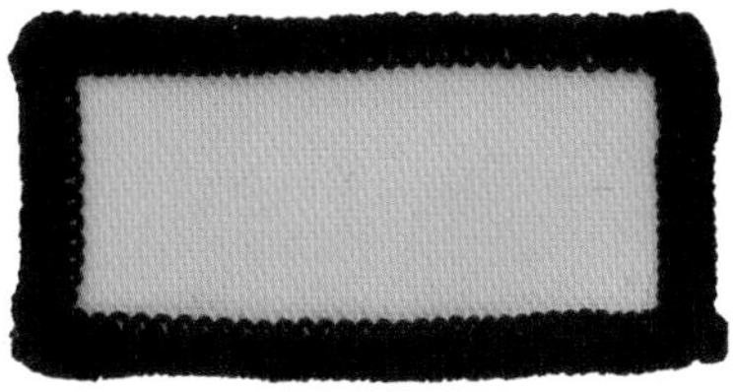

2

3

4

1 LCpl Bunny Bunn REME attached to the East of England Regiment and Captain Keith Spiers, Cpl Stephen Mee and Pte Ross Aitchison displaying the two regimental badges worn by soldiers of the East of England Regiment.
2 A Company EER Kohima arm badge 5 × 2.5 cm.
3 E Company EER arm badge 5 × 2.75 cm.
4 Colonel of the Regiment's rank slide.

Acknowledgement Captains Tam Steele and Paul Thurston

The Rifle Volunteers

The Rifle Volunteers was formed in 1999 by the amalgamation of 6th Battalion, The Light Infantry (V), 4th (V) Battalion, The Devonshire and Dorset Regiment and part 2nd (V) Battalion, The Royal Gloucestershire, Berkshire and Wiltshire Regiment.

The Rifle Volunteers companies wear the cap badges of their affiliated regiments; The Light Infantry, The Devonshire and Dorset Regiment and The Royal Gloucestershire, Berkshire and Wiltshire Regiment. Number 2 Dress is rarely worn but if required collar badges of the former regiments are also worn.

1

2

1 LCpl Dixie Dean, Pte Ashley Whelon and James Needs displaying the three regimental badges worn by soldiers of the Rifle Volunteers. They do not have a Tactical Recognition Flash, but are wearing the 43 (Wessex) Brigade badge below the Union Flag.
2 Major Stephen Higgs wearing combat kit with the D&D TRF and rank slide.

The East and West Riding Regiment

The East and West Riding Regiment was formed in 1999 by the amalgamation of 3rd Battalion The Prince of Wales's Own Regiment of Yorkshire (Yorkshire Volunteers), 3rd Battalion The Duke of Wellington's Regiment (Yorkshire Volunteers) and The King's Own Yorkshire Yeomanry (Light Infantry).

The East and West Riding Regiment companies wear the cap badges of their affiliated regiments; Light Infantry, Prince of Wales's Own Regiment of Yorkshire, and Duke of Wellington's Regiment. Number 2 Dress is rarely worn but if required collar badges of the former regiments are also worn.

1

The East and West Riding Regiment Tactical Recognition Flash adopted in 2004 was originally worn as an arm badge by the East and West Ridings District in 1948.

2

The Leeds Rifles

'Leeds Rifles' was an unofficial name given to the Rifle Volunteers in Leeds in 1859; in time the name became part of the official title. In 1908 there were two battalions of Leeds Rifles, one of which later served with the Royal Tank Regiment and the other with the Royal Artillery. Now reduced to a platoon, The Leeds Rifles retain the honours of a loop of green, yellow and dark blue ribbon worn on the shoulder straps, a Canadian Maple Leaf Battle Honour badge on the sleeves, the ribbon of the French Croix de Guerre worn below the Maple Leaf, and a Tank Battle Honour badge. As the TA is only issued combat dress only the Maple Leaf is now worn, as the Tactical Recognition Flash.

King George VI gave permission for officers of the Leeds Rifles to wear a cockade made from the ribbon of the Croix de Guerre on the left side of the Service Dress cap on ceremonial occasions. The medal had been presented by the President of France in honour of the gallantry of 8th Battalion The West Yorkshire Regiment at Bois de Petit Champ and Bligny between 20 and 30 July 1918.

3

4

5

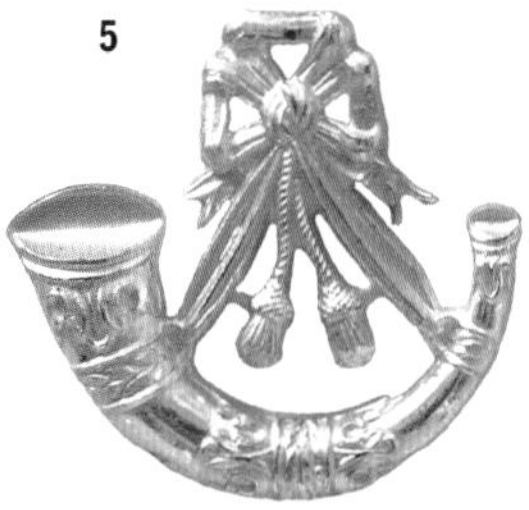

6

The Leeds Rifles was formed as the 11th Yorkshire West Riding Rifle Volunteer Corps in 1859, becoming the 3rd Volunteer Battalion, The West Yorkshire Regiment in 1887. In 1938 it converted as 45th (7th Battalion, West Yorkshire Regiment) Battalion, Royal Tank Corps. In 1956 it converted back to the West Yorkshire Regiment, was re-titled The Leeds Rifles, The Prince of Wales's Own Regiment of Yorkshire in 1961, reducing to a company and finally to the Leeds Rifles Platoon, Imphal Company (PWO), The East and West Riding Regiment in 1999.

previous page

1 East and West Riding Regiment TRF 5 × 5 cm.
2 OCdt Ben Clare wearing Light Infantry uniform.
3 The Leeds Rifles officer's silver cap badge 3.5 × 5 cm and silver and gilt collar badges 2.75 × 2.5 cm.
4 The Leeds Rifles officer's Battle Honour badge 5 × 4.75 cm.
5 Officer's silver pouch badge 3.5 × 3.25 cm.

this page

6 Officer's silver shoulder belt plate 7.25 × 9.5 cm.
7 The Leeds Rifles TRF 5 × 3 cm.

7

The Royal Welsh Regiment

The Royal Welsh Regiment was formed in 1999 by the amalgamation of 3rd (Volunteer) Battalion The Royal Welch Fusiliers and 3rd (Volunteer) Battalion The Royal Regiment of Wales

The Royal Welsh Regiment, or RWR, companies wear the cap badges of their affiliated regiments; The Royal Regiment of Wales and The Royal Welsh Fusiliers. Number 2 Dress is rarely worn but if required collar badges of the former regiments are also worn.

A regimental Tactical Recognition Flash, or TRF, was adopted in 1999.

1

2

3

4

1 OCdt Kevin Ferguson wearing his RWF beret and RWR TRF.
2 RWR TRF 6 × 6.25 cm.
3 RWR Second Lieutenant's rank slide.
4 OCdt Graham Parkhouse wearing RRW badges.

The Regimental Band of The Royal Welsh Regiment
Band Catrodol y Gatrawd Frenhinol Gymreig

The Royal Welsh Regiment has a Band, a Corps of Drums and a regimental choir.

1

2

3

Acknowledgement
WO2 Terry Young.

1 Goat Majors Sgt David Joseph BEM with Shenkin and Kevin Burke with Billy.
2 WO2 (BSM) Tim Baldwin wearing Full Dress.
3 WO1 (BM) Philip Coomer wearing Full Dress.

The Royal Irish Rangers

The Royal Irish Rangers was formed in 1993 as a TA battalion of The Royal Irish Regiment by the amalgamation of 4th Battalion and 5th Battalion, The Royal Irish Rangers.

The Royal Irish Rangers wears the cap badge of the former Royal Irish Rangers with the green hackle. The collar badges are the same as are worn by The Royal Irish Regiment except on Mess Dress where Royal Irish Rangers badges are worn.

1

2

3

4

5

6

7

previous page

1 Shoulder title 6.75 × 2.5 cm.

2 Royal Irish Ranger.

3 The Royal Irish Rangers anodised aluminium cap badge 3.5 × 5 cm and collar badges 2.25 × 2 cm.

4 Officer's silver and gilt cap badge 3.5 × 5 cm and silver collar badges 2 × 2 cm.

this page

5 Piper's bright metal cap badge 5.5 × 8 cm.

6 Lt Col Johnny Rollins wearing the Royal Irish Rangers badge and hackle in the caubeen.

7 Royal Irish Rangers officer's Mess Dress wire-embroidered collar badges 3.5 × 4 cm

Acknowledgement Capt Mark Hudson

51st Highland Regiment

The 51st Highland Regiment was formed in 1999 by the amalgamation of 3rd (V) Battalion, The Black Watch, 3rd (V) Battalion of The Highlanders and 7th/8th (V) Battalion The Argyll and Sutherland Highlanders, all of which were renamed in 1995 from battalions of the 51st Highland Volunteers, which had been formed in 1967. The name commemorated the 51st Highland Division, which fought during the First and Second World Wars.

51st Highland Regiment companies wear the cap badges of their affiliated regiments; The Black Watch, The Highlanders and The Argyll and Sutherland Highlanders. The Highlanders style of Tam o'Shanter has been adopted as the regimental pattern.

1

3

2

1 Sgt Wayne Young, LCpl Craig Frater and Pte Kevin Couper displaying the three regimental badges worn by soldiers of the 51st Highland Regiment.

2 Shoulder title.

3 OCdt Roger MacKay wearing his Highlanders Tam o'Shanter and the badge of the 51 (Scottish) Brigade on his left sleeve.

Acknowledgement WO1 (RSM) A Stewart

4th Volunteer Battalion The Parachute Regiment

4 PARA was originally formed in 1942 being re-designated the 1st Battalion in 1948. 4 PARA was re-formed by the amalgamation of the 12th/13th Yorkshire and Lancashire Battalion with the 17th (9DLI) Battalion in 1967. 15th (Scottish Volunteer) Battalion was reduced to 15 Coy 4 PARA in 1993 and 10th (City of London) Battalion became 10 Coy 4 PARA in 1999.

1

2

1 Major Ian Channon 4 PARA (V), wearing the battalion's black DZ flash on his right sleeve.
2 4 PARA (V) black DZ flash 7 × 7 cm.

Special Air Service Regiment

The TA SAS was formed in 1947 when The Artists Rifles, part of The London Regiment, was transferred to the Army Air Corps as 21 Special Air Service Regiment (The Artists' Rifles).

There is a sealed pattern anodised aluminium cap badge authorised for 21 and 23 SAS, and in 2003 101 were issued although the Territorial Army soldiers wear the SAS cloth beret badge. An issue of cloth badges to 23 SAS in 2002 is slightly larger than the sealed pattern and has faults in the embroidery to the side and below the left wing. A private purchase order by the regiment was produced with the same faults.

The issue rank slide for regular soldiers is embroidered SAS in black; that for Territorial Army soldiers is embroidered S.A.S., with punctuation between the letters.

The Regiment's mystique has led to any number of unofficial or downright spurious badges being produced and traded. With the exception of the anodized aluminium cap badge and rank slide with punctuation TA SAS badges are officially no different to those available to regular soldiers. Other badges are unofficial.

1

2

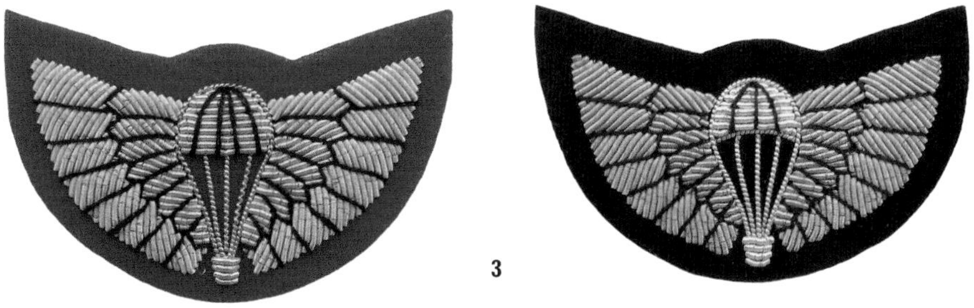

3

4

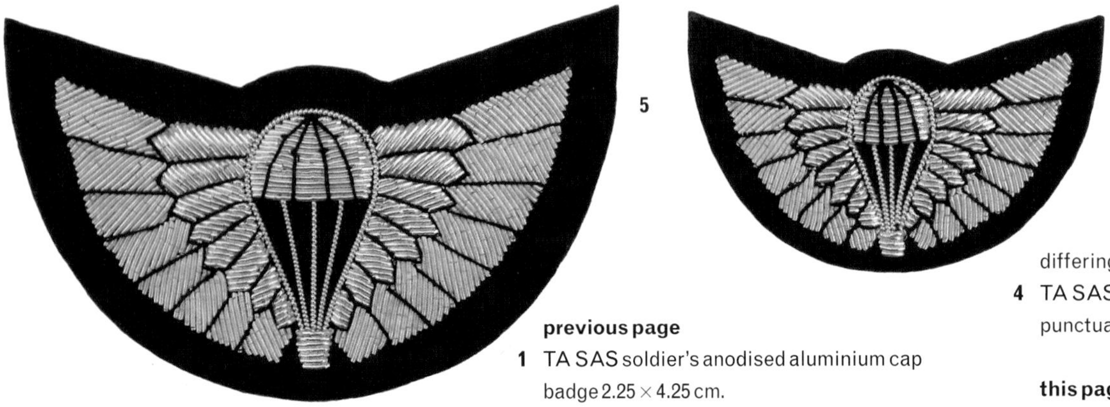

5

previous page

1 TA SAS soldier's anodised aluminium cap badge 2.25 × 4.25 cm.

2 23 SAS badly made but official soldier's beret badge 4.5 × 6 cm.

3 Mess Dress wings made for 23 SAS 5.5 × 3.5 cm differing from those of 22 SAS.

4 TA SAS corporal's rank slide identified by the punctuation between the letters.

this page

5 Unofficial SAS parachute wings made for a TA Light Infantry soldier No1 Dress 9 × 5.5 cm and Mess Dress 6 × 3.5 cm.

Army Air Corps (Volunteers)

AAC Volunteers wear the same badges as the Regular Army.

658 *Squadron AAC(V)*

The motto is *We see and destroy.* Originally an RAF Air OP squadron from 1943–1946, its badge represents the eagle which controls the accuracy required to hit the Gold at the centre of the target.

666 *Squadron AAC(V)*

The motto is *We ascend to observe.* 666 Squadron was formed as an RAF Air OP squadron with Canadian troops to support 1st Canadian Army in 1945 and disbanded in 1946. Reformed as a Royal Auxiliary Air Force squadron in 1949 and allocated to the AAC in 1957. The badge represents the Squadron's post-war role as Scottish Command's Auxiliary Air OP Squadron.

1

2

3

4

5

6

7

8

opposite page

1 7 Regiment AAC TRF 7 × 7 cm.
2 7 Regiment AAC new TRF 7 × 7 cm.
3 658 Squadron AAC(V) 9.5 × 11.5 cm.
4 666 Squadron AAC(V) 9.5 × 11.5 cm.

this page

5 666 Squadron unofficial arm badge 10 cm worn on the right sleeve.
6 3 Flight AAC arm badge 10 × 10 cm.
7 6 Flight AAC arm badge 10 × 10 cm.
8 Sgt Stew Milner wearing the 658 Squadron badge and Capt Tony Taylor-Roberts wearing the 666 Squadron badge.

Royal Army Chaplains' Department

TA RAChD chaplains wear the same badges as the Regular Army the exception being officiating chaplains to the TA who wear a T on the Preaching Scarf.

RAChD Preaching Scarf badge worn by TA officiating chaplains 2.5 × 2.5 cm.

Royal Logistic Corps (Volunteers)

The Royal Logistic Corps is the newest and largest Corps in the British Army, accounting for a third of all Specialist Volunteers. RLC Volunteers wear the same badges as the Regular Army except for special embellishments which are authorised to perpetuate either Battle Honours or historical antecedents.

RLC volunteer Ammunition Technicians, or AT, and Ammunition Technical Officers, or ATO, wear slightly different badges to those awarded to the Regular Army. The AT badges are issued whilst there are so few TA ATO that they are required to make their own badges by stitching a V onto Regular Army badges.

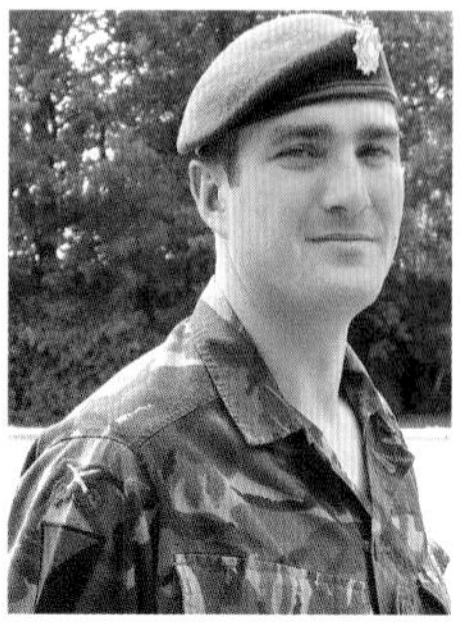
1

2

3

151 (Greater London) Logistic Support Regiment

151 Logistic Support Regiment's badge is based on the red oval badge of the 44th (Home Counties) Division, worn from 1940 to 1943. For many years it has been believed that the oval design represented the Kensington Oval cricket ground. Originally a white oval, the colour was changed to red after 44th Division was 'blooded' in France in 1940.

A contemporary sign writer said that when he painted the regimental signs during the Second World War the trident was made up of two numbers 4 reversed and conjoined. Officially the trident represented 'the united, sharp-ended brigades supported by the remainder and symbolising the maritime associations of the Division'.

Recent research indicates that the oval design was probably based on the shape of a 'Butter Osborne' biscuit, a play on words on the name of the General Officer Commanding at the time, Major General EA Osborne.

4

5

6

7

224 (Pembrook Yeomanry) Transport Squadron 157 (Wales and Midland) Logistic Support Regiment

The squadron was formed in 1969 with A Troop, representing the disbanded Pembrook Yeomanry, authorised to wear the Yeomanry collar badges. The privilege was extended to the whole squadron in 1987. The Commanding Officer 157 Logistic Support Regiment also wears the badges. Soldiers wear anodised aluminium collar badges, officers, silver gilt badges, and wire-embroidered badges on Mess Dress.

'Fishguard' was the first battle honour to be awarded to a volunteer unit, and the only one granted for service in the British Isles. In 1797 the Directory, the French revolutionary government, hoped that the English rural population would rebel if given armed support. A force of 1,400 mostly returned prisoners of war who had an understanding of English and volunteers from French prisons embarked on four transports with the intention of destroying Bristol but the fleet was blown off course and the troops landed off Carreg Wasted Point in Cardigan Bay. A Portuguese merchantman loaded with wine had been blown ashore and the cargo kept the invaders occupied. As a result they only managed to loot a church. After two days ashore the invading republican 'Legion Noir' surrendered to a small British force, including the Castlemartin Troop of the Pembrook Yeomanry which, raised in 1794, was the only effective troop of the Pembroke Yeomanry at the time.

In 1853 Queen Victoria granted the battle honour 'Fishguard' to the Pembrook Yeomanry.

8

158 (Royal Anglian) Transport Regiment

158 (R ANGLIAN) Transport Regiment was formed in 1996 from the 5th Battalion, The Royal Anglian Regiment, which had been formed from elements of the 5th, 6th and 7th Battalions. Because of the very strong regimental antecedents 158 Transport Regiment was allowed to retain the Royal Anglian title, beret and Minden Flash.

9

10

11

opposite page

1 OCdt James Martin a TA air despatcher.

2 TA ATO badge 3 × 4 cm.

3 TA Ammunition Technician badge 4 × 5 cm.

4 151 Logistic Support Regiment arm badge introduced in 1994.

5 Subdued arm badge, introduced in 1995 6 × 5 cm.

6 LCpl Neil McCrimmon AGC wearing the 151 Logistic Support Regiment arm badge.

7 WO1 (RSM) Sandra Robson MBE wearing the 151 Logistic Support Regiment arm badge.

this page

8 224 (Pembrook Yeomanry) Transport Squadron soldier's anodised aluminium collar badges 3 × 3.25 cm.

9 158 Transport Regiment arm badge 4.5 × 2 cm.

10 Cpl David Linley wearing the Royal Anglian beret with RLC cap badge. On his sleeve is the 49 (Eastern) Brigade 'Polar Bear' badge.

11 Major John Whatley wearing the Royal Anglian beret and Minden Flash arm badge with the RLC wire-embroidered cap badge

160 Transport Regiment RLC

The Pheonix was chosen as the Regiment's identification badge in 1998 not only because the bird symbolised the rebirth of the regiment but also because it forms part of the Arms of the Worshipful Company of Fuellers, to which the regiment is affiliated as a result of their role in transporting bulk fuel. A later version of the badge was circular. As with other 'regimental' badges it was to be replaced by the RLC TRF by April 2005.

1

2

168 Pioneer Regiment

The colours of the former Royal Pioneer Corps are worn on the left sleeve. As with other 'regimental' badges it was to be replaced by the RLC TRF by April 2005.

3

4

Scottish Transport Regiment

The Scottish Transport Regiment RLC (V) was formed in 1993 by the amalgamation of the 153 (Highland) Regiment RCT (V) and 154 (Lowland) Regiment RCT (V) but traces its history to the Highland Division Transport and Supply Company Army Service Corps, raised in 1908.

The Regiment wears the Red MacDuff tartan patch behind the RLC badge on berets and as a stable belt by officers and Warrant Officers. In the early 1930s 51 Highland Div RASC TA was in direct competition for recruits with the 6th/7th Battalion The Black Watch. The RASC unit needed a Scottish identity. The Adjutant, Captain NG Ducket suggested forming a Pipe Band. Application was made through the family of Duke of Connaught, Colonel-in-Chief RASC for a Tartan, and the Red MacDuff was authorised. In 1978 153 Transport Regiment RCT (V) was given permission to wear the Tartan as a badge backing. The authority has been passed to The Scottish Transport Regiment.

125 (Ration) Squadron has the authority to wear the Lamont Tartan patch behind the RLC cap badge. The historical background is lost but authority was given before the Squadron became part of the Regiment in 1999.

5

6

7

275 *Railway Squadron*

The Royal Corps of Transport took responsibility for military railways in 1965. 275 Railway Squadron was formed in 1967 from individual members of the Strategic Reserve and remnants of former volunteer units. Railway track remained a Royal Engineers responsibility. As with other 'regimental' badges the squadron badge was to be replaced by the RLC TRF by April 2005.

8

Catering Support Regiment

The Catering Support Regiment was formed in 1999 when the TA 'Pool of Chefs' was regimented. The regiment consists of 450 TA chefs recruited principally from the hospitality industry across the country. In order to provide a corporate identity the 'flaming cauldron' emblem, which had been the centrepiece of the Army Catering Corps badge from 1941 until the formation of the RLC in 1993, was issued as a cloth arm badge. As with other 'regimental' badges it was to be replaced by the RLC TRF by April 2005.

9

opposite page

1 LCpl Tony Duprose wearing the 160 Transport Regiment second pattern arm badge.
2 160 Transport Regiment arm badge 7 × 7 cm, now obsolete.
3 168 Pioneer Regiment arm badge introduced in 1994 6 × 2.25 cm, now obsolete.
4 168 Pioneer Regiment arm badge introduced in 2002 when TA soldiers began deploying regularly with regular troops 5.25 × 2.25 cm.
5 Pte Murray Kerr wearing the Scottish Transport Regiment Red MacDuff cap badge backing.
6 WO2 Sammy Wilson wearing Red MacDuff Tartan cap badge backing and stable belt.
7 Captain Tony McGuinness wearing Lamont Tartan cap badge backing and stable belt.

this page

8 275 Railway Squadron arm badge 5 × 5 cm.
9 Catering Support Regiment arm badge worn 1999–2005 5 × 6.25 cm.

Acknowledgement
Major Alvin Ward, Capt Claude Preira MBE and Jack Tarr, WO1 (RSM) AJ Fortuin and AW Honeyman

North Irish Territorial Army Band

The North Irish Territorial Army Band is the only unit to wear the Territorial Army badge. Formed as the Band of the 6th Battalion, The Royal Ulster Rifles in 1960, it was re-titled as The Northern Irish Territorial Army Staff Band in 1967. The Band was reorganised as a non-Staff band after 1988 but continues to use up stocks of the original white metal cap and cloth beret badges with the title Northern Irish Staff Band. There is an aspiration to apply for new badges and buttons in 2005.

1

2

3

4

5

previous page

1 Northern Irish Territorial Band white metal cap badge 3.25 × 4.75 cm and wire-embroidered collar badges 2.5 × 3.5 cm.

2 NITA Band button.

this page

3 Musician's Pouch badge, the same design as the helmet plate 9 × 11 cm.

4 North Irish TA Band uniforms based on those of the RLC. Photograph *NITA Band*

5 Cloth beret badge 4 × 5.75 cm.

Acknowledgement WO1 (BM) Chris Attrill

Royal Army Medical Corps (Volunteers)

RAMC Volunteers wear the same badges as the Regular Army except for special embellishments which are authorised to perpetuate either Battle Honours or historical antecedents.

B (220 1st Home Counties) Medical Squadron

The Volunteer Medical Staff Corps 5th Division was formed in 1886, being granted the title 1st Home Counties in 1908. A gilding metal shoulder title HOME COUNTIES was worn until the First World War. On the unit's 75th anniversary in 1962 the woven title, yellow letters representing the gilding metal title, on a blue background representing the original uniform colour, was authorised as a Special Embellishment.

1

205 *(Scottish) Field Hospital*

205 (Scottish) Field Hospital wear a tartan backing to the cap badge on the beret. The Graham of Montrose tartan was first worn by the Pipe Band 2nd Scottish General Hospital in 1919, commanded by Colonel David Graham OBE TD. In 1975 the tartan was adopted by the successor unit 205 (Scottish) General Hospital and a 2 × 2 inch square patch was approved as the beret badge backing in 1997.

2

3

4

207 *(Manchester) Field Hospital*

The 4th Division Volunteer Medical Staff Corps was formed in 1887 in Manchester from a Volunteer Medical Association, which had been formed by professors and lecturers at Owens College. In 1953, the unit now re-titled 7th (Manchester) General Hospital (TA) was granted the Eagle from the City Arms to be worn on the right sleeve of Number 2 Dress. The honour passed to 207 (Manchester) Field Hospital.

5

225 *(Scottish) Field Ambulance*

225 Field Ambulance is the only RAMC unit to wear theTam o'shanter. The unit was formed from the Black Watch in 1904 and wore that tartan. Following the First World War a Pipe Band was reformed by Colonel WA Robertson. It was disbanded in 1963 although when Lieutenant Colonel JSG Blair gained permission for the Tam o'Shanter in 1973 the Robertson tartan was selected as the badge backing.

6

opposite page

1 220 (1st Home Counties) Medical Squadron (Volunteers) cloth arm badge 10.75 × 2.5 cm.

this page

2 Pte John Bell wearing the Graham of Montrose beret badge backing.
3 205 (Scottish) Field Hospital badge backing.
4 Pte Heather MacDonald and Miki Canham 205 Scottish Field Hospital.
5 207 (Manchester) Field Hospital arm badge 5.5 × 5 cm.
6 225 Field Ambulance badge backing.

243 *(The Wessex) Field Hospital (Volunteers)*

243 Field Hospital wears the ribbon of the Croix de Guerre on the upper left sleeve of Number 2 Dress (see The Devonshire and Dorset Regiment p.142). The Croix de Guerre with Silver Gilt Star was awarded to 24th (Wessex) Field Ambulance RAMC, which was re-titled 128 (Wessex) Field Ambulance, then 211 (Wessex) Casualty Clearing Station in 1967, and finally 243 (The Wessex) Field Hospital in 1996.

From the 22nd to the 25th October, 1918, in a town fiercely bombarded by the enemy, the entire staff of the above medical unit, under the command of Lieutenant Colonel R Burgess, with incomparable devotion, went out, day and night, to the rescue of wounded civilians in various parts of the town; dressed their wounds and ministered to their wants before sending them behind the lines. Under dangerous conditions, operated in urgent cases and achieved the evacuation of 2,000 wounded, sick or disabled, after having administered first aid.

7

256 *Field Hospital*

217 (London) General Hospital formed a link with the Worshipful Societies of Apothecaries in 1970 and permission was granted for the unit to wear a *Rhynoceros Proper*. This device is taken from the Apothecaries Crest and dates to a description by Clarence King of Arms in 1634. The beast was drawn by Durer from a second-hand description and has a second forward curving horn behind the ears.

In 1999, 256 Field Hospital succeeded 217 General Hospital and adopted the London badge (see *The London Regiment* p. 396).

8

257 *Field Hospital*

9

10

11

257 Field Hospital existed from 1967 to 1995 and had a set of attractive arm badges made which are occasionally still worn by former members of the unit.

7 Pte Kristina Turner, 243 Field Hospital wearing the 2 Medical Brigade badge below the Union Flag.

8 217 Field Hospital rhinoceros arm badge 5 × 4.5 cm.

9 257 Field Hospital Mess Dress arm badge.

10 257 Field Hospital No2 Dress arm badge.

11 257 Field Hospital No1 Dress arm badge.

Acknowledgement
Capt Pete Starling, WO1 (RSM) JA A' Lee and AIJ Herrod, SSgt PG Darlington and Mr Graham Patterson

Royal Electrical and Mechanical Engineers (Volunteers)

REME Volunteers wear the same badges as the Regular Army except for the special embellishments which are authorised to perpetuate the historical antecedents of 102 Battalion. The Volunteer designation was removed from battalion titles in 2003.

102 Battalion REME

102 Battalion REME is the successor to REME units which have been associated with 'The Tynes' since 1947. The Tynes badge is worn on the left arm of Mess Dress by officers and senior non-commissioned officers in Battalion Headquarters, 124 and 186 (Tyne Electrical Engineers) Workshop Companies. Three officers have been promoted to the Staff from 102 Battalion and wear the wire-embroidered Tyne Engineers Mess Dress arm badge on a red backing to match the red Staff mess jacket.

Tyne Electrical Engineers Mess Dress arm badge 4 × 3.75 cm.

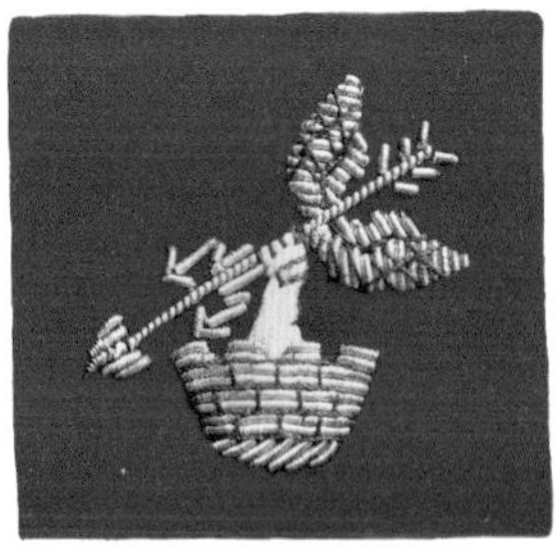

Staff Mess Dress arm badge 4 × 3.75 cm.

Tyne Electrical Engineers Pipe Band

In 1902 the Tyne Division Submarine Miners recruited a small Pipe Band which served until 1919. The Pipes reformed in 1932 and in 1957 transferred to the 105 Corps Engineer Regiment where they were known as The Tynes. In 1967 The Tynes transferred to the new 72 (Tyne Electrical Engineers) Engineer Regiment RE(V) which in 1999 was reduced to a squadron in 71 Engineer Regiment RE(V). The regiment already had a Pipe Band and The Tynes pipers, searching for a new home, were transferred to 102 Battalion REME(V).

1

2

3

4

5

Acknowledgement
Major Eric Ingram and Pipe Sergeant Arthur Middleton

previous page

1 Tyne Electrical Engineers Pipe Band, PMaj David Bark, Sgt David Harper, Mr Derek Elliott, LCpl Bryan Robinson, Cfn Adrian Brown, Mr Marty Levely and Sgt Arthur Middleton.

this page

2 REME hackle worn by the Tyne Electrical Engineers pipers 8 × 11 cm.
3 Tyne Electrical Engineers anodised aluminium cap badge and cross belt badge 5.75 × 6.5 cm
4 Cpl Gary Dodd wearing the pre-1999 Glengarry badge with the Argyle jacket worn at less formal occasions.
5 Pipe Major Dave Bark.

Small Arms School Corps

SASC Volunteers wear the same badges as the Regular Army.

WO2 Gary Fox a TA SASC soldier.

Intelligence Corps

Intelligence Corps Volunteers wear the same badges as the Regular Army.

OCdt Tom O'Sullivan a TA Intelligence Corps soldier.

Queen Alexandra's Royal Army Nursing Corps

The TA Medical Services play an essential part in supporting the British Army, providing 70% of its healthcare capability. QARANC Volunteers wear the same badges as the Regular Army

Lt Zayne Crow a QARANC TA officer. Uniform and insignia are the same as worn by regular officers.

The Royal Gibraltar Regiment

The Royal Gibraltar Regiment was re-titled in 1999 from The Gibraltar Regiment, which had been placed on the British establishment on the withdrawal of the British battalion from the Rock in 1991. It had originally been raised in 1939 as the Gibraltar Defence Force.

1

2

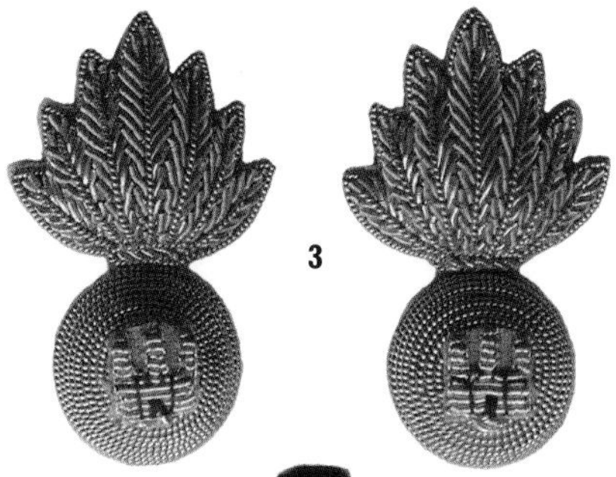

3

The Royal Gibraltar Regiment cap badge represents a shield bearing the Key and Castle superimposed on a decorative backing depicting the blue sky of the Mediterranean together with its sea.

The first version of The Royal Gibraltar Regiment's badge was worn by the Gibraltar Volunteer Corps from 1915 to 1920, and modified for the Gibraltar Defence Force from 1939 to 1958. The present badge was adopted in 1960.

The Royal Gibraltar Regiment wears the Key from the Arms of Gibraltar, where it represents the 'key to the Mediterranean', as an arm badge and Tactical Recognition Flash, or TRF. The Key badge was first worn during the Second World War by Gunners from the Gibraltar Defence Force together with the letters AA on either side of the Key indicating their role as anti-aircraft artillery. At the same time the Fortress Engineers from the Royal Engineers wore the Key on a dark blue diamond and Royal Artillery the Key on an upright blue and red diagonal. The Key badge was retained after the War until the mid-1960s when Number 2 Dress replaced Battle Dress although it continued to be worn by the staff of Fortress Headquarters. The Key badge in its present form was introduced in 1992. The yellow Key is copied from the Gibraltar flag and the red background represents the Infantry.

4

5

The Ceremony of the Keys has been carried out daily since 1783. Gibraltar was captured from Spain in 1704, and from 1779 to 1783 Spain and France unsuccessfully besieged The Rock. General Sir George Elliott remained concerned that a coup de main could seize one of the three gates and ordered them all locked each evening. He personally carried the keys, handing them to the Port Sergeant to lock the gates with an escort and drummers. Since 1927 a ceremonial parade has been conducted daily.

6

7

8

9

10

11

12

13

previous page

1 The Royal Gibraltar Regiment soldier's anodised aluminium cap badge 3.25 × 4.25 cm and collar badges 2.75 × 4.25 cm.
2 Royal Gibraltar Regiment button.
3 The Royal Gibraltar Regiment officer's wire-embroidered Mess Dress collar badges 2.75 × 4.25 cm.
4 Sgt David Porro wearing Combat Dress.
5 Officer's beret badge 4.5 × 5.75 cm.

opposite page

6 The Royal Gibraltar Regiment officer's silver and gilt cap and collar badges.
7 Lance corporal rank slide.
8 Pte Julian Mauro and Matthew Holgado wearing Full Dress.
9 Arm badge worn in most orders of dress 3.5 × 7.25cm.
10 TRF 3.5 × 7.25cm.
11 Officer's No1 Dress and Mess Dress wire-embroidered arm badge 3.25 × 6 cm.
12 The Royal Gibraltar Regiment officer and soldier's helmet plates, both 9 × 11 cm.

this page

13 The Royal Gibraltar Regiment waist belt clasp 7.25 × 5.75 cm.

The Royal Gibraltar Regiment Band

Pte Brian Buckley, Sgt Anselmo Ochello and LCpl Mark Alcantara wearing Winter Guard Order.

The Royal Gibraltar Regiment Band led by Drum Major Dylan Bocarisa.

Acknowledgement
Maj Wilfred Jurado and CSgt Danny Rowbottom

The Bermuda Regiment

The Bermuda Regiment was formed in 1965 from the Bermuda Volunteer Rifle Corps which had been raised in 1895, and the Bermuda Militia Artillery, raised in 1902. Two contingents of the Bermuda Rifles served with the 1st Battalion The Lincolnshire Regiment and the Artillery served as the Bermuda Battery, Royal Garrison Artillery during the First World War.

The Bermuda Regiment cap badge, introduced in 1965, combined the Maltese Cross and laurel wreath of the Bermuda Rifles with the Bermuda Militia Artillery gun badge. The collar badges reflect the Lion in the Arms of Bermuda.

As a result of its Service with the Royal Lincolnshire Regiment during both World Wars The Bermuda Regiment is now affiliated to The Royal Anglian Regiment.

1

2

3

4

5

6

7

8

9

1 The Bermuda Regiment bi-metal cap badge 4 × 4.5 cm and gilt collar badges 1.75 × 3.5 cm.
2 Anodised aluminium shoulder title 4.5 × 1.5 cm.
3 The Bermuda Regiment button.
4 OCdt Noel Pearman wearing No 2 Dress.
5 CSgts Craig Booth and Paul Rodrigues wearing Lightweight Combat Dress.
6 The Bermuda Regiment TRF 7.5 × 5.5 cm.
7 OCdt Clifford Powell wearing the officer's small beret badge
8 Officer's beret badge 2.75 × 3.5 cm.
9 Bermuda Regiment waist belt clasp 9.25 × 5.5 cm.

Officer Training Corps

The Officer Training Corps trace their origins to the volunteer movement of 1859. The first to be formed was the 1st Oxfordshire (Oxford University) Rifle Volunteer Corps in 1859, followed by the 3rd Cambridgeshire (Cambridge University) Rifle Volunteer Corps in 1860. Numerous schools and colleges also formed their own cadet corps.

The critical shortage of officers during the South Africa War, 1899–1902, led to the establishment of Officer Training Corps as part of the reform of the Army by Lord Haldane in 1908. The aim was the provision of as many officers as possible for the Special Reserve and Territorial Forces. The Officer Training Corps were organised into a Senior Division consisting of University contingents and the Junior Division made up of the college and school contingents. In 1940 the Senior Division became the University Training Corps, the title reverting to Officer Training Corps in 1955. The Junior Division joined contingents from the other services in 1948 to form the Combined Cadet Force. There are now nineteen Officer Training Corps, or OTC, established under a charter agreed between the Army and the Military Education Committees of the universities.

The OTC develop the leadership potential of selected university students through enjoyable and challenging training, and social activities in order to communicate the values, ethos and career opportunities of the British Army.

Undergraduates are ranked as Officer Cadets, wear special appointment badges on their rank slides and are paid Territorial Army rates.

Officer Training Corps Rank and Appointment Badges

As a general rule the rank badges indicate:
1 Senior Under Officer **2** Junior Under Officer **3** Passed Military Training Qualification 2, MTQ2 **4** Passed Military Training Qualification 1, MTQ1.

Aberdeen Universities Officer Training Corps

Aberdeen University OTC traces its history to the 1st Aberdeen Artillery Volunteers raised in 1885 by the Professor of Physiology, Captain William Stirling. In 1897 University Company was raised for 1st Volunteer Battalion The Gordon Highlanders. The OTC was formed in 1908 and now serves Aberdeen and Robert Gordons Universities.

The Aberdeen Universities Officer Training Corps, or OTC, cap badge was introduced in 1935 and approved in 1951 to replace the original badge based on the Arms of Aberdeen University. The Boar's Head is taken from the crest of Bishop Elphinstone, the founder of the university. The motto translates, as *I shall not be ashamed.*

The collar badges were replaced during 2004 by officer cadets' white gorgets.

1

2

3

4

5

6

7

1 Aberdeen UOTC aluminium Glengarry badge 7 × 5.5 cm, worn on a square of Gordon's tartan, and obsolete aluminium anodised collar badges 2.75 × 2 cm.
2 Senior Under Officer's rank slide.
3 Aberdeen UOTC button.
4 Gordon Highlanders sporran badge 3 × 4.25 cm worn by Aberdeen UOTC.
5 OCdts Chris Sylvan and Catherine Porterfield showing the difference between the No 2 Dress for males and females
6 OCdt Chris Sheldon wearing The Highlanders No2 Dress kilt and sporran.
7 Aberdeen Universities OTC Honorary Colonel, Brigadier Charles Grant OBE speaking to Pipe Major Mike Laing, with SUO Gail Fisher in the background.

Acknowledgement
WO1 (RSM) MJ White and WO2 (RQMS) LJ Thomson

Birmingham University Officer Training Corps

The Birmingham University OTC cap badge has remained unaltered in design, with the exception of the wording on the scrolls, since it was introduced. The ornamental escutcheon design bears the original Arms of the university. The university has redesigned its Arms but the OTC decided to retain its badges unaltered. The title on the cap badge is OTC whilst that on the collar badges is TC.

The OTC serves the Universities of Birmingham, Aston, Wolverhampton, Keele, Coventry, Warwick, Central England and Stafford.

William Slim, although not an undergraduate, joined Birmingham University OTC in 1912 and rose to the rank of lance corporal. In August 1914 he was commissioned into The Warwickshire Regiment. In 1948 he was appointed Chief of the Imperial General Staff and in 1949 promoted Field Marshal.

1

2

3

4

1. Birmingham UOTC cadet's anodised aluminium cap badge 4 × 4 cm and gilding metal collar badges 2.75 × 2.75 cm.
2. Officer's wire-embroidered beret badge 4 × 4 cm.
3. Second Lieutenant and Senior Under Officer's rank slides. All rank slides are woven with the title Birmingham UOTC except for those for Senior and Junior Under Officers, which have the abbreviated BUOTC.
4. OCdts Oliver Brindle and Thomas Clarke wearing No2 Dress.

Acknowledgement
WO1 (RSM) GJ Low and Mr Gary Evans

Bristol University Officer Training Corps

The Bristol University OTC originally had title scrolls below the shield but the present design still based on the Arms of the university has been worn for many years. Second year officer cadets, those who have passed MTQ1, may wear a woven cloth beret badge.

The OTC serves Bristol and Bath Universities and the University of the West of England.

1

2

3

1 Bristol UOTC anodised aluminium cap badge 4 × 4.5 cm. Officer's wire-embroidered beret badge 3.5 × 4 cm. Second Year Officer Cadet's woven beret badge 4.5 × 5 cm.
2 Junior Under Officer's rank slide.
3 OCdt Rob Cook and Rachel Nelson, with a poppy, wearing the cadets' anodised aluminium cap badge, and JUO Charlie Ring wearing the cloth badge.

Cambridge University Officer Training Corps

Cambridge University OTC use the Arms of Cambridge University granted in 1573 as its badge. Before the Second World War different collar badges were worn by each of the five sections, Cavalry, Artillery, Engineers, Signals and Infantry.

The Cambridge University OTC cap badge has not changed in design, with the exception of the wording on the scrolls and the Crown, since it was introduced. The present cap badge has remained unaltered since about 1955 except that from about 1958 it was produced in anodised aluminium.

There was a volunteer unit formed by Cambridge University for local defence from 1803 to 1808. The Officer Training Corps dates from the formation of the Cambridge University Rifle Volunteer Corps. The Volunteers had themselves emerged from the Cambridge University and Town Rifle Club in 1860; separating in order to form a financially independent corps of University members only, organised on military lines. A detachment served during the South Africa War with The Suffolk Regiment, gaining the Battle Honour *South Africa 1900–1901*. The OTC serves the University of Cambridge, Anglia Polytechnic University and the University of East Anglia.

3

1

2

4

5

6

7

opposite page

1 Cambridge University OTC anodised aluminium cap badge 3.5 × 4.5 cm and collar badges 2.75 × 3.5 cm.

2 No2 Dress cloth shoulder title 11 × 4 cm.

3 CUOTC button.

this page

4 Officer's wire-embroidered beret badge 4 × 5.25 cm.

5 Second Lieutenant's rank slide.

6 OCdts Jamie Hull and John Bethell wearing No2 Dress.

7 OCdts Doug Brain, Matthew Neave and Amber Roach wearing No2 Dress.

Acknowledgement
Captain Matt Heath and WO2 (SSM) CD Parkes

East Midlands Universities Officer Training Corps

The East Midlands Universities OTC badge is based on the design of the former badge of The Sherwood Foresters (Nottinghamshire and Derbyshire Regiment). Originally formed as the University College Nottingham OTC, there has always been a close connection between The Sherwood Foresters and the OTC and during the First World War 238 students from the OTC were commissioned into the regiment. The OTC was renamed the East Midlands Universities OTC in 1966.

The Maltese Cross, oak wreath, and stag on the cap badge are from the 95th Foot which amalgamated with the 45th Foot and the county militias in 1881. The Nottinghamshire Militia also had a wreath in their badge in allusion to Sherwood Forest, and two Royal Stags form the supporters to the Arms of the City of Nottingham. The Maltese Cross is said to have been adopted because many of those recruited into the 95th Foot on formation in 1823 had served in a former 95th Foot which became the Rifle Brigade in 1816 and had the same Cross as its badge.

The OTC serves the Universities of Nottingham, Leicester, Derby, Lincoln, and Loughborough University of Technology, Nottingham Trent University and De Montford University.

1

2

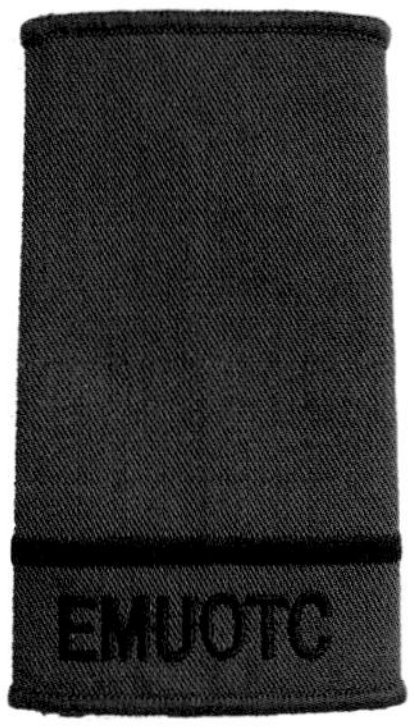

3

4

1 Officers' wire-embroidered beret badge 5 × 5.25 cm.

2 East Midlands UOTC anodised aluminium cap badge 4.75 × 4.5 cm.

3 First year cadet's rank slide.

4 OCdts Tom Mobbs, Giles Ernsting and Warren Allison wearing No2 Dress.

Acknowledgement WO1 (RSM) D Watts

City of Edinburgh Universities Officer Training Corps

The City of Edinburgh Universities OTC was originally Edinburgh University OTC and wore a shield bearing the Arms of the university as its badge. The badge was altered to the present design on the expansion of the OTC.

No 4 (University) Company Edinburgh Rifle Volunteers was formed in 1859, and Edinburgh University OTC formed in 1908. Renamed the Edinburgh and Heriot-Watt Universities OTC in 1966, and the City of Edinburgh Universities OTC when Napier gained university status in 1994.

1

2

3

4

5

6

7

1 The City of Edinburgh Universities Officer Training Corps anodised aluminium cap badge 5 × 5.25 cm and collar badges 2.75 × 2.75 cm.
2 City of Edinburgh UOTC button.
3 City of Edinburgh UOTC pipers, OCdt Andrew Hood, JUO Jaimie Baillie, 2Lt Marco Petrucci, OCdt Kirsty Mackintyre, JUO Mike Lawson, OCdts Kevin Masson, Ruaridh De Gruyther and Gregor Horn.
4 Junior Under Officer's rank slide.
5 OCdt Graham Brady wearing Number 2 Dress.
6 Piper's plaid brooch 9cm.
7 OCdts Gregor Horn and Kevin Masson, pipers with the City of Edinburgh Universities OTC.

Acknowledgement WO2 (CSM) Karen Smith

Exeter University Officer Training Corps

Exeter University OTC was raised in 1980 for the universities of Exeter and Plymouth. There had previously been an OTC at Exeter University until 1945.
The Exeter University OTC cap badge was introduced to replace The Wessex Regiment badge, which was worn from 1980 to 1982. The OTC badge design represents the castle from the Arms of Exeter and the Wessex Wyvern. The Wessex Regiment collar badges were retained.

1

2

3

4

5

1 Exeter University OTC officer cadet's anodised aluminium cap badge 4 × 4.5 cm and collar badges 2.5 × 2.5 cm.
2 Exeter UOTC button.
3 Officer's wire-embroidered beret badge 4.25 × 4.25 cm.
4 OCdts Rhianna Middleditch and John Santer wearing No 2 Dress.
5 Exeter UOTC officer cadet's rank slide.

Acknowledgement WO 2 (RQMS) AK Hincke

Glasgow and Strathclyde Universities Officer Training Corps

1

2

3

The Glasgow and Strathclyde Universities OTC badge was originally adopted by Glasgow University OTC. Slightly altered wording was adopted in 1951 and the present badge taken into use when the OTC included Strathclyde University. The design has St Mungo, or Kentigern, the patron Saint of Glasgow backed by St Andrew's Cross.

1 Glasgow and Strathclyde Universities OTC anodised aluminium cap badge 3.25 × 5 cm and collar badges 2.25 × 3.75 cm.
2 Junior Under Officer's rank slide.
3 OCdt Daniel Wessel wearing Combat Dress.

Acknowledgement WO1 (RSM) JA Piggott

Leeds University Officer Training Corps

Leeds University OTC was formed in 1909 and serves Leeds, Bradford, York and Hull Universities. The cap badge is a winged sphinx sejant. The issue anodised aluminium badge is only worn on the forage cap by cadets attending the commissioning course at the Royal Military Academy Sandhurst. A silver wire-embroidered beret badge is worn by officers and a gold wire-embroidered badge by officer cadets.

Unusually, Leeds has rank slides for the permanent staff as well as cadets.

2

3

4

1

1 The Leeds University OTC officer's silver wire-embroidered beret badge and officer cadet's gold wire-embroidered badge, both 4 × 4.5 cm.
2 The issue anodised aluminium badge 4 × 4.5 cm.
3 Leeds UOTC lieutenant colonel's rank slide.
4 3rd Year Officer Cadet's rank slide with three bars.

Liverpool University Officer Training Corps

The Liverpool University OTC wears the cap badge of The King's Regiment (Liverpool), which amalgamated with The Manchester Regiment in 1958. The badge is worn on a red backing to reflect its affiliation to The King's Regiment. In the past the OTC did not wear collar badges but now wears The King's Regiment collar badges.

Liverpool University serves the University of Liverpool, Lancaster University, Liverpool John Moores University, Hope College, University of Central Lancashire, Edge Hill University College, St. Martins College and Chester College.

1

2

3

4

5

opposite page

1 Liverpool University OTC anodised aluminium cap badge 4 × 4 cm and The King's Regiment collar badges.

2 OCdt Matthew Hammond. The practice of soldiers wearing metal rather than anodised aluminium cap badges is widespread throughout the Army and he wears a King's (Liverpool Regiment) cap badge from 1898–1926.

this page

3 Liverpool UOTC officer cadets rank slides for 1st year cadets, 2nd year cadets and 3rd year cadets not appointed as Under Officers.

4 Officer's wire-embroidered beret badge 5 × 4.75 cm.

5 OCdt Alison Sargeant wearing the anodised aluminium cap badge and Adam Stapley wearing the wire-embroidered beret badge.

Acknowledgement WO2 (RQMS) Billy Norris BEM

University of London Officer Training Corps

The first University of London OTC badge was designed by the adjutant, a Coldstream Guards officer who based the design on the Garter Star. The present design is based upon the Arms of London.

The University of London OTC was one the eight formed in 1908 with sections at Kensington, at London University, Kings and East London Colleges and St Bartholomew's and Guys Hospitals.

1

2

3

4

5

6

previous page

1 University of London officer cadet's anodised aluminium cap badge 3.75 × 4.5 cm and collar badges 2.75 × 3.5 cm based upon the arms of London University.
2 ULOTC button.
3 ULOTC officer's wire-embroidered beret badge 5 × 5.5 cm.
4 ULOTC third year officer cadet's rank slide.
5 OCdt Chris Excell wearing Combat Dress.

this page

6 OCdt Louise Moore Dutton wearing the cadet's cap badge, and Steve Carter, the Senior Under Officer, wearing the officer's wire-embroidered badge with Number 2 Dress.

Acknowledgement
Capt Andy Murray and WO1 (RSM) O'Grady

Manchester and Salford Universities Officer Training Corps

The Manchester and Salford Universities OTC uses a lion rampant, from the arms of Manchester University, as the badge. The badge is worn on the beret on a red backing to reflect its affiliation with The King's Regiment. The officer's wire-embroidered beret badge is padded.

Owens College Company was raised in 1898 at Victoria University of Manchester, transferring into the Officer Training Corps in 1908. Recruiting at the Royal College of Advanced Technology began in 1947, this became the University of Salford in 1967 and led to the change of title. The Officer Training Corps recruits from Manchester, Manchester Metropolitan and Salford universities and still includes Owens Company.

From 1939 until stood down in 1944 Manchester University OTC was re-titled 61st City of Manchester Battalion, Home Guard.

1

2

3

4

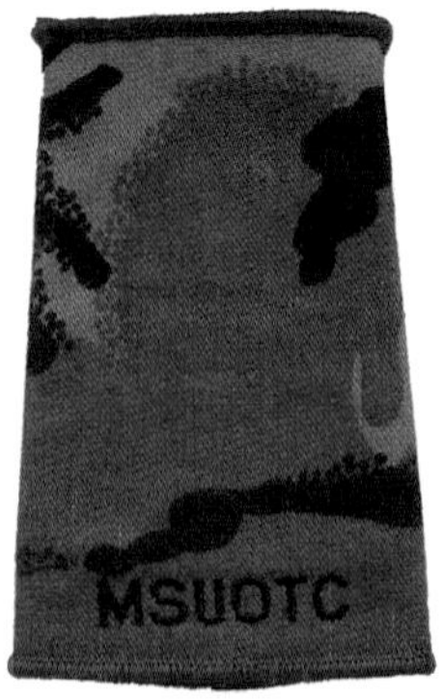

5

1 Officer Cadet's anodised aluminium badge 3.25 × 4 cm.
2 Officer's wire-embroidered beret badge 5 × 5 cm.
3 Manchester and Salford UOTC button.
4 Manchester and Salford UOTC first year officer cadet's rank slide.
5 OCdt Chris Gilbert wearing No2 Dress.

Acknowledgement Major Malcolm Gregory and Mr Ken Mills

Northumbrian Universities Officer Training Corps

The Northumbrian Universities OTC cap badge is the cross pattée quadrate from the Arms of Durham University and was introduced for Durham University OTC in 1950. There is a pattern for a wire-embroidered officer's beret badge for those granted a Territorial Army commission in the OTC. Those sponsored by a regiment or corps wear their own cap badge. There are no Northumbrian University OTC officers and no officer's badges held by the unit. Collar badges are not worn although the OTC has a stock of white plastic gorgets fitted with the former Women's Royal Army Corps button which can be sewn on to Number 2 Dress if required.

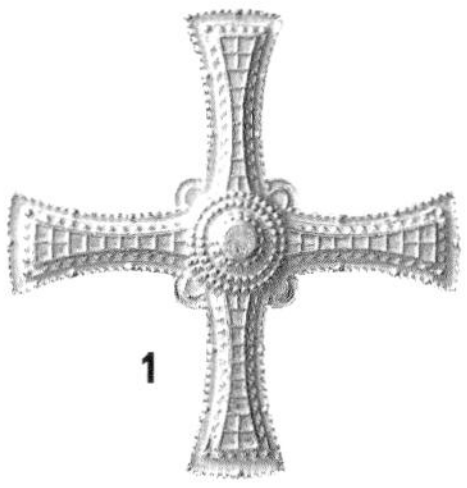
1

2

3

4

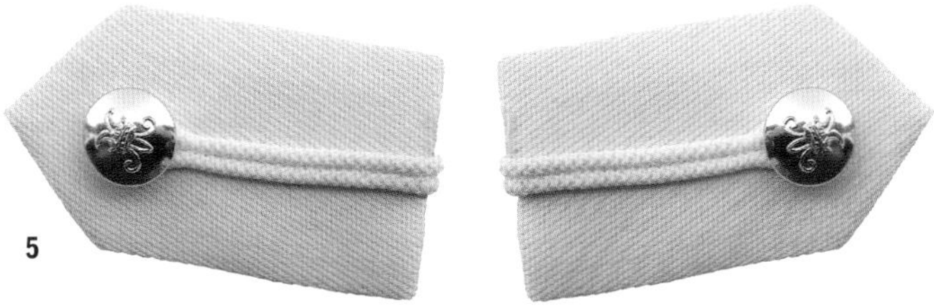
5

1 Northumbrian Universities OTC anodised aluminium cap badge 3.25 × 3.25 cm.
2 Northumbrian UOTC button.
3 Northumbrian UOTC Senior Under Officer's rank slide.
4 OCdt Frances McAuley wearing the Northumbrian UOTC cap badge.
5 Gorgets for Number 2 Dress 6 × 3.25 cm.

Acknowledgement WO1 (RSM) DT Stafford

Oxford University Officer Training Corps

The Oxford University OTC badge is based on the arms of Oxford University. As with many Officer Training Corps Oxford University OTC has a number of specialist platoons which officer cadets may elect to join after passing MTQ1. At Oxford the specialist troops and platoons are identified by specialist rank slides.

1

2

3

4

5

6

7

8

1 Officer's wire-embroidered beret badge 5 × 5.75 cm.
2 Oxford UOTC button.
3 Oxford University OTC officer cadet's anodised aluminium cap badge 4.25 × 5 cm.

Oxford UOTC rank and appointment slides
Lieutenant **4** First year cadet **5**
Junior Under Officers, Royal Armoured Corps **6**
Royal Artillery Troop **7** and the REME Platoon **8**.

Acknowledgement Captain Richard Sellwood

Queen's University Belfast Officer Training Corps

The Queen's University OTC cap badge with a flattened Imperial (or King's) Crown was introduced in 1950. The present badge with the St Edward's (or Queen's) Crown was introduced in white metal in 1957 and later produced in anodised aluminium. The ornamental escutcheon design bears the Arms of the university. The badge is worn in the caubeen with the Irish Guards piper's hackle

The OTC serves Queen's University Belfast and the University of Ulster.

1

2

3

1 Queen's University OTC anodised aluminium cap badge 3.5 × 4.25 cm and collar badges 2 × 3 cm.

2 Officer Cadet's rank slide.

3 OCdt Richard Scott wearing No2 Dress.

University of Sheffield Officer Training Corps

Sheffield University OTC badge is the Arms of Sheffield University.

1

2

3

5

4

1 OCdt Lewis Matheson wearing Number 2 Dress.

2 Sheffield University OTC anodised aluminium cap badge 4.5 × 4.5 cm and collar badges 2 × 2.5 cm.

3 Sheffield UOTC button.

4 Officer's wire-embroidered beret badge 5 × 5 cm.

5 Sheffield UOTC Senior Under Officer rank slide.

Acknowledgement
WO1 (RSM) Stuart Batey and SC Goodman

Southampton University Officer Training Corps

Southampton University OTC serves the Universities of Bournemouth, Portsmouth and Southampton, Southampton Institute and King Alfred's College, Winchester.

1

2

3

4

1 Southampton UOTC button.
2 Southampton University OTC anodised aluminium cap badge 3 × 5 cm.
3 First year cadet's rank slide.
4 OCdt Izi Boden wearing No2 Dress.

Acknowledgement
WO1 (RSM) S Day and WO2 (RQMS) M Hyde

Tayforth Universities Officer Training Corps

Two professors and 61 students at St Andrews University formed The Anstruther No 7 Battery, First Fife Brigade of Garrison Artillery in 1882, which became St Andrews University Officer Training Corps in 1908. Tayforth Universities OTC was formed in 1971 with A Company at St Andrews, B Company at Dundee and C Company at Stirling Universities.

1

2

3

4

5

6

previous page

1 The Tayforth Universities OTC anodised aluminium cap badge 4.75 × 7.5 cm and collar badges 3.25 × 4.25 cm.
2 2Lt Nilene Hennessey wearing the Tayforth UOTC badge.
3 OCdt Milan Bogunovic wearing the Tayforth UOTC badge.
4 Tayforth UOTC Second Lieutenant's rank slide.
5 Tayforth UOTC Officer Cadet's rank slide.

this page

6 Tayforth UOTC Piper's plated plaid brooch 9cm.

Acknowledgement Captain Mike Rowney

University of Wales Officer Training Corps

The OTC serves all the universities in Wales with companies based at Aberystwyth, Bangor, Cardiff and Swansea.

1

2

3

4

1 University of Wales OTC anodised aluminium cap 4 × 3.5 cm and Royal Regiment of Wales collar badges.
2 OCdt Daren Jones wearing Number 2 Dress without collar badges.
3 University of Wales OTC officer's wire embroidered beret badge.
4 University of Wales OTC Senior Under Officer's rank slide.

Acknowledgement Captain Manny Manfred

The Combined Cadet Force

The Combined Cadet Force, or CCF, is made up of 251 contingents based in schools, many with Royal Navy, Army and Royal Air Force Sections and only one without an Army Section. The contingents trace their origins to the Junior Divisions of The Officer Training Corps formed in 1908, and consequently are often known as the 'Corps'. Some wear issue badges whilst others wear school badges. The Ministry of Defence supports three schools with CCF contingents, the Duke of York's Royal Military School, Dover, Queen Victoria School, Dunblane and Welbeck College. Their badges are provided from official sources.

Adult Instructors wear a CCF shoulder title in Number 2 Dress and Barrack Dress in order that they may be identified from soldiers.

Army Sections wear the same qualification badges as the Army Cadet Force with the exception of the Proficiency badges.

1

2

3
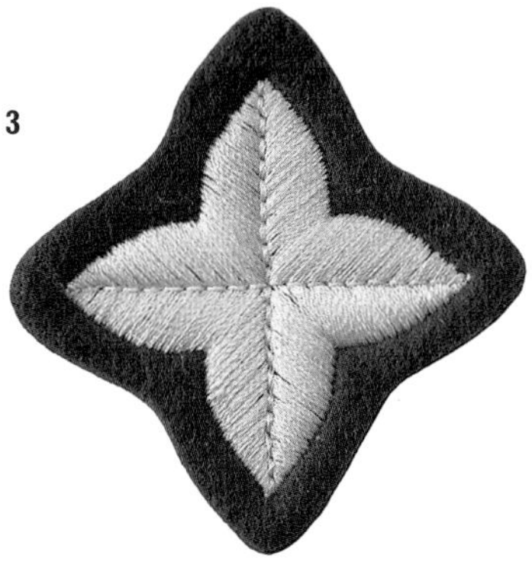

4

5

1 Adult Instructors anodised aluminium shoulder title 3 × 1.25 cm.

CCF Army Proficiency Certificate Badges

2 Half badge 6 × 3.25 cm.

3 Badge 4.75 × 4.75 cm.

4 Advanced badge 4.75 × 4.75 cm.

5 Queen Victoria School cadets Christopher Martin and Chris Milne.

The Duke of York's Royal Military School

Prince Frederick Augustus, Duke of York and Albany, son of King George III and Queen Charlotte, founded the Duke of York's Royal Military School in 1801. The establishment housed and educated orphans from the wars between Britain and Revolutionary France between 1793 and 1815. Named the Royal Military Asylum and located at Chelsea, in 1892 it was renamed The Duke of York's Royal Military School and in 1909 moved to Dover.

The Duke of York's Royal Military School provides co-educational admission to pupils whose parents are serving or were serving in any branch of the armed services at any rank. Pupils wear RMS cap badges and buttons. They also wear a cap badge of their parent's Service or regiment on their left breast.

1

2

1 Duke of York's Royal Military School anodised aluminium cap badge 2.75 × 4 cm.
2 RMS button.
3 Christopher Newns wearing RMS No1 Dress and his father's RE cap badge.

Acknowledgement Miss Caroline Cant

3

Queen Victoria School

Queen Victoria School is a co-educational boarding school for the children of Scottish Service personnel or those who are serving or have served in Scotland.

2

3

1

4

5

6

7

opposite page
1 Lt Gen Sir Alistair Irwin, the Adjutant General, with Mr Brian Raine, the Headmaster, speaking with Drum Major Philippa Roessler.
2 Queen Victoria School anodised aluminium cap badge 5.75 × 5.5 cm.

8

3 Chrome plaid brooch 7 cm.
4 Waist belt clasp 6.5 × 5 cm.
5 Queen Victoria School button.
6 School Sergeant Major Dougie Duthie, PMaj Gordon Ross, Boy PMaj Colin McInally and Ppr Callum Henderson.
7 James Birch, Jordon Cox and Helen McMillan.
8 Ciara Watson and Katy McIntyre wearing the plaid.

Welbeck College

Welbeck College is the Army funded sixth form college, established in 1953. Pupils are selected for a commission, mainly into technical Corps, study for A levels at Welbeck, then enter the Defence Technical Undergraduate Scheme and finally train for a commission at the Royal Military Academy Sandhurst. (See Defence Technical Undergraduate Scheme and Royal Military Academy Sandhurst).

1

2

1 Welbeck College anodised aluminium cap badge 3.5 × 4 cm and collar badges 2.75 × 2.75 cm.
2 Welbeck College button.

The Army Cadet Force

Cadet companies, which began with the unfunded Volunteer Rifle Corps in 1859, were authorised in 1863. Funding was withdrawn in 1924 and recognition withdrawn in 1930 although some cadet corps survived until, as a result of the Second World War, the Army Cadet Force was authorised in 1941.

1

2

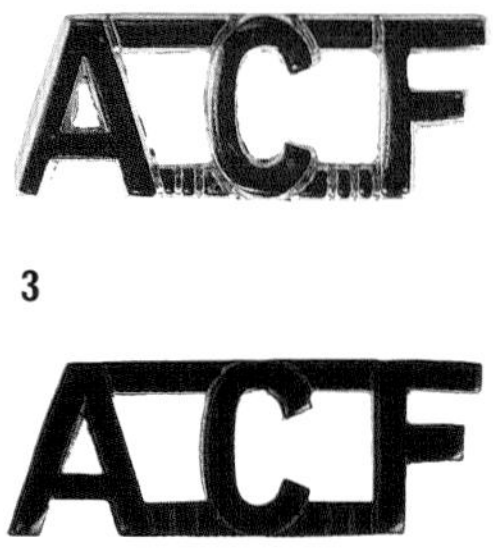

3

The Army Cadet Force, or ACF, is not part of the Army, it is a youth organisation sponsored by the Ministry of Defence and administered by the Reserve Forces and Cadet Associations, or RFCA. The membership of the ACF is in the region of 40,000, of which about 8,000 are adult instructors.

The ACF is organised on a county basis although, in some cases, counties are combined. County ACFs comprise a number of Detachments, which are grouped for administrative purposes into Areas. The organisation therefore operates at three levels: County, Area and Detachment.

Some latitude in nomenclature exists: in some cases the County ACF is called a Battalion and the Area, a Company. In London the county equivalent is the Sector and the Area equivalent is the Group. In a few counties the Area equivalent is termed a Regiment or Battalion.

Each Detachment has a regimental affiliation and wears the cap badge of the affiliated unit. Four cap badges from disbanded units are still worn by ACF Detachments.

The Scottish Yeomanry Detachment, C Squadron Angus and Dundee Battalion ACF, the Cupar Detachment, Burma Company The Black Watch Battalion ACF and the Belmont Detachment, D Company and the Girvan Detachment, E Company The West Lowland Battalion ACF wear The Scottish Yeomanry cap badge.

The seven detachments of A (Robin Hood Rifles) Company Nottinghamshire ACF wear the Robin Hood Rifles cap badge.

The Alderney Detachment, Dorset ACF wears the Royal Alderney Militia cap badge.

The Orkney and Shetland Independent Cadet Batteries ACF wear The Lovat Scouts cap badge.

Adult Instructors wear an ACF shoulder title in Number 2 Dress and Barrack Dress in order that they may be identified from soldiers.

The approved cloth shoulder title worn by cadets on a brassard on the right sleeve is woven

4

5

in gold on a scarlet backing, and referred to as the national title. The Cadet Shop at Frimley Park also stocks variations of the title; red on blue titles for Royal Artillery detachments, white on blue for Royal Signals detachments, white on red for Infantry detachments and yellow on blue for REME detachments. All reflect the colours of shoulder titles worn by the Army from about 1940 to 1962 on Battle Dress.

Each Lord Lieutenant has three cadets to accompany them on official engagements, one cadet each from the Sea Cadet Corps, Army Cadet Force and Air Training Corps.

The Scottish Yeomanry served as a TA regiment from 1992 until 1999.

The Robin Hood Rifles were formed in 1859 and were a TA battalion of The Sherwood Foresters until finally reduced to a cadre in 1969. A squadron of 73 Engineer Regiment preserves the regiment's traditions.

The Royal Alderney Militia, with militias on the other main Channel Islands was raised in the 10th Century and placed in suspended animation in 1929. The ACF detachment, the first on the Channel Islands was formed in 1983 and exceptionally authorised to take the title, style and traditions of the Royal Alderney Militia.

The Lovat Scouts was formed as independent reinforcement companies for the Boer War in 1900 the last of which disbanded in 1902. In 1903 The Lovat Scouts was formed as two yeomanry regiments which steadily reduced and converted until in 1999 it was reduced to one TA Infantry platoon. TA artillery badged as Lovat Scouts had been based on Orkney and Shetland since at least 1961 and the local ACF detachments followed the practice.

6

7

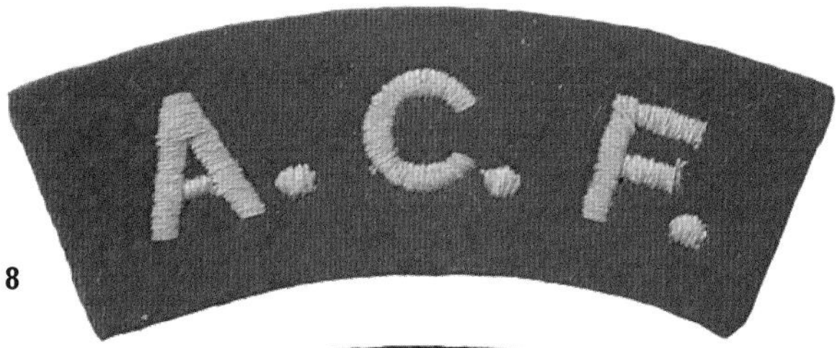

8

9

10

11

12

13

opposite page

1 The Scottish Yeomanry bimetal cap badge 4 × 4.75 cm.
2 The Robin Hood Rifles anodised aluminium cap badge 4.5 × 5.25 cm.
3 Adult Instructors anodised aluminium and black shoulder titles 3.25 × 1.25 cm.
4 The ACF is about fun – Cadet Ashley Abrahams tries not to laugh. Photograph *Wiltshire ACF*
5 Young cadets waiting for the armoury to be opened.

this page

6 The Royal Alderney Militia bimetal cap badge 4 × 4.5 cm.
7 The Lovat Scouts white metal cap badge 4.75 × 5.75 cm.
8 National shoulder title 8 × 3.5 cm.
8 Royal Artillery detachments shoulder title.
9 Royal Signals detachments shoulder title.
10 Infantry detachments shoulder title.
11 AAC detachments shoulder title.
12 REME detachments shoulder title.

East Anglia RFCA

There are 153 ACF detachments in East Anglia. There is a cloth arm badge for those cadets who have represented East Anglia at sports.

The 19 Bedfordshire ACF detachments, badged 9/12L, RA, RE, R SIGNALS, R ANGLIAN and RLC, wear the ACF shoulder title.

The 25 Cambridgeshire ACF detachments, badged RE, R SIGNALS, GREN GDS, R ANGLIAN, RLC and RAMC, wear a county shoulder title in different colours for cadets and adult instructors.

The 33 Essex ACF detachments, badged RA, RE, R SIGNALS, R ANGLIAN and PARA, wear a county shoulder title.

The 27 Hertfordshire ACF detachments, badged RA, R SIGNALS, IG, R ANGLIAN and RGJ, wear the ACF shoulder title. There is a badge for those who represent the county at sports.

The 27 Norfolk ACF detachments, badged H CAV, RA, RE and R ANGLIAN, wear a county shoulder title above a Royal Norfolk Regiment pattern cloth badge.

The 24 detachments in the Suffolk Battalion ACF, badged QDG, QRL, RTR, RA, R SIGNALS, GREN GDS, R ANGLIAN, PARA, AAC and REME, wear the ACF shoulder title above a cloth county badge.

1

2

3

4

5

6

7

8

1 East Anglia ACF sports badge 5.25 × 6.25 cm.
2 Suffolk ACF county badge 6.5 × 7 cm.
3 Norfolk ACF shoulder title 7.5 × 2.5 cm.
4 Norfolk ACF county badge 4 × 4.75 cm.
5 Hertfordshire ACF sports badge 7 × 6 cm.
6 Essex ACF shoulder title 7.5 × 3 cm.
7 Cambridgeshire AFC adult instructor's shoulder title 9 × 3 cm.
8 Cambridgeshire AFC cadet's shoulder title 8.5 × 2.75 cm.

East Midlands RFCA

There are 140 ACF detachments in the East Midlands.

The 33 detachments in the 5th Derbyshire Cadet Battalion (The Worcestershire and Sherwood Foresters) ACF, badged WFR, wear the ACF shoulder title and a battalion arm badge for those who have represented Derbyshire ACF at sport.

The 43 Leicestershire, Northamptonshire and Rutland ACF detachments, badged 9/12L, R ANGLIAN, REME and LDY, wear the ACF shoulder title.

The 34 Lincolnshire ACF detachments, badged QRL, RA, RE, GREN GDS, R ANGLIAN, PARA and RLC, wear the ACF shoulder title.

The 30 Nottinghamshire ACF detachments, badged RHA, QRL, WFR, SNH, SRY and RHR, wear a county shoulder title.

1

2

1 Derbyshire ACF sports badge 7.5 × 7.75 cm.
2 Nottinghamshire ACF shoulder title 6.75 × 2.75 cm.

Greater London RFCA

There are 102 ACF detachments in Greater London. The 19 City of London and North East London Sector ACF detachments, badged LG, RHA, RE, R SIGNALS, PWRR, RRF, R ANGLIAN, RGJ and RLC, wear the ACF shoulder title above the London shield badge in different designs for cadets and adult instructors. The 31 Middlesex and North West London Sector ACF detachments, badged RHG/D, RE, R SIGNALS, RRF, PWRR, PARA, RGJ, AAC RLC, RAMC, LONSCOT and LIR, wear the ACF shoulder title. The 25 Greater London South East Sector ACF detachments, badged RA, RE, GREN GDS, IG, PWRR, RRF, AAC, RLC, RAMC, REME, W DRGNS, LONSCOT AND LIR, wear the ACF shoulder title above a cloth Sector badge or numbered regimental cloth badge, none of which have been approved by the Deputy Inspector of regimental colours. The 27 Greater London South West Sector ACF detachments, badged RTR, RA, R SIGNALS, GREN GDS, PWRR, RRF, PARA, RGJ, RLC, RMP and KCLY, wear the ACF shoulder title above a cloth Sector badge.

1

2

3

4

5

6

7

1 City of London and North East London Sector ACF adult instructor's arm badge 3.75 × 4.75 cm.
2 City of London and North East London Sector ACF cadet's arm badge 3.75 × 4 cm.
3 Greater London South East Sector ACF arm badge 4 × 5.25 cm.
4 7 (London Yeomanry) Regiment arm badge 3.25 × 4.25 cm.
5 9 (London Artillery) Regiment arm badge 3.25 × 4.25 cm.
6 10 (Kent) Regiment RA arm badge 3.25 × 4.25 cm.
7 Greater London South West Sector ACF arm badge 6 × 4.5 cm.

Highland RFCA

There are 136 ACF detachments in the Highlands.

There are 21 detachments in the Angus and Dundee Battalion ACF, badged SCOTS DG, RA, RE, R SIGNALS, BW, PARA RAMC and SCOTS YEO. All wear the ACF shoulder title.

There are 36 detachments in The Argyll and Sutherland Highlanders Battalion ACF, badged RTR, R SIGNALS, A and SH and RLC. All wear the obsolete A and SH regimental arm badge above a cloth badge. The Army Dress Committee has ordered the regimental badge removed.

There are 22 detachments in the Black Watch Battalion ACF, badged R SIGNALS, SG, BW, PARA, RLC and SCOTS YEO. All wear the ACF shoulder title above individual company cloth badges. The Deputy Inspector of regimental colours has not approved the A Company badge.

There are 28 detachments in the 1st Cadet Battalion The Highlanders ACF, all badged HLDRS.

There are 25 detachments in the 2nd Cadet Battalion The Highlanders ACF, badged SCOTS DG, RE, HLDRS, PARA and RAMC.

The two detachments of the Orkney Independent Cadet Battery ACF are badged LOVAT SCOUTS and the two detachments of the Shetland Independent Cadet Battery ACF are badged RA. They all wear the ACF shoulder title above a cloth arm badge similar to that worn by the Orkney and Shetland Defences during the Second World War. The fouled anchor design denoted the close association between the Army and the Royal Navy at Scapa Flow.

1

2

3

4

5

6

7

1 A and SH Battalion ACF arm badge 6.25 × 2.5 cm.
2 A and SH Battalion ACF county arm badge 6.5 cm.
3 Orkney and Shetland Independent Cadet Batteries ACF arm badge 4.5 cm.

Black Watch Battalion ACF arm badges.
4 Alma Company 5.5 × 5.5 cm.
5 Burma Company 5 × 6 cm.
6 Korea Company 6 × 7 cm.
7 Ypres Company 5.75 × 7 cm.

Lowland RFCA

There are 90 ACF detachments in the Lowlands. There are 33 detachments in the Glasgow and Lanarkshire Battalion ACF, badged SCOTS DG, RA, RE, R SIGNALS, SG, RHF and KOSB. All wear a county cloth shoulder title.

There are 32 detachments in the Lothian and Borders Battalion ACF, badged SCOTS DG, RA, RE, COLDM GDS, SG, RS (with 26 Livingston Platoon as the RS Band Detachment), KOSB and RLC. All wear the ACF shoulder title.

There are 33 detachments in the West Lothian Battalion ACF, badged SCOTS DG, RA, RE, R SIGNALS, RHF, KOSB, A and SH, PARA, RLC and SCOTS YEO. All wear a county cloth shoulder title.

1

2

1 Glasgow and Lanarkshire Battalion ACF shoulder title 9 × 3.5 cm.

2 The West Lowland Battalion ACF shoulder title 8 × 3.5 cm.

North of England RFCA

There are 97 ACF detachments in the North of England.

The 27 Cleveland ACF detachments, badged RE, R SIGNALS, GH, LI, PARA and RLC, wear a county cloth shoulder title above an ACF badge.

The 37 Durham ACF detachments, badged LD, RA, RE, R SIGNALS, LI, PARA, RAMC and REME, wear a county cloth shoulder title above a small version of The Tyne Tees Regiment Tactical Recognition Flash, which had been the formation badge of 50th Northumbrian Division during the Second World War.

The 33 Northumbria ACF detachments, badged RA, RE, PARA, RRF, RAMC and QOY, wear a county cloth shoulder title and county badge.

5

6

1

2

3

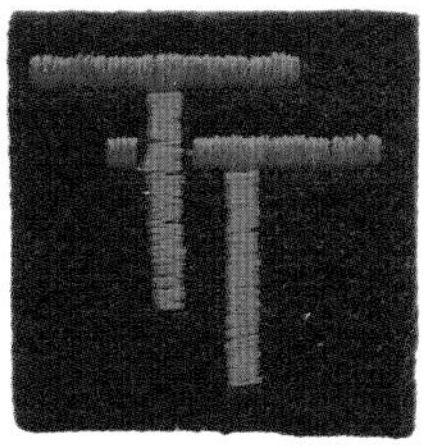
4

1 Cleveland ACF shoulder title 10.25 × 3 cm.
2 Cleveland ACF county arm badge 4.75 × 4.75 cm.
3 Durham ACF shoulder title 9.5 × 3 cm.
4 Durham ACF county arm badge 3 × 3 cm.
5 Northumbria ACF shoulder title 8.25 × 3.25 cm.
6 Northumbria ACF printed county arm badge 4.25 × 3.5 cm.

North West of England and Isle of Man RFCA

There are 162 ACF detachments in the North West of England and the Isle of Man. Many wear the 42 (North West) Brigade formation badge which has been ordered removed by the Army Dress Committee.

The 22 detachments of Cheshire ACF, badged RDG, RA, RE, R SIGNALS, KINGS, CHESHIRE, QLR, RLC, RAMC and QOY, wear a county cloth shoulder title above the 42 (North West) Brigade formation badge.

The 42 detachments of Cumbria ACF, badged KORBR, wear a county cloth shoulder title above the 42 (North West) Brigade formation badge.

The 42 detachments of Greater Manchester ACF, badged KRH, RTR, RA, RE, GREN GDS, RRF, KINGS, CHESHIRE, QLR, RLC, RAMC and REME, wear a county cloth shoulder title above the 42 (North West) Brigade formation badge.

The 6 detachments of Isle of Man ACF, all badged RA, wear the ACF shoulder title above a cloth Legs of Man badge in different designs for cadets and adult instructors.

The 32 detachments of Lancashire ACF, badged KRH, RA, R SIGNALS, KORBR, KINGS, QLR, RLC, RAMC and REME, wear a county cloth shoulder title above a county arm badge.

The 34 detachments of Merseyside ACF, badged RHA, RDG, RTR, RA, RE, R SIGNALS, IG, KINGS, CHESHIRE, QLR, R IRISH, RGJ, RLC, RAMC and LSCOTS, wear the ACF shoulder title above the 42 (North West) Brigade formation badge.

1

2

3

4

5

6

7

1 Cheshire ACF shoulder title 8 × 3.25 cm.
2 Greater Manchester ACF shoulder title 8.5 × 4.25 cm.
3 Cumbria ACF shoulder title 6.25 × 3.75 cm.
4 Lancashire ACF shoulder title 5 × 2 cm.
5 Lancashire ACF arm badge 4.75 × 5.75 cm.
6 Isle of Man ACF adult instructor's arm badge 5 × 6 cm.
7 Isle of Man ACF cadet's arm badge 4 × 4.5 cm.

Northern Ireland RFCA

There Are 68 ACF detachments in Northern Ireland.

The 32 detachments of 1st (Northern Ireland) Battalion ACF, badged RDG, RA, RE, R SIGNALS, IG, RLC, RAMC and RANGERS, wear the ACF shoulder title.

The 36 detachments of 2nd (Northern Ireland) Battalion ACF, badged QRH, RA, RE, R SIGNALS, IG, R IRISH, RLC and AGC, wear the ACF shoulder title.

South East RFCA

There are 208 ACF detachments in the South East.

The 20 detachments of Buckinghamshire ACF, all badged RGJ, wear a black on green ACF cloth shoulder title above a county arm badge. There is a different badge for those who have represented Buckinghamshire ACF at sport.

The 48 detachments of Hampshire and Isle of Wight ACF, badged RA, RE, R SIGNALS, PWRR, PARA, AAC, RAMC and REME, wear the ACF shoulder title above the appropriate cloth arm badge. The Deputy Inspector of regimental colours has not approved the Hampshire arm badge.

The 42 detachments of Kent ACF, badged RTR, RA, RE, PWRR, PARA and REME, wear county arm badges in different colours for detachments sponsored by different Arms and Services, RTR, RA, RE, Infantry and REME. There is a different badge for those who have represented Kent ACF at sport.

The 25 detachments of Oxfordshire (Royal Green Jackets Battalion) ACF, all badged RGJ except for one RLC detachment, wear a black on green cloth shoulder title in Royal Green Jacket colours above the obsolete 1 RGJ Tactical Recognition Flash. There is an extra cloth arm badge for those who have represented Oxfordshire ACF at sports. The Army Dress Committee has ordered the TRF be removed.

The 19 detachments of Royal County of Berkshire ACF, badged HCR, RGBW and REME, wear a county cloth shoulder title.

The 26 detachments of Surry ACF, all badged PWRR, wear the ACF shoulder title above a county cloth arm badge.

The 28 detachments of Sussex ACF, badged RA, RE, R SIGNALS, PWRR and REME, wear a county cloth shoulder title above a Royal Sussex Regiment arm badge. The Army Dress Committee has ordered the arm badge be removed.

1

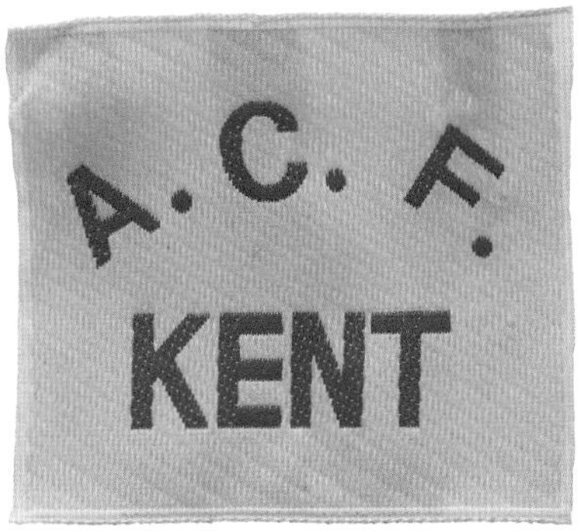

4

5

2

3

6

7

8

9

10

11

12

13

14

15

16

17

18

previous page

1 Buckinghamshire ACF shoulder title 8 × 3.25 cm.
2 Buckinghamshire ACF arm badge 4 × 5.25 cm.
3 Buckinghamshire ACF sports badge 4.75 × 5.5 cm.
4 RTR Detachments Kent ACF arm badge 5.5 × 5 cm.
5 RA Detachments Kent ACF arm badge 5.5 × 4.75 cm.
6 RE Detachments Kent ACF arm badge 5.5 × 4.75 cm.
7 Infantry Detachments Kent ACF arm badge 5.5 × 4.75 cm.

this page

8 REME Detachments Kent ACF arm badge 5.5 × 5 cm.
9 Kent ACF sports badge 4 × 5.25 cm.
10 Hampshire ACF arm badge 3.75 × 5 cm.
11 Isle of Wight ACF arm badge 4 × 5 cm.
12 Oxfordshire (RGJ) ACF 8.25 × 3.25 cm shoulder title.
13 Oxfordshire (RGJ) ACF 6 × 3.25 cm TRF.
14 Oxfordshire (RGJ) ACF sports badge 4.5 × 5.25 cm.
15 Royal Berkshire ACF shoulder title 8 × 3 cm.
16 Sussex ACF shoulder title 8.25 × 3.25 cm
17 Sussex ACF TRF 5 × 2 cm.
18 Surrey ACF arm badge 5 × 6 cm.

Welsh RFCA

There are 148 ACF detachments in Wales. There is a cloth arm badge for those who have represented Wales ACF at sport. There is also a badge for those who have taken part in the Cadet Cambrian Patrol Competition which is run concurrently with the annual Cambrian Patrol Competition in Wales.

The 20 detachments of 4th Cadet Battalion The Royal Welsh Fusiliers (Clwyd) ACF, all badged RWF except for one REME detachment, wear a county cloth shoulder title above a coloured square indicating the company to which the detachment belongs.

The 19 detachments of 6th Cadet Battalion The Royal Welsh Fusiliers (Gwynedd) ACF, all badged RWF except for two RA detachments, wear a county cloth shoulder title.

The 43 detachments of 3rd Cadet Battalion The Royal Regiment of Wales (Glamorgan Counties) ACF wears the ACF shoulder title.

The 23 detachments of Dyfed ACF, badged QDG, WG and RRW, wear the ACF shoulder title.

The 23 detachments of Gwent AFC, badged RA, RE and RRW, wear the ACF shoulder title above a county arm badge. There is a cloth arm badge for those who have represented Gwent ACF at sport.

The 20 detachments of Powys Battalion ACF, badged RA, WG and RRW, wear the ACF shoulder title above a cloth arm badge. There is a cloth arm badge for those who have represented Powys ACF at sport.

1

2

7

5

8

3

6

4

1 Wales ACF sports badge 6 cm.
2 Cadet Cambrian Patrol Competition 5.5 cm.
3 6 Cadet Battalion RWF (Gwynedd) ACF shoulder title 11 × 3.75 cm.
4 4 Cadet Battalion RWF (Clwyd) ACF shoulder title 8.5 × 3 cm worn above the company colour embroidered onto the brassard 3 × 2 cm.
5 Powys Battalion ACF cloth arm badge 4.5 × 3.75 cm.
6 Powys ACF sports badge 5 cm.
7 Gwent AFC sports badge 7.5 cm.
8 Gwent AFC county arm badge 4 × 5.5 cm.

Wessex RFCA

There are 178 ACF detachments in Wessex.

The 22 detachments of The City and County of Bristol ACF, badged RTR, RA, RE, R SIGNALS, GREN GDS, LI, RGBW, RLC and REME, wear the ACF shoulder title above a cloth arm badge.

The 22 detachments of The Cornwall Cadet Battalion (The Light Infantry) ACF, all badged LI, wear a county cloth shoulder title above a gold on blue cloth shoulder title.

The 35 detachments of Devon ACF, all badged D and D, wear the ACF shoulder title above a county cloth arm badge.

The 20 detachments of Dorset ACF, badged RTR, R SIGNALS, PWRR, D and D, RLC and RAM, wear the ACF shoulder title.

The 22 detachments of The Gloucestershire Cadet Battalion (The Royal Gloucestershire, Berkshire and Wiltshire Regiment) ACF, all badged RGBW, wear the ACF shoulder title.

The 22 detachments of Somerset Cadet Battalion (ACF) The Light Infantry, all badged LI, wear a gold on blue ACF shoulder title.

The 20 detachments of Wiltshire ACF, badged RA, R SIGNALS, RGBW and AAC, wear the ACF shoulder title above a county cloth arm badge.

1

2

3

4
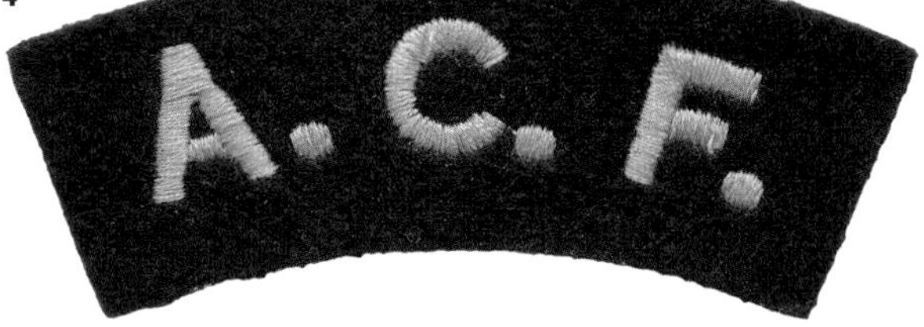

5

6

1 City and County of Bristol ACF cloth arm badge 5 × 4.75 cm.
2 The Maughan-Smith sisters, Karieanne wearing the new RGBW cap badge and Zeanne and Morantha wearing the old larger badge. Photograph *Wiltshire ACF*.
3 Cornwall Cadet Battalion (LI) ACF county cloth shoulder title 11.25 × 3.5 cm.
4 Cornwall Cadet Battalion (LI) ACF Somerset Cadet Battalion (ACF) LI shoulder title 8 × 3.25 cm.
5 Devon ACF county arm badge 4 × 5.25 cm.
6 Wiltshire ACF county arm badge 5 × 5.75 cm.

West Midlands RFCA

There are 115 ACF detachments in the West Midlands.

The 24 detachments of Hereford and Worcestershire ACF, badged QRH, RA, SG, LI and WFR wear the ACF shoulder title above a county cloth shoulder title.

The 21 detachments of Shropshire ACF, badged R SIGNALS, LI, RLC and RMLY, wear county cloth shoulder titles in different colours for Detachments sponsored by different Arms and Services; R SIGNALS, LI, RLC and RMLY each worn above the county cloth arm badge.

The 40 detachments of Staffordshire and West Midlands North Sector ACF, badged QRL, RA, RE, R SIGNALS, GREN GDS, STAFFORDS, RLC, RAMC, R MON RE and RMLY, wear the ACF shoulder title above the appropriate county cloth arm badge. The Staffordshire badge is The Staffordshire Regiment Tactical Recognition Flash that has been ordered removed by the Army Dress Committee. The Inspector of regimental colours has not approved the West Midlands badge.

The 30 detachments of Warwickshire and West Midlands South Sector ACF, badged RA, RE, R SIGNALS and RRF, wear the ACF shoulder title above the county cloth arm badge.

1

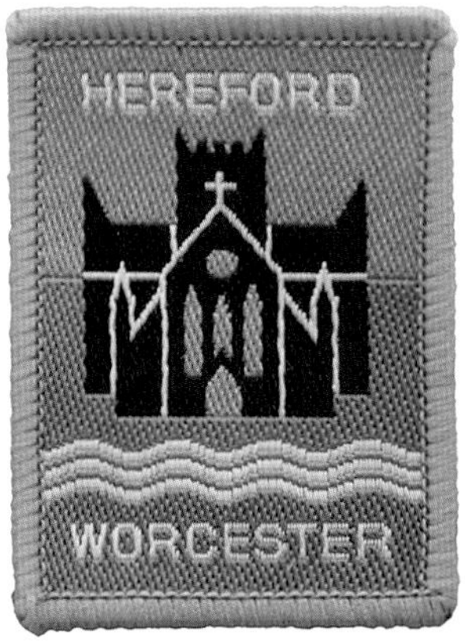

2

3

4

5

6

7

8

9

1 Hereford and Worcestershire ACF arm badge 4 × 5.5 cm.
2 Royal Signals ACF detachments shoulder title 8.25 × 3.5 cm.
3 The Light Infantry ACF detachments shoulder title 8.25 × 3.5 cm.
4 Royal Logistic Corps ACF detachments shoulder title 8.25 × 3.5 cm
5 Royal Mercian and Lancastrian Yeomanry ACF detachments shoulder title 8.25 × 3.5 cm.
6 Shropshire ACF county arm badge worn below the shoulder title 5 × 5.5 cm.
7 West Midlands ACF arm badge 4.5 × 6 cm.
8 Staffordshire ACF arm badge 4.5 × 3.75 cm.
9 Warwickshire ACF arm badge 4 × 5 cm.

RFCA for Yorkshire and Humberside

There are 97 ACF detachments in Yorkshire and Humberside.

The 50 detachments of Humberside and South Yorkshire ACF, badged RDG, LD, RA, RE, R SIGNALS, R ANGLIAN, PWO, DWR, PARA, RLC, RAMC, REME and QOY, wear the ACF shoulder title and is seeking approval for a county cloth badge.

The 47 detachments of Yorkshire (North and West) ACF, badged RA, RE, R SIGNALS, LI, PWO, GH, DWR, PARA, RLC and QOY, wear the ACF shoulder title and is also seeking approval for a county cloth badge.

1 Humberside and South Yorkshire ACF proposed county arm badge (approximately 6 × 6.5 cm).

2 Yorkshire (North and West) ACF proposed county arm badge (approximately 5 × 5 cm).

1

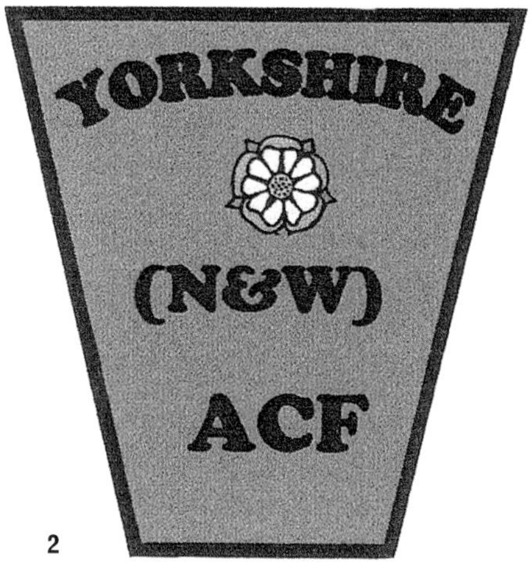

2

Army Cadet Force Training

Army Cadet Forces training and activities are of a challenging and exciting nature designed to foster and develop confidence, self-reliance and loyalty in the cadet both as an individual member of the community and as a member of a team. Military training is based upon the six levels of the Army Proficiency Certificate (APC) Syllabus.

Basic Training covers Drill, Turnout, Military Knowledge, Skill at Arms and Fieldcraft, and Expedition Training. The Basic Badge is awarded following successful competition of practical tests.

One Star Training extends basic knowledge. New subjects include first aid, shooting, map and compass and physical training.

Two Star Training covers the same subjects as the One Star but in more detail and expertise.

Three Star Training is usually undertaken when a cadet is a non-commissioned officer and may include a Methods of Instruction course.

Four Star Training is one of the milestones of a cadet's development. Emphasis is on leadership, including the Senior Instructors course.

Master Cadet requires attendance at the Cadet Training Centre course.

Cadets aged 16 and older may attend a formal leadership course. They are run both by Land Command and at the Cadet Training Centre, or CTC. The CTC was opened in 1959 at Frimley Park by the Ministry of Defence as the first national Cadet Training Centre. Cadets may also be selected to attend similar courses run by the Royal Canadian Army Cadets.

The Canadian Cadet Wilderness Instructors Course is run at the Argonaut National Army Cadet Camp. The Canadian Cadet Leadership Instructor Adventure Course is run at the Whitehorse National Army Cadet Camp and the Canadian Cadet Leadership and Challenge Course is run at the Rocky Mountain National Army Cadet Camp. All are marked by separate badges.

Cadets who qualify in First Aid may wear the badge of the Testing Authority; St Andrew's Ambulance Association, British Red Cross Society but only those for the St John Ambulance Association awards are available from the Cadet Supply Department.

Cadets also work towards The Duke of Edinburgh's Award, which was started in 1956. The Duke of Edinburgh's Award is a youth programme offering practical, cultural and adventurous activities relating to community service, physical achievement and expeditions. The similarities to Army Cadet training are clear and almost all the cadet activities are cross-credited with the Duke of Edinburgh's Award, so whilst cadets are training for first aid, drill, target shooting, expeditions and taking part in sports, they are simultaneously making progress towards their Duke of Edinburgh's Award.

Until 1986 Cadet Detachments trained with obsolete military weapons. Air Rifles and .22 inch calibre Number 8 rifles continue to be used but for Full Bore shooting the L98A1 Cadet General Purpose Rifle, made especially for the Cadets and visually similar to the Armed Forces SA80 was introduced, together with the Cadet Target Rifle. In 1994 the Detachments were issued with the Light Support Weapon. Until 2003 there were two sets of shooting badges; those with a khaki backing were awarded for Small Bore marksmanship (Air Rifles and .22 calibre rifles) and those with a red backing for Full Bore (7.62mm and 5.56mm). Only the red backed badges are now issued. Separate titles designating the weapon type are worn immediately underneath the rifle badge.

1

2

3

4

5

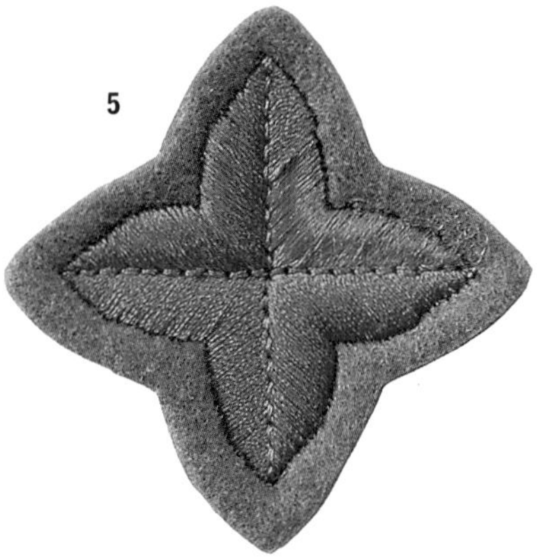

6

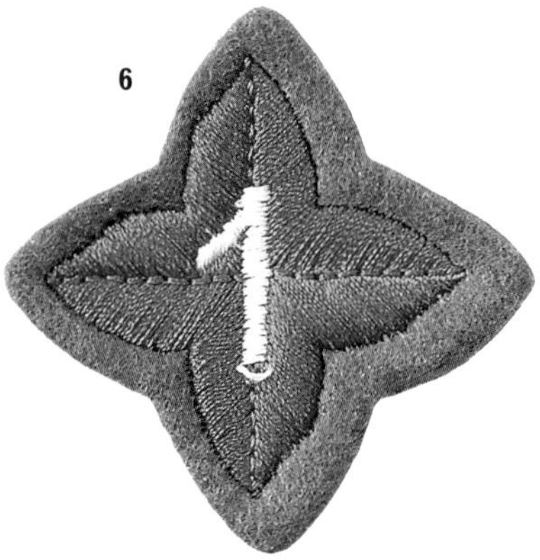

7

8

9

10

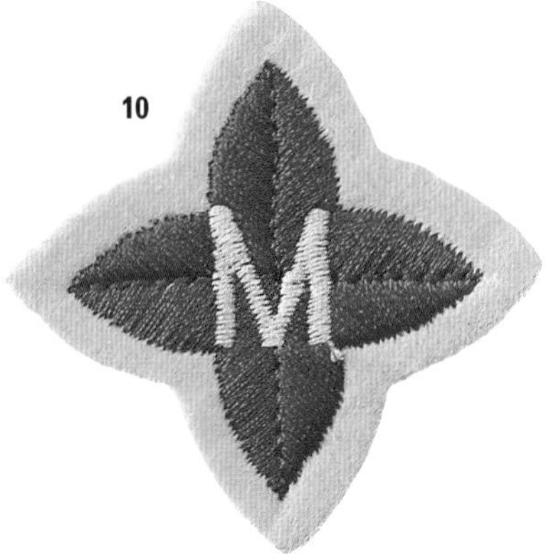

Shooting Badges

11

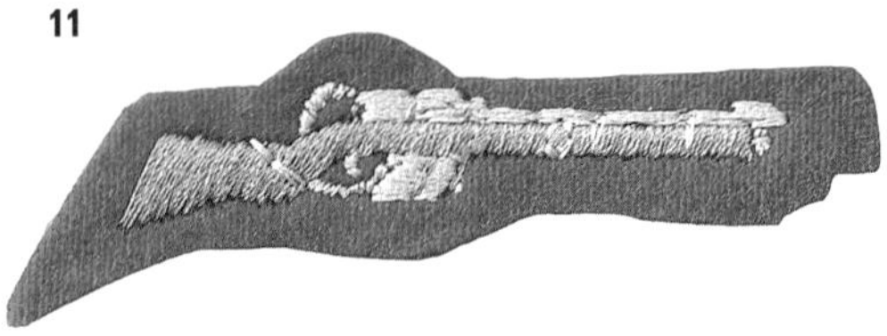

12

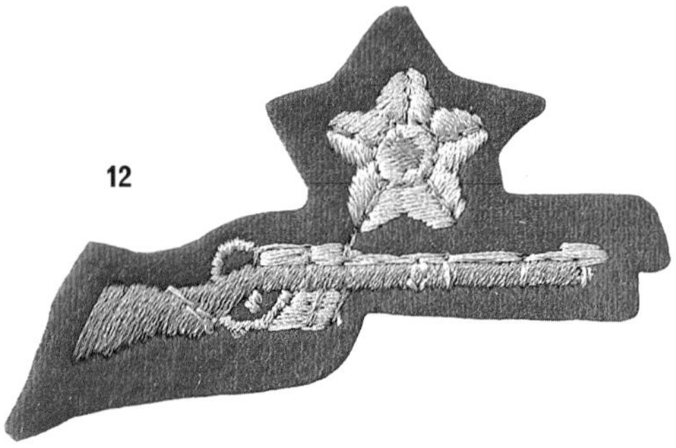

13

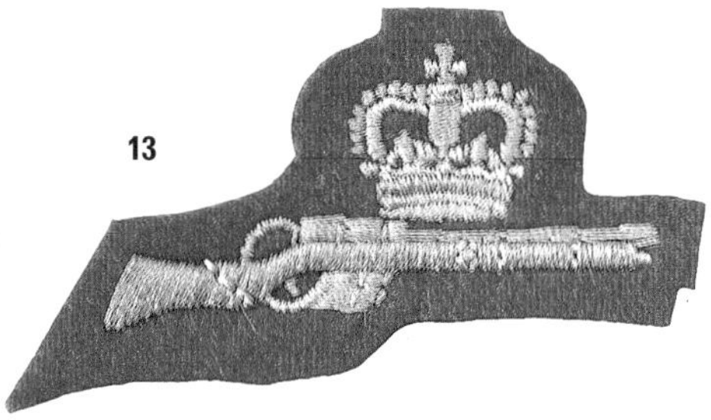

14

15

16

17

18

19

The Duke of Edinburgh's Award

The Duke of Edinburgh's Award, a registered charity, is a voluntary, non-competitive programme of activities for anyone aged 14–25. It offers an individual challenge and encourages young people to undertake exciting, constructive, challenging and enjoyable activities in their free time. Just over 7% of those in the UK aged 14–17 participate in the Award, through Award Groups in youth clubs, voluntary organisations, Open Award Centres, schools, colleges, young offender institutes and businesses.

The Award is a four Section Programme with three progressive levels: Bronze, Silver and Gold. The Sections involve: Service (helping the community); Skills (a hobby, skill or interest); Physical Recreation (sports, dance, fitness); Expeditions (on foot, cycle, horseback, or water); Residential Project – Gold only (an enterprise with people not known to the participant). Each year, Award Participants provide over one million hours of service to the community whilst, in the expeditions Section, they collectively covered over one million miles.

At any one time, around 225,000 participants are trying for an Award in the UK alone, with around 110,000 taking up its challenge each year. Approximately 70,000 volunteers share their skills, enthusiasm and time to help guide the participants through their Awards, learning new skills and making friends themselves along the way.

20

Leadership Course Badges

21

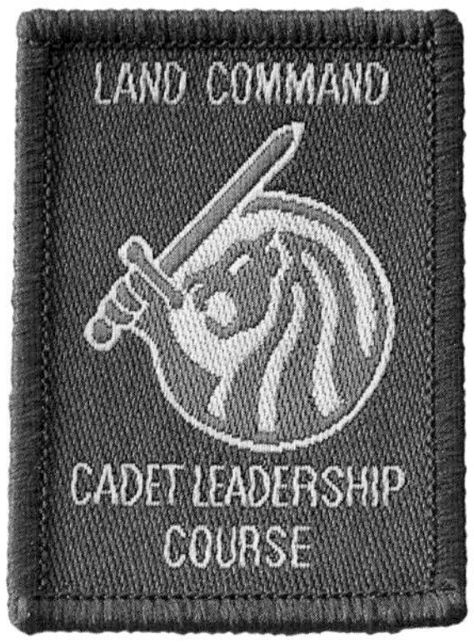

22

23

24

25

previous page

1 Craig Ratcliffe wearing the national shoulder title and Wiltshire ACF arm badge above his rank and the St John Ambulance Young Life Saver badge, the 1st Class Shot badge and an Army Proficiency Certificate badge.
2 Lord Lieutenant's Cadet badge 6.75 cm.
3 St John Ambulance Young Lifesaver 5 cm.
4 St John Ambulance Instructor 5 cm.

opposite page

5 Basic level, 5 × 5 cm.
6 Level 1, 5 × 5 cm.
7 Level 2, 5 × 5 cm.
8 Level 3, 5 × 5 cm.
9 Level 4, 5 × 5 cm.
10 Master Cadet, 5 × 5 cm.
11 2nd Class Shot 7 × 2.25 cm.
12 1st Class Shot 6.5 × 4.25 cm.
13 Marksman 6.25 × 3.75 cm.
14 Cadet 100 badge 6.75 cm.
15 Air Rifle 4 × 1.5 cm.
16 .22 Rifle 4 × 1.5 cm.
17 Cadet General Purpose Rifle 4 × 1.5 cm.
18 Target Rifle 4.5 × 1.5 cm.
19 Light Support Weapon 2.25 × 1.5 cm.

this page

20 Duke of Edinburgh Award Bronze and Silver Award badges 4.25 × 5 cm, Gold Award badge 3.5 × 4.5 cm.
21 Land Command Cadet Leadership Course 4.5 × 6 cm.
22 Cadet Training Centre Leadership Course 4.5 × 6 cm.
23 Canadian Cadet Wilderness Instructors Course Badge 3.5 cm.
24 Canadian Cadet Leadership Instructor Adventure Course Badge 3.5 cm.
25 Canadian Cadet Leadership and Challenge Course Badge 5 cm.

Acknowledgement
Lt Col Mike Watson, Major John Bradshaw, Captain David Fielding and John Richards BEM and Mr Mike McCauliffe

Staff

Appointments to the staff of the Army in the rank of colonel and above are made by the Secretary of State on the recommendation of the military members of the Army Board.

The names of officers selected to hold appointments in the rank of major general or above are submitted to The Queen for approval.

Field Marshals

There are seven Field Marshals and although there are no longer any serving in established posts all are provided with uniform and badges appropriate to their duties. On the centre of the cap badge are crossed batons, the staff of office of a Field Marshal. Field Marshals wear the same gorgets as generals.

The crossed batons of the Field Marshal first appeared on buttons and on the epaulette of State uniform in 1793.

Gorget patches were introduced in India in 1887 to distinguish generals and certain key staff officers and warrant officers. The gorget as it is recognised today was introduced in 1896. During the First World War they became known, as did their wearers, as 'red tabs'. In 1921 gorgets were restricted to officers on the Staff, defined as those of the ranks of colonel and above.

Officers of the Royal Army Medical Corps wear cherry red gorgets; those of the Royal Army Veterinary Corps, maroon; Royal Army Dental Corps, green; Royal Army Chaplains' Department, purple; and the Queen Alexandra's Royal Army Nursing Corps, grey with a scarlet cord.

1

3

2

4

5

6

7

opposite page

1 Field Marshal The Lord Inge KG GCB wearing The Green Howards khaki beret.
2 Field Marshal wire-embroidered cap badge 4 × 5.25 cm.
3 Field Marshal's full Dress rank badge worn on the Frock Coat 9 × 17.5 cm.
4 Field Marshal button.

this page

5 His Royal Highness Field Marshal The Duke of Kent KG GCMG GCVO ADC wearing The Royal Scots Dragoon Guards grey beret.
6 wire-embroidered rank badge 5.25 × 4.5 cm worn with a Crown.
7 Field Marshal anodised aluminium rank badges, wreath 3 × 2.75 cm, and Crown 1.5 × 1.5 cm.

Generals

The 'Gradation List of Officers of the Army on the Active List' includes four generals, eleven lieutenant generals, and forty four major generals. As officers of the Staff they are subject to Staff dress regulations but many continue to wear some regimental distinctions, particularly berets, in working dress and in a few instances in Service Dress. All wear the General's bullion cap badge which is produced in two sizes, one for the beret and a larger one for the Forage Cap.

The crossed Sword and Baton design was originally used in about 1780 on Generals' buttons. It was produced as a badge in 1828.

Gorget patches of gilt oak leaves and three acorns on scarlet cloth are worn in place of collar badges. In working dress, either shirt sleeve order or pullover order, 2 inches long patches are worn on the shirt collar. In Service Dress the patches are 3 inches long and in Number 1 Dress, 4 inches long with four acorns.

4

1

2

3

5

6

7

8

previous page

1 Maj Gen Andrew Richie CBE wearing the large Forage Cap badge and gorgets. As an officer promoted from the Royal Artillery he wears his cross belt rather than a Sam Brown belt.
2 General's wire-embroidered beret badge 4 × 5.5 cm
3 Forage Cap badge 5 × 25 × 7 cm.
4 General button.

this page

5 Field Marshals and General's gorget patches 7.5 × 3.5 cm.
6 Maj Gen David Leakey wearing his rank badges on RTR rank slides.
7 General's anodised aluminium rank badges worn on Number 2 Dress 3.25 × 2 cm.
8 Rank slide made for a General. The blue rank badges are of the style worn by officers of The Parachute Regiment, and the ER shows him to be an Aide-de-Camp General to the Queen.

Acknowledgement Captain Ross Haines

Brigadiers and Colonels

On promotion to the ranks of Colonel and Brigadier officers are transferred from their regiments and corps to the Staff. As with generals, many continue to wear some of their former regimental distinctions although all wear the Staff bullion cap badge, the exception being Colonels of Regiments, and their equivalents, who wear regimental uniform with colonel's rank insignia when representing their regiment.

Gorget patches of a red gimp on scarlet cloth are worn in place of collar badges. Gorgets are worn in the same circumstances as by generals. On Number 1 Dress the Staff patches are slightly shorter, at 3 inches long.

Since 1995 it has become common practice for all ranks to wear Number 8 Dress (Combat 95) as working dress. Many senior officers wear their rank badges sewn or embroidered onto regimental style 'slides'. Officially only ranks up to lieutenant colonel wear regimental pattern insignia. The only exceptions are Colonels of Regiments and if appropriate Colonels in Chief, who wear the rank insignia of a colonel.

Winter sports

Cresta is one of four winter sports which involve sliding down an ice slope. On the Cresta Run, the rider goes down by himself on a toboggan in a lying position on his tummy, head-first, using rakes on the end of special boots to brake and steer.

On Bob Runs, riders go down in pairs or teams of four in a metal capsule on runners. One person steers, another operates the brakes. Riders go down in a seated position.

The Luge. Riders lie on their backs on a toboggan, feet first. They ride on Bob Runs and Luge Runs, both singly and in pairs.

The Bob-Skeleton. As on the Cresta, individuals ride head-first, on similar toboggans, but without rakes. They ride on Bob Runs.

1

2

3

4

6

5

7

previous page

1 The Staff cap badge has been adopted as the badge worn on sports kit by those awarded Army Colours for sports.

this page

2 Staff wire-embroidered beret badge 3.54 × 5 cm and Forage Cap badge 4 × 5.75 cm.

3 Example of a rank slide of the Colonel of The King's Regiment.

4 Button.

5 Staff gorget patches (red tabs), 2 inches or 3 inches long.

6 Colonel Andrew Barnard OBE, an officer on the Staff. Although he wears a Staff cap badge and 'red tabs', as a former Royal Artillery officer he wears a cross belt rather than a Sam Brown belt.

7 Brigadier John Wolsey OBE wearing No1 Dress.

Aiguillettes

Field Marshals and Aides-de-Camp to The Queen wear aiguillettes on the right shoulder with the gilt brass ferrules decorated with the royal cypher. Other staff in representational posts wear the aiguillettes on the left shoulder.

1

2

3

4

5

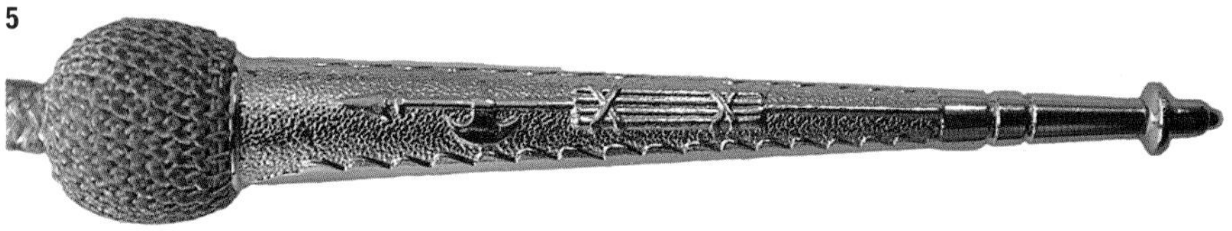

previous page

1 His Royal Highness Field Marshal The Duke of Kent KG GCMG GCVO ADC wearing the uniform of Colonel in Chief The Royal Regiment of Fusiliers with aiguillettes over the right shoulder as Aide-de-Camp to The Queen.

2 Major Charles Waters Coldstream Guards, riding Winston. As Adjutant of The Royal Military Academy Sandhurst he wears aiguillettes on his left shoulder.

this page

3 Aide-de-Camp to The Queen 12 cm.

4 Lady Aide-de-Camp to The Queen 5 cm.

5 Other representational posts 12 cm.

Cyphers

1

2

3

4

5

6

7

8

9

10

Royal Cypher badges worn by officers holding honorary appointments to the Sovereign

1 Full size dull silver Royal Cypher worn on Full Dress, Number 1, 3, 10 and 11 Dress, Frockcoat and Greatcoat.

2 Full size gilt Royal Cypher worn on Number 2, 4 and 6 Dress.

3 Full size Royal Cypher painted black for Royal Green Jackets, Brigade of Gurkhas and Chaplains, all 3.25 × 3.25 cm.

4 Small gilt Royal Cypher worn on Number 7, 13 and 14 Dress.

5 Small black Royal Cypher worn on Number 7, 13 and 14 Dress and the pullover.

6 Small silver Royal Cypher worn by former ADCs appointed before 1988, all 2.5 × 2.5 cm.

Cyphers worn by personal equerries

7 Equerry to Field Marshal His Royal Highness The Prince Philip Duke of Edinburgh KG KT OM GBE AC QSO 3 × 3.5 cm.

8 Equerry to Lieutenant General His Royal Highness The Prince of Wales KG KT GCB AK QSO ADC 3 × 3.25 cm.

9 Equerry to Field Marshal His Royal Highness The Duke of Kent KG GCMG GCVO ADC 2.2 × 3.25 cm.

10 Rank slide of the Commander in Chief of The Royal Gibraltar Regiment, who is also Governor of Gibraltar.

Acknowledgement WO2 (RQMS) Paul Orchard

Royal Military Academy Sandhurst

The Royal Military Academy Sandhurst cap badge was introduced in 1947 on the amalgamation of the Royal Military Academy Woolwich and the Royal Military College Sandhurst. Recently cap badges have identified the Sovereign's Platoon, the champion platoon of the Senior Intake, with a gold painted Cypher.

Cadets at the Royal Military College of Science at Shrivenham and students in Thunderer and Trojan Squadrons also wear the RMAS cap badge.

The Academy Sergeant Major, the only member of the Sandhurst permanent staff to wear RMAS badges, wears a wire-embroidered cap badge.

On the formation of the Royal Military Academy Sandhurst in 1947 it was decided to issue soldiers' uniforms to Officer Cadets; prior to 1939 Gentlemen Cadets at the Royal Military College had worn officers' pattern uniforms. In order to identify the cadets from privates, white gorget patches were adopted as collar badges, a practice already used by the Royal Navy and Royal Air Force. In the mid-1960s low maintenance plastic gorgets were introduced.

The Royal Military Academy Sandhurst Band Corps wore collar badges of the same pattern but smaller than the cap badge until it was disbanded in 1985. Collar badges are now only worn by the Academy Sergeant Major, on the brassards of the regimental police and the appointment slides of duty cadets.

1

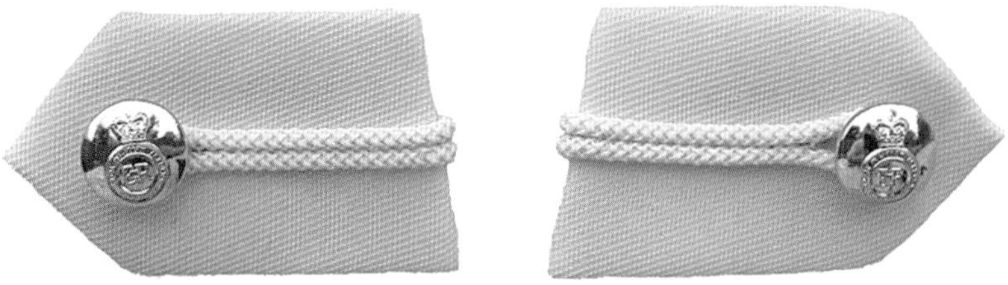

2

3

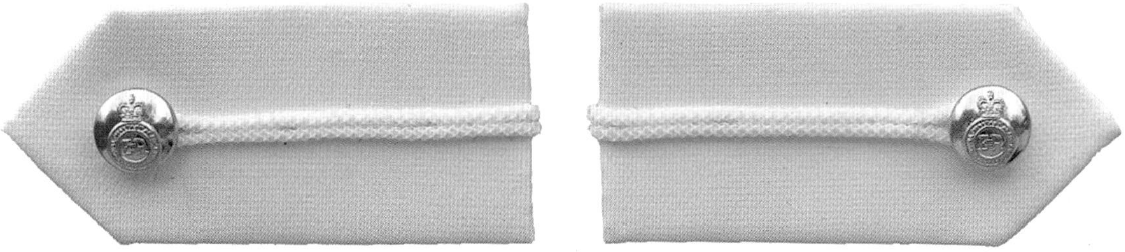

4

5

The Royal Military Academy Sandhurst was formed by the amalgamation of the Royal Military College Sandhurst, which trained cavalry and infantry officer cadets, with the Royal Military Academy Woolwich, which trained Royal Artillery, Royal Engineers and Royal Signals officer cadets. From 1940 war service officer cadets were trained at Officer Cadet Training Units, one of which was at Sandhurst. Mons Officer Cadet School, the last of the former OCTUs, was absorbed into RMAS in 1972. The Women's Royal Army Corps College was amalgamated with RMA Sandhurst in 1984.

Officer Cadets of the Senior Division wear slides decorated with the unique appointments of Senior Cadet and Under Officer.

7

8

At the conclusion of The Sovereign's Parade the Adjutant rides up the steps of the Grand Entrance following the officer cadets to be commissioned. The practice began with Lieutenant General Sir Frederick Browning KCVO KBE CB DSO when adjutant in 1925. It has been suggested that the parade commander had ridden up the steps after Pass off Parades before 1896 but the practice had ceased for 29 years.

9

10

11

12

previous page

1 Officer Cadet's anodised aluminium cap badge 3.5 × 5 cm and with a gold painted Cypher worn by the Sovereign's Platoon
2 Officer Cadets' gorgets worn by women 6 × 3.25 cm and men 8 × 3.5 cm on Number 1 and Number 2 Dress.
3 RMAS button
4 The Queen's Colour carried by OCdt Johnny Mackley and the Regimental Colour by OCdt Jim McAvan escorted by OCdts Tom Williams, Richard Clarke and Phil Roberts with WO1 (AcSM) Vince Gaunt.
6 College Duty Cadet appointment slide. A similar slide with a narrower coloured band is worn by the Company Duty Cadets and with a thin coloured band by the Platoon Duty Cadets.

opposite page

7 Stick Orderly's pouch 10.5 × 16 cm.
8 Senior Cadet, Junior Under Officer and Senior Under Officer appointment slides.
9 RMAS waist belt clasp 7.25 × 6 cm.
10 The Stick Orderlies at The Sovereign's Parade, Officer Cadets Sam Brown, Georgie Free, Thomas Cairncross and George Heyes wearing Number 1 Dress.

this page

11 '*Why we all do it*' Officer Cadet Edward Hodges wearing his King's Royal Hussars Mess Dress with Sarah, Anne, Sue, Marie and Katherine at his Commissioning Ball. Regimental coloured ribbons cover his rank badges.

The last evening at Sandhurst is marked by the Commissioning Ball at which the Officer Cadets who are to be commissioned wear their new Mess Dress but with the rank star of a Second Lieutenant covered until midnight.

12 OCdt Doug Bewley, Andrew Savery and Ross Drummond wearing Combat Dress.

Acknowledgement Lt Col Roy Parkinson

The Academy Sergeant Major

The Academy Sergeant Major is considered to be the senior sergeant major in the Army. He wears Royal Military Academy Sandhurst badges and a variation of the Foot Guards Regimental Sergeant Major's rank badge. The badge was designed by a former Commandant of the RMA Sandhurst, Major General Sir Philip Ward KCVO CBE, late of the Welsh Guards, and is thought to have been first worn by WO1 (AcSM) John Lord MVO MBE MSM who retired as the Academy Sergeant Major in 1963.

The Academy Sergeant Major wears a wire-embroidered cap badge. Always in recent years from the Foot Guards, he wears the badge on Household Division ribbon on a khaki beret. The Academy Sergeant Major is the only soldier to wear Royal Military Academy Sandhurst collar badges. From 1970–1980 the then Academy Sergeant Major, WO1 (AcSM) Ray Huggins, wore wire-embroidered collar badges on his Mess Dress. The practice did not become a custom.

The Academy Sergeant Major wears a cloth RMA SANDHURST shoulder title in Number 2 Dress and shirtsleeve order.

1

2

3

4

5

6

7

previous page

1 The Academy Sergeant Major's Foot Guards beret.

opposite page

2 Academy Sergeant Major's wire-embroidered cap badge 4.5 × 5.5 cm and anodised aluminium collar badges 2.5 × 3.5 cm.

3 Academy Sergeant Major's Number 2 Dress shoulder title 11 × 3.5 cm.

Academy Sergeant Major rank badges

4 Full Dress and Mess Dress 12.75 × 12.5 cm.

this page

5 Number 1 Dress rank badge 12.25 × 12 cm.

6 Number 2 Dress rank badge 12.75 × 12.5 cm.

7 WO1 (AcSM) Vince Gaunt.

Defence Technical Undergraduate Scheme

The Defence Technical Undergraduate Scheme, or DTUS, is not an OTC. Army scholars educated at Welbeck College have in recent years mainly proceeded to read for degrees at the Royal Military College of Science. RMCS is converting to a post-graduate university and the scholars now enter the DTUS and have studied at either Southampton or Newcastle Universities. Students are on the strength of Thunderer Squadron whilst at Southampton and Trojan Squadron whilst at Newcastle. Students are also now at Ashton, Loughborough and Northumbria Universities and it is anticipated that Taurus and Typhoon Squadrons will be formed. Officer Cadets wear the Royal Military Academy Sandhurst cap badge.

Thunderer Squadron at Southampton University and Trojan Squadron at Newcastle University students' rank slides.

OCdts Lawrence Till and Rob Ashton wearing the RMA Sandhurst cap badge with the Thunderer Squadron rank slide

Acknowledgement Lt Col Ian Parsons and Flt Lt Dave Vogel

Royal Military College of Science Officer Corps

The Royal Military College of Science, or RMCS, provides the training and administrative unit for Army undergraduates undertaking degree courses at Cranfield University. RMCS does not have an OTC but rather an officer corps. Students who are not commissioned rank as officer cadets and wear the cap badge of the Royal Military Academy Sandhurst. They wear rank slides with RMCSOC woven in black. Under Officers have their rank woven in fawn. Unusually the Senior Under Officer rank slide has three rather than the usual two bars below the Austrian knot.

Senior Under Officer's rank slide.

Acknowledgement WO2 (CSM) Tank Stalker

Recruiting, Training and Media Groups

Recruiting Group

The Army Recruiters badge of a Crown over crossed Union Flags was introduced for wear on Number 1 Dress in 1953 and the present badge, two-thirds the size of the original, was authorised in 1962 for wear on both Number 1 and Number 2 Dress. Army Recruiters now routinely wear Combat Dress on which they are not allowed to wear the full dress badge. Some recruiting offices, known as Army Careers Information Officers or Armed Forces Careers Offices, fund rank slides displaying miniature Recruiters badges.

1 CoH Steve Brown RHG/D wearing the recruiters' unofficial rank slide.
2 Army Recruiting Sergeant unofficial rank slide.
3 Recruiter's appointment badge 8.5 × 8.75 cm.

1

2

3

Initial Training Group

Initial Training Group is responsible for training recruits, except officer cadets who are trained at the Royal Military Academy Sandhurst and Infantry recruits who are trained at the Infantry Training Centre. All recruits complete a Common Military Syllabus as part of their initial training, the first milestone of which is 'passing off the square' after which a recruit is expected to salute officers. Each training unit has a way of identifying those who have and have not passed off the square. Several use coloured rank slides to identify recruits. Officers and non-commissioned officers selected to train recruits have all completed a number of skills courses which involve learning how to instruct the subject. However the particular skills needed to instruct the civilians during recruit training require additional skills which may be gained on specialist courses, the qualification Recruit Instructor being recognised by a qualification badge.

1

2

Army Foundation College

Formed in 1998 in Harrogate, the Army Foundation College trains 16 year olds. The gilded cast metal cap badge is worn by Junior Soldiers during their first six weeks of recruit training. Having 'Passed off the square' they wear their regimental badges.

When the Army Foundation College was established in 1998 it was intended that the junior soldiers, known then as Army Students, would wear AFC cap and collar badges throughout the year long training but practice has changed and they are not worn at present. The collar badges have the lugs removed from the back and were sewn onto Number 2 Dress in order to avoid punching holes into the lapels which might not match those required for the soldiers' regimental collar badges.

All Junior Soldiers at AFC wear rank slides with AFC woven in red. A coloured bar indicates the soldier's Company. Rank badges up to Warrant Officer Class 1 are awarded to the Junior Soldiers and special rank slides indicate those on duty.

6

3

4

5

previous page

1 Recruit Instructor qualification badge 4.5 × 3.75 cm.

2 WO1 (RSM) Stephen McGuire wearing the Recruit Instructor qualification badge below the Argyll and Sutherland Highlanders arm badge.

this page

3 Army Foundation College gilded cast cap badge 4.5 × 4.25 cm and collar badges 3.25 × 3.25 cm.

4 Junior Company Orderly Sergeant and Junior Company Orderly NCO appointment rank slides.

5 JS company identification slide.

6 JS Ben Smith wearing the AFC cap badge and rank slide.

Media Operations Group

The Media Operations Group (Volunteers) provides the Army with media and other specialist expertise in order to communicate key messages and create a positive image. During operations, the Group provides media advice to Commanders, press handling personnel and Combat News Teams.

Media Operations are conducted by a combination of Regular officers and soldiers, Government Communication Information Service staff and TA personnel. The Territorial Army Pool of Information Officers, or TAPIO, was formed in the early 1980s. An arm badge consisting of a sword, pen and electronic flash was introduced in 1995 but it appears to be almost obsolete.

During major operations media correspondents may be embedded with military units. They are treated as members of the unit and provided support ranging from uniforms to rations. They are identified in uniform by a Defence Correspondent appointment slide.

2

1

3

1 Major Cathy Ridge, a TA officer in the Media Ops Group.

2 Territorial Army Pool of Information Officers arm badge 5.75 × 7.25 cm.

3 Defence Correspondent appointment slide.

Army ranks

There are 18 ranks in the Army, seven non-commissioned ranks and 11 commissioned ranks.

NON-COMMISSIONED RANKS

Private There are four Grades of privates; recruits are Class 4, a soldier who has been trained but lacks experience and requires detailed supervision may become Class 3 after 6 months service. A Class 2 soldier has served 18 months and is experienced and capable of performing any task appropriate to his employment without detailed supervision, and Class 1, often known by the obsolete title Grade 1, is achieved by annual tests. Privates are known by a number of titles; Trooper in the Household Cavalry, Royal Armoured Corps and SAS; Gunner in the Royal Artillery; Sapper in the Royal Engineers; Signaller in the Royal Signals; Guardsman in the Foot Guards; Fusilier in The Royal Regiment of Fusiliers, Royal Welsh Fusiliers and Royal Highland Fusiliers; Kingsman in The King's Regiment; Ranger in The Royal Irish Regiment; Rifleman in The Royal Gurkha Rifles and Royal Green Jackets; Craftsman in REME, Air Trooper in the Army Air Corps; Musician in the Corps of Army Music. In addition the title Recruit is used at the Army Training Regiment Pirbright and several regiments use the titles Drummer, Bugler or Piper.

Lance Corporal Known in the Royal Artillery as Lance Bombardier.

Corporal Known as Lance Corporal of Horse in The Household Cavalry; Lance Sergeant in the Foot Guards and Bombardier in the Royal Artillery.

Sergeant Known as Corporal of Horse in The Household Cavalry.

Staff Sergeant Known as Staff Corporal in The Household Cavalry and Colour Sergeant in the Infantry.

Warrant Officer Class 2.

Warrant Officer Class 1.

COMMISSIONED RANKS

Second Lieutenant
Lieutenant
Captain
Major
Lieutenant Colonel
Colonel
Brigadier
Major General
Lieutenant General
General
Field Marshal

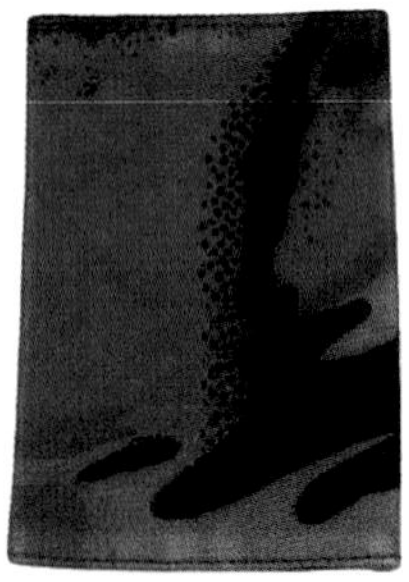
1

2

3

4

5

6

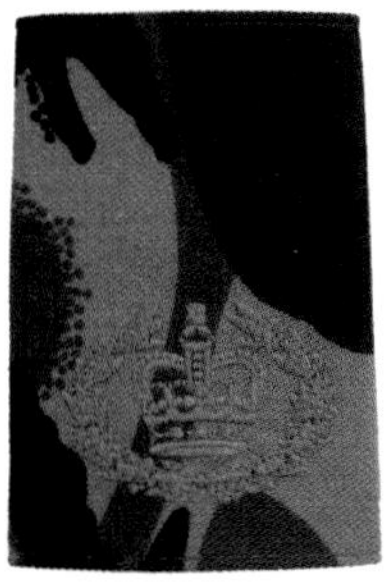
7

8

9

10

11

12

13

14

15

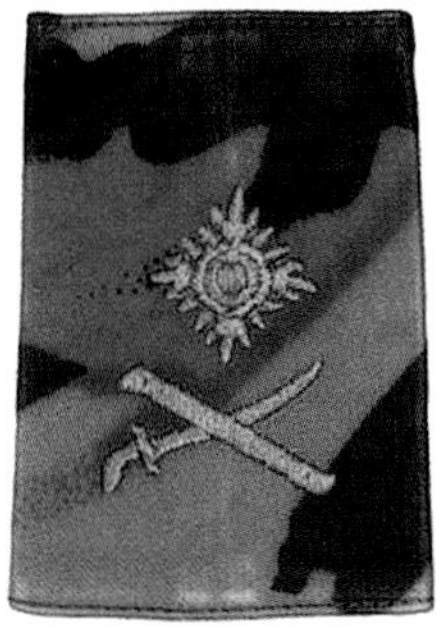
16

17

18

19

20

opposite page

Rank Badges Worn on Combat Dress

1 Private, no insignia.
2 Lance Corporal.
3 Corporal.
4 Sergeant.
5 Staff Sergeant.
6 Warrant Officer Class 2 (known as Sergeant Major).
7 Warrant Officer Class 2 (Quartermaster Sergeant, sometime known as Q).
8 Warrant Officer Class 1.
9 Second Lieutenant.
10 Lieutenant.
11 Captain.
12 Major.
13 Lieutenant Colonel.
14 Colonel.
15 Brigadier
16 Major General.
17 Lieutenant General (**NB** Major General as the junior of the two ranks has a lieutenant's 'pip' and the lieutenant general a major's Crown, and also that the swords are produced in facing pairs).
18 General.

this page

19 Field Marshal.
20 Retired major's rank slide

21

22

23

24

25

26

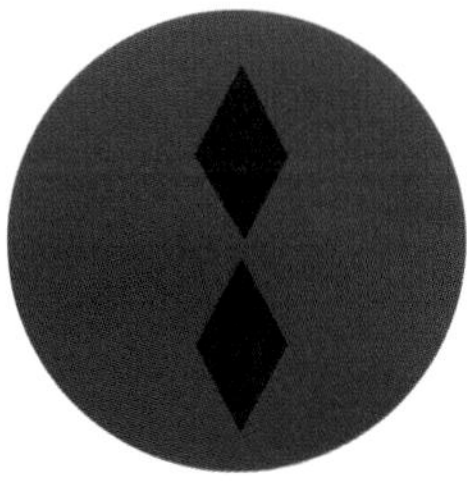

27

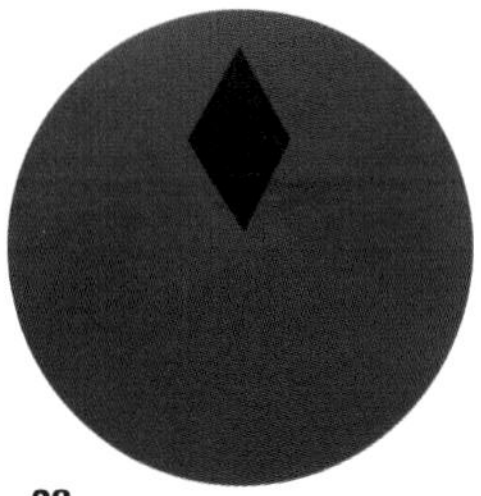

28

29

30

31

32

33

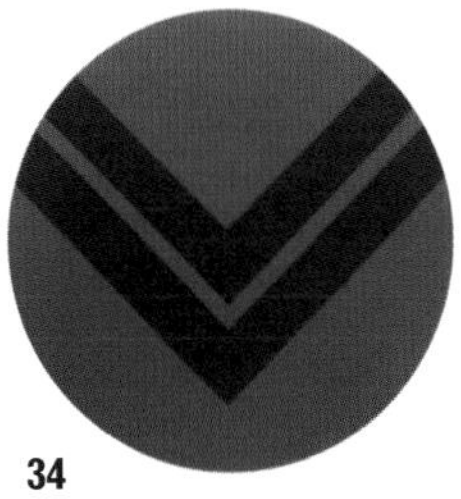

34

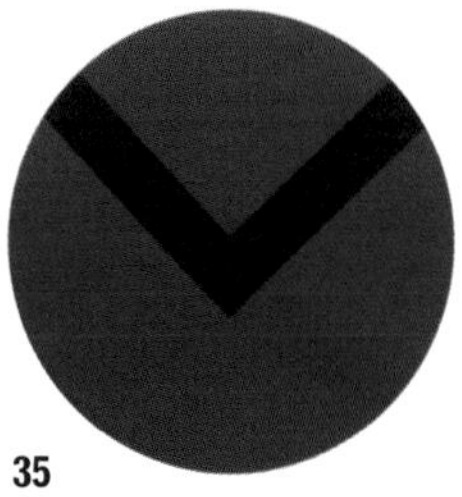

35

Private is thought to derive from the Latin *privare*, an individual without status and without responsibility for others. In the feudal army a private soldier served voluntarily with terms and conditions to reflect his professional status. A public soldier served in the levy drawn from a region, district, or town during a time of emergency. During the Middle Ages the feudal levy (along with the public soldier) was replaced by the militia, which eventually became the Territorial Force in 1908 and the Territorial Army in 1921.

Self Adhesive plastic rank and appointment badges worn on Nuclear, Biological and Chemical protection kit

21 Major General.
22 Brigadier.
23 Colonel.
24 Lieutenant Colonel.
25 Major.
26 Captain.
27 Lieutenant.
28 Second Lieutenant.
29 Warrant Officer Class 1.
30 Quartermaster Sergeant appointment badge.
31 Warrant Officer Class 2
32 Staff Sergeant
33 Sergeant.
34 Corporal.
35 Lance Corporal.
36 Blank badge for writing information

36

Regimental Sergeant Major Rank Badges

The Rank of Warrant Officer Class 1 is the senior non-commissioned rank within the Army. Regimental Sergeant Majors are all Warrant Officers Class 1, but not all Warrant Officers Class 1 are Regimental Sergeant Majors. The Queen's Regulations divide Warrant Officers Class 1 into four groups:

1 Conductor RLC, Royal Artillery Sergeant Major, Academy Sergeant Major RMAS and Garrison Sergeant Major London District,
2 Master Gunner Royal Artillery,
3 Garrison Sergeant Majors except London District,
4 all other.

Conductors and Staff Sergeant Majors RLC take their place on parade with the officers, whilst the Academy Sergeant Major is considered to be the senior sergeant major. Several of the Warrant Officers wear individual badges of rank. (See Royal Military Academy Sandhurst, The Household Division and Royal Artillery).

The appointment of sergeant major was created in 1680 when the Senior Sergeant of the Colonel's Company was to be the Sergeant Major. The rank of sergeant major was created for the Infantry in 1797 and for the Cavalry in 1800.

Badges of rank were introduced on 14 July 1803, four bars for Serjeant Majors and Quarter Master Serjeants, three bars for all other Serjeants and two bars for Corporals. In 1859 The Queen's Regulations stipulated that The Serjeant Major wore a Crown above his chevrons. In 1869 The Serjeant Major's rank was moved to the cuff below the elbow, in the style that continues to be worn by Drum Majors. The chevrons were removed in 1881 leaving the Crown on the cuff, in the present style of Warrant Officers Class 2.

The Serjeant Majors of the Guards had additional duties associated with royal events and were given the title Marshals of the Court. From about 1849 they were allowed the distinction of wearing the Royal Coat of Arms mounted on their four chevrons. When the chevrons were moved to the cuff the Royal Coat of Arms badge remained on the upper arm where it continues to be worn by a select few Guards Regimental Sergeant Majors (see The Guards Division). Sergeant Majors were given Warrant rank in 1881.

Warrant Officers Class 1 were authorised rank badges with coloured backing in 1945. In addition to those illustrated, until about 1992 there were Warrant Officers Class 1 in the Queen's Gurkha Signals and the Queen's Own Gurkha Transport Regiment. Their rank badge was embroidered black on blue. Although the badge remains extant there appear to be none available as the senior ranks in both regiments are now Warrant Officers Class 2.

1

2

3

4

5

6

7

8

9

10

11

12

13

14

15

opposite page

Warrant Officer Class 1 Rank Badges Worn on Number 2 and Number 6 Dress

1 WO1 Chris Tate, RSM 2 ROYAL ANGLIAN wearing the infantry Warrant Officer Class 1 rank badge when on parade with Lt Col Eddie Thorne MC the Commanding Officer.

2 Conductor RLC and Master Gunner RA; arms within the wreath 7.5 cm.

3 Household Division and Honourable Artillery Company, 8 × 8 cm.

4 RAC (except 9/12L); yellow border 8 × 8.5 cm. 9/12L wear the anodised aluminium badge on a black backing (see p292).

5 RA; red border 8 × 8 cm.

6 RE, Royal Signals and REME; blue border, 8 × 8 cm.

this page

7 Infantry (except LI, Royal Irish, PARA, RGR and RGJ), RLC and RMP; scarlet border 8 × 8.5 cm.

8 LI 6.5 × 6.75 cm.

9 Royal Irish Regiment 7.45 × 8.5 cm.

10 RGR 8.5 × 8.5 cm.

11 RGJ and 21 SAS 6.5 × 7 cm.

12 22 and 23 SAS 6.5 × 6.5 cm.

13 AAC and SASC; Cambridge blue border 8 × 8.5 cm.

14 RAMC; dull cherry border.

15 PARA, AGC, RAVC, GSC and CAMUS 6.5 × 7 cm.

16

17

18

19

20

21

16 RADC and Intelligence Corps; green border 8 × 8.5 cm.
17 APTC; black border 8 × 8.5 cm.
18 QARANC; 7 × 7.5 cm.
19 RLC (EOD) (TA) 6.5 × 6.75 cm.
20 Rank badge designed for wear on working dress, such a pullovers and coveralls, by all Arms and Services, but rarely worn, 6.5 × 7 cm.
21 Worn on the Atholl Grey Greatcoat 7 × 7 cm.

Acknowledgement Mr Scott Salter

Generic badges

Employment Badges not sponsored by a particular Arm or Service.

There are a number of badges which are common across the Army.

The German language badge in the Gernman national colours was authorised by British Army of the Rhine, or BAOR, in 1980 to be worn on working dress by soldiers stationed in Germany and able to speak colloquial German.

In 1944 soldiers were organised into four groups of Tradesmen, A to D. C and D trades were discontinued in the 1950s and the others were effectivly discontinued in the 1990s when the system of Common Employment Groups, or CEG, were introduced. The badges remain extant but are rarely seen.

The Crossed Flasgs badge was introduced in 1881 as a prize badge for Telegraphists Royal Engineers at the time when the telegraph was suplementing flags, heliograph and lamps for commications. The Army Order of 1887 awarded the badge with a prize of 15/- per annum to each qualified telegraphist. Signal Regulations 1914 describe the different flags as 'large flags 3 feet square; they are of two colours, white with a blue horizontal stripe for use with a dark background, and dark blue for use with a light background.' The badge is worn by Qualified Signallers on the left forearm and by instructors who have qualified on the upper right arm above their chevrons, or below the Warrant Officer's rank badge on the lower right arm. Instructors who have gained a Distinction on the course wear a small Star above the badge.

1 Cpl Sean Horn REME wearing the German language badge 3 × 3 on his right sleeve.
2 Obsolete A and B Trades badges 4.5 × 3.75 cm.
3 The Army waist belt clasp worn with the sword belt by Warrant Officers and by some regiments and corps without their own clasps.
4 Signaller badge 4.75 × 5.25 cm.
5 SSgt Nath Jones RLC wearing the crossed flags on his upper right arm as a Regimental Signals Instructor.

1

2

3

4

5

BRITISH FORMATION BADGES

Formation badges were introduced for the British Army during the First World War, initially as recognition signs on vehicles. It is claimed that Lieutenant 'Bonhomme' Goodman, the workshop officer of 49th Yorkshire Divisional Supply Column, started the practice in 1915 when he suggested painting the White Rose of Yorkshire on the unit's vehicles in order to recognise them when in trouble. General Percival was not impressed by the initiative, ordered the Roses removed and demanded an explanation from Major Kitson, the Officer Commanding. General Percival must have been convinced by the explanation because General Headquarters (GHQ) approved the idea and before long recognition signs were in use throughout the British Expeditionary Force. By 1920 the formation badges had almost all been removed, except for those worn by five Territorial Army divisions. Formation Signs were readopted in 1940 and re-titled Formation Badges in 1941. By 1945 over 500 different formation badges were in use. The continued use of Formation Badges was agreed in 1948.

Army

The Army flag was approved in 1938 and the badge developed from its design at the end of the 1990s. It is rarely, if ever, worn as a badge on uniform, its use being confined to sports teams.

The one badge that is common to all ranks whatever their regiment, corps or rank, is the Union Flag. In 2002 the Chief of the General Staff directed that the Union Flag badge was to be worn on the left sleeve of combat dress. The Union Flag badge has been worn since 1945 but was only available in small quantities to units deploying on specific operations, and the sewing required has never been a particularly high priority to a busy Army. In recent times a Union Flag badge was approved as an issue item in 1966 as a squarish design approximately 3.75 × 3.25 cm. This was not generally known about and except for the United Nations Honor Guard Platoon serving in Seoul, South Korea, who wore a larger woven version on the right sleeve of Number 6 Dress on parade, the Union Flag badge was not worn.

The Union Flag badge with a white border became common in the Balkans and with British Army Training Teams (BATT) in the mid-1990s and was reportedly bought from the Boy Scouts. (The Union Flag surrounded by a white border is known as the Pilot Jack and is hoisted at the fore by a ship summoning a pilot).

In 2002 the Royal Navy and Royal Air Force had also agreed to wear the Union Flag badge although in late 2004 the Royal Navy considered replacing Combat 95 with a dark blue uniform and the Union Flag with a White Ensign badge.

At the time of CGS' direction that Union Flag badges were to be worn on combat kit insufficient badges were available, and over a year later many soldiers still did not wear the badge. Before the Dress Committee instruction regularised the position some units required the badge to be worn on the right sleeve, and a lesser number wore the Flag on the rank slide. New stocks of Combat 95 shirts are being issued with the flags already sewn on, however there is some discussion about the sensitivity of the Union Flag badge being worn by troops in Northern Ireland where it may be seen by some as more of a sectarian emblem than national flag.

Some units, and individuals, particularly those serving in Sierra Leone, 3 Commando Brigade and 16 Air Assault Brigade have bought and worn 'subdued' green on black Union Flags and inevitably there are better quality private purchase Union Flag badges available.

Nametapes worn on combat dress may not be provided at public expense although they are worn by some units, most notably the Royal Military Academy Sandhurst. Some troops serving on exchange posting with US units wear a British Army nametape over the left breast pocket.

1

2

3

4

5

6

7

8

opposite page

1 Army badge 8.75 × 6.25 cm produced for the Recruiting Group and worn by some sports teams.

2 The Union Flag is still worn sewn onto a rank slide by some Territorial Army units which are not issued sufficient badges.

this page

3 Union Flag worn on the upper left sleeve 4.5 × 2.25cm.

4 Obsolete 'Boy Scouts' Union Flag badge 4 × 2.75cm.

5 Private purchase subdued Union Flag badge worn in Sierra Leone and occasionally elsewhere 4 × 2.75cm.

6 New good quality private purchase Union Flag badge 4 × 2.75cm.

7 Trial pattern White Ensign that may replace the Union Flag for the Royal Navy 4.5 × 2.5cm.

8 Name tape worn by troops serving on exchange with US units 12.5 × 2.5 cm.

Acknowledgement Maj Bruce Perkins

Permanent Joint Headquarters

PJHQ is the Tri-Service Headquarters which commands operational deployments. The badge is the Combined Operations badge superimposed on the Tri-Service colours. The circular design of the Combined Operations badge is worn as a Drop Zone flash by 148 (Meiktila) Commando Forward Observation Battery, (see p. 64) and a square version as a formation sign by Joint Force Headquarters (see p. 485).

1 PJHQ arm badge 6.5 × 5.25 cm.

Acknowledgement Cpl Jason Odisseos-Nilsson

Divisions

There are two deployable divisions in the Army, three regional division headquarters and also a number of other 'Two Star' headquarters which command Army units, including HQ Northern Ireland, the UK Amphibious Force and the Joint Helicopter Command. ('Two Star' is military shorthand for a major general and the equivalent in the other Services).

Formation signs are usually worn on the left sleeve of the Combat 95 shirt and the Field Jacket or smock by Headquarters staff and by troops of the Headquarters signal regiment.

1st (United Kingdom) Armoured Division

1st (UK) Armoured Division has used the symbol of the charging rhino, the strongest and best protected animal, since just before the Battle of El Alamein, 1942. The original design of a docile rhino is said to have been changed arbitrarily by a Royal Engineers sign-writer from 3 Troop, Cheshire Field Squadron who was repainting the Divisional HQ sign. The new aggressive rhino was approved of as being more in keeping with the Division's offensive spirit, and adopted as the Division's badge. The present subdued style badge was introduced in 1995 and is worn on the right sleeve in order that the rhino always appears to be charging to the front.

1st (UK) Armoured Division arm badge 6 × 5.25 cm.

2nd Division *The Army in Scotland and the North of England*

The 2nd Division uses the traditional badge of crossed keys. From the earliest times it was the practice to raise two armies in England, one in the north and one in the south. The crossed keys are derived from the arms of the Archbishop of York, which were borne on the shields and banners of the northern army, raised by the Archbishop. The present badges were introduced in 1996.

2nd Division printed arm badges 6 × 5 cm.

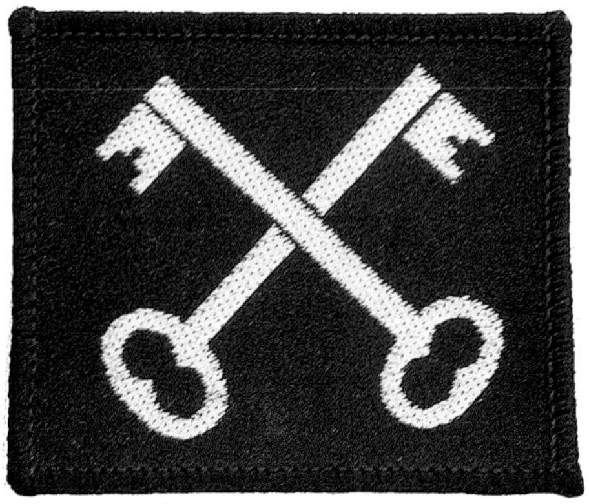

3rd (United Kingdom) Division

In 1940 Major General Bernard Montgomery chose the sign, representing the 3rd Division with its three infantry brigades each with three infantry battalions. The Staff's inspiration for the original design may have been the emblem on Bass bottled beer, or alternatively the shape may have represented the three corners of Great Britain, which the Division was preparing to defend against German invasion. The present badge was introduced in 1993.

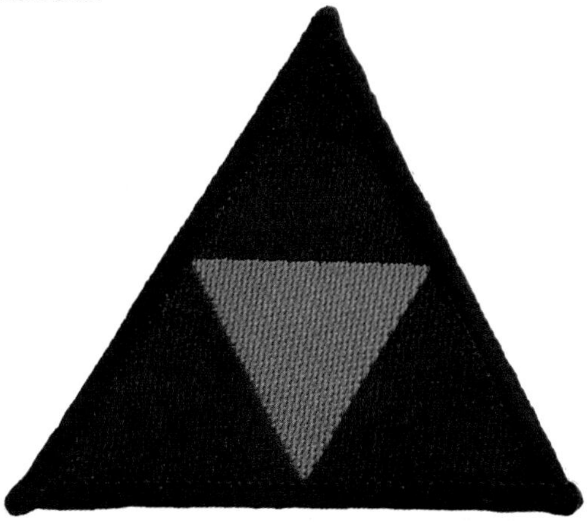

3rd (UK) Division arm badge 7.5 × 6.5 cm.

4th Division

Unusually the badge is worn with the design, a tiger's head, facing to the rear.

In 1992 4th Armoured Division was disbanded in Germany and South East District was renamed the 4th Division. Therefore the South East District badge has been retained rather than that of the 4th Armoured Division.

4th Division arm badge 5 × 5 cm.

Lawrence Irving was asked to design a badge by General Sir Bernard Paget during the Second World War for South East Command. He chose a stylised tiger's head. The present design is by the daughter of Lieutenant General Sir Richard Swinburn who was commanding HQ South East District.

Acknowledgement Major Phil Thomsett

UK Support Command (Germany)

HQ UKSC(G) was formed in 1994 as part of the restructuring of British Forces Germany following the collapse of the Warsaw Pact.

UKSC(G) is the descendent of the Second World War 21st Army Group which in 1945 was re-titled British Army of the Rhine (BAOR). The 21st Army Group badge continued in use by HQ BAOR and UKSC(G) on signs and letterheads and the badge was reintroduced for uniform in 2003.

HQ UKSC(G) 4 × 5.5 cm.

Headquarters Northern Ireland

The Headquarters Northern Ireland badge, based on the badge of the Royal Ulster Rifles, was introduced in 1948 to replace the design of a five barred gate worn during the Second World War.

HQNI arm badge 5 × 5.75 cm.

Acknowledgement Sgt AP Gatty AGC(SPS)

United Kingdom Amphibious Force

The UK Amphibious Force, commanded by Commandant General Royal Marines, is one of the Royal Navy's deployable formations. It commands Army Commandos and other Army units.

UK Amphibious Force arm badge 7 × 7 cm.

Joint Helicopter Command

The Joint Helicopter Command, or JHC, was formed in 2000 with Royal Marines and Army Air Corps helicopters and RAF support helicopters The Joint Helicopter Command Iraq 'desert' badge was introduced in 2004.

1 Joint Helicopter Command arm badges 5 × 5 cm.
2 JHC flying badge 9 × 11.5 cm.

1

2

Brigades

Until 1957 it was usual to wear Division arm badges but with the reduction in the size of the Army in 1957 Brigades were moved more frequently between Divisions and Brigade arm badges were adopted but have drifted in and out of favour. At present the Army Dress Committee has regularised the situation and most brigades, and similar 'one star' formations, have and wear an arm badge. They are usually worn on the left sleeve of the Combat 95 light jacket, with a subdued version sometimes worn on the left sleeve of the Field Jacket and smock.

Joint Force Headquarters

Joint Force Headquarters, or JFHQ, deploys from Permanent Joint Headquarters. Both wear the Combined Operations badge. The square shaped badge was worn as a Drop Zone flash by 148 (Meiktila) Commando Forward Observation Battery until the 1990s. The Battery now wears a circular version of the badge (see p. 64).

Joint Force Headquarters arm badge 7.5 × 7.5 cm.

Acknowledgement
Corporal Jason Odisseos-Nilsson

1st Artillery Brigade

1st Artillery Brigade wears the Ram's Head as a formation sign. It was first used as the sign of the 4th Division in 1916. The black on green subdued badge was introduced in 2004. The badge gained some notoriety in 2001 when farmers took exception to it being worn by soldiers involved in the cull during the Foot and Mouth epidemic.

1st Artillery Brigade arm badges 5 × 3.75 cm.

1 Mechanized Brigade

The 1 Mechanised Brigade badge was introduced for 1 Infantry Brigade in 1982. It was superseded by the ACE Mobile Force badge between 1988 and 1992. The present badge was introduced in 1996.

1 Mechanized Brigade arm badge 5 × 4.5 cm.

Acknowledgement Major Ian Cameron

1st Military Intelligence Brigade

1st Military Intelligence Brigade is a Theatre Troops brigade as yet not wearing a badge although the Army Dress Committee has registered the design based upon the colours of the Intelligence Corps.

1st (UK) Reconnaissance Brigade

The Allied Rapid Reaction Corps Recce Brigade was established in 1996 and considered adopting the Reconnaissance Corps badge from the Second World War as the brigade badge. Instead a yellow seahorse on a blue ground, the badge of the Second World War 27th Armoured Brigade, which had been formed as 1st Armoured Brigade, was selected. At the last moment the Commanding Officer The Queen's Own Yeomanry pointed out that the sea horse is now the international symbol for transvestites. The Fox's head badge of the Second World War 8th Armoured Brigade was chosen instead when the brigade was renamed 1st Recce Brigade in 1998. The fox was chosen as representing stealth, cunning and guile, all qualities expected of recce troops. Major Graham Wilding RTR redrew the fox's head for the final badge from an illustration on the cover of Country Life magazine. (It was not explained how CO QOY knew about the modern interpretation of the sea horse emblem).

Major Graham Wilding's sketch for the Recce Brigade badge.

The original 8th Armoured Brigade badge used as the model for the 1st Recce Brigade badge.

1st (UK) Reconnaissance Brigade arm badge 5 cm.

Acknowledgement Captain JR Tector

1st Signal Brigade and Rhine Garrison

1st Signal Brigade was formed in 1995 to command signals units deployed to the Former Yugoslavia. The brigade adopted the Second World War badge of 1st Corps Signals in 1996.

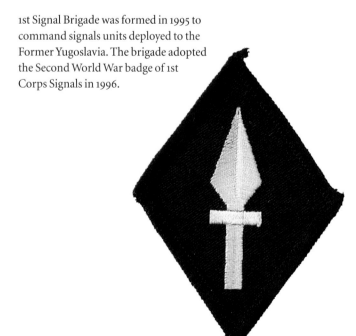

1st Signal Brigade arm badge 6 × 7.75 cm.

2nd (Infantry) Brigade

The coloured sign was produced for 2nd (South East) Brigade in 1994 with the subdued version introduced in 1996. There is a report that the coloured version was worn only by the Chief of Staff and by members of the Brigade Training Team before being superseded by the subdued version.

2nd (Infantry) Brigade arm badge 3.75 × 4.5 cm.

2nd (National Communication) Signal Brigade

The 2nd (National Communications) Signal Brigade was formed in 1968 to command the units which provide fixed communications within UK.

The Brigade badge was introduced in 1998. Brigadier Gordon Hughes, who commanded from 1997–2000, introduced the coloured badge. The subdued version was introduced by 39th (Skinners) Signal Regiment in 1998 and was later adopted by the Brigade Headquarters Staff but is actively discouraged by the present Brigade Commander.

25th Division used a red horseshoe as a formation sign during the First World War. Major General Sir Guy Bainbridge chose it to help restore esprit-de-corps after the heavy casualties suffered at the beginning of the Battle of the Somme in 1916. It was reintroduced for 13 Signal Group in 1967 and passed down in due course to 2 (NC) Signal Brigade.

2nd (National Communications) Brigade arm badges 5 × 5.25 cm.

13th Signals Group was formed in 1967 and the horseshoe with 13 nail holes adopted as a formation sign. It was renumbered as 2nd Signals Group in 1972. The present badge retains 13 nail holes as recognition of its antecedents. The first batch of badges had 12 nail holes and they were not officially issued.

Acknowledgement Major Tom Dean

2 Medical Brigade

The 2 Medical Brigade, redesignated from Headquarters Medical Group, commands medical units in UK and became operational in 2002. The cross represents the Geneva Red Cross and the four arms also represent the four Corps in the brigade; Royal Army Medical Corps, Queen Alexandra's Royal Army Nursing Corps, Royal Army Dental Corps and Royal Army Veterinary Corps. The central logo depicts the international symbol of medicine; Aesculapius's Rod and the serpent.

2 Medical Brigade arm badge 3.75 × 4.75 cm.

3 Commando Brigade

The Royal Marines 3 Commando Brigade includes supporting Army units. Army Commando units, known at first as Special Service Troops, were formed in 1940. Commando brigades wore a badge of a unsheathed red dagger now worn by all commando trained soldiers but not by the Royal Marines who wear a shoulder title on Combat Dress, ROYAL MARINES COMMANDO. The present badge was introduced in 1996.

3 Commando Brigade arm badge 7 × 7.25 cm.

3 Infantry Brigade

3 Infantry Brigade was an operational brigade in Northern Ireland until disbanded in 2004.

The design of the badge evolved from the brigade's service with the 1st Division during the Second World War when the white triangle was worn, representing the point of 1st Corps' spearhead badge. The red Roman numeral III and the red border represent the brigade's later service as an independent formation in Cyprus.

3 Infantry Brigade arm badge 4.5 × 4 cm.

Acknowledgement Major Ian Comber

4th Armoured Brigade

The sign of the black Desert Rat was introduced early in 1940 when 4th Armoured Brigade was formed from the Light Armoured Group in Egypt. The badge was reintroduced during Gulf War 1 in 1900 or 1991 on a sand coloured backing. The subdued version was then introduced in 1992, and the present sand coloured version in 2003.

4th Armoured Brigade arm badges 6.5 × 5.5 cm.

7th Armoured Brigade

7th Armoured Brigade was formed in 1940 in 7th Armoured Division. The General Officer Commanding, Major General PCS Hobart adopted the Jerboa or Desert Rat as the Divisional emblem, 'This little animal should become our emblem: we must learn to live as he does, the hard way in the desert.' The first Division badge had a red rat in a white circle; the second version had a brown rat outlined in white. 7th Armoured Brigade adopted a green rat badge when it was sent from North Africa to Burma in 1942, where it was known as the 'Jungle Rat'.

In 1991 several thousand badges were ordered and delivered whilst the Brigade was engaged in the Gulf War. The Desert Rat had been woven in orange rather than the correct red. The next batch of correctly coloured red Desert Rats was delivered after a break of 12 years, in 2003. It is worn on the right sleeve in order that the Rat faces forward.

There is a similar badge with a red rat on an olive green background with a black merrowed edge which was worn by 4 Field Squadron, 21 Engineer Regiment during operational tours in the Former Yugoslavia. The badge was introduced in 1995 but now appears to be obsolete.

7th Armoured Brigade arm badges 5 × 6cm. The 'orange rat' issued from 1991–2003, the Red Rat issued between 1980–1991 and reintroduced in 2003. Subdued badge worn on the Field Jacket.

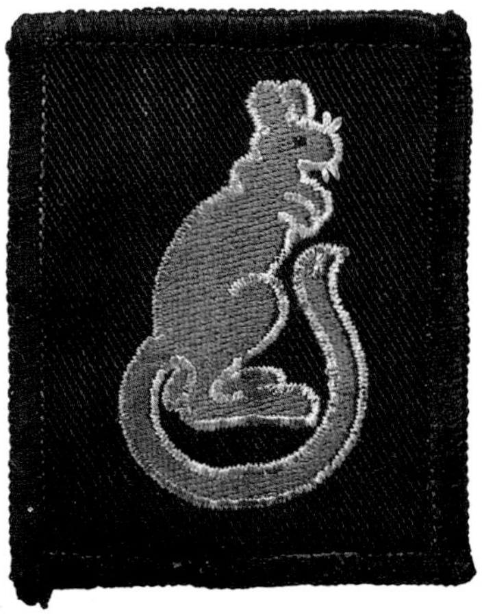

7 Air Defence Brigade

7 Air Defence Brigade adopted the Centaur badge when it was reformed in 1997. 7th Anti-Aircraft Brigade was formed in 1947; it was redesignated 7th Army Group Royal Artillery (Anti-Aircraft), or 7 AGRA, in 1955 and the Centaur adopted as the formation sign. At the time star signs were particularly popular amongst the AGRA then being formed. The Centaur is the seventh star constellation and the bow and arrow had been symbolic of air defence during the Second World War. The coloured badge, introduced in 1997, is reported to be unpopular with the regular troops in the Brigade and was replaced by the black and green subdued version in 2004.

7 Air Defence Brigade arm badge 6.5 × 5 cm.

7 Air Defence Brigade subdued arm badge 5.5 × 4.5 cm.

Acknowledgement
Major Nick Makin, Capt Jon Wheale and WO2 Ronnie Biggs

8 (Land Support) Engineer Brigade

8 (Land Support) Engineer Brigade is a Theatre Troops brigade renamed from Theatre Troops Royal Engineers in 2005 and as yet not wearing a badge.

8 Infantry Brigade

8 Infantry Brigade badge, representing Richmond Castle, was adopted when the brigade was reformed in Catterick in 1965. The present badge, representing Castle Tower, was adopted in 1999. There has been discussion amongst collectors that the badge represents the Gate of Jerusalem, the proverbial 'Eye of the needle', but the official description remains Castle Tower.

8 Infantry Brigade arm badge 5 × 5 cm

Acknowledgement Major Paul Tilley

11 (ARRC) Signal Brigade

11 (ARRC) Signal Brigade was formed in 1967 and the arm badge adopted in 1994. A subdued version of the badge was produced in 1998 but was not approved.

11 (ARRC) Signal Brigade arm badge 6.5 × 5 cm.

Acknowledgement Major Colin McGrory

12 (Air Support) Engineer Group

Renamed from 12 (Air Support) Engineer Brigade in 2005 having been formed as 12 Engineer Group in the 1960s the Group badge represents the Royal Engineers red and blue colours on a diamond. These are reproduced as black and green on the subdued version of the badge worn on uniform.

12 (Air Support) Engineer Brigade 4.75 × 5.5 cm

12 Mechanized Brigade

Brigadier Adrian Freer OBE chose the badge when the headquarters in Aldershot was redesignated from 5th Airborne Brigade to 12th Mechanised Brigade in 1999.

The Ace of Spades is a traditional sign of death. In 1966 United States Army Lt Charles W Brown serving with Company C, Second Battalion, 35th Regiment, 25th Infantry Division in Vietnam asked the United States Playing Card Company for packs of playing cards printed only with the Ace of Spades. The cards were left after actions on the bodies of dead Viet Cong. The action is famously depicted in the film Apocalypse Now (see 665 Squadron Army Air Corps). The practice became widespread and the so-called 'Death Cards' were banned by the US Army in 1967 but were common again in Viet Nam by 1971.

One version of the Ace of Spades card used by 101st Airborne Division in Vietnam in 1966 was reproduced by the Division during the war to liberate Kuwait in 1991.

Before the invasion of Iraq in 2003 a deck of cards identifying the 52 most wanted Iraqis was issued to coalition forces. The Ace of Spades featured President Saddam Husayn Al-Tikriti.

12 Mechanized Brigade Headquarters and Signal Squadron have a farewell presentation with the quotation, Don't dilly dally with the Ace of Spades; it is the mark of death.

The Ace of Spades was previously used as a badge by 25th Indian Division from 1942–1945. The coloured badge was introduced in 1999 and the subdued version in about 2003.

12th Mechanized Brigade arm badges 5 × 5 cm.

Acknowledgement WO1 K Marsh

15th (North East) Brigade

The badge of 15th (North East) Brigade introduced by Brigadier Andrew Farquhar MBE in 2001 is a Merlin, a small but ferocious bird of prey that roams the dales and moors of northeast England, on a red Infantry ground. Brigadier Michael Aris had adopted the original badge, a Merlin in the kill posture, when 15 Infantry Brigade was reformed in 1982. The approved badge faces to the right, or forward, when worn on the left sleeve.

64th (City of Sheffield) Signal Squadron wears a different version of the badge (see 38th Signal Regiment).

15th (North East) Brigade Obsolete arm badge 5 × 6 cm facing the wrong way, Approved badge facing the front when worn on the left sleeve.

Acknowledgement Major James Illingworth

16 Air Assault Brigade

The 16 Air Assault Brigade badge, adopted in 1999, combines the Army Air Corps eagle with the quartered colours of Airborne Forces and of the Army Air Corps. It is a copy of the Second World War badge of the Special Training Centre, Lochailort, the original commando training centre from 1940–1942, which had a golden eagle on a black and white quartered shield.

The badge is not popular with the older parachute trained soldiers of the brigade. The airborne insignia since the inception of airborne formations in 1941 had always been Bellerophon astride Pegasus, designed by Daphne du Maurier, the wife of Major General 'Boy' Browning and the first commander of 1st Airborne Division. Airborne troops, amongst others, have a piece of white material sewn under the collar of their smock or field jacket. At night the collar can be turned up giving troops moving in file a marker when following the man in front. Since the demise of the Pegasus badge it has become the custom of older soldiers to wear the Pegasus badge under the collar in place of the white patch.

In 1941 Brigadier 'Boy' Browning, commanding 24 Infantry Brigade (Guards) used his personal crest, red griffin wings on a blue background, as the brigade badge. The present style of badge was issued in 1993, a slightly different style with 'full Gryphons wings' was available to purchase from 1995. The badge was superseded on the formation of 16 Air Assault Brigade in 1999, but continues to be seen occasionally.

16 Air Assault Brigade was formed from 5th Airborne Brigade and 24th Airmobile Brigade in 2000. It combines parachute units, air assault units and Attack Helicopters. The Chief of the General Staff wrote:

> Our capability will also be enhanced by retaining the utility but increasing the potency of airborne forces. We will brigade all our 'airminded' forces, by embedding the smaller in-role parachute forces in a new air manoeuvre formation – together with the three aviation regiments that will be equipped with the Apache Longbow attack helicopter. This will have a number of advantages: the early entry capability of the Lead Parachute Battalion Group, combined arms support to complement the attack helicopter, and greatly increased tactical mobility and firepower in-theatre for parachute forces

Troops serving with airborne units are identified by a Drop Zone, or DZ flash worn on the right arm. Troops serving with air assault units wear a Landing Zone, or LZ, flash, which in some cases is the same as the Tactical Recognition Flash, or TRF. The flashes are listed with each unit as appropriate.

1

4

2

3

5

6

7

previous page

1 16 Air Assault Brigade arm badges 5.5 × 6.5cm.

2 Obsolete 24th Airmobile Brigade badge 5 × 6 cm worn by some AAC.

3 Obsolete 5th Airborne Brigade badge 4.5 × 4.5 cm worn unofficially under the collar of the smock.

4 Headquarters 16 Air Assault Brigade Landing Zone flash 7 × 7 cm.

5 Brigade Parachute Squadron RAF LZ 6.5 × 6.5 cm.

this page

6 Pathfinder Platoon Drop Zone flash 7 × 7 cm.

7 Corporal from the Pathfinder Platoon in freefall, the DZ badge visible on his right sleeve below the Parachute wings.
Photograph *Parachute Regiment*

19 Mechanized Brigade

A panther emblem was adopted in 1957 when it was planned that 19 Brigade became independent. The design represents Bagheera, the celebrated panther from Rudyard Kipling's Jungle Book, an animal representing alertness, strength and compassion.

The new badge was introduced in time for the Brigade's deployment to Iraq in 2003.

Obsolete 19 Brigade badges
Two obsolete Brigade badges, known for many years by the nickname 'spewing tiger', continue to be worn by a few of those who had served in 19 Brigade.

1

2

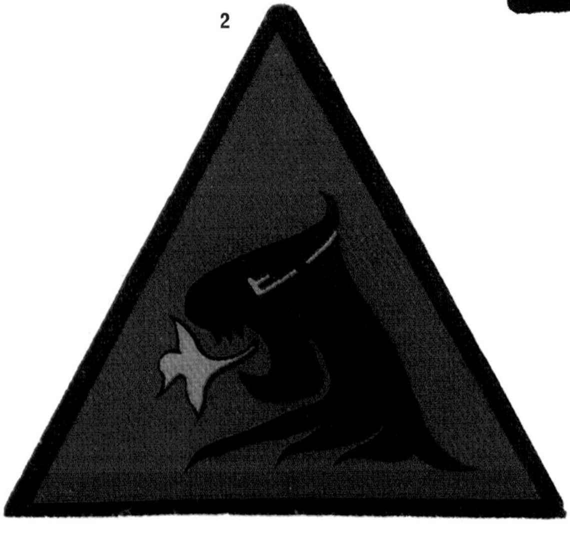

3

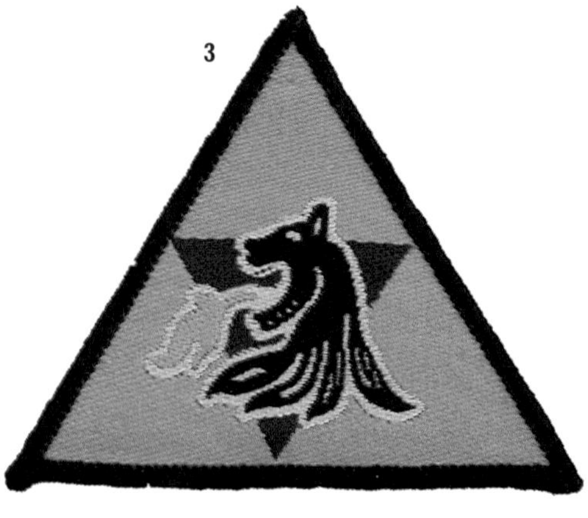

1 19 Mechanized Brigade arm badge 6.5 × 6 cm.

2 Obsolete badge 7.5 × 6.25 cm worn by 7 Field Force and 19 Brigade 1977–2003.

3 Obsolete badge 6.5 × 5.25 cm worn 1993–2003.

20th Armoured Brigade

20th Armoured Brigade copied the style of the Second World War badge originally introduced in 1940 by 6th Armoured Division. Its badge had been a white mailed fist on a black square. The present design was adopted in 1992 and altered to the present style in 1995 for a tour with the United Nations Protection Force, or UNPROFOR, in the Former Yugoslavia. The subdued badge with the black fist was introduced by Brigadier Jeff Cook MC for the Field Jacket in 1998.

20th Armoured Brigade arm badges 5.25 × 5.5 cm.

29 (Land Support) Engineer Group

Renamed from 29 (Corps Support) Engineer Brigade in 2005 the Group badge of the Scottish Lion on the Royal Engineers red and blue striped background is not worn as a badge. The subdued version of the badge is worn.

The Scottish Lion for the badge was chosen as the Group traces its origins to 264 (Scottish) Beach Brigade TA which had been formed in 1947.

29 (Land Support) Engineer Group arm badge 4.75 × 5.5 cm.

Acknowledgement Major Ian McCormick

39 Infantry Brigade

During the first years of 'The Troubles' in Northern Ireland Brigadier Frank Kitson wanted his operational brigade to have a badge with historical significance, and consequently adopted the Horseshoe badge in 1971. A black horseshoe was used as a formation sign by 13th (Western) Division, which included 39 Brigade, during the First World War and had been chosen to help counter any possible bad luck from the number 13. The Division gained the popular nickname the 'Iron Division'. The previous brigade badge in use in 1971 had no historical significance. It is said that the black and Brunswick green colours of the new badge were strongly influenced by the fact that both brigade commanders since the outbreak of violence in Northern Ireland had been from The Rifle Brigade. The subdued version of the badge is said to have been issued in 1971. The coloured version of the badge is issued and the subdued version is unofficial.

39 Infantry Brigade arm badges 4 × 4 cm.

Acknowledgement
Major Ben Hughes and WO1 (RSM) PM Downie

42 (North West) Brigade

The rose within a red diamond badge was originally introduced for the Lancashire Division in 1947 and eventually passed to 42 Infantry Brigade based in Chester. The brigade was later disbanded. North West District had been formed at Preston and in 1991 became 42 (NW) Brigade, adopting the 42 Infantry Brigade badge in 1995. The brigade covers four counties and the Lancashire centric badge did not prove popular and was rarely worn. The formation sign was changed in 2003 when the North West District badge was reintroduced, a gold sword pointing to the north west superimposed on the 1916 pattern 42 Infantry Brigade badge.

Subdued badge 5 × 5 cm introduced in 2004.

Acknowledgement
Major Tony Wilby and WO1 (RSM) R Glendinning

42 (North West) Brigade badge 5 × 5 cm introduced in 2003.

43rd (Wessex) Brigade

The badge of 43rd (Wessex) Brigade is the Wyvern, a creature with origins in both eastern and northern mythology. The dragon is attributed to the bringer of death and the serpent was the symbol of guile. The Saxons who landed in the West Country in the fifth century bore the symbol of the dragon painted on the shields and carved on the bows of their ships. The design evolved into the Wyvern during the Dark Ages as the warriors learnt the art of cunning in war. Alfred the Great used the symbol during his campaigns in Kent and Wessex, and the Bayeux tapestry shows that it was raised by Harold at the Battle of Hastings in 1066. It continued in use in the coats of arms of the fighting men of Wessex and was chosen in 1915 as the sign of 43rd (Wessex) Division from whom it was handed down to the Brigade and adopted as an arm badge in 1994

43rd (Wessex) Brigade arm badge 5.5 × 5.5 cm.

Acknowledgement Major Andy Jennings

49 (East) Brigade

The first polar bear badge was introduced as a play on words as the formation sign for VII Corps, commanded by Lieutenant General Sir T D'O Snow, in 1915.

The present polar bear badge was originally the second design chosen by the 49th (West Riding) Division whilst serving in Iceland between 1940–1943. The badge is said to have been based on the familiar logo of 'Fox's glacier mints'.
The present badges were introduced in 1993.

46th (City of Derby) Signal Squadron wears a different version of the badge (see 38th Signal Regiment, p.388).

49 (East) Brigade arm badges 7.5 × 5.5cm and 7 × 5.25 cm.

51 (Scottish) Brigade

Consideration of the options for a badge for the new 51 (Scottish) Brigade began in 2000 with the suggestion of a red lion Rampant on a blue background in order to reflect the colours of its forerunner, the 51st Highland Brigade. The use of the Lion Rampant meant that the badge had to be submitted to Lord Lyon King of Arms. The proposal was not accepted and instead Lion Court suggested the heraldically correct gold lion Rampant, which had been worn as an arm badge by Headquarters Scotland since 1996. The background to the new badge to be divided to represent the purple heather of the Highlands and the lush green of the Lowlands. The badge was originally introduced for the North Highland District during the Second World War and retained in 1948 by Highland District. It was authorised for 51 Brigade in 2002.

51 (Scottish) Brigade arm badge 4.5 × 4.5 cm.

Acknowledgement Mrs Eslea MacDonald

52 Infantry Brigade

52 Infantry Brigade wears the traditional Scottish badge of St Andrew's cross. First worn by 52nd (Lowland) Division during the First World War with a thistle on the centre, the present badge was adopted by the Division in 1940 and also worn by 155th Independent Brigade Group (TA) from 1948, and 30th (Lowland) Armoured Brigade from 1952 and eventually by 52nd Infantry Brigade. The present badge was introduced in 1998.

52 Infantry Brigade arm badges 5 × 5 cm.

101 Logistic Brigade

The badge, known as 'Sammy' was chosen for the Combat Service Support Group (UK) when formed in 1997 and retained when it was retiled 101 Logistic Brigade in 1999. (The designation 101 Logistic Brigade was given historical perspective as 101 Beach Sub-Area was under command 3rd Infantry Division, I Corps during the Assault Landings in Normandy on D Day, 1944).

The 'black adder' design of the badge was originally chosen by Brigadier Martin White commanding the Force Maintenance Area during the war to liberate Kuwait in 1991. His daughter asked him if he had 'a cunning plan' – a well known expression originally said by Baldrick in the popular *Blackadder* television series. The *Blackadder* theme was used throughout the FMA, which included Baldrick Lines and Meltchett Lines, Blackadder Camp and Camp Bob.

The black on sand version of the badge is worn on desert combat shirts.

101 Logistic Brigade arm badges 4x5.25 cm.

Acknowledgement WO1 Fray

102 Logistic Brigade

The halberd badge was chosen for 102 Logistic Brigade in 1999. (The designation 102 Logistic Brigade was given historical perspective as 102 Beach Sub-Area was under command 3rd Canadian Division, I Corps during the Assault Landings in Normandy on D Day, 1944).

The halberd appears in the Old Testament book of Jeremiah as the embodiment of strength, success and restoration. The dual capability of the halberd as weapon and hand tool represents the combination of artisan and technical skills combined with the war fighting skills. The badge is also symbolic of the spirit of the Crusader and was the badge of 78th Division from 1942.

The commercially produced black on sand version of the badge has not been authorised.

Acknowledgement Major Steve Carrington

102 Logistic Brigade arm badges 4.5 × 4.5 cm.

107 (Ulster) Brigade

107 (Ulster) Brigade (Volunteers) wears traditional Irish badges. The shamrock was worn by 38th Infantry Brigade during the Second World War and later by the North Irish Brigade. The Red Hand, the traditional Baronet's badge, had been the sign chosen by 36th (Ulster) Division during the First World War. The present badge was worn by 107th (Ulster) Infantry Brigade (TA) between 1950–1967 and readopted in 1988 until the Brigade Commander ordered the badges to be removed from uniforms in 2002.

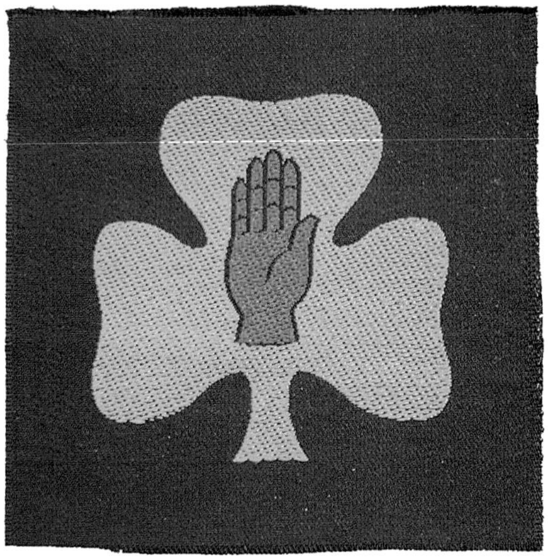

107 (Ulster) Brigade arm badge 7.5 × 7.5 cm.

143 (West Midlands) Brigade

143 (West Midlands) Brigade adopted the Macaw sign of 48 Division as its badge when reformed in 1984. 48 Division's original sign had been a white diamond but in October 1939 Major General Andrew Thorne, GOC 48th Division changed the design after entering Littlecote House, Berkshire where he was apparently greeted by a Macaw calling out what sounded like 'Good luck, good luck'. The present badge dates to 1994. It is told that when Prince Andrew, Duke of York first saw the brigade badge on the arm of a female soldier he asked 'What's that bird?' The escorting officer replied 'Private Williams, Sir.'

143 (West Midlands) Brigade arm badge 4.5 × 6.5 cm.

Acknowledgement Major Paul Armitage

145 (Home Counties) Brigade

Formed in 1902, the brigade was resurrected when 145 (HC) Brigade was formed as a Regional Brigade in 1995. The badge, adopted in 2004, has a Roebuck, an animal common across the Home Counties, on the RBGW red diamond on the PWRR blue backing. The badge was designed by committee with final authority being given by Brigadier John Deverell OBE. The second pattern issued to TA units has the Roebuck facing to the right, or forward when on the left sleeve. (See Royal Rifle Volunteers)

145 (Home Counties) Brigade first pattern arm badge 5.25 × 5.25 cm.

Second pattern 5.5 × 5.5 cm.

Acknowledgement WO1 (RSM) Brian Stoddart

160(Wales) Brigade *Pencadlys 160 Brigâd (Cymru)*

The badge of 160 (Wales) Brigade was originally designed by Major General BT Wilson CB DSO and worn by 53rd (Welsh) Division. The design is said variously to be; the W for Wales, a diagram of an assault, a Bardic Crown, or a Welsh woman's hat. It was adopted by 160 (Wales) Brigade in 1995.

160 (Wales) Brigade arm badge 4.5 × 4.25 cm.

Acknowledgement Major Lance Patterson

HQ Rhine and European Support Group

HQ Rhine and European Support Group was formed from 1st Signal Brigade in 2004. The badge was originally adopted in 1947 for Rhine Army Troops and worn from 1996 by Training Support Command Germany.

HQ Rhine and European Support Group arm badge 5 × 5 cm.

Training and Support Units

15 (UK) Psychological Operations Group

15 (UK) Psychological Group is a tri-service unit established in 1999. The title was 15 (UK) Psychological Operations Group in 1997 when some members of the unit wore a coloured arm badge featuring a caribou. In 2000 the renamed 15 (UK) Information Support Group adopted a subdued black on green version of the badge. The badge has been approved as a formation sign for 15 (UK) Psychological Group but is not being issued at present.

The unit traces its history to the Indian Field Broadcast Units formed in 1943 and tasked with reducing the enemy's will to fight. The present number 15 was chosen as it was a 'spare' number from the Second World War when Battlefield Psychological Support units 10–14 and 16–20 served in 21st Army Group. The number 15 also does not conflict with any number used by similar US units. The arm badge is based upon that of the IFBU.

15 (UK) Psychological Group arm badge 5.25 × 5.25 cm.

15(UK) Psychological Operations Group obsolete private purchase arm badge 6.25 × 5 cm.

British Army Training Unit Suffield

Canadian Forces Base Suffield, or CFB Suffield, was established in Alberta, Canada in 1971 in order to oversee British All-Arms Battle Group training, which, until Major Gadaffi seized power, had been conducted in the Western Desert in Libya. The co-located British training camp, Camp Crowfoot, was opened in 1972 and the first Exercise Medicine Man conducted by 4th Royal Tank Regiment the same year. The Medicine Hat News, the local town newspaper, gave permission for their Medicine Man's head logo to be used as the British Army Training Unit Suffield, or BATUS, badge. The use of the arm badge has depended upon the whim of Commander BATUS over the years and at present it is worn only by the Royal Military Police detachment on the right sleeve.

In 1995 the training was extended from live firing to Tactical Engagement Simulation using laser simulators and an Opposition Force has been stationed at BATUS for the nine months of each training season. The first OPFOR, 2nd Royal Tank Regiment, adopted a distinctive badge, which was passed on each year to succeeding OPFOR regiments. The stock is almost exhausted but a few badges remain.

1

2

3

opposite page

1 BATUS arm badges 5.25 × 6.25 cm.

this page

2 BATUS Opposition Force obsolete printed badge 8 × 9 cm.

3 Constable Gerald Sadlemyer of the Medicine Hat Police and Cpl Mark Bembrick wearing the BATUS badge above the MP TRF on joint patrol. The bulky shirts are worn over body armour. Photograph *PM(A)*.

Acknowledgement WO2 Darren Lole

British Army Training Liaison Staff Kenya

Under an agreement with the Kenyan Government, three infantry battalions train in Kenya each year. A Royal Engineer Squadron also deploys to Kenya over the same period to carry out a civil engineering project. A small permanent administrative element called The British Army Training and Liaison Staff Kenya, or BATLSK, provides the logistic support to visiting units.

Their arm badge is the second pattern badge worn by the former East Africa Command and adopted by BATLSK in 1995.

BATLSK arm badge 5 × 5 cm.

British Peace Support Team (Eastern Africa)

Based at the Kenyan armed forces' Peace Support Training Centre in the Defence Staff College campus, British Peace Support Team (Eastern Africa) co-ordinates UK support to East African countries with a view to improving the effectiveness and democratic accountability of their armed forces, and then increasing peace-keeping capacity in the region.

British Peace Support Team (Eastern Africa) arm badge 5 × 5 cm.

Acknowledgement Major Christopher Kuhle

Brunei Garrison

The Brunei Garrison badge combines the crest of the Sultanate of Brunei above the crossed kukris of the Brigade of Gurkhas.

Brunei Garrison arm badge 4 × 5 cm.

Acknowledgement
Captain Ed Rankin and SSgt Angus MacLellan

Colchester Garrison

All Garrisons have badges, those which differ from deployable or regional formations are usually only used on notice boards and letterheads. Colchester is the exception, with an arm badge worn by members of the small Staff.

Colchester Garrison arm badge 7 × 7 cm.

Defence School of Transport

The Defence School of Transport, or DST, was opened in 1996 with an Army commandant on a former RAF station.

Defence School of Transport instructor's title worn on the rank slide.

Jungle Warfare Wing

The Jungle Warfare Wing, or JWW, has its origins in the Far East Training Centre set up in Malaya in 1948 at Pulada. Renamed The Jungle Warfare School in 1959, its primary aim was to train instructors for battalions engaged on operations during the Malayan Emergency. From 1963 this emphasis changed to preparation for units serving in the Borneo Confrontation. The Jungle Warfare Wing closed in 1975. In 1976 a small cadre of Gurkha Jungle Warfare Instructors set up a jungle training team in Brunei, where they continued to run jungle courses and maintain the British Army's hard-won jungle warfare experience. In 1982 the team was formerly established as Training Team Brunei and in 2000 renamed the Jungle Warfare Wing

Jungle Warfare Wing arm badge 7 × 7.25 cm.

Land Warfare Centre

The Land Warfare Centre, or LWC, Warminster was formerly known as the Combined Arms Training Centre, or CATC, and before that the School of Infantry.

A CATC badge was introduced in 1998 and remained in use until 2003 when it was replaced by the LWC badge which is worn by the regimental police.

LWC regimental police arm badge 9 × 9.25 cm.

Reserves Training and Mobilisation Centre

Permanent Staff serving at the RTMC conduct drafts of reservists into operational theatres in order to ensure their successful transit to the units with which they are to serve. The RTMC arm badge is worn on the left sleeve.

Reserves Training and Mobilisation Centre arm badge 7 × 7.25 cm.

Acknowledgement Captain John Gregson

Joint Service Units

Defence Export Sales Organisation

The early 1960s was a period of uncertainty for the defence industry worldwide and British defence manufacturers clamoured for some form of Government assistance.

In 1966 the Defence Sales Organisation was formed, headed, by an industrialist on secondment to the Ministry of Defence, and initially supported by a Major General, a Wing Commander and a Major.

In 1985, following the privatisation of the Royal Ordnance Factories, the title of the organisation was changed to the Defence Export Services Organisation, or DESO, which employs a civilian/military mix of over 600 people, both at home and overseas.

In 1984 RAC, RA, RE and Infantry Export Support Teams were established to organise presentations and demonstrations of in-service and private venture equipments both in the UK and overseas, undertake trials and product evaluation, and provide customer training on equipments in the UK and overseas.

The DESO arm badge is almost obsolete.

Defence Export Sales Organisation arm badge 7.5 × 7.5 cm.

Armed Forces Parliamentary Scheme

A number of Members of Parliament are given the opportunity to visit military units throughout the year in order to better understand the working of the Armed Forces. The MPs do not hold military rank but wear rank slides which are more accurately appointment slides, embroidered with designs connected with both Houses of Parliament equating to the ranks of major up to brigadier.

Armed Forces Parliamentary Scheme wire-embroidered beret badge 4 × 4.5 cm.

Armed Forces Parliamentary Scheme appointment slide.

Joint Arms Control Implementation Group

The Joint Arms Control Implementation Group (JACIG) was formed in 1990 as a Tri-Service unit tasked with implementing the United Kingdom's arms control commitments under the Conventional Forces in Europe Treaty (CFE), the Vienna Document 1999 (VD 99), the Chemical Weapons Convention (CWC), the Anti Personnel Land Mines Treaty (APM), the Dayton Accords, and the Open Skies Treaty (OS). The arm badge was introduced in 1991 worn on the right sleeve and was later worn on both sleeves.

Joint Arms Control Implementation Group arm badge 6.5 × 6.5 cm.

Joint Arms Control Implementation Group pocket fobs. 'Inspector' is worn when visiting another country and 'Escort' is worn when escorting foreign inspectors to UK units and sites.

JACIG flying badge 8 × 10.25 cm worn by aircrew.

Acknowledgement
Lt Col John Wheeley RE and Sqn Ldr Jim Christie RAF.

Compulsory Drugs Testing Team

The Compulsory Drugs Testing Team, or CDT, sponsored by Headquarters Adjutant General, consists of Army and Air Force personnel. Major Tim Saunders MBE designed the Tri-Service arm badge in 1997 when the Royal Navy were included in the team. The badge is not being worn at present.

Compulsory Drug Testing Team arm badge 5 × 5 cm.

Operational Analysis

Civilians employed to carry out operational analysis, typically tasks such as Battle Damage Assessment, may wear military protective clothing, in which case they are identified by an appointment slide, the standard of embroidery of which are variable.

Operational Analyst's slide

Joint Air Transport Evaluation Unit

The Joint Air Transport Evaluation Unit, or JATEU, is a joint Army and RAF unit. It has its origins in the Second World War Army's Airborne Forces Development Centre (AFDC) and the RAF's Airborne Forces Tactical Development Unit which were amalgamated into the Army Air Transport Development Unit (ATDU). It was renamed the Joint Air Transport Establishment (JATE) in 1968. It became JATEU in 1998 responsible for Airportability, Engineering and Airborne Trials.
The JATEU arm badge was introduced in 1996.

Joint Air Transport Evaluation Unit arm badge 5 × 5 cm.

International and Multinational Formations
and British Military Missions

Operational Interpreter

There is a nametape identifying an interpreter working with British forces. It is worn either above the breast pocket if the interpreter is wearing British uniform, or sometimes on a brassard, occasionally with the TRF of the unit being supported. However the nametape is not much known about and is worn by only a few interpreters.

United Nations

Since 1964 the UK has contributed troops to 18 of the 56 UN Missions. At present 457 UK troops are serving in UNFICYP (Cyprus), NAMSIL (Sierra Leone), UNOMIG (Georgia), MONUC (Congo) and UNMEE (Ethiopia/Eritrea), and in the Department of Peacekeeping Operations in New York. The largest contribution is 415 to UNFICYP. There is no operational link between British soldiers serving in the Cyprus Sovereign Base Areas and the British UN contingent although logistic support is provided to the Mission from the SBAs.

The issue cap badge is white enamel and bright gilt with a pin back. Officers sometimes wear a private purchase wire-embroidered beret badge. Although troops assigned to a United Nations force are often known as the 'blue berets' other nations sometimes equip their troops with a pale blue baseball-type cap with an embroidered badge.

Peacekeeping soldiers wear their own national uniforms, with blue helmets, berets or soft peaked caps and the United Nations insignia. Blue helmets were first worn in Egypt in 1956 during the Suez crisis to distinguish between the peacekeepers, many equipped with British uniforms, and British troops who were involved in the war.

1

2

3

4

5

1 UN all ranks enamel and bright gilt cap badge 5.25 × 4.5 cm.
2 Captain Ben Hallatt RA wearing the officer's wire-embroidered beret badge.
3 Sgt Edward Corkhill wearing the United Nations beret badge and the arm badge on his left sleeve.
4 UN private purchase officer's wire-embroidered beret badge 6 × 6 cm.
5 UN arm badge 7.5 cm worn by all nationalities.

Allied Rapid Reaction Corps

The ARRC arm badge was introduced in 1992. The badge incorporates the spearhead of the British 1 Corps, which had been adopted whilst with the British Expeditionary Force in 1939–1940. The successor 1st British Corps served in Germany from 1945 until 1991 when it was replaced by the ARRC. The motto translates as *Fortune favours the brave.*

The ARRC, based in Rheindahlen, Germany is a NATO formation established in 1991 to meet the requirements of future challenges within the alliance. With a staff of 400 from 13 contributing nations commanded by a British lieutenant general, the Corps is assigned ten divisions, four of which could be placed under command for a specific operation.

The main British contribution to the ARRC is 1 (UK) Armoured Division, and there are also a considerable number of British troops assigned to HQ ARRC and to Corps Troops.

Allied Rapid Reaction Corps Arm badge
6.5 × 8.75cm

NATO Response Force

The first Response Force was established at RHQ AFNORTH in Brunssum in 2003. It provides NATO with a robust and credible high readiness capability able to deploy quickly wherever required. The NRF emblem is in the traditional NATO colours of white and dark blue, with a black belt representing the heraldic symbol for armour. The gold border represents the value of the Force to NATO. Three badges have been produced, a full colour pocket fob, a full colour uniform patch and a subdued uniform patch. Only the subdued patch is authorised for British troops.

NATO Response Force new arm badge authorised for future NATO operations 6.5 × 8 cm.

Acknowledgement Maj Derek Burton

Stabilisation Force Former Yugoslavia

SFOR arm badges were sold in Bosnia-Herzegovina from 1996; they were worn formally by some national contingents assigned to the NATO led force in the former Yugoslavia. They were rarely worn by formed bodies of UK troops but were worn on occasions by those assigned to HQ SFOR and multi-national specialist units. Badges were available for sale in various contingent shops on bases – the equivalent of NAAFI/EFI.

1

2

Mines Information Co-ordination Cell
Unofficial arm badges are worn by some troops involved in mine clearance in the former Yugoslavia.

MICC is a small multi-national team based at HQ SFOR. Unofficial badges based on the design of the international mines warning red triangle are sold in Bosnia.

Headquarters NATO Sarajevo
When SFOR ceased operations in 2004 a small team remained in Sarajevo co-located with HQ EUFOR. The team, which includes British personnel, wear a distinctive HQ NATO badge on the left sleeve. A similar badge is worn by the NATO team based in Skopja.

3

4

5

previous page

1 Mines Information Co-ordination Cell unofficial arm badge 10 × 4.75 cm.

this page

2 Unofficial arm badge worn by some troops involved in reconnaissance for mined areas 9 × 5.5 cm.

3 SFOR arm badges 6.5 × 8 cm.

4 HQ NATO Sarajevo arm badge 5 × 8.25 cm.

5 SFOR Psyops badge introduced in 1999 representing the national Psyops badges (clockwise) of Germany, US, France and UK and retained by EUFOR in 2004.

Multi National Brigade (North West)

UK forces have been deployed in the former Yugoslavia since 1992. The original contribution was 5,000 troops to the United Nations Protection Force (PROFOR); this was succeeded by 10,000 troops assigned to the Implementation Force (IFOR). Throughout 2004 about 1,500 UK troops were assigned to the Stabilisation Force (SFOR). UK troops served in HQ SFOR in Sarajevo, in HQ Multi-National Brigade (North West), originally designated Multi-National Division (South-West), at Banja Luka and with the UK Battlegroup. The MNB(NW) arm badge is worn by HQ staff. It features the NATO crest and the flags of the three principle contributing nations to the brigade; Canada, the Netherlands and the UK who each contribute a Battle Group. In June 2004 the Brigades were re-titled Multi-National Task Force. In December 2004 EU Force Althea replaced SFOR, although many of the troops were the same. The badge was replaced by the EUFOR badge.

HQ Multi-National Brigade (North West) arm badge 7.5 × 9 cm.

Military Police Company Multi National Brigade (Centre) Kosovo Force

The MNB(C) KFOR Military Police Company is a multi-national unit based at Pristina in Kosovo which supports Multi-National Brigade (Centre). It includes military police personnel from Austria, Czech Republic, Finland, Norway, Sweden and the UK.

There is a KFOR badge similar to the SFOR arm badge but it is not worn by British troops.

1

2

1 Norwegian and British military police wearing the KFOR military police badge in Kosovo.
2 KFOR military police company obsolete arm badge 6.75 × 6.75 cm.

EU Force Althea

The European Union, or EU, deployed Althea Force of 7,000 troops to replace SFOR in the Balkans in December 2004; the third occasion on which the European Union has deployed a force outside of the NATO framework. Previous deployments were to the Congo and Macedonia. Many of the troops serving with SFOR remained in place whilst the command and the badge changed. The EU Force is drawn from the EU nations, with other NATO nations and nations applying for EU membership welcome to contribute troops. The EU Force arm badge was designed by Lt Col Martin Lilly MBE.

There are two unofficial versions of the badge sold in Sarajevo. A reduced sized coloured badge is worn by one or two of the 33 nationalities above the right breast pocket. A subdued badge with black stars on a khaki background is made to order in Sarajevo. Soldiers have been ordered not to wear it although a version with a REME badge in the centre was worn for a day by a soldier serving with 653 Squadron AAC.

1

2

The title Althea is of classical origin that eliminates problems in translating its name and acronym into the many languages of the European Union.

1 EU Force arm badge 6cm.

2 Sgt Steve Graham wearing the EUFOR badge worn by all ranks in Bosnia since December 2004, below the Union Flag badge and the 16 Air Assault Brigade badge.

Acknowledgement SSgt SA Tickner

International Security Assistance Force Afghanistan

ISAF is the international force, established in 2002 following the fall of the Taleban, based in Kabul, Afghanistan where it supports the Interim Administration. There is a Kabul Multi-National Brigade arm badge, which is not worn by British troops. British troops are issued a green badge and a desert coloured badge both with Velcro fastenings

1

2

1 Bi-lingual badge 8.25 cm originally introduced in 2002 for those working with Afghan forces.

2 Fus Nanji Nijjar WMR serving with ISAF, wearing the bi-lingual badge on his left arm .

opposite page

3 ISAF obsolete square badge 8.5 × 8.5 cm issued when the UK was the lead nation in 2002;

4 ISAF badge issued in 2004, 8 cm.

3

4

Acknowledgement Capt Richard Blaney

Multi-National Division (South East) Iraq

Multi National Division (South East) replaced 1st Armoured Division in Iraq in 2003. The Division's arm badge is made in the Iraq's national colours, red, white and black. Soldiers have speculated that the Arabic script on the badge gives an instruction such as, 'other way up'. Personnel in Iraq working directly with local forces wore an Iraq National Guard arm badge between April 2004 and January 2005, when the Iraqi National Army was formed. The badge was produced with the outline of Iraq woven in red, white and green. Iraq's colours are red, white and black and British officers spent hours colouring the green section of 4,000 badges black with a marker pen.

The Army has a history of using foreign script, particularly on signs. In the post-Second World War years when the Army was used for crowd and riot control across the Empire it was discovered that the banner displayed before Chinese rioters in Hong Kong did not say as intended 'Disperse or we fire'. Its far more aggressive invitation actually translated as 'Fire or we disperse'.

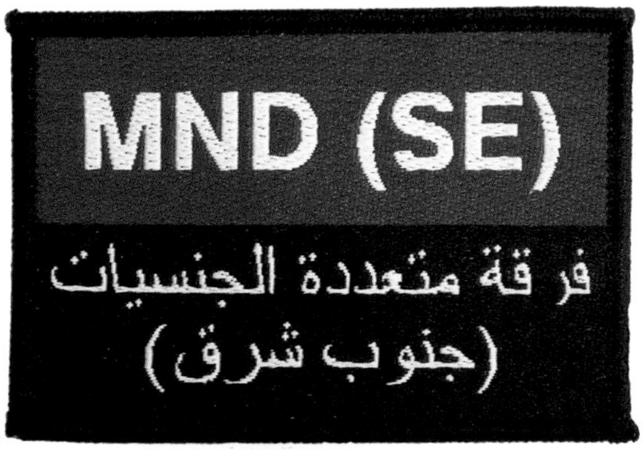

1

2

3

4

1 MND(SE) arm badge 7.5 × 5 cm.
2 WO1 (RSM) Brian Stoddart and Sgt Tim Neate wearing the MND(SE) arm badge. Photograph *RRV*.
3 Iraq National Guard arm badge 7.5 cm.
4 Proposed British badge for wear in Iraq.

Acknowledgement Major Richard Matters

International Military Advisory and Training Team

Until 2001 the Army provided Short Term Training Teams, or STTT, to the Sierra Leonean Army. In September 2001 the International Military Advisory and Training Team, or IMATT, was established with a significant British contribution, and continued with the training designed to create effective and democratically accountable armed forces.

British soldiers wear the IMATT badge on the right sleeve and Royal Sierra Leone Armed Forces cap badge and rank badges on British uniforms.

4th Battalion Sierra Leone Army was trained by a training team from the Royal Gurkha Rifles and adopted an arm badge with crossed kukris and the motto, *Brave, Fierce, Aggressive, Gurkha.*

1

2

3

6

5

4

1 International Military Advisory and Training Team Sierra Leone arm badge 6.25 × 8 cm.
2 CSgt Davie Mann CG wearing the IMATT badge below The Guards Division TRF. The beret badge backing is worn on the right side of his jungle hat.
3 Royal Sierra Leonean Armed Forces wire-embroidered cap badge 4.25 × 5.5 cm.
4 Brig David Santa-Olalla DSO MC wearing the Sierra Leonean cap badge and rank slide.
5 4th Battalion Sierra Leone Army arm badge 9 × 9.5 cm.
6 Royal Sierra Leonean Armed Forces colonel's and WO1 rank slides.

Acknowledgement Col Alistair Reid and WO2 Angela Arkwright

Foreign Formation Signs

In support of Defence Diplomacy officers and some Warrant Officers and senior non-commissioned officers serve with foreign armies, usually as liaison officers or exchange officers. Officers and senior ranks may also be seconded to foreign armies usually as instructors.

1

2

3

4

5

6

1 Lt Col Bob McKeegan RLC British Liaison Officer to the French logistic headquarters at Montlhery, wearing the French formation sign and both British and French parachute wings.
2 Colonel Clive Hodges MBE 24 Liaison HQ, British Liaison Officer to the US Army in Europe at Heidelberg, wearing the formation sign of HQ USAREUR, and his Staff cap badge on The King's Regiment's red patch.
3 Lt Col Simon Worsley RA British Liaison Officer to the German artillery school at Idar-Oberstein wearing the German formation sign.
4 Colonel Clive Mantell MBE UK Liaison Officer to HQ EUROCORPS at Strasbourg wearing the Corps formation sign on his left sleeve, and the Staff cap badge on a green Royal Irish Regiment beret.
5 Captain David Wilkins AAC serving as an exchange Attack Helicopter pilot with the US Army wears British uniform with the US 101st Airborne Division badge.
6 WO2 (QMSI) Ray Watson serving on Loan Service with the Sultan of Oman's Armed Forces wears Omani uniform and badges.

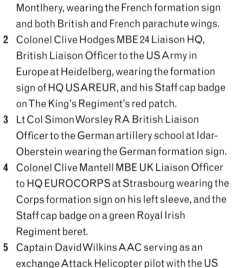

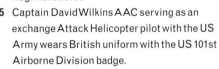

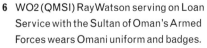

Body Guards and Royal Companies

Her Majesty's Body Guard of The Honourable Corps of Gentlemen-at-Arms

Her Majesty's Body Guard of the Honourable Corps of Gentlemen-at-Arms, the Sovereign's 'nearest guard' was instituted by Henry VIII in 1509. Originally formed from the younger sons of noble families, the Honourable Corps still consists of five Officers and 27 Gentlemen, all of whom, with the exception of the Captain, are retired officers of the Army and Royal Marines. They wear the insignia of their former military ranks but their Officers are promoted from amongst the Gentlemen notwithstanding their former rank, and receive Sticks of Office from the Sovereign on appointment. The Captain is appointed by the Government from the House of Lords.

The Honourable Corps carry out ceremonial duties about the Court only on State Occasions and Services of the Great Orders of Chivalry.

1

2

3

4

5

opposite page

1 Honourable Corps of Gentleman at Arms button.

2 Honourable Corps of Gentleman at Arms helmet worn with the swan feathers falling over the helmet plate.

3 Epaulette 15 × 20.5 cm, badge 5 × 7 cm. Members wear their former military rank, in this case a colonel.

this page

4 Coatee tail badges 7.5 × 8.25 cm.

5 Major Ivor Ramsden MBE, Major Sir Fergus Matheson of Matheson Bt and Colonel David Fanshaw LVO OBE.

Photograph *Honourable Corps of Gentlemen-at-Arms*

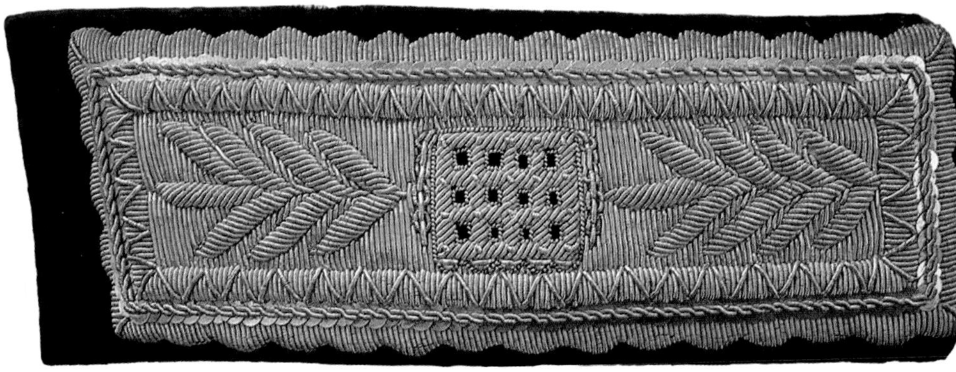

6

7

8

6 Collar insignia 13.5 × 5 cm.
7 Officer's pouch 18 × 10.5 cm.
8 Gentleman's pouch 18 × 10.5 cm.

Acknowledgement
Major Pat Verdon, Axe Keeper, and Mr Gary Carr of Gieves and Hawkes who look after the uniforms

The Queen's Bodyguard of The Yeoman of The Guard

In 1485 Henry VII created what is now the oldest Body Guard in the world from those who had fought for him at the Battle of Bosworth Field. The Queen's Body Guard consists of six officers and sixty-two Yeomen of the Guard. The Captain is appointed by the Government from the House of Lords whilst the Yeoman are chosen from retired senior ranks of the Army, Royal Marines and Royal Air Force who have completed twenty two years service and hold the Long Service and Good Conduct Medal.

The Yeoman of the Guard wears a uniform almost identical to that worn by the Yeoman Warders, with the addition of a musket sash. The Body Guard escort the Sovereign on certain State Occasions and because they are not permanently on duty are referred to by the Yeoman Warders as 'the TA', whilst they refer to the Yeoman Warders as 'the Gaolers'

1

2

1 Yeoman of the Guard button

2 Yeoman Bed Goer John Powell (late RGJ) and Charles Bouch (late MPSC), Yeoman Thomas Lee (late LG), Yeoman Bed Hanger Dennis Tubb (late WG) and Yeoman John Davies 28 (late WG).

Photograph *Yeoman of the Guard*

Acknowledgement Capt Chris Sayer

The Body of Yeoman Warders of Her Majesty's Tower of London

Yeoman Warders have guarded the Tower of London since the 11th Century. The Body owes many of its traditions to the Duke of Wellington, Constable of the Tower from 1826 to 1852. He changed the system whereby the Warders bought their positions to the present practice whereby Warders are recruited from retired deserving warrant officers and staff sergeants of the Army, Royal Marines and Royal Air Force who have completed a minimum of 22 years service and hold the Long Service and Good Conduct Medal. The strength is thirty-five Warders, all quartered with their families within the Tower.

Yeoman Warders are erroneously known as 'Beefeaters'. The most likely explanation is that Yeoman Warders were given a daily ration of meat for their duties. Even in 1813 the daily ration for 30 Warders on duty was 24lbs of beef, 18lbs of mutton and 16lbs of veal.

For daily duties the Yeoman Warders wear a blue Undress uniform designed by Sir Robert Peel in 1868. Those on duty wear a Watch coat at night, introduced by George III in 1761 to replace the coat descended from John of London's 'Rugg Gown' worn since 1321.

In 1552 Edward Seymour, Protector to Edward VI, made the Yeoman Warders Extraordinary members of the Sovereign's Body Guard, and they wear the same scarlet livery as The Queen's Bodyguard of The Yeoman of The Guard, the only difference being that the Yeoman Warders do not wear a bandolier. The State Dress is thought

The Yeoman Warders are sworn in on Tower Green with an oath of allegiance which dates from 1337. The Chief Yeoman Warder toasts new recruits with the words 'May you never die a Yeoman Warder.' Originally the post of Yeoman Warder was sold for 250 guineas. £250 went to the retiring Yeoman Warder and the balance to the Constable of the Tower who appointed him, but if the Yeoman Warder died in post the whole amount went to the Constable.

to have been designed by Hans Holbein. Wearing the uniform has been likened by a Yeoman Warder to being a three-dimensional king-sized playing card.

The Crown and Rose badges worn on the chest were the first badges, being embroidered at a cost of £88 9s 4 d in 1597. The thistle, motto and sovereign's cypher were added in 1761, and the Shamrock probably in 1801.

The Tudor (or King's) Crown is retained on the scarlet State Dress, whilst St Edward's (or Queen's) Crown is worn on the Blue Undress uniform; both with Queen Elizabeth II's Cypher.

As a full-time unit the Yeoman Warders have a working, rather than honorary command structure with six of the Yeoman Warders wearing four chevrons, in the Victorian style, on the right sleeve. The Chief Yeoman Warder carries out duties similar to those of a Regimental Sergeant Major and wears a Crown above the chevrons and crossed keys, recalling his original title of Yeoman Porter. His deputy is the Yeoman Gaoler, who was originally the senior appointment when the Tower was a prison. The Gaoler also wears a Crown above his chevrons and a magnificent embroidered badge of the White Tower. There are four Yeoman Sergeants who wear the four chevrons without other embellishments.

One of the Yeoman Warders holds the volunteer appointment of Raven Master, responsible for overseeing the well being of the Tower's ravens which, since the 1660s, or 1897 depending upon which version of the story is believed, will guarantee the continuation of the Monarchy.

2

3

4

5

6

7

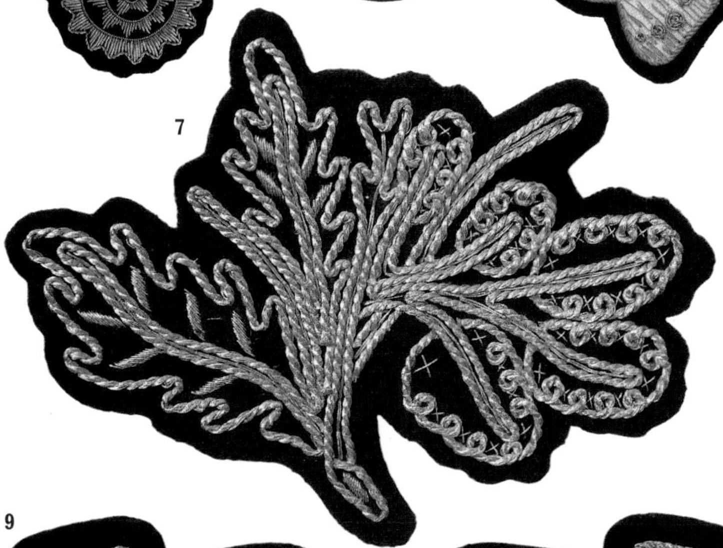

8

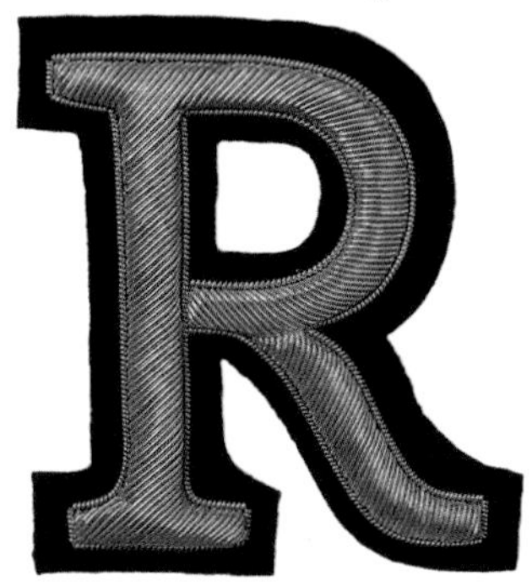

9

opposite page

1 Yeoman Gaoler John Kehone BEM, now Chief Yeoman Warder, with his ceremonial axe, and the then Chief Yeoman Warder Tom Sharp (now retired) with his wand of office, a silver replica of the White Tower on a wooden staff dating from 1792 (both late Royal Signals).
Photograph *HM Tower of London*

this page

Badges worn by Yeoman Warders, and the Yeoman of the Guard, on the scarlet State Dress.

2 Tudor (or King's) Crown 14 × 15.25 cm.
3 Thisle 5 × 7.5 cm
4 Rose 8.25 cm
5 Shamrock 5.5 × 5.75 cm.
6 E 7.5 × 8.25 cm
7 Oak leaves 17.25 × 13.5 cm.
8 R 8 × 8.5 cm.
9 Motto 16 × 6.5 cm.

10

11

12

13

14

15

16

10 Crown 7 × 7.5 cm worn by the Chief Yeoman Warder and the Yeoman Gaoler above four chevrons in the Victorian style of a sergeant major.
11 Yeoman Warder's name badge.
12 Yeoman Raven Master appointment badge 5.5 cm.
13 Chief Yeoman Warder's appointment badge 10.5 × 8.5 cm worn on four chevrons below a Crown.
14 Yeoman Raven Master Derrick Coyle (late Green Howards) and Yeoman Sergeant Alan Kingsholt (late Royal Hussars) wearing Blue Undress uniform.
15 Yeoman Warder button
16 Yeoman Gaoler's appointment badge 9 × 9.5 cm worn on four chevrons.

Military Knights of Windsor

There are thirteen Military Knights

Edward III founded the College of St George and appointed the 'Poor Knights' from amongst those who had been made penniless because of ransom payments made to the French. They were appointed as bedesmen to pray for the souls of their benefactors. Their uniform was introduced by William IV in 1833 at the same time as they were titled the Military Knights of Windsor.

The cocked hat does not have a badge, rather red over white swan feathers. The ancient badge of the College of St George, worn by the original 'Poor Knights' is embroidered on the epaulettes, on the skirts of the coat and is worn as a cap badge on the Forage Cap.

The shoulder belt plate and the buttons have the Garter Star introduced by Charles I in 1629 beneath the King's Crown. Both are dipped in gold to make cleaning easier.

1

2

3

4

5

6

7

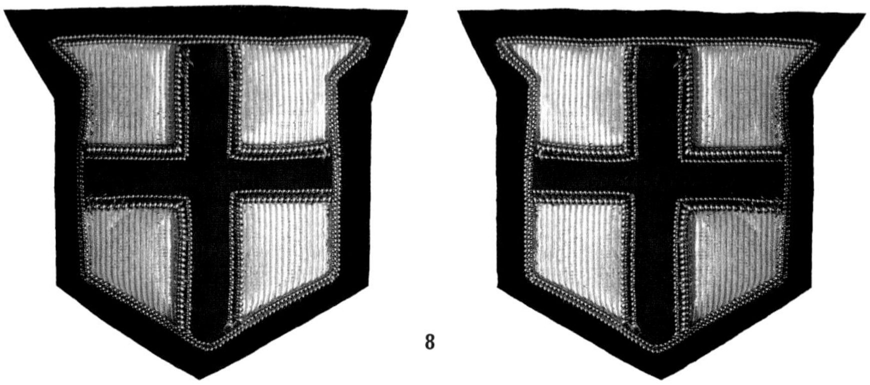

8

previous page

1 Lt Col Ray Giles, a Military Knight, in Full Dress worn annually between Easter and Remembrance Sunday.

2 The black silk cocked hat worn by the Military Knights, introduced in 1833.

3 Military Knights silver, gilt and enamel on gilt shoulder belt plate 7.75 × 9 cm of St George's Cross within the Garter. An attempt recently to have the Crown changed to the St Edward's (or Queen's) Crown was rejected.

4 Military Knights Garter and Star gold button.

this page

5 Swan feathers plume worn by the Military Knights in the cocked hat 21 × 12.25 cm.

6 Full Dress epaulette worn between Easter and Remembrance Sunday15 × 20 cm and the Undress epaulette worn during the winter between Remembrance Sunday and the Sunday before Easter 11 × 18.5 cm (both shown half size) The rank badges are those of a Household Cavalry lieutenant colonel.

7 St George's Cross Forage Cap badge 7 × 5.5 cm. The Forage Cap is worn in wet weather. Military Knights may use their regimental hat although the official pattern is the blue cap with scarlet band.

8 Military Knights dress coat St George's Cross skirt ornaments 5.75 × 5.25 cm.

The Queen's Body Guard For Scotland Royal Company of Archers

Organised in 1676 as an archery club, the Body Guard was reconstituted in 1703. The Company is commanded by the Captain-General and Gold Stick for Scotland and has 400 active members and a non-active retired list.

1

The original instruction on dress in 1676 directed that 'Members shall attend meetings with sufficient shooting graith and with the seal and arms in their hats or bonnets.' A white St Andrews badge with white and green ribbons was ordered in 1713. In 1789 it is recorded that there was to be a painted St Andrew on the bonnet. In 1813 a stamped copper badge was ordered, which was replaced in 1829 by a gilt Star of the Order of the Thistle badge, which in 1862 was transferred to the end of the Bowcase, where it is still worn.

Yellow gilt metal buttons were introduced in 1789 and a golden arrow adopted as collar badges in 1813. Rank and appointment badges are now worn on the collar.

There are seven appointments to which members of the Royal Company of Archers can be promoted. Members wear no collar badges and a single feather behind the cap badge. Officers' wear collar badges and two feathers and the Captain General three feathers. The Secretary wears a 'prodigious Condor's feather' presented by the Earl of Dalhousie when both Captain General of the Royal Company of Archers from 1830–1838, and Viceroy of India. The Adjutant is identified by gold spurs (an interesting choice when everyone else is counting feathers).

2

3

4

5

7

6

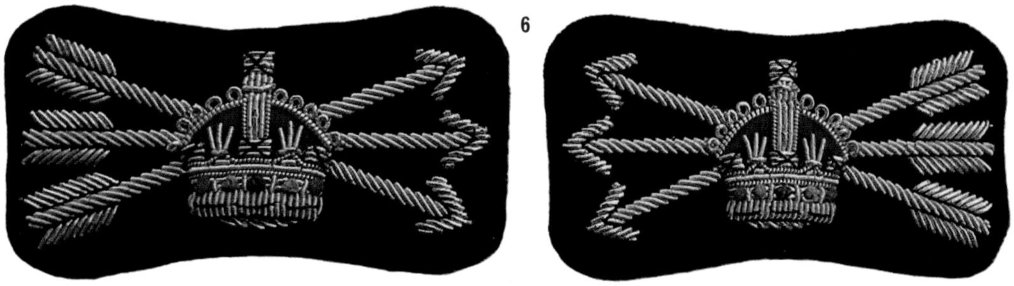

8

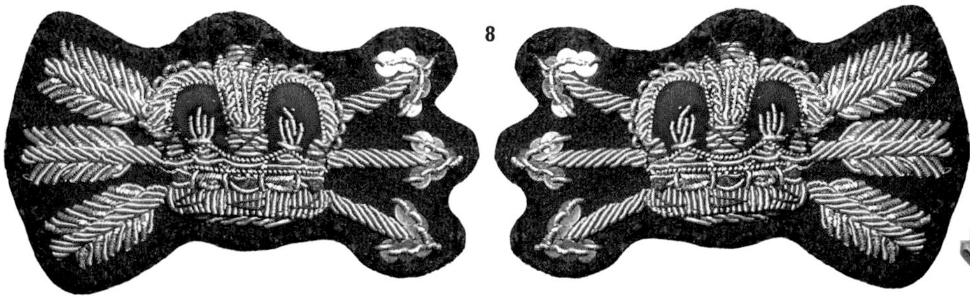

12

9

10

13

11

previous page

1 Royal Company of Archers gilt bonnet badge 5.25 × 7.75 cm worn on white and green cockades (older example with light gilt finish)
Rank badges worn on the collar
2 Captain 4 cm, **3** Lieutenant 2.75 × 4.5 cm, **4** Ensign 3.25 × 3.5 cm, **5** Brigadier (originally a French non-commissioned officer rank reflecting the Service of many Scotsmen in the service of France) 4 cm.

6 Shooting Judge badges with Tudor (or King's) Crowns 7.25 × 3.75 cm.

7 Secretary and Treasurer 7.25 × 4.25 cm.

this page

8 Queen's Body Guard for Scotland older wire-embroidered Shooting Judge badges 7 × 4 cm but with post-1953 St Edward's (or Queen's) Crowns.

9 Lt Gen Sir Alistair Irwin KCB CBE a member of the Royal Company of Archers.

10 Queen's Body Guard for Scotland gilt shoulder belt plate worn on the Bowcase 5.25 × 8.75 cm.

11 Queen's Body Guard for Scotland gilt waist belt clasp 10.5 × 6.25 cm with the Royal Crest of Scotland in the centre.

12 Copy of the original gilt cap star worn at the bottom of the Bowcase 9 × 9.25 cm.

13 Older gilt and enamel copy of the original cap star worn at the bottom of the Bowcase 9 × 9.25 cm.

Acknowledgement
Captain David Younger and Jonathan Bannister of Mayfield Jays Ltd.

Royal Hospital

Charles II founded the Royal Hospital Chelsea in 1682 for 'the succour and relief of veterans broken by age and war'

The Royal Hospital is not a hospital; the name was used in the 17th Century to mean almshouses. The Royal Hospital is a retirement home, albeit a rather special one for retired soldiers in receipt of a Service or disability pension, at least 65 years of age and free from the obligation to support a wife or family. The in-pensioners range in age from 65 to 99; the average age of the 310 residents is 80. About 90 of the in-pensioners work around the Royal Hospital and may hold Hospital Rank according to their duties. The in-pensioners are organised into six companies each commanded by a retired officer, titled Captain of Invalids.

In-Pensioners at the Royal Hospital wear a scarlet Full Dress uniform based upon that worn by the Army in 1704. They have three headdresses; a blue Lounge Cap, similar to the first World War soft forage cap, which is worn with their regimental cap badge. In-Pensioners have a month on joining the Royal Hospital in which to choose or change their badge providing it is one that they have worn during Army service. The Quartermaster's clothing store maintains a selection of obsolete as well as current badges obtained from a variety of sources. On leaving the Hospital grounds, when wearing Blues, the In-Pensioners wear a shako. Corporals and In-Pensioners wear a red embroidered RH badge, whilst those holding a Hospital Rank of sergeant and above wear a wire-embroidered badge. In scarlet Full Dress In-Pensioners wear a tricorn decorated with a leather Georgian cockade on the left side; corporals and below with a black ribbon, sergeants and above with a gold ribbon.

The uniformed staff, almost all retired senior Non-Commissioned Officers and Warrant Officers not in-pensioners, wear a gilding metal Royal Hospital cap badge on the forage cap. Officers do not wear cap badges.

Anodised aluminium collar badges are worn by uniformed Staff, not by In-Pensioners. The two Park Keepers, who wear livery on formal occasions, wear wire-embroidered collar badges.

1

3

4

5

2

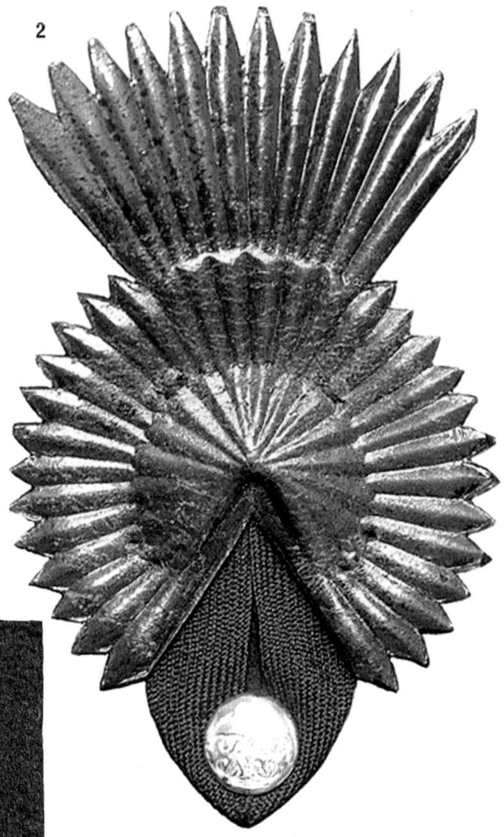

6

7

8

9

previous page

Royal Hospital In-Pensioners' Georgian leather cockades worn on the Tricorn in Full Dress

1 Sergeants, Colour Sergeants and Company Sergeant Majors with gold ribbon, 8.5 × 15 cm.

2 corporals and below with black ribbon 8.5 × 15 cm.

3 Royal Hospital button.

4 Sergeant, Colour Sergeant and Company Sergeant Major's wire-embroidered shako badge 6.5 × 3.75 cm.

5 Corporal's and below woven shako badge 8 × 4 cm.

this page

6 Royal Hospital uniformed staff gilding metal cap badge 4 × 5 cm and anodised aluminium collar badges 2.5 × 3 cm.

7 Hospital Sergeant Ken Williams SAS in Blues worn for walking out within one mile of the Royal Hospital. He wears the SAS parachute wings above his sergeant's 'Broad stripes' indicating that he was not a senior NCO in the Army but holds the rank of Hospital Sergeant having volunteered to carry out duties. Colour Sergeant Charles Liddle Queen's Own Highlanders in Full Dress, the gold lace edging to his cuffs and pockets indicates that he holds NCO rank within the Royal Hospital. AQMS Bill Slaney, late Scots Guards, a member of the uniformed staff wearing the Royal Hospital's cap badge in the forage cap. Those at the Royal Hospital may wear the Royal Hospital stable belt, or that of their former regiment, in this case Scots Guards.

8 David Williams, a civilian member of staff, wearing the Park Keeper's uniform for Founders Day.

9 Royal Hospital Park Keepers wire-embroidered collar badge 6 × 4 cm.

Acknowledgement
In-Pensioner Arthur Felstead (late REME) and Mr David Williams

Lords Lieutenant

Head of the Reserve Forces and Cadets of the county

The office of Lord Lieutenant is of military origin and dates from 1551 when responsibility for the maintenance of law and order and for local defence in the county was taken from the Sheriff.

A Lord Lieutenant is the permanent representative of the Crown in a county and is appointed by the Sovereign on the recommendation of the Prime Minister.

The Lord Lieutenant attends on Royalty during official visits to the county, is head of the Reserve Forces and Cadets of the county and makes presentations of honours and awards on behalf of the crown (as well as being Patron or President of a wide range of charitable organisations).

1

2

5

3

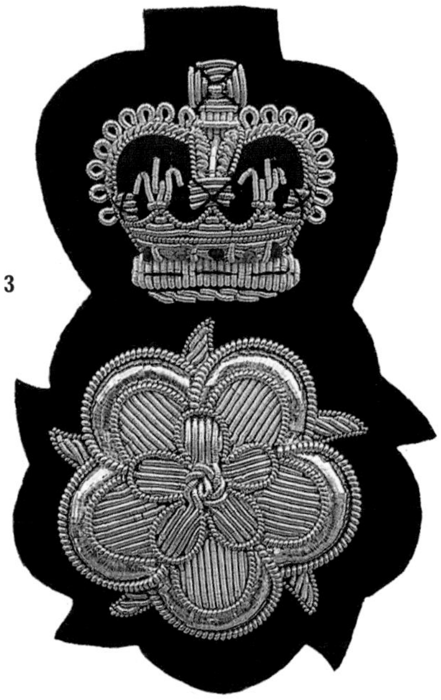

4

6

9

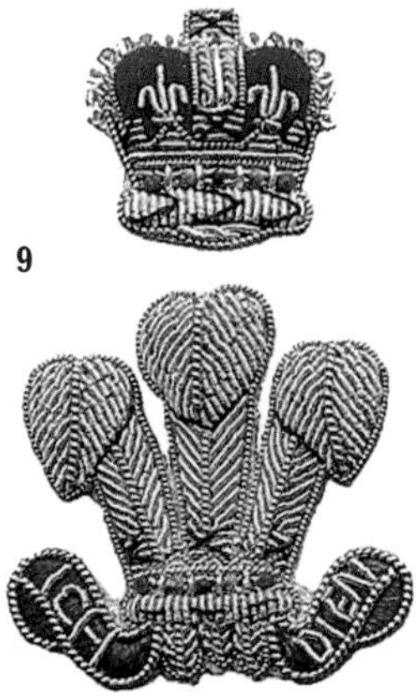

7

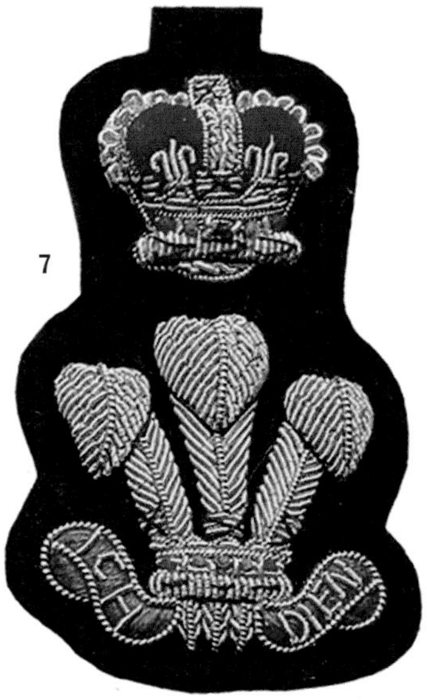

8

10

13

Lords Lieutenant and their Deputies do not all have to wear uniform, a few are so required and others choose to do so. When they do, Lords Lieutenant wear a Number 1 Dress uniform equating to that of a lieutenant general, and Deputy Lieutenants to a colonel. The shoulder boards and buttons are silver, following on from the Militia's tradition of silver insignia when the Regular Army had gold insignia.

There are 47 Lords Lieutenant of English counties and Shires, eight Lords Lieutenant of Welsh counties and Shires, 17 Lords Lieutenant of Scottish counties and Shires, with the Lord Provosts of the four principal cities ex-officio Lords Lieutenant and eight Lords Lieutenant of Northern Ireland counties.

11

12

18

14

17

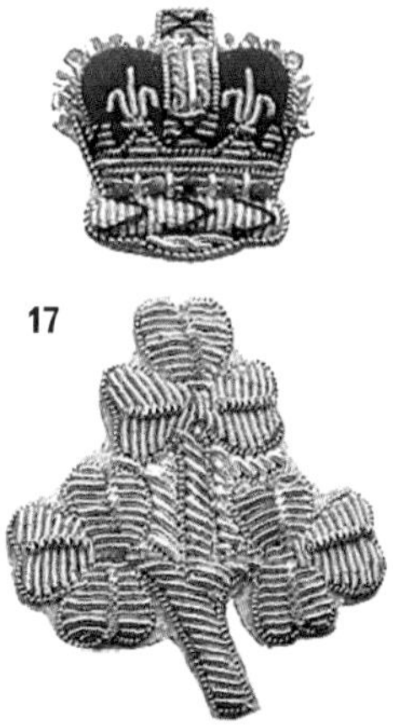

15

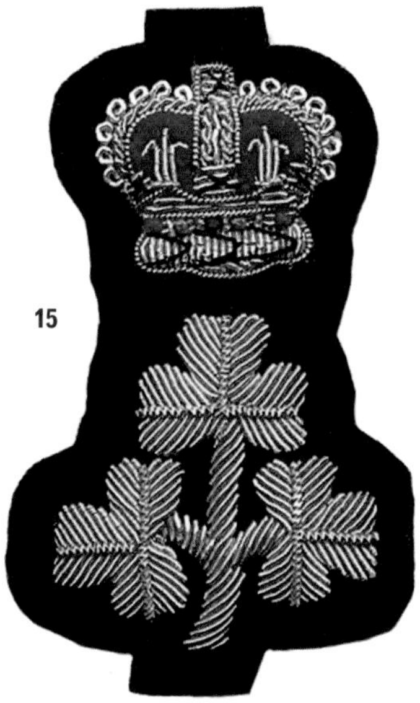

16

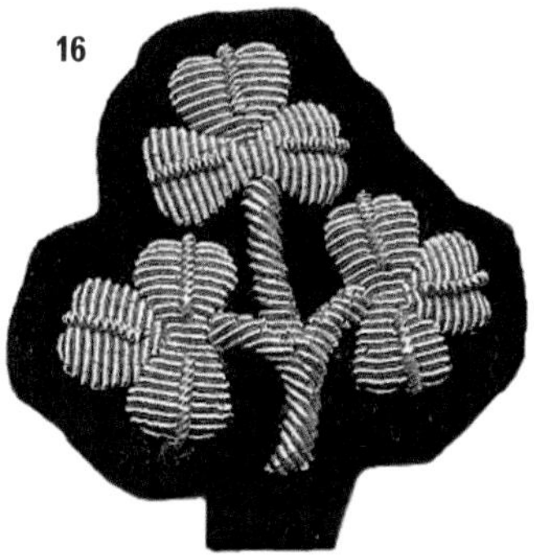

previous page

1 The Queen escorted by Lieutenant General Sir Maurice Johnston KCB OBE Lord Lieutenant of Wiltshire.
2 Lord Lieutenant of England button.
3 Wire-embroidered cap badge for Lord Lieutenant of England 5.5 × 8.5 cm.
4 Deputy Lord Lieutenant cap badge, 5 cm.
5 Shoulder badge, rose 3.75 and crown 2.5 × 2.5 cm.
6 Lord Lieutenant of Wales button.
7 Wire-embroidered cap badge for Lord Lieutenant of Wales 4.75 × 7.5 cm.
8 Deputy Lord Lieutenant cap badge, 4.5 × 4.75 cm.
9 Shoulder badge, Prince of Wales's plumes 4 × 3.5 and crown 2.5 × 2.5 cm.

this page

10 Wire-embroidered cap badge for Lord Lieutenant of Scotland 5.75 × 7.75 cm.
11 Deputy Lord Lieutenant cap badge, 6 × 5 cm.
12 Shoulder badge; thistle 4 × 4 and crown 2.5 × 2.5 cm.
13 Lord Lieutenant of Scotland button.
14 Lord Lieutenant of Ireland button.
15 Wire-embroidered cap badge for Lord Lieutenant of Ireland 4.5 × 7.25 cm.
16 Deputy Lord Lieutenant cap badge, 4.5 × 4.5 cm.
17 Shoulder badge; shamrock 3.5 × 3.75 and crown 2.5 × 2.5 cm.
18 Deputy Lord Lieutenant button.

Acknowledgment Lt Gen Sir Maurice Johnston KCB OBE

Other Corps

Soldiers' and Airmen's Scripture Readers Association

The Soldiers' and Airmen's Scripture Readers Association dates from 1818 when Sgt William Rudd distributed Bibles in Woolwich Garrison. In 1825 an Act of Parliament gave every soldier the right to access to a bible but many could not read and in 1838 concerned Christian officers formed the Soldiers' Friends Society and the Army Scripture Readers, who literally read the scriptures to soldiers. The Chaplain General placed the society on a more formal footing by issuing a Charter in 1854.

The Soldiers' Christian Association was formed in 1887, and renamed the Soldier's and Airman's Christian Association in 1918. In 1938 the Army Scripture Readers and the Soldier's and Airman's Christian Association amalgamated. In 1952 the name Soldiers' and Airmen's Scripture Readers Association was adopted.

It is understood that there are about 28 members, all ex-servicemen and women who undertake personal evangelism amongst the Forces. Those visiting Army barracks are issued Number 2 Dress with Service Dress cap and combat dress. Some also retain Barrack Dress.

The Army Scripture Readers, or ASR, cap badge was originally produced in bimetal, the last pattern, a few of which remain, was reduced in size from earlier versions (6 × 4.75 cm reduced to 4 × 3.25 cm). Anodised aluminium badges were procured in the late 1980s. Recently ASR have been authorised to wear the embroidered part of the title as a beret badge where appropriate.

There are no collar badges although from time to time ASR have worn a pair of the lapel badges usually worn in mufti as collar badges. The practice is actively discouraged.

ASR wore red titles in Barrack Dress but they were found to confuse the soldiers who could misidentify them as 'red tabs'; wire and cotton woven titles were recently introduced. With the demise of Barrack Dress the titles are now sewn on to rank slides for wear on Combat Dress. For visits to the field subdued titles have been produced. The new badges have in their turn been misidentified as Quarter Master Sergeant's rank badges. In Number 2 Dress cloth shoulder titles are worn.

1

2

3

4
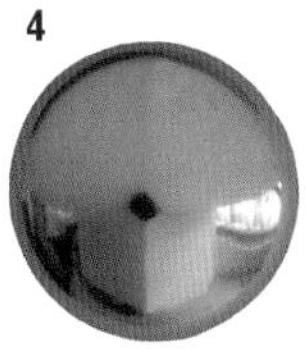

5

6

7

8

previous page

1 Obsolete bimetal cap badge 4 × 3.25cm.
2 No2 Dress shoulder title 11.5 × 2.25 cm.
3 Anodised aluminium cap badge 4.25 × 3.5 cm.
4 ASR button.
5 Beret badge cut from title 5 × 3.5 cm.
6 Lapel badge for mufti and sometimes misused as No2 Dress collar badges 2.75 × 2.25 cm.
7 Shoulder strap 14.5 × 1.5 cm formerly sewn on No2 Dress.

this page

8 Obsolete titles for ASR evangelising in Army barracks 6 × 4 cm and RAF stations 7 × 4 cm.
9 Title for ASR evangelising in Army barracks 5 × 5.5 cm.
10 Title for RAF stations 5 × 5.5 cm
11 Title for use in the field 5 × 5.5 cm.
12 Title on a slide, which has been mistaken for an RQMS or QMSI badge.
13 ASR plastic name badge worn on the left breast when with the Army and on the right with the RAF.

9

10

11

12

13

Acknowledgement Mr JG Tucker

First Aid Nursing Yeomanry (The Princess Royal's Volunteer Corps)

The First Aid Nursing Yeomanry, or FANY, cap badge was originally introduced shortly after the corps was raised in 1907 and altered to the present design in 1937. The wire-embroidered beret badge was altered when the title of the corps was changed in 2002.

The shoulder title and button also date back to the reorganisation before the Second World War.

FANY, although all recognised as officers, do not hold ranks, rather they are appointed to a position with a rank, according to their duties. When they relinquish the post they also relinquish the rank.

FANY supported a number of military formations during the Second World War including the Special Operations Executive, or SOE. Thirty-nine of the female agents parachuted into France were FANY; 12 were killed and three awarded the George Cross, two posthumously. The first two FANY SOE agents to parachute into France to work with the Resistance were commemorated by a visit to France by the unit on the sixtieth anniversary of their deployment in 1942. Those who attended were presented with the badge of the École Des Troupes Aéroportées; the French parachute school.

Subsequently FANY members, who are not permitted to parachute with the British forces, have trained and qualified as parachutists with the French army.

When operating in civilian clothes FANY are identified by an enamelled brooch. In 2004 silver replicas of the cap and collar badges were introduced for sale as brooches. The Commanding Officer has a special brooch passed down to each in succession, in enamel and marcasite.

1

2

3

4

5

6

7

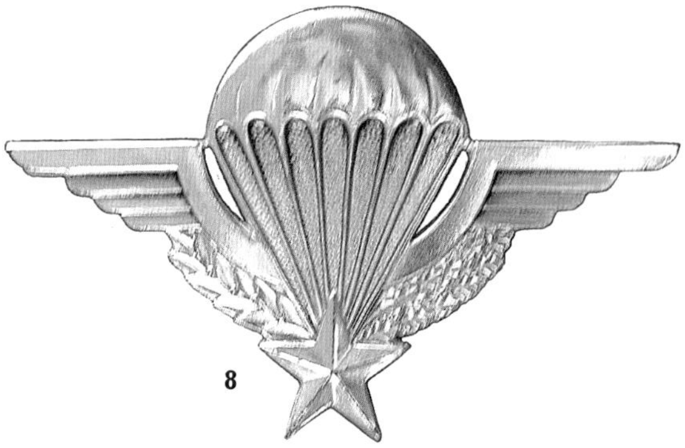

8

The First Aid Nursing Yeomanry was formed in 1907 with the intention of developing a corps of mounted nurses who would provide succour to the wounded on the battlefield. During the First World War FANY did serve with the medical services, but not riding sidesaddle around the front lines. During the Second World War FANY provided the nucleus of the Auxiliary Territorial Service, or ATS, Motor Companies and also worked with the SOE. The all female Corps was given its new title in 1999 and is affiliated to the Territorial Army, providing communications support to the police and Army during emergencies.

9

10

11

FANY ranks

FANY has unique ranks reflecting its voluntary status. The nurses are volunteers and are appointed to a position, which carries a rank, rather than being promoted. The junior appointments are Junior Cadet Ensign, wearing the rank of a maroon dot and bar, and Cadet Ensign, which equates to the rank of Midshipman in the Royal Navy. The rank indicated a degree of responsibility rather than being under training as with Officer Cadets at the Royal Military Academy Sandhurst.

Ensign, with a single pip, equates to Second Lieutenant. Lieutenant and captain wear the same rank badges as Army equivalents.

Officers are appointed not commissioned and therefore field officers wear the Coronet rather than Crown as a rank badge.

A Coronet, the gift of The Princess Alice, Countess of Athlone, represents a Commander, equivalent to major; a Staff Commander equates to a lieutenant colonel, the Deputy Corps Commander, to a colonel, and the Corps Commander, to a brigadier.

Coronet rank badge 2.75 × 1.25 cm worn as a rank badge equivalent to the Crown worn by Army officers.

previous page

1 First Aid Nursing Yeomanry bronze cap badge 3.5 cm and collar badges 2.75 cm
2 First Aid Nursing Yeomanry button.
3 Cloth shoulder title 8.25 × 2.5 cm.
4 Cadet Ensign Katie Garrod and Junior Cadet Ensign Annabel Anderson wearing Service Dress. Photograph Steve Dock
5 Wire-embroidered beret badge 4.25 cm.

this page

6 Cadet Ensign Alex Muir having been awarded her French parachute wings at the École Des Troupes Aéroportées.
7 École Des Troupes Aéroportées badge 5 × 5 cm presented to FANY who visited France on the sixtieth anniversary of the first parachute deployment by FANY SOE agents in 1942. The badge was worn on uniform when presented to the Commanding Officer in France.
8 French parachute wings 7.5 × 4.75 cm awarded to qualified FANY.
9 First Aid Nursing Yeomanry Cadet Ensign's rank slide.
10 FANY brooch 3 cm worn in civilian dress.
11 New silver brooches to the design of the cap badge 3.5 cm and collar badge 2.75 cm.

Acknowledgement Captain Joan Drummond.

The King's Fusiliers

Central Television produced the award winning drama *Soldier, Soldier* from 1991 to 1994. The four series were so successful that the 'regiment' on which the series was based was given unique insignia and even had a stand of Colours embroidered. Those badges survived the series and are now used in other dramas, such as episodes of *Silent Witness* in 2004, and *Holby City* and *The Last Detective* in 2005.

1 The King's Fusiliers anodised aluminium cap badge 2.5 × 4 cm and collar badges 2.75 cm.
2 Gilding metal shoulder title 3 × 1 cm.
3 The King's Fusiliers hackle 9 × 10 cm.

1

2

3

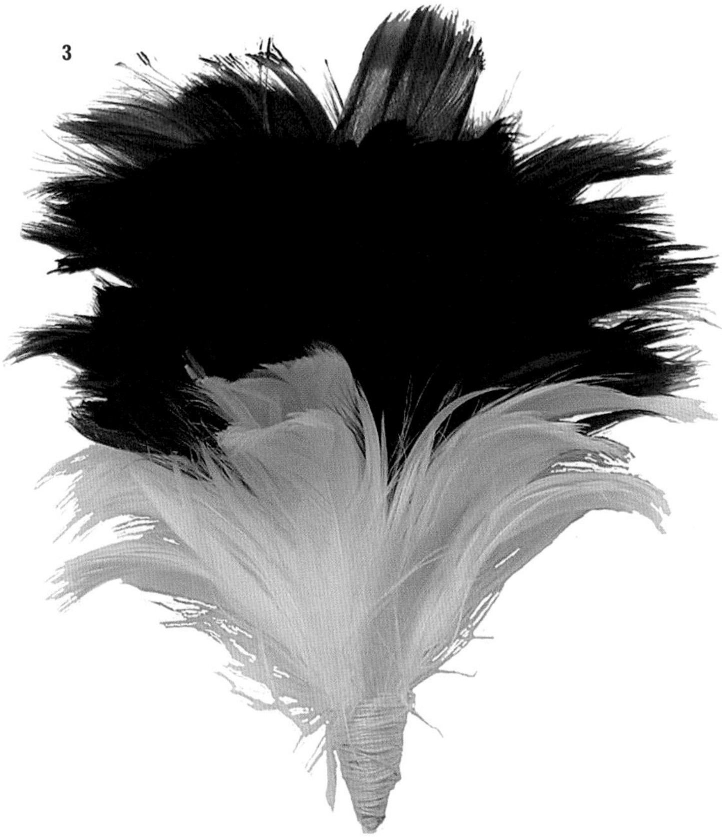

Badge identification

Index

Sources

The Army List 2004 Part 1, (London: The Stationery Office).
Badge Backings and Special Embellishments of The British Army, (The Ulster Defence Regiment Benevolent Fund, 1990, ISBN 0 9514342 0 9).
Beckett, Ian F., *Discovering British Regimental Traditions*, (Risborough: Shire Publications Ltd, 1999; ISBN 0 7478 0410 9).
Cook, H.C.B., *The Battle Honours of the British and Indian Armies 1662–1982* (London: Leo Cooper, 1987; ISBN 0 85052 0827).
Edwards, Denis and Langley, David, *British Army Proficiency Badges*, in association with the Victorian Military Society, (Wardley Publishing, 1984; ISBN 0 9509427 0 7).
Hobbes, Nicholas, *Essential Militaria*, (London : Atlantic Books, 2003).
Lawrence-Archer, Major J.H., (Formerly of the 60th KRRC etc), *The British Army: its Regimental Records, Badges, Devices etc.*, (London: George Bell and Sons, 1888).
Payne, Peter and MacDonald, Jim, *Tanks Again*, (privately published CD).
The Queen's Regulations for the Army 1975, (London: Her Majesty's Stationary Office 1976; ISBN 0 11 771880 7).
regiments.org author and webmaster T. F. Mills.

The record of a Regiment has
no ending. Its spirit can be seldom expressed
in words, only articulated in the bearing of
officers and men in the fierce competitive brilliance
of peace and the discipline and comradeship of
war. This spirit has been created by generation after
generation of soldiers, by men who fought at
Blenheim, in the Peninsula and at Waterloo, in
South Africa and India, in the mud of
Flanders, in North Africa, Burma, Italy
Korea and Iraq.

*

Anon